HTML 4.0 Sourcebook

IAN S. GRAHAM

WILEY COMPUTER PUBLISHING

John Wiley & Sons, Inc.
New York • Chichester • Weinheim • Brisbane • Singapore • Toronto

Publisher: Robert Ipsen
Editor: Cary Sullivan
Assistant Editor: Pam Sobotka
Managing Editor: Brian Snapp
Electronic Products, Associate Editor: Michael Sosa
Text Design & Composition: Benchmark Productions, Inc.

Designations used by companies to distinguish their products are often claimed as trademarks. In all instances where John Wiley & Sons, Inc., is aware of a claim, the product names appear in initial capital or ALL CAPITAL LETTERS. Readers, however, should contact the appropriate companies for more complete information regarding trademarks and registration.

This book is printed on acid-free paper. ∞

This publication is designed to provide accurate and authoritative information in regard to the subject matter covered. It is sold with the understanding that the publisher is not engaged in professional services. If professional advice or other expert assistance is required, the services of a competent professional person should be sought.

Library of Congress Cataloging-in-Publication Data:

Graham, Ian S., 1955–
    HTML 4.0 sourcebook / Ian S. Graham. -- 4th ed.
        p.   cm.
    Rev. ed. of: HTML sourcebook, 3rd ed, ©1997
    "Wiley Computer Publshing."
    Includes index.
    ISBN 0-471-25724-9 (pbk. / online)
        1. HTML (Document markup language) I. Graham, Ian S., 1955–
HTML sourcebook.
QA76.76.H94G73   1998
005.7'2--dc21   98-10106
                                                         CIP

Printed in the United States of America.
10 9 8 7 6 5 4 3 2

CONTENTS

Chapter 9 The HTTP Protocol   497

On the Companion Web Site

www.wiley.com/compbooks/graham

"Web Management and Maintenance Tools"

Appendix A Character Sets, Character Encodings,
    and Document Character Sets

Appendix B Multipurpose Internet Mail Extensions (MIME)

Appendix C Obtaining Software: Shareware Archives

Appendix D "Listening" and "Talking" at a TCP/IP Port

Appendix E Tags for Identifying Languages—RFC 1766

Appendix F Color Names and RGB Codes

ACKNOWLEDGMENTS

To my nephews, Cory and Matthew, who will do things with
this technology that I cannot possibly imagine. How I envy them!

No book (particularly one as comprehensive as this) is written in a vacuum, and I have many friends to thank for their roles in keeping the vacuum comfortably populated. First, I must thank Kelly Peters, my co-author for Chapter 5. Kelly's infectious enthusiasm for "all things Web" was a constant reminder that, indeed, this material is of interest to someone other than me. In addition, her perspective—that of a professional webmaster at Canada's largest Web site—provided a useful counterpoint to my academic experience and sensibilities! Second, I must thank Michael Lee, who researched the material on Web development resources such as link checkers, server log analyzers, and GUI-based imagemap editors. Unfortunately, much of this material did not make it into print—it is instead available on the supporting Web site. And, as far as I am concerned, that makes it as much a part of the book as the page you are now reading!

Many others made contributions for which I am truly grateful. In particular, I would like to thank Norman Wilson, for designing the programs *listen.c* and *backtalk.c*, and also for his helpful and concise reviews of chapters from previous editions. John Bradley and Sian Meikle were kind enough to review early drafts of Chapter 4, and their feedback helped improve the chapter enormously. In the same vein, I must thank Steve Rapaport, who proofread an early version of Chapter 3 and helped clarify some of my more confusing rants! And, of course, I must thank all my friends and coworkers at Groveware Inc., the Centre for Academic Technology at the University of Toronto, and University of Toronto Computing, whose friendship over these past months helped make the whole effort possible.

But most of all, I thank my wife, Ann, for her love, patience, and support throughout the long writing process. And now that it is finished—I *promise* to clean the basement!

INTRODUCTION
AND BOOK OUTLINE

In 1995, in the introduction to the first edition of this book, I stated that the World Wide Web had "taken the Internet by storm." At the time I hoped this was appropriate, but felt in my heart that I was probably overstating things. In retrospect, or course, it was a gross understatement. Over the past three years—and three editions of this book—the Web has grown far beyond everyone's expectations (well, perhaps not those of Marc Andreessen), to become one of the core technologies of the 1990s. Hundreds of thousands of companies now offer products and services via the Web, and the trickle of Web-related products available in late 1994 has grown, by late 1997, into a torrent. Purely Web-based companies such as Netscape Communications and Yahoo! are now market-valued in the billions of dollars—and these companies did not exist three years ago! Meanwhile, traditional software companies such as Oracle, Sun, and Microsoft have totally redesigned their product and business models, while noncomputer-related businesses, from news and entertainment to financial services, high technology, and manufacturing, are adopting these new technologies as a new paradigm for internal operations, and as a new way of communicating with clients and customers. This is not the simple swell of "a storm," but a tidal wave that threatens—and promises—to change our society in ways that we cannot yet imagine.

This is because the World Wide Web model makes distributing and accessing any form of digital data easy and inexpensive for anyone—company or consumer—with profound implications for business, culture, and society. Thus, it is no surprise that seemingly "everyone" is now buying or downloading the latest in Web tools and is madly learning how to build pages so that they too can join this new electronic world. Indeed, this is probably why you have picked up this book—to learn about the tools, and how to build Web pages!

The Web Model

A tool may be easy to use, but usually requires skill and training to be used well. This is certainly true of the tools involved in preparing and distributing information via hypertext documents and Internet Web servers. Just as designing a book or magazine requires experience and knowledge in the tools of design and typography, preparing well-designed, useful, and reliable Web resources requires an in-depth understanding of how the tools that deliver these resources work, and how to use them *well*. The intention of this book, as with the first three editions, is to help you develop this understanding. Given a basic feeling for what the Internet is—simply a system, rather like a courier service, for communicating digital information from one place to another—there are four essential concepts that you need to understand:

Uniform Resource Locators, or URLs. These are the means by which Internet resources are addressed in the World Wide Web. If you want to specify a resource on the Internet, you specify its URL.

The HyperText Markup Language, or HTML. This is the markup language with which World Wide Web hypertext documents are written and is what allows you to create hypertext links, fill-in forms, etcetera. Writing good HTML documents involves both technical issues (proper construction of the document) and design issues (ensuring the information content is clearly presented to the user).

The HyperText Transfer Protocol (HTTP) and HTTP client-server interactions. HTTP servers are designed specifically to distribute hypertext documents, and you must know how the underlying HTTP protocol works if you are to take advantage of its powerful features.

Server-side resource processing. This lets a user with a Web browser interact with resources lying on an HTTP server, by providing a tunnel through the server to these resources. This can be either through the so-called *Common Gateway Interface*, or through special modules built into the server.

The goal of this book and its companion Web site (www.wiley.com/compbooks/graham) is to explain these main concepts, and give you the tools you need to develop your own high-quality World Wide Web products. The remainder of this introduction looks briefly at these components and explains their basic features, and outlines the organization of the book. A figurative summary of these different components and the relationships between them is found in Figure I.1.

Uniform Resource Locators

Uniform Resource Locators, or URLs, are a naming scheme for specifying how and where to find any Internet server resource, such as those available from HTTP, FTP, or WAIS servers. For example, the URL that references the important file *bunny_hop.zip* in the directory */pub/web/browsers* on the FTP server *ftp.banzai.net* is simply:

```
ftp://ftp.banzai.net/pub/web/browsers/bunny_hop.zip
```

World Wide Web hypertext documents use URLs to reference other hypertext resources.

Figure I.1. Schematic diagram illustrating the essential components of the World Wide Web. The user's tool is the *browser*, or *user agent*— the program that understands and displays *HTML* documents. The browser can interpret *URLs* to determine where a resource is, and can use the URL-specified protocol to retrieve the resource. One of the most important protocols is *HTTP*—most WWW servers use this protocol and are called *HTTP* or *Web servers*. Using a Web server's *CGI* or *Common Gateway Interface* (or other, similar mechanisms), users can access other resources on the Web server, such as databases.

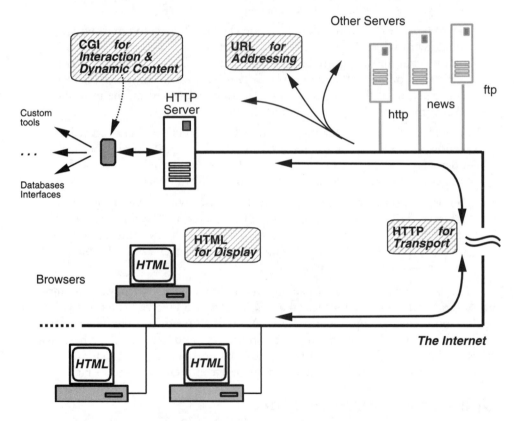

The HyperText Transfer Protocol

The *HyperText Transfer Protocol*, or HTTP, is an Internet communications protocol designed expressly for the rapid distribution of hypertext documents. Like other Internet tools such as FTP, WAIS, and Gopher, HTTP is a *client-server* protocol. In the client-server model a *client* program, running on the user's machine, sends a message requesting service to a *server* program running on another machine on the Internet. The server responds to the request by sending a message back to the client. In exchanging these messages, the client and server use a well-understood *protocol*. FTP, WAIS, and Gopher are other examples of Internet client-server protocols, all of which are accessible to a World Wide Web browser. However, the HTTP protocol was designed expressly for hypertext document delivery. Today, almost all Web services are delivered via HTTP servers.

Server-Side Resource Processing

At the simplest level, HTTP servers simply "serve up" files when clients request them. However, HTTP servers support additional important features:

- The ability to return to the client information generated by other programs running on the server.
- The ability to take data sent from the client and pass this information on to other programs on the server for further processing.

The special server-side utilities that implement these features are often called *gateway* programs, as they usually act as a gateway between the HTTP server and other resources accessible to the Web server, such as databases. Just as a server can access many files, an HTTP server can access many different gateway programs; in both cases you specify which (file or program) resource you want through a URL.

The interaction between the server and these gateway programs is governed by the *Common Gateway Interface (CGI)* specifications. Using the CGI specifications, a programmer can easily write simple programs or scripts to process user queries, interrogate databases, make images that respond to mouse clicks, and so on.

Many servers also let you program gateway-like functionality directly into the server, for increased speed and performance.

The HyperText Markup Language

The *HyperText Markup Language*, or *HTML*, is the language used to prepare Web hypertext documents. These are the documents you distribute on the World Wide Web and are what your human clients actually see. HTML contains commands, called *elements* or *tags*, to mark text as headings, paragraphs, lists, quotations, and so on. It also has tags for including images within the documents, for including fill-in forms that accept user input, and, most importantly, for including hypertext links connecting the document being read to other documents or Internet resources such as WAIS databases or anonymous FTP sites. It is this last feature that allows the user to click on a string of highlighted text and access a new document, an image, or a movie file from a computer thousands of miles away. And how does the HTML document specify where this other document is? Through a URL, which is included in the HTML markup instructions and which is used by the user's browser to find the designated resource.

What resources can URLs point to? They can be other HTML documents, pictures, sound files, movie files, or even database search engines. They can be downloadable programs in Java or other languages. They can be located on the user's computer or anywhere on the Internet. They can be accessed from HTTP servers or from FTP, Gopher, WAIS or other servers. The URL is an immensely flexible scheme, and in combination with HTML, yields an incredibly powerful package for preparing a web of hypertext documents linked to each other and to Internet resources around the world. This image of interlinked resources is in fact the vision that gave rise to the name, World Wide Web.

Overview of the Book

This book is an introduction to HTML, URLs, HTTP, and the CGI interface and to the design and preparation of resources for delivery via the World Wide Web. It begins with the HTML language. Almost every resource you prepare will be presented through an HTML document, so that your HTML presentation is your "face" to the world. It is crucial that you know how to write accurate HTML, and that you understand the design issues involved in creating attractive, useful documents, if you are to make a lasting impression on your audience and present your information clearly and concisely. It won't matter if your Internet resources are the best in the world if your presentation of them is badly designed, frustratingly slow to access, or difficult to use.

HTML is also an obvious place to start. You can write simple HTML documents and view them with a Web browser such as Internet Explorer, Netscape, Mosaic, or lynx without having to worry about CGI programs, HTTP servers, or other advanced features. You can also easily include, in your documents, URLs pointing to server resources around the world, and get used to how the system works: Browsers understand HTML *hypertext anchors* and the URLs they contain and have built-in software to talk to Internet servers using the proper protocols. You can accomplish a lot just by creating a few pages of HTML.

Chapter 1 is an elementary introduction to HTML and to the design issues involved in preparing HTML documents. This nontechnical chapter combines a brief overview of HTML with a discussion of some aspects of document design. The details of the HTML language and more sophisticated client-server issues are left to later chapters. Design issues are very important in developing good World Wide Web presentations. HTML documents are not like text documents, nor are they like traditional hypertext presentations, since they are limited by the varied capabilities of browsers and by the speed with which documents can be transported across the Internet. Chapter 2 discusses what this means in practice and gives guidelines for avoiding major HTML authoring mistakes. In most cases this is done using examples, with the important issues being presented in point form, so that you can easily extract the main points on first reading.

The issue of images and graphics also comes up often in Web page design: Images are an important addition to any Web page, either as simple images or as clickable imagemaps. However, they must be carefully processed to make them Web-friendly: The image files must be small, in the right format, and of the right "style" for display by computer. These and other image-related issues are discussed in Chapter 3.

At the same time, designing an HTML document *collection* is more than just writing pages—the design of a collection is critically important, and involves design issues that are not always apparent from the point of view of a single page. Chapter 4 looks in detail at the issues surrounding document collection design, and will help you through the process of designing a real document "web."

Chapter 5 takes a more practical look at Web design issues, and describes how to go about planning and implementing a site (determining why you are building a site defining your audience, planning the site layout, etc.), cost analysis (how to estimate the costs of different site components), and maintenance (how to maintain the site, and how to estimate the costs of this process). This chapter helps to connect the theory of Chapters 1 through 4 with the practical realities of designing, building, and maintaining a Web collection.

One point that is emphasized throughout the book is the importance of using correct HTML markup constructions when you create your HTML documents. Although HTML is a relatively straightforward language, there are many important rules specifying where tags can be placed. Ensuring that your documents obey these rules is the only way you can guarantee that they will be properly displayed on the many different browsers your site visitors may use. All too often, writers prepare documents that look wonderful on one browser but end up looking horrible, or even unviewable, on others.

Although some general rules for constructing valid HTML are included in Chapters 1 and 5, Chapters 6 and 7 and the references therein should be used as detailed guides to correct HTML. In particular, Chapter 6 presents a detailed exposition of the current "definitive" version of HTML, known as HTML 4, and of the allowed nesting of the different HTML markup instructions. Chapter 7 continues along this line, but looks at more advanced features, such as framed documents, advanced HTML forms and tables, proprietary HTML extensions by browser vendors, document scripting (JavaScript), cascading style sheets, font embedding, and experimental HTML features that are not yet formally part of the "standard" HTML language, or that are not yet widely supported. You can use Chapter 6 as a guide for writing universally viewable HTML documents, and Chapter 7 as a guide to advanced features, and as a preview of coming attractions.

Of course HTML is only a beginning. To truly take advantage of the Web you need to understand the interaction between browsers and HTTP servers, and be able to write server-side gateway programs that take advantage of this interaction. These topics are covered in Chapters 8 through 11. Chapter 8 describes the URL syntax in detail, while Chapter 9 delves into the specifics of the HTTP protocol used to communicate with HTTP servers, and discusses the basics of HTTP server operation. Chapter 10 then describes the details of the Common Gateway Interface (CGI) specification for writing server-side programs that interface with an HTTP server. Chapter 11 gives several concrete and clearly explained examples of real-world CGI programs, to show how the issues from Chapters 8 through 10 affect gateway program design. This chapter also contains a detailed reference list of resources useful in developing CGI or other server-based applications—many of these resources are available right over the Web, just waiting for you to go and get them.

Chapters 6 through 11 are the technical core of this book, and will be useful reference material when you are writing HTML documents, JavaScript scripts, or CGI programs.

Book Notation

In this book, HTML element names are generally given in boldface capital letters, for example, **DIV**. Similarly, the names of URL schemes are given in a boldface lowercase type, as in the phrase **http** URLs. A monospace font is generally used for explicit examples of HTML or other code, as in `<DIV CLASS="foo">` to denote a specific **DIV** element tag. Also, JavaScript and Cascading Style Sheet code, as well as system environment variable names, are given in a Courier font. Program, directory, and file names are often given in italics, to make them stand out from the text and to reduce confusion. However, this is not always the case, and in many situations the names are given in a regular, non-italicized font, to make the text easier to read.

URL references are written using the standard text font. However, to make the text shorter and easier to read, the http:// portion has been omitted from all **http** URLs. Most browsers (in particular, Netscape Navigator and Internet Explorer) assume that strings typed into the Location (Netscape) or Address (Microsoft) windows are **http** URLs, if no other protocol is specified. With some other browsers you will need to explicitly add the http:// portion. And, of course, you *always* need to add the http:// when you use a URL as an **HREF** value in an HTML document!

The Companion Web Site

www.utoronto.ca/ian/books/

www.wiley.com/compbooks/graham/

For those of you familiar with the previous editions, this fourth edition has been both significantly expanded and brought up-to-date. Indeed, there was so much new material, that not everything made it into print! Instead, the companion Web site, available at either of the URLs listed at the beginning of this section, has been used as an "adjunct" to the book, containing the more time-sensitive material (such as lists of software resources and descriptions, or lists of defined MIME types), plus additional content that simply didn't fit, or that simply "worked" better on the Web. For more information on what the site contains, go to the "About the Web Site" section at the end of the book.

INTRODUCTION TO THE HYPERTEXT

1

MARKUP LANGUAGE

What is a text markup language? A markup language is a way of describing, using instructions embedded within a document, what the different parts of the text mean or what they are supposed to look like. For example, suppose I want to indicate that the words "Frozen Albatross" should be displayed in boldface. A markup language might let you express this desire by typing

> *[beg_bold]* Frozen Albatross *[end_bold]*

meaning: "turn on boldface, write the words 'Frozen Albatross', and then turn off boldface." The text strings *[beg_bold]* and *[end_bold]* (in boldface italics for emphasis) are part of the markup language, which here turns boldface on and off. In general, a markup language has many such codes, or *tags*, to allow for a rich description of the document content and desired rendering.

Every electronic text processing tool uses some kind of markup language. Most of the time, this language is hidden from the user, although some word processors let you use a "reveal codes" command to display the actual markup commands—these commands are usually sequences of unprintable characters, unlike the printable characters used in the above example. Nevertheless, the idea is the same: A markup language is just a collection of codes, embedded in the document, that explain the meaning or desired formatting for the text.

Physical Versus Semantic Markup

There are two basic markup language approaches. The first is known as *physical markup*. In this approach, the markup tags explicitly say how the document should look, and contain commands such as: "*indent 0.5 inches, print the word 'Frozen Albatross' using an 18 point Arial font, . . .*" and so on. This is ideal for printing the text, but bad if printing is not the primary goal. Suppose, for example, you want to display the document on a computer that is not capable of the requested formatting. In this case, the physical formatting information is useless, and the computer has no easy way of determining a good alternative presentation for the text.

The second approach is known as *logical* or *semantic markup*. Here, the markup language defines the *meaning* of the text and not how it looks. Using semantic markup, the previous example might be written as

[beg_heading] Frozen Albatross *[end_heading]*

which means: "the enclosed text, 'Frozen Albatross', is a heading." The advantage is that the markup encodes the structural *meaning* of the text and not its physical representation. It is now easy to translate this heading into the formatting commands: "*indent 0.5 inches, print the word 'Frozen Albatross' using an 18 point arial font, . . .*" should you be printing the document to paper, or into other instructions should you be presenting the document on some other medium, such as a computer display or a Braille reader. Thus, although semantic formatting is more difficult (you have to think about what each part of the document means when you add the markup instructions), it is a much more powerful and flexible for describing text and has become the technique of choice for modern document processing systems. This includes modern word processors such as Word or WordPerfect that now incorporate many semantic markup features into their markup model. Indeed, Microsoft Word "Styles" are really just a way of defining semantic markup tags and relating that markup to desired physical formatting.

What is the *HyperText Markup Language,* or HTML? Despite all the hype, HTML is simply another markup language.* However, unlike the others, HTML is designed specifically for marking up electronic documents for delivery over the Internet and for presentation on a variety of different possible displays. As a result, HTML is very much a semantic markup language, designed to specify the *logical* organization of a text document; there are very few physical formatting commands in HTML. In addition, HTML has important extensions that allow for *hypertext links* from one document to another, as well as other extensions that allow for user input and user interaction.

It is important to stress these design principles, because they explain the large differences between authoring with HTML and writing documents using word processors. HTML was *not* designed to be the language of a "What You See Is What You Get" (WYSIWYG) word processor such as Word or WordPerfect. Instead, HTML takes a "What You Get Is What You Meant" (WYGIWYM) approach, such that authors must construct documents with sections of text (and/or images and other embedded objects, such as Java applets) marked as *logical* entities, such as titles, paragraphs, lists, quotations, and so on. The interpretation of these marked elements is then largely left up to the browser displaying the document. This approach builds enormous flexibility into the system and allows the same document to be displayed by browsers of very different capabilities.

---

*The rules of HTML are defined using a language called the *Standard Generalized Markup Language* or SGML. SGML is an extremely sophisticated tool for defining markup languages—HTML is just one example of this process. SGML is discussed in a bit more detail in Chapter 6.

Consequently, there are browsers for machines ranging from fancy UNIX graphics computers to plain-text terminals such as VT-100s or old 8086-based DOS computers. As an example, in viewing the same well-designed HTML document, a graphical browser like Netscape Navigator may present major headings in a large, slanted, and boldfaced font (since elegant typesetting is possible with graphics displays) and may include attractive inlined graphical elements indicated by the HTML markup, while a text-only browser like lynx may just center the title, use a single font for all the text, and display text alternative descriptions to the images; and a Braille browser would present the same text information in a completely different way. However, all these presentations will reproduce the logical organization and meaning of the original text document, since this information was built in using the HTML language.

Specifying Formatting—Cascading Style Sheets

Of course, a page designer can ignore the semantic markup approach and use embedded images, tables, and formatting-specific HTML tags to define quite precise page layout and design—albeit with a lot of hard work! However, this comes at the price of portability, accessibility, and speed—documents so designed will inevitably display poorly on some browsers or under some conditions (e.g., when image loading is disabled). Indeed, using large quantities of formatting-specific markup most often leads to large, slow-to-download documents. Clearly, a designer in the real world must make compromises between these issues, aware of the strengths and weaknesses of each design choice. The goal of this book is to give you the tools to make these choices wisely.

The modern approach is to use a second language (known as a *style sheet*) to define formatting details and to apply the instructions of this language to an HTML document while it is being displayed. The latest versions of the Netscape and Microsoft browsers (Versions 4) support a style sheet language known as *Cascading Style Sheets*, or *CSS*. Using CSS, an author can define how particular HTML elements should be formatted, positioned, and displayed, without having this information coded into the HTML markup. Then, when the page is displayed, the browser will use the instructions to adjust the formatting and layout according to the rules specified in the CSS style sheet.

CSS style sheets only work if the HTML markup is rigorously correct—that is, if the placement of the HTML elements follow the rules of the HTML language. Moreover, style sheets only work with the latest versions of Web browsers—the CSS instructions are totally ignored by Netscape Navigator 3 (and, for the most part, Internet Explorer 3) or earlier, so that HTML-specific formatting is needed for these older browsers.

This book focuses on HTML and on the structural layout control possible via HTML. It does so in the framework of accurate HTML markup, the goal being documents that will continue to work with future HTML standards or with CSS.

Indeed, with proper HTML markup, it is often quite easy to "add" style sheets on top of documents and define additional stylistic formatting without needing to change the underlying HTML markup.

CSS is described in a bit more detail in Chapter 7. However, CSS is complex, and the section in Chapter 7 provides no more than a brief (albeit useful) overview. If you are interested in learning more about style sheets, I suggest you buy a book on the subject—my own *HTML Stylesheet Sourcebook* would, of course, be an excellent choice. However, to be a little less biased, additional CSS book references are found at the end of Chapter 7.

HTML as an Extensible Language

HTML is designed to be *extensible*. This simply means that new features, commands, and functionality can be added to the language without "breaking" older documents that don't use these new features. In fact, HTML is a rapidly evolving language, with new features being added on a regular basis. This book summarizes most of the current and forthcoming commands, and provides references to other sources that will allow you to keep up with the changes.

Since HTML is constantly evolving, it is important to have a way of indicating the version of the language being used. This is done through the *version number* of the HTML specification. The very first definition of HTML was called Version 1, or HTML 1.0. This quickly evolved into the next "definitive" version of HTML, known as Version 2, or HTML 2.0, and from there to HTML 3.2. All browsers, at a minimum, support the HTML 3.2 standard. The newest "definitive" version of HTML is known as HTML 4.0. This standard is described in detail in Chapters 6 and 7. Note, however, that many of the newest features of HTML 4 are not widely supported. Chapters 6 and 7 are careful to note where this is the case.

As mentioned, HTML is a moving target, and there is much effort underway to add new features and improve old ones. Chapter 7 discusses many of these up-and-coming changes, in addition to advanced issues such as FRAMEs, document scripting (e.g., JavaScript and VBScript) and style sheets. However, authors should be aware that if they use some of the advanced features discussed in Chapter 7, there will be people who cannot properly view the document content.

Overview of the HyperText Markup Language

So what does an HTML document look like? A simple example is shown in Figure 1.1. As you can see, this looks like a plain text document. In fact, that is exactly what it is—an HTML document contains only the printable characters that you ordinarily type. Consequently, you can prepare an HTML document using a simple text editor, such as the NotePad editor on a Windows PC,

TeachText on the Macintosh, or vi on a UNIX workstation. You don't need a special word processor or fancy HTML editor to create HTML documents—although, of course, such tools can speed up the writing process!

Markup Elements and Tags

The things that make an HTML document special are the HTML markup *tags*. These are strings of text enclosed by a less than and greater than sign (<...>), and are the markup instructions that explain what each part of the document means. For example, the tag <H1> indicates the *start* of a level 1 heading, while the </H1> tag marks the *end* of a heading of level 1. Thus, the text string

```
<H1>This is a Heading</H1>
```

marks the string "This is a Heading" as a level 1 heading (there are six possible heading levels, from **H1** to **H6**). Note how a forward slash inside the tag indicates an end tag.

An HTML document is said to be composed of *elements*. For example, the string

```
<h1>This is a Heading</H1>
```

is an **H1** element, consisting of an **H1** start tag, the enclosed text, and an **H1** end tag. You will also often see an **H1** element referred to as the *container* of a heading, since the start and stop tags *contain* the text that makes up the heading.

Some elements, instead of being containers, are *empty*. This simply means they do not affect a block of text and do not need an end tag. An example is the **BR** element in Figure 1.1, in the line:

```
some kind of <STRONG> exciting <BR> fact</STRONG>...
```

The tag <BR> forces a line break at the location of the tag, just after the word "exciting" (see Figures 1.2 and 1.3). The **BR** element does not affect any enclosed text (a line break does not "contain" anything), so an end tag is not required.

Tag Names Are Case-Insensitive

Note that the names inside the tags are *case-insensitive*, so that <h1> is equivalent to <H1>, and <STRONG> is equivalent to <StROng>. However, capitalization is recommended to make the tags stand out clearly (to you, as Web page author) relative to the text being marked up.

Element Attributes

Sometimes, an element takes *attributes* that define properties or special information about the element. Attributes are much like variables and are usually assigned *values* that define these special properties. For example, the element

```
<H1 ALIGN="center">This is a Heading</H1>
```

takes an **ALIGN** attribute with the value "center," which states that, where possible, the heading should be centered on the display. Note that attributes only appear in the start tag of an element.

Another example is found in the **IMG** element, used to include an image within an HTML document. An **IMG** element appears via the tag:

```
<IMG SRC="filename.gif">
```

The **SRC** attribute specifies the name of the image file to be included in the document (actually a Uniform Resource Locator [URL] "pointing" to the image file—URLs are discussed in Chapter 2 and, in detail, Chapter 8). The attribute name, like the element name, is case-insensitive. Thus the above line could equally well be written as either of:

```
<iMg src="filename.gif">
<iMg SrC="filename.gif">
```

However, the value *assigned* to an **SRC** attribute is *case-sensitive*; case-sensitivity can be preserved by enclosing the string in quotation marks. As you may have noticed, the **IMG** element is empty (like the **BR** element), since it merely inserts an image and does not affect a block of text.

HTML as a Structured Language

HTML is a *structured* language, which means that there are rules for where elements can and cannot go. These rules are present to enforce an overall *logical structure* upon the document. For example, a heading element like `<H1>...</H1>` can contain text, text marked for emphasis, line breaks, inline images, and hypertext anchors (discussed in Example 2), but it cannot contain any other HTML element. As a result, the markup

```
<H1><H2>...text ... </H2></H1>
```

is invalid. Obviously, it does not make sense for a heading to "contain" a list or another heading, and the HTML language rules reflect this reality. In addition, elements can never overlap—this means that tag placement like

```
      ┌─────────────────────────────────────────┐
      │  ┌──────────────────────────────────┐    │
<EM> <H2>   EM and H2 overlap -- this is illegal </EM>  </H2>
```

is illegal. There are many such structural rules; they are given in detail in Chapters 6 and 7. This chapter and Chapter 2 illustrate the most obvious cases.

Summary

1. HTML documents are divided into elements. Elements are usually marked by *start* and *end tags*, and take the form `<NAME>.. some text ..</NAME>`, where the enclosed text is the content of the element.

Some elements do not affect a block of text and are hence called "empty" elements. Empty elements do not require end tags.

2. Some elements can take *attributes*, which appear within the start tag and define properties of the element. For example, heading elements can take the **ALIGN** attribute to specify how the heading should be aligned on the display (e.g. `<H1 ALIGN="center"> text .. </H1>` to center-align a heading).

3. Elements names and attribute names are *case-insensitive*. Thus, `<NAME ATTRIBUTE="string">`, `<NamE ATtRiButE="string">`, and `<name attribute="string">` are equivalent. However, the attribute value (here the string string) may be *case-sensitive*. If you suspect the value is case-sensitive, you should enclose it inside double quotation marks (`"..."`).

4. The placement of elements in a document must obey the HTML nesting rules that specify where elements can and cannot appear. For example, a heading element, such as **H1**, cannot contain a list or another heading, but can contain a hypertext anchor. In addition, elements *cannot overlap*. Details of the nesting rules for HTML elements are provided in Chapters 6 and 7.

Example 1: A Simple HTML Document

At this point, it is easiest to get a feel for the language and for HTML documents by looking at some examples; the details of the language are found in Chapter 6. Figure 1.1 shows a simple but complete HTML document and is designed to illustrate both the basic document structure and some of the simpler markup elements. This document was created using a simple text editor and was saved in a file named *ex1.html*. The *.html* filename extension is important, as browsers and Web/HTTP servers understand files with this suffix to be HTML documents as opposed to "plain" text documents. On PCs running Windows 3.1 or DOS (yes—some people still use DOS), the extension is *.htm*, since four-letter extensions are not possible. More will be said later about extension names and what they mean.

The rendering of Figure 1.1 by two different browsers is shown in Figures 1.2 and 1.3. All browsers allow you to load and view files created on your own computer, even if you are not connected to the Internet, simply by giving the browser the name of the local file. To view the example using the lynx browser, you type

```
lynx ex1.html
```

at the command prompt. With graphical browsers like Netscape Navigator and Microsoft Internet Explorer, start the program, select the "Open File..." or other similar menu, usually from the "File" pull-down menu at the top of the window, and then select the desired file.

Figure 1.1 Contents of the example HTML document *ex1.html*. The rendering of this document by different browsers is shown in Figures 1.2 and 1.3.

```
<HTML>
<HEAD>
<TITLE> This is the Title of the Document </TITLE>
</HEAD>
<BODY>
<H1> This is a Heading</H1>

<P>Hello.  This is not a very exciting document.
I
    bet you were expecting <EM>poetry</EM>, or

some kind of <STRONG>exciting <BR> fact</STRONG> about the Internet and
the World Wide Web.

<P>Sorry.  No such luck.       This document
does
contain examples of HTML markup, for example, here is an "unordered
list":
<UL>
    <LI>One item of the list,
    <LI>A second list item  <LI>A third list item that goes on and on and
    on to indicate that the lists can wrap right around the page and still
    be nicely formatted by the browsers.
    <LI>The final item.
</UL>
<p>Lists are exciting. You can also have ordered lists (the items are numbered)
and description lists.
<HR>
<p>And you can draw horizontal lines, which are useful for dividing
sections.
</BODY>
</HTML>
```

Figures 1.2 and 1.3 show this document rendered by two different WWW browsers. Figure 1.2 shows the document as displayed by the graphical Netscape Navigator browser, while Figure 1.3 shows what you get from the character-based browser lynx.

Figure 1.2 Netscape Navigator 3.0 rendering of the HTML document *ex1.html* (the HTML document is listed in Figure 1.1).

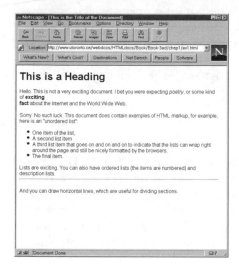

Figure 1.3 Lynx rendering of the HTML document *ex1.html* (the HTML document is listed in Figure 1.1).

Document Structure: The HTML Element

Since HTML is a structural language, the tags and elements are best analyzed by starting from the outside and working in. The outermost element, which encompasses the entire document, is named **HTML**. This element indicates that the enclosed text is an HTML document. This may seem unnecessary, but it is useful in some contexts where the content of a file cannot be determined from the file-name—there are actually several other markup languages that look superficially like HTML. The HTML tag lets software easily distinguish between these different types of documents.

The Document HEAD

The next element inside the **HTML** element is named **HEAD**. The **HEAD** element is a container for information *about* the document, such as the **TITLE**. **HEAD** information, if it is displayed, is not presented as part of the document. Looking at Figures 1.2 and 1.3, notice that the content of the **TITLE** element is displayed apart from the text. With Netscape Navigator the title is displayed in the frame of the window, while with lynx, the name is displayed at the top of the screen and to the right.

The **HEAD** must be the first element inside the document, right after the `<HTML>` tag.

Document TITLE—Short and Descriptive

Because it is displayed separately from the text and usually in a restricted space such as a window title bar, a small fixed-size text box, or as a single line at the top of a text screen, the **TITLE** should be both descriptive and short. If a **TITLE** is too long, it will simply not fit. The **TITLE** should be descriptive because when users store a visited location in a Web browser's *bookmark* or *favorites* list, they are actually recording the location of the document along with the **TITLE**. The **TITLE** is then the *only* stored information that describes the item referenced by the bookmark. Authors should thus create **TITLEs** to be descriptive of the documents, so that the pages can be easily located and identified in a bookmark list.

The Document BODY

After the **HEAD**, comes the **BODY**. This element contains *all* the text and other material that is to be displayed. Notice how this is true in Figure 1.1, where all the displayed material lies between the `<BODY>` and `</BODY>` tags.

Why a HEAD and a BODY?

Why bother with this **HEAD/BODY** separation? Recall that HTML is designed to organize documents in a logical way. It then makes sense to separate the document itself (the **BODY**) from information *about* the document (the **HEAD**). In addition to **TITLE**, there are several other **HEAD** elements (discussed in Chapter 6) that describe the relationships between a document and other documents (the **LINK** element) or provide indexing or other meta-information about the document (the **META** element). These can be extremely useful for indexing and cataloging document collections as well as for other organizational purposes.

Heading Elements

The first element in the **BODY** is an **H1** element. **H1** stands for a level 1 *heading* element. In HTML, headings come in six levels, **H1** through **H6**, with **H1** being the highest (most important) heading level, and **H6** the lowest. A browser must then take the **H1** element content and display it in a manner appropriate to a major heading. For example, Netscape Navigator (Figure 1.2) shows the heading

```
<H1>This is a Heading</H1>
```

as a large, boldfaced string of characters, left-justified and separated by a wide vertical space from the following text. Lynx, on the other hand (Figure 1.3), shows it as a capitalized text string, centered on the page. This comparison is designed to remind you of the point made at the beginning of this section: Different browsers may render the same elements in very different ways. HTML markup instructions are designed to specify the logical structure of the document far more than the physical layout. If documents take advantage of this feature, then the browser is free to find the best way to display items, such as headings, consistent with its own limitations.

Interpretation of Spaces, Tabs, and New Lines

Referring back to Figure 1.1, review the next few lines of text:

```
<P>Hello.  This is not a very exciting document.
I
    bet you were expecting <EM>poetry</EM>, or

some kind of <STRONG>exciting <BR> fact</STRONG> about the Internet and
the World Wide Web.
```

As shown in Figures 1.2 and 1.3, these lines are rendered as a continuous paragraph of text, ignoring the blank lines, extra spaces, and tabs that are present in the original file. The rendering of an HTML document largely ignores extra spaces, tabs, and blank lines, and treats any combination of these characters as a single word space. This means that extra space characters, line breaks, and indentations can be used to organize the logical layout of an HTML document, making it easier to see the placement of the tags relative to the text. This is done in the bottom half of Figure 1.1 (note how the `<LI>` list items are indented inside the list) and in most of the examples in this book. This concept will be familiar to anyone who has written computer programs or used typesetting languages such as TeX or Scribe and is equivalent to using spaces and tabs to make a computer program easier to read.

Character Highlighting

The first sentence in Figure 1.1 contains two additional elements: **EM** for *emphasis* and **STRONG** for *strong* emphasis. Note that these are *logical* descriptions of the enclosed text and do not directly specify a physical formatting style. The HTML specifications recommend that text marked with **EM** be italicized and that text marked with **STRONG** be rendered as bold. This is exactly what is done by Netscape Navigator, as shown in Figure 1.2. Lynx, on the other hand, renders both **EM** and **STRONG** as underlined text (Figure 1.3). Character-based programs such as lynx can really do only four things to text—underline it, boldface it, force it to capital letters, or display it in reverse video. Given these limitations, lynx cannot render as distinct all the different elements in HTML. It therefore renders **EM** and **STRONG** in the same way. On the other hand, a text-to-speech converter would have no problem distinguishing **EM** and **STRONG**, and could simply modify the spoken intonation to account for the specified emphasis. Unfortunately, it is hard to include a text-to-speech example in a book!

Highlighting elements, such as **EM** and **STRONG**, can be placed almost anywhere you find regular text, the only exception being within the **TITLE** element in the **HEAD**. The content of a **TITLE** element can only be text; there can be no HTML elements inside it. Recall that the text inside a **TITLE** is not part of the document, but simply a text string providing information about the document. Thus markup has no meaning here.

HTML has several other logical highlighting elements, such as **CODE** for computer code, **KBD** for keyboard input, **VAR** for a variable, **DFN** for the defining instance of a term, **CITE** for a short citation, and so on. HTML also has *physical* highlighting elements, such as **B** for boldfaced, **I** for italics, **TT** for typewriter font (fixed-width characters), and **U** for an underlined font. Where sensible, specify logical meaning for text strings rather than these physical styles: Logical styles assign true meaning to the associated text and give a browser more flexibility in determining the best presentation.

Physical highlighting tags are particularly useful when translating from a word processor format that already contains tags for boldface, italics, or other physical styles, since these styles can be directly converted to their HTML equivalents. They are also useful for specifying physical formatting that is purely decorative and for which there is no important structural meaning.

Paragraphs and Vertical Spacing

Look at the next line, beginning with the string <P> Sorry.:

```
<P>Sorry.  No such luck.     This document
does
contain examples of HTML markup, for example, here is an "unordered
list":
<UL>
```

The `<P>` tag marks the beginning of a paragraph and is best thought of as marking the start of a paragraph container. Most browsers interpret the `<P>` that starts a paragraph by skipping a line, as shown in Figures 1.2 and 1.3. Note also that a paragraph mark can be anywhere in a line. For example, the three lines (note the blank line between the two lines of text):

```
the World Wide Web.


<P>Sorry.  No such luck.       This document
```

can equally well be written as:

```
the World Wide Web.  <P>Sorry.  No such luck.  This document
```

Recall that the rendering of an HTML document depends only on where the markup tags are located relative to the text they describe. Of course, putting `<P>` at the beginning of a line makes it easier to read the "raw" HTML, and is thus a good idea.

Notice that Figure 1.1 does not include `</P>` ending tags to mark the ends of the paragraphs. In HTML, ending paragraph tags are optional. The rule is that a paragraph is ended by the next `<P>` tag that starts another paragraph or by any other tag that starts another block of text, such as a heading tag (`<Hn>`), a quotation tag (`<BLOCKQUOTE>`), or list tags (`<UL>`, `<OL>`, `<DIR>`, `<MENU>`, `<DL>`). Thus, the paragraph ending with the words unordered list is ended by the following `<UL>` tag that marks the beginning of an *unordered list* element.

Don't Use Empty Paragraphs

The HTML specification recommends that, if two or more adjacent elements describing the logical structure of the document require some special vertical spacing, only one of the spacing values (the larger) should be used and the other should be ignored. This implies that constructions like

```
<p><p><p><p>  This is a paragraph
```

should yield at most a single paragraph break. If you enter markup such as this, you will find that the spacing is rendered differently by different Web browsers: Some will leave extra space, and some will not.

Adding Extra Vertical Space

If you really need extra vertical space, try using consecutive line break elements:

```
<BR> <BR> <BR>
```

This is valid HTML, and it usually yields the extra spacing you require. The long-term solution for detailed formatting is found in *style sheets*, discussed in Chapter 7.

Lists

Having beaten paragraphs into the ground, we now move on to the next component, namely the list of items seen in Figures 1.2 and 1.3. HTML supports several types of lists, the example here being an unordered (bulleted) list. An unordered list element begins with the tag <UL> and ends with a </UL>:

```
<UL>
    <LI>One item of the list,
    <LI>A second list item  <LI>A third list item that goes on and on and
    on to indicate that the lists can wrap right around the page and still
    be nicely formatted by the browsers.
    <LI>The final item.
</UL>
<p> Lists are exciting. You can also have ordered lists (the items are numbered)
```

Both the start and stop tags are mandatory—unlike the closing tag for paragraphs the </UL> that ends an unordered list cannot be omitted. Other list elements include the *ordered* list element **OL** and the *description* or glossary list element **DL**. These elements are discussed in Chapter 6: The **DL** element is illustrated in Figures 6.25 and 6.26, while **OL** is illustrated in Figures 6.27 and 6.28.

Like paragraphs, lists cannot be empty. However, unlike paragraphs, **UL** or **OL** lists can contain only one thing—**LI** *list elements*. In turn, **LI** elements cannot be empty, as every list item must consist of some text; however, if you want a blank item, just put in a space character or a **BR** element. The ending </LI> tag is not required, as the end of a list item is implied by the next <LI> or by the </UL> tag that finally terminates the list, as illustrated in this example.

An unordered lists is simply that—an unordered lists of items, each item marked by an indentation of some type and a star or bullet. It is up to the browser to format list items nicely and, as you can see in Figures 1.2 and 1.3, lynx and Netscape Navigator do very similar things. However, you will also note that these browsers do different things to the spacing that surrounds the lists; such browser-to-browser variations are common.

As mentioned, the only thing that can go directly inside a **UL** element is an **LI** element. Thus, the following markup

```
<UL>
    here is some non-list text inside a list
    <LI>Here is list item 1.
</UL>
```

is invalid. An **LI** element, however, can contain lots of things. For example, an **LI** element can contain text, the **IMG** element (for inline images), text emphasis (such as the **STRONG** element), another list, paragraphs, and even a fill-in HTML form. It cannot contain a heading element. Heading elements can only be directly inside the **BODY**, or inside a **FORM** (for fill-in forms) or a **BLOCKQUOTE** (for quoted text) element. **FORMs** and **BLOCKQUOTEs** are discussed in Examples 6 and 7 in Chapter 2.)

TIP: Avoid Extra Spaces Inside Elements

Do not leave spaces between the `<LI>` tag and the content of the list item. This is because the space will be treated as a whitespace, which will affect the indentation for the particular list item. Thus, the two items

```
<LI>   Item 1
<LI>Item 2
```

will be indented differently due to the extra whitespace in front of "Item 1." This is a subtle point, but will come up often when you are trying to format list items (**LI**) or table cells (**TD**, **TH**, discussed in Examples 8 and 9 in Chapter 2). In general, it is safest to omit spaces between the tags and the enclosed text.

Lists Within Lists

You can include lists within lists. For example, the markup

```
<OL>
    <LI>ordered list Item 1
    <LI>ordered list Item 2
      <UL>
         <LI>unordered item under ordered list item 2
         <LI>unordered item under ordered list item 2
      </UL>
    <LI>ordered list Item 3
</OL>
```

indicates an ordered list that in turn contains an unordered list under the second ordered list item.

Horizontal Rules

The final element in Figure 1.1 is the **HR** or horizontal rule element. This element simply draws a horizontal dividing line across the page, and it is useful for dividing sections. This is also an empty element, since it does not act on a body of text.

Lessons from Example 1

1. Titles should be short and descriptive of the document content.
2. HTML is a hierarchical set of markup instructions. The outer layer of this organization, showing the basic document structure, is:

```
<HTML>
   <HEAD>
   .. document head ..
   </HEAD>
   <BODY>
   .. document body ..
   </BODY>
</HTML>
```

The **TITLE** goes inside the **HEAD**, while the text to be displayed goes inside the **BODY**.

3. Extra white spaces, tabs, and blank lines are irrelevant in the formatting of a document; the only thing that affects the display of the document by the browser is the placement of the HTML markup *tags*. You should, however, avoid spaces between start tags and the text being marked up by the tags—this can lead to extra space, for example, between a list bullet and the content of a list item.

4. Heading elements (**H1** through **H6**) can only go inside the **BODY**, **FORM**, or **BLOCKQUOTE** elements.

5. **UL** and **OL** lists can contain only **LI** (list item) elements. The **LI** elements can contain text, images, and other lists, but cannot contain headings.

Example 1 Exercises

It is time to start creating HTML documents! Using your favorite text or HTML editor (it doesn't matter which one), start creating Web pages—you can use the examples in this book as a starting point, if you wish. All the example documents in this book can be found at either of the URLs:

www.utoronto.ca/ian/books/html4ed/

www.wiley.com/compbooks/graham/

Once you've created a page, save it on your computer as a disk file. Make sure that you save it with the filename extension *.html* or *.htm*. Remember that a Web browser uses the filename extension to determine the type of the file, and these two extensions imply an HTML document. Once the file is saved to disk, you should start up a Web browser and view the document. All browsers provide an "Open File..." mechanism for loading in and viewing files from the local disk. If you have more than one browser, try viewing the document with these different programs—this helps you appreciate (and adjust for!) the different capabilities of the different browsers.

Once the file is created and can be displayed by the browser, it is time to start editing the document, adding headings, lists, and other elements. In this process, concentrate on following the rules of HTML. Chapter 6 gives these rules in detail, so you can check there if you are not sure about the placement of a given element.

Example 2: Simple Images and Hypertext Links

Example 1 illustrated how HTML can be used to mark up the logical organization of a single document. This second example illustrates the hypertext capabilities of HTML. The example consists of two documents, *ex2a.html,* and *ex2b.html*, with a hypertext link from one to the other. The documents are shown in Figures 1.4 and 1.9, respectively. *Ex2a.html* also includes inline images, here used to illustrate some of the issues involved when using images in your documents. Notice how space characters are used to indent and align the tags, in order to make the raw HTML easier to read.

The Example Document

We will first examine Figure 1.4, namely the contents of the file *ex2a.html*. The first paragraph contains only text. The second paragraph is similar, except that it contains three images, included via the **IMG** element `<IMG SRC="home.gif">`. *Home.gif* is a GIF format image file; I know this by the *.gif* filename extension (and, of course, because I created it). GIF files are one of the common image formats that can be included within HTML documents.

Rendering of the Example Document

Renderings of the document *ex2a.html* (listed in Figure 1.4) are shown in Figures 1.5 through 1.8. Figure 1.5 and 1.6 show the document as presented by the Netscape Navigator 4, while Figure 1.7 shows the view using the Internet Explorer 4 browser, and Figure 1.8 shows the view displayed by lynx. Many of the differences between these views are simply due to the different window sizes and fonts. Still, there are other differences that warrant mention.

Inline Images

Note the appearance of the images in Figures 1.5 and 1.7. By default, an image is included as if it were a large letter or word inline with the surrounding text, deforming the line spacing to ensure that no text overlaps the image. Also by default the bottom of the image aligns with the bottom of the line of text leading up to the image. Note that there is no wrapping or flowing of the text around the image and, since there is no way of guaranteeing how the document will be formatted and displayed, no guarantee that an image embedded in the middle of a sentence will appear in a particular place on the screen. Indeed, the only way to

Figure 1.4 Contents of the example HTML document *ex2a.html*. The rendering of this document by the Netscape Navigator, Internet Explorer, and lynx browsers is shown in Figures 1.5 to 1.8.

```
<HTML>
<HEAD>
    <TITLE> Example 2A, Showing IMG and Hypertext Links </TITLE>
</HEAD>
<BODY>

<H1> Example 2A: Image Inclusion and Hypertext Links </H1>

<P> Greetings from the exciting world of HTML Example documents. OK,
    so text is not so exciting.  But how about some pictures!

<P> There are many ways to fit in the image.  For example, you
    fit it in this way:
    <IMG SRC="home.gif" ALIGN="top">, this way
    <IMG SRC="home.gif" ALIGN="middle"> or this way
    <IMG SRC="home.gif" ALIGN="bottom">.

<P> Another important thing: you can make
    <a href="ex2b.html">hypertext links</a> to other files.<BR>
     This <a href="ex2b.html"> second link </a> has spaces
    between the start and stop tags, and the enclosed text.<BR>
    You can also place images inside hypertext links,  for example:
    <a href="ex2b.html"><IMG SRC="sright.xbm" ALIGN="middle"></a>.<BR>
    You can get rid of the border around the image by setting a
    BORDER="0" attribute on the IMG element. For example:
    <a href="ex2b.html"><IMG SRC="sright.xbm" BORDER="0" ALIGN="middle"></a>.

<P> Lastly, here is a row of images:
 <IMG src="home.gif" alt="[Home Icon]"> <IMG src="home.gif" alt="[Home Icon]">
 <IMG src="home.gif" alt="[Home Icon]"> <IMG src="home.gif" alt="[Home Icon]">
 <IMG src="home.gif" alt="[Home Icon]"> <IMG src="home.gif" alt="[Home Icon]">
 <IMG src="home.gif" alt="[Home Icon]"> <IMG src="home.gif" alt="[Home Icon]">
</BODY></HTML>
```

guarantee image placement is to make the image element the first item following a paragraph (or other) break; then, it will always be the first item on a line.

Figure 1.5 Netscape Navigator 4 rendering of the HTML document *ex2a.html* (the document is listed in Figure 1.4).

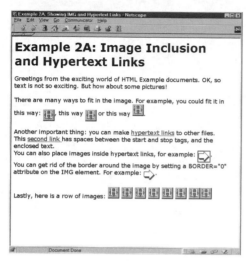

This point is illustrated by the last line of *ex2a.html* (Figure 1.4), which is simply a row of inline images. Note that these wrap to best fit the width of the screen, just as if they were a sequence of words (Figures 1.5 and 1.7). Consequently, if the

Figure 1.6 Netscape Navigator 4 rendering of the HTML document *ex2a.html*, but with image loading disabled (the document is listed in Figure 1.4).

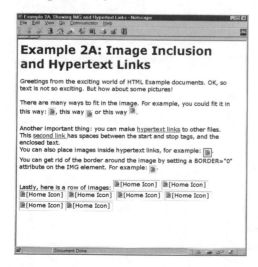

Figure 1.7 Internet Explorer 4 rendering of the HTML document *ex2a.html* (the document is listed in Figure 1.4).

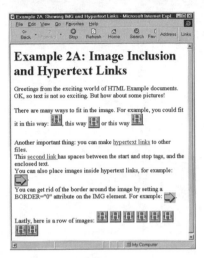

user changes the size of the browser window, these icons are repositioned. This is another example of the wide variation possible between different renderings of the same document.

Figure 1.8 Lynx browser rendering of the HTML document *ex2a.html* (the document is listed in Figure 1.4).

Fortunately, there are more sophisticated image placement mechanisms that permit better control of image positioning and alignment. Some of these are discussed later in this example, while others are described in Chapters 2 and 6.

Aligning Images with Text

The **IMG** element can take an optional **ALIGN** attribute to specify how the image should be aligned on the page. Several values control the placement of the image with respect to the surrounding text. The effects of the three most common values are illustrated in Figures 1.5 and 1.7, using the three "Home" icons (I am afraid I am not a great graphic artist). The first, **ALIGN**="top", aligns the top of the image with the top of the text, while the **ALIGN**="middle" value aligns the middle of the image with the bottom of the text, and **ALIGN**="bottom" aligns the bottom of the image with the bottom of the text. The latter is the default behavior when **ALIGN** is not specified.

The four additional values textop, absmiddle, baseline, and absbottom also control the positioning of the image with respect to the adjacent line of text. Also supported are the alignment attribute values **ALIGN**="left" and **ALIGN**="right", which cause an image to "float" with subsequent text flowing around the image. These aspects of layout control are described in detail in Chapters 2 and 6.

No Graphics?—The ALT Attribute

Most graphical browsers let the user disable the loading of images (although this feature may be hard to find, particularly in more recent versions of Navigator or Internet Explorer). Disabling image loading can substantially speed up the appearance of a page, since the browser does not need to wait for all the images before displaying the text. Figure 1.6 shows the display by Netscape Navigator when image loading is disabled, while Figure 1.8 shows the lynx interpretation—lynx is a text-only browser and cannot display images. Netscape Navigator replaces the missing images by symbols that denote a missing image, while lynx replaces each occurrence of an image with the text string [IMAGE]. In neither case is the replacement very descriptive, but at least it tells users that they are missing something.

A far better choice is to use the **IMG** element **ALT** attribute to provide a real text alternative to the image. This is essential for any browser that cannot display images and is extremely useful for graphical browsers with disabled image loading. The usage is simply:

```
<IMG SRC="image.file" ALT="[A text alternative to the Image]">
```

The string specified for **ALT** is case-sensitive and thus must be enclosed in double quotes. It is also common (but not necessary) to surround the string with square brackets, as is done at the bottom of *ex2a.html*, where the attribute **ALT**="[Home Icon]" is used with all the inline images. The resulting text rendering is shown in Figures 1.6 and 1.8. Note how the text effectively indicates the content of the missing image.

TIP: Purely Decorative Image?—Use an Empty ALT

Given a purely decorative image with no important meaning, you should use the **ALT** attribute to assign an empty description, that is:

```
<IMG SRC="decoration.gif" ALT="">
```

This means that a user with a text-only browser will see nothing. This is far better than seeing the string "[IMAGE]", or an image symbol, both of which leave a reader wondering if the author forgot to provide a description of an important part of the document.

ALT Text as Pop-up Help

Finally, with Netscape Navigator 4, as well as Internet Explorer 3 or 4, **ALT** attribute content is displayed as "pop-up" text (much like a tool tip in Windows and Mac programs) whenever the mouse pointer rests on top of an image. Thus, the **ALT** text can serve as a reminder of the role of an image—an example is shown in Figure 1.18. This is very useful when an image is used as the start of a hypertext link, as discussed later in this example.

Browser Loading of Images

How does the browser actually obtain images and complete the document? The browser first obtains the HTML document and then looks for **IMG** elements. If it finds **IMG** elements, the browser makes additional connections to the server(s), indicated by the **SRC** attributes, to obtain the required image files. Thus, a single document containing ten images will require 11 distinct connections to load the complete document content. Needless to say, this can be slow, particularly if the browser has a slow network connection to the server.

In addition, the way the browser formats the page can make the text rendering process incredibly slow. This is because browsers cannot properly format a page until they knows the sizes of the images being included—without this knowledge, the browser does not know how big a "box" to set aside for each image. For many browsers, the result is a blank display, with nothing being rendered until the browser knows the size of everything to fit on the page. This can be incredibly annoying to the reader. It would therefore be nice if the browser knew the size of the images before they actually arrived—in that way, the browser could format the document, leaving appropriate sized "boxes" on the page to be filled in by the arriving graphics. Indeed this is possible via **HEIGHT** and **WIDTH** attributes.

Image Size—WIDTH and HEIGHT Attributes

The **IMG** element supports optional **HEIGHT** and **WIDTH** attributes that define the size, in pixels, of the space to reserve on the display for the image. For example, if you have an image 500 pixels high and 230 pixels wide, you should include it in a document via the element

```
<IMG SRC="image.gif" HEIGHT="500" WIDTH="230" ALT="[alt text]">
```

where **HEIGHT** and **WIDTH** give the image size in pixels. In this case, the browser retrieving the document knows the size of the image *before* the data are actually received. As a result, it can start drawing the page immediately, leaving an appropriate empty space (500×230 in this example) for the yet-to-arrive image. This significantly speeds up the presentation of the page to the user and is particularly important for pages containing large, slow-to-download images.

Image Formats

There are many formats for storing digital images, each with various advantages and disadvantages. Unfortunately, Web browsers are able to display only a small subset of commonly understood image formats, so that images for Web pages must be converted into one of these formats.

On the World Wide Web, the most universally accepted image format is the Graphics Interchange Format, or GIF (filename extension *.gif*). This was the format used in the previous figures. GIF images can be displayed inline by all Web browsers. Another common format is JPEG (filename extensions *.jpeg* or *.jpg*), which is a format optimized for storing photographic images. Almost all browsers support JPEG. Both GIF and JPEG store images in a *compressed* format, which means that images can be stored in relatively small files. This is important, as images tend to require big files, which can be very slow to access over the Internet. On the Web, smaller is almost always better!

A third common format is the X-Pixelmap, or its black-and-white X-Bitmap equivalent (filename extensions *.xpm* and *.xbm* respectively). However, these store data in a non-compressed format and are thus inefficient at storing images. Fortunately, such images can easily be converted to GIF or JPEG. Finally, the newer Portable Network Graphics format (filename extension *.png*) is of growing importance. The different image formats and ways of converting images between formats are discussed in more detail in Chapter 3.

Hypertext Links

The third paragraph in *ex2a.html* shows a hypertext link. The form is straightforward:

```
<A HREF="ex2b.html">hypertext links</A>
```

The element marking a hypertext link is called an **A** or *anchor* element, and the marked text is referred to as a *hypertext anchor*. The area between the beginning <A> and ending </A> tags becomes a "hot" part of the text. With graphical browsers such as Netscape Navigator or Microsoft Internet Explorer, "hot" text is often displayed with an underline, and usually in a different color (this is configurable by the user), while with lynx, this region of text is displayed in bold characters. Placing the mouse over this region and clicking the mouse button, or, with lynx, using the tab key to move the cursor to lie over the hot part and pressing Enter, causes the browser to access the indicated document or other Internet resource.

Images Within Hypertext Anchors

You can also place images inside hypertext anchors, as illustrated in the third paragraph in the document *ex2a.html* (Figure 1.4). Here the image *sright.xbm* lies inside an anchor (recall that the *.xbm* means this is an X-Bitmap image). The relevant piece of HTML is:

```
<a href="ex2b.html"><IMG SRC="sright.xbm" ALIGN="middle"></a>
```

Graphical browsers indicate this by *boxing* the image with a colored or highlighted box, while lynx simply bolds the [Image] text string it uses in place of the image. However, adding a **BORDER**="0" attribute to the **IMG** element can make this border disappear, as illustrated in the second anchored image in this paragraph. Note, in Figures 1.5 and 1.7, there is no box around this second image.

The use of a hypertext anchor to enclose an image makes it possible to use small images as *button* icons, as is common in most computer applications. This doesn't do much good with lynx, of course, so if you do use images as navigation icons, you had better add an **ALT** attribute to let lynx (or Braille browser) users know what's going on.

Space Characters Inside Anchor Elements

You will note that there are no spaces between the anchor tags and the **IMG** element that they surround. If you have spaces at either end of the enclosed anchor string, the browser will assume that spaces are intentionally part of the anchor and will render them accordingly. This is not always pleasing and can leave an anchored image with small horizontal lines sticking out from the bottom of the image, or anchored text with underlines hanging out beyond the beginning or end of the text. The latter is illustrated by the second selection of linked text in paragraph 2 of *ex2a.html* (Figure 1.4). Note, in Figure 1.5, the hyperlink underline extends out past the end of the actual anchored text. The lesson once again is: Use tags around the text you want to mark up and don't include extra spaces unless specifically intended.

Uniform Resource Locators

The *target* of the hypertext link is indicated by the anchor attribute **HREF**, which takes as its value the *Uniform Resource Locator* (*URL*) of the target document or resource. As mentioned in the Preface, a URL is a text string that indicates the server protocol (HTTP, FTP, WAIS, etc.) to use in accessing the resource, the Internet domain name of the server, and the name and location of the resource on that particular server. Obviously, the **HREF** attributes in Figure 1.4 do not contain all this information! These URLs are examples of *partial* URLs, which are a shorthand way of referring to files or other resources *relative* to the URL of the document currently being viewed. For Figure 1.4, this means: Use the same mechanism used to retrieve the present document (*ex2a.html*) and retrieve the indicated file *ex2b.html* (see Figures 1.9 and 1.10) from the same directory. This works whether the files are on a local computer or on a Web server half-way around the world.

Figure 1.9 Contents of the example HTML document *ex2b.html*. This document is the target of a hypertext link from the file *ex2a.html* shown in Figure 1.4.

```
<HTML>
<HEAD>
<TITLE> Example 2B: Target of example Hypertext Link</TITLE>
</HEAD>
<BODY>

<h2> Target of Hypertext Link </h2>

<p> OK, so now that you are here, how do you get back?  This document
    doesn't have any hypertext links, so you have to use a "back" button (or the
    'u' key if using lynx) to move back to the previously viewed document.

</BODY></HTML>
```

Figure 1.10 Internet Explorer 4 rendering of the HTML document *ex2b.html* (the HTML document source is listed in Figure 1.9).

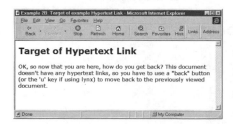

Figure 1.11 Netscape Navigator 4 rendering of the HTML document *ex2a.html* after returning from a hypertext jump to the document *ex2b.html*.

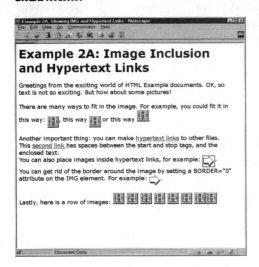

If you click the mouse button over the hypertext anchor, the browser downloads and displays the linked document, as shown in Figure 1.10. To return to the previously viewed document, press the Back button on the browser control panel (with lynx, press the letter "u", for *up*), which takes you back to the previously displayed document, namely *ex2a.html*. Figure 1.11 shows, for Navigator 4, what this document looks like the second time around. The document is now subtly different: The portion of text that served as the launching point for the hypertext link, previously underlined in blue, is now underlined by a faded, purple line (this does not show up well in this black-and-white figure). Graphical browsers use such highlighting changes to keep users oriented by letting them know where they have already been. Unfortunately, this is not possible with lynx, as there are too few text highlighting modes to allow this level of subtlety. With lynx, users must pay a bit more attention to what they have been doing and where they have been.

Relative Uniform Resource Locators: Linking Documents Together

As mentioned, the anchor

```
<A HREF="ex2b.html">hypertext links</A>
```

uses a partial URL, which references a location relative to the URL of the displayed document. This partial URL idea is great news, because it means that you need not specify entire URLs for simple links between files on the same computer.

Figure 1.12 Accessing neighboring files using partial URLs. The dotted lines and the associated text strings illustrate partial URLs relating the file *ex2a.html* to the files *ex2b.html*, *ex2c.html*, and *ex2d.html*. The grayed directory, *cgi-bin*, indicates a gateway program directory—this directory contains programs to be executed by the HTTP server. The figure shows these folders and files as lying in the *Document Directory*— the directory, on a Web server, that contains the resources available via the Web. Material not under the document directory, such as the file *file.html*, are inaccessible to the outside world.

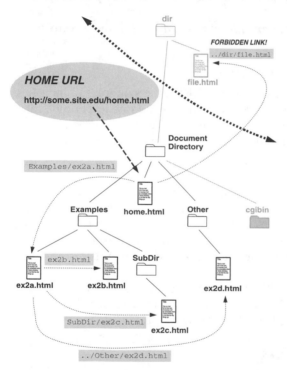

Instead, you need only specify their position on the file system relative to each other, as done in Figure 1.4.

Partial URLs can point to directories other than the one containing the current document. Specification of these relative directories is done using a UNIX-like path structure, as illustrated in Figure 1.12. Suppose that the example documents *ex2a.html* and *ex2b.html* lie in the indicated directory structure. That is, the files *ex2a.html* and *ex2b.html* are in the directory *Examples/*, while the file *ex2c.html* is in *Examples/SubDir/*, and *ex2d.html* is in */Other/*.

How do you reference the files *ex2c.html* and *ex2d.html* from the file *ex2a.html*? To reference *ex2c.html*, simply create a hypertext link that accesses the partial URL *SubDir/ex2c.html*:

```
<A HREF="SubDir/ex2c.html">hypertext links</A>
```

Notice that the pathnames use the forward slash characters to indicate a new directory. The URL specification states that the forward slash—and no other character—delimits directories or other hierarchical relationships (formally, URLs can reference not just files, but also programs or other resources). You *cannot* use backslashes (\) as you do with DOS and Windows or colons (:) as you do on Macintoshes.

If you want to create a link from *ex2a.html* to *ex2d.html* in the directory *Other/*, you write the URL as

```
<A HREF="../Other/ex2d.html">hypertext links</A>
```

since the file is one directory level up—in partial URLs, the symbol ".." indicates a resource one directory up from the current directory—and one level down into the directory Other. A single dot (.) in a URL indicates the current directory, so **HREF="./Subdir/ex2c.html"** and **HREF="Subdir/ex2c.html"** are equivalent.

Special Characters in a URL

Of course, this scheme will cause problems if you actually use a slash character as part of a filename, since the URL convention will try to interpret it as a directory change. It is therefore best to avoid directory or file names containing this character. The URL syntax does have a way of allowing this and other special characters within a URL. The required *encoding* mechanism is discussed in Chapter 8.

There are a lot of other partial URL forms and, of course, we have yet to properly discuss full URLs. More URL examples appear later in this chapter as well as in Chapter 2, while the details of the URL syntax is given Chapter 8.

Tips for Effective Hypertext Links

Hypertext links are easy and can be very useful—in fact, it is fair to say that they are the most important feature of an HTML document. However, it is easy to get carried away with hypertext links, and they can quickly become a source of irritation to readers of a document. The following sections outline a few suggestions for ways to include links in an HTML document without detracting from the presentation and readability of the text. Most of these issues are illustrated in Figures 1.13 and 1.14.

Create hypertext links that flow naturally from the text. Make the link appear as a natural part of the text, so as not to interrupt the flow of reading, Thus, it is better to write:

```
<p> The issue of hormone-controlled ostrich-feather
     growth has recently been a topic of
intense <A HREF="ostrich-paper.html">interest</A>
```

than:

```
<p> For information about current hormone-controlled
     ostrich-feather
growth press <A HREF="ostrich-paper.html"> here </A>
```

Keep linked text strings short. It is much more effective to link to a single word or selection of words than to a whole sentence. Thus such links as

```
<p> <A HREF="animal.html">The life cycle of the
     atlantic polar-bear ocelot</A>  is a complex and
interesting example of ...
```

are better written as:

```
<p> The life cycle of the  <A HREF="animal.html">atlantic
     polar-bear ocelot</A> is a complex and interesting example
of ...
```

Link text-related icons and text together. Occasionally, you will want to use a small icon to indicate a hypertext link. To make this clearer to the reader, it is sometimes useful to include the text adjacent the icon within the anchor.

Create menus of links for navigational purposes. It is easiest to navigate a collection of documents if the navigational links to adjacent pages or to the home page are grouped together and always appear at the same place on all pages. Figure 1.18 illustrates some simple ways this can be done.

There are no hard and fast rules for creating bad and good link presentations. In general, if you are adding links within a text document that you want easily read, it is best to make the links as unobtrusive as possible.

Using the URL as the Linked Text

It is sometimes appropriate to include the URLs as part of the text—you don't always have to hide the URL inside **HREF** attributes. This is particularly useful if a document is likely to be printed, since the URL references are otherwise not visible. For example, the Web FAQ (Frequently Asked Questions) document, a wonderful repository of useful information about the World Wide Web, contains sentences such as:

```
<p> ....The original home of the WWW F.A.Q. is
<A HREF="http://www.boutell.com/faq/">http://www.boutell.com/faq/</A>.
```

Figure 1.13 Listing for the document *badlinks.html*. This document illustrates good and bad examples of hypertext links. A Microsoft Internet Explorer rendering is shown in Figure 1.14.

```
<HTML>
<HEAD>
<TITLE> Examples of Bad Hypertext Links </TITLE>
</HEAD>
<BODY>
<H1> Examples of Good/Bad Hypertext Link Design</H1>

<p> <B> 1) Don't distort the Written Text  </B>
<P> <B> Good: </B>
<BR>The issue of hormone-controlled ostrich-feather growth has recently
    been a topic of intense <A HREF="ostrich-paper.html">interest</A>.

<P> <B> Not So Good: </B>
<BR> For information about current hormone-controlled ostrich-feather
    growth press  <A HREF="ostrich-paper.html">here</A>.
<p> <B> 2) Keep the linked text section short. </B>
<p> <B> Good: </B>
<br> The life cycle of the  <A HREF="animal.html">atlantic polar-bear
    ocelot</A> is a complex and .......

<p> <B> Not So Good: </B>
<br> <A HREF="animal.html">The life cycle of the atlantic polar-bear
    ocelot is a complex</A> and .......

<p> <B> 3) Link Icon and Text Together </B>
<p> <B> Good: </B>
<br> <A HREF="file.html"><IMG SRC="home.gif"> The latest</A> home
    security systems breakdown show......
<p> <B> Not so Good: </B>
<br> <A HREF="file.html"><IMG SRC="home.gif"></A> The latest home
    security systems breakdown show......

</BODY>
</HTML>
```

If you are reading the HTML document online, just click on the anchored text to view the referenced document. If reading the paper version, you can see the printed URL and have the information you need to access the site when you next have access to the Internet (go to www.boutell.com/faq/).

Figure 1.14 Microsoft Internet Explorer 3 rendering of the file *badlinks.html* (shown in Figure 1.13).

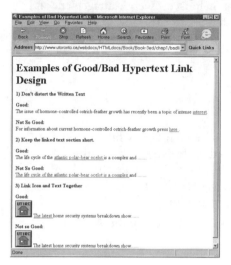

Lists, Paragraphs, or Menus of Links

If putting together a collection of links, think carefully about their organization. Should they be placed within in a paragraph? Probably not. More likely, they should go in a list or as a menu bar (a horizontal list of text or graphical buttons linked to the desired objects). A collection of links should also be arranged in a logical manner—a page full of random links is exceedingly frustrating to use. Link-mania pages containing seemingly random collections of links occur quite innocently, often when you have been slowly assembling lists of interesting URLs. The collection may be fine for personal use, but will be confusing to anyone else.

Figure 1.16 shows a simple home page constructed using some of the features of "bad" anchor design (the source for this document is in Figure 1.15), while Figure 1.18 shows an improved and better organized page using the suggestions given in the preceding paragraph (the source is in Figure 1.17.) Note that Figure 1.18 is much easier to understand than Figure 1.16, even though Figure 1.18 actually contains less textual information.

Validate All Hypertext Links

Finally and most important of all: Make sure all hypertext links work and go to the right place! There is nothing worse than clicking on a link, only to get "ERROR. Requested document not available" in response. Actually, that's not quite true. It is even worse to click on an anchor that indicates a particular destination, only to find that you have actually accessed something completely different and obviously incorrect. Errors like these tell a reader that the document developers did not bother to check their work, which immediately brings into question the accuracy of the documents themselves. It is easy to check links: Indeed, there are automated software packages that can help (see "Web Management and Maintenance Tools" on the companion Web site). So, as the *Nike* ads say: Just do it.

Lessons from Example 2

1. Images are included via the **IMG** element:

   ```
   <IMG src="prism-small.gif" ALT="[Text stuff]">
   ```

   SRC specifies the URL of the image file to be included, while the **ALT** attribute gives a text string to be displayed by browsers that cannot display images. The **ALIGN** attribute specifies how the image should be aligned with the surrounding text, while the **HEIGHT** and **WIDTH** attributes can specify the size (in pixels) of the image.

2. Hypertext links to another document are included using the **A** (anchor) element

   ```
   <A HREF="SubDir/example1.2B.html">hypertext links</A>
   ```

   where **HREF** is used to specify the URL of the target of the link. The examples here are of partial URLs: Partial URLs assume the same Internet site and protocol as for the document currently being viewed and look for the file (or resource) relative to it. In this regard the slash (/) and double dot (..) characters are special, representing relative positions in the directory (or other) hierarchy.

3. Images can also be hypertext anchors via constructs such as:

   ```
   <A HREF="someplace.html"><IMG SRC="image.gif"></A>
   ```

4. Don't use hypertext links gratuitously. If they are embedded in the text, try to make them flow with the text. If a paragraph has many links, try thinking of another way to present the material: Maybe it should be a list or a menu, or perhaps the hypertext anchors could be combined into a less intrusive form. Above all, make sure the links work; links going nowhere or to the wrong place are cardinal sins of HTML authoring.

Exercises for Example 2

As a first exercise, disable image loading on your browser and then access Web pages containing lots of images. If possible, do this from sites where you have a slow connection. Note how confusing sites can be when the designers do not bother with **ALT** attributes, and how slowly the page appears if the author did not include **HEIGHT** and **WIDTH** attributes on the **IMG** elements.

For the second exercise, create some hypertext-linked HTML files using partial URLs to link the pages together. Create these files on your personal computer's hard disk—your browser can access these files directly from the disk, without the need for a Web server. You can do this via the "File Open" tool, usually located below the "File" menu. Note that this means that you can create and test Web pages on any computer, without using a Web server—or even having an Internet connection.

Once you are satisfied with your pages, they can be copied onto a machine running an HTTP server, and from there make them accessible via the Web. And, because they were entered as partial URLs, the hypertext links will still work on the Web server—the files are still "next to" each other, even if they are on a different machine.

Example 3: Home Pages—Headings, ADDRESS, and Anchors

This example, illustrated in Figures 1.15 through 1.19, looks again at the **A** (anchor) and heading elements and introduces the **ADDRESS** (address information) element, all in the context of a practical document design problem, namely the construction of a document collection *home page*. A home page is designed to be the first document seen by visitors to a site and serves as the introduction for guests. It is most often used to direct people to other interesting resources at the site, and to provide an overview of the site content. This particular example is based on a page constructed for the Instructional and Research Computing Group at the University of Toronto. Figures 1.15 and 1.16 illustrate bad design features (don't imitate this page!), while Figures 1.17 through 1.19 exemplify good design. In terms of layout, however, both designs are rather simple—but then, they do not use any of the fancy structural and layout tools possible with advanced HTML tags. The more advanced layout tools will be discussed in the next chapter.

Figure 1.17 shows the example home page for the Instructional and Research Computing Group at the University of Toronto, while Figures 1.18 and 1.19 show how this page looks using the Netscape Navigator 4 and UNIX lynx browsers.

Appropriate Use of Heading Elements

Let's begin with the **TITLE** and **H1** headings in Figure 1.17. In both cases, these are clearly descriptive of the content and origin of this document or document collection. As mentioned previously, a **TITLE** should always be clearly descriptive of a page's content, since it is used to reference a page when a user bookmarks the location. You have much more flexibility with headings, but, in general, the main heading of a home page should also clearly reflect the contents of the collection, as this quickly lets your visitors know that they have reached the right place.

Figure 1.15 HTML document listing for the file *home_bad.html*, which contains a poorly designed home page. Figure 1.16 shows the rendering of this by the Microsoft Internet Explorer 4 browser.

```
<HTML> <HEAD>
<TITLE> Instructional and Research Computing </TITLE>
</HEAD> <BODY>

<H1 ALIGN="center"> Instructional and Research Computing </H1>

<P>This is the home page of the Instructional and Research Computing
    Group <STRONG>(IRC)</STRONG>, one of seven departments of the Division
    of Computing and Communications.  The IRC group provides support for
    <A HREF="MulVis/intro.html"> multimedia and visualization techniques</A>,
    access to and support for <A HREF="HPC/intro.html">high performance
    computing</A>, and support for <A HREF="AdTech/intro.html">adaptive
    technology</A>.  (aids for the physically challenged).  We also have
    some interesting links to <A HREF="Lists/Lists.html">WWW Starting
    Points</A>, a big list of <A HREF="Lists/Lists.html">WWW Search
    Tools</A>, another list of hypertext pointers to
    <A HREF="Lists/Libraries.html">Libraries</A> resources, and a
    link to the  <A HREF="http://www.utoronto.ca/uoft.html">Main
    University Home Page </A>.

<P>If you become lost in our documents use the navigation icons.
    The <EM> home </EM> icon brings you back here, while the <EM> up </EM>
    icon takes you up one level in the document hierarchy.  <EM> Info </EM>
    and <EM> help </EM> are also useful, while the <EM> letter</EM> icon
    lets you send us a message, and the <EM> search </EM> icon allows you
    to do a text search of our pages.
<HR SIZE="1" NOSHADE>
  <A HREF="home.html"><IMG SRC="home.gif"    ALIGN="TOP"></A>
  <A HREF="help.html"><IMG SRC="ic_help.gif" ALIGN="TOP"></A>
  <A HREF="info.html"><IMG SRC="ic_info.gif" ALIGN="TOP"></A>
  <A HREF="/cgi-bin/mail.pl"><IMG SRC="ic_mail.gif" ALIGN="TOP"></A>
  <A HREF="home.html"><IMG SRC="ic_up.gif"    ALIGN="TOP"></A> . . .
  <A HREF="cgi-bin/doc-search.pl"> <IMG SRC="ic_find.gif" ALIGN="TOP"></A>
<HR SIZE="1" NOSHADE>
<ADDRESS>
<A HREF="Staff/web_admin.html">webmaster@site.address.edu</A>
</ADDRESS>
</BODY></HTML>
```

Figure 1.16 Microsoft Internet Explorer 4 rendering of the HTML document *home_bad.html*.

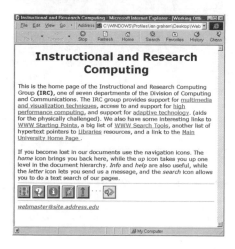

As mentioned earlier, headings can range from **H1** through to **H6**, in decreasing order of importance. In designing a collection of documents, you should use heading elements that retain this sense of relative importance, as it helps to build organizational structure within and between documents. There are useful programs that can build a table of contents for a large collection of HTML documents based on the contents and relative *levels* of the heading elements. This, of course, will work only if the headings elements were used correctly (i.e., **H1** for major sections, **H2** for subsections, **H3** for sub-subsections, and so on). Similarly, some of the Web indexing tools (such as *AltaVista*, *Lycos,* or *Excite*) weight heading element content as more important than regular text. This, of course, will result in useful indexing only if the document's headings contain sensible content.

Figure 1.17 Listing of the example home page document *home.html*.

```
<HTML> <HEAD>
<TITLE> Instructional and Research Computing </TITLE>
</HEAD> <BODY>
    [<A HREF="home.html">          Home   </A>]
    [<A HREF="help.html">          Help   </A>]
    [<A HREF="info.html">          Info   </A>]
    [<A HREF="/cgi-bin/mail.pl">    Mail   </A>]
    [<A HREF="home.html">          Up     </A>]
    [<A HREF="cgi-bin/doc-search.pl">Search</A>]
```

```
<HR>

<H1 ALIGN="center"> Instructional and Research Computing </H1>

<P>This is the home page of the Instructional and Research Computing
Group <STRONG>(IRC)</STRONG>, one of seven departments of the Division
of Computing and Communications.  We provide:

<UL>
<LI>support for <A HREF="MulVis/intro.html">multimedia and visualization
    techniques</A>
<LI>access to and support for <A HREF="HPC/intro.html">high performance
    computing</A>
<LI>support for <A HREF="AdTech/intro.html">adaptive technology</A>
    (aids for the physically challenged).
</UL>
<P>Some other useful University resources are:<BR>
   <A HREF="Lists/Lists.html"> WWW Starting Points </A> |
   <A HREF="Lists/Lists.html"> WWW Search Tools</A> |
   <A HREF="Lists/Libraries.html"> Libraries </A> |
   <A HREF="http://www.utoronto.ca/uoft.html"> Main University Home Page </A>
<P>If you become lost in our documents use the navigation icons.
   The <EM> home </EM> icon brings you back here, while the <EM> up </EM>
   icon takes up one level in the document hierarchy.  <EM> Info </EM>
   and <EM> help </EM> are also useful, while the <EM> letter</EM> icon
   let you send us a message, and the <EM> search </EM> icon allows you
   to do a text search of our pages.
<HR SIZE="1" NOSHADE>
  <A HREF="home.html"><IMG SRC="home.gif" ALIGN="TOP"
     ALT="Home"></A><A
     HREF="help.html"><IMG SRC="ic_help.gif" ALIGN="TOP"
     ALT="Help"></A><A
     HREF="info.html"><IMG SRC="ic_info.gif" ALIGN="TOP"
     ALT="Info"></A><A HREF="/cgi-bin/mail.pl"><IMG SRC="ic_mail.gif"
     ALIGN="TOP" ALT="Mail"></A><A
     HREF="home.html"><IMG SRC="ic_up.gif" ALIGN="TOP"
     ALT="Up"  ></A><A
     HREF="cgi-bin/doc-search.pl"><IMG SRC="ic_find.gif"
     ALIGN="TOP" ALT="Search"></A>
<HR SIZE="1" NOSHADE>
<ADDRESS>
<A HREF="Staff/web_admin.html">webmaster@site.address.edu</A>
</ADDRESS>
</BODY></HTML>
```

Figure 1.18 Netscape Navigator 4 rendering of the HTML document *home.html* **(the document is listed in Figure 1.17).**

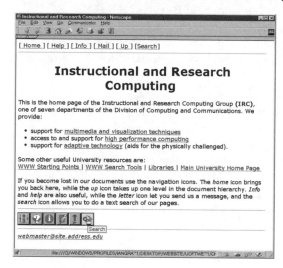

Figure 1.19 Lynx rendering of the HTML document *home.html* **(the document is listed in Figure 1.17).**

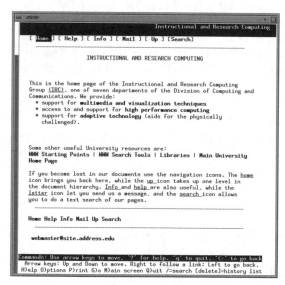

Heading Alignment with ALIGN

Note also the use of the **ALIGN** attribute in the heading. The **ALIGN** attribute can be used with a number of elements (Headings, **P**, **BLOCKQUOTE**, **ADDRESS**, etc.) to define the text alignment within the block; in Figures 1.15 and 1.17, it is used to center the heading on the page. Other possible alignment options are "left" (the default value) and "right," for right-margin aligned text.

Sign Documents with an ADDRESS

It is always a good idea to sign HTML documents, particularly the home pages or other major pages. This provides information allowing visitors to send feedback or comments regarding the site. The HTML **ADDRESS** element is specifically designed for address information and is used for this purpose in Figure 1.17. Here, the **ADDRESS** element contains an e-mail address suitable for feedback and/or commentary about the site. Also, this e-mail address is placed within an anchor element linked to a page (*web_admin.html*) containing additional information—for example, about the server and server administrator. For more personal projects, this might be an HTML document containing a brief biography of the document author. The link may also be a **mailto** URL containing the indicated email address—clicking on the link will let the reader send mail to the indicated person.

Horizontal Dividing Lines with HR

As shown in Figures 1.15 through 1.19, the **HR** element defines a horizontal divider, which is rendered on the display as a solid dividing line. In HTML 4, this element can take a **SIZE** attribute to specify the height of the dividing line, in pixels (the default is usually 2), as well as a **NOSHADE** attribute to specify a solid line (the default is a chiseled line). Note how **NOSHADE** does not take a value. Other attributes are also supported. These are discussed in Chapter 6.

Full Uniform Resource Locators

Looking at Figure 1.17, note that most of the URL references are relative references. There is one, however, that is not. This is the URL pointing to the *Main University Home Page*. This is a full URL that specifies the complete information needed to access the main University HTTP server:

```
http://www.utoronto.ca/uoft.html
```

A complete HTTP URL has three main parts, as in this example:

1. **http:**—The *protocol specifier*. The string http: indicates the HTTP protocol. This and other URL schemes are discussed in Chapter 8.

2. **//www.utoronto.ca**—The *Internet domain name* of the server. This gives the Internet name the client should contact. Sometimes, you will see this with a number after the name, for example: www.somewhere.edu:8080.

The trailing number is a *port number* and specifies the port at which the server is actually listening. (Port numbers are rather like local telephone extensions, and allow a single computer to run several different services [FTP, HTTP, etc.] each "listening" at a different port). Most HTTP servers listen at port 80. You can omit the port number from the URL if contacting the server at the default value.

3. **/uoft.html—The** *path and filename* **of the desired file** (or other resource). Here, the URL is to the file *uoft.html* that lies right at the top of the server's *document directory* which is the directory under which the HTTP server keeps the documents. If the file were in a sub-directory, then that information would be here, so that paths such as: */Examples/ex2a.html* (as in Figure 1.12) are possible.

The URL scheme allows for many protocols: ftp: for the FTP protocol; gopher: for the gopher protocol; wais: for the WAIS protocol, and so on. Consequently, using URLs, you can create hypertext links to anonymous FTP servers, Gopher sites, WAIS databases, and many other Internet resources. Web browsers are designed to understand these protocols. When they encounter a hypertext reference in an HTML element such as **HREF=**"*url*", where *url* points to an anonymous FTP or Gopher site, browsers are able to contact the site, using the appropriate protocol, and access the indicated resource.

General Home Page Design Issues

There are several things to consider when designing home pages for the Web. Typically:

Web pages should be *small*. In particular, a home page should be a small document with a minimum of extraneous graphics or text. Large images (meaning large image files) and the detailed resources of your site should be elsewhere. Many people have slow Internet connections and will not wait for thousands of kilobytes of gratuitous imagery. Icons or images on a home page should therefore be small image files, totaling less than 20 kilobytes (this will take approximately ten seconds to download for someone using a 28.8 Kbaud modem).

A home page should be *concise*. A home page is like an introductory map to a site or to a collection of documents, explaining what the site is and where to find the local resources. Thus, it should *briefly* outline the content of your site and provide hypertext links to those specific content resources. It should also (when necessary) provide a link to a "help" page that explains, in more detail, the organizational of the site, such as the meanings of icons or menus or the function of special tools, so that visitors will know how to navigate their way around. Avoid abbreviations, acronyms, or other wording that visitors are unlikely to understand. And, if your site is multilingual, the home page should display obvious, prominent links to the different language versions.

A home page should *not* be dependent on graphics. Make sure that a user can navigate from your home page without a graphical browser. Many users disable image loading while "surfing," and will quickly leave a site that does not make sense. Thus, if you use icons for navigation buttons, use the **IMG** element **ALT** attribute to provide a text description of the button. In general, if you decorate a home page with graphics, make sure that the content of the page is easily understood when image loading is disabled.

A home page should include *contact information*. At some point, someone will want to contact you or your Web server administrator, perhaps to point out a problem, or most likely to compliment you on your work. The home page should therefore include contact information for the administrator(s) of the resources. A common, generic e-mail address for the site administrator is webmaster@www.domain.name, where www.domain.name is the domain name of your server. Such information should be included on the home page, most commonly at the page bottom.

Clarity of Content

To make a home page small and compact, the content must be clear and concise. The text in the example home page document (Figure 1.17) fulfills these criteria, providing a clear, concise description of the site and the material it contains, with a minimum of extraneous detail. The content can be written in any style: polite and well mannered, or eclectic and off-the-wall. In the example in Figure 1.17, the first paragraph explains the reason for the site and provides links to the major areas of interest. Each of these areas may, in turn, have its own home page specific to the subject at hand. This hierarchical structure lets people quickly find what they are looking for, and also makes it easy for the site developer to organize his or her documents. For example, you can have independent subdirectories for each distinct area, with your main home page having hypertext links to introductory home pages located in each of these subdirectories. Other hypertext links can then provide alternative relationships between documents, within this overall hierarchical arrangement.

The home page in Figure 1.17 also contains a second, less detailed, list that provides a brief selection of alternative services. These items link to documents or services that are perhaps peripheral to the main purpose of the site, but that may be useful in directing the visitor to his or her destination. This figure also contains a collection of hypertext pointers to other resources that our group commonly uses. Such links are also often moved to a second page, to keep the home page as uncluttered as possible.

Referring to Figures 1.18 and 1.19, you can see how clean the organization looks. Since the document is written in correct HTML, both browsers display it clearly, subject to their own limitations. A comparison of Figure 1.19 with the less-well-thought-out version in Figure 1.16 illustrates the importance of good organizational design. A little thought about how the hypertext links should be organized makes an enormous difference in the clarity of the final presentation.

Image-Intensive Home Pages

Alternatively, you might consider an all-graphical home page. Some sites use as a home page a large *image map*, or a collection of images that appear elsewhere in the site, and that provide a graphical key to the site's pages. Usually, these images are placed inside hypertext links and are linked to the various resources on the Web site, much like the text buttons in Figure 1.18. However, if a site uses image maps, or image buttons, it is wise to provide a link to an alternative text-only version of the home page, to make the site accessible to as wide an audience as possible. An example of this approach is seen in Figure 4.13. (The link to the Screen Reader Friendly version of the site is to a text-only home page.)

Images: The "Right" Size

Although not included in Example 3, decorative images, such as a company or organizational logo, are often included within a home page. This can be very attractive, adding an appealing graphical impact to your site. Be careful, however, to ensure that such images are not too large, as long download times for the page will frustrate visitors. As mentioned previously, the sizes of all the images on a page should ideally sum to less than 20 KB. Even if the page is attractive, the impact of this elegance is lost on a user who has had to wait minutes for the images to arrive.

As mentioned in Example 2, use the **IMG** element **HEIGHT** and **WIDTH** attributes to specify the size of the images. This information lets the browser format the text, while setting aside space for the images that have not yet arrived. If you don't specify **WIDTH** and **HEIGHT**, most browsers will wait to load the images (and thereby determine the image sizes) before drawing the page. This can be very slow if there are lots of images, during which the user sees nothing at all, and curses you for having created such an irritating, slow-to-access page!

Images: Acceptable Color Depths

Always process home page images so that they do not contain too many distinct colors and that they contain the "right" set of colors! Many computer graphics displays can only display 256 colors (8-bit color), while some Web browsers limit each image in the browser window to fewer colors than this—the reasons why are discussed in Chapter 3. Most graphics editing programs let graphics developers process images to reduce the number of colors they contain, often with little loss of image quality (at least as displayed by the browser). This has the added bonus of making the image files smaller and faster to download.

Images: Navigation Icons

Look back to the bottom of the HTML document listed in Figure 1.17 and displayed in Figures 1.18 and 1.19. The feature to look at is the collection of small *icons*. These icons are attached by hypertext anchors to a collection of important reference documents of the collection; the paragraph preceding these icons explains what the icons mean. The intent is to place these icons on every HTML document to provide a universal cue for navigating through the local document collection. For example, the *home* icon always links back to this main home page, while the *up* icon links up to the top of whatever set of documents you are looking at. Thus, if you had chosen to visit the High Performance Computing section, then the *up* icon would bring you back to the High Performance Computing home page. In turn, the *Info* icon refers to a page giving a brief description of IRC and its mandate, while the *Help* icon connects to a page that briefly describes the meanings of all the icons. Finally, the *Mail* icon links to a gateway program on the HTTP server that allows the user to send mail to the server administrator, while the *Search* icon links to a different gateway program that allows the user to do keyword searches on the collection of HTML documents. Note that all these icons are equipped with an **ALT** attribute text alternative. If you are going to navigate with icons, be sure that people using a text-only browser know what the icons mean! Figure 1.18 also illustrates how the **ALT** attribute "tool tip" feature works with newer browsers—upon letting the mouse hover over the right-hand icon (the confusing one!), the browser displays the "pop-up" text, which explains the purpose of the link.

Having navigation icons is extremely important, particularly when there are a number of related documents. It is very easy to get lost when browsing through large collections. Hypertext is not like a *linear* book, where readers can always tell where they are by the page number or the thickness of the remaining pages. Navigation icons replace these tactile methods of navigation with symbols that link the user to reference points within the collection. In addition, icons can direct users to general services that may be useful wherever they are in a collection, such as a search tool for searching a database or a mail tool for sending an electronic message to the site administrator.

Navigation is a particularly thorny issue for hypertext design, and much has been written on the ways to design hypertext for easy navigability and searching. Indeed, Chapter 4 looks into these issues and provides some useful references for further reading on this topic.

Text-based Icons

The very top of this home page shows a text-only variant of the navigation icons (see Figures 1.17 to 1.19). This was added to contrast with the iconic approach.

Text and icons both provide the same functionality, and choosing one or the other is largely a matter of taste. Text-based navigation aids can take up less space on a page and do not require image loading. If you use image icons, the latter problem is mitigated by using the same icons in all your pages. All Web browsers *cache* (retain local) copies of images once they have been accessed and don't bother to retrieve them from the server when they are required on subsequent occasions.

Image downloading problems can be mitigated by using small icons and a reduced number of colors per image. Most of the GIF-format icons included in the document shown in Figure 1.17 and displayed in Figure 1.18 are only 36 pixels square and contain only 16 colors each (4 bits/pixel) and, as a result, they take up only 280 bytes each. Consequently, these icons download quickly, even over a dial-up connection.

Lessons from Example 3

1. A home page should be small and should not contain many large images. It should also be designed to be usable if accessed by a browser that has image loading disabled.

2. Home pages should clearly and concisely describe the contents of a Web site and should contain hypertext links to these resources.

3. All included images should contain appropriate **ALT** text descriptions and should use the **HEIGHT** and **WIDTH** attributes to specify the image size.

4. A home page should explain and introduce navigation icons if they are used and if their function is not obvious to the user.

5. Home pages should contain contact information for the administrator of the documents managed at the site.

Exercises for Example 3

Figure 1.17 was very simple, designed only to illustrate the basic design features of a home page. As an exercise, try visiting several Web sites, examining how they follow (or not!) these design principles. To test a page properly, first access it with you browser's image loading disabled (to check how well it works without images). Then load in the images and see how long it takes—and how good it looks or not! Here are some sample Web sites (from amongst millions):

home.netscape.com

www.microsoft.com

www.shift.com

www.cnet.com

www.nando.net

References

There is a great deal of HTML documentation available via the Web. The best place to start is the World Wide Web FAQ. Thanks to Thomas Boutell, the Web Frequently Asked Questions (FAQ) list is one of the most useful collections anywhere of up-to-date, Web-related information. Sections of this list are posted regularly on the various Web newsgroups, while the entire FAQ is available in hypertext form at the URL

www.boutell.com/faq/

and at many mirror sites. USENET newsgroups, devoted to World Wide Web and HTML issues, are also a good place to see announcements of new products or services, to ask questions, or to hear of the latest WWW happenings. There are also several Web sites offering introductions to the Web and HTML and lists of links to other useful resources.

Web USENET Newsgroups

The following is a list of the World Wide Web newsgroups, with short descriptions of the newsgroup topic. Please, post messages only to the appropriate groups and *cross-post* when sending the same message to more than one group!

comp.infosystems.www.advocacy	Political and advocacy issues
comp.infosystems.www.announce	Announcements of new sites or services (moderated)
comp.infosystems.www.authoring.cgi	CGI programming
comp.infosystems.www.authoring.html	HTML authoring issues
comp.infosystems.www.authoring.images	Images in Web documents including image formats, format conversions, and imagemaps
comp.infosystems.www.authoring.misc	Miscellaneous web authoring issues
comp.infosystems.www.authoring.site-design	Issues to do with site design
comp.infosystems.www.authoring.stylesheets	HTML and Cascading Style Sheets
comp.infosystems.www.authoring.tools	Discussion of authoring tools
comp.infosystems.www.browsers.mac	Macintosh browsers
comp.infosystems.www.browsers.misc	Miscellaneous browser issues
comp.infosystems.www.browsers.ms-windows	MS-Windows Web browsers
comp.infosystems.www.browsers.x	X-Windows Web browsers
comp.infosystems.www.marketplace	Miscellaneous marketplace musings ...
comp.infosystems.www.servers.mac	Macintosh HTTP servers
comp.infosystems.www.servers.misc	Miscellaneous HTTP server issues
comp.infosystems.www.servers.ms-windows	Windows 3.1/95/NT HTTP servers

comp.infosystems.www.servers.unix   UNIX HTTP servers
comp.os.os2.networking.www   Web issues related to IBM OS/2
bionet.software.www   WWW applications in the biological
                                                             sciences

User Surveys of WWW Resources

www.cc.gatech.edu/gvu/user_surveys/

Useful HTML and Web References

www.utoronto.ca/webdocs/HTMLdocs/
    NewHTML/intro.html
www.web-designer.com/~towheed/sswg/
    candy_style.html
WWW.Stars.com/Vlib/   (Web developer's virtual library)
www.sandia.gov/sci_compute/html_ref.htm   (HTML reference manual)
www.htmlhelp.com   (Web Design Group's guide to HTML)

A Guide to Browser Capabilities—Browsercaps

www.browsercaps.com/

Yahoo List of HTML-related Web Resources

www.yahoo.com/Computers_and_Internet/   (General Web resources)
    Internet/World_Wide_Web/
www.yahoo.com/Computers_and_Internet/   (HTML resources)
    Information_and_Documentation/
    Data_Formats/HTML/

HTML AND DOCUMENT DESIGN

Chapter 1 introduced the philosophy and design behind the HTML language. It also included example documents to illustrate the basic markup elements, such as headings, lists, character highlighting, images, horizontal rule dividers, and—most important—hypertext anchors. In this chapter, we look again at these elements, focusing on advanced features and document design issues. We also introduce the other important HTML elements—such as **BLOCKQUOTE, OL** (ordered list), **FORM,** and **TABLE** elements—that significantly enrich the vocabulary of HTML document authors.

The examples are designed to illustrate the proper use of these elements and to point out some common mistakes. Since most browsers do not check for incorrect HTML, it is easy to write badly formed HTML documents that look fine on one browser, but awful on another—document authors need to be careful to avoid this problem. In addition, these examples reflect design issues that are important when creating a page. For example, what are the best ways to include hypertext anchors or image files? Although there are no universal strategies, these examples help illustrate the characteristics and limitations of the Web, thereby showing why some design choices are often better than others.

This chapter is designed as a tutorial in HTML design, so the examples are relatively simple. Chapter 5 presents a discussion of Web site implementation and planning and includes several examples of page design that make use of more advanced aspects of HTML coding. In addition, Chapters 6 and 7, which provide detailed specifications for all HTML elements, also present advanced HTML coding examples.

Example 4: Linear Hypertext— PRE and BLOCKQUOTE

This example, illustrated in Figures 2.1 through 2.6, looks at a hypertext collection of text-based documents. One common use of HTML is to prepare on-line documentation or on-line collections of reference materials. These can be very large collections of documents, not only with some overall hierarchical structure (such as sections and subsections), but also with many hypertext links *cross-linking* these documents and linking them to other resources on the Internet. Frequently, the root structure of these documents is linear, reflecting their origins as a printed manual or their logical presentation as a readable, linear collection. This is not necessarily a bad thing—after all, books are a very successful form of communication. Furthermore, while hypertext allows for nonlinear representations of information, this does not mean that a nonlinear model is always more appropriate! Linear models may be the best match for user needs.

The PRE Element

Figures 2.1 and 2.2 introduce the **PRE** element. This element contains *preformatted* text for presentation as is, preserving the space characters and carriage returns typed into the HTML document and displaying the characters using a fixed-width typewriter font. You can use **PRE** to display computer codes, text examples, or verbatim text sequences. This is also one way you can create tables for display in an HTML document, since this element preserves the horizontal whitespaces needed to align columns.

You can include character emphasis within a **PRE**, and thus you can use **STRONG** and **EM** to emphasize text. You can also include hypertext anchors. Note that tags do not add width to the text, so you can use them to add highlighting or hypertext anchors without changing the vertical alignment of the text. The usefulness of the **PRE** element in this context is illustrated in Figures 6.15 and 6.16 (Chapter 6), where **PRE** is used to display both program code and a small table.

Anchors and text highlighting elements are the only HTML elements allowed within a **PRE**; other elements, such as **IMG, P**, heading elements, list elements, **BLOCKQUOTE** (for quotations), or **ADDRESS** elements, are prohibited.

The BLOCKQUOTE Element

Figures 2.1 and 2.2, as well as Figures 2.13 and 2.14, illustrate another element, **BLOCKQUOTE**. This element denotes block quotations, such as an extract from a book, or a speech. Since blockquoted text is often indented by browsers, Web authors often use this element to indent text (as done in the examples). This is not the true intent of **BLOCKQUOTE**—but it does work, and it is one of the few ways you can currently create indented sections. In the long run, the new *cascading style sheets* (*CSS*) language is the better way for applying indentation or other styles to paragraphs or other blocks of text. Style sheets are discussed in Chapter 7.

Document Collections: Some Design Issues

The design of document collections is discussed in more detail in the next chapter. However, some major points are apparent in this example, so it makes sense to discuss them here.

Each document should be small. Each document should display no more than two or three screens full of data. The advantage of the hypertext model lies in the linking of various components of the document web. This advantage is often lost if you are viewing a single, huge document containing hundreds or thousands of lines of displayed text. Although you can build hypertext links within a document to other points inside the same document, this is generally more difficult to navigate than a collection of smaller files.

Each document should have navigation tools. These are simply hypertext links that connect the document to other documents in the hierarchy and to general navigation points within the collection. Thus, each page should have links to *next* and *previous* documents (if there is an obvious order to the pages) and to a table of contents or the section heading. If the document is big, say more than two or three screens full of text, then it might be a good idea to place the navigation icons at both the top and bottom of the document to make them easier to find.

Every document should use a consistent presentation style. The documents should be consistently designed, with the same heading structure, the same navigation icons, and similar content outlines. This makes it easy to get the *feel* for the collection and also makes it possible to index or catalog the collection using programs that take advantage of this structure.

Artistic license is, of course, encouraged! But these general guidelines will help to make your work more pleasing and easier to use.

Figure 2.2 (the HTML listing is in Figure 2.1) shows an example HTML document from a large collection of related files. This particular example is one of approximately 80 documents that discuss various aspects of the HTML language. This collection of documents can be accessed at:

www.utoronto.ca/webdocs/HTMLdocs/NewHTML/htmlindex.html

Flat or Serial Document Collections

The documents in Figures 2.1 and 2.3 are a part of an essentially *flat* collection of documents, where all the files are linked together in a linear, or serial, fashion, like pages in a book. However, there are also many hypertext links relating the documents in non-serial ways; for example, one document discussing the **IMG** element has a sentence mentioning URLs, which, in turn, contains a hypertext link to a document giving a more detailed discussion of URLs. The documents are also ordered hierarchically. Thus, the document discussing the **HR** element is *under* the **BODY** document, which is, in turn, *under* the Table of Contents (see Figure 2.4). The Table of Contents page contains hypertext links to all the documents in the collection and is an easy tool for quickly finding and accessing a particular section.

Figure 2.1 HTML listing for the document *hrule.html*, a typical text-only HTML document.

```
<html>
<head><title> HR element in HTML </title></head>
<body>
[<a href="htmlindex.html">Index</a>]   [<a href="body.html">Up</a>]
[<a href="lists_reg.html">Back</a>]    [<a href="entities.html">Next</a>]

<H1> 4.7 Horizontal Ruled Line </H1>

<P>The HR element is used to draw a horizontal dividing line completely across
the screen. This can be used to logically separate blocks of text, or to separate
icon lists from the body of the text.

<p> The HR element is empty (you don't need a <code>&lt;/HR></code>).

<h2> Example </h2>
The following illustrates the use of &lt;HR>:
<blockquote>
<pre>
The following document is scanned from the back of
a cereal box.  To see the scanned image, press the
icon at the bottom of the text ....
&lt;HR>
&lt;H1> MIGHTY CHOKEE-OS! &lt;/H1>
The cereal of chocolate deprived kiddies everywhere!
&lt;p> Aren't you lucky your parents love you enough
to buy you CHOCKEE-OS!
&lt;p> Remember to ask Mom and Dad for NEW SUPER
CHOCKEE-OS, now with Nicotine!!
</pre>
</blockquote>
<p> <b> This is rendered as:</b>
<p> The following document is scanned from the back of
a cereal box.  To see the scanned image, press the
icon at the bottom of the text ....
<HR>
<H1> MIGHTY CHOKEE-OS! </H1>
The cereal of chocolate deprived kiddies everywhere!
<p> Aren't you lucky your parents love you enough to buy you CHOCKEE-OS!
<p> Remember to ask Mom and Dad for NEW SUPER CHOCKEE-OS, now with Nicotine!!!
<hr>
<p> [<a href="htmlindex.html">Index</a>] [<a href="body.html">Up</a>]
    [<a href="lists_reg.html">Back</a>]  [<a href="entities.html">Next</a>]
</body></html>
```

Figure 2.2 Netscape Navigator 4 rendering of a typical text-only document (*hrule.html*).

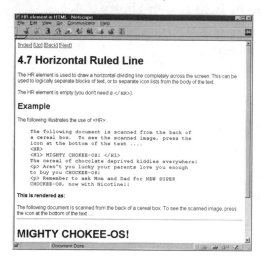

Navigation Buttons

Note the navigation text icons at the top of the page in Figure 2.2. There are four navigation buttons: *Index*, *Up*, *Back*, and *Next*. The *Index* button takes you directly to a Table of Contents page, while the *Up* button takes you one level up in the hierarchy, in this case, to the **BODY** page. The *Back* button takes you backward to the preceding document in the hierarchy, while the *Next* button takes you forward to the next document. The *Back* and *Next* buttons are the ones to use if you want to read the document straight through.

Table of Contents Page

Figure 2.4 shows the HTML table of contents document for this collection (the listing is in Figure 2.3), although only a portion of it appears within the window. Notice how this gives a complete overview of the document tree, including the relative placement of the sections in the hierarchy and the hypertext links to each section. This table of contents was constructed by hand—a tedious process to say the least. Fortunately, there are programs that can automatically generate a hypertext table of contents directly from the HTML documents, using the headings embedded in the documents to create both section names and the hierarchical organization. This is another good reason to use appropriate heading elements. Information about such indexing tools can be found in "Web Management and Maintenance Tools" on the companion Web site.

Figure 2.3 HTML source document for the Table of Contents Page
***htmlindex.html*. Some of this document has been omitted to save**
space. The rendering of the document is shown in Figure 2.4.

```
<html><head>
<title> HTML Documentation Table of Contents</title>
</head>
<body>
<h1> HTML Documentation Table of Contents </h1>
<dl>
  <dt><a href="htmlindex.html">Table of Contents (this page)</a>
  <dt><a href="about_the_author.html">About the Author</a>
</dl>
<ol>
  <li><a href="intro.html">Introduction to this Document</a>
  <li><a href="html_intro.html">Introduction to HTML </a>
  <ol>
    <li><a href="elements.html">HTML Elements</a>
    <li><a href="doc_struct.html">HTML Document Structure</a>
    <li><a href="naming.html">HTML Document Naming Scheme</a>
  </ol>
  <li><a href="head.html">HEAD</a> of an HTML Document
    <ol>
      <li><a href="title.html">TITLE</a>
      <li><a href="isindex.html">ISINDEX</a>
      <li><a href="nextid.html">NEXTID</a>
      <li><a href="link.html">LINK</a>
      <li><a href="base.html">BASE</a>
    </ol>
  <li><a href="body.html">BODY</a> of an HTML Document
    <ol>
      <li><a href="headings.html">Headings</a> (Hn)
      <li><a href="paragraph.html">Paragraphs</a> (P)
      <li><a href="line_break.html">Line Breaks</a> (BR)
. . .
    </ol>
. . .
    </ol>
</body></html>
```

General Design Issues: Offering Alternative Formats

There are several other organizational features that you may want to use. For
example, you might want to provide a printable version of a document collection.

Figure 2.4 Table of Contents page (*htmlindex.html*, listed in Figure 2.3) for the HTML document collection containing the file *hrule.html* (shown in Figure 2.1), as rendered by the NCSA Mosaic for X-Windows browser. This document collection is accessible at www.utoronto.ca/webdocs/ HTMLdocs/NewHTML/htmlindex.html

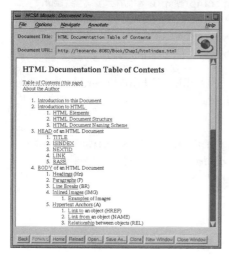

If so, you can join the documents together and present them as a single, large file that clients can download and read as HTML or print as a single file from their browsers. However, if you do this you should let users know what to expect. For example, you can add text to the table of contents (or some other page) that provides a link—plus related information—such as:

```
<p> This entire archive of documents is also available as a
    single <A HREF="alldocs.html">concatenated HTML document</A>
    (198 Kbytes), suitable for printing.  Note, however, that
    the hypertext links in this document have been removed.</P>
```

This guides users to a document that can be both viewed and printed, but also warns that the file is big, and that certain functions available in the discrete files are not present. The user can then decide whether to click on the phrase "concatenated HTML document" and access the resource.

In some cases, you might want to make the entire document collection available as an archive. Then, users who make extensive use of the documents can copy down the entire HTML collection and install it on their own machines, reducing the load on your server and increasing the speed with which they can access the material. If you are using a PC, you might make such an archive using the programs *PKZIP* or *WinZip*. This lets you archive multiple files and directories in a single compressed file, usually with the filename extension *.zip*. For example, you could archive all the files from a collection in a file named *alldocs.zip*. On Macintoshes, the *StuffIt* program serves a similar function: StuffIt creates archive files with the filename extension *.sit*. UNIX users will use a program called tar (for tape archiver), which could yield the archive file *alldocs.tar*. UNIX also has two programs for compressing programs: *compress*, which places a *.Z* at the end of the compressed filename, and *gzip*, which places a *.z* or *.gz* at the end of the compressed filename. This would yield the compressed archive files *alldocs.tar.Z* (using compress) or *alldocs.tar.gz* (using gzip), sometimes shortened to *alldocs.tgz*. If you were generous in preparing archives for multiple platforms, you might prepare a document section pointing to these files. An example of such a document is shown in Figures 2.5 and 2.6.

Most HTTP servers let you restrict access to certain files or directories on the server. You can then choose to control access to archives, should there be copyright problems associated with the archive content.

Figure 2.5 Example HTML document *src_link.html* that contains links to alternative formats of a document collection. Clicking on the items retrieves the archives to the client's machine.

```
<HTML>
<HEAD><TITLE> Archives of this Documentation </TITLE></HEAD>
<BODY>
<H2> Document Archives </H2>
<p> Archives of the document collection are available in the following
formats:
<OL>
<LI><A HREF="alldocs.zip">alldocs.zip</A>    (138 Kbytes) -- <EM> DOS PKZIP  </EM>
<LI><A HREF="alldocs.sit">alldocs.sit</A>    (532 Kbytes) -- <EM> Macintosh
      Stuffit</EM>
<LI><A HREF="alldocs.tar">alldocs.tar</A>    (527 Kbytes) -- <EM> UNIX tar </EM>
<LI><A HREF="alldocs.tar.Z">alldocs.tar.Z</A> (133 Kbytes) -- <EM> UNIX tar
    (compressed)</EM>
<LI><A HREF="alldocs.tar.z">alldocs.tar.z</A> (104 Kbytes) -- <EM> UNIX tar
    (gnuzipped) </EM>
<LI><A HREF="alldocs.html">alldocs.html </A> (523 Kbytes) -- <EM> Concatenated
      HTML documents </EM>
    <UL>
      <LI><EM>This is a concatenation of the HTML documents, suitable for
          printing from a browser. The Hypertext links have been removed.</EM>
    </UL>
</OL>
<HR NOSHADE>
<B>Last Update:</B> <EM>12 July 1996</EM> --
&lt;A HREF="mailto:prof.plum@clue.com">prof.plum@clue.com</a>&gt;
</BODY></HTML>
```

Figure 2.6 Rendering of the HTML document *src_link.html* (shown in Figure 2.5) by the Internet Explorer 3 browser.

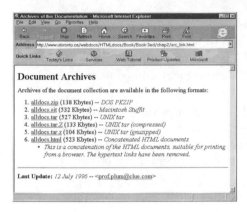

Nesting of List Elements

As a final HTML aside, note that Figure 2.6 illustrates how different types of lists can be nested. Here, an unordered list element (**UL**) is nested inside an *ordered list* (**OL**):

```
<OL>
   <LI><A HREF="alldocs.zip">.........

      .

      .

   <LI><A HREF="alldocs.html">alldocs.html</A> (523 Kbytes) .....
        Concatenated HTML documents </EM>
   <UL>
      <LI>(This is a concatenation of the .....
   </UL>
</OL>
```

The browser does exactly what you would expect, and simply nests one list inside the other. In HTML, any type of list can be nested within another list. Recall, however, that you cannot put lists inside headings or headings inside lists.

Lessons from Example 4

1. **PRE** surrounds blocks of preformatted text: This is displayed with a fixed-width font and preserves the spaces, tabs, and line breaks of the actual text. Text emphasis and anchor elements are allowed inside **PRE**; other elements, such as **Hn** and **IMG,** are not permitted.

2. **BLOCKQUOTE** is for block quotations, and usually displayed by browsers with indented margins. This element is often used to produce indented text.

3. Collections of documents should have a consistent design to make them easy to navigate. Where appropriate, you should create a hypertext table of contents. There are programs available that can help you do this, some of which are discussed in "Web Management and Maintenance Tools" on the companion Web site.

4. Use navigation icons (or text keywords instead of pictures) as hypertext links to help the user navigate through the document collection. However, if you use icons, make sure that you provide a text-only navigation option (use that **ALT** attribute!) for users with nongraphical browsers.

5. Single HTML documents should be small and self-contained. Larger documents should be broken up into smaller documents to best take advantage of the hypertext facilities.

6. Sometimes it is desirable to have a *flat*, printable text version of a collection. You can concatenate your HTML files together to make such a document and create a hypertext link from your collection to this document. But, be sure to include information about the size of this file (if it is large) so that the user knows what to expect.

Exercises for Example 4

There are several examples of book-like document collections—have a look at them, and see how they compare with the model described here. Some examples are:

www.utoronto.ca/webdocs/HTMLdocs/NewHTML/htmlindex.html

info.med.yale.edu/caim/manual/

Navigation icons are found in almost all document collections, not just book-like ones. Look for them the next time you are on the Web and note how their presence makes it easy to navigate within the collection.

Example 5: Linking to Data— Images, Movies, and Audio

As mentioned earlier, Web browsers can only display certain image formats and sometimes restrict GIF images to fewer than 50 or so displayed colors per image. Further, small images are advantageous, since large images can take a long time to download and are often irritating for that reason alone.

However, sometimes these image format restrictions are unreasonable. Often you need to include a large image that is an important part of your material—for example, a still from a movie (for a film publicity site), or a campus map that can be *clicked* on to access information about various campus buildings. For both of these cases, a tiny image is unacceptable. Furthermore, you may have truly high-quality GIF images containing 256 colors, or perhaps non-GIF format images, and want to make them available for viewing. Perhaps you even have movie or sound files. How can these options be included in a document and presented to your clients?

Large Images—Small Files

If you need a large image on a main page, the key is to make the image *file* small. Remember that GIF and JPEG store images in a compressed format and as a result, you can often process an image so that the file is small, even if the image itself is very large. Chapter 3 discusses these and other issues associated with processing images for use on the Web.

Linking to Large Images

If you have secondary pages containing large image files, the key to good design is simply to warn the user of what to expect and to place this warning near the hypertext anchors pointing to these secondary pages. This gives the user several options: accessing the page as is; disabling image loading when accessing the page; or not accessing the document altogether.

Thumbnail Sketches

A *thumbnail sketch* is a particularly useful way of linking to a large image. A *thumbnail* is just a reduced size icon of the actual image or of some characteristic portion of the image. Thumbnails are easy to make with any commercial or public-domain image editing program. You can then include the thumbnail in your document, and make a hypertext link from the thumbnail to the document containing the large image. This is done in Figure 2.7, where the small images are links to larger images or to movie files. In this example, the thumbnail of the larger GIF image is only 1,500 bytes in size, one-tenth the size of the original file. Note that sizes of the linked documents are also given—these are big files! Extra information such as this is useful to readers, as it lets them know what to expect.

Linking to Other Data Types

You may also want to indicate the data type of the file; in Figure 2.8, for example, the text indicates that the linked image file is a GIF and that the linked movie is in MPEG format. Anchors can indicate links to anything—not just HTML documents or images. There are many different audio, movie, multimedia, and image formats, and most browsers are capable of displaying only a few of them. Therefore, it is a good idea to indicate the format of large data files, so that users can avoid accessing files they cannot view or use.

Figure 2.7 The HTML document *vortex.html*, showing links from image icons to full-size images and video sequences. Figure 2.8 shows the rendering of this document by the Mosaic for X-Windows browser.

```
<HTML>
<HEAD>
<TITLE>Simulated Vortex Dynamics in a Porous-Body Wake</TITLE>
</HEAD>
<BODY>
<H1>Simulated Vortex Dynamics in a Porous-Body Wake</H1>
<P>This video presents the result of a numerical simulation on the wake
generated by a porous body.  The wake flow is simulated by inserting
small-scale discrete vortices into a uniform stream,  and  the colors
in the video represent the magnitude of vorticity.   The initial flow
field is subjected to a small perturbation based on experimental data.
The evolution of the wake flow is  manifested  by the merging  and
interactions of the small-scale vortices.
<P>The objective of this investigation is to study the merging and
inter-action processes of vortices and the formation of large eddies in
the flow.  Such an investigation is of importance to many flow-related
industrial and environmental problems, such as mixing, cooling,
combustion and dispersion of air-borne or water-borne contaminants.<P>
<HR>
<B> <A HREF="legend.gif"><IMG SRC="legicon.gif"
ALIGN=Bottom> Initial flow</A> and color legend for vorticity.</B>
(14.5 KB gif image)<p>
<HR>
<B> <A HREF="flow.mpeg"><IMG SRC="vortex.gif" ALT="[movie icon]"
ALIGN=Bottom> Visualization</A> of the evolution of the wake flow.</B>
(0.38 MB mpeg-1 movie)<p>
</BODY></HTML>
```

Helper Applications

So far our hypertext links have been to HTML documents or to HTML documents containing images via the **IMG** element. What happens if these links connect instead to other media, such as movies or sound files, or image files in special formats? Many Web browsers are not capable of displaying these data formats. So, what do they do?

With hypertext anchors, the answer lies in so-called *helper* or *viewer* applications. These are programs on the user's computer that can display images, movies, or sounds that cannot be handled by the browser itself. Thus, in Figure 2.8, the

Figure 2.8 Mosaic for X-Windows rendering of the document listed in Figure 2.7, showing thumbnail image icons linked to full-size image, movie, and sound files. The image overlaid on the browser (bottom left) resulted from clicking on the image icon at the top of the screen, while the movie-playing window (bottom right) was launched by pressing on the icon at the bottom of the screen.*

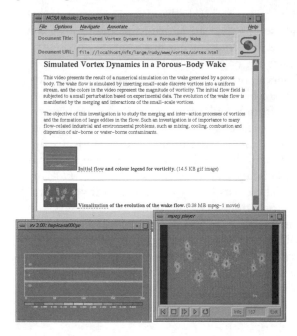

large-screen image was produced by clicking on the upper image icon in the browser window, which caused the browser to retrieve the data accessed by this link, acknowledge the data to be an image file, and launch the appropriate helper application to display the image (in this case, the UNIX image viewing program xv). In the case of the movie file, the browser recognized the data as an MPEG movie, so it started up the program *mpeg_play* to display the video information.

Downloaded Data and MIME Types

How does the browser know what a file contains, and what to do with it? Whenever data are retrieved from an HTTP server, the server, as part of the

---

* This page and the associated images and movies are courtesy of Rudy Ziegler of the University of Toronto's Centre for Academic Technology, while the data yielding the displayed image and movie frame were provided by Z. Huang, J. G. Kawall, and J. F. Keffer of the Department of Mechanical Engineering at the University of Toronto.

HTTP protocol, explicitly tells the browser the type of data being sent. It does this with a special message, sent to the browser just ahead of the actual data, called a *MIME content-type* header. The messages for GIF image files and MPEG movies, respectively, look like

```
Content-Type: image/gif
Content-Type: video/mpeg
```

When the browser receives this information, and if the browser cannot itself display the data, it searches in its database of *helper* applications to find a program that matches the indicated MIME type. If it finds such a program, the browser passes the data to the program and lets the helper do its job.

If the data comes from an FTP server, or if the browser is accessing the file from the local machine and not from an HTTP server, then the browser has to guess at the data content. It does this from the filename *extension*. Each browser has a database that matches filename extensions to the appropriate MIME type and uses this database to determine the MIME types of files accessed locally or via FTP. In general, this database will map the *.gif* suffix to the image/gif MIME type, the suffixes *.jpeg* or *.jpg* to JPEG images, and the suffixes *.mpeg*, *.mpg*, or *.mpe* to the video/mpeg MIME type. These lists have to be updated if you add a new filename extension. With Macintosh and Microsoft Windows browsers, the lists can be edited from a pull-down menu.

There are literally dozens of MIME types for data ranging from still images, audio, and video to compressed archives and executable programs. A detailed description of MIME types is given on the companion Web site in Appendix B, while the usage of MIME types is discussed in detail in Chapter 9.

Lessons from Example 5

1. Warn users when you present a link to a large image document or file, so that they can estimate how long it will take to download the data.

2. Identify the data format in any links to large image, audio, movie, or data archive files so that the users can tell if the file is in a format they can actually use.

3. You can use icons to link to larger image or movie files. This lets the users know what to expect and is often a good graphical addition to your document.

Exercises for Example 5

While you are Web surfing, try and keep track of how long it takes for a file to arrive—if you have a watch, actually measure this time. You will no doubt grow frustrated after only a few seconds. Now imagine how users will feel if they decide to download one of your files only to discover that they will need to wait *several minutes* for the data to arrive and be displayed. . . .

Example 6: Internal Links Within a Document

Up until now, we have looked at hypertext links that either connect one document to another or connect a document to other data resources. When these links are accessed, the browser retrieves the linked object and displays it, starting at the top of the HTML document or the beginning of the data file.

With HTML documents, this is not always desired. Sometimes, a document is quite long, and you want to link to a particular point in the document and not the beginning. Alternatively, you may want to link *between* different places in the same document—for example, from a short list of sections to the beginning of each section or to the top of the page. This is possible with HTML, but requires the use of an additional feature of the anchor element—the **NAME** attribute.

Anchor Element: The NAME Attribute

Links to particular locations in a document, or between locations in the same document, are made possible through the **NAME** attribute of the **A** (anchor) element. The **NAME** attribute lets you assign a unique name, called a *fragment identifier*, to a particular place in a document. You can then link to this named location using a special form of URL that contains this special name.

Figure 2.9 shows a document containing several named locations, illustrating one of the common uses of named locations to create a simple index for the contents of the page. The top of the page contains links that access the different sections of the document, while each section contains links that allow you to return to the top of the page and back to the contents listing. This page was originally developed by the author and Sian Meikle of the University of Toronto Library, and is part of a template document collection we distribute to university departments interested in developing their own document collections. The entire template is located at www.utoronto.ca/ian/Template/readme.html.

Figure 2.9 A Typical HTML document, *deptinfo.html*, that contains named anchor elements. Portions of the document have been omitted to save space. Comments are in italics, while markers indicating the named anchors are in boldface italics.

```
<HTML> <HEAD>
   <TITLE> Biology Department: General Information  </TITLE> </HEAD>
<BODY>
<A HREF="depthome.html" NAME="top"><IMG SRC="home.gif" ALT="[home]"></A>
<HR>
<IMG ALIGN="right" SRC="french2.gif" ALT="[Picture of our Building]">
```

Continued

Figure 2.9 *Continued*

```
<H1>Biology at the University of Toronto</H1>
<ADDRESS>
   University of Toronto          <BR>  150 St George Street, Room 213 <BR>
   Toronto Ontario M5S 1A1 CANADA <BR>   <B>Tel:</B>     (416)-978-7000   <BR>
   <B>Fax:</B>     (416)-978-9000   <BR>   <B>E-mail:</B>
<a href="mailto:infobiol@biology.utoronto.ca">infobiol@biology.utoronto.ca</a>
</ADDRESS>
<HR>
<B>On this page:</B>
[<A HREF="#general">General Information</A>]
[<A HREF="#facilities">Research Facilities</A>]
[<A HREF="#history">Department History</A>]   [<— References Named Anchor]
<HR>

<H2><A NAME="general">General</A></H2>
<BLOCKQUOTE>
 <P><EM> This example document ... [text deleted] ...
   There is one advantage, however, to keeping this material together — it
   allows the user to print the entire document for reading away from the
   computer.</EM>
</BLOCKQUOTE>

<P> The University of Toronto is the largest university in Canada
  with 2500 graduate faculty and more than 9000 full and part-time graduate
  students. ...
... [text1 deleted ...]
<H2><A NAME="facilities">Research Facilities</a></H2>

<P> The Department provides many facilities to aid astronomical research,
   and students and staff use national and international observatories
   all over the world ...
...   [text deleted]
[<a HREF="#top">... to top of page</A>
<H2><A NAME="history">History of the Department</A> </H2> [<—NAMED ANCHOR]

<P> Biology became a major department in 1905.  The first chair of
   the Department, Dr. Roland Fishburn, ...
.......[more text deleted]
[<a HREF="#top">... to top of page</A>
<HR>
<a HREF="depthome.html"><IMG SRC="icons/home.gif" ALT="[home]"></A>
</BODY> </HTML>
```

Figure 2.10 Netscape Navigator 3 rendering of the document deptinfo.html shown in Figure 2.9.

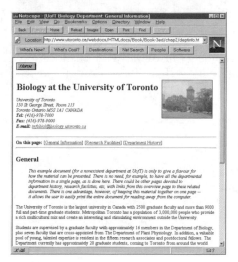

Figure 2.11 Netscape Navigator 3 rendering of the document deptinfo.html shown in Figure 2.9 after accessing the internal link referenced by the text string "Department History," shown at the top of Figure 2.10. Note how the browser has scrolled the page so that the link target (History of the Department) is visible.

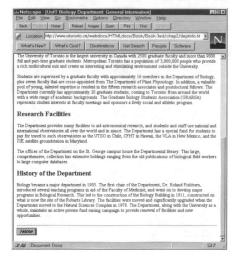

NAME Attribute and Fragment Identifiers

There are four named anchors in Figure 2.9, but for this discussion we will focus on the one for the history section. The relevant hypertext anchor is:

```
<A NAME="history">History of the Department</A>
```

This anchor associates a *fragment identifier*, namely "history," with this location in the document. Looking at Figure 2.10, you will see that this section of text is not rendered in any special way. In general, an anchor that contains only a **NAME** attribute is not specially displayed. From elsewhere in this document, this location can be referenced using a URL of the form

```
<A HREF="#history">Department History</A>
```

as illustrated in Figure 2.9. Note how the fragment identifier is indicated by *prepending* the hash character (#), to distinguish this from a regular URL. If the user clicks on the anchored text *Department History*, the browser will search for the named fragment identifier and scroll down (or up) the page to that location, as illustrated in Figure 2.11.

NAME and HREF Combined

A hypertext reference can simultaneously take both **HREF** and **NAME** attributes. An example is shown in the very first anchor in Figure 2.9, namely:

```
<A HREF="depthome.html" NAME="top"><IMG SRC="home.gif" ALT="[home]"></A>
```

Clicking on this anchor links the user to the document *depthome.html* (you will note in Figure 2.10, this image is highlighted as a linked hypertext anchor). At the same time, clicking on internal page links of the form

```
<a HREF="#top">... to top of page</A>
```

returns the user to the top of the page and to this same linked image. Thus, anchors can be both the start and destination of a hypertext link.

Fragment Identifiers and Full URLs

You can also access named locations from outside the document. This is done by *appending* the fragment identifier to the document's locator string. For example, if the full URL for the document *deptinfo.html* were

```
http://www.utoronto.ca/ian/Template/deptinfo.html
```

then the URL that explicitly references the history section is simply (with the fragment identifier in boldface):

```
http://www.utoronto.ca/ian/Template/deptinfo.html#history
```

Figure 2.12 schematically illustrates some of the more common uses of named anchors. Details about writing valid fragment identifiers and URLs are found in Chapter 8.

Figure 2.12 Schematic illustrating the use of NAME and HREF attributes. The dashed lines indicate hypertext links and their destinations. Links (A) and (E) are absolute URLs, while (B) and (D) are partial URLs between two documents in the same directory. (C) is an internal link within the document deptinfo.html. The base URL for both documents is: http://www.utoronto.ca/ian/Template/

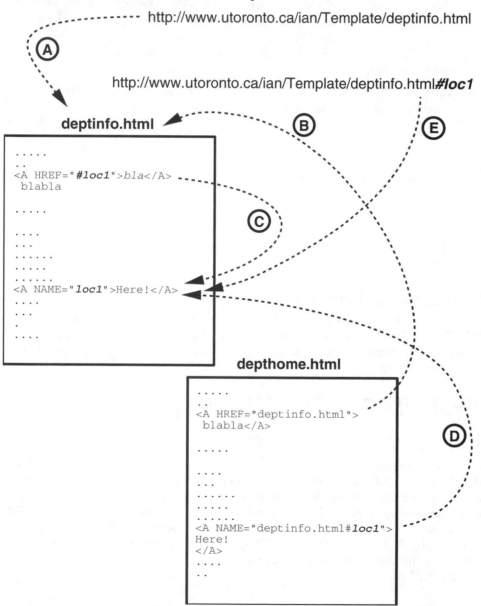

Lessons from Example 6

1. The **NAME** attribute assigns a name, called a *fragment identifier,* to an **A** (anchor) element. This allows an anchor to be the *destination* of a hypertext link, and allows for hypertext **HREF** anchors that target specific locations within a given document.

2. You can reference a **NAME**d location from within the same document, using an anchor element of the form `<A HREF="#`*frag_id*`">anchor text</A>`, where *frag_id* is the fragment identifier you wish to reference. The hash character is mandatory, and indicates the start of a fragment identifier.

3. You can reference a **NAME**d location from any other document by appending the fragment identifier to the URL of the document, for example:

   ```
   <A HREF="http://bla.bla.edu/Projects/doc2.html#frag_id">anchor text</A>
   ```

4. You can combine **HREF** and **NAME** anchors in the same anchor element:

   ```
   <A HREF="URL_string" NAME="frag_id" >anchor text</A>
   ```

   This means that the anchor is both the start and the possible destination of hypertext links.

Exercises for Example 6

Create a long HTML document (e.g., convert a word-processor document to HTML) and build some internal links between a contents list and the various sections. Note how much easier it is to read the document when these internal navigational tools are available.

Example 7: Image, Heading, and Paragraph Alignment

Example 2 presented some methods for obtaining very rudimentary control over the placement and alignment of images and text on the page. Fortunately, other attributes and attribute values allow for significantly more control over this aspect of document presentation. These extensions occur through the addition of **ALIGN** (alignment) attributes to most elements that contain text (i.e., Hn (heading), **P** (paragraph), **BLOCKQUOTE**, and **DIV**), and also additional **ALIGN** attribute values for the **IMG** element. These attributes, and their effects, are illustrated in Figures 2.13 through 2.16.

Heading and Paragraph Alignment

For elements that contain text, **ALIGN** defines the desired alignment for the text and can take the values "left" (left-justify the text: the default), "center" (center the text between the margins), "right" (right-justify the text), and "justify" (justify text between left and right margins). Currently, only *left*, *center*, and *right* alignment are widely implemented. Figure 2.14 shows the effect of these different alignment options on the heading and paragraph elements. If a browser does not understand the alignment value, it ignores the **ALIGN** attribute and uses the browser's alignment default (usually left-adjusted).

Image Alignment

Image alignment is more complex than text alignment, since the desire is to let the image "float" to some preferred location and then to let text flow around it. HTML supports the use of **ALIGN** values of "left" and "right" for this purpose, where *left* causes the image to float to the left margin and *right* causes the image to float to the right margin. Any text *following* the **IMG** element in the HTML markup, flows to the side of and below the image. Figure 2.16 (the HTML document is listed in Figure 2.15) shows the effect of the left and right alignment values. Here the images have floated to the indicated margins, with text flowing around them.

Almost all browsers support this type of image alignment; however, some older ones do not and simply place the image inline with the text. It is therefore a good idea to place an **IMG** element as the first item in a line or to precede it by a line break element. This guarantees that the image will appear as the first item in a line, regardless of the browser.

Image WIDTH and HEIGHT

To format the page, a browser must know the size of the image being inserted. In general, a browser does not know this size until the image is delivered, which means that it can't begin displaying the page until all the images have arrived. Since this can significantly delay the construction of the page, HTML supports the **IMG** element **HEIGHT** and **WIDTH** attributes, to specify the size of the image in pixels. Given this information, the browser can begin formatting the page, leaving an empty box for the image(s) still being downloaded. If an image is not of the specified size, the browser *resizes* the image to fit the defined box. This is illustrated in Figure 2.16, where the little home page icon has been zoomed to almost twice its actual size. Of course, with an image as ugly as this, shrinking the image would have been a better choice!

Image Padding: HSPACE and VSPACE

When inserting an image into a document, an author may wish to leave extra space between the image and the surrounding text. One way to do this is to create the image with a surrounding border, and use this border (perhaps *transparent*— see Chapter 3 for more information on image formats and transparency) to space

Figure 2.13 HTML code for the document *align.html*. This document illustrates some of the alignment features possible with the heading and paragraph elements.

```
<HTML>
<HEAD><TITLE>
Heading and Paragraph Alignment Options
</TITLE></HEAD>
<BODY>
<H2 ALIGN="center"> Alignment Options: Headings and Paragraphs</H2>
<HR NOSHADE>
<BLOCKQUOTE>
<H3 ALIGN="left">Left-Aligned Paragraph &amp; Heading</H3>
<P>
Alignment can take the four values "center", "left" (the default), "
right" and "justify". This paragraph is "left" (default) aligned, so that
the text lines up with the left margin, and the right side is ragged.
<H3 ALIGN="right">Right-Aligned Paragraph &amp; Heading</H3>
<P align="right">
Here is a right-aligned paragraph. This can look odd, but is useful for
special emphasis, or if placed against a left-aligned image. Note how
the right margin is straight, and the left is ragged.
<H3 ALIGN="center">Center-Aligned Paragraph &amp; Heading</H3>
<P align="center">
Here is a centered paragraph. In principle, this means both the left
and right margins will be ragged. This is a useful way of centering
images. For example:<BR><IMG SRC="sright.xbm">
<H3 ALIGN="justify">Justified Paragraph &amp; Heading</H3>
<P align="justify">
Here is a justified paragraph. In principle, this means both the left
and right margins should be smooth, with wordspaces being adjusted
to keep it that way.   If your browser does not understand
<CODE>ALIGN="justify"</CODE> (most do not), it will use the default
left-justification.
</BLOCKQUOTE>
</BODY></HTML>
```

the image from the text. However, this is not always possible or convenient, so HTML supports **HSPACE** and **VSPACE** attributes to define a spacing, in pixels, to be left around an image. For example, in Figure 2.16, the second image has been inserted using **HSPACE**="8" and **VSPACE**="5". This creates padding borders on all sides of the image—here 8 pixels on the left and right sides, and 5 pixels above and below.

Figure 2.14 Netscape Navigator 4 rendering of the document *align.html*, listed in Figure 2.13.

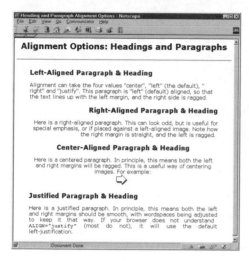

Image Borders

An image can be inside an anchor element, which turns the image into a clickable icon for accessing another resource. By default, most browsers will box an anchored image with a colored or shaded border, just as they underline anchored text. This is not always desired, as the borders can detract from the appearance of the icon, particularly in a toolbar menu, where the "button" nature of the image is obvious.

HTML supports a **BORDER** attribute to the **IMG** element, to specify the thickness, in pixels, of the border surrounding the image. The default value for an IMG inside an anchor element is **BORDER="1"**; borderless images can be created by specifying **BORDER="0"**. The navigational buttons at the top of Figures 2.15 and 2.16 illustrate this use of **BORDER**; note how the second arrow does not have a border, although it is an active anchor. Most graphical browsers indicate that an image is an active anchor by changing the mouse pointer to a special symbol (usually a hand) when the pointer passes over the image.

Clearing Margins for Text

Often, you will want text to appear after the bottom of an image and not beside it. To do this, you must *clear* the text so that subsequent text moves down unconditionally below the image. Since the image can be to the left or right, you must also be able to specify that the text should start only when the left margin is clear, when the right margin is clear, or when both margins are clear.

In HTML, this is accomplished using the **CLEAR** attribute, available only on the **BR** element. Thus, `<BR CLEAR="left">` ensures that the text following the **BR** is cleared to the left margin; while `<BR CLEAR="right">` ensures that the

Figure 2.15 HTML code for the document *alignimg.html*. This document illustrates some of the alignment features possible with the image element.

```
<HTML><HEAD>
<TITLE>
Heading, Paragraph and Image Alignment Options</TITLE>
</HEAD>
<BODY>
<A HREF="isindex.html"><IMG SRC="sleft.xbm" ALT="[Previous]"></A>
<A HREF="url.html"><IMG SRC="sright.xbm" BORDER=0 ALT="[Next]"></A>
<HR NOSHADE>
<H2 ALIGN="right"> Alignment Options —<BR>
    <em>Images</em></H2>
<P>
Here is some text that flows around the image. The
<CODE>ALIGN="left"</CODE>
<IMG ALIGN="left" ALT="[Example Image]" SRC="home.gif">
attribute value causes the image to float to the left hand margin, and
allows the text to flow around the image.  This results in much nicer
image—text placement, a better use of the page, and graphically more
attractive documents.
<P>
The following is the same example image, but with <B>HSPACE</B> and
<IMG VSPACE=5 HSPACE=8 ALIGN="left" ALT="[Example Image]" SRC="home.gif">
<B>VSPACE</B> attributes used to add spacings around the image.
Note how this improves the readability of both text and image. You
could get a similar effect by simply building this border into the image
file itself.
<P> To the right is the image with <B>HEIGHT</B> and <B>WIDTH</B> set
to 100—
<IMG ALIGN="right" HEIGHT=100 WIDTH=100 ALT="[Example Image]"
    SRC="home.gif">
the image is zoomed to this size. To clear text to follow the image,
we need <CODE>&lt;BR CLEAR="right"&gt;</CODE>.
<BR>
<em>after regular <CODE>&lt;BR&gt;</CODE></em>
<BR CLEAR="right">
<em>after <CODE>&lt;BR CLEAR="right"&gt;</CODE></em>
<HR>
</BODY></HTML>
```

Figure 2.16 Microsoft Internet Explorer 3 rendering of the document *alignimg.html*, listed in Figure 2.15.

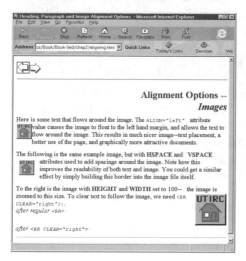

following text is cleared to the right margin; and `<BR CLEAR="all">` ensures that the following text is cleared to both margins. Figure 2.15 shows the effect of **CLEAR**="right" to clear the text that follows the large right-hand image. This attribute is understood by any browser that allows left- and right-aligned images.

Lessons from Example 7

1. The **ALIGN** attribute on headings and paragraphs can be used to modify the default alignment of the text content. Possible values are "left" (the default), "right", "center", and "justify".

2. On most browsers, the **ALIGN** attribute on **IMG** elements can float an image to the left (**ALIGN**="left") or right (**ALIGN**="right") of the display and allow text to flow around the image. An author can also use the **WIDTH** and **HEIGHT** attributes to specify the dimensions of the image being inserted (in pixels), as well as **HSPACE** and **VSPACE** attributes to specify the horizontal and vertical spacing (also in pixels) to be left at each border of the image. **BORDER** can be used to set the width of (or eliminate) the border drawn around images within anchor elements.

3. When text flows around image, an author can use the element **BR**, with an appropriate **CLEAR** attribute value, to clear subsequent text to start below the image.

Exercises for Example 7

Take the example document *align.html* and modify the alignment options. In particular, use the **HEIGHT** and **WIDTH** attributes to modify the size of embedded images. Note how you can use these to stretch and deform inline images.

Example 8: Tables and Backgrounds (1)

The next two examples look at HTML elements and attributes for modifying the background of the display window and for defining tables of items. These features are particularly used to define complex page layout and typography, and are perhaps the most used elements in an HTML page designer's repertoire. Several of the most common applications of these elements are illustrated here and in Example 9. Some additional table examples are found in Chapter 6.

Background Control

HTML 3.2 supports a **BACKGROUND** attribute to the **BODY** element to indicate an image file that the browser can use as a background for the displayed document. The form is:

```
<BODY BACKGROUND="url">
```

The value for **BACKGROUND** is the URL of an image file. If capable, the browser will load this image and use it to *tile* the background of the document being displayed. Figure 2.18 shows an example of a loaded background (the HTML document is given in Figure 2.17). This can be an attractive change to the document, but should be used with care—remember that not everyone has a good graphics display or a high color (16-bit color) graphics card.

Backgrounds can cause problems if the background color is similar to the default color of the text. Consequently, all browsers supporting BACKGROUND also support the attributes TEXT, LINK, ALINK, and VLINK for specifying the color of regular text, text within hypertext anchors, text within activated links (when the link is pressed), and text within visited hypertext anchors, respectively. Such browsers also support a BGCOLOR attribute to specify a single background color, which works even if image loading is disabled.

Figure 2.17 HTML code for the document *tables.html*. This document illustrates the TABLE element, as well as the BODY element BACKGROUND attribute.

```
<HTML><HEAD>
<TITLE>Table and Background Example</TITLE></HEAD>
<BODY BACKGROUND="paper01.jpg" TEXT="#000000"
```

Figure 2.17 *Continued*

```
                    ALINK="#ff0000" VLINK="#005050">
<H1> Simple Table Examples </H1>
<BLOCKQUOTE>
<P>This simple example demonstrates simple table layout. Note how the second
table does not have any borders, and is right-alignedon the page.
<HR>
<TABLE BORDER>
<CAPTION> <B>First Example <A HREF="tables.html">Table</A></B></CAPTION>
 <TR BGCOLOR="#ffffff">
      <TH ROWSPAN="2"> Segment </TH>  <TH COLSPAN="2"> Total Memory </TH>
 </TR> <TR>
                                        <TH>Bytes</TH>    <TH> Kbytes </TH>
 </TR> <TR>
     <TD> 005B5 </TD>    <TD ALIGN="right"> 78 </TD>   <TD> (OK)   </TD>
 </TR> <TR>
     <TD> 00780 </TD>    <TD ALIGN="right"> 175</TD>    <TD> 0K      </TD>
 </TR> <TR>
     <TD> 020B  </TD>    <TD ALIGN="right"> 88348 </TD>
                                      <TD BGCOLOR="#ffffff"> 510K </TD>
 </TR> <TR>
     <TD COLSPAN="2" ALIGN="left"><A
     HREF="memory.html">Total Free</A></TD>
                                      <TD BGCOLOR="#666666"> 510K </TD>
 </TR>
</TABLE>
<HR>
<TABLE BORDER="0" ALIGN="right">
<CAPTION> <B>Second Example <A HREF="tables.html">Table</A> </B></CAPTION>
 <TR>
     <TD COLSPAN="2"   ALIGN="center"
                   BGCOLOR="#ffff77"><EM><B>Note Well!!</B></EM></TD>
 </TR><TR>
     <TD BGCOLOR="#f1ffff">Here is some<BR>text in a cell      </TD>
     <TD BGCOLOR="#666666">Here is some<BR>text in the next cell</TD>
 </TR>
</TABLE>
<P>Text flows around this right-aligned  table, just as with images.
Thus you can create proper text documents and associated tabular
information (or images) without difficulty.
</BLOCKQUOTE>
</BODY></HTML>
```

BGCOLOR is also important because if image loading is disabled, the background image is not displayed. This can be a problem if, for example, the background image is dark and the TEXT attribute is used to change the text color to white. With image loading disabled, the background will be white (or gray, or whatever the default is for the user's browser), not black (since the background image was not loaded), so that the text is rendered in white against a white background—difficult to read, to say the least! Thus, if BACKGROUND is used, BGCOLOR should also be used, to specify a color that mimics the background due to the image.

TABLEs

Tables are defined using the **TABLE** element, while the content of the table is laid out as a sequence of table rows (**TR**), which, in turn, contain table headers (**TH**) and/or table data (**TD**). A table can also have a caption, defined by the **CAPTION** element. The caption can contain all forms of character formatting markup, including hypertext anchors. An example is shown in Figures 2.17 and 2.18. Tables can have borders and dividing lines or can be borderless. The start tag <TABLE BORDER> ensures that the table is drawn with borders and dividers— you can adjust the thickness of the border by assigning a value (in pixels) to the **BORDER** attribute.

HTML also allows tables to "float" on the page, like images. This is illustrated in Figure 2.18, where the second table was floated to the right-hand margin. Some older browsers do not support floating tables, in which case the tables always appear alone, with all images and text preceding or following the table.

Figure 2.18 Netscape Navigator 3.0 rendering of the document *tables.html*, **listed in Figure 2.17.**

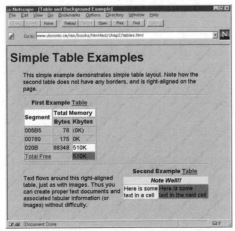

Rows and Columns

Tables are defined as a collection of rows, defined by the **TR** element. Each of these rows contains a collection of *cells*, defined by the **TH** or **TD** elements. **TH** (table header) elements are used for column or row headings, while **TD** (regular tabular entry) elements are used for everything else. The differences between the rendering of **TH** and **TD** content are small: In general, **TD** content is left-aligned, while **TH** content is centered within the cell and rendered in boldface. Both are nonempty elements, and end tags are required.[1] These elements can take several attributes to define the horizontal and vertical alignment of the element content (**ALIGN** and **VALIGN**), or the number of rows or columns (**ROWSPAN** and **COLSPAN**) occupied by the table cell.

Justification of Table Rows and Columns

When you design a table, you must ensure that the number of rows and columns sum to the correct number for your table; that is, all the rows must *span* the same number of columns and all the columns must span the same number of rows. For example, compare the markup in Figure 2.17 with the table rendering in Figure 2.18. The first table is defined with three columns and six rows. Note how the number of columns in each **TR** element always sums to three—a cell with **ROWSPAN="2"**, such as the first once in Figure 2.18, contributes an extra column to the following row, since this cell "spans" two rows. Keeping track of the rows and columns tends to be a bit tricky the first time you create a table, but you will quickly get the hang of it. Often it is easiest to sketch out the table design on a piece of paper—this helps you determine the required number of rows and columns, and also where and when cells should span multiple rows or columns. If you are then coding doing tables by hand, it is useful to lay them out structurally, as done in Figure 2.17, as this allows you to see the underlying tabular structure. You should also turn on the table borders, so you can see the actual structure of the table.

Of course, it is easier if you can find a program that will create HTML tables for you. This is possible with some modern HTML editors. Note, however, that most advanced table design is still done by hand—there are still some cases where software is no match for the expert designer.

Alignment Within Table Cells

Items within elements, or along entire rows, can be aligned using the alignment attributes. **ALIGN**, which can take the values **ALIGN="left"**, "center", or "right", aligns the cell contents horizontally within the cell. The attribute **VALIGN** is used to vertically align the content, and can take the values **VALIGN="top"**, "middle", or "bottom". The effects of some of these alignment options are illustrated in Figure 2.18. Note that you can use these alignment attributes with a **TR** element, to set the alignment for all **TD** or **TH** cells in a row.

---

[1] Officially, **TD, TH,** and **TR** end tags are optional, but omitting the end tags often leads to problems when the browser renders the table (i.e., the browsers have bugs), so you should always put them in.

TIP: Common TABLE Problems

Often, leaving out end tags (`</TR>`, `</TD>`, etc.) will cause the table to be improperly formatted. If you have problems, make sure all the end tags are in place.

Typing text inside a table, but outside a **TD** or **TH**, is illegal. If you do type text outside cell (For example, `<TR> error text <TD> ...`), the text that is improperly positioned will be displayed just above the table. Thus if you see text appearing magically above a table, it probably came from an error inside the table.

If you omit the `</TABLE>` to end a table, Netscape Navigator does not display any of the table content. Thus, look for missing `</TABLE>` tags if the table refuses to appear!

Row and Cell Properties

Finally, you can use the **BGCOLOR** attribute within a **TR**, **TD**, or **TH** element to change the background color of the cell or group of cells. This is illustrated in both example tables shown in Figures 2.17 and 2.18, where the background color has been modified to emphasize cell contents. Netscape Navigator 4 and Internet Explorer 3/4 also support a **BACKGROUND** attribute for specifying a background image for table cells.

Lessons from Example 8

1. The **TABLE** element permits formally defined tables in HTML documents. A few older browsers do not support this element, so you may want to offer a non-**TABLE** alternative for these users, if this is likely to pose a problem.

2. The **BACKGROUND** attribute to the **BODY** specifies an image file to be used as a background to the displayed text. Care should be taken to make sure that the background does not dominate or otherwise obscure the text or images lying on top. The additional **BODY** attributes **TEXT**, **LINK**, and **VLINK** allow for control of the color of the text and are described in Chapter 6.

Exercises for Example 8

Tables are complicated to design and are well worth some practice. As a first exercise, try modifying the tables in Figures 2.17 to create your own variants. You can, for example, take tabular information from a printed book or magazine and recreate the layout using HTML. Note that tables need not contain text, but can contain pictures, or even other tables—try including images, or entire tables, within a table cell.

Example 9: Tables and Backgrounds (2)

Tables are an important tool for structuring and organizing page content, and this second set of table examples illustrate some of the important tools and principles for controlling the layout of table content. Other examples are found in Chapter 6.

Table Padding, Spacing, and Borders

The **TABLE** element supports **BORDER**, **CELLPADDING**, and **CELLSPACING** attributes for specifying the size in pixels of the table border, the padding space within a cell, and the spacing between table cells, respectively. These different attributes are used in the six tables listed in Figure 2.19. Figure 2.20 shows the rendering of this document by both Netscape Navigator 3 and Internet Explorer 4. The structure and content of all six tables are the same: Each table consists of two rows, with three cells per row. In the first row, the first cell is "empty" (there is no text inside), while the remaining cells contain text; note that the third cell takes a **BGCOLOR** attribute to color the cell red. In the second row, the TR element takes the attribute **BGCOLOR="#b0b0b0"**, which colors the row a light gray. In this case, all the cells contain text content—note that the first cell contains only an * * (a non-breaking space entity reference—entities are described in more detail in Chapter 6 and on the companion Web site in Appendix A) so that there is no visible text in this cell.

Looking to Figure 2.20, we can see the effect of the **CELLPADDING**, **CELLSPACING**, and **BORDER** properties (set to values of "8" in the second, third, and fourth tables, respectively). Note how **CELLPADDING** adds space around the content of a cell, while **CELLSPACING** pads the space between the cells, and **BORDER** simply thickens the border around the entire table.

Netscape Navigator/Internet Explorer Differences

There are important differences between these two browsers in their handling of the spacing between cells, and the coloring of "empty" cells. As you can see in Figure 2.20, Netscape does not color the cellspacing region (space between the cells) and also does not color cells that are "empty"—that is, that do not contain characters (you can trick an empty cell into being colored by placing a single * * character in it, as illustrated in the first cell in the second row of each table). This should be contrasted with Internet Explorer, which colors the cell spacing region using the **TABLE** background color and which colors all cells—even those that are empty.

Note also the difference in vertical spacing between adjacent tables: Netscape leaves a space, while Internet Explorer 4 leaves no space. This must be accounted for when designing documents with adjacent tables.

If not specified, the default values of **CELLPADDING** and **CELLSPACING** are on the order of one or two pixels, depending on the browser. Thus, setting these two quantities to zero should bring the cells into contact with one another,

Figure 2.19 HTML document illustrating the table BORDER, CELLPADDING, and CELLSPACING attributes. See Figure 2.20 for an example rendering.

```
<HTML><HEAD><TITLE>Test of Table Spacings </TITLE></HEAD>
<BODY>
<TABLE BGCOLOR="yellow">
   <TR>
      <TD>        </TD>  <TD> One  </TD>  <TD BGCOLOR="red"> Two! </TD>
   </TR><TR BGCOLOR="#b0b0b0">
      <TD> </TD>    <TD> Four </TD>  <TD> Yahoo </TD>
   </TR>
</TABLE>

<TABLE BGCOLOR="yellow" CELLPADDING="8">
   <TR>
      <TD>        </TD>   <TD>  One </TD>   <TD BGCOLOR="red"> Two! </TD>
   </TR><TR BGCOLOR="#b0b0b0">
      <TD> </TD>     <TD> Four </TD>   <TD> Yahoo </TD>
   </TR>
</TABLE>
<TABLE BGCOLOR="yellow" CELLSPACING="8">
   <TR>
      <TD>        </TD>   <TD>  One </TD>   <TD BGCOLOR="red"> Two! </TD>
   </TR><TR BGCOLOR="#b0b0b0">
      <TD> </TD>     <TD> Four </TD>   <TD> Yahoo </TD>
   </TR>
</TABLE>
<TABLE BGCOLOR="yellow" BORDER="8">
   <TR>
      <TD>        </TD>   <TD> One </TD>   <TD BGCOLOR="red"> Two! </TD>
   </TR><TR BGCOLOR="#b0b0b0">
      <TD> </TD>     <TD> Four </TD>   <TD> Yahoo </TD>
   </TR>
</TABLE>
<BR>
<TABLE BGCOLOR="yellow" CELLPADDING="0" CELLSPACING="0">
   <TR>
      <TD>        </TD>   <TD> One </TD>   <TD BGCOLOR="red"> Two! </TD>
   </TR><TR BGCOLOR="#b0b0b0">
      <TD> </TD>     <TD> Four </TD>   <TD> Yahoo </TD>
```

Figure 2.19 *Continued*

```
    </TR>
</TABLE>
<BR>
<TABLE BGCOLOR="yellow"  CELLPADDING="0" CELLSPACING="0" BORDER="0">
    <TR>
        <TD>        </TD>   <TD> One </TD>  <TD BGCOLOR="red"> Two! </TD>
    </TR><TR BGCOLOR="#b0b0b0">
        <TD> </TD>    <TD> Four </TD>  <TD> Yahoo </TD>
    </TR>
</TABLE>
</BODY></HTML>
```

Figure 2.20 Rendering, by Netscape Navigator 3 (left) and Internet Explorer 4 (right) browsers, of the tables listed in Figure 2.19. The differences and similarities between the two renderings are discussed in the text.

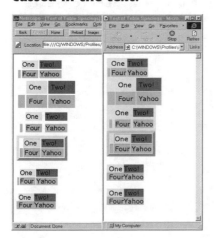

with no intervening space. This works with Internet Explorer, but not Netscape Navigator—Navigator still leaves a small space between the cells and around the table, as illustrated by the fifth table shown in Figure 2.20. This is because Navigator assumes a default "invisible" table border or width "1", which it inscribes around the entire table and around each cell. By setting **BORDER**="0", as done in the sixth example table, this border can be eliminated, bringing the cells into direct contact.

Tiling and Image Using Tables

Zero-width cell spacings and paddings are used in Figure 2.21 to create a composite image from four image tiles. The table consists of a two-column, two-cell table, with each cell containing one quarter of the total image. The rendered image, shown at the top of Figure 2.22, shows a single picture made up of the four parts, tiled next to one another. Extra space characters inside a table cell can add whitespace to the rendered cell and spoil the image alignment. This is illustrated in the second table in Figures 2.21 and 2.22; note how the space after the bottom-left-hand image causes whitespace to appear inside the rendered table.

The DIV Element

This example also introduced the **DIV** element: **DIV** denotes a block division of a document and can include almost any other element, including paragraphs, tables, and other **DIV**s. Here, the **DIV** takes the attribute **ALIGN**="center", which instructs the browser to center-align all content within the **DIV**. Thus, the enclosed headings are center-aligned on the display, as are the tables within the **DIV**.

Figure 2.21 HTML document illustrating the use of TABLEs to create a composite image. The comment on line 22 marks the line that has extra whitespace inside the table cell. The result is a "broken" tiled image, as shown in Figure 2.22.

```
<HTML><HEAD><TITLE>Test of Table Spacing -- Image Icons</TITLE>
</HEAD>
<BODY>
<DIV ALIGN="center">

<H3>Images In Table</H3>
<TABLE BORDER="0" CELLPADDING="0" CELLSPACING="0">
<TR><TD><IMG SRC="top-left.gif"></TD>
    <TD><IMG SRC="top-right.gif"></TD>
</TR>
<TR><TD><IMG SRC="bottom-left.gif"></TD>
    <TD><IMG SRC="bottom-right.gif"></TD>
</TR>
</TABLE>

<H3>Space Character Inside a TD Cell</H3>
<TABLE BORDER="0" CELLPADDING="0" CELLSPACING="0">
<TR><TD><IMG SRC="top-left.gif"></TD>
    <TD><IMG SRC="top-right.gif"></TD>
</TR>
<TR><TD><IMG SRC="bottom-left.gif"> </TD>     <!-- EXTRA SPACE in cell -->
    <TD><IMG SRC="bottom-right.gif"></TD>
```

Figure 2.21 *Continued*

```
</TR>
</TABLE>
</DIV>
</BODY></HTML>
```

Figure 2.22 Rendering, by Netscape Navigator 3, of the tables listed in Figure 2.21. Identical table rendering is found with Navigator 4 and Internet Explorer 3 or 4.

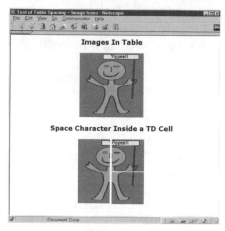

Table Widths and Alignments

Last, we look at controlling table widths. By default, a table "grows" to be just as big as required; note how the tables in Figures 2.20 and 2.22 are as small as possible, given their content. However, sometimes we wish to fix the size of the table, either in height or width, while at other times we wish to fix the size of a particular cell (or column) within the table. This is possible, to some degree, through the **WIDTH** attribute, supported by **TABLE**, **TD**, and **TH** elements. Some browsers also support a **HEIGHT** attribute for these elements to specify the height of the table or of the cells. This is less widely supported and is not discussed here. The behavior is similar to that of **WIDTH**—when it works!

On the **TABLE** element, **WIDTH** specifies the desired width of the table. This can be given as a percentage of the available width, or as a length in pixels. Thus **WIDTH**="100%" calls for a table that fully spans the available space.[2]

---

[2] For a table inside the document **BODY**, the available width is the full width of the display. Sometimes, however, a table lies within a table cell of another table, within a **BLOCKQUOTE**, or within another element that restricts the available horizontal space. In these cases, the *available* width is simply the width of the element the table lies within.

Alternatively, the value can be a number, as in **WIDTH**="200". This calls for a table 200 pixels wide. Note, though, that these are only guidelines to the browser—if the table content is too big for the specified table size, the browser will enlarge the table so that the content fits.

Figure 2.23 is a simple example document that illustrates these features. This document has two main structural tables. The first table, at the top of the page, generates the page caption (*Table Test Documents*) to the right and the navigation buttons to the left—notice how the **WIDTH**="100%" attribute causes the table to fully span the page width, while the **ALIGN**="right" attribute in the right-hand table cell aligns the page caption with the right-hand margin of the page. Note also the use of the **FONT** element to reduce the size of the text within these two cells: **FONT**, discussed in detail in Chapter 6, can modify text font size and color and can also suggest the font face (e.g. Arial or Times Roman) to use. Note, however, that the style sheet mechanism provides better ways of doing this, as discussed in Chapter 7.

The second table also has **WIDTH**="100%", and is used to structure the layout for the remainder of the page. This table has one row, consisting of three cells: The first cell, of **WIDTH**="40", introduces a left margin for the page. The third cell, of **WIDTH**="150", has a background color and could be used for sidebar graphics or text associated with the main content (here it simply has some placeholder text). The middle cell is of unspecified size and is sized to take up the remaining space, such that the table fills the full width of the browser. Note that this cell contains a second table.

How reliable are these **WIDTH** specifications? For **TABLE**, these values are quite reliable: The **TABLE** will generally be of the specified size, provided the content actually fits horizontally in the specified space. However, when specified for particular cells, **WIDTH** values are treated by many browsers (in particular, Netscape Navigator 3 and 4) as a "hint" to the browser, rather than as a hard rule: Such browsers often adjust cell sizes far from the **WIDTH** specified values. To actually fix the cell size at a particular value, you can place an **IMG** element whose **WIDTH** property is set to the desired size within the cell. Note, in Figure 2.23, how the left- and right-hand cells both contain **IMG** elements with **HEIGHT**="1" and **WIDTH** values equal to the desired cell width (you need to make allowances, in this width calculation, for the cell spacing and cell padding lengths). Here, the actual image file is a 1 pixel by 1 pixel transparent GIF image—this is invisible on the display and is there only to ensure the desired cell widths.

Although table elements can produce quite acceptable page layouts, the mechanism is rather crude and, to say the least, time-consuming—it takes a long time to figure out how to lay out a complicated page. The new cascading style sheets technology offers much improved mechanisms for controlling page layout, as discussed in Chapter 7.

Figure 2.23 HTML document illustrating the use of TABLEs to structure page layout. Browser rendering of this document is shown in Figure 2.24.

```
<HTML><HEAD><TITLE>Test of Table Width Specifications</TITLE>
</HEAD>
<BODY>
<TABLE BORDER="0" CELLPADDING="0" CELLSPACING="0" WIDTH="100%">
<TR>
   <TD VALIGN="top" ALIGN="left"><FONT SIZE="-1">
      <A HREF="home.html">Home</A>       ~ <A HREF="home.html">Next</A> ~
      <A HREF="home.html">Previous</A> ~ <A HREF="home.html">Index</A></FONT>
   </TD>
   <TD VALIGN="top" ALIGN="right"><FONT SIZE="-1">
      <B><I>Table Test Documents</I></B></FONT></TD>
</TR></TABLE>


<HR SIZE="2" NOSHADE>


<TABLE BORDER="0" CELLPADDING="8" CELLSPACING="0" WIDTH="100%">
<TR>
   <TD WIDTH="40"><IMG SRC="transparent.gif" ALT="" HEIGHT="1" WIDTH="40"></TD>
   <TD>
      <H1>This Is The Main Content</H1>
      <P>The table has three cells: the first cell, at the left,
         adds an artificial left margin. The second cell, in the
         middle, takes the main content of the page.The final cell,
         at the right, might contains a decorative sidebar.
      <TABLE HSPACE="10" ALIGN="left" CELLPADDING="4">
          <TR> <TD BGCOLOR="yellow"COLSPAN="2"><B>FLYING
               TURTLES</B></TD> </TR>
          <TR> <TD BGCOLOR="fuchsia"><B>Buy</B><BR> The Album</TD>
               <TD BGCOLOR="cyan"><B>See</B><BR> The Movie</TD>
          </TR>
      </TABLE>
      <BR> <B>Note that you can</B> also have tables within a table
      cell, for further substructure of the page. An example is the
      table to the left of this paragraph.
   </TD>
   <TD  WIDTH="150" VALIGN="middle"  BGCOLOR="#ffff66">
      <P>Here is some space for extra text, highlighted by
      the table cell's background color.
```

Continued

Figure 2.23 *Continued*

```
    <BR><IMG SRC="transparent.gif" ALT="" HEIGHT="1" WIDTH="150">
  </TD>
</TR>
</TABLE>
</BODY></HTML>
```

Figure 2.24 Rendering, by the Internet Explorer 4 browser, of the document listed in Figure 2.23.

Lessons from Example 9

1. The spacing within table cells can be controlled via the **TABLE** element **CELLPADDING** attribute, while the spacing between cells is controlled via **CELLSPACING**. The **WIDTH** attribute can set a preferred size for the entire table, either in pixels or as a percentage of the available width.

2. **BGCOLOR** can set the default background color for the entire table, for a row, or for a cell. Note that the effect of **BGCOLOR** applied to **TABLE** is different on Netscape Navigator and Internet Explorer.

3. The **ALIGN** and **VALIGN** attributes, applied to table rows or table cells, define how the cell content should be aligned. **WIDTH**, when applied to a cell, defines a preferred cell width, either in pixels or as a percentage of the full size of the table.

Exercises for Example 9

Visit a variety of Web sites with complicated page layouts and save the documents onto your hard disk. Then, go into each document with an editor and examine how the page is designed. Most likely the design uses table elements to position the page components on the display.

Example 10: Fill-in Forms

This example looks at the HTML **FORM** element. **FORM** elements let a document author solicit user input through documents containing fill-in forms. Using this element, a designer can build a document containing checkboxes, radio boxes, pull-down lists, text windows, and menus, and can configure this **FORM** to send the gathered data to a program on an HTTP server. For example, **FORMs** can be used to collect data for a database search, solicit data for an on-line questionnaire, accept electronic text for submission to a database, or solicit electronic messages for forwarding to a particular user.

The example in Figure 2.25 illustrates this last case; namely, a **FORM** that lets the user type in a message for forwarding to a recipient chosen from a list. Figure 2.26 shows this form rendered by Internet Explorer, while Figure 2.27 shows the rendering by lynx.

The FORM Element

Let's first look at Figure 2.25 and the **FORM** element start tag:

```
<FORM ACTION="http://side.edu/cgi-bin/send_note">
```

This line starts the **FORM** and ties the data of the form to a particular program (*send_note*) on the indicated HTTP server. All a **FORM** element does is collect data: It does only minimal processing of the data, so the only way you can get a form to do anything useful is to send the data it gathers to a program on a server. The **ACTION** attribute tells the browser where to send the data—in this case, to the program *send_note* at the indicated URL. Data is sent to this server-side program when the user presses the *Send Message* button at the bottom of the page. Of course, the program must be able to understand the message sent by the form. As a result, the **FORM** and the program *send_note* must be designed together.

The program *send_note* takes the data sent by the client and processes it to complete the task. Here, the program might take the data and send an electronic mail message to the intended recipient. The HTTP mechanisms for sending data to a server are described in Chapter 9, while gateway programs and the mechanisms by which data are sent to gateway programs are discussed in the **http** URL section in Chapter 8 and also in Chapter 10.

The FORM Input Elements

By comparing the HTML document in Figure 2.25 and its rendering in Figure 2.26, you can see some of the several input items that can go inside a form. This example shows a **SELECT** element pull-down menu (where the user selects the

Figure 2.25 The HTML source code for the document *form.html*.

```
<HTML><HEAD> <TITLE> Example of an HTML FORM </TITLE></HEAD>

<BODY>
<H1> Example of an HTML FORM  </H1>
<FORM ACTION="no_action">
<P>Data entered into a FORM is sent to a program on the server
for processing.  If you see a button at the end of this sentence
then your browser supports the HTML FORMs element.
-[<INPUT TYPE="checkbox" NAME="button" VALUE="on">]-
If you do not see a button between the square brackets go to the
<A HREF="text_only.html"> text-only interface </A>. </FORM>
<hr>
<FORM  ACTION="http://side.edu/cgi-bin/send_note">
  <p> <STRONG> 1) Send this note to: </STRONG>
  <SELECT NAME="mailto_name" >
    <OPTION SELECTED> Martin Grant </OPTION>
    <OPTION> Jack Smith </OPTION>        <OPTION> Bruce Lee </OPTION>
    <OPTION> Anna Mcgarrigle </OPTION>  <OPTION> Kate Bush </OPTION>
    <OPTION> Spike Lee </OPTION>         <OPTION> Diane Koziol </OPTION>
    <OPTION> Ross Thomson </OPTION>      <OPTION> Ann Dean </OPTION >
  </SELECT>

  <p> 2) <STRONG>Give your e-mail address: </STRONG>  This indicates who
      sent the letter
  <p> <INPUT TYPE="text"  NAME="signature"
                          VALUE="name@internet.address" SIZE="60">
  <p> <STRONG> 3) Message Body: </STRONG>
  <TEXTAREA COLS="60" ROWS="8" NAME="message_body">
Delete this message and type your message into this   textbox.  Press the
"Send Message" button to send it   off. You can press the "Reset" button to
reset the   form to the original values.
  </TEXTAREA>
  <P> <INPUT TYPE="submit" VALUE="Send Message">
      <INPUT TYPE="reset"> (reset form)
</FORM>
</BODY></HTML>
```

name of the person to whom he or she wishes to send the message—the possible names being given by the **OPTION** element); a single-line text **INPUT** element (here, where the user types in an e-mail address); and a **TEXTAREA** element

Figure 2.26 Microsoft Internet Explorer rendering of the document *form.html*, listed in Figure 2.25. The fill-in FORM elements are clearly evident.

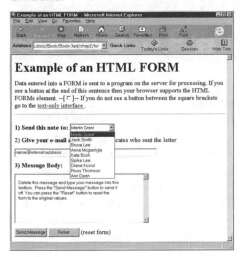

Figure 2.27 Lynx browser rendering of the *form.html* document, listed in Figure 2.25. The FORM fill-in elements are clearly evident. In general, lynx gives written instructions at the bottom of the screen to help the user properly manipulate the form.

(where the user types the body of the message). These are the three possible input elements allowed inside a **FORM**, although the **INPUT** element itself supports various types of input mechanisms, specified via a **TYPE** attribute. The details of the different elements and input types are described in Chapter 6 and also in Chapter 7.

The elements **SELECT**, **INPUT**, and **TEXTAREA** can only appear inside a **FORM**. Indeed, with all versions of Netscape Navigator, form input elements are displayed only when inside a **FORM**.

Input Element NAME and VALUE Attributes

Every **FORM** input element must take one key attribute. This is the **NAME** attribute, which associates a *variable name* with the data entered into the input element, for example *NAME="mailto_name"* or *NAME="message_body"*. These names differentiate between the data from different input elements in the same form. For example, in Figure 2.25, these names distinguish the recipient name (*mailto_name*—associated with the **SELECT** list) from the actual message to send (*message_body*—associated with the **TEXTAREA**).

INPUT elements can take a **VALUE** attribute, which assigns a default initial *value* to the named variable. An example is the element

```
<INPUT TYPE="checkbox" NAME="button" VALUE="on">
```

which assigns the value "on" to the name "button". These values can subsequently be changed by user input: by selecting a different entry from a pull-down menu, typing text into a box, or clicking on checkboxes or buttons.

Default values are also possible with **TEXTAREA** or **SELECT**. With **TEXTAREA**, any text entered between the start and stop tags is taken as the default value, while with **SELECT**, default values are set by placing a **SELECTED** attribute on the appropriate enclosed **OPTION** elements.

Submitting the FORM

When the user presses a special **INPUT** element of *TYPE="Submit"* (in Figure 2.25, this is the *Send Message* button), the data in the form are sent to the server. They can be sent in a number of ways, but in all cases are sent as a collection of *name/value* pairs, where *name* is the value of **NAME** attribute of an element, and *value* is the value assigned by the user's input or by **VALUE**. For example, the text input field accepting the e-mail address would send the pair *signature/name@ internet.address*. The details of the algorithms used to construct the messages sent to a server are discussed in Chapter 8 and in Chapter 10.

The server program sorts out the data by matching the *names* in the message to names the program is designed to recognize. Consequently, a form and the associated server-side gateway program designed to process form data must be designed together. Gateway program design is described in more detail in Chapter 10.

As with all HTML elements, **FORM** has restrictions on where it can be placed. A **FORM** cannot be inside a heading, inside another **FORM,** or inside character emphasis markup, such as a **STRONG** or **EM** element. However, a **FORM** can contain headings, character markup elements, lists, and even tables. Indeed, tables are commonly used to structure the input elements, as illustrated in Figure 4.10.

Figure 2.27 shows the **FORM** from Figure 2.25 as displayed by lynx. The lynx browser can display all the **FORM** elements and provides instructions at the bottom of the screen explaining how to fill in the different items.

FORMs Not Supported?

It is now very rare, but there are still a few browsers in use that do not support forms. The little checkbox enclosed in square brackets near the top of Figures 2.26 and 2.27 is designed explicitly to handle this situation—note that this button does not do anything, as it lies inside its own **FORM** and does not have an associated submit button. However, this checkbox does test a browser's support for forms. If the checkbox is absent, then the browser does not support forms, so the reader can see that there is a problem and select the text-only interface.

Lessons from Example 10

1. The document developer can use the HTML **FORM** element to solicit user input. However, each form document must send the data it gathers to a server-side gateway program designed to analyze the form data. This gateway program is specified by the **ACTION** attribute of the **FORM** element. The program and form must be designed together.

2. An HTML **FORM** can contain several input elements, namely **INPUT, SELECT,** and **TEXTAREA.** These elements can only appear inside a **FORM.**

3. A **FORM** cannot be inside a heading element or inside another **FORM**— **FORM**s cannot be nested. However, heading, list, character markup, **PRE,** and **TABLE** elements can be inside a **FORM.**

Exercises for Example 10

Constructing **FORM**s is a complicated compromise of structure and ease-of-use: You need to organize the input elements so that they are easy to use and understand, while keeping the form small enough that it does not get confusing. As an exercise, you can try creating HTML versions of some of the form-style interfaces of standard programs. You will find that **TABLE**s are one of the most useful tools for constructing well laid out input forms. Chapter 6 gives more details about how **FORM**s work. At this point, do not worry about the server-side processing of the data other than to give all the form input items appropriate **NAME**s. Additional details about forms are found in Chapter 6 and 7, while form-based data processing is discussed in Chapters 10 and 11.

Example 11: Inline Data Viewers— EMBED and OBJECT Elements

In Example 5, we looked at hypertext links to data other than other HTML documents and discussed how these data could be processed by external helper applications. Sometimes, however, you do not want exotic data types to be displayed away from the document, but rather want them displayed within the text. For example, you might want an audio or movie player to appear right within the page of a text document or perhaps an Excel spreadsheet to be displayed next to a description of the data.

This is possible using the **EMBED** element (nonstandardized, but supported by Netscape and most other browser vendors) and the newer **OBJECT** element (partially supported in Internet Explorer 3, more fully but still incompletely supported in Navigator 4 and Internet Explorer 4). These are designed for embedding objects of arbitrary data types *within* an HTML document, much in the same way that images are embedded using the **IMG** element.

For example, using **EMBED**, an author can include one of these nonstandard data types using a tag such as

```
<EMBED SRC="/dir/video/movie1.avi" WIDTH="200" HEIGHT="150">
```

which embeds the file *movie.avi* (a Microsoft AVI-format movie) in the document. How does the browser determine the data type of this file? The type is determined in the same manner described in Example 4: Either the HTTP server explicitly sends a MIME content-type header to indicate the type, or the browser guesses the type based on the filename extension, using its preconfigured database of filenames and MIME types.

This only works if the browser knows the filename extension—in fact, there are hundreds of extensions for which the browser has no default MIME type. Therefore, it is always best to serve data out using an HTTP server, since a properly configured Web server always sends the proper content-type MIME header. For example, the following **EMBED** element would insert a *Corel* CMX-format image into a document:

```
<EMBED SRC="cmx/canary.cmx" WIDTH="500" HEIGHT="200">
```

Current browsers do not know, by default, what this filename extension (*.cmx*) means and count on the server to provide the proper content-type information.

The **EMBED** element can take the three attributes **SRC**, **WIDTH**, and **HEIGHT**, which have the same meanings as with the **IMG** element. **SRC** gives the URL for accessing the data, while the **HEIGHT** and **WIDTH** give the size for the box that will display the data within the page. In addition, **EMBED** can take arbitrary user-defined attributes of the form *PARAM_NAME="value"*, where both *PARAM_NAME* and *value* are arbitrary, and depend only on the particular data type being displayed. This turns out to be a bad way of doing things and, as a result, the **EMBED** tag will soon be dropped in favor of the much more flexible **OBJECT** element. **OBJECT** is discussed in detail in Chapter 7.

Figure 2.28 shows a typical HTML document that uses **EMBED** to include a special data type—in this case, a Corel CMX image. Figures 2.29 and 2.30 show the display of this document by the Netscape Navigator browser.

Displaying Embedded Data—Browser Plugins

Of course, just getting data to the browser is not sufficient, as you also need a way of displaying it. The problem is that the browser does not know how to do this without help. As you may recall from Example 5, this is the same problem we encountered when linking to arbitrary data types—in this case, the problem was solved by helper applications that processed the data in place of the browser. For embedded data types, we again need the help of additional software, but in this case this help must be plugged right into the browser. Such software modules are thus called *browser plugins*.

Figure 2.29 shows the Netscape Navigator rendering of the page shown in Figure 2.28, where the browser is not equipped with the special plugin capable of displaying *Corel* CMX image files. The browser, unable to display this data type, substitutes a default symbol indicating this failure. Note also the pop-up menu that informs the user that the plugged-in data is of an unknown type (the type would be listed as "image/x-cmx," if the server understood this data type). Figure 2.30 shows the same document, but after the browser has been equipped with the Corel CMX plugin—the browser can now, via the plugin, display the image. In addition, the region displaying the CMX image supports special right-mouse button menu controls for processing and displaying the image. These controls are provided by the plugin module.

The bottom of Figure 2.29 and 2.30 show an additional plugin, in this case one that plays audio files. This plugin is a control panel: The slider on the bottom is a volume control, while the other buttons stop, pause, and play the audio file. More sophisticated controls are, of course, found in other plugins.

Finally, Figure 2.31 shows what users see when using a browser that does not support plugins. In this case they see nothing, which can lead to very confusing and/or misleading documents. The **EMBED** element does not allow for an alternative to the embedded data, which is a major weaknesses of the **EMBED** approach.

OBJECT Instead of EMBED

As mentioned earlier, **OBJECT** is the more fully functional successor to **EMBED**. As an example of how it works, consider an **OBJECT**-based equivalent to the **EMBED** element used in Figure 2.28 to play audio files. First the **EMBED**:

```
<EMBED  SRC="sound.au" WIDTH="145" HEIGHT="60"
                    HSPACE="10" VSPACE="5" ALIGN="LEFT">
```

and second, the equivalent **OBJECT**:

```
<OBJECT DATA="sound.au" TYPE="audio/aiff" WIDTH="145" HEIGHT="60"
                         HSPACE="10" VSPACE="5"  ALIGN="LEFT">
   <P>The audio says:
   <BLOCKQUOTE> The best, and most enjoyable, way to see ....
   </BLOCKQUOTE>
</OBJECT>
```

These are quite similar, although the **OBJECT** element has two obvious advantages. First, the element itself can indicate the MIME type of the resource being referenced (via the **TYPE** attribute). Second, the content of **OBJECT** is alternative markup that is displayed when the browser cannot display the specified data, or when it does not understand **OBJECT**.

Figure 2.28 Example HTML document *embed.html*, which uses the EMBED element to include arbitrary data types within the HTML document. The rendering of this document by the Netscape Navigator browser is shown in Figures 2.29 and 2.30.

```
<HTML><HEAD>
<TITLE> Example of the EMBED Element</TITLE></HEAD>
<BODY>
<H1>Example of the EMBED Element</H1>
<BLOCKQUOTE>
<P>These simple examples illustrate the  <B>EMBED</B> element,  as currently
implemented on the Netscape Navigator and some other browsers. <BR>

<EMBED SRC="canary.cmx" WIDTH=200 HEIGHT=150><BR>

<P> Here is another <B>EMBED</B>, this time for an audio file. The associated
 plugin is an audio control panel—
<EMBED SRC="sound.au" WIDTH="145" HEIGHT="60" HSPACE="10" VSPACE="5">
 the panel is treated like an image.
<P> You can also left and right-align the plugin, in the same way as images.
<EMBED SRC="sound.au" WIDTH="145" HEIGHT="60" HSPACE="10" VSPACE="5" ALIGN="LEFT">
<EMBED SRC="sound.au" WIDTH="145" HEIGHT="60" HSPACE="10" VSPACE="5" ALIGN="RIGHT">
Here are two examples: note how the text wraps around the panels, just as it
wraps around regular image files.
</BLOCKQUOTE>
</BODY></HTML>
```

Figure 2.29 Rendering of the document in Figure 2.28 by a Netscape Navigator browser that is not equipped with the appropriate plugin. The browser is consequently unable to display the embedded data.

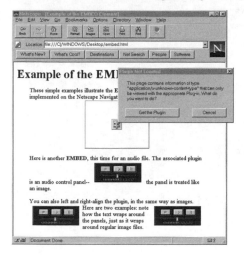

Figure 2.30 Rendering of the document in Figure 2.28 by a Netscape Navigator browser equipped with the appropriate plugin. The browser can now display the embedded data, with the plugin also providing a user interface that lets the user manipulate the data.

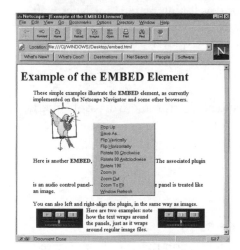

Figure 2.31 Rendering of the document in Figure 2.28 by the
***NetManage* WebSurfer 5.02 browser. This browser does not support**
Netscape plugins.

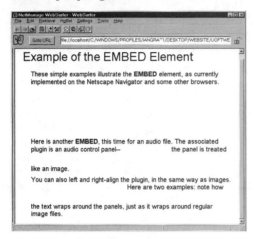

Of course there is much more to **OBJECT**; and refer to Chapter 7 for details.

Microsoft Plugins—ActiveX Controls

Needless to say, Microsoft has also pursued embedded object technology and defined the *ActiveX* technology as the tool for developing plugins for Microsoft's Internet Explorer. Software written according to the Microsoft ActiveX specifications will work as a plugin to Microsoft's Internet Explorer—but unfortunately will not work within Netscape Navigator or Communicator. However, plugins written for Netscape Navigator 3 (but not Navigator 4) will work with Microsoft's Internet Explorer 3 and 4.

Information about plugins for the Netscape Navigator and Microsoft Internet Explorer browsers can be found, respectively, at:

home.netscape.com/comprod/products/navigator/version_2.0/
plugins/index.html

www.microsoft.com/activex/

Plugins: Strengths and Weaknesses

Embedded data richly expands the types of information that can be presented by a Web browser. However, you must keep in mind that not everyone can display the data—most people will not have the required plugin, will be using a computer (e.g., Macintosh or UNIX as opposed to Windows-based) for which there is no appropriate plugin, or will simply be using a browser that does not support plugins. In addition, many plugins require advanced operating systems (Windows 95/NT, Macintosh System 7.5, etc.), fast processors (Pentium or faster), and lots of memory (16 MB or more). If the user's machine has too little memory or too slow a processor, the plugins will be at best slow and unresponsive.

If you decide to incorporate **EMBED/OBJECT** elements, you should provide instructions to the readers explaining how to obtain the required plugin. You might also want to provide an alternative to the embedded data should you want to service clients who simply cannot obtain the required software.

For now, plugins are most useful in a semi-controlled environment (such as a corporate intranet), where you can ensure that users will have the required hardware and software.

Lessons from Example 11

1. Arbitrary data types can be included inline in an HTML document using **EMBED** or **OBJECT** elements. **EMBED** works like the **IMG** element and takes the same **SRC**, **HEIGHT**, and **WIDTH** attributes, as well as arbitrary attributes specific to the plugin. **EMBED** is not supported by all browsers and is not part of "standard" HTML.

2. HTML is currently standardizing around the **OBJECT** element as a replacement for **EMBED**. **OBJECT**, which is more flexible than **EMBED**, is described in detail in Chapter 6. **OBJECT** is supported by Netscape Navigator 4 and Internet Explorer 4.

3. Embedded data types can only be displayed if the browser is equipped with the appropriate *plugin*. A plugin is a platform- and browser-specific software component that *plugs into* the browser, giving it the ability to display the associated data type. Most plugins are developed by software vendors responsible for the corresponding data type. Many plugins are available for only a limited number of browsers and/or platforms.

Exercises for Example 11

Examine your inventory of data (audio or video, spreadsheets, special image formats, etc.) and think about how these may or may not be incorporated into HTML documents. Then locate and install the plugin required for a particular data type you would like to use. Next, write some simple Web pages that embed this data type. If you know your intended audience, try polling them (by email, for example) to find out if they have a browser that supports a plugin for this data type. This helps you determine whether this will be an effective way to distribute your resources.

Example 12: Embedded Programs and Applets

In addition to embedding arbitrary data into an HTML document, HTML also supports the embedding of actual *programs*. Embedded programs are downloaded from a Web server and then run on your local computer. This exciting concept brings with it a host of security concerns: A user has no idea what the program is going to do when it arrives; and after it arrives, it is too late, since the program could have destroyed files, copied passwords to another computer, or done other despicable things.

This has led to the development of several so-called safe languages, the most well-known of which is *Java*. Java is designed to be both safe (such that running a downloaded Java program cannot damage your computer or access your computer's files and send them elsewhere) and platform independent. A compiled Java program can thus run on any computer—Windows, UNIX, or Macintosh, regardless of the processor or operating system. Almost all browser vendors now include support for Java programs within their Web browsers. HTML authors can then use the **APPLET** or **OBJECT** element to embed Java programs into their pages—the browser downloads the referenced Java program and executes it, using a built-in browser subsystem that supports Java. For security, a downloaded Java program can only run a small, restricted set of functions on the user's computer. For this and other reasons, the downloaded Java program is not considered a full application, but rather a mini-application or *applet*.

Current browsers let you include Java applets using the **APPLET** element, as illustrated in Figure 2.32. This element can contain two important parts: **PARAMETER** elements that define parameters required by the running applet and regular HTML markup that is displayed by browsers that do not understand **APPLET** or that are incapable of running Java programs. The **APPLET** element can take several attributes: **HEIGHT, WIDTH, HSPACE, VSPACE,** and **ALIGN** have the same meanings as with images, while **CODEBASE** indicates the URL where the applet software comes from, and **CODE** gives the name of the actual applet program at this URL.

Figure 2.33 shows the resulting document as displayed by the Microsoft Internet Explorer 3.0 browser—both Microsoft and Netscape support Java in their browsers. The applet appears as the graphic to the right, which is an animation that illustrates binary search tree rotations—an important concept in computer science. The reader can actually click on the balls causing these rotations and, in doing so, learn about this important database concept.

Like **EMBED, APPLET** is being replaced by the more flexible **OBJECT** element. **OBJECT** is supported by both Netscape Navigator 4 and Internet Explorer 4.

Java applets offer enormous promise for building dynamic, interactive Web pages. However, writing Java programs is not like writing HTML. Java is a full-blown programming language, comparable to C++, so that writing Java programs

Figure 2.32 Example HTML document *applet.html*, which uses the APPLET element to include a Java-language program within an HTML document. The rendering of this document by the Microsoft Internet Explorer 3 browser is shown in Figure 2.33.

```
<HTML><HEAD><TITLE>Example of an Embedded Applet</TITLE>
</HEAD><BODY>

<H1>Example of an Embedded Applet</H1>
<BLOCKQUOTE>

<P>To the right is a simple example of an embedded
<APPLET
   CODEBASE="http://www.dgp.toronto.edu/people/JamesStewart/378/notes/"
   CODE="bst.class" WIDTH=321 HEIGHT=151 VSPACE=10 HSPACE=10 ALIGN="right">
     <PARAM NAME=keys VALUE="50 42 43 15 6 23 17 30">
     <PARAM NAME=action VALUE="rotate">
     <PARAM NAME=alternate_nodes VALUE="15 42">
     <BLOCKQUOTE>
     <HR> If you were using a Java-enabled Web browser, you would
     see a binary search tree instead of this paragraph. <HR>
     </BLOCKQUOTE>
</APPLET>
applet, in this case a Java applet that demonstrates <EM>binary search tree (BST)
rotations</EM>. This is a  complicated concept in computer science, associated
with data storage and searching algorithms. The interactive applet (the user
can click on the balls to "select and rotate" the data) helps illustrate the
principles in an easy to use and effective manner.
<P>Note how the HTML <EM>content</EM> of the <B>APPLET</B>  element is not
displayed: the content is alternative markup,  that is displayed by browsers
that do not understand  the <B>APPLET</B> element or that are unable to run
Java applets.
<P>This applet example is courtesy of James Stewart, an Assistant professor
in the Department of Computer Science, University of Toronto.
</BLOCKQUOTE>
<HR NOSHADE></BODY></HTML>
```

is complex and not for the faint of heart! Also, Java applets, accessed over the Web, are often large files that take a long time to download—it is not uncommon to wait minutes for large applets to arrive. Also, as with plugins, you need modern, fast machines with lots of memory to run applets with acceptable speed and response times—a 100 MHz Pentium processor with 16 MB of memory is a good minimum configuration. Thus, be careful when jumping on the Java bandwagon

Figure 2.33 Rendering of the document in Figure 2.32 by the Microsoft Internet Explorer 3 browser.

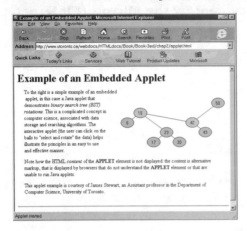

in case you find yourself delivering content that cannot be used by your users. Possibly the best environment for Java is inside a corporate intranet, where you can predict the types of equipment and software accessible to the users. Possibly the worse environment is one where you want to make Web resources accessible to the widest possible audience.

Document Scripting: Javascript and VBScript

If you can download programs and run them on the browser, why can't you also incorporate programs within the HTML documents?

This is now possible using two scripting languages: JavaScript, developed by Netscape and Sun Microsystems, and VBScript (Visual Basic Script), developed by Microsoft. Scripting languages are discussed in Chapter 7.

Lessons from Example 12

1. The **APPLET** element is used to embed a program applet within an HTML document. This element can contain HTML markup as well as **PARAMETER** elements to define parameters needed by the applet. The **APPLET** element also takes attributes needed to define the location (**CODEBASE**) and name (**CODE**) of the requested applet, and to specify the size and location for the applet on the window (**HEIGHT**, **WIDTH**, **HSPACE**, **VSPACE**, and **ALIGN**.)

2. The **OBJECT** element (see Chapter 6) is a likely successor to the experimental **APPLET** tag. Browsers will, however, be backward-compatible with the **APPLET** element.

Exercises for Example 12

Try visiting some sites containing applets to get a flavor for what they can do and also to get a flavor for the time it takes to download a large applet over the Internet. A large repository of Java applets can be found at:

www.gamelan.com

This is a good place to find Java examples. You might even find an applet you want to use.

GRAPHICS AND IMAGES IN HTML

DOCUMENTS

Inline images are one of the most appealing features of HTML, allowing the communication of important graphical information, as well as documents with colorful visual appeal. Images can be used in many contexts: as iconic buttons, as imagemaps, or purely as decorations. And they look so easy, you are probably itching to make some yourself.

However, the Web imposes important limitations on inline images that must be taken into account by any Web author who wants to design effective, usable documents. What are these limitations? First is bandwidth, or the speed at which data is sent from your server to a user's browser. As this is usually low, you must strive to keep image files small so that they are quick to download. Second is computer display quality. Readers will be using many different types of computers, with varied qualities of color monitors and graphics cards. You must design your images to look good on a variety of displays. Third, you must be sure to use image formats that are widely supported. There is no point in including an image if few browsers can display it. Finally, you must make allowances for users who do not see the images, either because they are using a text-only browser or because they have disabled image loading.

This chapter provides an overview of image use within HTML documents, taking into account these four important factors. The beginning of the chapter is a review of the **IMG** element—the element used to include images in a document. The remainder looks at some of the details of image preparation and processing, beginning with a brief introduction to computer graphics, followed by a description of the image file formats supported on the Web. Watch for the section that discusses basic image processing tricks and tools, and some of the particular features of some of the supported image formats, such as transparency and animated GIFs. This is followed by an overview of active images and imagemaps. Finally, the chapter concludes with a list of useful image icon archive sites and a list of references.

Including Images in HTML Documents

As discussed in Chapters 1 and 2, images are included via the **IMG** element. All **IMG** elements should minimally have the following attributes:

```
<IMG SRC="image-url" HEIGHT="y_pixels" WIDTH="x_pixels"
    ALT="text alternative">
```

Here, *image-url* is the URL pointing to the image file, *y_pixels* is the height of the image in pixels, and *x_pixels* is the width of the image, also in pixels. By including the size of the image in the HTML markup, a browser can begin formatting the document before the image arrives, as it knows how much space to set aside on the display for the image. The string *text alternative* is a text description of—or alternative to—the image, used by browsers that do not display the pictures. Also, most newer graphical browsers display this as a text "pop-up" on top of the image (see Figure 1.18). You should always have **ALT** values to explain a picture's meaning; if it is purely decorative and has no meaning, you can use **ALT=""** (i.e., assign an empty string to **ALT**) to indicate this fact.

Web Graphics Introduction

When designing Web graphics, a designer must be aware of the types of displays used by the users. These will vary from low resolution 640×480 pixel displays capable of at most 256 colors, to high resolution 1280×1024 displays capable of displaying full 24-bit ($2^{24} = 16.8$ million) color. Unfortunately, the majority of users fall closer to the bottom of this range than the top, so a Web graphics designer must prepare pages that display well on low-resolution displays with a limited color palette.

The size constraint implies the need for small graphics to fit on the display. For example, a page banner should be no more than 570 pixels wide and less than 100 pixels high. Similarly, the raw images must be designed using a limited color palette, so that the browser does not "run out" of colors while trying to display multiple images. However, understanding how to work within these limitations requires a basic knowledge of computer graphics and of a computer's representation of colors. This, coincidentally, is the subject of this section.

Color Representations—The RGB System

The science and technology of color is actually very complicated—far more complicated than you are likely to want to understand! Fortunately, for basic graphics work, a Web developer need only understand a few details, the most important of which is the RGB color system.

On a computer, colors are usually defined using what are called *RGB* (Red-Green-Blue) codes. This coding scheme expresses a color as a mixture of the primary colors red, green, and blue, with the *intensity* of each color ranging from 0 (no intensity) to 255 (as bright as possible). As a result, the strength of each primary color can be expressed in a single byte (8 bits), so that any color can be expressed as a 24-bit sequence containing the intensity of the red, green, and blue components. This is why very high-resolution color displays are called 24-bit color graphics systems.

RGB codes are usually expressed as numbers in the hexadecimal numbering system. In this system, a complete color specification looks like

RRGGBB

where *RR* is the hex code for the red intensity (ranging from 00 to FF), *GG* is the hex code for the Green intensity (ranging from 00 to FF), and *BB* is the hex code for the blue intensity (you get the idea). For example, the code 000000 corresponds to black, FFFFFF corresponds to white (as bright as possible), and AAAAAA corresponds to a rather light shade of gray.

Limited Numbers of Colors—The *Colormap*

To display true, full-color images on a display, a computer must have 24 bits of memory for each pixel on the screen (this is what is meant by the phrase "24-bit color"). However, most computers do not have this many bits per pixel—many, in fact, have only 8 bits per pixel and support what is known as 8-bit color. In this case, a pixel can display at most 256 different colors, a far cry from the millions that are possible with 24 bits.

At the same time, a number shorter than 24 bits is too short to specify how much red, green, and blue to use in making the color—recall that you need 24 bits to fully specify a color. Thus, a system that has less than 24 bits per pixel needs a way of relating the number associated with a given pixel to the desired RGB color. The mechanism for doing so is called a *colormap* or *colormap table*.

Let's take the example of an 8-bit color system. In an 8-bit system, each pixel can contain an integer value ranging from 0 to 256. To determine the color each of these integers corresponds to, we create a *colormap table* that relates each possible position in the colormap (referenced by the colormap *index*) to a full RGB color code. An example table is:

Colormap Index (Integer)	RGB Color (Decimal)	RGB Color (Hex Code)
0	00 00 00	000000
1	00 00 51	000033
2	00 00 102	000066
...	.. .. ..	. . .
216	255 255 255	FFFFFF
...	.. .. ..	. . .

Each 8-bit number in a pixel now corresponds to one of the colors in the table. Thus, if a pixel is set to the number 2, the graphics system will look to the color table, pull out the RGB hex code 000033, and paint the pixel with this color.

Default System Colormaps

Most computers that only have 8-bit color hardware have a *default* colormap—that is, they come preconfigured with a colormap that relates pixel codes to specific RGB colors. On Microsoft Windows systems, this is known as the *Windows colormap*. The Windows colormap defines 232 (16 values from the VGA color palette, plus an additional 216 colors, for a total of 232) out of the 256 possible colors. The group of 216 colors is defined using the individual primary color codes 0, 51, 102, 153, 204, 255—the 216 comes from having 6 different shades of red, 6 different shades of green, and 6 different shades of blue, for a total of 6×6×6=216 different colors. The other 16 are from the colors defined in the VGA color palette—these are the 16 colors originally defined on old DOS and Windows machines that only supported 16 colors (the colors and RGB codes are listed on the companion Web site in Appendix F). The remaining 24 colors can sometimes be dynamically set by programs needing specific colors—for example, a Web browser, when trying to display an image, may set these entries to the colors needed by the image being displayed.

Obviously, this scheme omits a lot of colors! But, it does evenly cover the range of possible colors and provides a reasonable set of default values.

With Microsoft Windows, the 24 undefined positions are the only ones that can be modified by software—Windows 3.1, 95, or NT do not let user programs change the other 232 colormap entries. Thus, on 8-bit Windows systems, you're essentially stuck with the colors defined by the Windows colormap. Other systems (Macintosh or UNIX) with 8-bit color are generally more forgiving, and can dynamically modify the system colormap to account for the colors desired by an application. Thus, for Web applications it is best to use the Windows colormap when creating images, since this will work best on Microsoft Windows systems and will also work acceptably well on other machines.

Displaying Images—Color *Dithering*

Problems arise if an image contains a color that is not available in the system colormap. For example, you might have an image that contains the color 00102F, but a user's 8-bit color system can only get as close as the colors 000000, 000033, and 003333. How, then, will the system display the desired color?

There are two approaches. First, the computer can look in the system colormap for the color "nearest" the color in the image and use this color instead. Given the Windows colormap, the computer might then take all pixels of color 00102F and paint them with color 000033. Unfortunately, the concept of "nearest" can lead to truly bizarre replacement colors, so this is often not an ideal replacement scheme.

The second way is known as *color dithering*. With dithering, the program displaying the image tries to find colors in the local colormap that are close to those in the actual image and then replaces *blocks* of the original color by a *mixture* of the colors actually available on the computer. You can often detect dithering by looking at regions of an image that "should" appear as a solid color. If the area appears mottled, with lots of dots of slightly different colors, then the image has been dithered.

Dithering is illustrated in Figure 3.1. The chosen color, illustrated at the upper left, is not defined in the 8-bit color palette. Thus, when the color is displayed on a 256 color system, the color is dithered, as illustrated by the figure labeled "Dithered." The bottom of the figure shows an expanded view of a dithered region and more clearly illustrates how the original color is mimicked via a mix of other colors. In this case, the original color (pale aquamarine) is dithered using a mix of white, gray, and aqua.

Dithering is sometimes better than taking the closest color and sometimes not. Both cases are not ideal, and a better choice is to make sure that images use the colors that are available in the system colormap. This is most easily accomplished by selecting an appropriate colormap when the images are created. For the Web, this means choosing the Windows colormap mentioned previously.

Selecting an Image Colormap

Most Web browsers, including Netscape Navigator, support the Windows colormap for 8-bit displays. Thus, if you are creating an image (an icon or line graphic, as opposed to a photograph), it is best to create it using the Windows colormap (most graphics editors let you choose the colormap you wish to use), as opposed to a colormap customized for the occasion.

Storing Images in Files

Once image data have been processed and stored on a computer, a graphics designer needs a way of storing this information as a computer file. There are literally hundreds of *image file formats* for doing so, each with its own strengths and weaknesses. For the Web, the most important criterion is file size—the file must be as small as possible, so that it can be quickly transmitted over the Internet. For this reason, the image formats listed in the following sections are the only ones widely implemented in Web applications, with GIF and JPEG being the most popular choices.

Supported Image Formats

Although most browsers support a variety of different image formats, there are only four that are universally acceptable: the GIF (GIF87 and GIF89A), JPEG, X-Bitmap, and X-Pixelmap formats. The different types can usually be inferred by the filename suffix: GIF image files usually have the suffix *.gif*, JPEGs usually *.jpg* or *.jpeg*, X-Bitmaps usually *.xbm*, and X-Pixelmaps usually *.xpm*. A fifth format, PNG, for Portable Network Graphics (usually with extension *.png*), while gaining popularity, is not yet universally supported. The MIME types corresponding to these five formats are image/gif, image/jpeg, image/x-bitmap, image/x-pixelmap, and image/png, respectively.

Figure 3.1 An illustration of color dithering. The first figure
(Original) illustrates the original color (a pale aquamarine), while
the second figure (Dithered) shows the display of this color when
dithered for a 256-color display. The third figure (*expanded view*)
shows an expanded view of a dithered region, showing the individual pixels: The original color is dithered using a mixture of gray,
white and aqua, which appear here as white and two shades of gray.

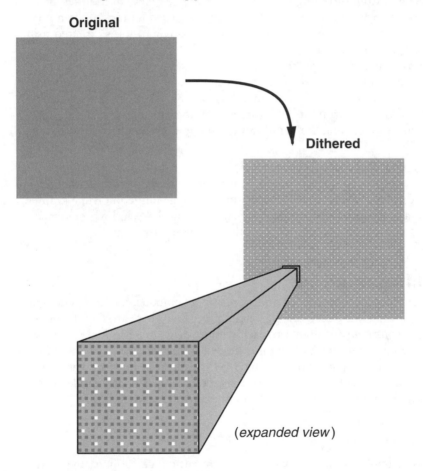

Original

Dithered

(*expanded view*)

X-Bitmap/Pixelmap

X-Bitmaps are a common format on UNIX workstations and are often found in
older image and icon libraries. An X-Bitmap assigns a single bit to each image
pixel, and therefore supports only black-and-white images. Simple bitmaps are
useful, however, as browsers treat the white portion as *transparent*—the black
part of the image is displayed in black, while the white part is replaced by the

color or image of the underlying background. This permits attractive black icons, since the surrounding white background is not visible. However, X-Bitmaps are inefficient at storing images and are uncommon outside the UNIX environment. As we shall see, GIF is a better choice.

X-Pixelmaps are similar to X-Bitmaps but assign 8 bits to each pixel, as opposed to 1, and can consequently support images with 256 distinct colors. However, like X-Bitmaps, X-Pixelmaps are an inefficient way to store an image. Again, it is better to use GIF—you get the same picture, but in a much smaller file.

GIF

GIF (an abbreviation for Graphics Interchange Format) is the most common image format in World Wide Web applications. This format can store black-and-white, grayscale, or color images, although it is limited to a maximum of 256 colors (or shades of gray) per image. Somewhat like the X-Pixelmap, the GIF format encodes the image information using a color indexing scheme. When you create a GIF image, the software uses an image analysis algorithm to find the set of 256 (or fewer) colors that best describe the color content of the raw image and creates a *color table* mapping these colors onto integers ranging from 0 to 255. The software then examines each pixel in the original image, finds the color in the color table that is closest to the actual color, and assigns the corresponding color index value to this pixel. The resulting GIF image file consists of an array of these color indices plus a color table that maps each of the 256 indices onto the chosen color.

The color table can be optimized for each image. For example, if a picture is of a red sunset, this table will contain mostly reds, whereas if it is a picture of a forest, it will be mostly greens. This technique can yield a quite successful rendering of the original image, even though there are at most 256 different colors. As mentioned previously, however, it is best for Web applications to use the Windows colormap for this color table whenever possible.

GIF stores the images in a *compressed* format. The compression algorithm is relatively simple: Basically, it looks for repeated sequences of the same color and encodes long sequences using a much shorter string. For example, if there were 50 pixels in a row with the same color (lets call this color "Q"), this might be encoded as:

```
QQQQQ . . . QQQQ    ==   50Q
```

That is, instead of having 50 Qs one after the other, the string is compressed into the color index plus a number indicating how many times the color repeats.

GIF compression works very well on images with large blocks of solid colors, such as logos and icons. The compression is not, however, efficient for photographic images, where there are no large single-color regions and the image is highly irregular. For this type of image, JPEG is a better choice.

There are two common versions of the GIF format—GIF87 and GIF89A—the latter having several important features not possible in GIF87. For example, GIF89A lets you make one of the colors *transparent*, so that the background shows through. This is equivalent to the transparency of X-Bitmap images. GIF89 also lets you place more than one image in a single GIF file; most Web browsers take this sequence of images and play them as a crude animation, known as an *animated GIF*. Both features are discussed in more detail later on.

JPEG

The JPEG (for Joint Photographic Experts Group) format was designed expressly for storing photographic images in a compact digital form. JPEG is an extremely sophisticated compressed image format that can support an almost infinite number of colors, instead of only 256. JPEG also supports a *lossy* image compression technique—the greater the compression, the poorer the quality of the stored image. In general, JPEG is far better than GIF at storing photographic images, both in terms of image quality and file size, while GIF is better for images containing few colors and/or that have large single-colored regions, such as buttons, logos, clip art, and so on. Also, JPEG does not support animated sequences nor image transparency.

Recently, the JPEG group introduced a variant of the JPEG format, known as progressive JPEG or P-JPEG. This format supports progressive rendering of images as the data arrives, similar to the "wiping in" of an interlaced GIF. This image format has its own MIME type, image/pjpeg. PJPEG is supported by most modern browsers.

PNG

PNG (Portable Network Graphics) is designed as a public-domain successor to GIF. Like GIF, PNG allows for transparency, interlacing, and image compression, the latter via a nonproprietary compression algorithm (the GIF method is patented). However, PNG is also much enhanced relative to GIF, as it supports greater color depth than GIF (up to 24-bit color), 8-bit transparency (so that images can "fade in"), as well as features for color and gamma correction.

PNG is supported by Internet Explorer 4, but not Netscape Navigator 4 (there is, however, a free Netscape Navigator 4 plugin that adds support for PNG graphics). It is not supported by earlier versions of either browser.

Image Processing—Basic Issues

This book is not intended to be a graphics manual. If you are planning on doing intensive graphics work, you should hire a graphics expert—or buy a real book on graphics! However, there are some relatively simple tricks that will help you make images work effectively on the Web, and these bear mentioning here.

Reducing or Rescaling Images

You will often want to reduce the size of an image, either because the original is too big or because you want to create a small icon of the image and link it to the bigger version. You can create reduced image sizes with many graphics programs, including the ones listed later in this chapter.

When you *shrink* an image, you may want to *smooth* it beforehand—smoothing reduces edge breakup, or *aliasing*, created by the size reduction process. Some programs do this automatically when you shrink an image, while others let you turn smoothing on and off and expect you to do the smoothing yourself. Note that you want to smooth before or during the size reduction, but not after: Once the image is shrunk, smoothing simply blurs what's left. This combination of shrinking and smoothing is also called *resampling*.

Note that it is extremely difficult to rescale images that contain text, as the text is almost always blurred to the point of being unreadable. A better choice is to remove all text from the image, resize the image, and re-enter the text using the desired font and size.

Smoothing Colors

Sometimes you will have an image that appears to have large, uniformly colored regions, only to find that, when you look closely, these uniform regions actually contain many dozens of very similar colors patterned in a non-smooth way—this often results from image dithering. Some graphics programs let you smooth the colors, which reduces this irregularity and makes it easier to compress the image in GIF or PNG format. Often this can be accomplished by reducing the number of colors in the image, also known as *flattening* the image or reducing the *color depth*.

Reducing Color Depth

Most image processing tools let you reduce the number of colors. This is useful with the GIF and PNG formats, as the process can substantially reduce the size of the image file, without significantly affecting the appearance on most computer displays. Color depth reduction is particularly useful with icons, which often use fewer than 10 colors. Color depth reduction should not be done with JPEG images, however, as the reduced color depth actually impairs the JPEG compression technique.

Composed Images

Quite often you will find yourself reusing parts of an image over and over again—for example, part of a button in a button bar, a corporate logo attached to different section headings, and so on. In these cases, it is best to construct these images from a collection of image components that are *tiled* together on the page to make the desired total image. In this way, the user does not keep downloading this part of the image. Once the logo is downloaded, it can be reused by appending it to different section headings, with only the headings changing from document to document. An example is shown in Figure 3.2, which displays a section heading from one of the University of Toronto pages. The top image is actually

Figure 3.2 A page from the University of Toronto Web site navigational collection. The graphic at the top of the screen consists of two images, tiled together. The right-hand portion is reused on a number of different pages.

two images tiled together—a large image, consisting of the title plus the picture of the lecture theater, and a second, smaller image containing a photograph of the campus. The markup is:

```
<IMG SRC="img1.gif" . . . ><IMG SRC="img2.gif" . . . >
```

Because the **IMG** tags are flush next to each other, the images appear together without intervening space, giving the impression of a single graphic. Alternatively, the images can be tiled together using a **TABLE**, as illustrated in Example 9 in Chapter 2.

Special GIF Image Properties

Since GIF is still the most common format on the Web, this section looks at some of GIF's most important properties. The references at the end of the chapter point to sources of additional information, as well as sites listing useful GIF utilities not discussed in the text.

Reducing GIF Image File Size: The Colormap

You can reduce the size of a GIF image file by reducing the number of colors used in the image. The GIF format can take up to a full byte to store color information about a pixel, which is why GIF is limited to 256 different colors ($256=2^8$). However, you don't always need a full byte for a pixel—the GIF format is clever enough to know, if an image has only 8 colors instead of 256, that it needs fewer bits per pixel to index all the colors. This reduces the amount of data needed to store the image. Also, as discussed previously, reducing the number of colors can make it easier to compress the image, further reducing file size. Some tools particularly suited to this task are *BatchMaster* (Windows PCs) and *Debabelizer* (Macintoshes—the freeware version *Debabelizer Lite* is also suitable). However, most image-processing programs, such as Adobe *Photoshop*, *PaintShop Pro* (a shareware program for Windows PCs), *Lview Pro* (another shareware program for PCs), and *Graphic Converter* (a shareware program for the Macintosh), or the *pbmplus*, *GIMP*, and *ImageMagick* packages (shareware programs for UNIX workstations) have tools for reducing the number of colors in the image.

You also should want to reduce the number of colors because of the limited display capabilities (the 256-color limit) of many computers. Ideally, the fewer the colors the better, as this frees up space in the color table for other images. And, as mentioned, it is also a good idea to create image icons using the Windows colormap as the default color palette.

Interlaced GIF Images

The GIF format stores images as a sequence of thin (1 pixel high) horizontal strips. Usually these are stored one after the other, so that when a browser receives an image file, it receives the first (top) strip, followed by the second, the third, and so on. If your browser displays the image as it is being downloaded, the image appears to "wipe" in, starting at the top and wiping downwards.

However, as you have certainly noticed, this does not always happen. Sometimes the image opens rather like a venetian blind—a rough outline of the image appears first and detail is gradually added. This occurs due to an optional GIF89 feature called *interlacing*. With interlaced GIF images, the strips are stored in nonconsecutive order. For example, the strips might be stored in the order 1, 11, 21, 31, 41, and so on, followed by 2, 12, 22, *et cetera*. A rough outline of the image is obtained from the first batch of slices, while subsequent batches fill in the gaps and refine the image. In the end, both kinds of images take nearly the same time to arrive, but to the user the presentation of an interlaced GIF can be more appealing, since the outline of the entire image appears more quickly. However, interlaced images are slightly larger than non-interlaced ones. Whether or not they are appropriate then depends on the nature of the image and speed requirements.

Most standard image processing programs, including those mentioned at the beginning of this section, are capable of producing interlaced GIFs. The image processing tool *GIFtool*, described later in this chapter, can add interlacing to your GIF images should your other tools not be able to do so.

Transparent GIF Images

Unlike X-Bitmaps, GIF images have no implicit transparent color. This is inconvenient if the image is simply a black-and-white logo, a colored bullet on a plain background, or an equation to be presented inline with the text. Fortunately, the

GIF89 format lets you declare one of the color indexes as *transparent*—as with X-Bitmaps, these transparent pixels let the background underlying the pixel show through. For this to be useful, you must find the color index value corresponding to the color you want to make transparent (usually the background) and use a program to modify the image file and make this color transparent. Some ways of doing this are outlined in the following sections.

Transparency (Macintosh)

Aaron Giles of Cornell University Medical College has developed an elegantly useful program called *transparency*, which is a simple graphical tool for editing GIF images and making one of the colors transparent.

You operate *transparency* either by dragging a file to the program icon or by double-clicking on the icon and opening the desired GIF image file. To select the transparency color, you simply place the mouse pointer inside the image and hold down the mouse button. You are presented with the color palette for the image and can select the color you wish to make transparent by putting the mouse pointer over the desired color and releasing the button. You can choose to have no transparent color by selecting the "NONE" bar at the top of the palette. Upon releasing the mouse button, there is a short pause, after which the image is redrawn with the selected color rendered transparently. You now select the "Save as GIF89 . . ." menu from the pull-down File menu to save the newly transparent version.

Transparency is available at a number of anonymous FTP sites, including:

ftp://uiarchive.cso.uiuc.edu/pub/systems/mac/info-mac/gst/
    grf/transparency-10.hqx

ftp://ftp.uwtc.washington.edu/pub/Mac/Graphics/

Giftrans (UNIX and PC-DOS)

Giftrans is a simple command-line C-language program, written by Andreas Ley, that can convert any GIF files into the GIF89A format, making one of the colors transparent in the process. *Giftrans* is available in source code (for compilation on any platform, but most specifically for UNIX workstations) and as an executable program for PCs running DOS or a DOS session under Windows.

Typically, *giftrans* is used as follows

```
giftrans -t xx image.gif > transp_image.gif
```

which translates the file *image.gif* into *transp_image.gif* and makes the color labeled by *xx* transparent. There are several ways of labeling the color, the most common being:

- Specify the absolute RGB value for the color (as a 24-bit RGB value). For example, the command

```
giftrans -t #ffffff image.gif > transp_image.gif
```

makes the color white transparent (ffffff is the RGB code for white).

- Specify the color index value. For example, the command

```
giftrans -t 21 image.gif > transp_image.gif
```

makes the color found in color index 21 transparent.

How do you find the color index or RGB value of the color you want transparent? To find this information, you need a graphics program that can tell you the color indices or RGB values for a given pixel. Several shareware graphics programs can do this—*xv* is a common UNIX program suitable for this task. With *xv*, you load the image file, place the mouse over the desired color, and depress the left mouse button. This gives the mouse coordinates with respect to the upper left-hand corner of the image, plus color information for the pixel. This is presented in the following format:

```
132, 34  5 = 203, 203, 203 (0, 1, 79 HSV)
```

The first two numbers are the x and y coordinates of the pixel. The number just before the equals sign is the color index, while the next three numbers are the RGB values for this color (in decimal numbers). The numbers in parentheses are an alternate color coding scheme. Similar information is available from common tools for PC (*Paint Shop Pro*, *PhotoShop*, *Corel Draw*) and Macintosh (*Graphic Converter*, *PhotoShop*, etc.).

Now that you know the color you want to make transparent, *giftrans* provides two ways to do so—using the color index:

```
giftrans -t 5 image.gif > transparent_image.gif
```

or the RGB value:

```
giftrans -t #cbcbcb image.gif > transparent_image.gif
```

where cb is the hexadecimal code for the decimal number 203. If you run *giftrans* without arguments, the program prints a list of the possible arguments and their meanings.

Giftrans is available from many anonymous FTP sites. Its original home is:

ftp://ftp.rz.uni-karlsruhe.de/pub/net/www/tools/

The file *giftrans.exe* is the DOS/Windows executable, *giftrans.os2.exe* is the OS/2 version, and *giftrans.c* is C source code (you will also need the file *getopt.c* if compiling on a PC). Last, *giftrans.1* is the UNIX-style manual page.

The program *xv* is available from many anonymous FTP sites. You will need both a C compiler and the standard X11 libraries to compile *xv* on your machine. *Xv* is available at:

ftp://ftp.cis.upenn.edu/pub/xv/

GIFtool (UNIX, MS-DOS)

GIFtool is a multipurpose shareware GIF manipulation program from HomePages (www.homepages.com) that lets you add interlacing or transparency to GIF images. *GIFtool* can be used in batch mode to convert multiple files at the same time. The program is available at:

    ftp://ftp.ies.lafayette.in.us/pub/dos/giftool.exe   (DOS)

    ftp://sunsite.unc.edu/pub/Linux/apps/graphics/convert/   (UNIX)

PhotoShop Transparent GIF Plugin

Oddly enough, commercial programs such as *PhotoShop* and *CorelDraw* cannot create transparent GIF images. Fortunately, Adobe provides a free *PhotoShop* plugin that does these tasks. This plugin can be obtained (in Macintosh, Windows, and UNIX versions) at:

    www.adobe.com/supportservice/custsupport/LIBRARY/psmac.htm

    www.adobe.com/supportservice/custsupport/LIBRARY/pswin.htm

    www.adobe.com/supportservice/custsupport/LIBRARY/psunix.htm

Similar plugins are available for other commercial packages—check with your software vendor for details.

Animated GIFs

Netscape Navigator 2.0 introduced support for animated GIF images: GIF images that display like short movie sequences. GIF89A lets a single GIF file contain a sequence of images of the same height and width—the file can be an *archive* of images, stored sequentially. Of course, if the stored files are subsequent frames of a short animation sequence, and you can display them one after the other, then . . . *voila!*—you have an animation. In fact, the GIF format lets you specify: the time delay (in 100ths of a second) between subsequent frames; whether the animation should start automatically or upon user selection of the image; and how the sequence should be treated after it has been displayed (should it cycle in a loop, or stop). The latter is a special extension implemented by Netscape—the GIF89A format allows for such proprietary extensions of the file format.

Browsers that can't display GIF animations ignore all this—when such browsers encounter an animated GIF file, they simply display the first or last picture in the file.

Creating Animated GIFs

You need special software to create an animated GIF sequence. In general, you prepare the animation as a collection of single GIF images, and paste them together using a GIF animation tool. In general, you want the frames to be small, and as with all GIF images, you want to use as few colors as possible—animated GIF files are much larger than single-frame pictures, so you want to reduce the size of the frames as much as possible. URLs listing GIF animation software are given at the end of this section, while most commercial HTML editors (e.g., SoftQuad *HoTMetaL*, Microsoft *FrontPage*, Adobe *PageMill*, or Sausage Software's *HotDog*) come equipped with animated GIF tools. These tools are in general quite easy to use.

NOTE: Animated GIF Problems with Older Browsers

Animated GIFs require extra processing to run the animation process. This is not a problem on newer machines with fast processors and lots of memory (16 MB or more). Users with slower machines will find that GIF animations significantly slow down their computers. The moral: Don't get carried away with animated GIFs!

Placing Animated GIFs in HTML Documents

This is easy—you insert an animated GIF using our friend, the **IMG** element. For example, if your animated GIFs are in the file *anim.gif*, then the **IMG** tag is:

```
<IMG SRC="anim.gif" ALT="animated button" HEIGHT=54 WIDTH=45">
```

Browsers that do not support the animated GIF format will display a single frame from the animation. Be warned that some display the first frame, while others display the last—there's nothing like consistency, is there? One way around this problem is to make the first and last frames identical. This is also useful for looping animations, as making the first and last frames identical (or nearly so) makes the sequence loop smoothly.

Additional Animated GIF Information

There is a wonderful collection of animated GIF resources, provided by Royal Frazier, containing a detailed tutorial on the GIF97 and GIF89A file structures, tutorials on creating animated GIFs, lists of software to help you in this process, and a gallery of animated GIFs created by Royal and others. The URLs for this reference (the second URL lists mirror sites) are:

> user.aol.com/royalef/gifanim.htm
>
> user.aol.com/royalef/mirrors.htm
>
> user.aol.com/royalef/toolbox.htm

Background Images and Colors

As discussed in Chapters 2 and 6, most browsers support background images via a **BACKGROUND** attribute to the HTML **BODY**, **TD**, or **TH** elements. Background images can use any of the supported image formats. However, care must be taken when selecting a background, so that it does not impair the readability of the actual content. In addition to a **BACKGROUND**, an author can specify the background color for the document using the **BGCOLOR** attribute. In both cases, here are some important design points:

Use low-contrast backgrounds. You don't necessarily want the background to overshadow or obscure the text or images.

Use small colormaps. You don't want to use up all the colors in the background and have none left for the actual images. This is particularly important for 256-color displays. Also, you should use the Windows colormap if at all possible—dithering looks particularly bad when applied to the background.

Contrast strongly with text colors. You don't want the background color to be similar to any of the regular text colors. As described in Chapter 6, you can use the body element **TEXT** (regular text), **LINK** (nonvisited link), **VLINK** (previously visited link), and **ALINK** (link selected by user) attributes to reset the text colors, so that text is clearly visible.

Make sure the color choices look good on different machines/browsers. Again, you want to ensure that your choices work on poorer-quality computer displays—not everyone has a 16-million color graphics card and a $2,000 monitor!

If using BACKGROUND, also use BGCOLOR. This is particularly important when the text color contrasts poorly with the default background gray. In this case, the text will be unreadable until the background image arrives. An appropriate **BGCOLOR** will make the text readable, and also makes for a smoother transition once the background is loaded.

BGCOLOR values can be either RGB hexadecimal codes (e.g., #FF0000 for the color "red") or a color name chosen from a defined list of names. Go to Appendix F on the companion Web site for a list of all the defined color names and their RGB hex code equivalents.

The references at the end of this chapter list sites on the Web that archive useful background images. Additional information about backgrounds is found at:

www.sci.kun.nl/thalia/guide/color/faq.html

This site also provides links to databases containing color and background examples.

Active Images and Imagemaps

Active images, clickable images, imagemaps—whatever they are called—you have certainly seen them, and most authors want to use them. An active image means that users can click their mouse pointer on top of the image and have different things happen, depending on where they clicked. For example, the active image could be a city map, such that clicking on different locations returns information about particular buildings, transportation routes, or historic monuments.

There are two ways of implementing active images. The original way, known as *imagemapping*, stores information about the active image on an HTTP server. When the user clicks on the image, the Web browser measures the location of the click, and sends this information to an HTTP server. The server uses these coordinates to determine which information to return to the browser.

This requires special processing by both the client and the HTTP server. First, the client must be able to measure the coordinates of the mouse pointer when the user clicks on the active image, and must be configured to send this information to an HTTP server for interpretation and action. Second, there must be resource on the server—often a gateway program—capable of interpreting this coordinate data. Finally, there must be a database on the server relating, for each image, the click coordinates to the appropriate URL. This means that the imagemap designer must take the image, mark out the desired regions, link these regions to particular URLs, and store this information in an imagemap database.

The second approach, called *client-side imagemapping*, includes the imagemap database within the HTML document. This eliminates the need to contact a server and offers many substantial advantages. However, not all browsers support this approach. Fortunately, you can use both methods for the same imagemapped image: If the browser understands client-side imagemapping, it will use the map within the document, and if it does not, it will access the HTTP server instead.

NOTE: Allowed Formats for Active Images

It is best to use the GIF format for active images, as some older browsers cannot handle active JPEGs. Also, do not use **HEIGHT** and **WIDTH** attributes to change the size or shape of the image—these values, when present, *must* be equal to the actual image size.

Things to Think About Before Starting

Before you get carried away with active images, stop and think about your audience. First recall that some users will not be able to view your active images, because they are using a text-only browser, such as lynx, or because they have disabled image loading because of a slow network connection (quite common). Consequently, you should make the image files as small as possible, and you might also wish to provide a text-only alternative for accessing the same information. For example, your document can have a line of text explaining what the image does and offering a hypertext link to a page providing a text-only approach. In particular, every active image element must have an **ALT** text string to explain the image's purpose and to explain what to do if the image is not visible.

Server-based *Imagemap* Active Images

You must do two things to mark up a server-side imagemapped image. First, add the **ISMAP** attribute to the **IMG** element, which this tells the browser that this is an active image. Second, surround the **IMG** element with a hypertext anchor that points to the program on the server that will process the selected coordinate data. Thus, the minimal HTML markup (the extra markup for the active image is shown in boldface) is:

```
<A HREF="http://some.site.edu/cgi-bin/imagemap/my_database"><IMG SRC="image.gif"
    ALT="[Imagemap: The author, and a Large, Hairy Llama - an ACTIVE image]"
    ISMAP></A>
```

which tells the browser that this is an active image and that, when a user clicks inside the image, the coordinates of the click should be sent to the server and to the program *imagemap* at the given URL. The coordinate information is sent to this URL using the HTTP GET method. Thus, once the image is selected, the accessed URL will look like

```
http://some.site.edu/cgi-bin/imagemap/my_database?x,y
```

where *x* and *y* are the *integer pixel coordinates* of the mouse pointer measured from the *upper left-hand corner* of the image.

Note that the path *my_database* is included at the end of the URL. As discussed in Chapters 8 and 10, URLs that point to program resources are treated in a special way, and any directory-like information appended to the URL after the program name (like *my_database*) is treated as "extra path" information and is passed as a parameter to the gateway program. In this example, *my_database* is path information used by *imagemap* to find the imagemap *database* for this particular image. Thus, *imagemap* can be used with any number of active images, each image having its own personalized database.

Imagemap is an actual CGI program for handling active image data, distributed with the current NCSA and Apache HTTP servers. Since it is CGI-compliant it should, in principle, run on any server. This program comes with all versions of the NCSA and Apache servers.

Built-in Server Imagemap Support

The Apache, Netscape, NCSA, and most other servers are now equipped with built-in modules that work in exactly the same manner as *imagemap*. If you have this feature, then you do not need the *imagemap* program. However, if you do need it, the following section describes how to obtain, create, and install the package.

Installing Imagemap

If you don't have the program and wish to install it, simply download the files

    ftp://ftp.ncsa.uiuc.edu/Web/httpd/Unix/ncsa_httpd/cgi/cgi-src/imagemap.c

    ftp://ftp.ncsa.uiuc.edu/Web/httpd/Unix/ncsa_httpd/cgi/cgi-src/util.c

and compile with your C compiler—note that the program requires the CGI-utility package *utils.c*. You then install the *imagemap* executable in your server's CGI program directory. By default, this is often *cgi-bin*, located in the directory structure containing the server executable, server support directories, and configuration files. (This is *not* the directory that contains the HTML and other documents made available via the server.) The program is now accessible through URLs of the form:

```
http://some.site.edu/cgi-bin/imagemap
```

where the *cgi-bin* directory is a *virtual* name used by the server to reference the directory containing CGI programs. Check your server configuration files (or with your server administrator) to verify that this name is correct.

Creating an Imagemap Database

The imagemap database file relates a region of the image with a URL to be accessed when a user clicks inside that region. You can specify regions as circles, rectangles, polygons, or points. You can also include comments in a map database file by placing a hash character (#) as the first character in the line. Figure 3.3 shows a simple map file, named *blobby.map*, while Figure 3.4 shows the figure and the areas associated with the mapped regions.

This file declares that clicks within the circle centered at coordinates 226,40 (and with an edge at 5116,10) are linked to the designated URL and makes similar declarations for a rectangle (indicated by rect) and a polygon (indicated by poly). These coordinates are measured in pixels from the upper left-hand corner of the image. The "default" method indicates the URL to access if the user clicks in places not falling inside any of the mapped regions.

The general form of a map file entry is

```
method  URL  x1,y1 x2,y2 ... xn,yn
```

where *method* specifies the manner in which the region is being specified (one of circle, rect, poly, point, or default), *URL* is the URL to be accessed if the click occurs inside this region, and *xn* and *yn* are the integer coordinates of a point, measured from the upper left-hand corner of the image. The coordinates are measured in pixels, so you will need some way of measuring the pixel coordinates in an image. Tools for doing this are presented later.

Note that mapped regions can overlap. The imagemap program reads the map file from the beginning, and if a click occurs at a point lying within two mapped regions, the program takes the first region it encounters.

The URLs specified in a map file can be complete URLs, or partial URLs of the form

```
/path/stuff/file
```

which references a file or gateway program relative to the HTTP server *document directory*. With the NCSA, Apache, and certain other servers, you can also use the form

```
/~user/stuff/file
```

Figure 3.3 The example imagemap map database file *blobby.map*. The meanings of the different region types (circle, rect, etc.) are discussed in the text.

```
# Imagemap file for blobby.gif
circle        /dir1/blob2/his_head.html    116,40 116,10
rect          /dir1/blob2/his_hand.html    36,30 84,90
poly          /dir1/blob2/his_foot.html    86,154 64,170 76,188 104,184 112,166
default       /cgi-bin/nph-no_op.sh
```

Figure 3.4 A schematic of a 240x200 pixel image (*mr_blobby.gif*) showing the locations of the regions mapped by the database in Figure 3.3.

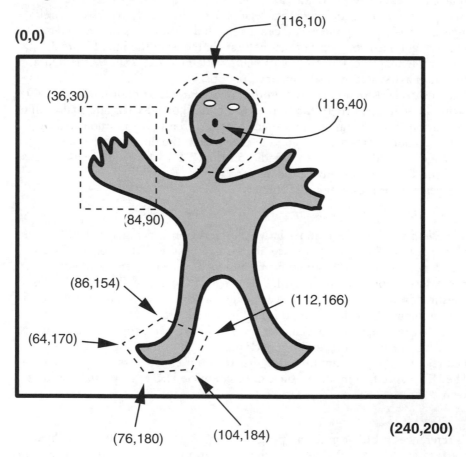

where user is the name of a user on the system. This references a file or gateway program relative to the user's personal HTML area.

Table 3.1 gives the specifications of the five methods for declaring active regions in an imagemap database.

Table 3.1 Methods Specifications for Imagemap Databases. The string *link_URL* is the URL to which the selected region is linked.

circle	*link_URL xc, yc xe, ye*
	This maps the region inside the indicated circle to the given URL. Two coordinate pairs are required: one for the circle *center* (xc,yc) and the other for an *edgepoint* (xe,ye) lying on the edge of the circle. An example entry is: circle /path/file.html 50,40 20,30
point	*link_URL x,y*
	This declares a specific *point* in an image as active. When you click on the image, and the click is not inside a circle, rectangle, or polygon, the imagemap program locates the point closest to the coordinates of the click and accesses the indicated URL.
poly	*link_URL x1,y1 x2,y2 . . . xn,yn*
	This maps the region inside the indicated polygon to the given URL. Each coordinate pair represents a vertex of the polygon. You should make sure that the line segments do not cross one another (no bow ties!). The polygon is automatically closed by linking the last point xn,yn to the first coordinate x1,y1. The current NCSA program limits you to 100 corners in a given polygon.
rect	*link_URL xul, yul xlr, ylr*
	This maps the region inside a rectangle to the given URL. The coordinates of the upper left (*xul,yul*) and lower right (*xlr,ylr*) corners of the rectangle are required, in that order. An example entry is: rect http://banzai.com/booger.html 20,20 40,50
default	*link_URL*
	This URL is accessed if the click did not lie inside any other region. This is never accessed if you define a point, since a clicked location will always be *closest* to a defined point, even if it's the only one!

Referencing the Imagemap Database

Now that you have a database—for example the *blobby.map* database of Figure 3.3—where should you put it, and how does the *imagemap* program know where to find it? This database can go anywhere you can put regular HTML documents or data files. You indicate its location to the imagemap program via extra path information in the URL. For example, let us suppose that the Web server document directory is */u/Web* and that the collection of documents and images related to Mr. Blobby is found in the directory */u/Web/weird/blobby*. One choice is to put the map file in the same directory as the image, so that the absolute path for the map file is */u/Web/weird/blobby/blobby.map*. You access this map file from *imagemap* by using the markup

```
<A HREF="http://some.site.edu/cgi-bin/imagemap/weird/blobby/blobby.map">
    <IMG SRC="blobby.gif" ISMAP>
</A>
```

where *some.site.edu* is the site containing the documents and the extra path information that references the imagemap database is in boldface. Note that the path to *blobby.map*, relative to the document directory of the HTTP server (*/u/Web*), has been added to the imagemap URL (it is shown in boldface). The string "/weird/blobby/blobby.map" is passed to *imagemap* and is used by the program to locate the database *blobby.map*.

With most servers, this method is not restricted to the regular document directory. If a user has a personal HTML directory, he or she can place map files in this directory and access the maps using URLs like

```
<A HREF="http://some.site.edu/cgi-bin/imagemap/~user/path/blobby.map">
<IMG SRC="blobby.gif" ISMAP>
</A>
```

where **user** is the username of the person with the personal public HTML directory and *path/blobby.map* is the path leading to the map file from the root of his or her personal document directory.

Getting a Click to Do Nothing

Sometimes, you want a click to do nothing. For example, your image could be a map of buildings, and you don't want anything to happen if the user clicks on nonmapped objects, like roads or trees. In this case, you might want the browser to keep the current document on the browser window screen. This can be accomplished by linking the default method in your imagemap file to a server CGI program that returns a response message to the client. In Figure 3.3, the default method references the UNIX shell script *nph-no_op.sh*, designed to do exactly this. This script, along with an equivalent program written in perl, is listed in Figure 3.5.

Figure 3.5 Listing for (A) the Bourne shell script *nph-no_op.sh*, and (B) the perl script *nph-no_op.pl*. Both return HTTP headers that tell a browser to continue displaying the currently displayed document.

(A) *nph-no_op.sh*—Bourne shell script

```
#!/bin/sh
echo "HTTP/1.0 204 No response -- server CGI-script output"
echo "Content-type: text/plain"
echo "Server: $SERVER_SOFTWARE"
echo
```

(B) *nph-no_op.pl*—Perl script

```
#!/bin/perl
print "HTTP/1.0 204 No Response -- CGI script output \r\n";
print "Content-type: text/plain\r\n";
print "Server: $ENV{"SERVER_SOFTWARE}\r\n";
print "\r\n";   #Blank line ending the header
```

Output from scripts having an *nph-* prefix is sent directly to the client without being parsed by the server (see Chapter 10 for more information on *non-parsed header* gateway programs). This script sends the HTTP status code 204, which tells the client that there is no server message and that the client should continue displaying the current document.

Tools for Generating Imagemap Files

Generating a map file is not difficult and only requires some concentration, a piece of paper, and an image viewing program that gives the pixel coordinates of the mouse pointer. On UNIX systems, the program *xv* is often used to do this (found at many anonymous FTP sites by searching for the string xv-3.00 or xv-3.10). You load the image into *xv*, locate the coordinates, and type the numbers into a map file. A similar procedure can be followed with typical Macintosh or PC image editing programs, such as *PhotoShop* (all platforms), *GraphicConverter* (Macintosh), or *Paint Shop Pro* (Windows).

Of course, it is much easier if you have a graphical tool to view the images and automatically generate the map files. Thomas Boutell has satisfied this need with his shareware program *mapedit,* which lets you read the GIF image into a display window; use the mouse to draw circles, rectangles, and polygons on top; and specify a URL for each of the marked regions. You can also insert comments, which is important if you want to understand the content of the map file at a later date.

Mapedit is available for UNIX systems, Windows PCs, and for Macintoshes. The executables and additional information are found at:

www.boutell.com/mapedit/

There are, of course, other programs that can help you create imagemap database files. The shareware programs *WebMap, Mapper* and *ImageMapper* are useful for Macintosh users, while for Windows users there are the programs *Coffee Cup Image Mapper++, LiveImage,* and *Web Hotspots*. Information about these packages is found at:

shareware.unc.edu/shareware/home /ftp/pub/mac/comm/	(WebMap)
tucows.myline.net/mac/htmlacc.html	(WebMap, Mapper)
www.coffeecup.com/mapper/	(Image Mapper ++)
www.mediatec.com	(LiveImage)
www.cris.com/~automata/index.html	(Web Hotspots)

Most of these programs support client-side imagemaps, discussed later in this chapter. Also, most commercial HTML editors include an imagemap editor as one of their software "extras."

Other Server Imagemap Gateway Programs

There are other imagemapping CGI programs, designed for different platforms or taking a different approach to mapping. *Mac-ImageMap*, for example, provides imagemap capabilities for the Macintosh *WebSTAR* (formerly MacHTTP) server, using the NCSA imagemap approach. *Glorglox*, on the other hand, takes a completely different approach and maps individual pixels onto URLs. Others programs are available; you should inquire at standard archive sites, such as Yahoo, for information about other tools. However, as a document creator your best bet is to stick with the CERN or NCSA default imagemapping programs, since these are well tested with development tools widely available.

Information about *Mac-ImageMap* and *glorglox*, respectively, can be found at:

weyl.zib-berlin.de/imagemap/Mac-ImageMap.html

www.net/~tomr/glorglox/

Client-Side Imagemaps

As discussed in Chapter 6, HTML also allows imagemapping information within the HTML document. The advantages are many: The link is faster, since the browser does not need to use a server to resolve the destination; imagemaps are not server dependent, so the documents are portable (you can run client-side imagemaps from a CD-ROM); and destination links can be shown as the mouse moves across the image, as all the relevant information is coded into the HTML.

An example of a client-side imagemap is shown in Figure 3.6. A client-side imagemap stores the mapped coordinate data within a **MAP** element, where each **MAP** element takes a **NAME** attribute to identify the map: consequently that a single HTML document can contain more than one map. The regions inside the map are indicated by **AREA** elements. These elements take four main attributes: **SHAPE** to indicate the shape (possible values are "rect" for rectangle, "circle" for circle, or "poly" for polygon), **COORDS** for the coordinates (in integer pixels from the upper left-hand corner of the image), **HREF** for the URL reference, and **ALT** for a text description of the link. In place of **HREF,** an area element can take the **NOHREF** attribute, which takes no value and simply means that the region is not linked to anything. The allowed shapes and a description of the required coordinate values are summarized in Table 3.2.

As with regular server-side imagemaps, regions can overlap, in which case the browser simply selects the first region that fits when looking down through the list of **AREA**s.

You can combine client-side and server-side imagemaps in the same image; a browser that understands client-side imagemaps will use the local map information, while other browsers will revert to the server-side database. Figure 3.7 shows how this is done using the client-side example in Figure 3.6 as a reference. The required additions are shown in boldface italics—all that is needed is an appropriate anchor element surrounding the image, and an **ISMAP** attribute in the **IMG** element.

Figure 3.6 Extract from an HTML document that uses a client-side imagemap for the image shown in Figure 3.4 (*mr_blobby.gif*). The new elements and attributes used by the client-side approach are shown in bold. Italics represents the omitted document content.

```
. . . standard HTML stuff . . .
<IMG SRC="mr_blobby.gif" USEMAP="mapname">
. . . more HTML stuff . . .
<MAP NAME="mapname">
   <AREA SHAPE="circle" COORDS="116,40,30"
        HREF="/dir1/blob2/his_head.html" ALT="text explanation">
   <AREA SHAPE="rect" COORDS="36,30, 84,90"
        HREF="/dir1/blob2/his_hand.html" ALT="text explanation">
   <AREA SHAPE="poly" COORDS="86,154,64,170,76,188,104,184,112,166"
        HREF="http://egghead.com/foot.html" ALT="text explanation">
</MAP>
. . . rest of HTML document . . .
```

Table 3.2 Possible Shape Attribute Values and Corresponding Coordinate Specifications for Client-Side Imagemap AREA Elements All coordinate values are given in pixels.

SHAPE="rect"	COORDS="xul, yul, xlr, ylr"
	Where *xul,yul* are the pixel coordinates of upper-left corner of rectangle, and *xlr,ylr* are the pixel coordinates of lower-right corner of rectangle
SHAPE="poly"	COORDS="x1,y1, x2,y2, . . . xn,yn"
	Where *xn,yn* are the *x*- and *y*-coordinates of the polygon vertices (in pixels)
SHAPE="circle"	COORDS="xc, yc, r"
	Where *xc,yc* are the *x*- and *y*-coordinates of the circle center, and where *r* is the circle radius (all in pixels)

Most of the imagemap generation programs described earlier will create both client- and server-side databases. Additional details of the client-side mechanism are found in the discussion of the **MAP** and **AREA** elements in Chapter 6.

Figure 3.7 Extract from an HTML document that simultaneously references server-side and client-side imagemaps (the changes from Figure 3.6 are shown in boldface italics). A browser that understands client-side imagemaps will use the local map data. A browser that does not understand client-side imagemaps will use the HTTP server.

```
. . . standard HTML stuff . . .
<A HREF="/cgi-bin/imagemap/path/blobby.map"><IMG
    SRC="mr_blobby.gif" USEMAP="mapname" ISMAP></A>
. . . more HTML stuff . . .
<MAP NAME="mapname">
    <AREA SHAPE="circle" COORDS="116,40,30"
          HREF="/dir1/blob2/his_head.html" ALT="text explanation">
    <AREA SHAPE="rect" COORDS="36,30, 84,90"
          HREF="/dir1/blob2/his_hand.html" ALT="text explanation">
    <AREA SHAPE="poly" COORDS="86,154,64,170,76,188,104,184,112,166"
          HREF="http://egghead.com/foot.html" ALT="text explanation">
</MAP>
. . . rest of HTML document . . .
```

Image and Icon Archive Sites

There are several Web sites that maintain extensive archives of publicly available images and icons, and these are useful places to find icons for your own documents. The following is a list of some of the more popular sites.

Public Domain Icon Archives

www-ns.rutgers.edu/doc-images/	
www.dsv.su.se/~matti-hu/archive.html	
www.cli.di.unipi.it/iconbrowser/icons.html	(Iconbrowser archive)
www.cli.di.unipi.it/iconbrowser/icons/mirrors.html	(List of mirrors of above site)
www.cit.gu.edu.au/~anthony/icons/index.html	(Anthony's archive)
bsdi.com/icons/AIcons/	(Mirror of preceding site)
www.hlt.uni-duisburg.de/AIcons/	(Mirror of preceding site)
ftp://ftp.cs.indiana.edu/pub/AIcons/	(Mirror of preceding site)
hobbes.nmsu.edu/pub/multimedia/icons/	(OS/2-related icons)
hobbes.nmsu.edu/pub/multimedia/images/	(OS/2-related images)
www.eecs.wsu.edu/~rkinion/lines/lines.html	(Dividing lines)
www.cco.caltech.edu/~cherish/images/	(Miscellaneous images)
www.erinet.com/jelane/families/index.html	(Jelane's graphics archive)
beseen.com/beseen/free/	(Beeseen free icons)
mich.pixelsight.com/PS/clipart/clipart.html	(Pixelsight free clipart)
www.geocities.com/Heartland/1448/main.htm	

Background Images

cpcug.org/user/jlacombe/backgrnds/johnback.html	
www.algonet.se/~dip/photoshop/PS_index.html	(Tips for PhotoShop users)

Other Lists of Image Archives

www.yahoo.com/Computers_and_Internet/Internet/World_Wide_Web/
    Page_Design_and_Layout/Graphics/

www.yahoo.com/Computers_and_Internet/Graphics/Clip_Art/

www.yahoo.com/Business_and_Economy/Companies/Computers/Software/Graphics/
    Clip_Art/

oneworld.wa.com/htmldev/devpage/dev-page3.html#doc-i

References

General Issues in Web Graphics

www.inforamp.net/~poynton/Poynton-articles.html	(Articles on computer graphics)
www.inforamp.net/~poynton/Poynton-colour.html	(Color and computer displays)
www.sci.kun.nl/thalia/guide/color/faq.html	(FAQ on computer color)
www.vtiscan.com/~rwb/gamma.html	(An explanation of monitor gamma)
lynda.com/hex.html	(Index of RGB hex codes and colors)
news:comp.infosystems.www.authoring.images	(Web graphics newsgroup)

Designing Web Graphic 2, by Lynda Weinman, New Riders Publishing (1997)

Transparent/Interlaced GIFs

user.aol.com/royalef/gifabout.htm	(About GIF in general)
members.aol.com/htmlguru/transparent_images.html	(Tutorial)
www.best.com/~adamb/GIFpage.html	

Animated GIFs

user.aol.com/royalef/gifanim.htm

www.yahoo.com/Computers_and_Internet/Graphics/Computer_Animation/Animated_GIFs/

Client-Side Imagemaps

www.spyglass.com/techspec/tutorial/img_maps.html

Server-Side and General Imagemap Information

www.yahoo.com/Computers_and_Internet/Internet/ World_Wide_Web/Programming/Imagemaps/	(Resource lists)
www.webcom.com/~webcom/html/tutor/ imagemaps.html	(Online tutorial)
hoohoo.ncsa.uiuc.edu/docs/tutorials/ imagemapping.html	(Online tutorial)

THE DESIGN OF WEB COLLECTIONS   4

Chapters 1 and 2 provided a gentle (I hope!) introduction to HTML and to good design habits for creating HTML documents, while Chapter 3 outlined important issues associated with Web page graphics. This chapter takes a broader approach and looks at the issues involved in designing *collections* of Web documents and associated resources. In the printed world, there is a difference between designing a single page and designing a complete magazine, book, or library. Such document collections require organizational and design elements that are neither necessary nor apparent from the perspective of a single page. The same is true of hypertext collections, although here the required design elements are quite different from those needed in the purely printed world.

Why such differences? The reasons lie in the nature of the presentation media: Books are spatial, physical, static collections, with a fixed, *linear* structure, while hypertext is nonspatial, nonphysical, possibly dynamic, and often *nonlinear*. Good hypertext design must embrace these differences, while preserving the easy navigability of printed books. This chapter looks at some ways of accomplishing this goal and provides references for additional reading on this subject.

Paper and Books

The easiest way to appreciate the main issues is to start with the familiar example of a book. This lets us introduce, using a familiar model, the ideas behind structured document collections. The issues that arise in *hypertext* design can then be introduced and analyzed with respect to this more familiar case.

In simplest terms, a book is a collection of related, printed pages. Of course, there is much more to a book than that! A large collection of unbound and unnumbered pages is, to say the least, a cumbersome format (rather like the floor of this author's office as he sits writing this chapter). Given a pile of printed pages, a reader cannot distinguish between pages arising from different books or documents (should there be pages present from more than one collection), and cannot, even within a collection of associated pages, determine the proper reading sequence without explicitly checking for page-to-page continuity. The problems are essentially navigational: There is no easy way for the reader to figure out how to read the pages as a coherent whole.

Book or magazine design solves such problems by giving the pages a uniform design (top and bottom page banners, typeface, and so on), so that pages have a distinctive look; by numbering the pages to give *linear order* to the collection; and by binding the pages together to enforce the correct order. If there are many pages, or if there are organizational requirements, there is often a table of contents listing the page numbers of important starting pages and perhaps an index providing references to other significant locations. By convention, such content-listing or indexing tools are placed at the beginning or end of the volume (the exact location varies according to linguistic and national conventions), to make them easy to find. Additional cross-referencing is possible through internal page references, footnotes, bibliographies, and so on, while additional indexing components are present within specialty books, such as dictionaries. Indeed, the organizational technology of printed material is very sophisticated, covering everything from simple pamphlets to multivolume encyclopedias. This is not surprising, given that this technology has been refined over 500 years of practical experience.

Linear Documents

Books and other printed media are all, essentially, *linear*. By linear, I mean that they have an obvious beginning and end as well as a fixed sequence of pages in between. Indexes, tables of contents, or cross-references exist superimposed on this linear framework—they provide added value and are often critically important—but they do not change the underlying structure. In fact, they depend on the underlying linear structure, page numbers, and so on, to provide reference points within the book.

The reasons for the near universality of this linear model are both physical and psychological. Physically, the only reliable way to organize printed pages is as a bound, linear entity—it is hard to create a book as a random collection of connected but nonlinearly accessible documents! Psychologically, a linear, well-defined structure is comfortable, familiar, and convenient, since the result is easy to read, easy to reference, and easy to communicate to others. The goal of all publishing is *communication*, and a book is a robust collection that can be reliably communicated to others (through duplicate copies) and reliably referenced and compared (through page number references), since everyone with the same book has the same information, at the same location within the book.

It is also important to note that the physical nature of a book provides a psychological comfort zone to readers, by letting them know both the exact size of the book and where they are *within* the book. This makes it easy to browse a book, for example by jumping from the table of contents to a selected location or by simply selecting pages at random, all the while retaining a sense of location with respect to the beginning, end, table of contents, or index.

Other traditional media, such as music, video, and film, are also linear in this sense, being predetermined presentations of sounds or images, created by a musician or director. This, in part, reflects the temporal nature of these media—music and film move dynamically (and usually forward!) in time in a linear way. This also reflects the technical limitations of the media, as it is almost impossible to make nonlinear presentations with traditional film, video, or audio technology, just as was formerly the case with printed text.

Figure 4.1 illustrates both the structure of a book and how the table of contents and index merely provide referencing on top of the underlying linear structure.

Nonlinear Media

The advent in recent years of inexpensive, yet extremely powerful, computers and graphical displays has made it possible to step beyond the linear approach and has opened up enormous—and still largely unexplored—possibilities in the organization and presentation of information. This is because a computer has no preferred organization for stored data and can easily store, index, relate, and access data in a number of different ways, subject to the design of the database holding the data and the capabilities of the database software. In addition, a computer can create a representation of the underlying data quickly, efficiently, and *inexpensively*, according to

Figure 4.1 The structure of a linear document collection, in this case a book. The ordering is implicit in the page numbering. Tables of contents and indexes simply provide referencing on top of this underlying structure.

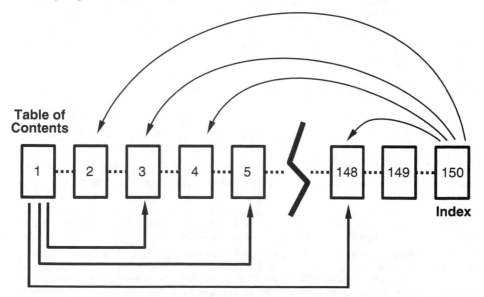

instructions provided by software and/or user input. In a sense, you can think of the stored data as a collection of book pages or page components (paragraphs, images, etc.) that can be shuffled and rearranged almost instantaneously by the computer at practically no cost. This is in stark contrast to the difficulty and high cost of modifying the order of printed material, or material on tape or film.[1]

At the same time, modern computer interfaces can directly, and again at low cost, present these data to a user—a Web browser is just one instance of this process. This also is a new phenomenon, since high-resolution computer display systems capable of rapidly displaying finely formatted text and graphics have only become affordable in the last few years. Thus, not only can a computer rapidly organize data, it can also nearly instantly present the data to a user, in almost any format (text, graphics, audio and video, etc.). A computer can consequently act much like a customizable printing press, capable of organizing and presenting data in decidedly nonlinear ways, limited only by the capabilities of the underlying software and the interests of a user.

Computer Games as Media

This has led, in the past 15 or so years, to the birth of several new media. The first (and still most popular) was video games. Games are inherently nonlinear in the sense described above, since they evolve in an unpredictable way according to the input (i.e., "play") of the user. Video games preserve this model through an environment that incorporates both the game scenario and rules—the user "plays" in this environment and can explore nearly endless game variants, the number of possible variations depending on the sophistication of the game. The first games were very simple, with primitive graphics and limited scenarios, but today's games, such as *Myst*, *Doom*, or *Quake* (my favorites), provide enormously rich environments and enormous flexibility in the way a player can explore the game's virtual world. Indeed, anyone interested in understanding the possible future directions of digital media should spend time playing with modern computer games—even if it is hard to convince your friends that this really is "work"!

Hypertext and Multimedia

At the same time, it was apparent from the earliest days of computers that this new technology could realize the long-dreamed notions of hypertext and multimedia.[2] Inexpensive computers and easy-to-use programs like HyperCard and Macromedia Director opened up exciting new ways of presenting combinations of otherwise weakly connected media. Very quickly, hypertext and multimedia

---

[1] This flexibility and speed also applies to audio and video, which in large part explains why text, audio, and video editing are now commonly performed on computers.

[2] *hypertext*: a collection of text and graphics that can be explored, by the reader, in a nonlinear way; *multimedia*: the mixture of text, graphics, sound, and video in a single presentation. Note that many multimedia presentations are often *linear*. The combination of multimedia in a nonlinear hypertext format is often called *hypermedia*. In this book, the term hypertext can be taken as synonymous with hypermedia.

became the basis of new media design, with products ranging from multimedia wine guides and hypertext encyclopedias to multimedia/hypertext training packages. Indeed, today many corporations commission multimedia promotional presentations instead of the more traditional videos or films.

Designing linear multimedia is relatively straightforward, whereas the design of *hyper*text or *hyper*media introduces enormous design complexities. This is because each hypertext presentation must incorporate, *within* the presentation's structure, the tools to let a user successfully and comfortably explore the collected material. Since, in hypertext, the components can be related in decidedly non-linear ways, there are no simple organizational schemes, such as page numbering, that can serve as ubiquitous and commonly understood tools for navigation and location. And, unlike those in a game, the rules must be nonintrusive and easy to follow, since the goal is to communicate *content*, without the reader having to worry about navigation. Designers and researchers are still exploring ways of designing easy-to-use hypertext and hypermedia structures, and it is not a surprise that good design is something of an art, as opposed to a science.

Web Collections as Hypertext

Most design problems are apparent in large collections, or webs, of HTML documents. Web collections are a form of hypermedia, limited of course by the technologies of the Web and the Internet (a web collection is clearly not as dynamic or multimedia-oriented as a Macromedia Director presentation), but at the same time enriched by the ability to interconnect with resources around the world. Most importantly, the Web is inherently nonlinear, since there can be a nearly (and often frustratingly) endless number of ways of getting from one page to another. Figure 4.2 shows a simple figure of a possible Web document collection—as in Figure 4.1, the solid lines indicate the links (in this case, hypertext links) between the pages, with the arrows indicating the directions of the links.

Do you see the problem inherent in Figure 4.2? Suppose you are reading document *A*, and want to proceed to a topic discussed in document *B*. How do you get there? The answer is that you have absolutely no idea. If a collection were to have no structure other than the links indicated in Figure 4.2, the reader would be forced to move randomly through the collection until he or she happened, largely by chance, upon the desired page. In the absence of additional navigational cues, the reader does not know where to find the table of contents (or even if there is one), the index, or even the beginning of a section. Even if the links are sequential (the documents connected one after the other, like a book), a reader would not be able to find these places as, with the Web, there is no way to step back, "see" the entire book, and just "turn" to the "front" for the table of contents. Indeed, a reader has absolutely no idea of the size of the collection: There could be one page or a thousand. A book gives you both a local and global feel for its size and for your location in it. The page number tells you where you are and where the next and previous pages are, while the feel of the book tells you approximately

Figure 4.2 An illustration of a web of documents—the arrows show the links between documents. The collection is *nonlinear*, in that there are a number of different routes by which the collection can be explored. It is very easy to get lost in such a web.

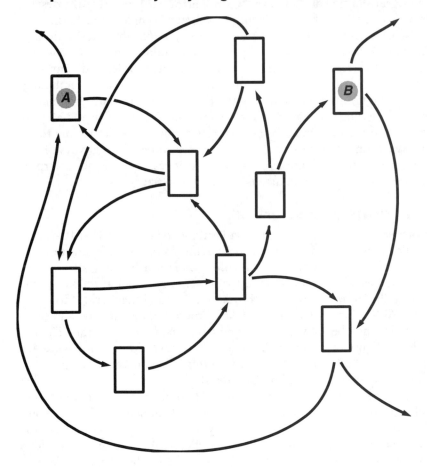

where you are with respect to the entire book (e.g., halfway through) and also tell you exactly where to find the table of contents (at the front) or the index (at the back). The reader's ability to see the whole picture, plus conventions for the location of contents pages and indexes, are part of the technology of books that makes them so easy to use. And, it is the absence of these views that can make hypermedia design so difficult. It is your goal, in designing a Web, to include navigational tools to allow visitors to easily explore and find what they are looking for without becoming lost or frustrated.

Types of Web Collections

Now that we've given this introduction, it is time to look at some practical examples of Web collection design and at the issues that a web designer must take into account in managing and maintaining such collections.

We will first look at a linear model for a Web—just because the Web is nonlinear doesn't mean you have to give up linearity completely! A linear approach is perfectly appropriate when converting a printed document to hypertext, for online documentation, or when you have a particular sequence that you want followed by your readers, such as a sequence of slides.

Of course, most webs are not linear, and later examples look at nonlinear collections, in particular, at the possible organization of collections of documents at a Web site. These sections will include design pointers for larger collections, as well as administrative suggestions for managing large collections developed by groups of authors.

Next, we look at design and planning issues that are independent of the layout of your web. Some examples are: how to plan the web layout, how to organize the documents, and how to incorporate multimedia components.

Finally, we look at tuning a design to make a Web site attractive to visitors to encourage their return. This is an issue both of hypertext design and of public relations/marketing. You must always remember that a Web site is a dynamic place, which *encourages* interaction with its visitors. You must be aware and take advantage of this character, if you are going to develop a site that attracts and retains visitors.

Marketing and site design are further examined in Chapter 5, where we look at some real-world Web sites and examine the site features that are used to ensure a persistent base of regular visitors.

Linear Document Collections

Figure 4.3 shows a schematic layout for a linear document collection—the solid lines with directional arrows show the critical navigational links. Figures 4.4 and 4.5 show a possible design for a page in this collection; Figures 2.2 and 2.4 are other examples of pages from a linear collection. The structure in Figure 4.3 very much follows the book layout shown in Figure 4.1, except that there are now explicit links to places such as the index and table of contents. Recall that, in a book, the reader could easily find these components because of their physical place in the book. This is not possible with hypertext, so that Web documents must have explicit links to these navigational aids.

It is easiest to start by looking at the structure of a single page, such as the example in Figures 4.4. and 4.5. Here, the important navigational features are in the banner at the top and bottom of the pages. The first feature is the title graphic. This quickly identifies the page as part of a particular collection (the "Information Commons" collection), so that users immediately know, from page to page, where

Figure 4.3 A linear collection of hypertext documents. Lines show the main navigational links; the thin lines illustrate secondary links superimposed on the linear structure. (A) illustrates the basic linear structure—note the links to the *Next, Previous, Index,* and *ToC* (Table of Contents) pages. To make the figure easy to follow, links from the Index to the individual pages are omitted. (B) shows a possible linking structure for section headings. *Up* links connect each page to the top page of the section—for simplicity, the links to the *ToC* and *Index* are omitted.

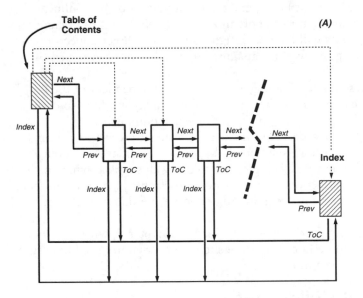

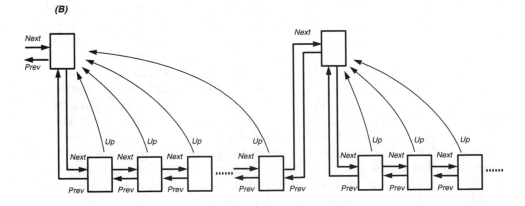

they are. (The text "INFORMATION COMMONS" and "Help with E-Mail" are part of the graphic itself.) Every collection should carry an identifying title graphic such as this or, alternatively, an identifying string of text. It is then possible to use variations of a particular graphic to indicate which section is being examined. For example, the graphic in Figure 4.5 could be varied from section to section—each section would still show the logo and the name "Information Commons," but might also show a smaller-font string with section names or headings. Some examples of this are shown later in this chapter.

Navigational Links

The second navigational feature is the collection of text buttons linked to important related documents. These buttons replace the navigational cues available in a printed book and let readers quickly find their place in the collection. Using the "Prev" and "Next" buttons, the document can be read sequentially; or it can be accessed nonsequentially, using "ToC" or "Index." The "Up" button is linked to the top page of the local section—for example, if this were a page from Section 2, the "Up" button might link to the first page of Section 2. Part (B) of Figure 4.3 shows how such pages could be organized. For convenience, a top-of-section page might contain a brief section introduction, and perhaps a contents listing for the section. This lets the user move "Up" for an overview of the section, without having to return all the way to the full table of contents.

Simplified Authoring—HTML Page Templates

Adding all this navigational and design information to a page need not be a lot of work. When building a large collection, you can use HTML document *templates*. Such templates contain all the generic markup, but not the text, image, or other content. You then make a copy of the template, edit the template to insert the desired content, and quickly prepare the desired document. Since all your pages need navigation tools, you can create the template with these components built-in; then to create pages, all you need do is edit the templates and add the correct URLs.

Some *informational* hypertext links are provided in this example linear collection—these connect to resources that are not really part of the collection, but that provide information useful to the user. For example, the "Feedback" link might connect to a gateway program (or simply a mailto URL) that lets the visitor send feedback to the document author(s), while the "Info" link could provide information explaining the meaning and function of the navigation buttons/bar. Both features should be present in a well-designed collection.

Clean Design and Dated Content

The last thing to stress is the importance of clean page design and the use of a similar design for all pages in the collection. Thus, if you decide to use centered **H2** headings for main sections and left-justified **H3** headings for subsections, you should do this for all pages. This reinforces the familiar pattern implied by the

Figure 4.4 Template HTML document for a linear collection, illustrating the use of navigational links within the page design. Each page in a collection should have a similar banner and labeling text or graphics that uniquely identify the pages within the collection. Figure 4.5 shows this document as displayed by Netscape Navigator. Note that the text adjacent to the logo ("INFORMATION COMMONS" and "Help with E-Mail") is part of the header graphic.

```
<HTML><HEAD>
<TITLE> REL and REV Attributes for Hypertext Links</TITLE>
</HEAD><BODY>
<P ALIGN="center"><IMG ALIGN="bottom" SRC="iclogo.gif"
      ALT="{Information Commons — HTML Docmentation]"><BR>
[<A HREF="page2_1.html">Prev</A>]
[<A HREF="page2_3.html">Next</A>]
[<A HREF="page2_0.html">Up</A>]
. . .
[<A HREF="contents.html"     REL="contents"><B>ToC</B></A>]
[<A HREF="/cgi-bin/index.pl" REL="index"><B>Index</B></A>]
. . .
[<A HREF="info.html"><EM>Info</EM></A>]
[<A HREF="/cgi-bin/feedback.pl"><EM>Feedback</EM></A>]
<HR>
<H2> REL and REV Attributes </H2>
<P> REL and REV attribute are used, with LINK and A (anchor)
elements, to describe the relationship between the document
containing the element, and the document referenced by the
 hypertext link .....
<P> And yet more babble about REL and REV...
<HR>
<CENTER> <EM><A HREF="mailto:ic_html_doc@ic.utor.ca">IC
HTML Documentation</A> . . . . . .</EM>
<EM>Last Update:</EM> 12 September 1995 </CENTER>
</BODY></HTML>
```

graphic and banner design, and makes it easy for a reader to navigate within each page, as well as across the collection.

Note also in Figure 4.5 that the page is dated and contains a hypertext link to the author or maintainer of the page. Although such features are not necessary on every page, dating pages lets visitors know when the material was last modified, while the feedback mechanism lets the author hear what the readers think. You should use a dating scheme that will not be misinterpreted internationally—

Figure 4.5 Display, by the Netscape Navigator browser, of the document listed in Figure 4.4.

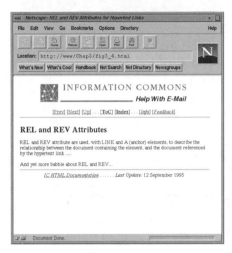

thus the form 8/9/98 is not ideal, since some countries use the order day/month/year, while others use month/day/year. If you don't want feedback, you can omit the feedback link—but my experience is that feedback is overwhelmingly positive and constructive, and helps enormously when building and maintaining large document collections.

If you use cascading style sheets, you can use the style sheet to define many of the desired layout features—which will then be adopted by all pages that use the style sheet. However, this will still only work if you have been consistent in your use of the HTML elements within the documents.

Structured Tree-Like Collections

The next hypertext model is that of a tree or hierarchical document collection. An example is shown in Figure 4.6, which shows a single, extended tree. A real-world example is the Yahoo! collection—a list of Web-accessible resources—found at www.yahoo.com. The Yahoo! documents are organized hierarchically. For example, the Yahoo! page covering aids for people with disabilities, shown in Figure 4.7B, lies under the category "Companies," listed in Figure 4.7A. This page in turn lies under the category "Disabilities," which in turn lies under the category "Health." If you have information that organizes itself in a hierarchical manner, this is your obvious approach. Of course, the hierarchy is useful even for small collections (the Yahoo! site is very large). Another more modest example is presented later in this chapter.

Figure 4.6 An illustration of a *hierarchical* document web. The documents are organized in a tree-like structure, descending from a single home document.

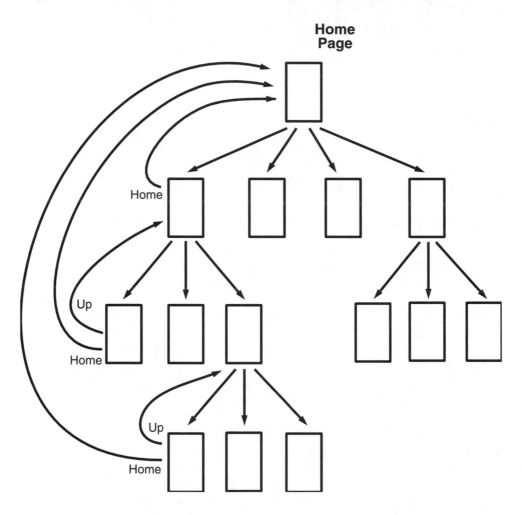

The navigation tools required within a hierarchy are different from those needed in a linear collection. For example, the linear concepts of *next* and *previous* are no longer meaningful, while links to "Up" are usually equivalent to the browser's "back" button, and are often not necessary. Instead, you want links back to a number of locations such as the root of the tree (the link to "Yahoo" in Figure 4.7—the image is clickable), perhaps to a "Search" or "Index" tool (essentially a searchable index), and also to important informational pages. The document in Figure 4.7 also

Figure 4.7 Example page from the Yahoo! hierarchical catalog of Web sites. (A) is an example of an index page from this collection—you can find this page by accessing the site: *www.yahoo.com* and selecting the category "Health," followed by the category "Disabilities." Note the boldface items, which indicate links that go an additional level down the hierarchical tree—the number afterwards gives the number of items in the linked index page. An "@" indicates that the link is to a document that can be reached from more than one Yahoo! category page—a "leaf" attached to more than one "branch." (B) shows the document returned by selecting the "Companies (@)" link in the document shown in part (A).

(A)   (B)

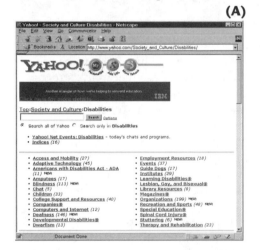 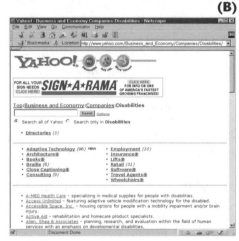

These screen captures are courtesy of Yahoo! Inc.

has links to a feedback utility ("Write Us") and to general information—here about the Yahoo! hierarchical resource list ("Info"). Finally, the special-purpose link "Add URL" lets a visitor register new URLs for inclusion in the collection. Obviously, each collection will have its own special-purpose utilities and links, depending on the site's function and purpose.

At Yahoo!, the page *layout* also contains important information. In all the Yahoo! index pages (e.g., Figure 4.7A), links to additional subcategories are indicated by boldface hypertext anchors, while the bracketed numbers after each such anchor indicate the number of items listed in that subcategory. A trailing "at" (@) character means that the subcategory is actually accessible from more than one place in the hierarchy, implying that the node has *multiple parents*—the hierarchy is not a simple tree, but contains cross-linked branches. In this case, the top of the page lists the primary route through the hierarchy to the document; in Figure 4.7B, these are "Business and Economics," followed by "Companies," followed by "Disabilities." The label "Disabilities" is not an active anchor, as this is the label for the document being displayed—the others provide links back to the indicated pages. This feature can be confusing, and an inexperienced Yahoo! user, unfamiliar with this nonlinear structure and with the meaning of the character "@", can sometimes get lost by selecting one of these alternative links upwards.

The Yahoo! design undergoes constant evolution, as better page layout models are developed, and as the collection of references grows—the Yahoo! tree(s) keep growing new document "branches" and "leaves" to account for the ever-increasing list of resources stored in the Yahoo! database. Overall, the design has evolved comfortably (at least as far as a user is concerned!) within the original structure, which is a good indication of the robust nature of the hierarchical approach.

Designing an Effective Hierarchy

The hierarchical approach can be extremely useful, but you must be careful to make it easily navigable. Particularly, you do not want the hierarchy to be too deep (too many levels) or too shallow (too few levels). If the hierarchy is too shallow, then there will be too many categories at each level and it will be difficult for visitors to find what they are looking for. At the same time, if there are too many levels in the hierarchy, it will also be hard for visitors to find what they want. After four or five selections down into the hierarchy they will lose confidence (or patience!) that they are on the right track. You should strive to keep the tree depth as shallow as possible, without making each level too unwieldy. A depth of 3 to 5 is ideal, while anything greater than 6 is likely to cause navigational problems.

Most importantly, your design—the number of levels and the names and labels of your categories—must reflect the material you wish to present and the way you wish to present it: There is no one universally appropriate hierarchical structure. Thus the Yahoo! layout, which works well for Yahoo!, is not where you should start—you should start by looking at *your* data and determining how you want *it* to be organized and accessed.

A Web Document Hierarchy

Another example of a well-organized hierarchy is found at the URL:

www.utoronto.ca/webdocs/HTMLdocs/tools_home.html

which is the top node for a document collection describing Web browsers, HTML editors, and support tools available on Mac, UNIX, and PC platforms. This collection is organized hierarchically, first by platform (Windows, Macintosh, OS/2, UNIX, Miscellaneous tools) and second by subcategories based on tool type (TCP/IP Software, WWW Browsers, Browser Helper Applications, HTML Editors, HTML Translators/Filters). Figure 4.8 shows a typical page from this collection—in this case, from the top-level page of this hierarchy. Note how this page has navigational links

Figure 4.8 A page from a hierarchical list of Web software resources, illustrating important design features in a hierarchical collection. This page is available at: www.utoronto.ca/webdocs/HTMLdocs/tools_home.html

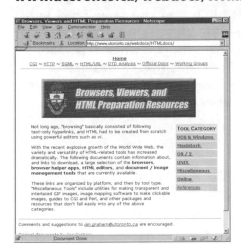

This page was designed by Michael Lee of the University of Toronto's Information Commons.

to the documents one level down in the hierarchy, namely to tools specifically for DOS and Windows, Macintosh, OS/2, UNIX, and so on. This organization makes it extremely easy to navigate through the hierarchy and find the desired information. Although not apparent from this page, the hierarchy is only three levels deep.

Note also that there is a link from this page all the way back to the home page for this Web site ("Home"), which is the top node or home page for the entire document collection. The overall design and organization of a Web site is discussed later in this chapter.

Hierarchies and Linear Components Together

Obviously, it is easy to include linear collections within a hierarchical model: A particular node within the hierarchy simply becomes the starting page for the linear collection. The hierarchy then gives an overall and easily navigable structure to the entire collection, rather like shelf labels in a library.

Web Site Collections

A Web site usually follows the hierarchical approach, but with a few twists. Figure 4.9 illustrates a possible organization of a large site's Web collection. In general, a Web has a single top node, or *home page*, which is the publicly advertised location

Figure 4.9 Schematic layout of a large web collection, showing the hypertext links between the home page, the top-level organizational nodes, and other documents. Solid lines indicate main links between items within the hierarchical (or linear) structures, while long-dashed lines indicate links between "siblings" at the same level in a hierarchy. The arrows indicate the possible directions of the links, as coded into the HTML anchor elements. The short-dashed lines indicate links to general-purpose pages—note that these links are unidirectional, since it is unreasonable to code in all the possible return paths. Typical home pages from large collections are shown in Figures 4.10 and 4.11.

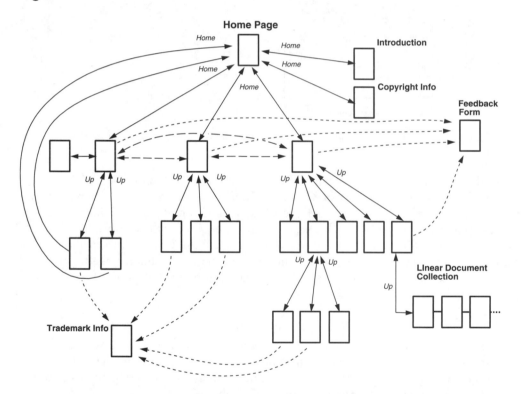

for the document collection. The home page then has links to other pages that lead down to the remaining resources. In this example, the home page has links to small introductory documents that explain the origins of the site and that outline copyright rules associated with the site content. There are also links to the top-level nodes of the various hierarchical collections beneath the home page. Figures 4.10 and 4.11A and B show three example home page that illustrate these features. Despite their superficial dissimilarity, both pages follow precisely this model.

Figure 4.10 An early mock-up for the official home page for the University of Toronto. The page has links to single documents describing the university organization and mandate as well as links to the main organizational areas. These latter links are to top-level nodes of subsequent hierarchical trees.

Distinguishing Branches in a Large Web

Often, a Web site will have many different main sections rooted in the home page, as seen at both the University of Toronto (Figure 4.10) and Silicon Surf (Figure 4.11A). The Web manager may want to use similar document layouts and design models in the different branches, since this makes it easier for users to navigate through the collection. At the same time, the designer will want to give each section a distinctive look, so that the readers have a sense of location and know where they are.

One way to do this is to modify the banner text graphic at the top of the page to reflect the identity of the site and the specific features of the local tree—this is just what we prescribed for linear collections earlier in this chapter. Consider, for example, the "Information Commons" Web site. For this site, the banner graphic shown in Figure 4.5, which contains the Information Commons logo and name, could be modified for each section at the Web site, retaining the logo and name, but adding a subtitle appropriate to each section. The logo immediately communicates that the page belongs within the Information Commons collection, while the subtitle quickly indicates the particular subsection or topic. In addition, different-sized or differently styled logos can be used for sections and subsections to give a graphical feel for the hierarchical location of the document in the overall collection. Finally, the **BACKGROUND** attribute to the **BODY** element can be used to tile the background with a "watermark" reflecting this same information. This is not sufficient on its own, however, as the information provided by the graphic is lost with a text-based browser or if image loading is disabled.

Figure 4.11 Part (A) shows the home page of *Silicon Surf*, the electronic publication of Silicon Graphics Inc, while (B) shows the home page for *The Nando Times*, an electronic newspaper. Both pages are strongly graphically oriented, with links to the main site areas. Despite the very different looks, the organization of these pages is very similar to that of Figure 4.10. Note that the *Silicon Surf* home page has a prominent link to a text-only version, while the *Nando Times* has a link to a "no frames" alternative: Both sites were carefully designed to support a wide range of users.

(A)   **(B)**

(A) is used by permission of Silicon Graphics (www.sgi.com); copyright 1997 Silicon Graphics Inc. All rights reserved. (B) is used by permission of The Nando Times (www.nando.net). All rights reserved.

Figure 4.12 shows some possible banner designs, based on the ideas just presented, that were created for the Information Commons Web site. Note how they preserve a common look and feel, while quickly communicating the function of the page and its location within the overall hierarchy.

Use the ALT Attribute!

If you use graphical banners to distinguish your pages, you must also use **IMG** element **ALT** attributes to assign alternative text strings to the images. Then, the important organizational information contained within the image is available to a visitor who is not able to view graphics. As an example, an Information Commons banner for a document describing e-mail services should have an **ALT** attribute value such as *"INFORMATION COMMONS—Help With E-Mail."*

Figure 4.12 Possible page banners for Web pages at the Information Commons. Note how the banner graphics preserve the identity of the site, while also communicating the subcategories of each page. Here, major section banners are bigger than minor page banners, allowing for easy determination of place in the hierarchy.

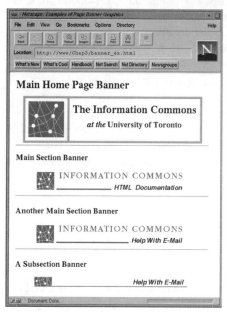

Multiple Document Versions

Ideally, you should design all your pages, including the home page, so that they can be understood on any Web browser. However, sometimes this is not possible, or it is inconvenient—for example, you may be presenting information both to users who have learning disabilities and prefer graphics over text, and to users who are blind, and can *only* use text. To deal with this type of conflict, some Web sites offer *multiple* home pages.[3] A good example of this is found at the University of Toronto's Adaptive Technology Resource Centre site home page, shown in Figure 4.13. This page is graphically rich, but offers an alternative home page designed for users with screen readers and those who want to avoid graphics. Note also how the Silicon Graphics Web site (Figure 4.11A) offered this same alternative view.

---

[3] This is also useful for sites that use imagemaps, Java applets, etcetera, on their home pages—such resources do not work for visitors using lynx, who have disabled image loading, or who cannot run Java, so these visitors need an alternative, graphics- and applet-free home page. The SGI home page, shown in Figure 4.11A, provides these options.

You may also want to offer alternative navigational pages that structure the underlying content of a site from a different point of view. For example, a collection of material on Adaptive Technology (aids for persons with disabilities) can be organized either as a tree presenting important issues and technologies or as a problem-solving tree, where the various hypertext links represent options, in a decision-tree, for obtaining technology solutions for particular user disabilities. A schematic for this type of structure is given in Figure 4.14, which illustrates two organizational trees linked to the same underlying content.

You must be careful with this type of design, since the documents at the bottom of the tree (the actual data in your collection) will display identically no matter if they were accessed from tree *A* or tree *B*. The navigational icons on each document must therefore point to both trees and to the appropriate places on each tree. This presents difficulties similar to those at the Yahoo! site, where several list categories appeared below multiple nodes in the tree. At Yahoo!, the referenced page lists all the possible parent nodes. Unfortunately, accessing these alternative parents can be quite disorienting for an inexperienced user, unless their nature as optional routes is well explained—note all the efforts the Yahoo! administrators have made to make this as easy to navigate as possible. You should visit Yahoo! and try this out for yourself.

Of course, one way to improve the readability of the pages is to customize the page layout, dependent on the pages previously seen by the visitor. This is possible

Figure 4.13 Home page for the Adaptive Technology Resource Centre at the University of Toronto. Note how this page offers, via the text link at the top of the page, an alternative home page designed for those using text-to-speech screen readers. This page is available at www.utoronto.ca/atrc/.

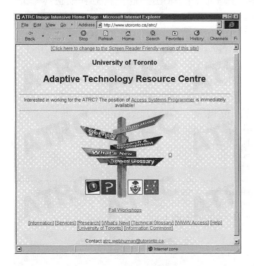

when the pages are generated by special software on the server, as discussed in the next section.

Gateway Filtering of Delivered Documents

Although the Web is a dynamic medium, HTML documents by themselves are static and unintelligent—as just noted, a retrieved page contains no information about the history of the user's interaction and cannot respond in a customized manner depending on the page(s) previously viewed. This means that, if you use multiple home pages, all documents that link back to the home pages must have multiple "Go to HOME" buttons to account for each possible origin—or these links must be omitted to avoid disorienting visitors.

In principle, you can in part deal with this issue by using a *gateway* program (gateway programs are discussed in a Chapters 10 and 11), or some other server-side processing mechanism, to dynamically modify *every* document returned from the server. For example, suppose there are two alternative structures for a document collection, labeled *pathA* and *pathB*, each path starting from a different home page. You can implement this collection so that the home pages do not

Figure 4.14 Possible structure of a Web site having two home pages and two parallel organizational structures, labeled *A* and *B*. Both trees access the same underlying collection of documents, shown at the bottom of the figure.

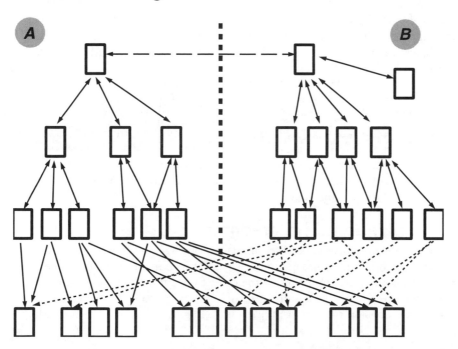

access the remaining documents directly, but instead access them *through* a gateway program. This program processes the documents so that they include the navigational icons and other information that reflects the path being explored. Suppose the first page to be explored from home page *A* is the document *monsters.html*. In this example, the page is accessed via the URL:

```
http://www.we.edu/cgi-bin/docfilter/dir1/dir2/monsters.html?path-a
```

where the gateway filtering program is `docfilter`, the path to the desired document is `/dir1/dir2/monsters.html`, and the query string `path-a` indicates which path is being explored. The `docfilter` program retrieves the indicated document, and edits all URL strings in the document so that they also use `docfilter` to access documents from the local collection, and so that they also contain the query string `path-a` to indicate the path being explored. In addition, `docfilter` could modify the document banner, inserting the navigational icons and hypertext links appropriate to this path.

This is not a trivial exercise, since the filtering process is complicated and must take into account the structure of the entire document collection. Thus, to date, use of this approach is limited to sites where the documents are largely delivered from a database. A good example of this approach can be found at the Electronic Books Technology Inc. site (EBT was, however, recently purchased by *Inso Inc.*, so this URL may soon change):

www.ebt.com/

These documents are entirely served from an underlying database of non-HTML documents—filtering programs dynamically convert the database entries (coded in markup language defined, like HTML, using SGML) into HTML and automatically configure the presentation dependent on many variables, including the path being explored by the reader.

Designing and Managing a Web Site

Large Web sites are usually designed and maintained by more than one person. As a site becomes large, maintenance and development become major issues, so it is useful to have a model for management that allows for distribution of management as the site grows and for a well-defined delineation of responsibilities amongst authors, editors, and managers.

Site Organization: The Webmaster

A Web site should have an overall Web manager, or *webmaster*, who organizes the home page and the main navigational pages. This manager is responsible for ensuring valid links to the top pages of the collection, but cannot be responsible for the internal consistency or details of those underlying collections. This makes for a reasonable division of responsibilities and obligations, giving the individual project groups full control over their own document collections, while leaving the overall management of the site in the hands of a site manager.

A site manager can prepare a collection of HTML document templates for use by groups developing their own resources. This template can contain a generic graphical logo for the site, some document templates that reflect a generic page or collection design and, finally, a list of URLs that link to the main navigational pages maintained by the site manager. Each project group can integrate these links into their own project pages to create links back to the site main home page. They can also use the logos and page templates to preserve, if they wish (or are mandated) to do so, a common look and feel for the entire site.

Individual Project Directories

Each major document subcollection should be placed in its own directory or subdirectory, distinct from the directory housing the Web site home page and main organizational pages. Users responsible for maintaining each collection can then be given permission to create and modify files in their particular directory, but nowhere else. This isolates the projects from each other and ensures that no user can accidentally modify another group's pages.

Test and Production Directories

In most cases, it is best to give each group two directories—one for the finished and publicly available material, the other as a development or test area. In this way, the development team can develop and modify documents in the test directory, without worrying about affecting the documents being seen by visitors to the site. Once the new material has been fully developed and tested, it can be formally "published"—that is, collectively copied into the public directory, making it available to the general public.

There are several Web development packages—for example, Microsoft *FrontPage*, Adobe *SiteMill*, SoftQuad *HotMeTaL*, and Silicon Graphics *WebMagic*—that support this type of development and "publication," while several HTTP servers integrate database management of the document collection with the server. Many of the newer *intranet*[4] software suites also include this type of functionality. You can expect more tools such as these to become available in the near future.

Revision Control and Document Management

In many cases, a single collection will be designed collaboratively by many different users. In this case, it is often convenient to use revision control or document management software to manage the collaborative development process. Such

---

[4] *Intranet*: an Internet network designed to work *internally* within a company or organization and provide a suite of network-based services, such as e-mail, document management, and workflow monitoring.

software can archive the changes made to a collection and can also ensure that only a single person can modify a given document at a time. To some degree, the tools mentioned in the previous section support this functionality.

There are also many standalone revision and document management packages available on every platform (most were originally designed for software development projects, for which similar issues are important) that can be adapted to Web applications. Some, such as *rcs* (Revision Control System) and *sccs* (Source Code Control System), often come bundled with UNIX systems and were designed to manage large software development projects. If you are developing a large project involving many document developers, you should definitely consider one of these tools. Sites such as Yahoo! have links to information about other similar packages. If you are interested in this option, you should search Yahoo! (or other) sites, using search strings such as "revision control" or "document management."

Document Management Tips

In the absence (or even in the presence) of document management software, you will want to use the following useful rules when designing and maintaining a large document collection:

- Keep your documents well organized on disk, using subdirectories to appropriately organize the material by topic or workgroup.

- Use HTML comments (`<!-- comment -->`), **META** elements, or some other mechanism, to record modifications to the documents. Document management systems often maintain a secondary database for these data. HTML comments and **META** elements are described in Chapter 6.

- Use partial URLs to reference documents on the same server. This makes the collection transportable, as relative references are correct regardless of the absolute location of the collection.

- Preserve the original high-resolution image files used to create page graphics, logos, and buttons. Then, at a later date, you can easily create new document graphics from these original data.

Design and Maintenance of a Web Collection

In designing a collection of any type, there are several general rules you should follow—these rules are presented in the following sections. Although most of these rules will seem like common sense, they are often overlooked or unimplemented unless you (a) incorporate them into your design model and (b) implement them early in the design phase for your Web site. It is usually very difficult to back up and fix mistakes once a site is up and running, and these simple rules will help you reduce the number of mistakes you make.

Storyboard the Collection

You have probably noticed the usefulness of schematic drawings in picturing the interrelationships and linkages between web documents. In fact, such drawings are extremely useful in *designing* web collections—it is always a good idea to sketch out the web layout on paper (or on a computer, if you have a suitable drafting program) and work out the desired relationships *before* you actually begin preparing the documents. Storyboarding is enormously flexible and lets you experiment with many possibilities before you even start to prepare the pages. Design and navigation problems quickly become apparent when you lay out the overall organization of the pages, as do the choices for the navigational links that must be built into each page. Storyboarding is easy to do and will save you time and effort in the long run.

Prototype the Page Layout and Design

Once you have a Web site design, you now need to implement the technical design elements described in Chapters 1 and 2; each page must contain the required navigational tools and should have a recognizable and well-designed layout. In the latter regard, you should take advantage of the typographic and design principles well-known in the print world. To paraphrase Robin Williams (the graphics designer, not the actor), these principles are:

> **Contrast.** Elements on a page that are not the same should be *very different*.

> **Repetition.** Elements that repeat through the page or collection should repeat with the *same design layout* to show the unity of the content and to indicate the organizational structure.

> **Alignment.** Page layout is not arbitrary, and everything placed on the page should have a *visual* connection to something else.

> **Proximity.** Elements *related* to one another should be placed *close together*.

For additional information on this topic, you are referred to Williams's excellent introductory book on typography and design, listed in the bibliography at the end of the chapter.

Plan for Future Growth and Features

This may seem obvious, but it is not—or, at least, many people seem to ignore this aspect of design. A well-designed collection will age and grow well. Aging well means that pages can be redesigned, with new graphics and a different layout, without affecting the underlying hypertext structure. The same is true for growth. A well-designed collection will have room for new nodes, new trees, and new branches, without requiring the pruning, dismemberment, or outright destruction of the original structure. You must plan ahead—you can do this while storyboarding the first version of your collection—because any good Web site will grow quickly, at which time it is exceedingly difficult to go back and fix basic design flaws.

Make Navigation Easy

This may seem needless repetition, but it is essential that you consistently use good design to make the collection easy to explore. All pages should have links back to master navigational pages, such as the local linear collection's table of contents or the home page of the local document tree. Also, all pages must have obvious exit points—you don't want users guessing at what to do next. And, finally, make sure that the links work! All the navigation buttons in the world won't help if they don't lead anywhere useful. On the companion Web site, "Web Management and Maintenance Tools" lists some useful utilities for testing hypertext links in a collection of documents, while many publishing systems (such as those mentioned earlier in this chapter) include link checkers as part of the publishing package.

Never Move the Main Pages

Once you have built a popular site, your visitors will bookmark your major navigational pages so that they can return directly to these locations. Therefore, once these pages are put in place, you must *never*, *ever*, move them. Doing so will break all your visitors' stored hotlist or bookmark entries and will cause no end of grief. If you must move pages, make sure to provide server redirection for the main pages[5] or provide temporary pages in place of the ones that have been deleted, pages that point to the new location. A CGI program that can help with this task is discussed in Chapter 11.

When expanding a collection, you should avoid eliminating pages—only add new ones. This avoids the problem just mentioned and reiterates the importance of properly thinking out the organization of your collection before you start. A well-organized collection has room for easy expansion, whereas an ill-thought-out jumble of pages will not grow easily and will lead to problems when reorganization is required.

Get an Appropriate Internet Domain Name

If you are setting up a major site, you should also obtain a suitable domain name for your HTTP/Web server—names of the form *www.mydomain.edu*, *www.companyname.com*, or *home.companyname.com* are quite common, with the strings *www*, *web*, or *home* quickly identifying this as a Web server site. Once obtained, a domain name can easily be moved from one machine to

---

[5] All servers can be configured to redirect a request from a specific URL to a different location.

another, without affecting your visitors. For example, you might initially have the domain name *www.myfirm.com* referring to a shared machine or a temporary location. Later on, the domain name can be moved to a machine dedicated to your Web services, without affecting the URLs that reference the resources.

Commercial domain names (ending with *.com*) are registered through the Internet Network Information Centre (InterNIC). This is accessible over the Web at:

www.internic.net

There is currently a registration fee of around $US 100. Many Internet providers will help you obtain domain names, for a small additional fee. Given the technical issues involved, this is probably worth the extra expense. And if you want a commercial name, you should hurry—most of the good names are already taken!

Make Resources Easy to Find

Your collection is there to be read, so make it easy for users to find what they are looking for. A visitor should be able to get to the primary content after only a couple of clicks—most visitors will give up if the resources they are searching for are too deeply embedded. Ensuring easy accessibility of pages requires a careful analysis of the intent of the site, the available content, and content usage. You can monitor how your documents are being used by analyzing the Web server log files. If you find that a particular resource is very popular, you can then add direct links from your home (or other) page to this resource to make it more easily accessible. Many commercial servers come with simple analysis tools, while a number of commercial, shareware, and freeware analysis packages are also available. Go to "Web Management and Maintenance Tools" on the companion Web site for a list of some of the more popular utilities.

Making information easy to find *also* means letting people know when resources are *not* available. For example, a visitor to an airline Web site will probably be looking for airline flight information and ticket prices. However, since ticket prices are notoriously variable, it is hard to keep Web-based data up-to-date. If this is the case, the site should have a page that says exactly this, and that provides an alternative (yes, even a 1-800 number) for further inquiries regarding fares.

Note Changes and Updates

Indicate on your Web pages when you make changes or additions. It is then easy for frequent visitors to know when content has been added and furthermore lets new visitors know that the collection is being continuously improved—visitors will keep coming back if they know you are keeping the site up-to-date.

Retain Site Visitors

No doubt you want people to stick around at your site once they arrive and, of course, if you have followed all my design pointers, they are bound to do so! However, one easy way to unwittingly send visitors away is to explicitly give them, just after they have arrived, links to locations outside your local web. It is generally a bad idea to include, on your home (or other high-level) pages, links to "KooL SiTEs" or "Important Resources" elsewhere on the Web, as your visitors will be tempted to head right there—and never come back. Instead, put this information further down in your collection, thereby forcing users to step through and see some of your own work before arriving at these external references.

Solicit User Feedback

Your pages should allow for user feedback—so that users can make inquiries, point out problems (broken links, non-functional search tools, etc.), or provide commentary. This can be done by using mailto URLs or fill-in feedback forms. Of course, if you use such a tool, you must also be ready to deal with the mail. You must make sure to respond to the mail you receive—after all, if a visitor goes to the trouble of sending you commentary, it would be very impolite not to respond!

Preserve Individual Privacy

You must guard your visitor's privacy. No user would be happy knowing that you were directly monitoring his or her access to information, just as you would be unhappy to find that someone was monitoring the books or magazines you were reading. If you analyze the log files, you should do so in a way that preserves user anonymity; for example, by hiding the domain names of the clients or by looking at aggregate information averaged over many users.

Creating an *Attractive* Web Site

This is clearly an open-ended section, as the design of a popular and attractive Web site depends enormously on both the material being presented and the intended audience. This section summarizes those features that, in the author's opinion, apply in most cases.

Useful, Timely, and Interesting Information

If your site does not provide something newer, better than, value-added, or different from other Web sites, no visitor will bother coming back. Before you design a site, think about how your material will be novel, different, or better than already existing resources. If you can't, then you should try thinking of something else to do. And, if you are presenting something new and different, be sure to explain why it is better or different.

Make the Site *Dynamic*

The Web is dynamic and encourages communication. Your site should recognize and embrace these facts by encouraging user feedback and user interaction and by providing information that is updated on a regular (that is, daily or weekly) basis. Some of the more attractive Web resources, such as daily cartoons (Dilbert), Web contests, newspapers, the amazing Fishcam (try searching for *Fishcam* at your favorite Web search engine!), browsable archives of mailing lists, and so on, do exactly this (you can find these examples by searching the Yahoo index). You should strive to implement similar dynamic and interactive features at your site.

Make the Site *Fast*

You must make sure that your visitors can quickly access your information. As a first test, you should access your content using a 14.4 or 28.8 Kbaud modem— after all, this is what most of your visitors will be doing. If the pages seem slow and irritating to you under these conditions, imagine how irritating they will be to real visitors!

Your Web server should have a high-speed connection to the Internet, so that any delays in delivering content are not due to your own low-speed link. This is particularly important if your site contains a lot of images, which are notoriously big files and correspondingly slow to download. At a minimum, you should have an ISDN-speed connection (128 Kbps), and really you should have something much faster, such as a T1 (1.44 Mbps) line.

You don't necessarily need to lease high-speed bandwidth all for yourself— instead, you can choose to lease space on a commercial Web server (usually through an Internet Service Provider, or ISP), which in turn has a fast network connection. However, you should make sure that the ISP has a fast Internet connection that is not saturated by heavy use—just like a superhighway, even the fastest network connection slows dramatically when heavily used. You can check the "effective" speed of the connection by accessing a server from networks serviced by other Internet Service Providers—this will tell you if there are significant network bottlenecks between the server and your prospective visitors.

Make the Site *Accessible*

It is easy to get carried away designing a Web site by incorporating audio and video data, multimedia or other plugins, or complicated JavaScript scripts or Java applets. But remember that these objects require high bandwidth to be effective and that users with older PCs or inappropriate browsers will simply not be able to view these resources, regardless of bandwidth. Many Web sites have started with home pages filled with applets and gorgeous embedded multimedia components, only to remove these components due to complaints from visitors. This is not to say that these components are bad things; rather, you should be careful in their use and aware of the your users' limitations.

Listen—and Respond—to Your Visitors

As mentioned previously, if users bother to comment on your collection, you should pay attention to what they say. Almost universally, such letters either point out problems with your collection (perhaps a broken link), contain suggestions for improvements or changes, or contain requests for additional information. You should respond to these notes—after all, if they have bothered to send you a comment, the least you can do is send a note of thanks. This is both polite and will complement your public relations.

Watch for New Ideas

There are thousands of people creating new and exciting Web resources, every day of the week. Certainly, much of what I have learned has been the result of surfing around the Web and seeing what others are doing. You must do the same! The design possibilities are growing quickly, as a result of novel design by talented individuals and as a result of new Web technologies that permits new design elements (backgrounds, tables, animation, and so on). You must explore the Web, and see how these tools are implemented elsewhere, before you can intelligently implement them yourself.

Planning and Implementation

This chapter has covered basic issues related to the structure of good hypertext collections, but has not discussed aspects of Web site planning and implementation. These issues are discussed in the next chapter.

Annotated Bibliography

info.med.yale.edu/caim/manual/—This site contains an excellent on-line discussion of hypertext design issues and their relevance to the Web. This resource has a large and very useful annotated bibliography. The authors of the collection are Patrick J. Lynch, director of the Center for Advanced Instructional Media at the Yale University School of Medicine, and Sarah Horton, a Multimedia Applications Specialist for Academic Information Resources at Dartmouth College.

Multimedia and Hypertext: The Internet and Beyond, by Jakob Nielsen, Academic Press, Cambridge, Mass. (1995)—Jacob Nielsen's book is an expansive overview of multimedia and hypertext, with important discussions of usability and design issues. With its almost 70 pages of references, you will never again be at a loss for what to read!

The Non-Designer's Design Book, by Robin Williams, Peachpit Press (1994)—This small, outstanding book covers all the basic elements of good typography, page layout, and book design. Although written for the printed page, this is a must-read book for anyone who wants to design Web pages and who does not have a background in design and/or typography.

Designing Visual Interfaces: Communication-Oriented Techniques, by Kevin Mullet and Darrell Sano, Prentice-Hall (1995)—An excellent book on visual interface design concepts for computer graphical user interfaces.

Designing and Writing Online Documentation, Second Edition, by W. K. Horton, John Wiley and Sons (1994)—An excellent book that covers in detail all aspects of electronic document design. There are also many useful references.

Visual Design of the User Interface, by E. R. Tufte, IBM Corporation (1989)—An excellent review of the issues involved in designing usable interfaces for users.

Envisioning Information, by E. R. Tufte, Graphics Press (1990)—Simply a lovely book that illustrates the many ways in which information can be graphically communicated, with some reflections on computer interface issues. This is a must-have book for any serious interface designer.

The Visual Display of Quantitative Information, by E. R. Tufte, Graphics Press (1983)—This is considered by many to be the best book ever written on the graphical presentation of data. An outstanding book that nicely compliments his later work, *Envisioning Information*.

Understanding Hypermedia, by Bob Cotton and Richard Oliver, Phaidon Press (1993)—A somewhat glitzy and visual introduction to hypermedia and an excellent addition to any coffee table. This will be of particular interest to those with a background in design.

Hypertext, by George P. Landow, Johns Hopkins University Press (1992)—This is a discussion not of the technical aspects of hypertext, but of the literary meaning of hypertext and of its impact on our understanding of text and literature. If "critical theory" or the name Michel Foucault means anything to you, then this is the book to read.

The Gutenberg Elegies, by Sven Birkerts, Fawcett Columbine (1994)—Some thoughts on the usefulness of hypertext and hypermedia and on the advantages of print. A much easier book than *Hypertext*.

STRATEGIC WEB SITE DESIGN

BY IAN GRAHAM AND KELLY PETERS[1]

The preceding four chapters looked at technical and theoretical issues associated with Web site design. This chapter takes a complementary approach and looks at the *strategic* issues behind developing a site. These are issues of intention and goal, rather than design, so this chapter does not have as many figures as the preceding chapters. It does, however, use URLs to reference sites illustrating the points raised. Indeed, this chapter can be usefully read while sitting next to a Web browser, so that the reader can access the referenced URLs and "follow along" with the book. To help with this process, the book's supporting Web site has a document that lists these URLs, which you will find at either of:

> www.compbooks.com/graham/html/chap5/links.html
>
> www.utoronto.ca/ian/books/html4ed/chap5/links.html

The first step in a site's development should be is to determine the *goal* of the site—indeed, this should be done well before the first HTML page has been coded. To help you analyze your own goals, this chapter looks at four characteristic goal-based site models, namely: marketing, customer service, e-commerce, and content-driven. Each of these four sections provides guidelines for developing such sites, and references example sites. Although the quoted examples are commercial Web sites, most of the guidelines apply equally well to sites developed for educational or nonprofit organizations.

Once the purpose of a site is known, the next step is to understand the customers—who they are, what they are already getting, and what they are likely to want. The next two sections of this chapter look at approaches for obtaining this information. The first of these looks at performing a competitive analysis, and

---

[1] Kelly Peters is a professional Webmaster and has worked at CANOE, Canada's largest Web site, since December 1995. Ms. Peters has been an active organizer, speaker, teacher, and writer on Web topics since 1994, and has made numerous presentations at conferences such as Comdex Canada and Internet World. Ms. Peters is on the board of directors of the Association of Web Professionals and is the current director of Toronto Webgrrls. She wishes in particular to acknowledge the kind support of Hugh Stuart and Tamara Atkin.

attempts to convey the importance of researching the sites already on the Web. The next section looks at ways to analyze your target group. Knowing what is already available and understanding the intended audience will strongly affect a site's layout and design.

The last third of this chapter explores some of the issues involved in designing a site's architecture. Subjects discussed include: choosing the development team, creating a storyboard, determining the right number of links off the home page, designing a site metaphor and navigational scheme, testing the site before launch and, last, planning for ongoing maintenance.

Marketing Web Sites

With over 90 million users, there is no doubt that the Web is a worthwhile marketing venue. A Web site can serve as a 24-hour-a-day sales marketing arm, with a well-designed site yielding greater consumer awareness of a company's brands, products, and services. Indeed, many companies and other organizations have already started to use a Web presence as a "next-generation" marketing tool. Perhaps this helps explain why, according to the authoritative *Internet Wizards'* 1997 Internet Domain Survey (www.nw.com/zone/WWW/top.html), the number of Internet sites has doubled since January 1996, to a total of nearly 20 million hosts.

Presentation

The design and presentation of a marketing site must be of the highest quality, since they must both attract and retain visitors. Internet users have become very discriminating Web "browsers," and expect well-designed HTML documents and well-designed, quick-to-load images—and if they don't get this, they will leave! As with television, first impressions really count. Competing for hits amongst a plethora of Web sites, each one newer than the last, a Web site needs to effectively engage the viewer on the very first page.

Once visitors are past the first page, the quality of a site will determine their perception of the accuracy of the information they are reading and of the quality of the company behind it. Thus, the high quality of the site must be maintained throughout—at a marketing site, there is no room for poorly designed pages, broken links, inaccurate material, or stale content.

It is also important to tie the Web site into an existing corporate identity, for example by incorporating existing graphics or logos—suitably processed for the Web—into the pages. It is also important to integrate the Web site into other marketing or advertising media, either by cross-relating the media (e.g., by publishing URLs in print material) or by including print or video-based themes in the Web site. However, it is a mistake to push these relationships too hard, and if the print or video material do not transfer well to an on-line format, it is best to use a design created exclusively for the Web.

Design Tip: Graphics and Fast Downloads

Although the aesthetics of presentation on the Web are crucial just as they are for interactive multimedia on CD-ROMS and for print materials, designing for the Web presents very different technical challenges. Indeed, most commercial graphic and illustration software packages are not designed for this medium and do not work easily with it, while most designers are unfamiliar with the special requirements of Web presentations and graphics. Some of the most important issues were discussed in Chapter 3.

The first challenge is that on the Web, only two graphics formats are widely supported: GIF and JPEG. These formats, not commonly used by graphics designers, dominate the Web because they offer extremely good compression—the image files can be small, even if the images are physically large. The size of the image files is a second major challenge—even with GIF and JPEG, there are many image processing tricks that can be used to produce smaller files. Unfortunately, many print designers are unfamiliar with these tricks. Creating small files is important, as this allows for images that download quickly from server to browser—a consideration that artists working in other media find difficult to understand. This point must be stressed over and over again with the design team, since Internet users repeatedly state that "waiting" is the most frustrating aspect of the Web—and waiting is almost always caused by large, slow-to-download image files.

The design strategy for the Web is also different from that of multimedia or print, and does not emphasize graphics design at all costs. The goal should always be to first produce a functional site layout, and only then to incorporate "Web-appropriate" graphical design. As a counterexample, one of the most universally disappointing page designs, still far too prevalent on the Web, is a home page containing a single, giant imagemap. It is imperative to remember that if the page takes long to download, many people will simply press "stop," and will neither see the image nor be able to access the linked site resources.

Ideally, the entire page—including graphic and text files that load with the page—should be no more than 50 KB in size, and it should be functional to the user even in the absence of the page graphics.

Design Tip: Useful, Current Content

Content is critical to impact and should be dynamic, conveying a sense of freshness and relevancy. Not every page needs to be constantly updated, but key pages—such as the home and second-level pages—should include frequently updated content. For example, a "What's New" blurb pointing to what's new on the site, or a small collection of links that are referencing various resources on the site and are changed on a regular basis, can keep the pages up to date and encourage a user's return.

In a Forrester Research (www.forrester.com) report entitled *Web Best Practices*, 60 percent of companies surveyed said that the marketing team was responsible for the development of content. It is therefore critical that the marketing department have an informed sense of what type and style of content is appropriate for the Web and that they venture beyond the material available in brochures and press releases. If other divisions of the company can contribute interesting and useful content, they should be given the opportunity to do so. After all, the nonmarketing people are probably closer to the newer material and are probably able to maintain updated content about it. Such timely knowledge is a valuable resource and should not be wasted.

Design Tip: Go Beyond Brochure-Ware

A frequent complaint of Internet users is that many Web sites are little more than "brochure-ware"—namely, simple scanned versions of brochures or videos dumped onto the Web. Content *must* be designed for the Web—scanning brochures will create giant image files that are slow to download, visually dull, and insulting to your visitors. Often such sites are created under the guise of "protecting corporate identity." Guarding a corporate identity is an important aspect of site design, but it should not be done to the detriment of a site's effectiveness. Michael Strangelove, publisher of the *Internet Business Journal*, has described how an early effort by MCI " . . . takes a mediocre 60-second TV commercial and transforms it into a painful 30-minute on-line experience."[2] Such sites are guaranteed to receive very few regular visitors, while those who do visit will be left with a very poor impression of the company.

Design Tip: Tie into Interesting Content

One goal for a marketing site can be to create a *destination* on the Web—such an approach will attract potential customers that traditional advertising methods cannot reach. A *destination site* is filled with content about a particular subject area and can attract a wide cross-section of readers, who, in visiting the site, will see associated information about the company sponsoring the content. This "good citizen" approach can point readers to products of interest, and the pages themselves can contain advertising for relevant services or products provided by the sponsoring company.

An example of such a destination site is found at the Chase Manhattan Bank (www.chase.com/loans/rvadventures.html). In the United States, Chase Manhattan is one of the largest lenders to recreational vehicle (RV) purchasers. Thus, instead of creating "another" boring banking Web site, Chase Manhattan chose to create a comprehensive site for RV owners—the site includes information about RV clubs and associations, several RV FAQ (frequently asked questions) lists, and even a place where visitors can enter first-hand accounts of their RV travels. Of course, information about Chase Manhattan banking services and RV purchasing loans is only a click away!

---

[2] *Internet World*, May 1995.

Interactivity can also be a key component in a marketing Web site. Since the Web is the first truly interactive publishing medium, opportunities exist to feature a product and solicit immediate reader response. Thus, the Web can be ideal for promotions such as contests, sweepstakes, and surveys, all of which can be used to attract readers, collect information about them, and promote customer loyalty.

In general, all marketing-based Web sites need to provide ways for the public to contact staff, and companies need to develop customer service channels to facilitate the immediate processing of these requests. Indeed, it is critical that those planning the site take into account all the extra work that will arise when people start mailing in queries and requests for Web site or product information. Visitors will expect quick responses to their messages, and the goodwill created by providing inquiry addresses will soon fade if you don't quickly answer the letters you receive!

Customer Service Web Sites

Developing a Web site to serve as an extension to customer service can be both rewarding to your customers and a cost-saving venture to your company. The Web allows you to easily and inexpensively "push out" your services around world, through tools such as searchable content (for example, allowing visitors to search your product database), "expert" e-mail and newsgroup forums, and applications that permit real-time interaction between visitors and staff (allowing users to ask questions of company experts). For such sites, elegant site design is nice, but is less important than providing effective and simple tools—since users are there for a specific purpose, the goal should be to make the functions and features of the site as easy to use as possible.

The Federal Express (www.fedex.com) Web site is an ideal example of this approach. Federal Express was an early adopter of the Web when they launched their Web site in the fall of 1994. Although their site initially had very little content, it supported *package tracking*. By entering a Federal Express package waybill number into a Web form, anyone could see the status and location of the package without having to telephone FedEx and wait for an available agent to search the database on their behalf. This was an extremely useful tool for users, and brought Federal Express much publicity—and many site visitors.

Indeed, at present, over half a million packages are tracked each month via the Web. Not only is this good for the customers, it has also led to substantial cost reductions for Federal Express. In practice, each 1-800 call costs the company approximately 50 cents, when the cost of staffing and infrastructure are taken into account, so that costs can be significantly reduced by simply reducing the number of calls. Thus, even if only half of the packages tracked via the Web are done in place of a phone call, the cost reductions are substantial. Indeed, recent estimates indicate savings to Federal Express on the order of $125,000 per month.

Creating a large-scale application such as the Federal Express package tracking mechanism is beyond the budget of many Web sites. But then, not every company is the size of Federal Express! The key to providing a customer service site is simple: Provide Web-based accessibility to support resources and staff, and give customers the opportunity to receive timely answers to their questions.

E-commerce Web Sites

On the Web, even a small company can use electronic commerce technology, or *e-commerce*, to deliver an effective international presence. Indeed, e-commerce has become a "fourth channel" of sales, after phone, mail, and sales agents, significantly extending the sales capabilities of the traditional three. For example, phone access is limited by time of day—either a customer can't be reached, or a customer can't get a question answered when no one is available after office hours. On the other hand, a Web site is open 24 hours a day, seven days a week. Print sales material can be hindered by time lines—the material is useless if prices and availability change and is expensive to produce and distribute. Web content can be instantly updated, at minimal cost. Finally, much of the content relayed by a sales agent can also be handled or facilitated by an interactive, on-line exchange—indeed, some sales agents can effectively "move on-line," and use the on-line medium to supplement their other tools for contacting customers.

Although relatively small at present, the size of the on-line market is expected grow rapidly over the next few years. Indeed, by the year 2000, estimates for the amount of public commerce that will take place via the Web range from a conservative $6.6 billion (Forrester Research Inc.), to a middle-of-the road $7.3 billion (Jupiter Communications, www.jupiter.com), or to a maximum of $12 billion (Price Waterhouse, 1997 *Technology Forecast*).

Using the Web, on-line companies can often move quickly into new markets, even outflanking larger competitors. The on-line bookstore Amazon.com (www.amazon.com) exemplifies such e-commerce possibilities. By offering over 2.5 million book titles and a simple, secure on-line ordering system, Amazon.com generated more than $16 million US dollars in sales in 1996, with steady increases each quarter. Although other booksellers have now moved to on-line ventures, Amazon.com has continued to innovate to maintain a leading position. To build interactivity and a sense of community, Amazon.com offers unique features, such as forums whereby authors and readers contribute profiles and reviews for books sold through the site—this becomes value-added content for the Web site.

The Amazon.com "Associates" program is another interesting and uniquely Web-based approach to building a client base. This program encourages other Web sites, particularly those that list or describe books, to create "Associate" links from their documents to the pages at Amazon.com associated with the described books. This makes it easy for a site visitor to purchase the book—by following the link to Amazon.

Many small Web sites are unable to afford on-line transaction mechanisms, so that "associating" to Amazon.com is an easy way for a site to provide an on-line purchasing venue. Of course, a site needs a good reason to offer such a link, and to provide this incentive, Amazon.com offers to remit, to registered Associate partners, up to 8 percent of the revenue of each sale arising from the Associate's site link. Needless to say, this is a significant incentive! Indeed, a quick check, using the AltaVista search engine (www.altavista.com), shows that over 100,000 Web pages now contain links to Amazon.com. An analysis of some of these sites indicates that most are small sites wanting to provide readers with a convenient way to purchase books they recommend or have reviewed. Such cross-marketing arrangements are likely to become more common amongst e-commerce sites.

Of course, customer sales is only one aspect of Web-based commerce. Indeed, according to *CommerceNet*, an international industry consortium dedicated to e-commerce issues, business-to-business transactions will be one of the largest e-commerce growth areas. In an analysis of business-related e-commerce, Paul Regan, Director of the Networking Solutions Group at Tandem Canada, states that while 15 percent of retail electronic commerce will have moved to the Internet by the end of the century, he expects that up to 30 percent of business-to-business transactions will occur on-line.[3] At the same time, Forrester Research estimated that business-to-business trade will have reached $8 billion in 1997, a figure that will increase to $327 billion by the year 2002.

Fruit of the Loom (www.fruitactivewear.com) has already made the shift to business-to-business e-commerce. To encourage the use of the Web for their business-to-business relationships, Fruit of the Loom builds customized Web sites for all of their *Activewear* distributors. These sites include an ordering system integrated with the Fruit of the Loom back-end accounting and inventory databases. Then, if a distributor's client needs to order 10,000 shirts, the distributor can check the Web site for special price options such as deals on overruns, place the order, and produce and print a proper record on the transaction.

Design Tip: Make the Web Interface Easy to Use

An e-commerce site is essentially a computer application interface to be used by relatively naïve users. Thus, the primary design goal must be to create a simple, easy-to-use interface. Users must be able to navigate through the site efficiently, with a minimum of confusion. If this is not the case, then navigating the site becomes more like solving a puzzle—and the last thing you want to do is puzzle potential customers!

The second main goal is to provide security—you must be sure to protect private information provided by users during a transaction (such as credit card information) and must make sure that the Web site itself is protected from hackers.

---

[3] *Reality Check*: *Commerce on the Internet*, General Content Corporation, in association with CommerceNet Canada, 1997.

This generally means hiring software developers who are expert in these issues and purchasing commercial e-commerce software packages.

It is also important to reassure users about the security methods used in on-line transactions. Many users are justifiably nervous about sending private information over the Internet, and it is important to alleviate their concerns. Providing a page outlining the secure transactions methods used at the site, along with a clear statement highlighting the high priority of security in the commerce environment, can help ease consumer concern. Highlighting partnerships with established banks and on-line commerce security vendors is also be beneficial, should such relationships be an important part of your site's security and transaction-processing technologies.

The third goal is to have timely and accurate content. On-line catalogs *must* be up to date, with changes being immediately integrated into the Web environment—a successful Web site will always present the most current available information. Although people are willing to make allowances for dated prices in print media, Internet users do not have the same tolerance for out-of-date price or product information. Indeed, it is not just users who lack this tolerance. According to Alan Gahtan, an attorney specializing in cyberlaw with Borden and Elliot, Virgin Atlantic Airlines was recently fined US $15,000 for advertising an expired fare on its Web site.[4]

Once an order has been submitted, it is important to provide clear confirmation that it has been processed—customers need reassurance that their order has been received and will be filled. A Web page response confirming an order and providing a confirmation number is certainly necessary, while follow-up e-mail to the customer is also a valuable option. Many current commerce sites do not clearly confirm completed transactions, leaving users uncertain as to the state of their order. The result is a reduction in on-line customers (because the interface is unclear, and users are reluctant to use it) and increased costs of telephone or e-mail support (for customers who are confused, and who are not sure if they actually bought anything!).

Finally, although the goal is to develop an autonomous on-line commerce application, customers need to be able to reach a *real* person, by phone or by some other means. In general, Internet users will have only modest skills relative to your e-commerce application, and your customers may need assistance when using the site or may want the chance to make additional inquiries. The traditional requirements of good customer service—namely, establishing good communication channels with customers to properly determine customer needs—is still of primary importance.

Content-Driven Web Sites

It is generally accepted that those under thirty will soon be looking to the Web as their primary source of "newspaper"-style information. Thus it is not surprising

---

[4] www.borden.com/techlaw/website2.htm

that almost every newspaper or magazine has already constructed a significant, content-driven Web presence. Indeed, Wayne Parrish, vice-president of strategic development for the Sun Media Group and CANOE, said, "[By going on-line] you're investing to protect your future and you're investing for the potential to become a player in what will be a fundamentally new and different medium."[5]

However, it is less clear how to turn such a presence into a profitable venture. Some sites have tried to develop revenue via on-line subscription services, but most of these have met with only limited success. Others sites, particularly those associated with news organizations, have developed a "free" content service, and use advertising or collateral product sales to generate revenue. Again, results are mixed, and very few such sites are profitable on their own. In most cases, they are cross-subsidized by their corporate parent.

On-line Fee-based Publications

The day Playboy (www.playboy.com) launched its site, it received over 100,000 visitors—a significant feat, leveraged in part by the strong *Playboy* brand name. Today, the same (but larger) site serves over 40 million page views per month.[6] Playboy's primary focus is to use the site to drive readers to the newsstand to purchase copies of the magazine. The site attempts to do so by providing a small amount of content for free, as a "teaser" to the print publication. However, the site also hosts an on-line *Cyber Club* service containing the full content of the print magazine, plus significant extra content. This extra content is only available on an electronic subscription basis. At present, some 16,000 members pay a $60 annual fee to access this adults-only library. This is a significant revenue stream, but it is unlikely that it actually covers the annual costs of maintaining the *Cyber Club* site.

On-line Publications as a Complement to Print

In contrast, the Web site for Canada's largest circulation women's magazine, Chatelaine (www.chatelaine.com), is purely content-driven and contains on-line versions of every article printed in the magazine, integrated into an extensive, searchable (and free) archive. Indeed, Chatelaine sees the Web and print magazines as complementary, and goes so far as to integrate content from the Web site into the print magazine by quoting from users who post to Chatelaine-sponsored discussion forums. In addition, Chatelaine uses the information gathered via the Web site to help define magazine content—for example, by following users' comments in on-line discussion groups and writing magazine articles that address the concerns expressed in the on-line forums.

Chatelaine's strategy is to provide, via the Web site, a value-added reader service that complements the print magazine. Thus, although the print content is

---

[5] "Newspapers Enter the New, Wired World," *Globe and Mail,* Toronto, July 23, 1996.

[6] www.ijumpstart.com

available on-line, the emphasized on-line features are the popular discussion forums and the "Chatelaine Seal of Approval" Web site reviews. According to Paula Gignac, the on-line director for the *Chatelaine Connects* Web site, the correspondence received to date indicates that the Web site has not led to a loss of subscribers and, in fact, has increased actually increased magazine readership and brand awareness.

Design Tip: Design for the Readers

When designing a content-based Web site, it is important to determine the identity and characteristics of the audience, so the design properly matches the audience's expectations. Thus for technically sophisticated audience, the design can use more advanced design features, as they are likely to challenge rather than intimidate the readers. On the other hand, a site designed for relatively unsophisticated Internet users should not be challenging and should strive to be as straightforward as possible.

Word magazine (www.word.com) is an example from the former category. This literary Web site "pushes" the envelope of Web design and depends on the use of cutting edge technology to attract and retain visitors. Shift magazine (www.shift.com) falls into the same category. On the other hand, the New York Times Co. (www.nytimes.com) takes a very conservative approach. Their Web site uses a large imagemapped image to make the home page look almost exactly like the front page of the "physical" *New York Times* newspaper, although the site is also careful to offer a text-based alternative for those who disable image loading. This design apparently gives Internet newcomers a sense of confidence about how to handle the information presented—or perhaps the New York Times was unable to find another design that sufficiently preserved the newspaper's identity.

Note that although there may be valid reasons for using graphics-intensive designs, many users will be frustrated by the time it takes to download the resulting pages. This is true independent of the style of the site. For example, the New York Times and Shift magazine home pages are very slow to download, as both designs incorporate large image files.

Design Tip: Confronting Design Limitations

The range of possible Web page designs is limited by several issues, most importantly browser compatibility, limited network bandwidth, and the design constraints imposed by the needs of the target audience. It is important to test your design against these limits. In particular, you should preview the pages using as many browsers—and versions of browsers—as possible and also view the pages using a browser connected to the site via a slow Internet connection (for example, using a 14.4 KB modem). This will help to illuminate design problems that were not detected on the machine you used to create the pages or internally within your organization's high-speed network.

The page design must also reflect download times and computer screen sizes. Thus, each page should not contain more than 1500 words of text—larger pages should be broken into multiple pages, connected by hypertext links. The content does not necessarily need to be rewritten for the Web, but it should be *designed* to fit within the constraints of the medium.

Design Tip: It Isn't TV

Reaching past the hypertext model of the Web, some companies are experimenting with the concept of "Web broadcasting" and are applying this approach to their on-line presence. The Microsoft Network (MSN) is betting hundreds of millions of dollars that it can adapt the "feel" of the television model to the Web, complete with its infrastructure of channels, programs, directors and producers, by developing animated content to be passively "watched" by the user. MSN believes that this model will eventually attract a mass audience, which will then allow MSN to generate large advertising revenues in the manner of today's television networks.

It is possible that, one day, this model will become the reality. However, today's users are saddled with slow bandwidth, insufficiently powerful computers, and insufficient technical sophistication to keep up with the installation and configuration of the dozens of new applications required to "catch the experience." Thus it will be quite some time before the Web is able to match television's major strength—the ability to rapidly deliver real-time animated content. This situation will change as the digital bandwidth to homes increases, but these changes will not happen in the near (or even not so near) future.

Aside from the obvious bandwidth problem, there are also deeper issues that call into question the appropriateness of the "Broadcast Web" approach. In particular, the Web offers more than television, since the Web model can in principle support many different media and significant user interaction. Indeed, most of the more popular Web applications have revolved around tools, such as on-line discussions groups, that build a sense of community. Such issues are simply not relevant in the standard broadcast model.

Design Tip: Advanced Technology

The applications used in the development of a Web site should be based on the priorities of the readers. CANOE (www.canoe.ca) is Canada's largest Web site and is purely content-driven. The priority at CANOE is to provide content as quickly and effectively as possible. Thus, CANOE regularly adds applications to the site, such as chat tools or special information services, and is constantly updating and adding to the available content. However, the site does not incorporate JavaScript, Java, Shockwave, or other advanced technologies into the site. The experience at CANOE is that such use of advanced technology tends to slow the delivery of content and decrease the *accessibility* of the content. Indeed, CANOE users frequently praise the site's "content-first" approach.

Design Tip: Distribute Content Maintenance Tasks

At CANOE the content is maintained by a team of journalists, trained in HTML coding. Although a portion of their job is simple cutting and pasting stories downloaded from the newswire, their journalism training gives them a professional understanding of newsworthy timing and pithy headlines; they quickly adapted this expertise to the development of sophisticated, rapidly changing news articles tailored for the Web. "For two weeks Princess Diana was our top news story," according to Dave Moore, on-line editor of CANOE CNews. "The story changed more than six times a day. What's in a newspaper box is out of date before it's even daylight. On CANOE we were able to coordinate and maintain more depth, more pictures, more information than anything CNN and Newsworld could do."

Given the speed with which content can (and should) be updated, it is important to allow as many people as possible to participate in the content-development process. HTML editing tools can convert content into (basic) Web pages, while the site designer can provide content developers with predesigned HTML templates that simplify the authoring process. What actually goes on the site will be chosen and approved by the editorial staff, who can filter the stories and select those that are most appropriate.

Finally, be sure that hyperlink references to other Web sites are both *accurate* and *active*. Accuracy is always an issue—there is nothing more annoying to a reader than an erroneous or broken link. However, users are also deeply annoyed by inactive links—that is, URLs given as text references, but where this text is not an active link. While it is understandable that a company may not want visitors to leave their site and thus may wish to "leave out" such external links, this approach should be avoided: All implicit hypertext references should be made explicit via active links—even when the link is to a competitor's site.

Design Tip: Build a Community

Through newsgroups or other discussion forums, a Web site can become a type of virtual community in which users can meet, shout, laugh, and talk. Such a sense of community helps to build loyalty amongst site visitors and to define the "sentiment" of the site.

Special-purpose forums can be established for discussions related to a special event, or to particularly moving news stories. As an example, the Princess Diana newsgroup on CANOE, created for writing condolences to the Princess's family, quickly received over 1000 postings.

At the same time, it is important to take an active role in these discussion groups. Thus, the site should designate a newsgroup moderator, whose role includes maintaining civility in the forums, initiating discussion by posting questions to the group, and soliciting responses from visitors.

It is also important to establish an efficient process for handling e-mail queries. Users tend to mail in questions covering a wide range of topics, from requests for assistance in the use of a specific site application, to a request for help in locating content for a term paper. A content site is in the business of providing information and must be able to handle all such e-mail questions.

Design Tip: Advertising

The designers of an advertising-supported site must accommodate ad placement within the overall page layout. Although it is often difficult to integrate the desires of the design and marketing teams, it is important to do so early on in the design process. If this is not done, then the design team will later be forced to rework their design, as they will not have properly allowed for the placement of advertising content.

It is important that the page design be flexible enough to accommodate a range of possible advertising strategies, in order to ensure that advertising graphics can be successfully placed in the pages. While in print, radio, and television, there are standardized dimensions and position placements for advertising, on the Web such standards are still being established. While the Internet Advertising Bureau (www.iab.net) now advocates a set of standard banner sizes, these are not yet widely adopted.

Another advertising tactic involves creating *sponsorship areas*, whereby the advertising client buys the marketing rights to a complete section of the Web site. The section is then branded with the sponsor name, and the pages in that section are given graphics that advertise products from the site sponsor. Colgate-Palmolive recently made the largest Canadian on-line sponsorship buy in history when they purchased a $300,000 three-year agreement for exclusive Colgate-Palmolive branding of the CANOE Web site Hockey Pool section.

Competitive Analysis

Once the goal(s) of a Web site have been established, the next step is analyzing—on a continuous basis—the competition. The webmaster of the Federal Express Web site told author Evan Schwartz that she regularly "has to spend time looking at [UPS's] site" because it is "an ultra-competitive industry." Similarly, you should be constantly asking the following questions about each competitor's Web site: How does their Web site look? What novel features are they employing, and are people using them? What kinds of technology features are employed and how useful are they? As Schwartz summarized, "the Web economy is a world in which a competitive advantage may only last a few months, if not weeks. Webmasters must act quickly and take a proactive stance toward employing new technologies before competitors do."[7]

---

[7] *WEBONOMICS*, Evan Schwartz, Broadway Books, 1997, page 118.

Analyzing the Target Group

The next stage is to analyze the target group for the site and to determine how well this group is represented on the Internet. While the Internet is now breaking into mainstream usage, many groups are still under-represented. Recent Canadian demographic surveys reveal that Internet users are predominately college-educated males between the ages of 24 and 44, with household incomes exceeding $60,000 annually. Consequently, a site trying to appeal to women must recognize that 60 percent of today's Internet users are male, and the number of sites focusing on female users is small. On the other hand, this might reveal the opportunity to fill an under-serviced niche.

Understanding the target group should also affect a site's design. For example, a colorful and typographically creative layout will appeal to a younger audience, while a more staid design would be the most effective approach for a financial services site. Thus, general rules of design relevant to the print world can also serve as useful guidelines on the Web.

Site Design: The Site Architecture

Once the objectives of a Web site have been established, it is time to begin design and construction. The first step is to choose the team and to define the responsibilities of its subgroups. The content group can include people from across the company or organization. For example, the artists and programmers can come from existing creative and information technology departments. However, it is important to have a core of staff who are experienced in Web site management and design, so that those new to the Web can be trained in the technical details and can be properly managed. Ideally, the site architect should be a Web expert and a skilled organizer. Large projects will also need a project manager to coordinate the different groups and to serve as a bridge between the content, technical, and marketing/advertising groups.

Storyboarding the Site

The next step is to create or sketch out the site storyboard—a schematic diagram which graphically represents the site's topical categories and corresponding content. Before the first page is coded, this site blueprint must be developed. Storyboarding allows a variety of site structures to be assessed before one is selected. The storyboard defines the major content areas and should illustrate the navigational paths.

Creating a Navigation Scheme

Graphics do more than just add visual aesthetics to a Web site—they also play an important role in the development of a navigational scheme. A Web site as a whole should have a consistent look, but individual sections should also have customized graphical features, such as different background colors or unique graphical elements. For example, each of the three key areas of Chatelaine uses a different dominant color. Thus, as the user moves through pages in the *Destinations Web Links* section, the pages have a purple background, the graphics are purple, and in the global navigation graphics, the Destinations piece is highlighted.

Most Web sites support two different navigational mechanisms and two different navigational bars. *Global* navigation refers to those links that point to the major areas of a Web site, such as the home page and the help and feedback areas. These links provide users with a strong sense of how the site is organized and how they can navigate through it. Often, these navigational elements are combined into a graphical or text-based bar, placed across the top or bottom of the page. In the Chatelaine site, a global navigation toolbar—a collection of labeled puzzle pieces— is placed on every page. This is illustrated in Figure 5.1.

The second navigational tool, *local* navigation, provides links to the content within a particular section. Each page in a section should contain links to the other pages in that section, so that when the user finishes reading one piece there is a convenient link to related content. Increasing the number of click options can increase the average number of pages viewed by users before they leave the site.

Figure 5.1 Rendering of the bottom of one of the pages at the Chatelaine Web site. Notice that the puzzle pieces are used as global navigation buttons, while the links inside the page are used for local navigation within the current section ("Destinations").

*Screen capture used by permission of Chatelaine and copyright Maclean Hunter Publishing.
All rights reserved.*

Determining the Content and Owners of the Content

All items destined for the Web site, including pages for help, feedback, and the site index, should be added to a document maintenance list. The Web site architect should then determine who will create the content for the different pages and who will be responsible for maintaining the pages. At this time, it is also useful to look into creating other, default pages. For example, the site managers may wish to create a custom page to return when a visitor requests a nonexistent resource. A "customized" mini site-index page in place of the otherwise cryptic "404 not found" message can serve as a useful way of guiding the visitor towards the site content.

Determining Home Page Content

The content for the home page should reflect the key topic categories of the site and should provide links to those categories and the underlying content. Beyond that rather obvious statement, there are two main schools of thought on how best to organize the links. Many designers follow a model called "chunking," wherein the content is organized as small logical sections, with each page containing on the order of seven such sections. This approach is based on the work of cognitive psychologists, who have shown that people are best able to remember unrehearsed lists if they contain no more than seven items. Designers following this approach create home pages with a small number of links, carefully chosen to represent the broad categories of information—these links are connected to pages that summarize the contents for each of these categories. The power of creative copywriting comes to play in devising a naming scheme for these sections that is easily understood by the site visitor, that is memorable, and that works well with a graphical theme for each area.

A second school recommends placing as many links as possible on the home page. This approach is based on some early page design work by the developers at CNET (www.cnet.com), an on-line electronic newspaper. In 1995, CNET was experimenting with the number of links on their home page and found that the more links they offered, the greater the chance of users finding something that interested them, thereby increasing traffic.

A good design will often contain a mix of these two approaches, by having a collection of main links to the site's broad categories (i.e., chunking), plus an additional collection of links to recently added, or notably topical, content.

Making an Entrance: Tunnels and Flash Pages

A site entrance can be made more visually exciting through the use of a flash page or an entrance tunnel. An entrance tunnel is a linear collection of Web pages that exists at the beginning of a Web site—the user clicks through the tunnel pages, until finally arriving at the "real" home page. David Siegel, author of *Creating*

Killer Web Sites, argues that an entrance tunnel "...help[s] build anticipation as people approach the heart of the site. An entrance tunnel uses a game or some other device to hook the viewer." An entry tunnel can be enticing, if well designed and fast to traverse—which means that the tunnel must be short and must contain minimal copy and graphics. A tunnel also can frustrate users who have to wade though these preliminary pages before arriving at the real content. There is, however, more forgiveness for this type of effect when the site's focus is marketing or entertainment, and not content delivery. Siegel also makes clear the importance of providing a direct link to the home page from the pages in the tunnel, so that the site does not frustrate repeat visitors who wish to bypass the "experience."[8]

A slightly different approach is a flash page—this is a page that appears for only a few seconds, to be replaced by the regular home page. Such a page is easily created using the client-pull technique outlined in Chapter 11. Like an entry tunnel, a flash page must download quickly and must have content that is changed frequently, so that it does not become boring to the reader. A flash page should contain a real hypertext link to the home page to account for browsers that do not support client-pull and to let users "skip" the flash page by selecting the link by hand.

Figure 5.2 shows a typical storyboard for a site with a lead-in flash page or entry tunnel (structurally, the two look the same). The flash pages/entry tunnel are grayed out, to show that the content is dynamic and variable. The URLs corresponding to the associated pages are shown on the left.

Flash pages can also separate a home page from areas containing site content. In this model, a link from the home page is followed by a flash page, which quickly disappears to be replaced by the actual content. This is commonly implemented on advertising-driven sites and is used to showcase a particular advertiser before the actual "content" page downloads. An example is found at www.word.com.

The Image: Graphical Design and Page Layout

Given a plan for a site and its content, the next hurdle is to develop a distinctive page layout and graphic theme. Although textual content is usually the heart of a Web site, imagery is important for making a strong impression and an important component of good site design. Certainly it is important to follow good design principles to present a professional image. Conversely, an amateurish design will hinder, or even cripple, your efforts.

A Web site can be given character through the creative use of graphics and through careful choices of typography and page layout. However, at the design stage, proposed designs need to be tested in the real world of Web browsers. For example, for users with 640-by-480-pixel displays and Windows-based PCs, the Netscape Navigator browser produces a window 600 pixels. This width then can serves as a useful upper bound on the width of Web graphics. Once the design has

---

[8] Creating Killer Web Sites, by Dave Siegel, Hayden Books, Indianapolis, 1996

Figure 5.2 A storyboard illustration of a Web site entrance tunnel or entrance flash page. The entry pages are grayed to distinguish them from the regular documents.

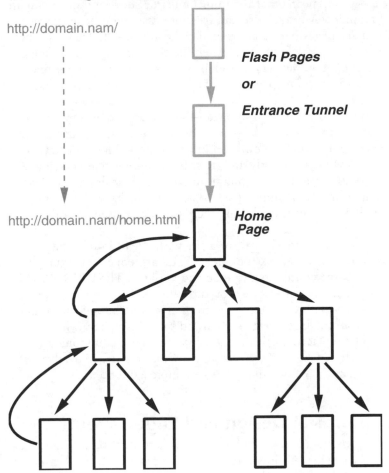

been created, prototype pages should be developed and tested on the various platforms likely to be used by site visitors. For an intranet, this may be an easy task since most (if not all) users will have the same browser. This is not true for a publicly accessible Web site, for which the pages need to be tested on several different browsers. The pages should be tested for proper functioning (functional links, expected text formatting, proper functioning of any JavaScript programs) and for consistent quality of graphics across different computer displays. Last, it may be useful to bring in outside parties (for example, a focus group) to put your site through its paces and provide nonpartisan appraisal of the site's effectiveness.

Design Details

Given a well defined set of site design parameters, it is time to look for a site design metaphor or theme. As stated earlier, the design can be tied in with an existing corporate identity; it can be integrated with a specific advertising campaign; or it can be a design created exclusively for the Web. In all three cases, the team needs to determine how chosen graphical design should be adapted to provide a theme for the pages.

In the case of Chatelaine, the design was created exclusively for the Web— Chatelaine wanted to create a Web site that had a look and attitude very different from the magazine and did not want to be bound to the layout of the magazine. After much design work, puzzle pieces were chosen as a site metaphor, to emphasize the "connection" theme which drives the site. Consequently, puzzle pieces were incorporated throughout the site as navigation buttons, banners, and home page icons, providing a unifying visual theme for the entire site.

All pages within a site should be branded with the designated site logo graphic (to enforce brand identity). All pages should also contain a link to the home page. Users that arrive at a page of your site from a Web search engine or from some other outside reference will have no way of visiting the rest of the site—or of identifying what your site is—unless explicit site navigational links are provided on every page. The intended audience's knowledge of the Internet should be considered when establishing a site's overall design. If your site is being designed for new users, the layout and the links should be straightforward and obvious—new users often complain that they cannot identify links in a page, unless they are clearly identified as such. Novices could be made more comfortable through the use of "Click here" text associated with links, simple page design, and extra explanatory text.

Develop a Style Guide

The image of a site must be consistent. Once the desired design has been determined, the site managers should create a content preparation guide, for use by users creating or updating content. This is critical if the site is to maintain a consistent look and feel, particularly when there are many people involved in the maintenance of the site. HTML document templates, built using the style guide and any default graphics, can also help in maintaining a consistent look.

Different Audiences, Different Versions

If radically different audiences are being served by the Web site, different home pages should be created for these different groups. For example, one of the authors recently analyzed a major automotive Web site, and found that the main design flaw was the attempt to reach too broad an audience from a single home page. This page provided links for customers searching for information about cars, as well as links to shareholder reports and other corporate information.

Content that doesn't address the needs of a larger (perhaps consumer) group should not crowd the home page. A simple solution is to create separate home page URLs for each target category. Different teams can then be responsible for the content of each site.

Java or Multimedia Content?

JavaScript, Java applets, VRML, and browser plug-ins can all enhance the look and functionality of a Web site—but they do so at a cost. In general, such components work only on a limited number of browsers and are only effective and efficient on powerful computers equipped with the newest system software. Consequently, documents that depend on these components can be unusable to some visitors to your site. It is important, therefore, to check the target audience profile and determine if the users are likely to have the equipment required to use this advanced content.

Component Testing

A component should always be examined to determine if it is necessary for the basic functionality of the site. In some cases, such as in a Java-database interface, there will be no alternative, but for noncritical components a prototype should be developed and then tested on various platforms. Such testing should be conducted against well-specified criteria, developed *before* the component is created—it is all to easy to "adjust" the requirements if they have not been defined before testing begins. It is important to be rigorous in this process; and if the component does not pass the tests, it should not be used.

Testing and Launching the Site

After the site has been internally tested, the next step is to have a *soft launch*. In a soft launch, the site is made publicly accessible, but is not actively promoted. This provides for a time period during which people can visit and test the site, while the site developers can monitor system usage and user feedback, and use them to resolve any problems prior to going "live" to the world.

In particular, this is a good time to test any access control or secure transaction technology. It is also a good time to test system performance, by exercising the site as heavily as possible. There are several programs, accessible via the Web, that can simulate multiple and rapid requests for documents from a Web server, to help you to understand conditions under which the system will respond poorly. This may lead to a redesign of certain components, or it may simply lead to the development of "alarms" that can warn the administrator of potential upcoming problems.

Long-Term Maintenance

All Web sites contain content that is to some degree transient, with new material being added and old material being archived, updated, or deleted. As a general rule, pages of a marketing or sales-oriented site should be updated on a regular, almost daily basis. Recall that one of the key things keeping users at the site is their sense that the information is recent and accurate. You should also be prepared to handle user e-mail about everything from questions regarding content to faulty links. All users should receive some sort of quick reply, regardless of how short.

Maintenance also means monitoring and keeping up with the changing technologies of the Internet. Although the aesthetic image of the site many not be tied to the latest Web technology, it is important that site managers be aware of the upcoming technologies, so that they can determine if, and when, these technologies are relevant for their site. It is thus important that one or more people on the team have "Web technology research" as a formal part of their job description.

HTML IN DETAIL

6

This chapter and Chapter 7 provide a detailed exposition of the *HyperText Markup Language,* or *HTML*. These chapters are written from a document developer's point of view and are designed to help authors create well-designed, *valid* HTML documents. The two chapters present detailed descriptions of every HTML element and of the allowed hierarchical relationships amongst these elements. Although relatively straightforward, the material is most easily followed by those who already have a basic understanding of HTML, at the level outlined in Chapters 1 and 2 of this book. If things seem confusing, you should probably go back to these earlier chapters and review the examples given there.

This chapter is divided into 14 sections. The first explains the structural rules and design principles behind HTML and outlines specific features of the HTML markup model. The second section defines the terminology used, in this chapter and Chapter 7, for explaining the details of the HTML element specifications. The subsequent 12 sections break the elements into the following categories:

- Basic Structure (**HTML, HEAD,** and **BODY**)
- Head Meta-Information Elements (**BASE, ISINDEX, LINK, META, SCRIPT, STYLE, TITLE**)
- Body Text Block and Heading Elements (**ADDRESS, BLOCKQUOTE, CENTER, P,** etc.)
- Fill-In Forms (**FORM** and related elements)
- Lists and List-Related Elements (**DL, UL, OL, DIR, MENU, DT, DD, LI**)
- Tables and Tabular Structures (**TABLE** and related elements)
- Inclusion Elements (**APPLET, IMG, OBJECT,** etc.)
- Hypertext Relationship Elements (**A, LINK**)
- Inline Text-Formatting Elements (**STRONG, CITE, B, I,** etc.)
- Character-Like Elements (**BR**)

- Phrase-Level Meta-Information Elements (**BASEFONT, MAP, AREA, SCRIPT**)
- Special Elements (**DEL, INS, NOSCRIPT**)

Note that Figure 6.3 provides an alphabetical element-specific Table of Contents for Chapters 6 and 7, as a complement to the index at the back of the book.

This chapter focuses on the markup elements of HTML 4, which is the current, definitive version of HTML, and is the language version you should use to design universally viewable documents. However, several extensions to this version of HTML are in common use—some proprietary (Netscape- or Microsoft-specific, for the most part) and some part of the ongoing HTML standardization process. These elements—**EMBED, FRAMEs, SPACER, BLINK, MARQUEE,** and so on (there *are* a lot of them)—are described in Chapter 7. Similarly, some aspects of the HTML 4 specification (for example, Internationalized HTML, and new elements for **FORM** input mechanisms) are not yet widely supported. Discussion of these features is also deferred to Chapter 7. Chapter 7 also outlines other Web technologies that are strongly related to HTML, such as scripting languages (e.g., JavaScript), style sheets, and markup languages for mathematics. Note, however, that many of these more advanced/experimental features will not function on many of the browsers currently in use. This is an important consideration if you want your documents to be accessible to the widest possible audience.

The Basics of Markup Languages

As mentioned in Chapter 1, the HyperText Markup Language is designed to specify the *logical* organization and formatting of text documents, with extensions to include inline images, fill-in forms, embedded objects or programs, and hypertext links to other Internet resources. The goal of this approach has been a language that:

- Is not bound to a particular hardware or software environment
- Represents the logical structure of a document and not its presentation

This approach reflects the fact that, in a distributed environment like the Web, individuals viewing a document may use many different "browser" programs with very different formatting capabilities. For example, it is not terribly useful specifying that a portion of text must be presented with a 14 point Times Roman font, if the person "viewing" the document is using a Braille reader. For this reason, HTML does not specify details of the document typesetting and instead marks text according to its logical meaning, such as heading, list, or paragraph. The details of the presentation of these *elements* are left to the browser, which uses the logical description of the document to present the material in the best possible way. Thus, a well-designed HTML document can be intelligibly presented by graphical and nongraphical browsers, or even by nonvisual browsers, such as one that presents the content via Braille.

Defining HTML: The Document Type Definition

The rules of HTML are defined using the *Standard Generalized Markup Language*, or *SGML*. SGML, an international standard specified by the International Standards Organization (ISO), is an extremely sophisticated tool for defining markup languages that describe structured documents—HTML is just one of many languages that are defined using SGML. The details of SGML are complex, and fortunately not critical to an HTML document developer. One component that is useful, however, is the *definition* of the HTML syntax, contained in a special SGML document called a *Document Type Definition,* or *DTD.* This is a simple text file, often having an imaginative name like *html.dtd*. The HTML DTD can be used, in combination with SGML parsing programs such as *sgmls*, to *validate* the syntax of any HTML document—that is, it can check for HTML markup errors in a document and let the author know where they are. The "References" section at the end of this chapter suggests places where you can obtain the official DTD file for HTML, while "Web Management and Maintenance Tools" on the companion Web site discusses document validation using *sgmls*.

This book is a guide to authoring HTML documents, and although it provides a quite complete description of HTML, it should not be considered the definitive reference for the language. For comprehensive details, you should read the Internet Engineering Task Force (IETF) and World Wide Web Consortium (W3C) documents listed in the "References" section at the end of this chapter and at the end of Chapter 7.

Typing Characters in HTML Documents

As discussed in Chapter 1, an HTML document is just a text document containing printable characters and can be created and edited with any text editor. Of course, when a text editor creates a file, it stores the characters as binary codes, where the relationship between the typed characters and the binary codes is called the *character encoding*. On current computers, the most common character encoding is known as ISO Latin-1 (also known as ISO 8859-1—see Appendix A on the companion Web site for more information about ISO Latin-1 characters, character encodings, and character sets in general). Latin-1 is an 8-bit character encoding that encodes 256 different characters ($2^8=256$): These characters, listed in Table A.1, consist of the 128 ($2^7=128$) characters defined in 7-bit US-ASCII character encoding (also known as ISO 646) plus 128 additional characters that use the eighth bit. The ASCII characters are essentially those found on standard US keyboards, while the additional 128 consist of accented and other characters common in western European languages.

There are many other character encodings, optimized for different languages or writing systems (e.g., Cyrillic, Arabic, Japanese, Chinese, Korean, etc.).

However, Latin-1 is by far the most common encoding in Web documents—indeed, until recently, it was the only encoding formally supported by the Web protocols. For these reasons, when receiving an HTML document, most Web browsers assume the document to be encoded using Latin-1, unless explicitly told otherwise. Appendix A on the companion Web site describes how a server (or a document) can indicate that a document was created using a different encoding system.

Character and Entity References

Even when using Latin-1, it is often difficult (due to keyboard limitations) to type non-ASCII characters, while in some cases an author may wish to use a character that is not represented in the character set being used to type the document (for example, a Greek letter cannot be explicitly typed if a document is being written using the ISO Latin-1 character encoding). For these reasons, the HTML language has mechanisms for representing any character using special sequences of ASCII characters. These mechanisms are called *character references*, which reference characters using decimal numbers, and *entity references*, which reference them using symbolic names. For example, the character reference for the character é is `&#233;` (the semicolon is necessary and terminates the special reference), while the entity reference for this same character is `&eacute;`.

These references are useful with computers such as Macintoshes or PCs running DOS—these operating systems do not use ISO Latin-1 for their internal representation of characters (Microsoft Windows does use ISO Latin-1) and instead use proprietary mappings between binary codes and characters. Fortunately, these proprietary systems are differ from ISO Latin-1 only for the 128 non-ASCII characters, so that restricting yourself to ASCII ensures a valid HTML document, while character and entity references let you include characters from the full ISO Latin-1 character set.

Character References and ISO 10646

For character references to be useful, there must be a universal list that relates a reference of the form `&#233;` to the character é, independent of the actual encoding used to write a document. This list, defined as part of the HTML specification, is known as the *document character set*.

The HTML specification defines the document character set to be the 16-bit set known as the Universal Character Set (*UCS*) portion of ISO 10646 (this is formally equivalent to the Unicode 2.0 character set). This set defines up to 65,536 characters (2^{16}=65,536; but not all the possible positions in this set are assigned characters), encompassing the symbols used by most of the world's languages. In an HTML document, character references refer to the *position* of the character in the UCS character set. Thus, the reference é refers to the 233rd character in UCS (the character é), while the reference δ refers to the 948th character (the Greek lower-case letter δ). Appendix A on the companion Web site lists some of the common characters and the corresponding character references.

Entity References

The HTML specification also defines a collection of *entity references*: Symbolic ASCII-character names that also can indirectly reference characters from the document character set. An example entity reference is `&delta;`, which references the Greek lowercase letter δ. Entity references are often easier to use than character references, since the entity names are easier to remember than the actual code positions. For example, you can probably guess that the entity reference `&Delta;` corresponds to the uppercase Greek letter Δ, but would have trouble determining the correct decimal code (it's `&#916;`). The tables in Appendix A on the companion Web site list entity references defined as part of HTML 4. Note, however, that many of these names are not understood by current browsers.

Special Characters in an HTML Document

Certain ASCII characters codes are treated as special in an HTML document. For example, the ampersand character (&) indicates the start of an entity or character reference, the left and right angle brackets (< and >) denotes the markup tags, and the double quotation mark (") marks the beginning and end of strings within the markup tags. Since an HTML parser interprets these characters as special commands or directives, you cannot use the characters themselves to type in an ampersand, greater-than or less-than sign, or a double quotation mark. If you want these characters to appear as regular text, you must include them as character or entity references. The character and entity references for these special characters are given in Table 6.1.

When a browser interprets an HTML document, it looks for the special character strings and interprets them accordingly. Thus, when it encounters the string

```
<H1> Heading string </H1>
```

it interprets the strings inside each pair of angle brackets (H1 and /H1) as markup tags and renders the text lying between these bracket pairs and their tags (Heading string) as a heading. However, when the browser sees the string

```
&lt;H1&gt; Heading string &lt;/H1&gt;
```

Table 6.1 Special Characters in HTML

Character	Character Reference	Entity Reference
Left angle bracket (<)	`&#60;`	`&lt;`
Right angle bracket (>)	`&#62;`	`&gt;`
Ampersand sign (&)	`&#38;`	`&amp;`
Double quotation sign (")	`&#34;`	`&quot;`

it interprets < and > as entity references, and displays the characters

`<H1> Heading string </H1>`

as a string of regular text.

Comments in HTML Documents

In HTML documents, comments are surrounded by the special character strings `<!--` and `-->`. The text between `<!--` and `-->` is a comment and should not be displayed by a browser. There can be spaces between the `--` and the `>` that ends a comment, but the string `<!--` that starts a comment declaration must have no spaces between the characters. The following is an example of a simple comment:

`<!-- This is a comment --  >`

Comments can span multiple lines, but cannot nest or overlap. You should also be careful when using comments to *hide* HTML markup that would otherwise be displayed, as some older browsers will mistakenly use the greater-than sign (>) of a regular HTML markup tag to prematurely end the comment. Also, some older browsers do not properly handle multi-line comments and only hide the first line.

Here are some examples of comments:

```
<!-- This is a comment --
  -- This is a second comment within the same comment declaration -- >

<!-- This is also a comment
    This comment spans more than one line. Some old browsers improperly
    interpret comments that span multiple lines.
  -- >
```

NOTE: Full Details of SGML Comments

Formally, a comment consists of a comment *declaration* (consisting of the start string `<!` and the end string `>`) that, in turn, can contain any number of comments. Each comment is a text string surrounded by the strings `--` and `--` (two adjacent hyphens). Thus the string `-- this is a comment --` is a single comment when inside a comment declaration. However, there must be no whitespace between the starting string of the comment declaration (`<!`) and the start of the first comment, so that all comments must begin with the string `<!--`. (Pathologically, you can have empty comments of the form `<!   >`.) Whitespace is allowed *after* every comment, so that the string `--` marking the end of the last comment inside a comment declaration can be separated by whitespace from the `>` character marking the end of the declaration, for example: `<!-- This is also a comment -- >`.

HTML as a MIME Type

As discussed in Example 5 in Chapter 2, all data communicated over the Web have an associated *MIME content-type* to indicate the *type* of the data. In particular, the HTTP protocol uses these content types to communicate the *type* of data being sent out (or received) by a server—-the appropriate *content-type header field* is included within the header message that precedes the data being sent. For example, a JPEG format image file being sent from an HTTP server to a client would have the message string

```
Content-Type: image/jpeg
```

as part of the *HTTP header* (see Chapter 9) that precedes the actual data. Similarly, when an HTML document is served, the header that precedes it contains the string

```
Content-Type: text/html
```

to indicate that the data are an HTML document and not just plain text. HTTP and MIME types are discussed in more detail in Chapter 9 and Appendix B found on the companion Web site.

DOCTYPE Public Text Identifier

As mentioned several times, HTML is an evolving language. You can (and should!) formally specify the version of the language used in a document by including, as the first line in the text, a string known as a *public text identifier*. The declaration for HTML 4 is

```
<!DOCTYPE HTML PUBLIC "-//W3C//DTD HTML 4.0//EN">
```

where the text inside double quotation marks is the identifier for the DTD that applies to the document. DOCTYPE specifications are placed at the start of a document by HTML editors (such as SoftQuad's *HoTMetaL*) that rigorously enforce correct markup as defined by the DTD.

Elements and Markup Tags

The overall structure of the HTML language was covered in Chapter 1. The following is a review of the basic concepts, using the document in Figure 6.1 as an example, with Figure 6.2 showing typical rendering of this example.

An HTML document is simply a text file in which certain strings of characters, called *tags*, delimit regions of the document and assign special meanings to them. In the jargon of SGML, these regions and the enclosing tags are called *elements*. The tags are strings of characters surrounded by the less-than (<) and greater-than (>) characters. For example

```
<H1>
```

is the *start tag* for an **H1** (a heading) element, while the similar tag with a leading slash character

```
</H1>
```

is the corresponding *end tag*. The entire **H1** *element* is then the string:

```
<H1> Environmental Change Project </H1>
```

Each element has a name,[1] which appears inside the tags and which defines what the element means. For example, the **H1** element marks a level one heading. Elements that mark or contain blocks of text (such as **H1**) are also called *containers*. Most elements are containers and mark regions of the document into blocks of text, which in turn may contain other elements containing other blocks of text, and so on. You can think of a document as a nested hierarchy of these elements, with the complete hierarchy defining the entire document.

Figure 6.1 An example of a simple HTML document.

```
<HTML>
<HEAD>
  <TITLE> Environmental Change Project </TITLE>
</HEAD>
<BODY>
<H1> <A NAME="env-change"> Environmental </A> Change Project </H1>

<P>Welcome to the home page of the Environmental Change Project.
This project is different from other projects with similar
names.  In our case we actually wish to change the climate.
For example, we would like hot beaches in Northern
Quebec, and deserts near Chicago.

<P> So how will we do this.  Well we do the following:
<UL>
  <LI><A HREF="burn.html"><EM>Burn down</EM></A> more forests
  <LI>Destroy the <A HREF="http://who.zoo.do/ozone.html">Ozone</A> layer
  <LI>Breed more <A HREF="ftp://foo.do.do/cows.gif">cows</A> (for extra
      greenhouse gas)
</UL>
</BODY>
</HTML>
```

[1] In SGML terminology, the name of an element is formally called a *generic identifier*, or *GI*.

Figure 6.2 Display, using the Internet Explorer 3 browser of the document listed in Figure 6.1.

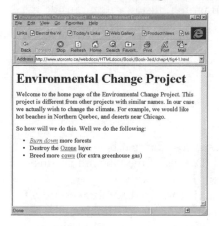

Optional End Tags

In some cases, element end tags are optional. This is so when the end of an element can be unambiguously determined from subsequent tags. As an example, look at the **LI** elements in Figure 6.1. These elements define a single list item inside the **UL** unordered list element but do not require `</LI>` end tags. This is because the end of a given item is implied by the next `<LI>` start tag or by the `</UL>` end tag ending the list.

Empty Elements

Some elements (such as the **IMG** [insert an inline image], **HR**, and **BR** [line break] elements) do not "contain" anything and are called *empty* elements. In HTML, empty elements cannot have end tags.

Element Attributes

Most elements have *attributes*, which are quantities that specify properties for a particular instance of an element. For example, the **A** (hypertext anchor) element can take the **HREF** attribute, which specifies the target of a hypertext link. Most attributes are assigned *values*. For example, **HREF** is assigned the URL of the target document, as in:

```
<A HREF="http://who.zoo.do/Ozone.html"> Ozone </A> layer
```

Attributes are always placed inside the start tag. Attributes are often optional, in which case they can be left out.

Element Nesting

Elements are always *nested*, with this nesting reflecting the structure of the document (for example, emphasized text inside a paragraph, inside a form, inside the **BODY**). However, elements can *never* overlap. Thus the structure

```
<A HREF=..><EM>Burn down</EM></A> more forests
```

is valid HTML markup, while (comment in italics)

```
<A HREF=..><EM>Burn down</A></EM> more forests <!-- Illegal markup!-->
```

is not. In addition, all elements have restrictions as to what can be nested inside them and where they, themselves, can be nested. Details of the allowed nestings are presented later in this chapter as each element is discussed.

Some browsers can recover from simple nesting errors, so that mistakes are often hard to spot. If you are lucky, you will get mail from someone questioning why he or she cannot properly view your document. A better choice is to use a validation tool, such as *sgmls,* to check your documents for mistakes. This option is discussed in "Web Management and Maintenance Tools" on the companion Web site.

Case-Insensitive Element and Attribute Names

Element and attribute names inside the markup tags are *case insensitive*. Thus, the strings <H1> and <h1> are equivalent, as are

```
<a HreF="Dir1/foo.html"><EM>Burn down</eM> </a> more forests
```

and

```
<A href="Dir1/foo.html"><em>Burn down</eM> </A> more forests
```

Element and attributes names are nevertheless usually written in uppercase, so that document developers can more easily see the markup tags and attributes.

Case-*Sensitive* Attribute Values

While element and attribute names are case insensitive, the *values* assigned to attributes are often case sensitive. An obvious example is a URL assigned to an **HREF** attribute. A URL can contain both directory and filename information. Many computers allow both upper- and lowercase characters in file and directory names, so it is crucial that case be preserved. For a document author, this is ensured by enclosing the attribute argument in double quotes, as done in Figure 6.1.

Attribute Values as Literal Strings

Formally, HTML has two main mechanisms for handling values assigned to attributes: *literal strings* and *name tokens*. A literal string is just that—a string of characters to be accepted literally as typed by the author, including the preservation of case. Literal strings must be surrounded by double quotation marks, since otherwise the string may be prematurely ended at a space or other character. Literal strings can contain any sequence of printable characters, including HTML character and entity references—a browser will turn these references back into the desired characters. Clearly, you must use character or entity references to include the double quotation mark (e.g., `&quot;`) inside an attribute value, since this character would otherwise be interpreted as marking the end of the string.

Most attributes that can be assigned arbitrary, author-defined strings, such as **HREF** and **SRC** (uniform resource locators), **ALT** (**IMG** elements), and **NAME** (fragment identifiers for anchor elements), are handled as literal strings.

Attribute Values as Name Tokens

Name tokens are restricted character strings that can only contain the letters a–z or A–Z, the numbers 0–9, periods (.), and hyphens (-), and must begin with a letter. Unlike literal strings, name tokens are *case insensitive*, so that the token `abba` is equivalent to `ABbA`. Because they are simple, name token attribute values do not need to be surrounded by quotation marks, as in the string "text" in the assignment **TYPE**=text. However, since it is never an error to include quotation marks, it is safest to leave them in.
Name tokens are used for values defined as part of HTML, such as the value "text" in the element `<INPUT TYPE="text"...>`.

The HTML DTD specifies whether an attribute value is a literal string or a name token and defines the allowed values for those attributes that take name tokens. For example, the HTML DTD states that the **ALIGN** attribute of an **H1** element can take the values "left," "right," and "center," but no others. Consequently, HTML *validators* (tools that check the validity of an HTML document) can check for incorrect values. This is not true with literal strings, and a validator has no way of knowing if a specified literal string is valid or not.

In this book, attribute values are, in general, placed inside quotation marks, since name tokens are always valid inside quotation marks, and the added quotation marks help them stand out from the regular text.

Browser Handling of HTML Errors, Unknown Elements, and Unknown Attributes

On the World Wide Web, browsers are generous in their handling of HTML documents. Thus, even if a document is badly constructed, for example with missing or misplaced tags, a browser will do the best it can to present the content. Often the document looks odd, due to the resulting formatting decisions, but from a user's point of view this is infinitely better than seeing nothing at all. This emphasizes the importance, on the author's side, of designing valid HTML documents that can be properly viewed by any browser.

At the same time, HTML is an evolving language, and new elements and attributes are constantly being added, either as part of the formal language development process (HTML 2.0, HTML 3.2, HTML 4, etc.) or as customized extensions introduced by browser designers. For such an evolution to work, there must be ways for browsers to handle HTML elements, or element attributes that they do not understand.

In general, browsers *ignore* elements, or element attributes, that they do not understand. For example, the **BLINK** element is Netscape-specific—on other browsers, the `<BLINK>` ... `</BLINK>` tags are usually ignored, and the enclosed text is rendered as regular text (given whatever other elements the string is inside). Similarly, in HTML 4, paragraphs can be centered using the **ALIGN** attribute, that is, `<P ALIGN="center">`. If a browser does not understand this attribute or the value assigned to it, it simply ignores the attribute and use its own preferred paragraph alignment.

However, many elements will not produce readable documents if the browser does not understand the relevant tags. Particular examples are the **FRAME** (discussed in the next chapter) and **TABLE** elements. In general, you can assume that any new element that implies both logical and physical structure will be poorly displayed by a browser that does not understand the element.

Basic HTML Document Structure

Every HTML document has two main parts: a *head*, which contains information about the document, but which is not displayed to the reader; and a *body*, which contains the part of the document to be displayed by a browser. These parts are defined by the **HEAD** and **BODY** elements, respectively. The basic structure of *all* HTML documents is then (commentary in italics):

```
<HTML>
   <HEAD>
   ...elements valid in the document HEAD
   </HEAD>
   <BODY>
   ...elements valid in the document BODY
   </BODY>
</HTML>
```

Note how Figure 6.1 follows this outline. The outer **HTML** element declares the enclosed text to be an HTML document. Directly inside this lie the **HEAD** and the **BODY**. The **BODY** contains the text and associated HTML markup instructions of the material to be displayed. The **HEAD**, which must appear before the **BODY**, contains elements that define information *about* the document, such as its title. Certain elements can only appear in the **HEAD**, while others can only appear in the **BODY**.

The preceding structure is modified somewhat for **FRAME**-based documents. For these, the basic document structure is:

```
<HTML>
    <HEAD>
    ...elements valid in the document HEAD
    </HEAD>
    <FRAMESET ..>
        .....FRAME and FRAMESET Elements ...
    </FRAMESET>
    <NOFRAMES>
        <BODY>
        ...elements valid in the document BODY
        </BODY>
    </NOFRAMES>
</HTML>
```

where the special markup due to the frame-related elements is shown in boldface. Note how a **BODY** can be included within the **NOFRAMES** element—the content is displayed by browsers that do not understand **FRAMESET**. Frame elements are discussed in detail in Chapter 7.

BODY Content: Block and Inline Elements

BODY content elements are divided into two broad categories: *block* and *inline*. Block elements define blocks of text, such as paragraphs or tables, while inline elements define sections of text or inserted objects such as images or applets that appear inline within the text. In general, inline elements can appear inside a block element, but not vice versa: For example, an **H1** heading (a block element) can contain an **EM** element (an inline element), whereas the opposite is not true.

The distinction between block and inline is particularly important for *internationalized* documents—that is, those containing a mix of different languages and writing systems—since the two groups of elements inherit text layout directionality (text laid out from left to right, or right to left) in different ways. Furthermore, the block or inline nature of an element can be altered using Cascading Style Sheets— CSS lets an author change the basic formatting characteristics of an element to be either block or inline. These issues are discussed in more detail in Chapter 7.

The new **INS** and **DEL** elements are an exception to this block/inline distinction. **INS** and **DEL** can appear anywhere within the **BODY** of the document or within any element lying inside the **BODY** and denote content that has been inserted or deleted relative to some other version of the document. Thus **INS** or **DEL** can be either inline or block elements, depending on context. Please see the sections describing these elements for more details.

Elements-based Table of Contents

Figure 6.3 lists all the HTML elements mentioned in this book and provides page references to the sections in Chapters 6 and 7 that describe each element—you can use this as an "element-oriented" table of contents to Chapters 6 and 7.

Figure 6.3 Index to all HTML elements described in Chapters 6 and 7. New HTML 4 elements are in italics, while proprietary extensions are underlined. Struck-through elements are *deprecated*—these are likely to be dropped in future versions of HTML and should be avoided in new documents.

Element	Description	Page Number	
		Chap. 6	Chap. 7
A	Hypertext anchor	314	437
ABBR	An abbreviation	298	
ADDRESS	Address information	226	
APPLET	Embedded applet	301	
AREA	Imagemap data	334	
B	Bold	326	
BASE	Base URL of the document	213	
BASEFONT	Base font for document	333	
BDO	Bidirectional override	325	451
<u>BGSOUND</u>	Background audio/sound		368
BIG	Bigger text	327	
<u>BLINK</u>	Blinking text		369
BLOCKQUOTE	Block quotation	229	
BODY	Document body	211	
BR	Line break	337	
BUTTON	Form-content push button	242	383
CAPTION	Table caption	291	
~~CENTER~~	Centered text	230	
CITE	Citation	325	
CODE	Typed computer code	325	
COL	Column properties specifier	292	
COLGROUP	Column group specification	294	

Figure 6.3 Continued.

Element	Description	Page Number Chap. 6	Chap. 7
DD	Description	264	
DEL	Deleted markup or text	339	
DFN	Definition	325	
~~DIR~~	Directory list (obsolete)	268	
DIV	Block division of a document	233	
DL	Description/glossary list	261	
DT	Term	263	
EM	Emphasized text	326	
<u>EMBED</u>	Embed arbitrary data		370
FIELDSET	Group related input elements		389
~~FONT~~	Font size/face/color	327	
FORM	User input form	242	437
FRAME	Specify frame contents		359
FRAMESET	Declare framed regions		356
H1–H6	Headings (1–6)	234	
HEAD	Document meta-information	210	
HR	Horizontal divider	235	
HTML	An HTML document	209	
I	*Italics*	329	
IFRAME	Insert floating document frame		364
<u>ILAYER</u>	Overlay presentation layer		408
IMG	Inline image	305	
INPUT	Input fields	248	
INS	Inserted text or markup	340	
~~ISINDEX~~	Searchable document	215	

Continued

Figure 6.3 *Continued.*

Element	Description	Page Number Chap. 6	Chap. 7
KBD	Keyboard input	326	
KEYGEN	Generate encrypted key for a **FORM**		387
LABEL	Label for input elements		388
LEGEND	Label or legend for a **FIELDSET**		390
LAYER	Overlay presentation layer		408
LI	List item	270	
LINK	Relationships to other resources	216	
MAP	Client-side imagemap	333	
MARQUEE	Scrolling marquee text		373
~~MENU~~	Menu list (obsolete)	268	
META	Meta information	218	
MULTICOL	Multicolumn text		377
NOBR	No line breaks		378
NOEMBED	HTML alternative to **EMBED**		379
NOFRAMES	Markup for nonframe browsers		362
NOLAYER	HTML alternative to **LAYER, ILAYER**		417
NOSCRIPT	HTML alternative to **SCRIPT**	341	
OBJECT	Embed data and handler		404
OL	Ordered list	264	
OPTGROUP	Grouping of **OPTION** elements		390
OPTION	Option in selectable field	256	
P	Paragraphs	238	
PARAM	Parameter for applet	304	407
PRE	Preformatted text	239	
Q	Inline quotation	326	
S	Struck-through text	329	

Figure 6.3 *Continued*.

Element	Description	Page Number Chap. 6	Chap. 7
SAMP	Sample text	326	
SCRIPT	Program scripts	222	
SELECT	Selectable fields	255	
SERVER	Server-side scripting		380
SMALL	Smaller text	329	
SPACER	Horizontal or vertical space		380
SPAN	Stylesheet-specified styling	329	
~~STRIKE~~	Struck-out text	329	
STRONG	Strong emphasis	326	
STYLE	Document stylesheet	224	
SUB	Subscript	332	
SUP	Superscript	332	
TABLE	Table	283	
TBODY	Table body grouping	296	
TD	Table data cell	298	
TEXTAREA	Text input region	257	
TFOOT	Table footer grouping	296	
TH	Table header cell	298	
THEAD	Table header grouping	295	
TITLE	Document title	225	
TR	Table row	297	
TT	Fixed-width font	332	
U	Underline	332	
UL	Unordered list	265	
VAR	A variable	326	
WBR	Optional word break		382

HTML Element Specifications

This section describes each HTML element, complete with a description of the purpose of the element, a list of where the element can be used, and examples of its use. This section describes elements from the HTML 4 specification, although a few non-HTML 4 elements and attribute extensions are mentioned where appropriate. Some HTML 4 elements, namely the frame-related elements (**FRAME, FRAMESET, IFRAME,** and **NOFRAMES**), **OBJECT,** and the advanced form input elements (**BUTTON, FIELDSET, LABEL, LEGEND** and **OPTGROUP**), are discussed in Chapter 7. Chapter 7 also covers the remaining, commonly supported, non-HTML 4 elements.

Key to Element Specifications: Content Rules and Allowed Attributes

Because HTML is a hierarchical language, is it important to know not only *how* to use an element, but also *where* it can be used. This information is given in the four lines at the beginning of each element's description. The format is:

Usage:	<NAME> ... </NAME>
Can Contain:	*element list*
Can Be Inside:	*element list*
Attributes:	*attribute list*

where **element list** is a list of allowed elements and **attribute list** is a list of allowed attributes. Figure 6.4 shows an example, using the **TD** *table data* element where the four fields in Figure 6.4 define the rules for using the different elements. A detailed description of the fields is found in Table 6.2.

Special Case: INS and DEL Elements

The new HTML 4 elements **INS** and **DEL** denote inserted and deleted content. These elements can appear anywhere inside the **BODY**, including anywhere within any nonempty element lying inside the **BODY**, with the exception of **SCRIPT** and **TEXTAREA**.

Because **INS** and **DEL** do not define document structure, it is confusing to discuss them in the same context as the structure-related elements. Thus, in this chapter and Chapter 7, **INS** and **DEL** are not explicitly mentioned in the content-rules given at the beginning of each element's description. For details regarding the correct use of **INS** and **DEL**, please see the sections at the end of this chapter describing these two elements.

Table 6.2 Meanings of Fields in Element Definitions (*see also* Figure 6.4)

Usage:	Shows how the element is used. An end tag indicates that an element is a container (the *Can Contain* field lists what can go inside the element). If the end tag is enclosed by parentheses, then it is optional. If no end tag is given, then the element is empty.
Can Contain:	Indicates what elements can go inside this element. This is given as two lists: a list of block elements (if any are allowed), followed by a list of inline elements. In the latter category, the string "**characters**" indicates elements that can contain text. If the element is empty and takes no content, the word "empty" appears here. In several places, the **ISINDEX** name appears enclosed by square brackets. This indicates that the element is allowed, but that it should more appropriately appear in the **HEAD**. Elements that are proposed as part of the HTML standardization process are shown in boldface italics. Underlined elements are proprietary extensions by browser vendors.
Can Be Inside:	Indicates the elements inside which this element can be placed. This is given as two lists: a list of block elements (if any are allowed as content), followed by a list of inline elements. The example in Figure 6.4 indicates that the **TR** element can be inside **TABLE**, **TBODY**, **TFOOT**, or **THEAD** elements, but nowhere else.
Attributes:	This lists the names of the attributes that can be taken by the element. The word "none" means that the element takes no attributes. Attributes proposed as part the HTML standardization process are shown in bold face italics. Underlined attributes are proprietary extensions by browser vendors.

Element and Attribute Notation

Element and attribute names are shown in capitalized boldface. Elements that are new as of HTML 4 are shown in italics, while underlined elements are proprietary to certain browsers vendors. Element names with a line struck through them are *deprecated*—these elements will probably be dropped in a future version of HTML and should consequently be avoided in new documents where possible. The following table summarizes this notation, with examples:

INPUT	Standard element or attribute; widely supported.
OBJECT	New element or attribute, added to standard as of HTML 4. Such elements or attributes are not universally supported.
~~**STRIKE**~~	Deprecated element or attribute; avoid this element in new documents.
BORDERCOLOR	Proprietary element or attribute; only supported on specific browsers.

Special Element and Attribute Abbreviations

For ease in reading, several abbreviations representing groups of elements or groups of attributes are used in the element descriptions. These abbreviations are defined in Table 6.3 and illustrated in Figure 6.4.

Attribute Value Notation and Definitions

Attribute values are either arbitrary strings selected by the user, such as URLs in hypertext anchors, form variable names and values, and so on (generally literal strings); or particular values (generally, but not always, name tokens) defined as part of HTML. To distinguish between these two types, user-definable values are presented in quoted italics (*"value"*), while values defined as part of HTML are presented as quoted regular text ("value"). The notation is summarized in Table 6.4.

In addition, user-defined values are often restricted in some way; for example, color specifications must be given as RGB color codes or as special named colors, while lengths may need to be integer numbers, and so on. Notation used with attribute value assignments to indicate these requirements is outlined in Table 6.5.

Table 6.3 Key to Abbreviations Used in Element Descriptions

Hn	The six heading elements **H1**, **H2**, **H3**, **H4**, **H5**, and **H6**.
characters	Any valid printable character, character reference, or entity reference.
character highlighting	*ABBR*, *ACRONYM*, *BDO*, CITE, CODE, DFN, EM, KBD, Q, SAMP, *SPAN*, ~~STRIKE~~, STRONG, VAR; and **B**, **BIG**, ~~FONT~~, **I**, ~~S~~, **SMALL**, **SUB**, **SUP**, **TT**, **U**
	These are the logical (**ABBR** through **VAR**) and physical (**B** through **U**) text/phrase markup elements that mark text for meaning or special formatting. Note that **STRIKE**, **FONT**, **S**, and **U** are *deprecated* elements, likely to be dropped in a future version of HTML.
Standard event handlers	*onClick*, *onDblClick*, *onKeyDown*, *onKeyPress*, *onKeyUp*, *onMouseDown*, *onMouseMove*, *onMouseOut*, *onMouseOver*, *onMouseUp*
	These are the "event" handler attributes supported by most HTML elements. See also Table 6.7 and Chapter 7.

Figure 6.4 Explanation of notation used to describe elements.

Element Name
Name plus a brief description

Tag Usage
Tags inside brackets are optional

Italicized Values
Indicate element or attribute extensions developed as part of the standards process

TR Element: Table Row

Usage:	`<TR> ...(</TR>)`
Can Contain:	**TH, TD**
Can Be Inside:	**TABLE, *TBODY, TFOOT, THEAD***
Attributes:	*CLASS, DIR, ID, LANG, STYLE, TITLE, standard event handlers, ALIGN, BGCOLOR, CHAR, CHAROFF, VALIGN,* (<u>BACKGROUND</u>: Netscape Navigator 4 and Internet Explorer 3 only), (BORDERCOLOR, BORDERCOLORDARK, BORDERCOLORLIGHT: Internet Explorer only)

Not Shown--Struck-through values
(e.g.: ~~STRIKE~~) Indicate elements or attributes marked as *deprecated*, and likely to be dropped in a future version of HTML.

Underlined Values
Indicate *proprietary* elements or attributes. Browsers supporting this element or attribute extension are listed when the extension is not widely supported.

Table 6.4 Explanation of Attribute Value Assignments

ATTRIBUTE="value"	Nonitalicized strings indicate attribute values that are defined as part of HTML and that are not arbitrary: for example, **ALIGN**="center", or **METHOD**="post".
ATTRIBUTE="*value*"	*Italicized* strings indicate arbitrary user-defined values. The value may be limited by context; for example, in **BGCOLOR**="*#rrggbb*", the string references an RGB color code, which restricts the allowed value of the string *rrggbb*. The special meanings of these strings are described in Table 6.5.

Table 6.5 Meaning of User-Specified Attribute Value Assignments

#rrggbb	Represents a color as an RGB (Red-Green-Blue) value—this describes the color in terms of its of red, green, and blue components. Each color can be in the range 0–255 (eight bits), and each color is referenced, in the RGB value, by its hexadecimal code. Thus the color red, which is full red (255), zero blue, and zero green, is coded as `"#ff0000"`, while white (all colors on full) is `"#ffffff"`. The default colors are determined by a browser's internal configuration. See also Appendix F on the companion Web site.
c	Represents a single typeable character.
color	Represents a *named color*. Several browsers support text strings to indicate particular colors. The commonly supported values are "aqua", "black", "blue", "fuchsia", "gray", "green", "lime", "maroon", "navy", "olive", "purple", "red", "silver", "teal", "white", and "yellow". If a browser does not understand the color name, it will ignore the associated attribute and use the default color.
	Color names are not supported by early versions of Netscape Navigator or Internet Explorer (Version 2 or earlier). See also Appendix F on the Web site.
lang-code	Represents a *language code* (e.g. "fr-ca", or "en-US") as defined in Appendix E on the companion Web site. This identifies the language used by the text inside the element.
mime-type	A MIME type, for example: text/html. See also Appendix B on the Web site.
name	Represents an arbitrary, user-defined *name token* string—a name token is a string of letters (a–z or A–Z), digits (0–9), periods (.), or hyphens (-), and which must begin with a letter. Although such names are sometimes case-insensitive, it is safest to assume that they are case-sensitive (i.e., the name "*Fix23*" is not equal to the name "*fix23*").
names	Represents an arbitrary, user-defined collection of name tokens, separated by spaces (e.g., "*name1 name2*").
number	Represents an arbitrary *integer number*.
pixels	Represents an arbitrary *integer number* corresponding to a number of pixels, either horizontally or vertically.
real	Represents a positive *real number*. Decimals (e.g., 2.3) are allowed, but not exponentials.
String	Represents an arbitrary, user-defined text string.
Url	Represents an arbitrary, user-defined URL.

Important "Generic" Attributes

HTML 4 introduces six "generic" attributes that are valid with almost all HTML body content (and some **HEAD**-level) elements. These attributes were introduced for four reasons: to provide mechanisms for linking HTML documents to formatting style sheets (**CLASS, ID, STYLE**); to add support for internationalization— that is, documents that use multiple languages on the same page (**DIR, LANG**); to provide for more flexible hypertext linking between parts of a single document (**ID**); and to provide better "tool-tip" style help facility, for easier interface design and also as an aid to non-graphical browsers (**TITLE**).

This section describes the use and function of these attributes, while Figures 6.5 and 6.6 show the use of these attributes, in practice, to relate specific HTML elements to style sheet formatting rules (the struck-through and underlined text) and to provide "tool-tip" style help via the **TITLE** element. Table 6.6 summarizes the level of support for these attributes by Internet Explorer 4 and Netscape Navigator 4—they are not supported by earlier versions of either browser.

CLASS="*string*" (optional) Specifies a subclass name for the element. *Subclassing* is used to define the special nature of an element, such as `<DIV CLASS="introduction">` , `<DIV CLASS="verse">`, and so on. Style sheets can bind to specific classes, so that an author can specify special formatting for different classes of the same element. This is discussed in Chapter 7. This functionality is provided by Netscape Navigator 4 and Internet Explorer 4.

DIR="ltr," "rtl" (optional) **DIR** defines the direction in which the text inside the element should be drawn onto the display. There are two possible values: "ltr" for text that is drawn from left to right (e.g., English, French) and "rtl" for text that is drawn from right to left (e.g., Arabic, Hebrew). DIR can be used to override the intrinsic directionality of text as implied by the language (**LANG** attribute). At present, this attribute is only understood by the *Tango* Web browser from Alis Technologies (www.alis.com). Internationalized HTML is discussed in more detail in Chapter 7.

ID="*name*" (optional) Specifies a unique name token identifier for the element. Within a given document, no two elements can have the same **ID** value. In principle, **ID**-labeled elements can be the targets of hypertext links, as **ID** plays the same role as the **NAME** attribute of the anchor element. This aspect of **ID** is not supported by Netscape Navigator 4, but is supported by Internet Explorer 4. Style sheets can also reference **ID**s and can apply formatting instructions to specific **ID**-labeled elements. This aspect of **ID** is supported by Internet Explorer 4 and Netscape Navigator 4. Style sheets are discussed in more detail in Chapter 7.

LANG="lang-code" (optional) Specifies the *language* of enclosed text, using a well-defined language code, for example "en-US" for U.S. English, or "fr-CA" for Canadian French. See Appendix E on the companion Web site for details of language code specifications. At present, this attribute is only understood by the *Tango* Web browser from Alis Technologies (www.alis.com).

STYLE="string" (optional) Contains style sheet instructions that should be applied to the content of the element. This attribute is understood by Netscape Navigator 4 and Internet Explorer 3 and 4. Style sheets are discussed in more detail in Chapter 7.

TITLE="string" (optional) Specifies advisory or descriptive information about the associated element. This is a general-purpose equivalent to the **ALT** attribute of the **IMG** element, except that **TITLE** can annotate almost all HTML elements. For example, **TITLE** can be used, within an **A** element, to describe the resource targeted by the link. A browser might then, for example, use this text to produce a "pop-up" text description. This functionality is provided by Internet Explorer 4, but not by Netscape Navigator 4.

Table 6.6 The Six General-Purpose Attributes Introduced in HTML 4

Element	Function	Supported by Netscape Navigator 4	Supported by Internet Explorer 4
CLASS	Define a subclass of an HTML element, or elements, for use with formatting style sheets	yes	yes
DIR	Change the text directionality (left-to-right or right-to-left) for an element	no	no
ID	Label an HTML element; for use with formatting style sheets	yes	yes
ID	Label an HTML element; for identifying target IDs for hypertext references	no	yes
LANG	Identify the language of the text within the elements	no	no
STYLE	Specify a specific style sheet rule for the element	yes	yes
TITLE	Specify a text title or label for the element	no	yes

Figure 6.5 Document illustrating the new "generic" attributes. The attributes CLASS="under" and ID="through" associate the style sheet rules (at the top of the document) to the formatting of the associated element. The TITLE attribute of the third paragraph element associates a "tool-tip" text pop-up with the paragraph text. The hypertext link at the top of the document is linked to the final paragraph (ID="label1"). This link is supported on Internet Explorer 4, but not Netscape Navigator 4.

```
<HTML>
<HEAD><TITLE> Attribute Tester: TITLE, CLASS, ID, STYLE,
              ID, STYLE, DIR </TITLE>
</HEAD>
<STYLE>
<!--
.under   {text-decoration: underline}    /* rule for underline     */
#through {text-decoration: line-through}  /* rule for strike-through */
-->
</STYLE>
<BODY BGCOLOR="white">
<H3>Attribute Tester: TITLE, CLASS, ID, STYLE, and DIR</H3>

<P>Here is a paragraph. This paragraph contains a
<A HREF="#label1">hypertext anchor</A> pointing to the
reference "label1".  </P>

<P ID="through">Here is a paragraph with <B>ID</B>="through".
There is a CSS rule associated with this ID value, such that
a browser should render this paragraph with a line struck
through the text.</P>

<P TITLE="Funny Paragraph">This paragraph contains an
<EM CLASS="under">EM element</EM> of <B>CLASS</B>="under".
The associated CSS rule should underline the section of
emphasized text. The paragraph also has the attribute
<B>TITLE</B>="Funny Paragraph". </P>

<P>This paragraph has two <B>SPAN</B> elements that use the
<B>DIR</B> attribute to change text directionality.Here
they are:<BR>
<B><TT>DIR</TT>="ltr":</TT></B> <SPAN DIR="ltr">A span of left to right
text</SPAN><BR>
```

Continued

Figure 6.5 *Continued*.

```
<B><TT>DIR="rtl":</TT></B> <SPAN DIR="rtl">A span of right to left
text</SPAN></P>

<P ID="label1">A final paragraph, of <B>ID</B>="label1". The
hypertext reference at the top of the page should link to
here.</P>

</BODY></HTML>
```

Figure 6.6 Internet Explorer 4.0 rendering of the document listed in Figure 6.5. Notice the struck-through and underlined text, formatted according to the style sheet rules. Note also the "tool-tip" text above the third paragraph—the text is from the paragraph element's TITLE attribute.

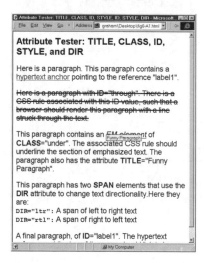

"Event-Handler" Element Attributes

HTML 4 defines 18 special "event-handling" attributes, listed in the following section. Event handling attributes relate HTML elements to script programs that should be run when the corresponding "event" happens to the element. For example, an *onMouseOver* event occurs whenever the mouse pointer moves on top of an element. Thus if an element has the attribute

onMouseOver="*handler_program*()"

then the program *handler_program()* will be run whenever the mouse moves over the element. The programs themselves must be included within the document and are written in either JavaScript or VBScript.

To mark the special nature of the event handling attributes, they are written in this book in mixed upper- and lowercase. The different HTML 4 attributes are listed in Table 6.7, alongside a list of elements to which they apply. Note, however, that most current browsers do not support all these attributes/element pairs, and also do support several other, nonstandard event handling attributes. For a more detailed description of the level of support for event-handling attributes by current browsers, please read the "Scripting in HTML Documents" section in Chapter 7.

Basic Structure: HTML, HEAD, and BODY

The basic structure of an HTML document is laid out by the **HTML**, **HEAD**, and **BODY** elements.

HTML Element: An HTML Document

Usage:	`<HTML> ... </HTML>`
Can Contain:	**HEAD, BODY, FRAMESET, NOFRAMES**
Can Be Inside:	nothing
Attributes:	*DIR*, *LANG*, ~~VERSION~~

Table 6.7 Event Handler Attributes and the Associated HTML Elements, as Defined in HTML 4

Attribute Name	Relevant HTML Elements
onLoad, onUnload	BODY and FRAMESET only
onBlur, onFocus	A, *BUTTON*, *LABEL*, INPUT, SELECT, and TEXTAREA
onReset, onSubmit	FORM
onChange, onSelect	INPUT, SELECT, and TEXTAREA
onClick, onDblClick, onKeyDown, onKeyPress, onKeyUp, onMouseDown, onMouseMove, onMouseOut, onMouseOver, onMouseUp	most BODY-content elements

The **HTML** element declares the enclosed text to be an HTML document. In a standard document, HTML can directly contain only two elements: **HEAD** and **BODY,** while in a frame-document, HTML can directly contain the elements **HEAD, FRAMESET,** and **NOFRAMES,** but cannot directly contain a **BODY.** The optional **LANG** and **DIR** attributes specify the language used in the document, as well as the direction in which the text should be laid out on the display. The optional **VERSION** attribute takes as its value a URL that points to the DTD, which encodes the HTML version corresponding to the document. This attribute is not currently supported, and indeed is deprecated, since the DOCTYPE declaration (discussed earlier) contains exactly the same information. Two simple examples illustrating the use of **HTML** are:

```
<HTML>
    <HEAD>
    ... head content....
    </HEAD>
    <BODY>
    ... body content....
    </BODY>
</HTML>
```

```
<HTML>
    <HEAD>
    ... head content....
    </HEAD>
    <FRAMESET>
    ... frame document content
    </FRAMESET>
    <NOFRAMES>
    ... noframe content
    </NOFRAMES>
</HTML>
```

Frame documents and the **FRAMESET, FRAME,** and **NOFRAMES** elements are discussed in Chapter 7.

HEAD Element: Document Meta-information

Usage:	`<HEAD> ... </HEAD>`
Can Contain:	**BASE, ~~ISINDEX~~, LINK, META, SCRIPT, STYLE, TITLE**
Can Be Inside:	**HTML**
Attributes:	*DIR, LANG, PROFILE*

HEAD contains general information about the document. This information is not displayed as part of the document text; consequently, only certain elements are appropriate within the **HEAD**. These elements (**BASE, ISINDEX, LINK, META, SCRIPT, STYLE,** and **TITLE**) can appear inside **HEAD** in any order. The only mandatory **HEAD** element is **TITLE**; all others are optional. All the head elements except **TITLE, SCRIPT,** and **STYLE** are empty.

The optional **PROFILE** attribute takes as its value a URL (or multiple space-separated URLs) pointing to a document containing metadata describing the document or the document collection. However, the format for such metadata documents is still being developed, so that this attribute is not in current use.

The division between the **HEAD** and the **BODY** is important, as there are mechanisms for retrieving just the information in the document **HEAD**. Since the **HEAD** is always much smaller than the body, this is faster than accessing an entire document and can be extremely useful for generating fast catalogs or indexes.

BODY Element: The Document Text Body

Usage:	`<BODY> ... </BODY>`
Can Contain:	**ADDRESS, BLOCKQUOTE,** ~~CENTER~~, ~~DIR~~, **DIV, DL,** *FIELDSET,* **FORM,** Hn, **HR,** [**ISINDEX**], ~~MENU~~, *NOFRAMES, NOSCRIPT,* **OL, P, PRE, TABLE, UL,**
	characters, character highlighting, **A, APPLET,** *BASE-FONT,* **BR,** *BUTTON, IFRAME,* **IMG, INPUT,** *LABEL,* **MAP,** *OBJECT,* **SCRIPT, SELECT, TEXTAREA**
Can Be Inside:	**HTML**
Attributes:	*CLASS, DIR, ID, LANG, STYLE, TITLE, standard event handlers,*
	onLoad, onUnload, (<u>onBlur</u>, <u>onFocus</u>: Netscape Navigator 3/4; Internet Explorer 4),
	ALINK, BACKGROUND, BGCOLOR, LINK, TEXT, VLINK, (<u>BGPROPERTIES</u>, <u>LEFTMARGIN</u>, <u>TOP-MARGIN</u>: Internet Explorer only), (<u>MARGINHEIGHT</u>, <u>MARGINWIDTH</u>: Netscape Navigator 4 only)

The **BODY** contains the document proper, as opposed to the meta-information found in the **HEAD**. Formally, the **BODY** should not directly contain text; instead, it should contain elements that in turn contain the text. Recall that **BODY** states simply "this is the body of the document" and supplies no additional meaning to its content. It is the job of elements nested within the **BODY** to organize the text and assign it meaning. This is accomplished by the elements that define headings, lists, addresses, paragraphs, and so on.

The contents of the **HEAD** and **BODY** are largely exclusive—elements that belong inside the **HEAD** do not belong inside the **BODY**, and vice versa.

BODY can take the optional default attributes such as **CLASS** and **DIR**, as well as the listed event-handling attributes (**onClick**, etc.): These attributes were described previously in the sections entitled "Important 'Generic' Attributes" and "'Event-Handler' Element Attributes." HTML 4 supports several other attributes for specifying properties of the document body, such as the default text colors and page background properties. Some proprietary attributes are supported by Microsoft Internet Explorer. In general, these properties are better (and much more easily) specified by style sheets, as described in Chapter 7. Indeed, these attributes will likely be dropped in a future version of HTML, in favor of the style sheet approach.

ALINK=*"#rrggbb"* or *"color"* (optional) Specifies the color for text within *active* (i.e., selected) links. The default color varies from browser to browser (red with Netscape Navigator).

BACKGROUND=*"url"* (optional) Specifies the URL of an image file (generally GIF or JPEG) that should be used to *tile*, or *wallpaper*, the background of the browser window. A background acts like a watermark and scrolls with the text.

BGCOLOR=*"#rrggbb"* or *"color"* (optional) Specifies the background color for the display window, either as an RGB color value or as a named color. If a **BACKGROUND** image is also specified, the background will first be tiled with the **BGCOLOR** color, and then with the image. If the **BACKGROUND** image is transparent, the color behind the background is given by **BGCOLOR**.

BGPROPERTIES=*"fixed"* (optional; Internet Explorer only) Takes the single value "fixed," which indicates a fixed (non-scrolling) background. The default is for the background to scroll with the text.

LINK=*"#rrggbb"* or *"color"* (optional) Specifies the color for text within unvisited hypertext links (the default is usually blue).

LEFTMARGIN=*"pixels"* (optional; Internet Explorer only)

MARGINWIDTH=*"pixels"* (optional; Netscape Navigator 4 only) Specifies, in pixels, the left and right margins to leave for the entire body of the document. If set to zero, the text will be flush with the left-hand border of the browser window. Netscape Navigator 3 and earlier always have a default margin, around 10 pixels in width.

TEXT=*"#rrggbb"* or *"color"* (optional) Specifies the default color for the document text (the default is black).

TOPMARGIN=*"pixels"* (optional; Internet Explorer only)

MARGINHEIGHT=*"pixels"* (optional; Netscape Navigator 4 only) Specifies, in pixels, the margin to leave at the top of the browser window. If set to zero, the text will be flush with the top window border.

Netscape Navigator 3 and earlier always have a default margin, around 10 pixels in height.

VLINK="*#rrggbb*" or "*color*" (optional) Specifies the color for text within *previously visited* hypertext links (the default is often a pale purple).

HEAD Meta-information Elements

There are only seven elements that can appear in the document **HEAD**. These elements (and their associated meanings/content) are shown in Table 6.8.

All these elements are empty, except for **TITLE**, **SCRIPT**, and **STYLE**. As you can tell by the descriptions, these elements provide information about the document, such as the title, the relationship to other documents, or a style sheet that should be *applied* to the document. To support older, less well-designed documents and software, the DTD actually allows **ISINDEX** and **STYLE** elements within the **BODY**. However, you are best advised to keep them within the head, where they belong.

BASE Element: Base URL

Usage:	`<BASE>`
Can Contain:	empty
Can Be Inside:	**HEAD**
Attributes:	**HREF**, *TARGET*

Table 6.8 Elements Allowed in the Document HEAD

TITLE	Provides the title of the document.
ISINDEX	Indicates that the document is searchable.
BASE	Records a record of the original URL of the document.
LINK	Defines a relationship between the document and another document.
META	Provides meta-information about the document that cannot be expressed in the preceding elements.
SCRIPT	Embeds executable program scripts, or references an external file that contains a program script. In both cases the script should be applied to the current document.
STYLE	Embeds style sheet instructions. The style sheet information should be used to format the document **BODY**.

BASE is an empty element and is optional. **BASE** has a single mandatory attribute, **HREF,** which is assigned the *base URL* of the document. The base URL references where the document was originally located. Consequently, a document can have at most one **BASE** element.

BASE is useful for documents moved away from their original URL—after moving the document, partial URLs that referenced neighboring documents are no longer valid. However, if the original URL address is specified in a **BASE** element, relative URLs from this document are evaluated relative to this "base" URL and are correctly referenced at the original location.

If the **BASE** element is absent, the browser determines partial URLs relative to the URL used to access the document.

NOTE: Possible Problems with BASE

Be aware that browsers differ in their interpretation of **BASE** when it comes to "bookmarking" a document or to accessing **FORM** or **ISINDEX**-referenced resources: Some browsers use the **BASE** URL in these cases, while others use the actual URL needed to retrieve the displayed document.

The following is an example of the appropriate use of **BASE**. If a document was originally found at the URL:

http://somewhere.org/Dir/Subdir/file.html

the appropriate **BASE** element to include in this document is:

```
<HEAD>
   <TITLE> some sort of title.... </TITLE>
   <BASE HREF="http://somewhere.org/Dir/Subdir/file.html">
</HEAD>
```

BASE Support for Netscape Frames

Browsers that support the frame elements support *targeted* links—this lets a document author direct the data returned, upon selecting a hypertext link, to a particular *named* browser window or named pane within a window—all browsers can produce multiple copies of themselves, while frame-capable browsers can create multiple window panes within a single browser window. *Named* windows are produced by using a **TARGET** attribute to the **A** (anchor) element or by using the **FRAMESET** element, as discussed in Chapter 7.

Browsers that support frames also support a **TARGET** attribute with the **BASE** element. Analogous to the value of **HREF, TARGET** defines the default name of the target window for all hypertext links within the document. For example, the element

```
<BASE TARGET="window3">
```

means that all accessed hypertext links will be displayed in (sent to) the window named `window3`. If a pane by this name does not already exist, then a new browser window will be created, and will be assigned this name.

A **BASE**-specified target is overridden by an explicit **TARGET** within an anchor, such as:

```
<A HREF="/path/file.html" TARGET="window2">anchor text</A>
```

The document returned upon accessing this anchor will be directed to the window named "window2," overriding any target implied by the **BASE** element **TARGET** value. The default target is always the window or frame containing the document currently being displayed.

ISINDEX Element: Searchable Document

Usage:	`<ISINDEX>`
Can Contain:	empty
Can Be Inside:	**HEAD**
	[BLOCKQUOTE, BODY, ~~CENTER~~, DD, DIV, *FIELDSET*, FORM, LI, *NOFRAMES*, *NOSCRIPT*, TD, TH,
	APPLET, *IFRAME*, *OBJECT*]
Attributes:	*CLASS, DIR, ID, LANG, STYLE, TITLE,*
	<u>ACTION</u>, PROMPT

ISINDEX is an optional, empty element. Because there are many older documents that have **ISINDEX** in the **BODY**, HTML allows this placement; ideally, **ISINDEX** should be inside the **HEAD**. This element informs the browser that the document can be examined using a keyword search and that the browser should query the user for a search or query string. The attribute **PROMPT**, which takes as its value an arbitrary author-specified string, specifies the prompt that should be presented for this query; for example:

```
<ISINDEX PROMPT="Please enter your favorite ice cream flavor:">
```

ISINDEX does *not* mean a search of the text being read. Documents containing **ISINDEX** elements are usually sent to the client from server-side gateway programs designed for database searches. You can think of such a document as a front end to a gateway program and the document you search as the database *represented* by the document you see.

By default, **ISINDEX**-accepted data are returned to the same URL that was used to retrieve the document containing the **ISINDEX** element. Several browsers support an **ACTION** attribute, which takes as its value a URL to which the query should instead be directed. This is supported by both Navigator and Internet Explorer.

NOTE: ISINDEX to Be Dropped from HTML

The **ISINDEX** element is marked for deletion from the HTML specification and should not be used in new documents. **ISINDEX** queries can instead be mimicked using the following **FORM** markup:

```
<FORM action="url-for-query" method="get">
Enter your search phrase: <INPUT type="text">
</FORM>
```

where *url-for-query* is the URL to which the query string should be sent. Note that, to properly emulate **ISINDEX,** you must omit the **NAME** attribute from the **INPUT** element.

The encoding mechanism by which ISINDEX query data are appended to a URL is discussed in the **http** URL section of Chapter 8 and also in Chapter 10.

LINK Element: Relationship to Other Documents

Usage:	`<LINK>`
Can Contain:	empty
Can Be Inside:	**HEAD**
Attributes:	*CLASS, DIR, ID, LANG, STYLE, TITLE, standard event handlers,*
	CHARSET, HREF, *HREFLANG, MEDIA,* REL, REV, *TARGET, TYPE*

LINK describes a *relationship* between a document and other documents or objects. For example, **LINK** can indicate a related index, a glossary, or perhaps different versions of the same document. Alternatively, **LINK** can point out likely *next* or *previous* documents. This information could be used by a browser, among other things, to predict and preload documents it is likely to need, or to configure customized navigational buttons or menus. A document may have any number of **LINK** elements to represent these various relationships to other documents.

LINK is an empty element and is optional. The **HREF** attribute (a URL that points to the linked resource) is mandatory, as is at least one of **REL** or **REV**: **REL** or **REV** take text string values that define the nature of the relationship between the linked resources. All other attributes are optional. Indeed, most other attributes are not understood by current browsers.

In general, **REL** defines the relationship of the *targeted* document to the current document. For example, **REL**="next" would indicate that the targeted document is the next document after the current one. **REV** defines the relationship of the current document relative to the target document, which is often just the converse of **REL**. Thus, **REV**="next" would indicate that the *current* document is the "next" document following the targeted one. In fact, **REL** and **REV** are not always the converse of one another—for example, **REL**="image" indicates that the targeted resource is an image file, but the converse **REV**="image" is not possible, since the current document is by definintion an HTML document and not an image.

The following are some commonly used **LINK** elements:

```
<LINK REL="made" HREF="mailto:igraham@utoronto.ca">
```

> **HREF** points to information about the creator of the document containing the **LINK**.

```
<LINK REL="stylesheet" HREF="./styles/stylesheet.css">
```

> **HREF** points to a document containing a style sheet. The style sheet should be retrieved and applied to the document being rendered. This use of **LINK** is understood by Internet Explorer 4 and Netscape Navigator 4.

```
<LINK REL="fontdef" HREF="/url/to/filenam.pfr">
```

> **HREF** points to a document containing a Bitstream *TrueDoc*-format Portable Font Resource (*PFR*) file. This is a downloadable font that can be used within the document. This font format (and this **LINK** mechanism) are only supported by Netscape Navigator 4.

```
<LINK REL="begin" HREF="/usr/to/begin/file.html">
```

> **HREF** points to a document that is at the "beginning" of the collection containing the current document. This is often used by Web indexing tools, to help determine the structure of a Web site, and a collection's preferred home page.

```
<LINK REL="alternate" LANG="fr" HREF="file-fr.html">
```

> **HREF** points to an alternative version of the current document. Here, the **LANG** attribute indicates that the alternate document is in French. Alternately, the TYPE attribute could indicate that the linked resource is an alternative document, in a different format.

In addition to **HREF**, **REL**, and **REV**, **LINK** also takes the "generic" and "event-handling" attributes noted earlier in this chapter. Notably, **ID** can be used to create *indirected* links: An **ID**-labeled **LINK** element can, in principle, be referenced by a hypertext anchor referencing the **ID** value. Thus this anchor references the **LINK**ed resource indirectly, via the element's **ID**. This behavior is not supported by current browsers.

LINK also supports several other newer (currently unsupported) attributes. These are:

> *CHARSET*="*string*" (optional; not currently supported) Specifies the character set used by the linked resource. Character set specifications are described in Appendix A found on the companion Web site. This attribute is not understood by current browsers.

HREFLANG="*lang-code*" (optional; not currently supported) Specifies the language of the resource specified by the **HREF** attribute. Language codes are described in Appendix E on the companion Web site. This attribute is not understood by current browsers.

MEDIA="*comma-separated-strings*" (optional; not currently supported) If the referenced resource is a style sheet, the **MEDIA** attribute can specify the presentation media for which the style sheet should be used. Some possible values are "screen" (for a computer display), "print," "projection" (for projection displays), "Braille" (for Braille readers), or "aural" (for text-to-speech synthesizers). This attribute is not understood by current browsers.

TARGET="*string*" (optional; not currently supported) Specifies the name of the target frame or window to which the **LINK**ed resource should be sent, upon retrieval. This attribute is not understood by current browsers.

TYPE="*mime-type*" (optional; not currently supported) If the referenced resource is a style sheet, the **TYPE** attribute defines the MIME type for the style sheet: for example, text/css for cascading style sheets. This attribute is not understood by current browsers.

LINK elements, with **REL** (or **REV**) attributes, are only useful given well-understood meanings for the values assigned to them. The process of defining a set of values is currently underway: Some of the commonly understood relationships are given in the examples below. In the absence of well-defined meanings, **LINK** is largely unused. The document

www.utoronto.ca/ian/books/html4ed/chap6/relrev.html

at the book's supporting Web site describes some efforts at establishing well-accepted values.

META Element: Document Meta-information

Usage:	`<META>`
Can Contain:	empty
Can Be Inside:	**HEAD**
Attributes:	*DIR, LANG,*
	CONTENT, HTTP-EQUIV, NAME, *SCHEME*

The **META** element provides a place to put meta-information about a document that does not fit inside other **HEAD** elements. This lets an author more richly describe the document content for indexing, parsing, or cataloging purposes, as illustrated in the following discussion.

The **META** element is optional. If present, it must take the **CONTENT** attribute and one of the **NAME** or **HTTP-EQUIV** attributes (but not both). The meanings of the attributes are:

NAME=*"name"* (one of **NAME** or **HTTP-EQUIV** must be present) This specifies the meta-information name (ideally as a name token). The client program (browser) must understand what this name means. HTML does not currently define any values for **NAME**. **META** must contain one of **NAME** or **HTTP-EQUIV**, but not both.

HTTP-EQUIV=*"name"* (one of **NAME** or **HTTP-EQUIV** must be present) This indicates meta-information equivalent to that communicated by the HTTP protocol within HTTP *response header fields*. HTTP response headers are discussed in Chapter 9. **META** must contain either **NAME** or **HTTP-EQUIV**, but not both.

CONTENT=*"string"* (mandatory) This assigns the content associated with the **NAME** or **HTTP-EQUIV** value of the **META** element.

SCHEME="string" (optional; not currently supported) This attribute names the scheme used to determine the appropriate value, given the indicated **NAME**d property: Thus, this is valid only when **NAME** is used. This provides additional information for identifying the meanings associated with the **NAME** and **CONTENT** values. For example, the attributes **NAME=**"description" and **CONTENT=**"c32e1: Biological Surveys" are not terribly meaningful, but the added attribute **SCHEME=**"HumanGenomeProject-Index" indicates that the format for the description is specified by the indicated indexing scheme. There is, unfortunately, no current software that processes this information.

NAME Attribute Usage

An example using the **NAME** attribute is:

```
<META NAME="keywords" CONTENT="pets dogs cats rocks lizards">
```

This tells the client that the words "pets," "dogs," "cats," "rocks," and "lizards" are keywords useful for indexing the current document. The client or indexing program that is accessing the **HEAD** of this document must consequently understand the meanings behind the names.

HTTP-EQUIV Attribute Usage

HTTP-EQUIV lets the document contain HTTP-header information, which can be accessed (and used to generate the HTTP response) either by the server delivering the document, or by the browser receiving the document. An example is:

```
<META HTTP-EQUIV="Creation-Date" CONTENT="23-Sep-94 18:28:33 GMT">
```

which indicates the creation date of the document, in the context of the appropriate HTTP header field `Creation-Date`. If the server actually parses the document head, then it will create an HTTP header field

```
Creation-Date: 23-Sep-94 18:28:33 GMT
```

and include this with the HTTP *response header* that precedes the document during an HTTP transaction (see Chapter 9). Even if the server does not create such a header, a browser or other program can still obtain this information directly from the **META** element.

NOTE: Do Not Use META to Override HTTP Headers

You should not use `<META HTTP-EQUIV...>` to override server response header fields normally returned by the server. According to the HTML specifications, a browser will use the information in an HTTP header and ignore equivalent information found in a **META** element.

Important Uses of META

Most servers do not parse a document for **META** elements, although several browsers parse documents for specific **META** elements and their content. In particular, most Web indexing tools (Lycos, AltaVista, etc.) check for specific **META** elements to guide them in their indexing. The most common cases are:

1. Specifying document character set:

   ```
   <META HTTP-EQUIV="content-type" CONTENT="text/html; charset="EUC-2">
   ```

   Gives the content-type of the document, as the HTTP content-type header field, but also lists the character set in which the document is written. This is useful, as most servers cannot currently indicate character set information relevant to the documents they serve out.

2. Specify expiry time for a document:

   ```
   <META HTTP-EQUIV="expires" CONTENT="Tue, 01 Jan 1981 01:00:00 GMT">
   ```

   Gives the expiry date for the document—a browser or server will not cache a document past its expiry date. Giving an expiry date in the past (as in the example) will hopefully prevent the document from being cached by a browser or proxy server.

3. Special document "refresh" request:

   ```
   <META HTTP-EQUIV="refresh" CONTENT="10; URL="http://foo.org/bx.html">
   ```

   This widely supported extension asks the browser to wait 10 seconds, and then access the indicated URL. Chapter 11 describes this *client-pull* feature in more detail.

4. Specify PICS page content-rating information:

`<META HTTP-EQUIV="PICS-Label" CONTENT="`*PICS-1.0 label information*`">`

References a PICS (Platform for Internet Content Selection) label for the document. PICS is a rating scheme for Web pages, and provides a way of censoring content that might be unfit for young children. Some browsers understand PICS, and will refuse to display documents that are PICS-rated as unsatisfactory. PICS information is available from the references at the end of this chapter.

5. Specify keywords for Web search engine:

`<META NAME="keywords" CONTENT="`*space separated keywords list*`">`

Several Web-based search engines will preferentially index a document using keywords specified by **META** elements of this form. A careful choice of keywords can make your documents much easier to find at search engines such as Lycos, AltaVista, Yahoo!, and OpenText.

6. Specify text description of content for Web search engine:

`<META NAME="description" CONTENT="`*A short resource description*`">`

AltaVista indexes the content of **META** elements with **NAME**="keywords" or **NAME**="description." The latter value is also used by the search engine as a brief description of the resource . If this is absent, AltaVista uses the first few sentences of the document.

7. Tell Web robots not to index the page or follow links from the page:

`<META NAME="robots" CONTENT="noindex, nofollow">`

This tells a Web robot that the robot should not index the document and that it should not explore any hypertext links going out from the document.

8. Indicate author of page:

`<META NAME="author" CONTENT="`*Author's name*`">`

This encodes, within the document, the name of the author.

9. Give name of software that created the document:

`<META NAME="Generator" NAME="`*name and version of software*`">`

This encodes, within the document, the name of the software tool that generated the document. Many HTML editors include this **META** element.

10. Indicate the default MIME type of any script programs in the document:

`META NAME="Content-script-type" CONTENT="`*mime/type*`">`

This indicates the default scripting language for the document. This can be overridden by explicit script language declarations in a **SCRIPT** element.

SCRIPT Element: Include a Program Script

Usage:	`<SCRIPT> ... </SCRIPT>`
Can Contain:	script program code (**characters**)
Can Be Inside:	**HEAD,**
	ADDRESS, BLOCKQUOTE, BODY, CAPTION, ~~**CENTER**~~**, DD, DIV, DT,** *FIELDSET,* **FORM, Hn, LI,** *NOFRAMES, NOSCRIPT,* **P, PRE, TD, TH,**
	character highlighting, A, APPLET, *BUTTON, IFRAME, LABEL, LEGEND, OBJECT*
Attributes:	*CHARSET, DEFER,* <u>*EVENT*</u>*,* <u>*FOR*</u>*,* LANGUAGE, SRC, *TYPE,* (<u>ID</u>, <u>IN</u>: Internet Explorer 4 only)

SCRIPT is used to include program scripts within an HTML document. If there is no **SRC** attribute, the content of the element is treated as script program code and is executed, if possible, by the browser. If **SRC** is present, then the resource specified by this attribute is retrieved and executed as script program code—in this case, the content of the element is ignored. Browsers that do not understand **SCRIPT** elements or the language in which the script is written will ignore this element and its content.

SCRIPT is usually nonempty, the content being the program script. To hide this content from browsers that do not understand **SCRIPT**, the actual code can be placed inside an HTML comment. This is illustrated in the following example, with the HTML comment markers shown in boldface (the dots indicate omitted code). Note that the ending comment string `-->` must be preceded by the string `//`—this is the string used by JavaScript to denote the start of a JavaScript comment.

```
<SCRIPT LANGUAGE='JavaScript'>
<!--
.
.
.function opentip() {
        str="/comprod/news/todaystip.html";
        tipWin = window.open(str,'tipWin','width=175,height=175');
        window.open(str,'tipWin','width=175,height=175');
        tipWin.opener = self;
}
.
.
// -->
</SCRIPT>
```

SCRIPT is allowed in the body as well as the **HEAD**: The **HEAD** portion should be used to define any functions used elsewhere in the document, while **SCRIPT**s in the **BODY** should be used to print script-generated text into the HTML document. This is described in more detail Chapter 7.

Inside the **BODY**, the element **NOSCRIPT** can contain HTML markup to use in place of the **SCRIPT** content, should the browser not understand **SCRIPT** or the scripting language.

SCRIPT can take a number of attributes. **LANGUAGE** indicates the language of a script placed inside a **SCRIPT** element—this is required as there are multiple scripting languages, and also multiple versions of each scripting language. **SRC** specifies the **URL** of a file containing a script program, and is used to include an external script into an HTML document. **TYPE** specifies the MIME-type of this file—HTML 4 recommends using **TYPE** in place of **LANGUAGE**, although at present only **LANGUAGE** is widely supported. The detailed specifications for these and other defined attributes are given below.

CHARSET=*"string"* (optional; valid only when **SRC** is specified; not currently supported) Specifies the character set used in the linked JavaScript program file. This is not supported by current browsers.

DEFER (optional; not currently supported) Indicates that the script does not affect the rendering of the document, and lets the browser defer execution of the script until the document is rendered. This is not supported by current browsers.

EVENT=*"string"* (optional; Internet Explorer 4 only; **FOR** must also be present) Indicates the event type that this script is bound to—the value of **EVENT** must be the name of a valid event handler, such as "onclick" or "onmouseover." This attribute allows for **SCRIPT**s that are explicit handlers of specific events. For example, `<SCRIPT EVENT="onclick" FOR="z23">` means that this script element is the event handler for onclick events arising from the element with **ID**="z23."

FOR=*"string* " (optional; Internet Explorer 4 only; **EVENT** must also be present) Indicates the identity of the element to which the **SCRIPT** is bound as an event handler. See **EVENT** for further details.

ID=*"string"* (optional; Internet Explorer 4 only) Indicates the identity of the element to which the **SCRIPT** is bound as an event handler. See **EVENT** for further details.

IN=*"string"* (optional; Internet Explorer 4 only) Indicates the name of an element within which the script can apply (i.e., defines the *scope* for the script). For example, to restrict a script to be valid only inside a FORM, you could set **IN** equal to the **NAME** of the form.

LANGUAGE=*"string"* (optional) Specifies the language of the script contained within the **SCRIPT** element. The only commonly supported values are **LANGUAGE**="JavaScript" for JavaScript and **LANGUAGE**="VBScript" for Visual Basic Script. Internet Explorer supports both languages, while Netscape Navigator 3 supports only JavaScript. Navigator also supports the names "JavaScript1.1" and "JavaScript1.2," corresponding to the JavaScript language implemented in Navigator 3 and Navigator 4, respectively.

SRC="*url*" (optional) Specifies the URL of a file that contains a script. The browser should access the file and load the script as if it were included inline with the document.

TIP: SRC Not Properly Supported in Netscape 3

Using external script programs can lead to problems with early versions of Netscape or Internet Explorer. It is thus safest to develop script applications with the script firmly embedded inside the **SCRIPT** element and then to try moving them to an external file once the script is debugged.

TYPE="*string*" (optional; not widely supported) Gives the MIME type for the script referenced by the **SRC** attribute. For example, an external JavaScript program from the file *prog.js* would be referenced by the markup:

```
<SCRIPT SRC="http://scripts.ian.com/prog1.js"
       TYPE="application/javascript">
</SCRIPT>
```

Some common MIME types are text/x-javascript (JavaScript) and text/vbscript (VBScript).

STYLE Element: Style Sheet or Rendering Information

Usage:	`<STYLE> ... </STYLE>`
Can Contain:	**characters**
Can Be Inside:	**HEAD**
Attributes:	*DIR, LANG, TITLE, MEDIA, TYPE*

STYLE contains style sheet rendering instructions to be applied to the document when displayed by the browser. **STYLE** allows rendering information to be placed within the document and not as a second file referenced through a **LINK** element. The latter may be accomplished using **LINK** elements of the form:

```
<LINK REL="stylesheet"
     HREF="http:some.where.dom/path/stylesheet"
     TYPE="mime/type">
```

where `mime/type` is the MIME type of the indicated style sheet (`text/css` for cascading style sheets). The **STYLE** element allows for browsers that do not support linked style sheets. In this instance, **STYLE** is best thought of as an interim mechanism for including style sheet information, as it has several disadvantages compared with linked style sheets. In particular, a linked style sheet can be shared between many documents, while the **STYLE** element forces every document to contain the style sheet data.

However, **STYLE** has a second use—for local customization of an external style sheet. In this regard, you can use a linked style sheet to specify the broad details of the layout, with the content in the **STYLE** element providing small-scale, local modifications.

The following is a simple **STYLE** example; styling mechanisms are discussed in more detail in Chapter 7.

```
<HEAD>
<STYLE>
  BODY { background: url(waves.gif) black; }
  H1 {   margin-top: 10px;
         color:      #4F;
         text-align: left;
         font: 30px Arial, gill, helvetica, sans-serif; }
...
</STYLE>
....
</HEAD><BODY>
```

TITLE Element: Document Title

Usage:	`<TITLE> ... </TITLE>`
Can Contain:	**characters**
Can Be Inside:	**HEAD**
Attributes:	*DIR, LANG*

The title of a document is specified by the **TITLE** element. Every document must have a **TITLE**, and can only have one. The text inside a **TITLE** should indicate the document content in a concise but general way. A **TITLE** serves several purposes:

1. To label the display window or text screen

2. To serve as a record in a history or bookmark list marking documents you have viewed

3. To allow quick indexing of a document in place of indexing the entire text

The **TITLE** is not part of the document text and cannot contain hypertext links or any other markup commands—it can contain only text, including entity or character references.

The **TITLE** should be short—preferably less than 60 characters—so that it can easily label a window or fit in a history list. You should be able to determine the content of the document from the **TITLE** itself. Otherwise, a person reviewing his/her bookmarks will see the title, but not know to what it refers. Here are some examples:

Good TITLEs:

```
<TITLE>Paper on Rings by Baggins and Gandalf, 1989</TITLE>
<TITLE>Introduction to MIME types </TITLE>
```

Bad TITLEs:

```
<TITLE>Introduction</TITLE>
<TITLE>A Summary of the Ring-Ring Interaction Cross-Section
Measurement of B. Baggins, et al. in both Low-Temperature and
High-Temperature Studies, including Water Immersion and
Non-Destructive Testing: A Brief Review plus Commentary on
the "Missing Ring" Problem.</TITLE>
```

Block and Heading Elements

Block elements divide a document into logical blocks of text, such as paragraphs (**P**), block quotations (**BLOCKQUOTE**), lists (see the following section), address information (**ADDRESS**), and so on. The block elements **FORM**, which defines a fill-in interactive form, and **TABLE**, which defines tabular structures, are more complex than the others and are described in detail later in this chapter.

Several proprietary block-like elements, such as **FRAMESET, FRAME,** and **IFRAME** (Netscape frame documents), **MULTICOL** (multicolumn text), and **NOBR** (no line breaks), are supported by a number of browsers. These are described in Chapter 7.

ADDRESS Element: Address Information

Usage:	`<ADDRESS> ... </ADDRESS>`
Can Contain:	**P,**
	characters, character highlighting, A, APPLET, *BASE-FONT,* **BR,** *BUTTON, IFRAME,* **IMG, INPUT,** *LABEL,* **MAP,** *OBJECT,* **SCRIPT, SELECT, TEXTAREA**
Can Be Inside:	**BLOCKQUOTE, BODY, CENTER, DD, DIV, DT,** *FIELDSET,* **FORM, LI,** *NOFRAMES, NOSCRIPT,* **TD, TH,**
	APPLET, *BUTTON, IFRAME, OBJECT*
Attributes:	*CLASS, DIR, ID, LANG, STYLE, TITLE, standard event handlers*

ADDRESS denotes information such as addresses, electronic signatures, lists of authors, and so on. Typically, document authors would use **ADDRESS** to sign his or her documents. In this case, the **ADDRESS** is often placed at the bottom of the

HTML document to keep it separate from the main text. In a family of documents, the **ADDRESS** may contain just the author's initials or name connected by a hypertext link to a biographical page. Alternatively, a collection of documents may have an introductory document that has **ADDRESS** elements containing detailed contact information for the author or authors, with the remaining documents having **ADDRESS** elements containing hypertext links back to this page.

As with all semantic markup elements, the rendering of the contents of **ADDRESS** is left up to the browser. By default, most browsers render **ADDRESS** content in italics.

ADDRESS supports the standard "generic" and "event-handler" attributes described earlier in this chapter. Note that the event handlers are only partially supported by Internet Explorer 4 and are not supported by Netscape Navigator 4.

Figures 6.7 and 6.9 show some typical applications of the **ADDRESS** element. Browser rendering of these documents are shown in Figures 6.8 and 6.10, respectively.

Figure 6.7 HTML example document illustrating heading, BLOCK-QUOTE, and ADDRESS elements. Figure 6.8 shows this document viewed by Internet Explorer 3.

```
<HTML>
<HEAD>
<TITLE> Examples of ADDRESS and BLOCKQUOTE elements</TITLE>
</HEAD>
<BODY>
<H1>The Meaning of Life </H1>

<P> How many times have you sat down and asked yourself "What is
the meaning of life?."  I certainly have.  I've
even read many of the good books, from C.S. Lewis, to Kant, to
Sartre to Zoltan the Magnificent.  But I think the most profound
statement about life was made by Jack Handey, who said:
<BLOCKQUOTE>
<P>I can still recall old Mister Barnslow getting out every morning and
nailing a fresh load of tadpoles to that old board of his.  Then he'd
spin it around and around, like a wheel of fortune, and no matter where
it stopped he'd yell out, "Tadpoles!  Tadpoles is a winner!"
We all thought he was crazy.  But then, we had some growing up to do.
</BLOCKQUOTE>
<P>That pretty well sums it up.
<HR>
<ADDRESS>   <A HREF="about_the_author.html"> C.S.O </A> </ADDRESS>
</BODY>
</HTML>
```

Figure 6.8 Display, by the Internet Explorer 3 browser, of the document shown in Figure 6.7.

Figure 6.9 HTML example document illustrating TITLE, heading, and ADDRESS elements. Figure 6.10 shows this document viewed by Internet Explorer 3.

```
<HTML>
<HEAD>
<TITLE> Some examples of ADDRESS and heading elements </TITLE>
</HEAD>
<BODY>

<H1 ALIGN="center"> Example 3: The Truth About Santa  </H1>
<P> Breaking the news to a small child that Santa Claus is
merely a tool of the modern capitalist is one of
the saddest moments in raising children.  Nevertheless, such
truths must be brought to life, for fear that your child
become another Pangloss lost in the idealism so prevalent
amongst our youth. Here are some different methods to
introduce this topic.

<H2 ALIGN="left"> Santa's Exploitation of the Working Class </H2>
<P>  Begin by talking about Santa's enslaved workforce.  How
can those poor gnomes make all those gifts?  Clearly
by driven overwork.....

<H3> Elves and the Union Movement </H3>
<P> and so on.......

<H4> Elf Exploitation </H4>
<P> And still more text.
```

Figure 6.9 *Continued*.

```
<HR>
<ADDRESS>
Santa Claus<BR>
Christmas Holiday Specialist <BR>
North Pole, CANADA H0H 0H0<BR>
Tel: (555) 555 POLE
</ADDRESS>
</BODY> </HTML>
```

Figure 6.10 Display, by the Internet Explorer 3 browser, of the document shown in Figure 6.9.

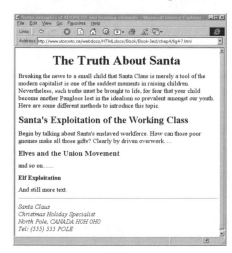

BLOCKQUOTE Element: Block Quotations

Usage:	`<BLOCKQUOTE> ... </BLOCKQUOTE>`
Can Contain:	ADDRESS, BLOCKQUOTE, CENTER, DIR, DIV, DL, *FIELDSET*, FORM, Hn, HR, [ISINDEX], MENU, *NOFRAMES*, *NOSCRIPT*, OL, P, PRE, TABLE, UL,
	characters, character highlighting, A, APPLET, *BASE-FONT*, BR, *BUTTON*, *IFRAME*, IMG, INPUT, *LABEL*, MAP, *OBJECT*, SCRIPT, SELECT, TEXTAREA
Can Be Inside:	BLOCKQUOTE, BODY, CENTER, DD, DIV, *FIELD-SET*, FORM, LI, *NOFRAMES*, *NOSCRIPT*, TD, TH,
Can Be Inside:	APPLET, *BUTTON*, *IFRAME*, *OBJECT*

Attributes:	*CITE, CLASS, DIR, ID, LANG, STYLE, TITLE, standard event handlers*

BLOCKQUOTE marks a block of text as a quotation. Browsers can render this in various ways: for example, by indenting the **BLOCKQUOTE** content and by offsetting it from the preceding and following text. A **BLOCKQUOTE** also causes a paragraph break and terminates preceding paragraphs.

Ideally, you should not place text directly inside a **BLOCKQUOTE**; rather, the HTML 4 specification recommends that text be placed inside other elements (such as paragraphs and lists) that are in turn inside the **BLOCKQUOTE**. Thus, the form:

```
<BLOCKQUOTE>
<P> This is the quotation. ...
.....
</P>
</BLOCKQUOTE>
```

is better than:

```
 <BLOCKQUOTE>
This is the quotation. ...
.....
</BLOCKQUOTE>
```

BLOCKQUOTE supports the standard "generic" and "event-handler" attributes described earlier in this chapter. Note that the event handlers are only partially supported by Internet Explorer 4 and are not supported by Netscape Navigator 4. **BLOCKQUOTE** also supports an optional **CITE** attribute, which takes as its value a URL that references the source of the citation. There are no current Web browsers that support the **CITE** attribute.

A typical **BLOCKQUOTE** is shown in Figures 6.7 and 6.8. Because **BLOCK-QUOTE** usually introduces left-margin indentation, it is often used to indent blocks of text, such as the paragraphs following a heading. An example is shown in Figure 2.17 and 2.18. A much better approach is to use style sheets, as discussed in Chapter 7.

CENTER Element: Center the Enclosed Text

Usage:	`<CENTER> ... </CENTER>`
Can Contain:	ADDRESS, BLOCKQUOTE, CENTER, DIR, DIV, DL, *FIELDSET*, FORM, Hn, HR, [ISINDEX], MENU, *NOFRAMES, NOSCRIPT*, OL, P, PRE, TABLE, UL,
	characters, character highlighting, A, APPLET, *BASE-FONT*, BR, *BUTTON, IFRAME*, IMG, INPUT, *LABEL*, MAP, *OBJECT*, SCRIPT, SELECT, TEXTAREA
Can Be Inside:	BLOCKQUOTE, BODY, CENTER, DD, DIV, *FIELD-SET*, FORM, LI, *NOFRAMES, NOSCRIPT*, TD, TH,

APPLET, *BUTTON, IFRAME, OBJECT*

Attributes: *CLASS, DIR, ID, LANG, STYLE, TITLE, standard event handlers*

CENTER center-aligns text enclosed within the element, including any enclosed blocks of text, with the exception of left- or right-aligned images or tables, or block elements for which the alignment is specified by the element's own alignment attribute. In particular, **CENTER** is often used to center a **TABLE**. **CENTER** introduces a line break both before and after the centered text, so that only the enclosed text is centered. Note that **CENTER** does not introduce any extra vertical spacing beyond that of a regular line break.

NOTE: CENTER to Be Dropped from HTML

CENTER is to be dropped in a future version of HTML and should be avoided in new documents. Instead of **CENTER**, use

```
<DIV ALIGN="center"> ... </DIV>
```

which yields equivalent formatting.

Formally, **CENTER** is a block element, equivalent to a **DIV**. However, you must be careful about assuming that **CENTER** provides a line break, since browsers that do not understand this element will ignore the tags and will neither introduce a break, nor center the text.

    CENTER (or **DIV** with **ALIGN**="center") can be used to center-align text between two **HR** elements, as in:

```
<center>
<hr width=80%>
These simple notes form a useful, single document
  explaining the rationale and organization of the Web Document
  template collection. Please print this out for off-line
  reference.
<hr width=80%>
</center>
```

    If the browser does not support **CENTER,** the text will still be broken from the preceding or following material because of the **HR**. Figures 6.11 and 6.12 show how this differs from the following (which includes a **P** element):

```
<center>
<hr width=80%>
<P> These simple notes form a useful, single document
  explaining the rationale and organization of the Web Document
  template collection. Please print this out for off-line
  reference.
<hr width=80%>
</center>
```

Figure 6.11 HTML example document illustrating CENTER and HR elements.

```
<HTML>
<HEAD><TITLE>Example of CENTER and HR</TITLE></HEAD>
<BODY>
<H2>Example of CENTER and HR</H2>
It is always better to use <B>ALIGN</B>="center" to align
things, but sometimes <B>CENTER</B> does have advantages.
For example, look at the following: text centered between
two <B>HR</B> elements:
<CENTER>
<HR WIDTH="60%">
This is a single-page document -- why not <BR>
  print it out for future reference?
<HR WIDTH="60%">
</CENTER>
<P>The <B>CENTER</B> element centers any enclosed, text,
including lists ...
<CENTER>
<UL>
  <LI>Lists
  <LI>Centering the text, and not the bullets
  <LI>Which is sometimes useful
  <LI>But not always.....
</UL>
</CENTER>
<HR NOSHADE>
Note that CENTER tags do not add extra vertical spacing. Observe
what happens when an extra <B>P</B> is added inside a <B>CENTER</B>:
<CENTER>
<HR WIDTH="60%">
<P>This is a single-page document -- why not <BR>
  print it out for future reference?
<HR WIDTH="60%">
</CENTER>
Note how the extra <B>&lt;P></B> in the second example of text
centred between HR elements  adds extra vertical space between
the text and the rule.
<HR SIZE=2 NOSHADE>
<DIV ALIGN="right">
<I>Another Exciting HTML Example</I>
</DIV>
</BODY> </HTML>
```

Figure 6.12 Rendering of the HTML document in Figure 6.11 by the Netscape Navigator 3 browser. Note the control of spacing around the HR elements.

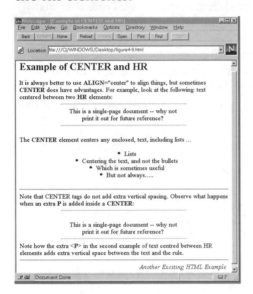

DIV Element: A Block Division of the BODY

Usage:	`<DIV> ... </DIV>`
Can Contain:	ADDRESS, BLOCKQUOTE, CENTER, DIR, DIV, DL, *FIELDSET*, FORM, Hn, HR, [ISINDEX], MENU, *NOFRAMES*, *NOSCRIPT*, OL, P, PRE, TABLE, UL,
	characters, character highlighting, A, APPLET, *BASEFONT*, BR, *BUTTON*, *IFRAME*, IMG, INPUT, *LABEL*, MAP, *OBJECT*, SCRIPT, SELECT, TEXTAREA
Can Be Inside:	BLOCKQUOTE, BODY, CENTER, DD, DIV, *FIELDSET*, FORM, LI, *NOFRAMES*, *NOSCRIPT*, TD, TH,
	APPLET, *BUTTON*, *IFRAME*, *OBJECT*
Attributes:	*CLASS*, *DIR*, *ID*, *LANG*, *STYLE*, *TITLE*, *standard event handlers*, ALIGN

DIV marks a block of the document as a logical group or *division* and is used to specify generic properties for an entire block. **DIV** supports the standard "generic" and "event-handler" attributes described earlier in this chapter. Note that the event handlers are only partially supported by Internet Explorer 4 and are not supported by Netscape Navigator 4.

DIV can also take an **ALIGN** attribute, to specify the desired text alignment within the block or within any other block element within the block. The allowed values are "left," "center," "right," and "justify," which call for left-aligned, center-aligned, right-aligned, and fully justified text, respectively. Note that many browsers do not support justified text. Text alignment can also be specified using a style sheet, as discussed in Chapter 7.

DIV implies the end of any paragraph and will cause a line break in the text. Other than this, **DIV** does not affect the formatting or presentation of a document (i.e., it does not add any extra vertical spacing) and is simply used to more formally organize the document content. Figure 6.13 and Figure 6.14 show an example of this use of DIV.

Hn Elements: Headings

Usage:	`<Hn> ... </Hn>`
Can Contain:	characters, character highlighting, A, APPLET, *BASE-FONT*, BR, *BUTTON*, *IFRAME*, IMG, INPUT, *LABEL*, MAP, *OBJECT*, SCRIPT, SELECT, TEXTAREA
Can Be Inside:	BLOCKQUOTE, BODY, CENTER, DD, DIV, *FIELD-SET*, FORM, LI, *NOFRAMES*, *NOSCRIPT*, TD, TH, APPLET, *BUTTON*, *IFRAME*, *OBJECT*
Attributes:	*CLASS, DIR, ID, LANG, STYLE, TITLE, standard event handlers*

The elements **H1** through **H6** denote *headings*. There is no forced hierarchy in these headings, but for consistency you should use the top level (**H1**) for main headings and lower levels for progressively less important ones. You should also avoid skipping heading levels within a document, as this breaks the logical structure and may cause problems when converting the document into another form or when automatically generating HTML table of contents documents.

TIP: Avoid Using Headings Just to Get Large Text

Because headings are often used to construct document indexes and databases, you should not using headings simply to obtain large-font text. The **FONT** element, or **SPAN** (plus style sheets), provide much better ways of accomplishing the same thing, without affecting the indexing of your work.

Renderings of headings are very much browser-dependent. Most graphical browsers left-adjust headings and use progressively smaller fonts as heading importance decreases (from **H1** to **H6**). Others, such as lynx, render **H1** headings as capitalized strings centered on the page. Examples are shown in figures throughout this chapter.

As a general rule, hypertext documents should be broken up such that each page does not occupy more than one or two browser screen areas. Across the collection of pages, you can then use **H1** or **H2** elements to mark the main headings for the collection and **H3** and greater to mark subheadings. Using heading elements consistently across the documents makes it easy for a user (or indexing software) to distinguish the relative position of a section—or an entire document—with respect to the entire collection.

Heading elements support the standard "generic" and "event-handler" attributes described earlier in this chapter. Note that the event handlers are only partially supported by Internet Explorer 4 and are not supported by Netscape Navigator 4.

Headings also support an optional **ALIGN** attribute, which can take the values "left," "center," "right," and "justify." The value "left" left-justifies the title flush with the left margin (this is the default), while the value "right" flushes the title to the right window margin. The value "center" causes the heading to be centered on the display window. The value "justify" calls for text to be justified between the left and right margins, falling back to left alignment when the heading is too short—this alignment is not widely supported. Examples of aligned headings are shown throughout this chapter. Note that HTML 4 recommends using a style sheet, rather than the **ALIGN** attribute, to define alignment.

HR Element: Horizontal Rule

Usage:	`<HR>`
Can Contain:	empty
Can Be Inside:	**BLOCKQUOTE, BODY, CENTER, DD, DIV, *FIELD-SET*, FORM, LI, *NOFRAMES, NOSCRIPT*, TD, TH, APPLET, *BUTTON, IFRAME, OBJECT***
Attributes:	***CLASS, ID, STYLE, TITLE, standard event handlers***
	ALIGN, (**COLOR**: Internet Explorer only), **NOSHADE, SIZE, WIDTH**

The empty **HR** element draws a horizontal line across the screen and is often used to divide sections within a single document. An `<HR>` terminates any preceding paragraph, so a new paragraph mark should follow an `<HR>` if there is subsequent text that is part of a paragraph. One common design is to place an `<HR>` at the bottom of a document, followed by an **ADDRESS** element containing address information for the document maintainer or owner. This is illustrated in Figures 6.7 through 6.10.

HR supports the standard "generic" and "event-handler" attributes described earlier in this chapter. Note that the event handlers are only partially supported by Internet Explorer 4 and are not supported by Netscape Navigator 4.

HR also supports several other attributes that define formatting properties of the rule. These attributes are:

ALIGN="left," "right," "center" (optional) If an HR does not span the page, then it can, like a heading, be aligned on the page. The alignment is controlled by the ALIGN attribute, which can take the values "left," "right," or "center" (center is the default).

Figure 6.13 Example HTML document illustrating use of the DIV element.

```
<HTML><HEAD><TITLE>Example of DIV</TITLE></HEAD>
<BODY>
<DIV ALIGN="left">
   <H1>A Left-Aligned Heading</H1>
   <P>A left-aligned paragraph....If you actually read this
      example you will realize that that the author is a
      raving idiot.
    ... more paragraph text ...
   </P>
   <DIV ALIGN="right">
      <H2>A right-aligned heading</H2>
      <BLOCKQUOTE>
      <P>A paragraph inside a block quotation -- the entire
         quotation is right-aligned. Note, however, that this
         is a formatting issue, and not a political statement
         on the part of the author.</P>
      </BLOCKQUOTE>
   </DIV>
   <P>Another left-aligned paragraph. Again, this is not a
      political statement.<BR>
       ...
   </P>
</DIV>
<HR NOSHADE>
<DIV ALIGN="right">
<I>Another Incredible HTML Example!</I>
</DIV>
</BODY></HTML>
```

Figure 6.14 Rendering of the document listed in Figure 6.13 by the NetManage WebSurfer 5 browser.

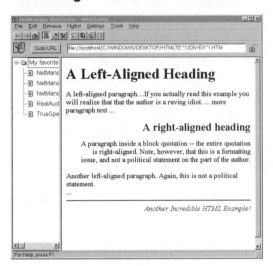

COLOR=*"#rrggbb"* or *"color"* (optional; Internet Explorer only) Specifies the desired color for the horizontal rule, either as an RGB color code or as a color name. If **COLOR** is specified, then the rule takes on this color uniformly and is not shaded.

NOSHADE (optional) By default, browsers usually render an **HR** as a shaded, chiseled bar drawn across the page. The attribute **NOSHADE** (which takes no value) indicates that the bar should be rendered in a solid color (usually black), with no shading.

SIZE=*"number"* (optional) Specifies, in pixels, the vertical thickness of the horizontal rule. The default is 2 pixels.

WIDTH=*"number," real%"* (optional) Specifies the horizontal width of the **HR** element. The form **WIDTH**=*"number"* specifies the absolute width in pixels (note that the displayed result will depend on the screen resolution of the display), while **WIDTH**=*"real%"* specifies the width as a percentage of the possible full width of a horizontal rule (e.g., **WIDTH**=*"80%"*).Note that percentage width is determined relative to the maximum allowed width, which depends on the location of the **HR**. For example, inside a **BLOCKQUOTE** or **TD** (table cell), the full width of an **HR** (**WIDTH**=*"100%"*) is limited by the width of the parent blockquote region, or the width of the parent table cell, respectively.

A style sheet can specify the alignment, size, and width of an **HR**: Thus the attributes **ALIGN**, **SIZE**, and **WIDTH** are marked as *deprecated* and should be avoided when possible.

P Element: Paragraphs

Usage:	`<P> ... (</P>)`
Can Contain:	characters, character highlighting, A, APPLET, *BASE-FONT*, BR, *BUTTON*, *IFRAME*, IMG, INPUT, *LABEL*, MAP, *OBJECT*, SCRIPT, SELECT, TEXTAREA
Can Be Inside:	ADDRESS, BLOCKQUOTE, BODY, ~~CENTER~~, DD, DIV, *FIELDSET*, FORM, LI, *NOFRAMES*, *NOSCRIPT*, TD, TH, APPLET, *BUTTON*, *IFRAME*, *OBJECT*
Attributes:	*CLASS*, *DIR*, *ID*, *LANG*, *STYLE*, *TITLE*, *standard event handlers*, ALIGN

P marks a paragraph block: `<P>` marks the start of a paragraph and ends any previous paragraph. This is different from **BR**, which represents a simple line break, possibly within a paragraph. A paragraph should be thought of as a logical block of text, similar to **BLOCKQUOTE**, **ADDRESS**, or **Hn** heading, whereas a **BR** is simply a "character" that causes a line break.

Typically, a paragraph is rendered with extra vertical space separating it from the previous and subsequent blocks of text. In some cases, the first line is indented.

For historical reasons, an end tag `</P>` is not required. Instead, the end of a paragraph is implied by the start of another paragraph or by the start of another element marking a block of text. However, an end tag definitively marks the paragraph end, and this is the recommended form.

P supports the standard "generic" and "event-handler" attributes described earlier in this chapter. Note that the event handlers are only partially supported by Internet Explorer 4 and are not supported by Netscape Navigator 4.

P can also take the optional **ALIGN** attribute to specify text alignment. The allowed values are "center," "left," "right," or "justify," which call for the indicated text alignment within the paragraph. Note that the "justify" alignment option (to justify the text between the left and right margins) is not widely supported.

HTML 4 recommends using a style sheet to specify text alignment within **P** elements.

Creating Extra Vertical Spacing

If you wish to leave extra vertical space, you should use a paragraph containing multiple `<BR>` tags—for example:

```
... text
<P> <BR><BR><BR>
<H2>Heading, with lots of space above it</H2>
```

You should *not* use empty paragraphs to add vertical spacing, as in:

```
....text
<P><P><P>
<H2> And another thing of Interest </H2>
```

NOTE: </p> Can Introduce Extra Vertical Space

Some browsers introduce extra vertical spacing after a paragraph ending with a `</P>`. For example, the markup

```
..... some text
<HR>
```

and

```
 ... some text </P>
<HR>
```

will be rendered differently: In the second example, there is extra space between the text and the **HR**. With Netscape Navigator 3/4 and Internet Explorer 3/4, this occurs when paragraphs are followed by **ADDRESS**, **HR**, **CENTER**, **DIV**, and **TABLE** elements. Internet Explorer 3 also leaves extra space in front of list elements, but Internet Explorer 4 does not.

Formally, a paragraph cannot be empty, so this is illegal. Most browsers will tolerate this, but their interpretations will vary—some will leave extra spaces, while most (Internet Explorer 3/4 and Netscape Navigator 3/4) ignore the extra `<P>` tags completely. The latter is formally the recommended behavior.

PRE Element: Preformatted Text

Usage:	`<PRE> ... </PRE>`
Can Contain:	characters, *ABBR*, B, *BDO*, CITE, CODE, DFN, EM, I, KBD, Q, ~~S~~, SAMP, SMALL, *SPAN*, ~~STRIKE~~, STRONG, TT, ~~U~~, VAR,
	A, BR, *BUTTON*, *IFRAME*, INPUT, *LABEL*, MAP, SCRIPT, SELECT, TEXTAREA
Can Be Inside:	BLOCKQUOTE, BODY, ~~CENTER~~, DD, DIV, *FIELD-SET*, FORM, LI, *NOFRAMES*, *NOSCRIPT*, TD, TH,
	APPLET, *BUTTON*, *IFRAME*, *OBJECT*
Attributes:	*CLASS, DIR, ID, LANG, STYLE, TITLE, standard event handlers,*
	(<u>COLS</u>, <u>WRAP</u>: Netscape Navigator only)

The **PRE** element marks text to be displayed with a fixed-width typewriter font. In particular, the **PRE** environment preserves the line breaks and space characters of the original text—this is the only HTML element that does so. **PRE** is therefore useful for presenting text that has been formatted for a fixed-width character display, such as a plain text terminal or for presenting program code or HTML markup examples that should be presented with a fixed-width font.

PRE supports the standard "generic" and "event-handler" attributes described earlier in this chapter. Note that the event handlers are only partially supported by Internet Explorer 4 and are not supported by Netscape Navigator 4.

PRE content is restricted to inline elements, with the exception of those inline elements that affect character font size or spacing (**BASEFONT, BIG, FONT, SMALL, SUP,** and **SUB**) or that insert arbitrary data (**APPLET, IMG, OBJECT**). Most browsers will allow these "forbidden" inline elements inside **PRE**, but the behavior is unpredictable.

An example of **PRE** is shown in Figures 6.15 and 6.16. Note the use of character highlighting. Character highlighting elements inside a **PRE** contribute zero character width.

Netscape Navigator supports two additional attributes, to control the rendering of **PRE** content. These attributes are defined in the following—note that these are nonstandard attributes and that equivalent formatting control is possible using style sheet instructions, as described in Chapter 7.

> COLS="*number*" (optional; Netscape Navigator 4 only) Specifies the maximum number of characters per line within the displayed **PRE**. If a line is longer than that specified by **COLS**, then the line is automatically wrapped. This attribute was introduced with Netscape Navigator 4 and does not work in earlier versions of the browser.

> WRAP (optional; Netscape Navigator) Enables word wrapping of the **PRE** element content—the default is to not allow word wrapping and to have **PRE** content extend past the edge of the browser window if the line is larger than the display region. If **WRAP** is present, then the text is automatically wrapped at the edge of the display area.

TIP: PRE Element—Things to Avoid

You cannot use elements that define paragraph formatting within the **PRE** element. This means you cannot use <P>, <ADDRESS>, <Hn>, and so on. You also cannot use <BR>. You should also avoid tab characters, since different browsers interpret the size of a tab differently. Instead, you should use space characters to control horizontal spacing.

TIP: Useful Features of PRE

You can use the **A** (anchor) element to create hypertext anchors inside **PRE**. You can also use the character highlighting elements (**STRONG**, **EM**, etc.), although these highlighting elements may be ignored by the browser if appropriate rendering is not possible.

Figure 6.15 HTML example document illustrating the use of the PRE element. Figure 6.16 shows this document as displayed by the Netscape Navigator browser.

```
<HTML>
<HEAD>
<TITLE> Example of the PRE Element </TITLE>
</HEAD>
<BODY>
<H1 ALIGN="center"> Example of the PRE Element</H1>
<P ALIGN="center"> <B><I>The PRE element is often used to
include blocks of plain text.  For example you can use it
to include examples of typed code, such as the following
extract from a C program:</I></B>
<HR>
<PRE>
/* main program for fitting program */

extern int *sharv;
static char boggle[100];

main (int argc, char *argv)
double x_transpose, y_transpose, f_ack=2.3;
{
   ....
</PRE>
<HR>
<P> PRE is also useful for simple tables, as in:
<PRE>
   Item          Price     Tax    Total        Category

   fileserver    10000     300    10300             <A HREF="cat_a.html">A</A>
   disk drive      900      30      930             <A HREF="cat_b.html">B</A>
  <STRONG>transmission</STRONG>     4400    110    4510            C
  <EM>fertilizer</EM>       5500    100    5600            F
</PRE>
The markup tags take up no space: if you delete everything alt the tags
inside the <B>PRE</B>, you will see that all the columns line up.
</BODY>
</HTML>
```

Figure 6.16 Display, by the Netscape Navigator 3 browser, of the document shown in Figure 6.15.

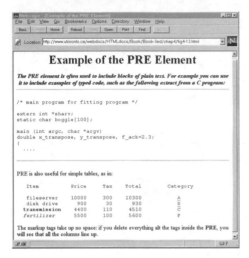

Fill-in Forms

HTML 3.2 supported interactive forms via the **FORM** element and the special elements **INPUT**, **SELECT**, **OPTION**, and **TEXTAREA**—these four elements define a form's user input mechanisms and can only appear inside a **FORM**. The **FORM** element, in turn, specifies how the data collected by the form should be encoded and where the encoded data should be sent.

Advanced FORMS: BUTTON, FIELDSET, LABEL, LEGEND, and OPTGROUP

HTML 4 introduced five new form-content elements—**BUTTON**, **FIELDSET**, **LABEL**, **LEGEND**, and **OPTGROUP**, plus several new attributes, to support improved rendering of form content and better control over the input mechanisms. These elements are not supported by Netscape Navigator 4, but are partially supported by Internet Explorer 4. Since this chapter focuses on generally supported HTML markup, discussion of these newer elements is deferred to Chapter 7.

Page Layout with INPUT Elements

A designer has little control over the look of these different form input elements: In general, the **FONT** element affects text-labeled input elements (**TYPE**="text," "password," buttons with text labels, or **TEXTAREA** elements) in very different ways, depending on the browser, as illustrated in Figures 6.17 and 6.18. Both Netscape Navigator 3 and Internet Explorer 3/4 ignore **FONT** or other text-highlighting elements surrounding form input elements (although, for some strange reason, the **SUP** element works with Navigator 3). With Navigator 4, however, these elements do affect the characteristics of the input elements, as shown at the bottom of Figure 6.18—note, however, that the browser miscalculates the size of the text input box when the **FONT** element changes the font face to a non-fixed-width font.

Alternatively, a cascading style sheet can set some of the display properties. An example is shown in Figures 6.19 and 6.20, where CSS rules are used to change the font size, family, and text color of text input elements and INPUT buttons. There are still important differences between the Netscape Navigator 4 and Internet Explorer 4 rendering of these elements, as shown in Figure 6.20: Only Internet Explorer can change the text color on buttons, while both browsers have trouble determining the correct width for text input regions. Note also that the default font for text input regions (**INPUT** or **TEXTAREA**) is Arial for Internet Explorer and Courier for Netscape Navigator.

FORM Element: Fill-in Forms

Usage:	`<FORM> ... </FORM>`
Can Contain:	ADDRESS, BLOCKQUOTE, ~~CENTER~~, ~~DIR~~, DIV, DL, *FIELDSET*, Hn, HR, [ISINDEX], ~~MENU~~, *NOFRAMES*, *NOSCRIPT*, OL, P, PRE, TABLE, UL,
	characters, character highlighting, A, APPLET, *BASE-FONT*, BR, *BUTTON*, *IFRAME*, IMG, INPUT, *LABEL*, MAP, *OBJECT*, SCRIPT, SELECT, TEXTAREA
Can Be Inside:	BLOCKQUOTE, BODY, ~~CENTER~~, DD, DIV, *FIELDSET*, LI, *NOFRAMES*, *NOSCRIPT*, TD, TH,
	APPLET, *IFRAME*, *OBJECT*
Attributes:	*CLASS, DIR, ID, LANG, STYLE, TITLE, standard event handlers,*
	onReset, onSubmit,
	ACCEPT-CHARSET, ACTION, ENCTYPE, METHOD, NAME, *TARGET*

FORM encompasses the content of an HTML *fill-in form*. This is the element you use to create fill-in forms containing checkboxes, radio boxes, text input windows, and buttons. Data from a **FORM** *must* be sent to server-side gateway programs for processing, since a **FORM** collects data, but does not process it. In general, a **FORM** and the server-side program handling the **FORM** output must be designed together so that the program understands the data being sent from the **FORM**. Some simple examples showing the variety of possible **FORM**s are shown in Figures 6.21 through 6.24. Note that **FORM**s do not nest—you *cannot* have a **FORM** within a **FORM**.

The **FORM** element takes three main attributes. These determine where the **FORM** input data is to be sent (**ACTION**); what HTTP protocol to use when sending the data (**METHOD**); and the data type of the content (**ENCTYPE**).

Figure 6.17 Document employing FONT and text highlighting elements to modify the presentation of form INPUT elements. See also Figure 6.18.

```
<HTML><HEAD>
<TITLE>Test of FONT and form INPUT Elements</TITLE>
</HEAD><BODY BGCOLOR="white">
<FORM ACTION="accesskey.htm">
<P><B>Three buttons: (1) Normal,  
     (2) Arial Font,     (3) Bold + Arial font,  
and (4) Superscript</B></P>

       <INPUT TYPE="button" NAME="y" VALUE="Button 1">
<FONT FACE="arial">
    <INPUT TYPE="button" NAME="y" VALUE="Button 2">
</FONT>
<FONT FACE="arial">
    <B><INPUT TYPE="button" NAME="y" VALUE="Button 3"></B>
</FONT>
   <SUP><INPUT TYPE="button" NAME="y" VALUE="Button 4"></SUP>
<BR>
<BR>
<INPUT TYPE="text" NAME="f"
       VALUE="12345678901234567890">        ... <B>Standard Text Box</B><BR>
<B><INPUT TYPE="text" NAME="f"
          VALUE="12345678901234567890"></B> ... <B>Boldface</B><BR>
<FONT FACE="arial" SIZE="+1">
    <INPUT TYPE="text" NAME="f"
          VALUE="12345678901234567890"></FONT>
                                        ... <B>Arial Font,
                                            SIZE="+1"</B><BR>
</FONT>
<FONT FACE="courier new" SIZE="-1">
    <INPUT TYPE="text" NAME="f"
          VALUE="12345678901234567890"></FONT>
                                        ... <B>Courier New Font,
                                            SIZE="-1"</B><BR>
</FORM>
</BODY></HTML>
```

Figure 6.18 Rendering by Netscape Navigator 3 (top), Internet Explorer 4 (middle), and Netscape Navigator 4 (bottom) of the document listed in Figure 6.17. Note how Internet Explorer 4 largely ignores HTML-based formatting when applied to form INPUT elements.

There are several additional attributes that provide additional functionality. All these attributes are described in the following:

ACCEPT-CHARSET=*"string"* (optional; not currently supported) Specifies the list of allowed character set encodings that the server, referenced by the **ACTION**, will accept. The value is a space- or comma-separated list of character set names—see Appendix A on the companion Web site for details on character set names and character encodings. The default value is "UNKNOWN," in which case the browser should encode data typed into the browser using the same character encoding used in the document containing the form. This attribute is not currently supported.

ACTION=*"url"* (mandatory) Specifies the URL to which the **FORM** content is to be sent. Usually this is a URL pointing to a program on an HTTP server, since only HTTP servers allow significant interaction between the client and the server. However, the **ACTION** can specify other URLs. For example, in the case of a **mailto** URL, the **FORM** content could be mailed to the indicated address. In this case, the **METHOD** must be set to "POST."

Action is formally mandatory, but if is omitted, some browsers (e.g., Netscape but not Internet Explorer) will attempt to recontact the URL

Figure 6.19 Document employing CSS rules to modify the presentation of form input elements. See also Figure 6.20.

```
<HTML><HEAD>
<TITLE>CSS Rules Applied to FORM Elements</TITLE>
<STYLE>
.b2 {font-family: Arial;          color: red}
.b3 {font-family: Arial;          font-weight: bold}
.t2 {font-weight: bold; }
.t3 {font-family: Arial;          font-size: 125%;}
.t4 {font-family: "courier new"; font-size: 75%}
</STYLE>
</HEAD>
<BODY BGCOLOR="white">
<FORM ACTION="accesskey.htm">

<INPUT TYPE="button" CLASS="b1" NAME="y" VALUE="Button 1">
<INPUT TYPE="button" CLASS="b2" NAME="y" VALUE="Button 2">
<INPUT TYPE="button" CLASS="b3" NAME="y" VALUE="Button 3">

<BR>
<BR>
<INPUT CLASS="t1" TYPE="text" NAME="f"
      VALUE="12345678901234567890">    ... <B>Standard Text Box</B><BR>
<INPUT CLASS="t2" TYPE="text" NAME="f"
      VALUE="12345678901234567890">    ... <B>Boldface</B><BR>
<INPUT CLASS="t3" TYPE="text" NAME="f"
      VALUE="12345678901234567890">    ... <B>Arial Font, and
                                             bigger </B><BR>
<INPUT CLASS="t4" TYPE="text" NAME="f"
      VALUE="12345678901234567890">    ... <B>Courier New Font,
                                             smaller </B><BR>
</FORM>
</BODY></HTML>
```

from which the document containing the form was retrieved and will use the specified **ENCTYPE** and **METHOD** to encode and send the data.

METHOD= "GET" or **"POST"** (optional) Specifies the **METHOD** for sending the data, the default value being GET. When **ACTION** indicates an **http** URL, the **METHOD** is just the HTTP *method* for sending information to the server. HTTP methods are discussed in Chapter 9. With GET, the content of the form is then appended to the URL in a manner similar to query data from an **ISINDEX** search (as discussed in Chapter

Figure 6.20 Rendering by Netscape Navigator 4 (top) and Internet Explorer 4 (bottom) of the document listed in Figure 6.19.

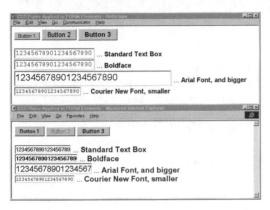

10). With the POST method, the data are sent to the server as a message body and encoded as specified by the **ENCTYPE** attribute value. The situation with **mailto** URLs is not fully specified—in practice you must specify **METHOD**="POST," and the data are sent as a mail message body and encoded as specified by **ENCTYPE**. Some browsers do not support **mailto** URLs in **FORM**s.

ENCTYPE= "*mime-type*" (optional) Specifies the MIME-type encoding used for data sent via the POST method. The default value is "application/x-www-form-urlencoded." The only other supported value is "multipart/form-data." These encoding formats are described in Chapters 8 and 9.

NAME= "*string*" (optional) Specifies a symbolic name by which the form can be addressed from within a script program. For example, if a **FORM** element has the attribute **NAME**="myForm," then this form can be referenced, from JavaScript, using the notation `document.myForm`. Note that JavaScript treats **NAME** values as case-sensitive, while VBScript treats these values as case-insensitive. **ID** values can in principle be used instead of **NAME**s; however, Netscape Navigator does not support **ID** values for this purpose.

TARGET="*string*" (optional) Specifies the name of the *frame* or window to which the data returned by the submitted form should be sent. This attribute is used to the same purpose with the **A** (anchor) element. Please see the anchor (**A**)element section for further details. This attribute is supported by all browsers that support **FRAMES**.

INPUT Element: Text Boxes, Checkboxes, and Radio Buttons

Usage:	`<INPUT>`
Can Contain:	empty
Can Be Inside:	ADDRESS, BLOCKQUOTE, BODY, CAPTION, ~~CENTER~~, DD, DIV, DT, *FIELDSET*, FORM, Hn, LI, *NOFRAMES*, *NOSCRIPT*, P, PRE, TD, TH,
	character highlighting, A, APPLET, *IFRAME*, *LABEL*, *LEGEND*, *OBJECT*
Attributes:	*CLASS, DIR, ID, LANG, STYLE, TITLE, standard event handlers,*
	onBlur, onChange, onFocus, onSelect,
	ACCEPT, ACCESSKEY, ALIGN, *ALT,* CHECKED, *DISABLED,* <u>HEIGHT</u>, <u>HSPACE</u>, MAXLENGTH, NAME, *READONLY,* SIZE, SRC, *TABINDEX,* TYPE, *USEMAP,* VALUE, <u>VSPACE</u>, <u>WIDTH</u>

INPUT specifies a variety of *editable fields* and is only allowed inside a **FORM**. It takes several attributes that define the type of input mechanism (text field, buttons, checkboxes, etc.), the *variable name* associated with the input data, and the alignment and size of the input element when displayed. Although the **INPUT** element can appear only inside a **FORM** many other elements (lists, blockquotes, etc.) are also allowed inside a **FORM** and can be used to structure **INPUT** elements into a well-organized interface. Some examples of **INPUT** elements, and the organization allowed by other elements are shown in Figures 6.21 through 6.24.

The most important attribute to the **INPUT** element is **NAME**, which assigns a *variable name* to the *value* entered into the element. The data entered into a **FORM** are sent to the server as a collection of strings of the form *name=value*, where *name* is the variable name and *value* is the value that is input or selected by the user (the *name* and *value* strings are encoded prior to being sent to the server, as discussed in Chapters 8 and 10). The program parsing the **FORM** data uses the variable *name* to interpret the contents of the corresponding *value* and must therefore understand the different *names*. For this reason, a **FORM** and the gateway program that handles the **FORM** data must be designed together.

The other main attribute is **TYPE**, which selects the type of the **INPUT** element. There are several other attributes, but their usage and relevance depends on the **TYPE**.

The attributes are:

ACCEPT = *"string"* (optional; valid with **TYPE**="file" only; not currently supported) Specifies a comma-separated list of MIME-types that are acceptable for input by **TYPE**="file" input elements. This proposed element is not widely implemented.

ACCESSKEY="*c*" (optional; Internet Explorer 4 only)   Specifies a typeable character that can be used to access the area. For example, three **INPUT** elements could be labeled, using **ACCESSKEY,** by the letters "a," "b," and "c." If the user then references the letter "b" on the keyboard (using some defined typing sequence), the browser will select the **INPUT** element with with **ACCESSKEY**="b." In the case of radio button or checkboxes, the browser will also change the state of the button or checkbox.

This functionality is supported by Internet Explorer 4—the labeled elements are accessed by typing ALT-*c*, where *c* is the letter assigned to the **ACCESSKEY** attribute, and ALT is the ALT key. Note that **ACCESSKEY** is also supported by **A** and **AREA** elements. This attribute is not supported on Netscape Navigator 4.

ALIGN="top," "middle," "bottom," "left," "right" (optional; **TYPE**="image" only)   Specifies the alignment of the element, for the case **TYPE**="image." The attribute values have the same meaning as for the IMG element, and you are referred there for details. This attribute has no effect on the element position for other input types.

ALT="*string*" (optional; **TYPE**="image" only; Internet Explorer 4 only) Specifies a short text description of the input image to be used by nongraphical browsers or as tool-tip (pop-up) help when the mouse is over of the image. This is supported by Internet Explorer 4—Netscape Navigator 4 displays the value of the **NAME** attribute as tool-tip help.

CHECKED (optional; **TYPE**="radio" or checkbox" only)   Specifies whether or not the radio button or checkbox is checked—this applies only to **TYPE**="radio" or **TYPE**="checkbox" input elements. Only one of a connected set of radio buttons should be checked. With linked radio buttons, the behavior if multiple buttons are "checked" is undefined—Netscape Navigator checks all the buttons, while Internet Explorer only checks the last element marked as **CHECKED.**

DISABLED (optional; Internet Explorer 4 only)   Disables user-control ofthe **SELECT** list. Also, the user cannot use the tab key to select this element. Last, the data content of the element is not sent when the form is submitted to a server. Note that disabling a single radio button does not disable any related radio buttons: To disable a collection of radio buttons, all buttons in the group must be marked **DISABLED.**

HEIGHT="*pixels*" (optional; **TYPE**="image" only)   Defines the height of the displayed image, in pixels. If the image is of a different size, it will be rescaled to fit the defined height. Authors should avoid resizing images, since this will distort the coordinates of the mouse pointer when the user clicks on top of the image.

HSPACE=*"pixels"* (optional; **TYPE**="image" only; Netscape Navigator only)   Defines a padding space, in pixels, to leave to the left and right of the image. This attribute applies only to elements of **TYPE**="image."

MAXLENGTH=*"number"* (optional; **TYPE**="text" or "password" only)   Specifies the length of the character buffer for a text box, where *number* is the buffer length. **MAXLENGTH** can be larger than the displayed text box, in which case, arrow keys may be used to scroll the text. The default buffer length is unlimited. **MAXLENGTH** simply restricts the maximum size of the string input by the user. This may also apply to **TYPE**="file," if the browser presents a type-in field for entering filename information. This is largely unimplemented.

NAME=*"string"* (mandatory for all **TYPE**s not equal to "reset") Associates the variable name *"string"* with the data content of this **INPUT** element. Values for this attribute are chosen by the document author, and should best be strings that logically relate to the purpose of the input quantity. If no name is entered, some browsers will ignore the associated data, while others will assume the name simply to be an empty string.

READONLY (optional; Internet Explorer 4 only)   As with **DISABLED**, this attribute disables user-control of the **TEXTAREA** content. However, in this case, the user can select the element using the tab key, and the element content is included when the form is submitted to a server. This attribute only applies to input elements of **TYPE**="text" or "password."

SIZE=*"number"* (optional; **TYPE**="text" or **TYPE**="password" only) Specifies, in characters, the actual size of the displayed text input field. This may also apply to **TYPE**="file," if the browser presents a type-in field for entering filename information.

SRC=*"url"* (mandatory; **TYPE**="image" only)   Specifies the URL of the image to be included *inline* and is valid only with **TYPE**="image."

TABINDEX=*"number"* (optional; Internet Explorer 4 only)   Specifies the *tabbing order* for the linked region. By default, a user can use the tab key to switch between the various anchor elements, active images, and **FORM** input elements, starting from the top of the document and working down. **TABINDEX** lets an author change this default order and explicitly set the order of tabbing: Tabbing is ordered from the smallest integer to the largest integer. Elements with negative tabbing indices are never accessed in the tabbing sequence. This is not supported on Netscape Navigator 4.

TYPE = "button," "checkbox," "file," "hidden," "image," "password," "radio," "reset," "submit," "text" (mandatory)   Determines the type of input element, from amongst a list of nine possible types. The meaning and function of these different types is given below. This is mandatory, although browsers will usually assume a default value, typically "text."

Definitions of Different TYPEs

TYPE="button"   Specifies an input button; the label of the element is obtained from the VALUE attribute value. *Button data are never sent when a FORM is submitted*—the button type is designed purely as an interface between **FORM** content and script programs within the HTML document containing the form. This is discussed in more detail in Chapter 7.

TYPE="checkbox"   The input element is a *checkbox*. A checkbox defines a Boolean (on/off) quantity, the default state of which is *off* (this is changed to *on* if a **CHECKED** attribute is present). **VALUE** sets the *value* assigned to an *on* checkbox. When you submit a **FORM,** the *name/value* pair is sent only if the checkbox is *on*. If there is no **VALUE** attribute to a **TYPE=**"checkbox" input element, then the browser uses the string "on" as the default value "on."

Different checkboxes may associate different *values* with the same variable *name*. This is convenient, for example, if you have six different databases to search and want to allow the user to select one, two, or all of them. When the **FORM** is submitted, the browser sends all the *values* from the *on* checkboxes, yielding several *name/value* pairs with the same *name*. An example is shown in Figure 6.21.

TYPE="file"   The **INPUT** element is a file-selection tool or widget, with which the user can select an arbitrary file to be sent to the server, as part of the submitted form data. This type is allowed only when the **FORM** element specifies **ENCTYPE=**"multipart/form-data." Note that this may cause problems if the **ACTION** indicates a **mailto** URL and if the file contains binary data: The encoding make no special provisions for binary data, and such data are often corrupted when sent by e-mail.

TYPE="hidden"   The **INPUT** element is not displayed to the user, although the content of a "hidden" element (set by the **NAME** and **VALUE** attributes) is always sent to the server when the **FORM** is submitted. This is useful for passing information back and forth between the client and server, and is typically used to record the state of the client-server interaction. Recall that the HTTP protocol is stateless, so that without such passed information, the gateway program handling the **FORM** data has no record of any past interaction. Thus, a "hidden" **INPUT** element is typically placed in a **FORM** by a server-side program

Figure 6.21 HTML example document illustrating several FORM INPUT elements and the SELECT element. Figure 6.22 shows this document as displayed by the Netscape Navigator 3 browser.

```
<HTML>
<HEAD>
<TITLE> Example of an HTML FORM </TITLE>
</HEAD>
<BODY>
<H1>HTML FORM Example </H1>
<BLOCKQUOTE>

<FORM  ACTION="http://side.edu/cgi-bin/script">

<P><B>Search String:</B> <INPUT TYPE="text" NAME="search_string" SIZE=24>
<P><B>Search Type:</B>
<SELECT NAME="search_type">
  <OPTION> Insensitive Substring
  <OPTION SELECTED> Exact Match
  <OPTION> Sensitive Substring
  <OPTION> Regular Expression
</SELECT>
<P><B> Search databases in:</B>
  [<INPUT TYPE="checkbox" NAME="servers" VALUE="Canada" CHECKED>Canada]
  [<INPUT TYPE="checkbox" NAME="servers" VALUE="Russia">Russia]
  [<INPUT TYPE="checkbox" NAME="servers" VALUE="Sweden">Sweden]
  [<INPUT TYPE="checkbox" NAME="servers" VALUE="U.S.A.">U.S.A.]
  <BR><SMALL><EM>Multiple items can be selected.)</EM></SMALL>
<P><B>Niceness: </B>
<MENU>
<LI> <INPUT TYPE="radio" NAME="niceness" VALUE="nicest" CHECKED > Nicest
<LI> <INPUT TYPE="radio" NAME="niceness" VALUE="nice" >   Nice
<LI> <INPUT TYPE="radio" NAME="niceness" VALUE="not nice"> Not Nice
<LI> <INPUT TYPE="radio" NAME="niceness" VALUE="nasty" >  Nasty
</MENU>
<P> <INPUT TYPE="submit" NAME="sub" VALUE="Start Search">
    <INPUT TYPE="reset" VALUE="Reset Form">

</FORM>
</BLOCKQUOTE>
<HR>
<ADDRESS>  Form by <A HREF="about_the_author.html"> I.S.G</A> </ADDRESS>
</BODY> </HTML>
```

Figure 6.22 Display of the document shown in Figure 6.21 by the Netscape Navigator 3 browser.

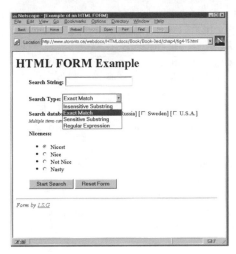

that assembles the **FORM**. This is discussed in more detail in Chapters 10 and 11.

TYPE="image"   The **INPUT** element is an inline active image (analogous to an **ISMAP** active **IMG** element). The **SRC** attribute specifies the URL of the image to include.

Clicking on the image immediately submits the **FORM** data, including the coordinates of the mouse pointer (measured in pixels from the upper left-hand corner of the image). The coordinates are sent in two name/value pairs. The name is created by taking the **NAME** attribute and appending the strings ".x" and ".y" to indicate the x or y coordinate. Thus, if the **NAME** is "king," the coordinates are sent as the name/value pairs `king.x=xval` and `king.y=yval`, where `xval` and `yval` are the pixel coordinates selected by the user.

TYPE="object" (Netscape Navigator 4 only) The **INPUT** element references a *JavaBean* object that will pass data to the form for inclusion in the form message. The **NAME** attribute then corresponds to the **ID** attribute of an existing JavaBean object previously created using an **OBJECT** element. When the form is submitted, the data sent by the object are included with the form and are associated with the specified **NAME**. Note that the connection between the **OBJECT** and the form is managed using Netscape's *LiveConnect* extensions to JavaScript.

TYPE="password"   The **INPUT** element is a single-line text field, but the text typed into the field is obscured by asterisks or by some other method. This is used for password entry. An example password field is shown in Figures 6.23 and 6.24.

TYPE="radio"   The **INPUT** element is a radio button. Radio buttons are only meaningful when there are multiple buttons taking the same **NAME** attribute value. Sharing a common **NAME** links the buttons together, such that when a user selects or turns on one of the radio buttons, all other buttons associated with the same **NAME** are automatically turned off. Thus, only one button can be selected at a time. Each radio button must have a value, so that every **INPUT** element of **TYPE=**"radio" must have a **VALUE** attribute. However, if a value is left off, the browser will assume a default value, typically the string "on."

TYPE="reset"   The **INPUT** element is a reset button. When this element is selected, all the fields in the **FORM** are reset to the values given by their respective **VALUE** attributes, thereby erasing all user input. **RESET** can itself have a **VALUE** attribute, the value of which is used as the button label. Data from **TYPE=**"reset" buttons are never sent to the server when the form is submitted.

TYPE="submit"   The **INPUT** element is a submit button. Pressing the submit button sends the **FORM** data to the specified URL. A form can have more than one such button, each with different **NAME** and **VALUE** attributes: The **FORM** sends only the name/value pair associated with the pressed submit button. The value is displayed as the button label.

NOTE: Possible INPUT Element Problems with Older Browsers

Some older browsers do not support multiple submit buttons with different name/value pairs. Also, Netscape Navigator 2, as well as early versions of Internet Explorer 3, do not support the **TYPE=**"file" input element.

TYPE="text"   The **INPUT** element is a single-line text entry field. The **SIZE** attribute determines the width of the input box, in characters—the default value is typically 20.

Note that with Netscape Navigator 3, you *cannot* use FONT elements to change the font size or font family of text displayed within form input elements (buttons or text input); However, with Netscape Navigator 4 or Internet Explorer 4, you can use either **FONT** or style sheets to modify the font style, size, or color of the text within the input field, to a limited degree. Please see Chapter 7 for details.

USEMAP="*url*" (optional; valid only with **TYPE=**"image"; not currently supported)   Specifies a URL referencing a **MAP** element. When the user presses on the mapped image, the browser uses the MAP element to select a URL and sends the form content to the specified URL using the method indicated by the **FORM** element **METHOD** attribute. This is not supported on current browsers.

VALUE=*"string"* (mandatory with **TYPE**="radio")   Specifies the initial value of the input element. If absent, a null value is assumed. This is a mandatory attribute for **TYPE**="radio" input elements.

VSPACE=*"pixels"* (optional; valid only with **TYPE**="image"; Netscape Navigator only)   Specifies the space to be left above and below the image, in pixels.

WIDTH=*"pixels"* (optional; valid only with **TYPE**="image")   Defines the width of the image, in pixels. If the image is of a different size, it will be rescaled to fit the defined width. Authors should avoid resizing images, since this will distort the coordinates of the mouse pointer when the user clicks on top of the image.

Figures 6.21 through 6.24 give typical examples of **INPUT** element usage. **FORM**s are also discussed in Chapters 2 and 10.

SELECT Element: Select from Among Multiple Options

Usage:	`<SELECT> ... </SELECT>`
Can Contain:	*OPTGROUP*, OPTION
Can Be Inside:	ADDRESS, BLOCKQUOTE, BODY, CAPTION, ~~CENTER~~, DD, DIV, DT, *FIELDSET*, FORM, Hn, LI, *NOFRAMES*, *NOSCRIPT*, P, PRE, TD, TH,
	character highlighting, A, APPLET, *IFRAME*, *LABEL*, *LEGEND*, *OBJECT*
Attributes:	*CLASS, DIR, ID, LANG, STYLE, TITLE, standard event handlers,*
	onBlur, onChange, onFocus, (<u>onSelect</u>: Internet Explorer 4)
	DISABLED, MULTIPLE, NAME, SIZE, *TABINDEX*

SELECT contains a list of selectable string values, the *values* of which are specified by **OPTION** elements lying within the **SELECT**. A browser provides a way for the user to select from amongst these values: for example, a selectable list or pull-down menu. The attribute **MULTIPLE** permits selection of multiple values; otherwise, only one value can be chosen. As with **INPUT** elements, the selected data are sent as *name/value* pairs. The attributes are:

DISABLED (optional; Internet Explorer 4 only)   Disables user-control of the **SELECT** list. Also, the user cannot use the tab key to select this element. Furthermore, the data content of the element is not sent when the form is submitted to a server. This is currently only supported by Internet Explorer 4.

MULTIPLE (optional)   Allows the user to select multiple items from a single **SELECT** element. If **MULTIPLE** is absent, the user can select only a single item.

NAME=*"string"* (mandatory)   Specifies the variable name associated with the **SELECT** element.

SIZE=*"number"* (optional)   Specifies the number of displayed text lines to be presented. The default value is 1 and, consequently, a list is often presented as a pull-down menu. For other values, the list is usually presented as a scrollbox. If **MULTIPLE** is present, browsers choose a default **SIZE** greater than 1 (so that multiple selections are possible) and will not permit a smaller value, regardless of the value assigned to **SIZE**.

TABINDEX=*"number"* (optional; Internet Explorer 4 only)   Specifies the *tabbing order* for the linked region. By default, a user can use the tab key to switch between the various anchor elements, active images, and **FORM** input elements, starting from the top of the document and working down. **TABINDEX** lets an author change this default order and explicitly set the order of tabbing. Tabbing is ordered from the smallest integer to the largest integer. Elements with negative tabbing indices are never accessed in the tabbing sequence. This attribute is not supported on Netscape Navigator 4.

Figures 6.23 and 6.24 show typical examples of **SELECT** (and **OPTION**) elements.

OPTION Element: List of Options for SELECT

Usage:	`<OPTION> ... (</OPTION>)`
Can Contain:	**characters**
Can Be Inside:	*OPTGROUP*, SELECT
Attributes:	*CLASS, DIR, ID, LANG, STYLE, TITLE, standard event handlers*,
	DISABLED, LABEL, SELECTED,VALUE,

OPTION sets the character-string options for a **SELECT** element. This element is not empty, but the terminating `</OPTION>` is optional, as the element is by default terminated by the next `<OPTION>` tag or by the `</SELECT>` tag ending the list. **OPTION** can contain characters, character references, or entity references only; it cannot contain markup. The content of **OPTION** is used as the *value* unless a **VALUE** attribute is explicitly set. In addition to the "generic" and "event handler" attributes, **OPTION** supports the following attributes:

DISABLED (optional; not currently supported) Disables user-control of the **OPTION**. Also, the user cannot use the tab key to select this element. Furthermore, the data content of the element is not sent when the form is submitted to a server. Please see Chapter 7 for a detailed discussion of **DISABLED**.

LABEL="*string*" (optional; not currently supported) When **OPTGROUP** elements break a **SELECT** list into a hierarchical menu, then the regular label for the list item (set by the content of the element) may be too long. Thus, if hierarchical menus are used, the browser can use the value of the **LABEL** attribute to label each of the options, instead of the element content. **LABEL** is only relevant for **OPTION** elements inside an **OPTGROUP**. **OPTGROUP** is not currently supported.

SELECTED (optional) This marks the **OPTION** as selected—by default, items are not selected. If the **SELECT** element has the **MULTIPLE** attribute, more than one **OPTION** can be marked as **SELECTED**. Figures 6.23 and 6.24 show examples. **SELECTED** items can be deselected by the user. Consequently, **SELECTED** is often used to set default selection values.

VALUE= "*value*" (optional) Specifies the *value* assigned to the **OPTION**. If **VALUE** is absent, then the text content of **OPTION** is used as the value.

TEXTAREA Element: Text Input Region

Usage:	`<TEXTAREA> ... </TEXTAREA>`
Can Contain:	**characters**
Can Be Inside:	**ADDRESS, BLOCKQUOTE, BODY, CAPTION,** ~~**CENTER**~~**, DD, DIV, DT,** *FIELDSET*, **FORM, Hn, LI,** *NOFRAMES, NOSCRIPT*, **P, PRE, TD, TH,**
	character highlighting, A, APPLET, *IFRAME, LABEL, LEGEND, OBJECT*
Attributes:	*CLASS, DIR, ID, LANG, STYLE, TITLE, standard event handlers,*
	onBlur, onChange, onFocus, onSelect
	COLS, *DISABLED*, **NAME,** *READONLY*, **ROWS,** *TABINDEX*, <u>WRAP</u>

TEXTAREA provides a mechanism for the user to input a block of text. Usually this is done by providing a text input window. The text input by the user can grow to almost unlimited size, and is not limited, either horizontally or vertically, by the size of the displayed input window. Scrollbars are often presented if the text entered into a **TEXTAREA** grows to be (or initially is) bigger than the displayed region.

Figure 6.23 HTML example document illustrating FORM INPUT, SELECT, and TEXTBOX input elements. Figure 6.24 shows this document as displayed by the Netscape Navigator 3 browser.

```
<HTML><HEAD><TITLE> HTML FORM Example (2)</TITLE></HEAD>
<BODY>

<H2>HTML FORM Example (2) </H2>
<P>Submit your abstract for registration in the appropriate databases.
<FORM  ACTION="http://side.edu/cgi-bin/submit_abstract">
<B>1. Please give Name and Password </B>
<BLOCKQUOTE>
   <B>Name:</B>      <INPUT TYPE="text"     NAME="userid" VALUE="guest" SIZE=20>
   <B>Password:</B> <INPUT TYPE="password" NAME="password" VALUE="bozo..." SIZE=8>
</BLOCKQUOTE>
<B>2. Select Appropriate Database(s)</B> <BR>
<BLOCKQUOTE>
    <B>Physics: </B>
     <SELECT NAME="physics_database" MULTIPLE SIZE=3>
        <OPTION SELECTED> Condensed-Matter
        <OPTION> High Energy
        <OPTION> Solid-State
        <OPTION> Quantum Cosmology
        <OPTION> Astrophysics
    </SELECT>
    <B>Chemistry: </B>
    <SELECT NAME="chemistry_database" MULTIPLE SIZE=3>
        <OPTION> Surface Dynamics
        <OPTION> Quantum Chemistry
        <OPTION SELECTED> Polymer Dynamics
        <OPTION> Biochemistry
        <OPTION> Nuclear Chemistry
    </SELECT>
</BLOCKQUOTE>
<B>3. Enter Abstract: </B>
<BLOCKQUOTE>
    <TEXTAREA NAME="abstract" COLS=50 ROWS=4>
If you are submitting an abstract, select the
desired databases from the above list, delete
this text, type (or paste) the abstract into
this box and press the "Deposit Abstract" button.
    </TEXTAREA>
</BLOCKQUOTE>
```

Figure 6.23 *Continued.*

```
<B>4. Submit Form or Reset --</B>
<INPUT TYPE="submit" NAME="depo" VALUE="Deposit Abstract">
<INPUT TYPE=reset VALUE="Reset Form">
</FORM>
<HR>
<ADDRESS>  Form by <A HREF="about_the_author.html"> I.S.G</A> </ADDRESS>
</BODY></HTML>
```

Figure 6.24 Display of the document shown in Figure 6.23 by the Netscape Navigator 3 browser.

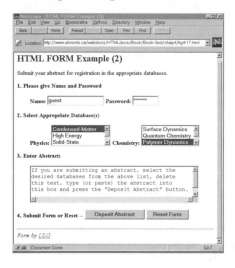

The size of a **TEXTAREA** is set by the **COLS** and **ROWS** attributes (the default size in the absence of these attributes is browser-specific). Since **TEXTAREA** windows usually display characters using a fixed-width font, **COLS** specifies the input box width as a number of characters, while **ROWS** specifies the height as the number of displayable text rows. **TEXTAREA** input can include any printable characters: The **TEXTAREA** data are simply characters to be sent elsewhere. Thus a person typing text into a **TEXTAREA** can in principle send an entire HTML document to a server by typing (or cutting and pasting) the document into the **TEXTAREA**.

By default, text in a **TEXTAREA** does not wrap—lines can be as long as desired, with line wrapping only occurring at carriage returns explicitly typed in by the user. In some cases, it is more convenient if the **TEXTAREA** element itself automatically wraps the text, either virtually (the lines are displayed with wrapping, but the software-imposed new-line characters are not sent as part of the **TEXTAREA** data) or physically (the new-line characters introduced by the **TEXTAREA** formatting are sent as part of the **TEXTAREA** data). Netscape Navigator supports a special **WRAP** attribute that allows for these options.

The attributes are:

COLS=*"number"* (mandatory)   Specifies the display width of a **TEXTAREA,** in columns.

DISABLED (optional; Internet Explorer 4 only)   Disables user-control of the **TEXTAREA** content. Also, the user cannot use the tab key to select this element. Furthermore, the data content of the element is not sent when the form is submitted to a server. Please see Chapter 7 for a detailed description of **DISABLED.**

NAME=*"string"* (mandatory)   Specifies the variable name associated with **TEXTAREA** contents.

READONLY (optional; Internet Explorer 4 only)   As with **DISABLED,** this attribute disables user-control of the **TEXTAREA** content. However, in this case, the user can select the element using tab key, and the element content is included when the form is submitted to a server. Please see Chapter 7 for a detailed description of **READONLY.**

ROWS=*"number"* (mandatory)   Specifies the display height of a **TEXTAREA,** in rows.

WRAP="off," "soft," "hard" (optional)   Specifies the handling of word-wrapping within the **TEXTAREA** element. **WRAP**="off" disables word-wrapping completely—the only new-line characters are those explicitly typed or included with the input data. **WRAP**="soft" causes virtual word-wrapping—new-line characters are introduced to ensure that the text fits within the specified area, but these characters are *not* included with the data when the **FORM** is submitted. According to the Netscape specifications, **WRAP**="hard" should cause word-wrapping equivalent to **WRAP**="soft," but in this case the extra new-line characters should be included with the data when the **FORM** is submitted. The default behavior is **WRAP**="off."

Text placed inside a **TEXTAREA** element is displayed as an initial value: A browser provides some way to edit the displayed text. Note that HTML markup tags are not interpreted inside a **TEXTAREA**, and are displayed as plain text. However, entity and character references inside a **TEXTAREA** element *are* interpreted and are converted to their respective characters prior to being displayed.

Figures 6.23 and 6.24 show a typical example of a **TEXTAREA** element.

Lists and List-Related Elements

There are two broad categories of list elements. Description lists (DL) define glossary-like lists, and can only contain two elements: DT (description term) and DD (the description). Regular lists define numbered or bulleted items. There are four regular list elements—DIR, MENU, OL, and UL. These elements can contain one thing: LI elements, which define the items within the list.

NOTE: Avoid DIR and MENU Lists

In HTML 4, the elements **DIR** and **MENU** are marked as deprecated and are likely to be dropped in a future version of HTML. You should thus avoid **DIR** and **MENU** and use **UL** lists instead.

The list elements support nesting of lists: DD and LI elements can contain any of the list element types, in addition to regular block elements such as paragraphs or tables.

DL Element: Glossary List

Usage:	`<DL> ... </DL>`
Can Contain:	DT, DD
Can Be Inside:	BLOCKQUOTE, BODY, ~~CENTER~~, DD, DIV, *FIELD-SET*, FORM, LI, *NOFRAMES*, *NOSCRIPT*, TD, TH, APPLET, *BUTTON*, *IFRAME*, *OBJECT*
Attributes:	*CLASS, DIR, ID, LANG, STYLE, TITLE, standard event handlers*
	COMPACT

This list type, known as a definition or glossary list, is designed for a list of items each with an associated, descriptive paragraph. This can be used, for example, for traditional glossaries. A DL list can contain two elements:

- DT—The *term* being defined
- DD—The *definition* of the term

Logically, DT and DD elements should appear in pairs. However, the specification does not require this, so that you can have DT and DD elements in any order you like. In general, DT elements are rendered flush with the left margin, while DD elements are placed one line below the DT and slightly indented.

In addition to the standard attributes, DL can take the optional attribute COMPACT, to signify that the list should be rendered in a physically compact way—this attribute takes no value. This is useful for compacting a list of small items or to compact a large list that would be easier to read if rendered in a compact manner. This tends to close up text, for example by placing the **DT** and **DD** text content on the same line. **COMPACT** is understood by Netscape Navigator 3/4 and Internet Explorer 4.

Figures 6.25 and 6.26 show an example of a **DL** list, and illustrate the effect of **COMPACT** on list rendering.

Figure 6.25 HTML example document illustrating the DL glossary list elements, and a UL unordered list nested inside a glossary list. Figure 6.26 shows this document as displayed by Internet Explorer 4.

```
<HTML> <HEAD><TITLE> Example of Glossary List elements </TITLE>
</HEAD><BODY BGCOLOR="white">
<H2> Example Glossary Lists </H2>

<P>The third <B>DD</B> has an unordered (<B>UL</B>) list inside it.
Note that the first term (<B>DT</B>) does not have a matching
description (<B>DD</B>). This is perfectly legal.
You can use <B>BR</B> elements to add extra vertical spacing --
here it is done after the first <B>DT</B>.</P>
<HR NOSHADE>
<DL>
   <DT>Things to do: <BR><BR>
   <DT>Things to Avoid:
   <DD>Writing examples for HTML books that make you look like an
        idiot!  In particular, spelling your wife's name incorrectly
        is not a good idea.
   <DT>Things to worry about:
   <DD>People you should never let format lists include:
        <UL>
           <LI>Bozo the Clown
           <LI>Uncle Fester
           <LI>Knights that go nii
        </UL>
        as they generally do a poor job.
</DL>
<HR NOSHADE>
<TABLE CELLPADDING="3" CELLSPACING="6"WIDTH="100%">
<TR><TD BGCOLOR="#dddddd" VALIGN="top" WIDTH="50%">

<H3>A Simple DL List</H3>
<DL>
   <DT>Etc.      <DD>Et Cetera
   <DT>HTTP      <DD>HyperText Transfer Protocol
```

Figure 6.25 *Continued*.

```
    <DT>HTML      <DD>HyperText Markup Language
</DL>


</TD><TD  BGCOLOR="#dddddd" VALIGN="top" WIDTH="50%">


<H3>Same List -- With <B>COMPACT</B></H3>
<DL COMPACT>
    <DT>Etc.      <DD>Et Cetera
    <DT>HTTP      <DD>HyperText Transfer Protocol
    <DT>HTML      <DD>HyperText Markup Language
</DL>


</TD></TR></TABLE></BODY></HTML>
```

Figure 6.26 Display, by Internet Explorer 4, of the document shown in Figure 6.25.

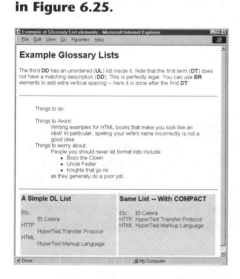

DT Element: Term in a Glossary List

Usage:	`<DT> ... (</DT>)`
Can Contain:	characters, character highlighting, A, APPLET, *BASEFONT*, BR, *BUTTON*, *IFRAME*, IMG, INPUT, *LABEL*, MAP, *OBJECT*, SCRIPT, SELECT, TEXTAREA
Can Be Inside:	DL

Attributes: *CLASS, DIR, ID, LANG, STYLE, TITLE, standard event handlers*

The **DT** element contains the term part of a glossary or description list entry. The contents of a **DT** element should be short—typically, a few words, and certainly shorter than a line. The element can contain standard character markup, images, line breaks, and hypertext anchors, as well as form input elements.

The **DT** element is not empty, but the terminating </DT> is optional, as it is implied by the start of another <DT> or <DD> element or by the </DL> ending the list.

DD Element: Description in a Glossary List

Usage: <DD> ... (</DD>)

Can Contain: ADDRESS, BLOCKQUOTE, ~~CENTER~~, ~~DIR~~, DIV, DL, *FIELDSET*, FORM, Hn, HR, [ISINDEX], ~~MENU~~, *NOFRAMES, NOSCRIPT*, OL, P, PRE, TABLE, UL,

characters, character highlighting, A, APPLET, *BASEFONT*, BR, *BUTTON, IFRAME*, IMG, INPUT, *LABEL*, MAP, *OBJECT*, SCRIPT, SELECT, TEXTAREA

Can Be Inside: DL

Attributes: *CLASS, DIR, ID, LANG, STYLE, TITLE, standard event handlers*

The **DD** element gives the description corresponding to the previous **DT** element or elements. It can be a long description, broken into paragraphs and containing other lists, **FORM**s, quotations, and so on. A **DD** element should follow a **DT** element and should not occur alone.

Most browsers render **DD** content a line below and slightly indented relative to the **DT** content. This may be changed if the **DL** element took the **COMPACT** attribute—in this case, the **DD** content may be tab-indented relative to the **DT** content, and on the same line.

DD is not empty, but the terminating </DD> is optional, since the end is implied either by the <DT> or <DD> tag starting another element or by the </DL> tag terminating the list.

OL Element: Ordered List

Usage: <OL> ... </OL>

Can Contain: LI

Can Be Inside: BLOCKQUOTE, BODY, ~~CENTER~~, DD, DIV, *FIELD-SET*, FORM, LI, *NOFRAMES, NOSCRIPT*, TD, TH,

	APPLET, *BUTTON, IFRAME, OBJECT*
Attributes:	CLASS, *DIR, ID, LANG, STYLE, TITLE, standard event handlers,*
	COMPACT, START, TYPE

OL defines an ordered list. Each item in the list is contained within an LI (list item) element— LI elements are the *only* elements that can appear inside OL. Items can be paragraphs of text, but should be kept reasonably short, as otherwise, the idea of a list is lost. If the list items are big, perhaps it is not really a list: Try paragraphs with appropriate section headings. A typical ordered list is shown in Figures 6.27 and 6.28.

A browser indicates item ordering by numbering the items, by assigning them ascending letters, et cetera. OL can take three attributes: COMPACT to render the list in compact format, and TYPE and START to control how items are numbered and ordered.

COMPACT (optional)   Indicates that the list should be rendered in a compact format, for example by reducing the space between items or by arranging the items horizontally across the display. This attribute is not widely supported.

START="*number*" (optional)   Specifies the starting number for the first item in the list, where *number* is an integer specifying the starting number.

TYPE="A," "a," "I," "i," "1" (optional)   Specifies the type of the marker by which the items should be numbered. Thus, TYPE="A" and TYPE="a" imply ordering via capital or lowercase letters respectively, while TYPE="I" and TYPE="i" imply ordering with uppercase or lowercase roman numerals respectively. TYPE="1" invokes standard numerical ordering and is the default.

UL Element: Unordered List

Usage:	<UL> ... </UL>
Can Contain:	LI
Can Be Inside:	BLOCKQUOTE, BODY, ~~CENTER~~, DD, DIV, *FIELDSET,* FORM, LI, *NOFRAMES, NOSCRIPT,* TD, TH,
	APPLET, *BUTTON, IFRAME, OBJECT*
Attributes:	CLASS, *DIR, ID, LANG, STYLE, TITLE, standard event handlers,*
	COMPACT, TYPE

UL defines an unordered list of items; a graphical browser will present each list item with a special leading symbol, such as a bullet or asterisk. Each *item* in a UL list is contained within an **LI** (list item) element—LI elements are the *only* things that can appear inside a UL. Items can be paragraphs of text, but should be kept reasonably short; otherwise, the idea of a list is lost. If the list items are big, perhaps it is not really a list: Try paragraphs with appropriate section headings.

The **UL** element can take two optional attributes, namely:

COMPACT (optional)   Requests that the list be presented in a compact way, for example, by reducing whitespace between list entries. This attribute is not widely supported.

TYPE="circle," "disc," "square" (optional)   Specifies the desired type of bulleting symbol. The allowed values are **TYPE**="disc" (for a small circular disc), **TYPE**="circle" (for a small open circle), or **TYPE**="square" (for a small square). The default value varies, depending on the level of the list: Most browsers use different symbols for list items nested inside other list items.

Figures 6.27 to 6.30 show examples of unordered lists.

Figure 6.27 HTML example document illustrating UL and OL lists and the nesting of list elements. Figure 6.28 shows this document as displayed by the Internet Explorer browser.

```
<HTML>
<HEAD>
<TITLE> Example of Regular List elements </TITLE>
</HEAD>
<BODY>
<H2> Examples of Regular Lists </H2>
<H3> Ordered Lists </H3>
<P>This shows an ordered list, with another ordered list nested
   within it.
<OL>
  <LI>First item -- items can contain images, blockquotes, and
      other lists, among other things
  <LI>A Second item in the list
  <LI VALUE="6">And a third item (but a <B>VALUE</B> attribute sets it
to numeral 6). And now.... a nested ordered list, with the type
attribute <B>TYPE</B>="i":
      <OL TYPE="i" START="2">
```

Figure 6.27 Continued.

```
        <LI>The first sub-item
        <LI>The second sub-item, and so on.....
    </OL>
</OL>
<H3> Unordered Lists </H3>
<P>This examples illustrates and unordered list containing another
unordered list.
<UL>
   <LI>A list item
   <LI>Another list item; again these can contain IMG elements,
       paragraphs, and so on
   <LI>List items can also contain lists, for example:
       <UL>
        <LI TYPE="circle">An item in the list
        <LI TYPE="square">Something else that is
            important, and so on
       </UL>
       Which is simply a list within a list
</UL>
</BODY> </HTML>
```

Figure 6.28 Display, by the Internet Explorer 3 browser, of the document shown in Figure 6.27.

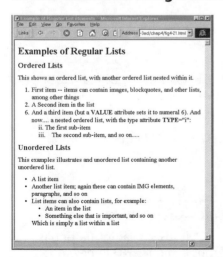

DIR Element: Directory List

Usage:	`<DIR> ... </DIR>`
Can Contain:	LI
Can Be Inside:	BLOCKQUOTE, BODY, ~~CENTER~~, DD, DIV, *FIELDSET*, FORM, LI, *NOFRAMES*, *NOSCRIPT*, TD, TH, APPLET, *BUTTON*, *IFRAME*, *OBJECT*
Attributes:	*CLASS, DIR, ID, LANG, STYLE, TITLE, standard event handlers,* COMPACT

NOTE: DIR To Be Dropped from HTML—Use UL Instead

The **DIR** element is to be dropped from HTML, as similar formatting is possible using the **UL** element. You should thus avoid **DIR** in new documents, in favor of **UL** lists.

DIR defines a directory list—a list of short items, each usually no more than about 20 characters. If possible, a browser may display the items in columns across the screen, rather than one above the other (most browsers do not do this, however, and format **DIR** and **UL** lists identically). Each item in a **DIR** list is contained within an **LI** (list item) element—**LI** elements are the *only* things that can appear inside a **DIR** list. An example of a directory list is shown in Figures 6.29 and 6.30.

MENU Element: Menu List

Usage:	`<MENU> ... </MENU>`
Can Contain:	LI
Can Be Inside:	BLOCKQUOTE, BODY, CENTER, DD, DIV, *FIELDSET*, FORM, LI, *NOFRAMES*, *NOSCRIPT*, TD, TH, APPLET, *BUTTON*, *IFRAME*, *OBJECT*
Attributes:	*CLASS, DIR, ID, LANG, STYLE, TITLE, standard event handlers,* COMPACT

NOTE: MENU To Be Dropped from HTML—Use UL Instead

The **MENU** element is to be dropped from HTML, as similar formatting is possible using the UL element. You should thus avoid **MENU** in new documents, in favor of **UL** lists.

MENU defines a list of short menu items, each item preferably less than a sentence long. **MENU** is designed to work like **UL** but to be formatted in a more compact manner similar to a `<UL COMPACT>` list, except that formatting may be optimized to favor short list items (most browsers do not do this, however, and format **MENU** and **UL** lists identically). Each item in a **MENU** list is contained within an **LI** (list item) element—**LI** elements are the *only* things that can appear inside a **MENU** list. Figures 6.29 and 6.30 give an example of a **MENU** list.

Figure 6.29 HTML example document illustrating the MENU and DIR lists. Figure 6.30 shows this document as displayed by the Netscape Navigator browser.

```
<HTML><HEAD>
<TITLE> More Examples of Regular Lists </TITLE>
</HEAD>
<BODY>
<H2 ALIGN="center"> Lists, Lists and Yet More Lists </H2>

<H3> Regular UL Lists </H3>
<UL>
    <LI>A list item.
    <LI>another list item
    <LI>and still more items
    <LI>What ... still more?
</UL>
<HR SIZE="5" WIDTH="20%">
<H3> DIR Lists </H3>
<DIR>
    <LI>Abraham - Carbon
    <LI>Cardshark - Elegant
    <LI>Elegiac - Food
    <LI>Foot - Hogs
</DIR>
<HR SIZE=5 WIDTH="20%">
<H3> MENU Lists </H3>
<MENU>
    <LI>First item    <LI>Second item
    <LI>Third item    <LI>Fourth item
</MENU>
</BODY></HTML>
```

Figure 6.30 Display of the document shown in Figure 6.29 by the Netscape Navigator 3 browser. Note how the UL, MENU, and DIR lists are rendered in the same way. Very few browsers distinguish between these three list types. MENU and DIR are deprecated elements and shoud not be used in new documents.

LI Element: List Item

Usage:	`<LI> ... (</LI>)`
Can Contain:	ADDRESS, BLOCKQUOTE, ~~CENTER~~, ~~DIR~~, DIV, DL, *FIELDSET*, FORM, Hn, HR, [ISINDEX], ~~MENU~~, *NOFRAMES*, *NOSCRIPT*, OL, P, PRE, TABLE, UL,
	characters, character highlighting, A, APPLET, *BASEFONT*, BR, *BUTTON*, *IFRAME*, IMG, INPUT, *LABEL*, MAP, *OBJECT*, SCRIPT, SELECT, TEXTAREA
Can Be inside:	~~DIR~~, ~~MENU~~, OL, UL
Attributes:	*CLASS, DIR, ID, LANG, STYLE, TITLE, standard event handlers,*
	TYPE, VALUE

LI marks a list item within DIR, MENU, OL, or UL lists. The item can contain text, character markup, and hypertext anchors, as well as subsidiary lists and text blocks.

LI supports two attributes for defining the type of the bullets in unordered lists, and for controlling numbering in ordered lists. These are:

TYPE="disc," "circle," "square" (within **UL** unordered lists), or "I," "i," "A," "a," "1" (within **OL** ordered lists)   Defines the type of marker to use with the item. Within unordered lists, the values "disc," "circle," and "square" produce closed discs, open circles, and squares respectively. In ordered lists, "I" and "i" produced uppercase and lowercase roman numerals respectively; "A" and "a" produce upper- and lowercase alphabetized lists respectively; and "1" produces numbered lists. Note that selecting a **TYPE** for a list item sets this type for all subsequent list items, unless another **TYPE** attribute is present.

NOTE: TYPE Not Supported on Internet Explorer 3

Internet Explorer 3 does not support **TYPE** attributes for **LI** elements inside **UL**, **MENU**, or **DIR** lists.

VALUE="*number*" (optional; valid only inside **OL** lists)   Sets the numeric counter for the current list item, where *number* is an integer. Thus **VALUE**=5 sets the current list item to be item number 5. Subsequent numbered items are incremented from this value. This attribute has no meaning inside **UL** lists.

Some example list items are shown in Figures 6.27 and 6.30.

Tables and Tabular Structures

The HTML **TABLE** element, and the elements allowed inside **TABLE** are used to define tables or other tabular structures. This first section gives an overview of the table model and introduces some of the basic elements. The next two sections describe additional details and features, as well as more advanced aspects of the table specification.

The design of HTML **TABLE**s will be familiar to those who have used tabular environments in typesetting languages such as LaTeX. A table is defined as a collection of *cells*, where a cell is simply an item (a box) within the table. For regular tables, the content of a cell might be a number, a word, or a small image. However, the HTML table model allows paragraphs, headings, blockquotes, and even other tables within a table cell, so that **TABLE** is not limited to describing ordinary tabular structures. Indeed, **TABLE** is commonly used to create multicolumn text, sidebar notes within multi-column tables, and so on. Some examples of these uses are illustrated in the next few paragraphs.

Individual table cells are specified using the **TD** (table data) and **TH** (table header) elements, which contain the contents of a cell. Cells are, in turn, organized into *rows*, each row defined by a **TR** (table row) element—a table row can contain any number of **TD** and **TH** elements. However, the **TD** and **TH** cells in every row of a given table must sum to the same number of *columns*, otherwise the table will not align vertically. Thus, if the first row contains two **TD** and two

TH elements (by default, each cell spans one column), then every other row in the table must also contain cells that span four columns.

Finally, a table can take an optional caption, via the **CAPTION** element.

The following small, captioned table has four rows, each row containing three cells, each cell spanning one column. This table is shown in Figures 6.31 and 6.32.

```
<TABLE BORDER>
<CAPTION>Here is the caption to this exciting table</CAPTION>
  <TR>  <th> Heading 1 </th>   <th> Heading 2 </th>    <th> Heading 3</th> </TR>
  <TR>  <td> item 1    </td>  <td> item 2    </td>   <td> item 3   </td> </TR>
  <TR>  <td> item 4    </td>  <td> item 5    </td>   <td> item 6   </td> </TR>
  <TR>  <td> item 7    </td>  <td> item 8    </td>   <td> item 9   </td> </TR>
</TABLE>
```

Note how each row contains three cells, defined either by **TH** header or **TD** data cells. In this example the first row contains the three headings, while subsequent rows contain data.

Multirow or Multicolumn Table Cells

Tables are made somewhat more interesting by letting a **TH** or **TD** cell occupy more than one row or column. This is accomplished through two special attributes. The **ROWSPAN** attribute specifies how many *rows* are occupied by a cell, counting down from the cell, while the **COLSPAN** attribute specifies how many *columns* are occupied by a cell, counting to the right. A multicolumn or multirow cell means that some **TR** row definitions will contain fewer **TD** or **TH** items in the row than you might expect, since some of the cells are occupied by the cell "hanging down" from the row above or pushing over from the cell to the left. It is the table designer's responsibility to make sure that all the items in a row sum to the correct number of columns.

The use of **ROWSPAN** and **COLSPAN** is shown in the following markup (the table cell tags are highlighted in boldface) and is also illustrated in Figures 6.31 and 6.32.

```
<TABLE BORDER>
<TR>
    <TH COLSPAN="2"> Heading 1                  </TH>    <TH> Heading 3</TH>
</TR>
<TR>
    <TD ROWSPAN="2"> item 1 </TD>   <TD> item 2 </TD>   <TD> item 3   </TD>
</TR>
<TR>
                                     <TD> item 4 </TD>   <TD> item 5   </TD>
</TR>
<TR>
    <TD> item 6            </TD>   <TD> item 7 </TD>   <TD> item 8   </TD>
</TR>
```

```
<TR>
    <TD> item 9            </TD>   <TD ROWSPAN=2 COLSPAN=2> item 10   </TD>
</TR>
<TR>
    <TD> item 1            </TD>
</TR>
<TR>
    <TD COLSPAN=3> a big wide item 11                                </TD>
</TR>
</TABLE>
```

The first row indicates that this table has three columns; the first **TH** cell spans two of these columns, so that there are only two **TH** elements in this row. The second row contains the required three cells, but the **ROWSPAN**="2" attribute in the first cell indicates that this cell spans two rows and, hence, hangs down into the next row. Consequently, there are only two cells declared in the third row, since the first column is occupied by the cell that started in the preceding row.

The fourth row is a regular row with three single-column and single-row cells. The fifth row, however, contains only two cells; the second of these occupies two rows and two columns. Consequently, the sixth row contains only one cell, as the second and third columns are occupied by the two-column-wide cell hanging down from row 5. Finally, the last row contains a single cell that spans the entire table (**COLSPAN**="3").

The last examples are shown in Figures 6.33 and 6.34. These show some convenient uses of tables, such as for boxing images and text and creating double-column text. Although the latter looks quite nice here, just imagine how it would look with a larger font size or a smaller display window!

Figure 6.31 HTML example document illustrating the TABLE elements. See Figure 6.32, which shows this document as displayed by the Internet Explorer browser.

```
<HTML><HEAD>
<TITLE> HTML TABLEs </TITLE>
</HEAD><BODY>

<H2 ALIGN="center"> HTML Tables</H2>
<P> The following two examples look at basic HTML tables.
<H3> First Example -- A Simple Table </H3>
<TABLE BORDER>
 <TR>  <TH> Heading 1 </TH>  <TH> Heading 2 </TH>  <TH> Heading 3 </TH> </TR>
  <TR>  <TD> item 1    </TD>  <TD> item 2    </TD>  <TD> item 3    </TD> </TR>
```

Continued

Figure 6.31 Continued.

```
 <TR>  <TD> item 4    </TD>  <TD> item 5    </TD>  <TD> item 6    </TD> </TR>
 <TR>  <TD> item 7    </TD>  <TD> item 8    </TD>  <TD> item 9    </TD> </TR>
</TABLE>
<HR NOSHADE>
<H3>Second Example with COLSPAN and ROWSPAN </H3>

<TABLE BORDER ALIGN="right">
<CAPTION>Here is the caption to this exciting table</CAPTION>
 <TR>  <TH COLSPAN=2> Heading 1                </TH>  <TH> Heading 3</TH> </TR>
 <TR>  <TD ROWSPAN=2> item 1</TD>  <TD> item 2 </TD>  <TD> item 3   </TD> </TR>
 <TR>                              <TD> item 4 </TD>  <TD> item 5   </TD>
</TR>
 <TR>  <TD> item 6    </TD>  <TD> item 7 </TD>  <TD> item 8    </TD> </TR>
 <TR>  <TD> item 9    </TD>  <TD ROWSPAN=2 COLSPAN=2> item 10  </TD> </TR>
 <TR>  <TD> item 1    </TD>
</TR>
 <TR>  <TD COLSPAN=3> a big wide item 11  </TD>                      </TR>
</TABLE>
</BODY></HTML>
```

Figure 6.32 Display, by the Internet Explorer 3 browser, of the document shown in Figure 6.31.

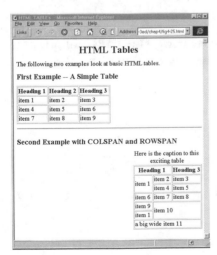

Figure 6.33 A second HTML example document illustrating the TABLE elements. Figure 6.34 shows this document as displayed by the NetManage WebSurfer 5 browser.

```
<HTML><HEAD>
<TITLe> HTML TABLEs (part 2)</TITLE>
</HEAD><BODY>
<H2 ALIGN="center"> More Table Examples</H2>

<H3>First Example: Images in Tables</H3>
<TABLE BORDER=5 CELLSPACING=5 CELLPADDING=10>
<TR><TD>
    <IMG SRC="./logo.gif" ALT="[Information Commons Logo]" ><BR>
</TD><TD>
    <H2 ALIGN="center">The Information Commons
    <BR><EM>at the</EM>
    <BR>University of Toronto </H2>
</TD></TR>
</TABLE>

<H3 ALIGN="center">Second Example: Text in two columns</H3>
<TABLE CELLPADDING=5>
<TR> <TD>
  <P> Here is the first column of text. This could go on, and on, and on
  and on, and on, and on, which is to say that I have completely lost any
  any sense of what to type for these examples. Oh, I know --
  how about throwing in a list:
  <UL>
    <LI> here's a nice item
    <Li>and here's another
  </UL>
  <P> But that's enough, now for the second column.
</TD><TD>
  <P> Here we go with the second column. This column sits nicely next to
  the other one, and is separated by the invisible cell border. Cells can
  contain all sorts of markup elements, so you can create very sophisticated
  things inside these cells, such as:
  <H3>Heading</H3>
  <P> If a browser does not understand tables, then this will be presented as
  a single page of single-column text: this is one example where things will
  still be readable, even if the browser does not understand tables.
</TD></TR>
</TABLE>
</BODY> </HTML>
```

Figure 6.34 Display, by the NetManage WebSurfer 5 browser, of the document shown in Figure 6.33.

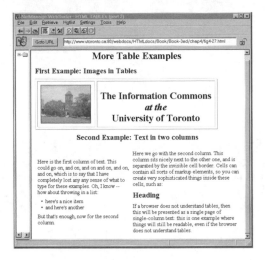

Table Presentation: Borders, Spacings, and Colors

The display and rendering of tables can be controlled through several **TABLE** attributes. The universally supported attributes are **BORDER, CELLSPACING,** and **CELLPADDING**, which specify, in pixels, the border width, the cell dividing line width (width between cells), and the padding space within table cells (between the cell content and the cell edges), respectively. Most browsers also support a **BGCOLOR** attribute, which specifies a background color for the table cells. With Netscape Navigator, this does not change the color of the table border or the space between the cells, which retains the background color of the display. With Internet Explorer, **BGCOLOR** colors both the cell content and the dividers between the cells. However, Internet Explorer supports some proprietary attributes that can directly control the color of the cell and table borders; these attributes, described later, are not supported by other browsers.

Internet Explorer 3/4 and Netscape Navigator 4 also support a (nonstandard) **BACKGROUND** attribute, which takes a URL value that references an image file—this image is used as a background for the table content. Note, however, that Netscape Navigator 4 tiles each cell with a new copy of the background image, whereas Internet Explorer tiles the entire background of the table. This difference is illustrated in Figures 6.35 and 6.36, which show the rendering, by Netscape Navigator 4 (top) and Internet Explorer 4 (bottom), of a 3-by-3 table with a background image. Note how Internet Explorer tiles the whole background space of the table, while Netscape restarts the tiling within each cell. Note also that Netscape does not tile the background behind the cell borders, and also does not apply background tiling to "empty" cells: The bottom right-hand cell in the HTML table is empty.

Figure 6.35 Example document illustrating the TABLE element BACK-GROUND attribute. Rendering of this document by Netscape Navigator 4 and Internet Explorer 4 is shown in Figure 6.36.

```
<HTML><HEAD>
<TITLE>Test of TABLE BACKGROUND Attribute</TITLE>
</HEAD>
<BODY BGCOLOR="white">

<TABLE  BACKGROUND="maptest.gif"        WIDTH="100%"
        CELLSPACING="5" CELLPADDING="5" BORDER="3">
<TR>
   <TD HEIGHT="40" WIDTH="33%">  <BR>     </TD>
   <TD HEIGHT="40" WIDTH="34%">      </TD>
   <TD HEIGHT="40" WIDTH="33%">      </TD>
</TR>
 <TR>
   <TD HEIGHT="40">                  <BR>     </TD>
   <TD HEIGHT="40">                      </TD>
   <TD HEIGHT="40">                      </TD>
</TR>
 <TR>
   <TD HEIGHT="40">                  <BR>     </TD>
   <TD HEIGHT="40">                           </TD>  <!-- EMPTY CELL -->
   <TD HEIGHT="40">                      </TD>
</TR>
</TABLE>
</BODY></HTML>
```

Figure 6.36 Browser renderings of tables with a BACKGROUND attribute applied to TABLE. The top shows the results with Netscape Navigator 4, and the bottom shows the result with Internet Explorer 4.

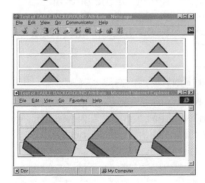

The HTML 4 specifications recommend against using the **BGCOLOR** (or **BACKGROUND**) attributes, and suggests instead that authors use cascading style sheets to specify these properties of tables or table cells. Unfortunately, with Netscape Navigator 4, CSS does not work properly with table elements, so it is best, for the present, to use attributes.

Table Cells: Backgrounds and Cell Content Alignment

The alignment of data within table cells can be controlled using the **ALIGN** (horizontal alignment) and **VALIGN** (vertical alignment) attributes. These attributes are supported by **TD** and **TH** elements, as well as **TR** elements; in the latter case, the alignment is applied to all cells in the row. However, any attribute specified in a **TR** element can be overridden by a value specified in a **TD** or **TH.** Thus you can use **TR** attributes to describe overall row properties and attributes within each **TD** or **TH** to set properties specific to a cell. The allowed values for these elements are described later.

The **TD** and **TH** elements can also take an optional **NOWRAP** attribute, which indicates that text lines within a cell may not wrap—the browser cannot introduce line breaks between words. This can cause odd-looking tables and should be used with caution!

Most browsers support a **BGCOLOR** attribute for the **TR, TH,** and **TD** elements to specify the background color for a cell or group of cells. In addition, Internet Explorer 3 and Netscape Navigator 4 support a **BACKGROUND** attribute for specifying a background image for a row (**TR**) or a table cell (**TD** and **TH**). Note, however, that Internet Explorer 4 supports **BACKGROUND** only for **TD** and **TH,** but not **TR.** A background image or color applied to a specific cell is painted on top of any background image or color set for the row, which is in turn painted on top of any background or color set for the entire table (set in the **TABLE** element).

There are some important differences between the different browser's renderings of table cell background colors, as illustrated in Figures 6.37 and 6.38. Figure 6.37 contains a simple table with a background color and with no drawn borders (**BORDER="0"**). Figure 6.38 shows the rendering of this table by Netscape Navigator 4 and Internet Explorer 4. Note how Netscape does not color the spacing between the cells or the single empty cell (middle of the bottom row), while Internet Explorer does. If you wish to create tables that reproduce the Netscape-style transparent borders, then you must apply the background color to each of the cells and not to the **TABLE** element.

NOTE: Differences in Background Color Renderings

When **BGCOLOR** is applied to the **TABLE** element, Internet Explorer colors cell content as well as the spacing between cells, whereas Netscape Navigator colors only the cell content and leaves the boundary regions untouched. Also, Internet Explorer colors empty cells (cells containing only whitespace characters), whereas Netscape Navigator does not color empty cells.

Internet Explorer 3 and 4 support some proprietary attributes for more refined control of cell border color. These attributes are discussed later in this section.

Cell Heights and Widths

By default, a browser chooses cell heights and widths according to a table-generation algorithm, which tries to find an optimal, minimum size for the table. Often, however, an author desires specific control over the layout of the table; for example, he or she may want a particular cell to occupy 50% of the entire table width or a group of columns to all be of the same width. Or, there may be a need for a column with an explicit absolute width, in pixels.

Cell widths can, to some degree, be controlled by the **WIDTH** attribute. This attribute can in principle specify the width in three ways: absolute width (pixels), percentage width (percentage of total table width), and relative width (width relative to other cells in the table). Cell heights are specified by the **HEIGHT** attribute, which takes as a value the height, in pixels, for the cell. Some examples of the use of these attributes are shown in Figures 6.39 and 6.40. The specification for the allowed values (and their meanings) are:

> **HEIGHT**=*"number"* (optional)   Specifies, in pixels, the height of the cell. Note that all cells in a row must have the same height, so that if more than one cell in a row takes a **HEIGHT** attribute, the largest value will be applied to all cells in the row.

> **WIDTH**=*"number," "real%," "real*"* (optional; The form *"real*"* is not currently supported)   Specifies the width of a cell. Note that all cells in a column must have the same width, so that if more than one cell in a column takes a **WIDTH** attribute, the largest resulting width is applied to all cells in the column. The value *"number"* specifies an absolute cell width, in pixels, while the value *"real%"* specifies the width as a percentage of the entire table width. Here, *real* is a decimal or integer value (e.g., 1, or 1.5), but not an exponential quantity. If you specify widths for all cells in a row, be careful that the sum for all cells adds up to 100%. The value *"real*"* defines the cell width relative to other cells in the table, the default relative width value being 1. Note, however, that the *"real*"* notation is not supported by current browsers.

Advanced Tables—Border Layout Control

The HTML development process has proposed several extensions to **TABLE**s, several of which are implemented on the Internet Explorer 3 and 4 browser. Notable among these extensions are the additional **TABLE** element attributes **FRAME** and **RULES**. **FRAME** specifies how the external border of the should be rendered (all borders, or only some of them), while **RULES** specifies how the internal borders between cells should be drawn. The use of these attributes is illustrated in Figures 6.41 and 6.42. The **RULES** attribute uses structural information about the table to

Figure 6.37 A simple HTML document illustrating table background colors. The rendering by Internet Explorer 4 and Netscape Navigator 4 browsers is shown in Figure 6.38.

```
<HTML><HEAD><TITLE>Test of Table BGCOLOR Properties</TITLE></HEAD>
<BODY BGCOLOR="white">

<TABLE  BGCOLOR="#cccccc"  WIDTH="100%"
         CELLSPACING="5"    CELLPADDING="5" BORDER="0">

<TR ALIGN="center" VALIGN="center">
    <TD  HEIGHT="40" WIDTH="33%">    1  </TD>
    <TD  HEIGHT="40" WIDTH="34%">    2  </TD>
    <TD  HEIGHT="40" WIDTH="33%">    3  </TD>
</TR>

<TR ALIGN="center" VALIGN="center">
    <TD HEIGHT="40" WIDTH="33%">     4  </TD>
    <TD HEIGHT="40" WIDTH="34%">     5  </TD>
    <TD HEIGHT="40" WIDTH="33%">     6  </TD>
</TR>

<TR ALIGN="center" VALIGN="center">
    <TD HEIGHT="40" WIDTH="33%">     7  </TD>
    <TD HEIGHT="40" WIDTH="34%">        </TD>     <!-- EMPTY CELL -->
    <TD HEIGHT="40" WIDTH="33%">     9  </TD>
</TR>

</TABLE>
</BODY></HTML>
```

decide where to draw dividing lines—this extra structural information is provided by the **TBODY**, **TFOOT**, and **THEAD** elements, which divide the rows into body rows (the table body), footer rows (the table footer), and header rows (the table header), as well as the **COL** and **COLGROUP** elements, which group columns rather than rows. The function of these newer elements is described in the next section. Their use is illustrated in Figures 6.41 and 6.42.

Advanced Tabular Structure

In the simple table model, a **TABLE** contains just **TR** (table rows) elements and optionally a **CAPTION**. In the advanced table model, a **TABLE** instead contains **THEAD**, **TFOOT**, and **TBODY** elements, which in turn group **TR** elements into a table header (**THEAD**), body (**TBODY**), and footer (**TFOOT**). Also, the **TABLE**

Figure 6.38 Rendering, by the Netscape Navigator 4 and Internet Explorer 4 browsers, of the document listed in Figure 6.37.

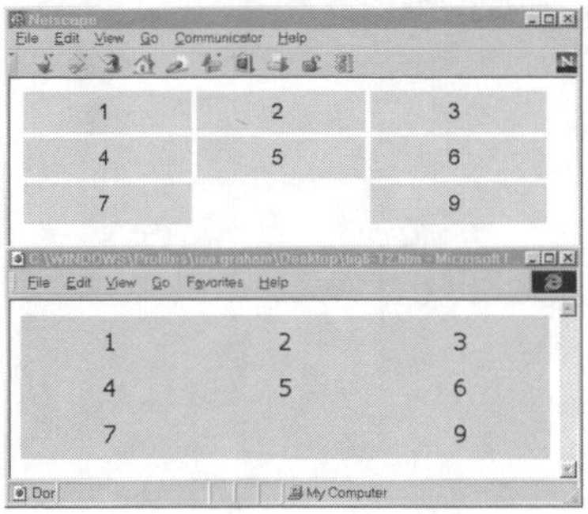

element can contain **COL** and **COLGROUP** elements, which define properties, such as cell alignments and/or widths, for individual columns (**COL**) or groups (**COL-GROUP**) of columns. **COL** and **COLGROUP** elements must precede all table rows, headers, or footers, since the program rendering the table must know this column-specific information before it begins formatting the table. These elements are illustrated in the example tables in Figures 6.41 and 6.42. At present these elements are only supported by Internet Explorer 3 and 4—not by Netscape Navigator 4.

The **THEAD**, **TFOOT**, **TBODY**, **COL**, and **COLGROUP** elements can all take alignment, background color, and other properties to define how the associated cells should be formatted. It is thus important to know how to handle cases where a cell is affected by formatting specifications coming from one or more of these elements. For example, should an alignment specified by a **COL** element override that specified by a **TFOOT**?

Internet Explorer 4, the only browser to support these elements, uses the following rules:

1. Use the value set by an element inside the table cell (e.g., a **P** or a **DIV**).

2. If the above does not set a value, then use the value set by a **TD** or **TH**.

3. If the above does not set a value, then use the value set by a **TR**.

4. If the above does not set a value, then use the value set by a **THEAD**, **TBODY**, or **TFOOT**.

5. If the above does not set a value, then use the value set by a **COL**.

6. If the above does not set a value, then use the value set by a **COLGROUP**.

7. If the above does not set a value, then use the value set by **TABLE**.

8. If the above does not set a value, then use the default value, which may depend on language.

Figure 6.39 Example tables illustrating use of HEIGHT, WIDTH, ALIGN, and BGCOLOR attributes. The rendering of this document by the Netscape Navigator browser is shown in Figure 6.40.

```
<HTML><HEAD>
<TITLE> HTML TABLEs (part 3)</TITLE>
</HEAD><BODY>
<H2 ALIGN="center"> Yet More Table Examples</H2>

<H3>Simple Table</H3>
<TABLE BORDER=2>
<TR>
    <TD>Item 1
    <TD>A
    <TD>Item 3 is much longer than the other items
</TR>
<TR>
    <TD>Fred
    <TD>B
    <TD>Wilma!
</TR>
</TABLE>

<H3>Same Simple Table with WIDTH, HEIGHT, ALIGN and BGCOLOR</H3>
<TABLE BORDER=2>
<TR>
    <TD WIDTH="20%">Item 1
    <TD WIDTH="20%">A
    <TD WIDTH="190">Item 3 is much longer than the other items
</TR>
<TR>
    <TD HEIGHT="80" VALIGN="top">Fred
    <TD ALIGN="middle" BGCOLOR="#bbbbbb">B
    <TD VALIGN="bottom">Wilma!
</TR>
</TABLE>

<H3>Another Simple Table with Table Alignment</H3>

<DIV>In this case, the simple table is right-aligned: consequently
<TABLE BORDER=0 BGCOLOR="#dddddd" ALIGN="right" VSPACE="5" HSPACE="5">
<TR>
    <TD ALIGN="center"><B><I>NOTE!</I></B>
</TR>
```

Figure 6.39 *Continued*.

```
<TR>
   <TD>My Dog Has Fleas!
</TR>
</TABLE>
the text flows around the table, just as it can flow around
left or right-aligned images. This is very useful for embedding
text in the document the text relates with, and is also
useful for embedding notes, sidebars, etc. within regular
text.
</DIV>
</BODY> </HTML>
```

Figure 6.40 Display, by the Netscape Navigator 3 browser, of the document listed in Figure 6.39.

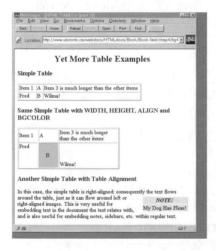

The HTML 4 specifications specify slightly different rules for setting cell content properties—these rules are summarized in Table 6.9. Some of these attributes (**LANG, DIR, STYLE**) were described earlier in this chapter, while the **CHAR** and **CHAROFF** properties are described a bit later. Note that **LANG, DIR, CHAR**, and **CHAROFF** are not supported by Internet Explorer 4.

TABLE Element: Tables and Tabular Structures

Usage: `<TABLE> ... </TABLE>`

Can Contain: CAPTION, *COL, COLGROUP, TBODY, TFOOT, THEAD*, TR

Table 6.9 HTML 4 Rules for Determining Formatting Properties for Table Cell Content (Differences between the left and right-hand rules are noted in italics. Note that Internet Explorer 4 uses the left-hand rules for all supported properties, as discussed in the text.)

ALIGN (also, CHAR, CHAROFF)	VALIGN (also LANG,DIR, STYLE)
1. The value set by an element inside the table cell (e.g., a **P** or a **DIV**).	1. The value set by an element inside the table cell (e.g., a **P** or a **DIV**).
2. The value set on a **TD** or **TH** element.	2. The value set on a **TD** or **TH** element.
3. *The value set by a* **TR**, *THEAD, TBODY, or TFOOT element.*	3. *The value set by a* **COL** *or* **COLGROUP**.
4. *The value set by a* **COL** *or* **COLGROUP**.	4. *The value set by a* **TR**, *THEAD, TBODY, or TFOOT element.*
5. The value set by the **TABLE**.	5. The value set by the **TABLE**.
6. The default value, which may depend on language.	6. The default value, which may depend on language.

Can Be Inside: BLOCKQUOTE, BODY, ~~CENTER~~, DD, DIV, *FIELD-SET*, FORM, LI, *NOFRAMES, NOSCRIPT*, TD, TH, APPLET, *BUTTON, IFRAME, OBJECT*

Attributes: *CLASS, DIR, ID, LANG, STYLE, TITLE, standard event handlers,*

ALIGN, <u>BACKGROUND</u>, *BGCOLOR*, BORDER, CELLPADDING, CELLSPACING, *FRAME*, <u>HEIGHT</u>, <u>HSPACE</u>, *RULES, SUMMARY*, <u>VSPACE</u>, WIDTH,

(<u>BORDERCOLOR</u>, <u>BORDERCOLORDARK</u>, <u>BORDERCOLORLIGHT</u>: Internet Explorer only)

TABLE specifies a table or other tabular structure. A basic **TABLE** can only contain two elements: a single **CAPTION**, to define a table caption, and one or more **TR** elements, which define the table rows. The **TR** element, in turn, can contain **TD** (table data) and **TH** (table header) elements that contain the actual content of the table. The construction of tables, using this model, is discussed later in the **TD** and **TH** sections.

Internet Explorer supports the more advanced HTML 4 table model, which includes extra elements for grouping rows into the table header (**THEAD**), body (**TBODY**), and footer (**TFOOT**). In addition, the **COLGROUP** and **COL** elements permit grouping of columns: for example, to assign them common properties (widths, alignment, borders). These newer elements are compatible with the older

Figure 6.41 Example HTML table illustrating the use of COL and COLGROUP elements and the FRAME and RULES attributes to the TABLE element. The rendering of this document by the Internet Explorer browser is shown in Figure 6.42.

```
<HTML><HEAD>
<TITLE> Advanced HTML TABLEs -- HEAD, FOOT and COL Elements</TITLE>
</HEAD><BODY>

<H3>Example Table</H3>
<TABLE ALIGN="center" WIDTH="80%" BORDER="2">
<THEAD>
    <TR><TH ROWSPAN=2>                  </TH>
        <TH ROWSPAN=2>Heading1        </TH>
        <TH ROWSPAN=2>Heading2        </TH>
        <TH COLSPAN=2> Main Heading </TH>
    </TR>
    <TR><TH>Subhead1                   </TH>
        <TH>Subhead2                   </TH>
    </TR>
</THEAD>
<TBODY>
  <TR><TH>Title1 </TH>
       <TD>Item 1 </TD>    <TD>Item2     </TD>
       <TD>Item 3 </TD>    <TD>  SubT-1 </TD>
  </TR>
  <TR><TH>Title2 </TH>
       <TD>Item 5 </TD>    <TD>Item6     </TD>
       <TD>Item 7 </TD>    <TD>  SubT-2 </TD>
  </TR>
</TBODY>
<TFOOT>
  <TR><TH>MAIN-T </TH>
       <TD>MAIN-A </TD>    <TD>MAIN-B    </TD>
       <TD>MAIN-C </TD>    <TD> SubMAIN </TD>
  </TR>
</TFOOT></TABLE>

<H3>Same Table, With:</H3>
<UL><LI><B>COL</B>,<B>COLGROUP</B>, <B>THEAD</B> etc., elements
     <LI><B>TABLE</B> element <B>FRAME</B> and <B>RULES</B> Attributes</UL>
```

Continued

Figure 6.41 Continued.

```
<TABLE FRAME="hsides" RULES="groups"
       ALIGN="center" WIDTH="80%" BORDER="2">
<COLGROUP>
  <COL ALIGN="left" BGCOLOR="#cccccc">   <!-- Column background color -->
</COLGROUP>
<COLGROUP>                                <!-- Group columns for rules -->
  <COL SPAN="2" ALIGN="middle">
  <COL ALIGN="center">
</COLGROUP>
<COLGROUP>
  <COL ALIGN="right">
</COLGROUP>
<THEAD>
   <TR><TH ROWSPAN=2>               </TH>
       <TH ROWSPAN=2>Heading1      </TH>
       <TH ROWSPAN=2>Heading2      </TH>
       <TH COLSPAN=2> Main Heading </TH>
   </TR>
   <TR><TH>Subhead1                </TH>
       <TH>Subhead2                </TH>
   </TR>
</THEAD>
<TBODY BGCOLOR="yellow">                  <!-- Color for table body    -->
  <TR><TH>Title1 </TH>
      <TD>Item 1 </TD>   <TD>Item2    </TD>
      <TD>Item 3 </TD>   <TD>  SubT-1 </TD>
  </TR>
  <TR><TH>Title2 </TH>
      <TD>Item 5 </TD>   <TD>Item6    </TD>
      <TD>Item 7 </TD>   <TD>  SubT-2 </TD>
  </TR>
</TBODY>
<TFOOT>
  <TR><TH>MAIN-T </TH>
      <TD>MAIN-A </TD>   <TD>MAIN-B   </TD>
      <TD>MAIN-C </TD>   <TD> SubMAIN </TD>
  </TR>
</TFOOT>
</TABLE>
</BODY> </HTML>
```

Figure 6.42 Display, by Internet Explorer 4, of the document listed in Figure 6.41.

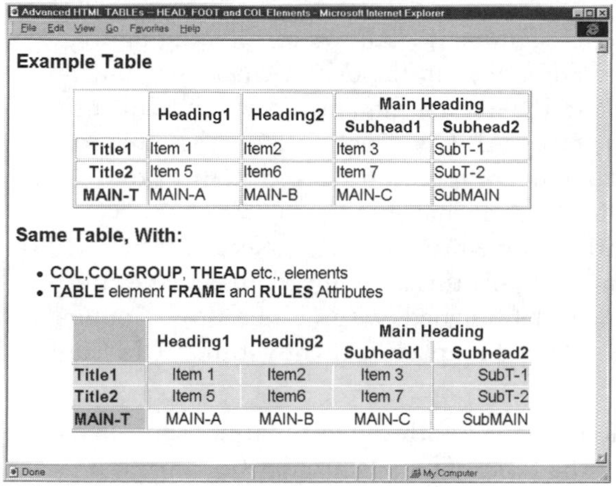

table approach, so that a browser that does not understand these elements can still render the table content correctly, albeit without the extra implied structure.

By default, tables are drawn without borders, with a predetermined spacing between items in the table, and with a table width that depends on the table content and that is calculated by the table-generation program. Finally, tables are, by default, left-aligned on the page and break all text flow. This means that text preceding a **TABLE** appears above the rendered table, and text following a **TABLE** appears below it.

TABLE supports the standard "generic" and "event-handler" attributes described earlier in this chapter. Note that the table-related event handlers are only supported by Internet Explorer 4 and are not supported by Netscape Navigator 4.

TABLE can take several additional and optional attributes that modify the presentation details of the table. **BORDER, CELLPADDING,** and **CELLSPACING** describe how borders should be drawn around the table and how much spacing should be left between items in the table. **WIDTH** specifies the desired width of the table, either as an absolute width in pixels or as a percentage of the full window width. Last, **ALIGN** allows for *floating tables*, which can float to the left or right margins, and which can have text flow around them. The details of these five attributes are provided here.

The more advanced table model supported by Internet Explorer supports additional attributes, **FRAME** and **RULES**, for further specifying how borders should be drawn. The use of these attributes is explained in the following descriptions.

Proprietary extensions to **TABLE** allow for control of the table cell background color (**BGCOLOR**). Microsoft supports additional extensions to control the color of the table borders, and to apply a background image for the table content.

ALIGN="center," "left," "right" (optional)   Allows for floating tables, analogous to floating images as described in the **IMG** element section. **ALIGN**="left" floats the table to the left margin and allows subsequent text to flow to the right of the table. **ALIGN**="right" floats the table to the right margin and allows subsequent text to flow to the left of the table. **ALIGN**="center" should float the image to the center of the window, with text flowing around it. Some browsers (e.g., Netscape Navigator 3 and earlier) do not support this attribute value and assume in its place the default alignment (left-aligned, with no text flow around the table). Tables can also be centered by placing them within a **DIV** element with **ALIGN**="center."

If **ALIGN** is absent, the table is aligned with the left margin, with text allowed only above or below the table. There is no text flow around the table.

BACKGROUND="#*url*" (optional)   Specifies a background image to be used to tile the background of the table. This attribute is supported by Internet Explorer 3 and 4 and by Netscape Navigator 4. Note that Navigator 4 independently tiles the background of each table cell, while Internet Explorer treats the entire background of the table as a single region to be tiled (see Figure 6.36).

BGCOLOR="#*rrggbb*," or "*color*" (optional)   Specifies a background color for the table—with Netscape Navigator this only changes the background color for the table cells, while with Internet Explorer this also changes the color of the space between cells specified by the **CELLSPACING** attribute (the width of the dividing lines and border). Note that Internet Explorer supports special border color attributes to change the colors of the borders. Note also that with Netscape Navigator, this color does not affect the spacing between cells or cells that are empty (contain only whitespace). However, adding a single   (non-breaking space) entity to an otherwise empty cell will cause the cell background to be colored.

Be careful that you allow sufficient contrast between the text and background color or else the text will not be legible.

BORDER="*number*" (optional)   Tells the browser to draw a box around each cell in the table and a border around the entire table. The default behavior in the absence of **BORDER** is a table without borders. Note that, when **BORDER** is not present, Netscape Navigator leaves an "invisible" padding space in place of the border—in a sense, Netscape Navigator leaves invisible borders. Internet Explorer, however, assumes zero-width "invisible" borders in this case.

The value assigned to **BORDER** specifies the width of the borders, in pixels—if a value is not specified, the default width value is typically 1 (this may vary from browser to browser). **BORDER**="0" draws a borderless table, with zero-width assigned to the border. You should thus use **BORDER**="0" to produce border-free tables that render equivalently on Internet Explorer and Netscape Navigator.

BORDERCOLOR="*#rrggbb*" or "*color*" (optional; Internet Explorer only)   Specifies the desired color for the cell border: This affects the outer, chiseled border of the table (outside the border width affected by the **CELLSPACING** attribute), as well as the thinly chiseled lines drawn around each cell. It has no effect if there are no borders. This is only supported by the Internet Explorer browser.

BORDERCOLORDARK="*#rrggbb*" or "*color*" (optional; Internet Explorer only)   Specifies the desired color for the darker portion of the cell border: This affects the bottom and right-hand side of the outer border of the table and the upper and left-hand side of the thinly chiseled lines drawn around each cell. It has no effect if there are no borders. This is only supported by the Internet Explorer browser.

BORDERCOLORLIGHT="*#rrggbb*" or "*color*" (optional; Internet Explorer only)   Specifies the desired color for the lighter-colored portion of the cell border: This affects the top and left-hand side of the outer border of the table, and the bottom and right-hand border drawn around each cell. It has no effect if there are no borders. This is only supported by the Internet Explorer browser.

CELLPADDING="*number*" (optional)   Specifies the horizontal and vertical space, in pixels, to leave between the edge of a table cell and the cell contents (image or text) on all four sides. The default value is 1.

CELLSPACING="*number*" (optional)   Specifies the horizontal and vertical space, in pixels, left between individual cells in a table (that is, on all four sides of a cell) —this is the "width" of the dividing lines. The default value is 2.

FRAME="void," "above," "below," "hsides," "lhs," "rhs," "vsides," "box," "border" (optional; implemented only on Internet Explorer 3 and 4)   Specifies which sides of the framing border should be rendered—this does not affect the borders drawn between table cells. The possible values and their meanings are:

FRAME Value	Meaning
above	draw a border only at the top of the table frame
below	draw a border only at the bottom of the table frame
box (or border)	draw borders on all four sides of the table frame
hsides	draw borders only at the top and bottom of the table frame
lhs	draw a border only on the left-hand side of the table frame
rhs	draw a border only on the right-hand side of the table frame
void	draw no borders for the table frame
vsides	draw borders only on the left- and right-hand sides of the table frame

HEIGHT=*"number,"* or *"real%"* (optional) Prescribes the desired height of the table, either as an absolute height (*number*) in pixels or as a percentage height (*real%*) in the range 0% to 100%. Percentage heights are calculated relative to the available height: For example, if a table lies within a cell of another table, the height is calculated relative to the height of this enclosing cell. Note, however, that a browser is free to ignore these height specifications, should the table content not fit in the designated space. Note also that fixing a table to a particular height may introduce formatting difficulties, should the content not fit in the defined space.

HSPACE=*"number"* (optional) Specifies a horizontal padding, in pixels, to leave to the left and right of the table. This is useful for providing spacing around tables that are left- or right-aligned and is only relevant for floated tables. **HSPACE** has no effect on tables that are not left- or right-aligned.

RULES=*"none,"* "groups," "rows," "cols," "all" (optional; Internet Explorer only) Specifies which cell dividing lines should be drawn within the table—this does not affect the external table border. The meanings of the five values are:

RULES Value	Meaning
all	draw dividing lines between all rows and all columns. A browser may use heavier lines between groups of columns or between **THEAD**, **TFOOT**, and **TBODY**. This is the default.
cols	draw only the vertical dividing lines between columns. A browser may use heavier lines between columns grouped within a **COLGROUP** grouping.

RULES Value	Meaning
groups	draw only the borders between table groups—groups are specified by **THEAD**, **TBODY**, **TFOOT**, and **COLGROUP**.
none	do not draw any interior dividing lines
rows	draw only the horizontal dividing lines between table rows. A browser may use heavier lines between **THEAD**, **TFOOT**, and **TBODY** than between regular cells.

VSPACE=*"number"* (optional)   Specifies the vertical padding, in pixels, to leave above and below the table. This only applies to floated (left-or right-aligned) tables and is useful for providing spacing between the table and the surrounding text.

SUMMARY=*"string"* (optional; not currently supported)   This attribute contains a text description of the table's purpose and structure and is designed to be used by software that renders the table in a nonvisual way, such as a text-to-speech synthesizer, or a Braille output device. This is not supported by either Netscape Navigator or Internet Explorer.

WIDTH=*"number,"* or *"real%"* (optional)   Prescribes the desired width of the table, either as an absolute width (*number*) in pixels or as a percentage width (*real%*) in the range 0% to 100%. Percentage widths are calculated relative to the available width: For example, if a table lies within a cell of another table, the width is calculated relative to the width of this enclosing cell. Note, however, that a browser is free to ignore these width specifications, should the table content not fit in the designated space. Note also that fixing a table to a particular pixel width may introduce formatting difficulties, should the table not fit easily within the specified size.

CAPTION Element: Table Caption

Usage:	`<CAPTION> ... </CAPTION>`
Can Contain:	**characters, character highlighting, A, APPLET,** *BASE-FONT,* **BR,** *BUTTON, IFRAME,* **IMG, INPUT,** *LABEL,* **MAP,** *OBJECT,* **SCRIPT, SELECT, TEXTAREA**
Can Be Inside:	**TABLE**
Attributes:	*CLASS, DIR, ID, LANG, STYLE, TITLE, standard event handlers,* **ALIGN**

CAPTION specifies an optional table caption or title. A TABLE can have at most one CAPTION. A CAPTION can contain text, character highlighting, IMG, and hypertext anchors elements, but not block content. CAPTION supports the standard "generic" and "event-handler" attributes described earlier in this chapter. Note that the event handlers are only partially supported by Internet Explorer 4 and are not supported by Netscape Navigator 4.

CAPTION can also take the optional attribute ALIGN to specify how the caption is aligned relative to the TABLE. The allowed values and their meanings are:

ALIGN="top," "bottom," "left," "right," (optional; "left" and "right" supported only by Internet Explorer) ALIGN specifies the desired location for the caption relative to the table. ALIGN="top" (the default) places the caption above the table, while ALIGN="bottom" places the caption below it. Internet Explorer 3 supports the additional values "left" and "right," which place the caption on top of the table, but left- or right-adjust the title relative to the left or right edge of the table. Note that Netscape Navigator 4 does not support the values "left" or "right."

Figures 6.31 and 6.32 illustrate an example table caption.

COL Element: Specify Properties of a Column (Internet Explorer Only)

Usage:	<COL>
Can Contain:	empty
Can Be Inside:	COLGROUP, TABLE
Attributes:	CLASS, DIR, ID, LANG, STYLE, TITLE, standard event handlers, ALIGN, BGCOLOR, CHAR, CHAROFF, REPEAT, SPAN, VALIGN, WIDTH

COL is an optional element and is used to specify default properties for a column or a group of columns. A table will generally have multiple COL elements to specify properties of the different columns. For example,

```
<COL ALIGN="left">
<COL ALIGN="right">
<COL ALIGN="center">
```

indicates that the first column content should be left-aligned, the second column content right-aligned, and the third column content center-aligned. The number of columns affected by a COL is set by the SPAN attribute. The default value for SPAN is 1. The SPAN attribute is only supported by Internet Explorer 4, which currently implements only partial support, as discussed in the following.

ALIGN="left," "center," "right," "justify," "char"   Specifies how the cell contents should be horizontally aligned within the cell. The values "left," "center," "right," and "justify" have the obvious meanings. Internet Explorer also supports the value "middle" as a synonym for "center"—for consistency with the standard, use "center." The value "char" indicates that the contents should be aligned on a particular alignment character, such as a decimal or comma (the alignment character is defined by the **CHAR** attribute). **ALIGN** is only supported by Internet Explorer 3 and 4, neither of which support the values "justify" or "char."

BGCOLOR="#*rrggbb*," "*color*" (optional)   Specifies the background color for the column of cells: This sets the color only for the cells and does not affect the boundary between cells. Note that this is an Internet Explorer-specific extension to HTML. For forward compatibility, you should use cascading style sheets to set table cell background colors.

CHAR="*c*" (optional; not currently supported)   Specifies the character upon with the cell contents should be column-aligned, given that **ALIGN**="char" is specified. The value can be any valid character, character reference or entity reference. The default value is the decimal point character as determined from the LANG attribute (e.g., a period in English and a comma in French). If the text to be aligned does not contain the alignment character, then the text is positioned such that the leading portion of the text is aligned with the vertical alignment position. This attribute is not currently supported.

CHAROFF="*number*," "*real%*" (optional; not currently supported) Specifies the offset of the line of vertical alignment relative to the edge of the cell: The edge (left or right) is determined from the directionality of the text flow, as defined by **DIR** or **LANG**. The value is given either in pixels, or as a percentage of the cell width. This attribute is not supported on current commercial browsers.

REPEAT="*number*" (optional; not currently supported)   Repeat is a synonym for **SPAN** and sets the number of columns affected by a **COL** element. This attribute will replace **SPAN**, discussed below. For backwards (and forwards) compatibility, **COL** elements that use **SPAN** should also use **REPEAT**, for example

```
<COL ALIGN="left" SPAN="2" REPEAT="2">
```

SPAN="*number*" (optional)   The number of columns affected by a **COL** is set by the **SPAN** attribute. Thus, **SPAN**="3" means that the properties specified by the **COL** element apply to three adjacent columns. For example,

```
<COL ALIGN="left">
```

```
<COL SPAN=3 ALIGN="center">
<COL ALIGN="right">
```

indicates that the second, third, and fourth columns should be center-aligned and that the fifth column content should be right-aligned. The value **SPAN**="0" is special, and *should* indicate that the properties apply to all columns from the current column up to the last column in the table. This special meaning for **SPAN**="0" is not, however, supported by Internet Explorer 3 or 4.

VALIGN="top," "middle," "bottom," "baseline" (optional) Specifies how the cell contents should be *vertically* aligned within the cell. The values "top," "middle," and "bottom" have the obvious meanings. The value "baseline" aligns the baseline of the content (text baseline or image bottom) with the baseline of adjacent cells in the row. At present, the only supported values are "top," "middle," and "bottom." Current browsers also support the value "middle" as a synonym for "center." For consistency with the standard, use "center."

WIDTH="*number*," "*real%*," "*real**"(optional) Specifies the desired width of a column, in three ways: as a length in pixels; as a percentage value (relative to the full width of the table) or as a "star" value (in which case the width is determined relative to the widths of the other table cells). This value can be ignored if the resulting table does not fit within the browser window. Current browsers do not support values ending with an asterisk (*), but do support percentage and pixel values.

COLGROUP Element: Properties of a Collection of Columns (Internet Explorer Only)

Usage:	<COLGROUP> ... (</COLGROUP>)
Can Contain:	*COL*
Can Be Inside:	TABLE
Attributes:	*CLASS, DIR, ID, LANG, STYLE, TITLE, standard event handlers,*
	ALIGN, <u>*BGCOLOR*</u>*, CHAR, CHAROFF, SPAN, VALIGN, WIDTH*

When laying out a table, it is often useful to *group* columns together, particularly where there is a logical structure associated with a group. For example, the left-most two columns might be a vertical collection of subject headings, or the two rightmost columns might correspond to spreadsheet totals. Such groupings are possible using **COLGROUP**, which lets you group columns and assign default alignment or other settings to this group. An example is

```
<COLGROUP  VALIGN="baseline">
   <COL ALIGN="left">
   <COL ALIGN="center">
</COLGROUP>
<COLGROUP ALIGN="center">
   <COL SPAN="2">
<THEAD> ....
```

which defines two column groups: the first with baseline vertical alignment, the second with horizontal centering. Note that **COLGROUP** properties apply to *all* columns specified within the **COLGROUP**.

COLGROUP takes the same layout control attributes as **COL**, and you are referred to the **COL** element section for a description of these attributes. There are two differences, however. With **COLGROUP**, **SPAN** specifies the default number of columns in the group and is ignored if there are any **COL** elements inside the **COLGROUP** (it applies only when there are no **COL** elements inside the group), while the **WIDTH** attribute defines the width for each column in the group.

The **RULES** attribute of the **TABLE** element allows for special rendering of the borders between grouped columns, as illustrated in Figures 6.41 and 6.42.

An example table illustrating **COLGROUP** is also shown in Figures 6.41 and 6.42. Note that this attribute is currently only supported by Internet Explorer 4.

THEAD Element: Table Header (Internet Explorer Only)

Usage:	<THEAD> ... (</THEAD>)
Can Contain:	**TR**
Can Be Inside:	**TABLE**
Attributes:	*CLASS, DIR, ID, LANG, STYLE, TITLE, standard event handlers,*
	ALIGN, <u>*BGCOLOR*</u>*, CHAR, CHAROFF, VALIGN*

THEAD defines the table header. A table header consists of rows that make up the header of the table (for example, a **THEAD** might contain one or more rows of **TH** table header cells). The **TABLE** element **RULES** attribute can specify special rendering for the borders between the **THEAD** and **TBODY** regions, as illustrated in Figures 6.41 and 6.42. In principle, **THEAD** could act as a non-scrolling header, such that if a table is longer than the display, the **THEAD** cells stay at the top of the displayed region as the user scrolls through the table body. There are no browsers that currently implement **THEAD** and **TFOOT** in this way.

THEAD takes the same layout control attributes as **COL**, and you are referred there for a detailed description of these attributes. In the case of **THEAD**, the layout controls apply to all the cells within the table head.

THEAD must precede the **TBODY**, which in turn must precede the **TFOOT**. An example employing **THEAD** is shown in Figures 6.41 and 6.42. At present, **THEAD** is only supported by the Internet Explorer browser—it is not supported by Netscape Navigator. Note also that the **CHAR** and **CHAROFF** attributes, discussed in the **COL** section, are not implemented.

TBODY Element: Table Body (Internet Explorer Only)

Usage:	(<TBODY>) ... (</TBODY>)
Can Contain:	**TR**
Can Be Inside:	**TABLE**
Attributes:	*CLASS, DIR, ID, LANG, STYLE, TITLE, standard event handlers,*
	ALIGN, <u>BGCOLOR</u>, CHAR, CHAROFF, VALIGN

TBODY defines the body of the table. Formally, you do not need to insert **TBODY** if there are no **THEAD** or **TFOOT** elements, since in this case the entire table is the table body, by default. An example employing an explicit **TBODY** is shown in Figures 6.41 and 6.42.

TBODY takes the same layout control attributes as **COL**, and you are referred there for a detailed description of these attributes. In the case of **TBODY**, the layout controls apply to all the cells within the defined table body.

TBODY must follow the **THEAD**, and must precede the **TFOOT**. An example employing **TBODY** is shown in Figures 6.41 and 6.42. At present, **TBODY** is only supported by the Internet Explorer browser—it is not supported by Netscape Navigator. Note also that the **CHAR** and **CHAROFF** attributes, discussed in the **COL** section, are not implemented.

TFOOT Element: Table Footer (Internet Explorer Only)

Usage:	<TFOOT> ... (</TFOOT>)
Can Contain:	**TR**
Can Be Inside:	**TABLE**
Attributes:	*CLASS, DIR, ID, LANG, STYLE, TITLE, standard event handlers,*
	ALIGN, <u>BGCOLOR</u>, CHAR, CHAROFF, VALIGN

TFOOT defines the table footer. A table footer consists of table rows that make up the footer of the table. **TFOOT** content is designed to act like a table banner, so that if the table is longer than the display, then the **TFOOT** cells stay at the bottom of the displayed portion of the table as the user scrolls through the table body. There are, however, no browsers that support this functionality.

TFOOT takes the same layout control attributes as **COL**, and you are referred to that section for a detailed description of these attributes. In the case of **TFOOT**, the layout controls apply to all the cells within the defined table footer.

TFOOT must be the final element in a table, just after **TBODY**. An example employing **TFOOT** is shown in Figures 6.41 and 6.42. **TFOOT** is only supported by Internet Explorer—it is not supported by Netscape Navigator. Note also that the **CHAR** and **CHAROFF** attributes, discussed in the **COL** section, are not implemented.

TR Element: Table Row

Usage:	`<TR>...(</TR>)`
Can Contain:	**TH, TD**
Can Be Inside:	**TABLE**, *TBODY, TFOOT, THEAD*
Attributes:	*CLASS, DIR, ID, LANG, STYLE, TITLE, standard event handlers,*
	ALIGN, BGCOLOR, *CHAR, CHAROFF, VALIGN,* (<u>BACKGROUND</u>: Netscape Navigator 4 and Internet Explorer 3 only), (<u>BORDERCOLOR</u>, <u>BORDERCOLORDARK</u>, <u>BORDERCOLORLIGHT</u>: Internet Explorer only)

TR marks out a row of a table. For example, a row in a table might be coded

```
<TR>
    <TH> Heading </TH>  <TD> data 1 </TD>
    <TD> data2   </TD>  <TD> data3  </TD> <TD> data4  </TD>
</TR>
```

which indicates a row containing five columns: the first column being a table heading and the rest containing table data. Note that although the ending `</TR>` is optional, you should always put it in—many browsers will improperly render tables when the end tags are absent.

TR takes the same layout control attributes as **COL** (**ALIGN, VALIGN, CHAR,** and **CHAROFF**), and you are referred to that section for a detailed description of these attributes. In the case of **TR**, the layout properties apply to all cells within the defined row.

NOTE: Internet Explorer 3 Bug

With Internet Explorer 3, **ALIGN** in a **TR** element does not properly override the default center-alignment of enclosed **TH** cells.

Current browsers support a number of proprietary attributes to control background coloring of the cells in a table row. These attributes are:

BACKGROUND="#*url*" (optional; Internet Explorer 3 and Netscape Navigator 4 only)   Specifies a background image to be used to tile the background of the row. Note that this attribute is not supported by Internet Explorer 4.

BORDERCOLOR="#*rrggbb*" or "*color*" (optional; Internet Explorer only)   Specifies the desired color for the cell border: the thinly chiseled lines drawn around the edge of each cell. This has no effect if there are no borders. This can be overridden by **BORDERCOLORDARK** and **BORDERCOLORLIGHT**, or by color specification within a given cell.

BORDERCOLORDARK="#*rrggbb*" or "*color*" (optional; Internet Explorer only)   Specifies the desired color for the darker portion of the cell border: This affects the bottom and right-hand side of the outer border of the table and the top and left-hand side of the thinly chiseled lines drawn around each cell. It has no effect if there are no borders. This attribute is overridden by color specification within a given cell.

BORDERCOLORLIGHT="#*rrggbb*" or "*color*" (optional; Internet Explorer only)   Specifies the desired color for the lighter portion of the cell border: This affects the top and left-hand side of the outer border of the table and the bottom and right-hand side borders drawn around each cell. It has no effect if there are no borders. This is overridden by color specification within a given cell.

TD and TH Elements: Table Data and Table Headings

Usage:	`<TD> ... (</TD>)`
	`<TH> ... (</TH>)`
Can Contain:	ADDRESS, BLOCKQUOTE, CENTER, DIR, DIV, DL, *FIELDSET*, FORM, Hn, HR, [ISINDEX], MENU, *NOFRAMES*, *NOSCRIPT*, OL, P, PRE, TABLE, UL,
	characters, character highlighting, A, APPLET, *BASEFONT*, BR, *BUTTON*, *IFRAME*, IMG, INPUT, *LABEL*, MAP, *OBJECT*, SCRIPT, SELECT, TEXTAREA
Can Be Inside:	TR
Attributes:	*CLASS, DIR, ID, LANG, STYLE, TITLE, standard event handlers,*
	ALIGN, *ABBR, AXIS,* <u>BACKGROUND</u>, BGCOLOR, *CHAR, CHAROFF,* COLSPAN, *HEADERS,* HEIGHT, NOWRAP, ROWSPAN, *SCOPE,* VALIGN, WIDTH, (<u>BORDERCOLOR</u>, <u>BORDERCOLORDARK</u>, <u>BORDERCOLORLIGHT</u>: Internet Explorer only)

TD and TH elements specify the cells in a table. The only difference between the two is their meaning: TD specifies a Table Data cell—a cell containing table data, while TH specifies Table Heading cell—a cell containing a table heading. In both cases, the element is not empty but the end tag is optional, as the end is implied by the next <TH>, <TR>, or <TD> tag. A cell can have empty content, which simply means that the cell is blank. Note that although the ending </TD> and </TH> tags are optional, you should always put them in—many browsers will improperly render tables when end tags are absent.

TD and TH elements have several attributes that define the formatting and layout of the cell and the cell content. All of these attributes are optional. In particular, the attributes ALIGN, CHAR, CHAROFF, BGCOLOR, VALIGN, and WIDTH have the same meanings as with the COL element, and you are referred to the COL element section for detailed descriptions.

Note that all cells in a table row must have the same height, while all cells in a column must have the same width; thus, if there are two WIDTH or HEIGHT specifications in the same column or row respectively, the largest value is used.

TR and TD also support several additional optional attributes. These attributes, and their meanings, are described in the following.

ABBR="string" (optional; not currently supported)   This contains an abbreviated string corresponding to or describing the cell content, which may be rendered by the browser in place of the content, for example, when the content is used repeatedly as a heading. In the absence of this attribute, the default description is taken to be the actual content of the cell. This attribute is not supported on current browsers.

AXIS="string" (optional; not currently supported)   This contains a comma-separated list of *category names*—these are used to define groups of cells, where a group consists of cells that are assigned the same category name. This allows for additional description of the table content beyond that implied by the table structure. In practice, a browser may let the user query the table, for example by specially rendering those table items that share a selected category name. The value of this attribute may also be used by screen readers, which may use this label to describe the table to the listener. This attribute is not supported on current browsers.

BACKGROUND=*"url"* (optional; not supported by Netscape Navigator 3) Specifies a background image to be used to tile the background of the cell. This attribute is supported by Internet Explorer 3 and 4 and by Netscape Navigator 4.

BORDERCOLOR=*"#rrggbb"* or *"color"* (optional; Internet Explorer only)   Specifies the desired color for the cell border—the thinly chiseled lines drawn around each cell. It has no effect if there are no borders.

This can be overridden by **BORDERCOLORDARK** and **BORDERCOL-ORLIGHT**.

<u>**BORDERCOLORDARK**</u>=*"#rrggbb"* or *"color"* (optional; Internet Explorer only)   Specifies the desired color for the darker portion of the cell border. This affects the bottom and right-hand side of the outer border of the table and the top and left-hand side of the thinly chiseled lines drawn around each cell. It has no effect if there are no borders.

<u>**BORDERCOLORLIGHT**</u>=*"#rrggbb"* or *"color"* (optional; Internet Explorer only)   Specifies the desired color for the lighter portion of the cell border. This affects the top and left-hand side of the outer border of the table, and the bottom and right-hand borders drawn around each cell. It has no effect if there are no borders.

COLSPAN=*"number"* (optional)   Specifies how many table *columns* are spanned by the cell—the default value is 1. Counting of columns starts from the left side of the table. It is the author's responsibility to ensure that the cells in each row sum to the correct number of columns.

HEADERS=*"names"* (optional; not currently supported)   Specifies a space-separated list of **ID** values referencing the **TH** heading cells that provide information, or are related to, the current table cell. For example, the markup

```
<TD HEADERS="ref1 ref2"> ... </TD>
```

would mean that the heading cells `<TH ID="ref1">` and `<TH ID="ref2">` are headings appropriate to the data cell. This is designed to aid nongraphical rendering of the table (for example, by a Braille or text-to-speech browser), but may also be used by a style sheet to present cell-specific rending. See also the **SCOPE** attribute. This attribute is not currently supported.

HEIGHT=*"number"* (optional)   Specifies the desired height for the cell, in pixels. Note that all cells in a row must have the same height: Thus, if two cells in a row specify different heights, the larger value will be used for the entire row. Care must be taken to ensure that the cell content will fit within the specified region.

In the absence of a **HEIGHT** value, the browser will determine a (hopefully) appropriate height. Note that percentage cell heights are not supported.

NOWRAP (optional)   Indicates that text lines within a cell may not wrap; the browser may not introduce line breaks between words. However, you can add **BR** elements to force hard line breaks, where desired. **NOWRAP** should be used with caution, as it can lead to extremely wide cells.

ROWSPAN = "*number*" (optional)   Specifies how many table rows are spanned by the cell—the default value is 1. Counting of rows is downward from the top of the table. It is the author's responsibility to ensure that the cells in each column sum to the correct number of rows.

SCOPE="row," "col," "rowgroup," "colgroup" (optional; not currently supported)   Specifies the set of cells for which the current heading cell provides heading information. This is designed for use in place of the **HEADERS** attribute, when the table is simple enough that this is possible. The value "row" means that the cell provides heading information for all remaining cells in the row, while "col" means that the cell provides heading information for all remaining cells in the column. "Rowgroup" means that the cell provides heading information for all remaining cells in the *row group* (defined by **THEAD, TFOOT,** or **TBODY**), while "colgroup" means that the cell provides heading information for all remaining cells in the column group (defined by **COL-GROUP**). This attribute is not currently supported.

WIDTH="*number*," or "*real%*" (optional)   Specifies the desired width for the cell, in pixels or as a percentage of the full width of the table. Note that all cells in a column must have the same width; thus, if two cells specify different widths, the larger value will be used for the entire column. In the absence of a **WIDTH** value, the browser will determine a (hopefully) appropriate width.

NOTE: Internet Explorer 3 WIDTH Bug

Internet Explorer 3 does not properly calculate widths of table cells when percentage widths are specified.

Inclusion Elements

These elements include nontext content or data within an HTML document. In HTML 4 there are five such elements: **APPLET** (include a program applet), **IFRAME** (include a frame containing an HTML document), **IMG** (include an image), **OBJECT** (include an arbitrary data object and its software handler), and the proprietary element, **EMBED**. This section will only discuss **APPLET** and **IMG**—the other three are discussed in Chapter 7.

APPLET Element: Include an Embedded Applet

Usage: `<APPLET> ... </APPLET>`

Can Contain: **ADDRESS, BLOCKQUOTE, ~~CENTER~~, ~~DIR~~, DIV, DL,** *FIELDSET*, **FORM, Hn, HR, [ISINDEX], ~~MENU~~,** *NOFRAMES, NOSCRIPT*, **OL, P, PRE, TABLE, UL,**

Can Contain:	PARAM,
	characters, character highlighting, A, APPLET, *BASE-FONT*, BR, *BUTTON*, *IFRAME*, IMG, INPUT, *LABEL*, MAP, *OBJECT*, SCRIPT, SELECT, TEXTAREA
Can Be Inside:	ADDRESS, BLOCKQUOTE, BODY, CAPTION, ~~CENTER~~, DD, DIV, DT, *FIELDSET*, FORM, Hn, LI, *NOFRAMES*, *NOSCRIPT*, P, TD, TH,
	character highlighting, A, APPLET, *BUTTON*, *IFRAME*, *LABEL*, *LEGEND*, *OBJECT*
Attributes:	*CLASS*, *ID*, *STYLE*, *TITLE*, (<u>onBlur</u>, <u>onFocus</u>: Internet Explorer 4 only),
	ALIGN, ALT, ARCHIVE, CODE, CODEBASE, HEIGHT, HSPACE, <u>MAYSCRIPT</u> (Netscape only), NAME, *OBJECT*, VSPACE, WIDTH

APPLET is used to include an inline applet—at present, Java applets are the only supported cases. The attribute **CODE** specifies the URL at which the applet is located (analogous to the **SRC** attribute of the **IMG** element), while the attributes **WIDTH** and **HEIGHT** specify the height and width required by the applet, in pixels. Parameter values required by the applet are obtained from **PARAM** elements contained within the **APPLET** element. An example showing the use of **APPLET** was given in Example 12 in Chapter 2. The following is another, simple example:

```
<APPLET CODE="HuntingMammoths.class" WIDTH="300" HEIGHT="300">
    <PARAM NAME="x_offset" VALUE="0.224">
    <PARAM NAME="image" VALUE="images/hairy_mammoth.gif">
    <PARAM NAME="weapon" VALUE="rubber biscuit">
</APPLET>
```

NOTE: APPLET to Be Replaced by OBJECT

APPLET has some annoying limitations and is destined to be replaced by the **OBJECT** element. **OBJECT**, which is supported by Internet Explorer 3/4 and Netscape Navigator 4, is discussed in Chapter 7.

The supported attributes and their meanings are:

ALIGN="top," "middle," "bottom," "left," "right" (optional)
Specifies the alignment of the applet with respect to the surrounding text. The values "top," "middle," and "bottom" align the top of the applet with the top of the text, the middle of the applet with the middle of the text, and the bottom of the applet with the bottom of the

text, respectively. The values "left" and "right" let the applet float to the left and right margins, respectively, and enable text flow around the applet frame.

ALT=*"string"* (optional)   Specifies a text string to be use in place of the applet by browsers that are unable to run the applet.

ARCHIVE=*"url"* (optional; not supported by Internet Explorer 3)
Specifies an *uncompressed* ZIP-format archive of classes. If specified, the browser will download the specified ZIP file and will search there for the **CODE**-specified applet and supporting classes. Classes not in the ZIP file will still be accessed from the server, following the traditional manner.

CODE=*"url"* (optional; one of **CODE** or **OBJECT** must be present)
Specifies the URL of the applet to be run. If referencing an applet from your local computer, this must point to a file with a name ending in *.class*. Internet Explorer 4 will not recognize applets if the names end in *.cla*—thus you cannot load local applets if you are using Windows 3.1.

CODEBASE=*"url"* (optional, depending on **CODE** value)   Specifies the *code base* for the applet selected by the **CODE** attribute, where the code base is simply the directory or location containing any supporting class libraries required by the applet. If the supporting libraries are at the same location as the program itself, then **CODEBASE** can be omitted.

HEIGHT=*"number"* (mandatory)   Specifies the *height* required of the embedded applet, in pixels. This is required, as a browser has no other way of knowing how big the applet is.

HSPACE=*"number"* (optional)   Specifies a padding space, in pixels, to be left to the left and right of the applet. This creates an extra space between the applet and the surrounding document. This is not supported by Netscape Navigator.

<u>**MAYSCRIPT**</u> (optional; Netscape Navigator 3+ only)   Lets the applet communicate with JavaScript programs running in the browser, and vice versa. If absent, then JavaScript programs cannot communicate with the applet.

NAME=*"string"* (optional)   Specifies a name which identifies the applet for external reference. This lets other programs (such as script programs within the document) reference and communicate with the named applet.

OBJECT=*"url"* (optional; one of **CODE** or **OBJECT** must be present; not currently supported)   Specifies a resource containing a *serialized* representation of an applet's state, but not the code implementation. The location is determined relative to the **URL** specified by **CODE-BASE**. The serialized data contains the applet's class name—the browser must use this name to retrieve the implementation from a class file or archive. The browser will then combine the class and the serialized data to restart the applet.

Note that one of **CODE** or **OBJECT** must be specified. Both may be specified, but it is an error if they reference different class names.

VSPACE=*"number"* (optional)   Specifies a padding space, in pixels, to be included above and below the applet. This creates an extra space between the applet and the surrounding document. This is not supported by Netscape Navigator.

WIDTH=*"number"* (mandatory)   Specifies the *width* required of the embedded applet, in pixels. This is required as a browser has no other way of knowing the appropriate size for the applet region.

PARAM Element: Define an Applet Parameter

Usage:	<PARAM>
Can Contain:	empty
Can Be Inside:	**APPLET,** *OBJECT*
Attributes:	*ID*, NAME, *TYPE*, VALUE, *VALUETYPE*

PARAM assigns a value to any required applet-dependent variable. The variable name is specified via the **NAME** attribute, while the value for this variable is specified by **VALUE**. **NAME**s and **VALUE**s are, of course, entirely specific to the applet being invoked: The applet must understand the names so that it knows what to do with the values. The attributes are:

NAME=*"string"* (mandatory)   Specifies a name to be associated with this parameter when the object or applet is run. Thus, **NAME**s must be understood by the associated applet or embedded object. Names may or may not be case-sensitive, depending on the applet.

TYPE=*"mime-type"* (optional)   Specifies the MIME type of the resource specified by **VALUE** for the cases where VALUE is a URL.

VALUE=*"string"* (optional)   Specifies the *value* to associate with the given name. Again, the value must be meaningful to the specified applet. If a value is not needed, this attribute can be left out.

VALUETYPE="data," "ref," "object" (optional; valid only for **PARAM** inside **OBJECT**)   Specifies the type of the value attribute and determines how the browser parses the data before passing it to the object. **VALUETYPE** has no meaning inside an **APPLET**. The value "data" means that the **VALUE** string is data to be passed to the object and that HTML entity and character references must be replaced by the referenced characters before the string is sent. The value "object" means that the assigned string is a reference pointing to another (possibly running) **OBJECT** within the same document. The value "ref" indicates that the value is a proper URL referencing a resource. If **VALUETYPE**="ref," then the optional **TYPE** attribute can specify the MIME type of the referenced object.

NOTE: Limited Support for TYPE and VALUETYPE

Microsoft Internet Explorer 3 does *not* support the **TYPE** and **VALUETYPE** attributes.

IMG Element: Inline Images

Usage:	`<IMG>`
Can Contain:	empty
Can Be Inside:	ADDRESS, BLOCKQUOTE, BODY, CAPTION, ~~CENTER~~, DD, DIV, DT, *FIELDSET*, FORM, Hn, LI, *NOFRAMES, NOSCRIPT*, P, TD, TH,
	character highlighting, A, APPLET, *BUTTON, IFRAME, LABEL, LEGEND, OBJECT*
Attributes:	*CLASS, DIR, ID, LANG, STYLE, TITLE, standard event handlers,*
	onAbort, onError, onLoad,
	ALIGN, ALT, BORDER, HEIGHT, HSPACE, ISMAP, *LONGDESC*, LOWSRC, NAME, SRC, USEMAP, VSPACE, WIDTH, (SUPPRESS: Netscape Navigator 4), (CONTROLS, DYNSRC, LOOP, START: Internet Explorer only)

IMG includes an image file *inline* with the document text, the image file being specified by the **SRC** attribute. There are currently four common image formats used for inline images. These are: GIF format (with the filename suffix *.gif*); X-Bitmaps (with the filename suffix *.xbm*); X-Pixelmaps (with the filename suffix *.xpm*); and JPEG format (filename suffix *.jpeg* or *.jpg*). A fifth format, Portable Network Graphics or PNG (with the filename suffix *.png*), is expected to be widely supported by the next generation of browsers. It is currently supported only by Internet Explorer 4.

To a large extent, images within a document are treated like words or characters, and you can place an image almost anywhere you have regular text. The exception is the **PRE** (preformatted text) element, which should not contain **IMG** elements. Images can also "float" on the page, allowing text to flow around them. This is facilitated with special **ALIGN** attribute options, outlined in this section.

IMG supports the standard "generic" and "event-handler" attributes described earlier in this chapter. Note that the event handlers are only partially supported by current browsers.

The **IMG** element takes three main attributes. **SRC** is mandatory and specifies the URL of the image file to be included. **ALIGN** specifies the alignment of the image with respect to the surrounding text, and **ALT** gives an alternative text string for browsers that cannot display images. There are several other attributes, as well as some Netscape- and Microsoft-specific extensions as discussed in this section. Some examples of **IMG** elements and image alignment are shown in Figures 6.43 and 6.44.

Note that the attributes **ALIGN, BORDER, HEIGHT, HSPACE, VSPACE,** and **WIDTH** are purely presentational and that equivalent formatting can be specified using a style sheet. Thus, HTML 4 recommends dropping these attributes in favor of using style sheets.

> **ALIGN**="bottom," "left," "middle," "right," "top, ("texttop,"
> "absmiddle," "baseline," "absbottom": Netscape extensions) (optional)
> Specifies the alignment of the image with the neighboring text.
> "Bottom" aligns the bottom of the image with the baseline of the sur-
> rounding text—this is the default. "Middle" aligns the middle of the
> image with the baseline of the text, and "top" aligns the top of the
> image with the top of largest item in a line (including other images).
> Note that text does not wrap around an image aligned using the "top,"
> "middle," or "bottom" attribute values, so that images within a sentence
> can create big gaps between adjacent lines.
>
> The values "left" and "right" allow for text flow around an image.
> **ALIGN**="left" floats the image below any text that precedes the **IMG**
> element and over to the left margin and allows subsequent text to flow
> around the right side of the image. **ALIGN**="right" floats the image to
> the right side of the window and allows subsequent text to flow around
> the left side of the image. Browsers that do not understand these values
> assume the **ALIGN**="bottom" default.
>
> Netscape Navigator (and several other browsers) support additional
> align values to better control alignment within a line of text.
> **ALIGN**="texttop" aligns the top of an image with the top of the sur-
> rounding text, independent of any other images that may appear inline.
> **ALIGN**="middle" aligns the middle of the image with the baseline of the
> adjacent line of text, while **ALIGN**="absmiddle" aligns the middle of an
> image with the middle of the region defined by the line of text plus
> any other inline images. **ALIGN**="baseline" aligns the bottom of an
> image with the baseline of the line of text—this is the same as
> **ALIGN**="bottom," but with a clearer meaning. **ALIGN**="absbottom"

aligns the bottom of the image with the bottom of the line (for example, the bottom tip of a letter such as "q," or the bottom of another inline image that hangs down below the text baseline).

ALT=*"string"* (optional)   Specifies a text alternative to the image, for use by text-only browsers. *This should always be included* to let users with text-only browsers know what they are missing, or to let graphical browsers preview the image using this text description. If the image is purely decorative and warrants no description, you should enter a null string using the form **ALT**=*"."*

BORDER=*"number"* (optional)   Specifies the border width, in pixels, around images that are marked as hypertext anchors (recall that images are generally surrounded by a colored border, if they are inside an anchor). **BORDER**=0 implies no border around the image and allows for clickable imagemaps or buttons without surrounding border. **BORDER** is illustrated in Figures 6.45 and 6.46. Note that **BORDER** can also be used to draw borders around images that are not inside **A** elements.

In general, element borders are better handled using style sheets, and this is the recommended mechanism.

CONTROLS (optional; Internet Explorer only)   Indicates that a set of video or VRML controls should be displayed along with the inline viewer. If **CONTROLS** is absent, then the controls are not displayed. Note that the use of **IMG** to display video or VRML data should be avoided, in favor of using **OBJECT**.

DYNSRC=*"url"* (optional; Internet Explorer only)   Specifies the URL of an AVI-format video clip or a VRML world description file to be included inline with the document. The attributes **CONTROLS**, **LOOP**, **LOOPDELAY**, and **START** are used to control the behavior of the video clip or VRML scene. Both **DYNSRC** and **SRC** can be specified in the same **IMG** element, so that **DYNSRC**-incapable browser can display a regular image file in place of the VRML data or video sequence.

Note that the use of **IMG** to display video or VRML data should be avoided, in favor of using **OBJECT**.

HEIGHT=*"number,"* *"real%"* (optional)   Specifies the height of the image to be displayed—a browser will scale the image to fit this height if the image is actually a different size. Percentage heights are calculated relative to the available space; thus, if the image is inside a table cell, this should be a percentage of the table cell's height. Unfortunately, when percentage heights are used on an **IMG** element, Netscape Navigator 3/4 and Internet Explorer 4 improperly render the element when it is placed inside table cell. Thus, percentage values should be avoided on **IMG** elements used within table cells.

Figure 6.43 HTML example document illustrating the IMG *inline* image element. Figure 6.44 shows this document as displayed by the Netscape Navigator browser.

```
<HTML>
<HEAD>
<TITLE> Example of IMG Element </TITLE>
</HEAD>
<BODY>
<H1>Examples of IMG Elements</H1>

<P> <IMG SRC="icon-help.gif" ALT="[Test image]" ALIGN=TOP> Here is
some text related to the test image.   The text is aligned with the
top of the image. Note that the text does not flow around the image.

<P> <IMG SRC="icon-help.gif" ALT="[Test image]" ALIGN=MIDDLE> Here is
some text related to the test image.   The text is aligned with the
middle of the image. Note that the text does not flow around the image.

<P> <A HREF="http://www.bozo.edu/test.html"><IMG SRC="icon-help.gif"
ALT="[Test image]" ALIGN=BOTTOM> Here is some text</A>  related
to the test image.   The text is aligned with the bottom of
the image, and is also part of the <EM> hypertext link</EM>.

<P>  Here is a <IMG SRC="icon-help.gif" ALT="" ALIGN="left">
left-aligned image. Note how the text flows around this image,
unlike the top, middle and bottom aligned images shown above. The
element <CODE>&lt;BR CLEAR="left"></CODE> (there is one just
coming up, right after the closing bracket....)
<BR CLEAR="left">
(....there it was) creates a line break that clears the text to
follow the left-flushed image.
</BODY>
</HTML>
```

If only one of **HEIGHT** or **WIDTH** is specified, then the entire image is resized, with the aspect ratio (ratio of height to width) kept constant—thus the image is not distorted. However, an author can use specific **HEIGHT** and **WIDTH** values to stretch and distort an image to any desired size. This is commonly used, with a transparent 1 pixel by 1 pixel image, to create fixed-width table columns.

Figure 6.44 Display, by the Netscape Navigator 3 browser, of the document shown in Figure 6.43.

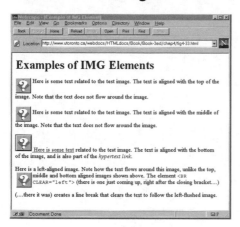

The use of **HEIGHT** is illustrated in Figures 6.45 and 6.46.

HSPACE=*"number"* (optional; floated images only)   Specifies, in pixels, the horizontal space to be left between a floated image and the surrounding text. Note that this spacing is added both to the left and the right of the image. Finer control of spacing is provided by the style sheet *padding* property. Indeed, HTML 4 recommends dropping the **HSPACE** attribute in favor of using style sheet properties to control spacing and image positioning. The use of this attribute is illustrated in Figures 6.45 and 6.46.

ISMAP (optional)   Denotes the image as an *active* image: When the user clicks the mouse over the image, the coordinates of the mouse pointer are measured by the browser. The **ISMAP**-activated **IMG** element must, consequently, be enclosed within an anchor element, specifying the URL to which the data should be sent. Typical markup for an active image is:

```
<A HREF="http://www.utirc.ca/cgi-bin/imagemap/map_bozo">
    <IMG SRC="bozo.gif" ISMAP>
</A>
```

where *imagemap* is a server-side gateway program that can interpret the map coordinates. When the user clicks on the image, the browser uses the HTTP GET method to access the URL, indicated by the anchor element, and appends the coordinates of the mouse click (relative to the upper left-hand corner of the image) to the accessed URL. The details of this procedure were discussed in Chapter 3.

Figure 6.45 Example HTML document illustrating IMG border, image size rescaling, and spacing control. Browser rendering of this document is shown in Figure 6.46.

```
<HTML>
<HEAD>
<TITLE> More Examples of IMG Elements </TITLE>
</HEAD>
<BODY>
<H2 ALIGN="center"> More Examples of IMG Elements</H2>

<P>Here is a left-aligned image
<IMG SRC="icon-help.gif" ALT="[Test image]" ALIGN="left"> with
text flowing around it.  Note how tight the text is to the image.
The next example has attributes <B>HSPACE</B>="15" and
<B>VSPACE</B>="15": <BR CLEAR="all">

<P>Here is a left-aligned image
<IMG SRC="icon-help.gif" ALT="[Test image]" ALIGN="left"
HSPACE="15" VSPACE="15"> with text flowing around it.
Note how there is extra space around the image, due
to the <B>HSPACE</B> and <B>VSPACE</B>
attributes added to the IMG element. <BR CLEAR="all">

<P>Here is a right-aligned image
<IMG SRC="icon-help.gif" ALT="[Test image]" ALIGN="right"
HEIGHT="60" WIDTH="120"> with the image size rescaled
using the <B>HEIGHT</B> and <B>WIDTH</B> attributes.
Note that you <EM>must not</EM> use these attribute to
resize imagemapped images.
<BR CLEAR="all">

<P>Here are three images inside anchor elements:
Note how the <B>BORDER</B> attribute controls the
border drawn around the images</P>
<CENTER>
<TABLE WIDTH="60%" CELLPADDING=5>
<TR>
  <TD ALIGN="center"> No Specification
  <TD ALIGN="center"> <TT>BORDER="0"</TT>
  <TD ALIGN="center"> <TT>BORDER="8"</TT>
</TR>
```

Figure 6.45 *Continued*.

```
<TR>
   <TD ALIGN="center"><A HREF="icon-help.gif"><IMG SRC="icon-help.gif"
                          ALT="[Test image]"></A>
   <TD ALIGN="center"><A HREF="icon-help.gif"><IMG SRC="icon-help.gif"
                          ALT="[Test image]" BORDER="0"></A>
   <TD ALIGN="center"><A HREF="icon-help.gif"><IMG SRC="icon-help.gif"
                          ALT="[Test image]" BORDER="8"></A>
</TR>
</TABLE>
</CENTER></BODY></HTML>
```

Figure 6.46 Display, by the Internet Explorer 3 browser, of the document shown in Figure 6.45.

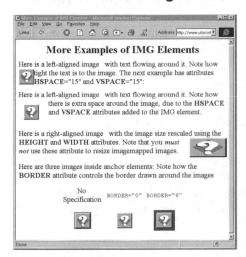

LONGDESC="*url*" (optional; not currently supported)   Specifies a URL that contains a long text description of the image. This is not supported by current browsers.

LOOP="*number*," "infinite" (optional; Internet Explorer only) Specifies how many times the video clip should be looped before stopping. **LOOP**="-1" or **LOOP**="infinite" means that the loop will play indefinitely. The default value is 1. The use of **IMG** for video display should be avoided, in favor of using **OBJECT**.

LOOPDELAY="*number*" (optional; Internet Explorer only)   Specifies the delay, in milliseconds, between subsequent replays of the video clip.

The default value is 0. The use of **IMG** for video display should be avoided, in favor of using **OBJECT**.

LOWSRC=*"url"* (optional)   Specifies the URL of an image file to be loaded and displayed prior to loading and displaying the image indicated by the **SRC** attribute. **LOWSRC** usually references a placeholder image that can be loaded and displayed more rapidly than the full-resolution version (specified by **SRC**).

NAME=*"string"* (optional)   Specifies a name identifier for the image element. The image element is then accessible, via this name, to a JavaScript program. JavaScript (as of Netscape Navigator 3) can then modify the content of the **IMG** element, for example to change the image element content when the mouse pointer passes over the image.

OnAbort=*"string"* (optional)   Specifies the JavaScript event handler to run if the user aborts the loading of the image file, for example, by pressing "Stop" before the image has arrived. The value string is script program code to run if the *onAbort* event occurs. See also Chapter 7.

OnError=*"string"* (optional)   Specifies the JavaScript event handler to run if an error occurs while loading the image file, for example, if the image file is corrupted. The value string is script program code to run if the *onError* event occurs. See also Chapter 7.

onLoad=*"string"* (optional)   Specifies the JavaScript event handler to run upon successfully loading the image file. The value string is script program code to run if the *onLoad* event occurs. See also Chapter 7.

SUPPRESS="0," "1" (optional; Netscape Navigator 4 only)   Suppresses the display of the placeholder image icon that appears prior to image loading. The possible values are "1" (true) and "0" (false). If true ("1"), then the placeholder image is not displayed. If false ("0"), then the placeholder is displayed. The default value is "0."

SRC=*"url"* (mandatory)   Specifies the URL of the image file to be included inline.

START="fileopen," "mouseover" (optional; Internet Explorer only) Indicates when a video clip should begin playing: **START**="fileopen" implies the movie starts as soon as the video file is downloaded, while **START**="mouseover" implies that the movie should start playing when the mouse pointer is moved over the viewing window. Both can be specified, separated by commas. For example, **START**="fileopen,mouseover" will invoke both behaviors. Note that, in general, the use of **IMG** for video display should be avoided, in favor of using **OBJECT**.

USEMAP=*"url"* (optional)   Specifies a URL pointing to a client-side imagemap MAP element. A document can contain, within a **MAP** element, imagemap coordinate data. This lets a browser itself determine which link to access when a user clicks the mouse over an active image, as opposed to the traditional (**ISMAP**) method of sending the click coordinates to a server gateway program for subsequent processing. An **IMG** element references a **MAP** element via the **USEMAP** attribute, which takes, as its value, either a fragment identifier (the **MAP** is in the same file as the **IMG** element) or a full URL plus a fragment identifier (the **MAP** is in a separate document). Each **MAP** element must consequently be identified by an appropriate **NAME** attribute value.

A developer can specify both **USEMAP** and **ISMAP** in the same **IMG** element, with **USEMAP** having precedence. Thus, if a browser understands **USEMAP**, it will use the local **MAP**, while if the browser does not understand **USEMAP**, it will access the standard server-side imagemap program referenced by the surrounding hypertext anchor. For example:

```
<A HREF="/cgi-bin/imagmep/mapfile1"><IMG SRC="image.gif"
        USEMAP="#map1"  ISMAP></A>
...
<MAP NAME="map1">
<AREA SHAPE="rect" COORD="10,20,50,50" HREF="stuff.html">
<AREA SHAPE="rcct" COORD="30,40,60,60" HREF="otherstuff.html">
...
</MAP>
```

If the browser interpreting this document understands **USEMAP**, it will use the local map `<MAP NAME="map1">` when the user clicks on the active image. If the browser does not understand **USEMAP**, it will revert to **ISMAP** and will send the click coordinates to the referenced server-side program, as per standard practice.

VSPACE=“*number*” (optional)   Specifies, in pixels, the vertical space to be left between a floated image and the surrounding text (above or below). The use of this attribute is illustrated in Figures 6.45 and 6.46. Note that this extra space is applied both above and below the image. Finer control of spacing is provided by the style sheet *padding* property. Indeed, HTML 4 recommends dropping the **VSPACE** attribute in favor of using style sheet properties to control spacing and image positioning.

WIDTH=“*number*,” “*real%*” (optional)   Specifies the width of the image to be displayed—a browser will scale the image to fit this width if the image is actually a different size. Percentage widths are calculated relative to the available space: Thus if the image is inside a table cell, this should be a percentage of the table cell's width. Unfortunately, when percentage widths are used on an **IMG** element, Netscape Navigator 3/4 and Internet Explorer 4 improperly render the element when it is placed inside a table cell. Thus, percentage widths should be avoided on **IMG** elements used within table cells.

If only one of **HEIGHT** or **WIDTH** is specified, then the entire image will be resized, with the aspect ratio (ratio of height to width) kept constant—thus the image is not distorted. However, an author can use specific **HEIGHT** and **WIDTH** values to stretch and distort an image to any desired size. This is commonly used, with a transparent 1 pixel by 1 pixel image, to create fixed-width tables.

Most importantly, specified **HEIGHT** and **WIDTH** values let a browser format the text before actually loading the image, since it already knows the size that the image requires.

The use of **WIDTH** is illustrated in Figures 6.45 and 6.46.

Hypertext Relationship Elements

These elements define active hypertext relationships between document content and another resource. There is only one such element in HTML, namely **A**.

A Element: Hypertext Anchors

Usage:	`<A> ... </A>`
Can Contain:	**characters, character highlighting, A, ~~APPLET~~, BR, *IFRAME*, IMG,*OBJECT*, BASEFONT, MAP, SCRIPT, *BUTTON*, INPUT, *LABEL*, SELECT, TEXTAREA**
Can Be Inside:	**BLOCKQUOTE, BODY, ~~CENTER~~, DD, DIV, *FIELDSET*, FORM, *IFRAME*, LI, *NOFRAMES*, *NOSCRIPT*, *OBJECT*, TD, TH, ADDRESS, ~~APPLET~~, CAPTION, DT, Hn, *LABEL*, *LEGEND*, P, PRE, character highlighting**
Attributes:	*CLASS, DIR, ID, LANG, STYLE, TITLE, standard event handlers,*
	onBlur, onFocus,
	ACCESSKEY, CHARSET, COORDS, HREF, HREFLANG, NAME, REL, REV, *SHAPE, TABINDEX,* TARGET, TITLE, *TYPE*

The **A**, or *anchor*, element marks a block of the document as a hypertext link. This block can be text, highlighted text, or an image. More complex elements, such as headings, cannot be inside an anchor. In particular, note that an anchor element *cannot* contain another anchor element.

A supports the standard "generic" and "event-handler" attributes described earlier in this chapter. Note that the event handlers are only partially supported by Internet Explorer 4 and Netscape Navigator 4.

A can take several attributes. At least one *must* be either **HREF** or **NAME**—these specify the destination of the hypertext link (**HREF**) or indicate that the marked text can itself be the destination of a hypertext link (**NAME**). Both can be present, indicating that the anchor is both the beginning of one link and the end of another.

Text within anchors containing **HREF**s is usually rendered differently than plain text. Often, such text is underlined, boldfaced, or rendered with a different color. Similarly, images within anchors containing **HREF**s are usually rendered with a special border by default. Some browsers change this rendering once a link has been accessed, to inform the user that the link has been *explored*. Anchors with only a **NAME** attribute are usually not rendered in a special way.

Some examples of **A** elements are given in Figures 6.1 and 6.2, as well as 6.43 and 6.44. The element attributes are:

In HTML 4, an **A** can play a special role within an **OBJECT**—it can define anchor reference that are linked to specific regions within an image referenced by the **OBJECT**. The details of this mechanism are discussed in the **OBJECT** element section, in Chapter 7. The relevant attributes, *COORDS* and *SHAPE*, are described in the following.

ACCESSKEY="*c*" (optional; Internet Explorer 4 only)   Specifies a typeable character that can be used to access the hypertext link. For example, different anchor elements could be labeled, using **ACCESSKEY**, by the letters "a," "b," and "c." If the user then references the letter "b" on the keyboard (using some defined typing sequence), the browser will explore the link with **ACCESSKEY**="b." This functionality is supported by Internet Explorer 4—the labeled links are accessed by typing ALT-*c*, where *c* is the letter assigned to the **ACCESSKEY** attribute and ALT is the ALT key. This feature is not supported by Netscape Navigator 4.

CHARSET="*string*" (optional; not currently supported)   Specifies the character set used by the document referenced by the value of **HREF**: This attribute is thus meaningless in the absence of **HREF**. There is no default value, and in the absence of a specified **CHARSET**, the browser must determine the character set from the HTTP header or by examining the document content. There are currently no browsers that understand this attribute.

COORDS="*string*" (optional: mandatory if **SHAPE** is present and not equal to "default"; valid only inside **OBJECT**; not currently supported) Specifies the coordinates associated with the designated **SHAPE**, measured from the upper left-hand corner of the image. Coordinates can either be integer quantities, in which case they are measurements in pixels from the upper-left hand corner, or percentage values in the range (0%,0%) (the upper left-hand corner) to (100%, 100%) (lower right-hand corner).

The following table illustrates the appropriate use of coordinates for the different possible SHAPEs

SHAPE	COORDS
"circle"	"x, y, r"—A circle centered at (x,y) and of radius r.
"default"	No specified coords. Corresponds to the default behavior upon selecting a point inside the object.
"rect"	"$x\_top, y\_top, x\_bot, y\_bot$"—A rectangle with upper-left hand coordinates (x_top, y_top) and lower right-hand coordinates (x_bot, y_bot).
"poly"	"$x1, y1, ... xn, yn$"—A polygon, where the coordinates $(x1,y1)$ .... (xn,yn) are the *vertices* of the polygon (minimum of three vertices). The polygon is closed by connecting the point $(x1,y1)$ to (xn, yn).

HREF="*url*" (mandatory if **NAME** is absent)   Gives the target of a hypertext link, where "*url*" is the uniform resource locator referencing the target object.

HREFLANG="*lang-code*" (optional; not currently supported)   Specifies the language of the resource specified by the **HREF** attribute. Language codes are described in Appendix E on the companion Web site. This attribute is not currently supported.

NAME="*string*" (mandatory if **HREF** is absent)   Marks the anchored text as a possible specific destination of a hypertext link. The value "*string*" identifies this destination. For example, the element

```
<A NAME="poison"> Deadly Toadstools </A>
```

marks "Deadly Toadstools" as a possible hypertext target, referenced by the string poison. This string is called a *fragment identifier*. Within the same document, the location is referenced by the hypertext anchor

```
<A HREF="#poison">Poisonous non-mushrooms</A>
```

where the hash character indicates that the remaining text is a fragment identifier. Selecting "Poisonous non-mushrooms" links the user back to the place in the document marked by the `<A NAME="poison">...</A>` anchor.

This location can be accessed from another document via an anchor of the form:

```
<A HREF="http://www.site.edu/slimy/toads.html#poison">Poisonous</A>
```

assuming http://www.site.edu/slimy/toads.html to be the URL of the document in question. Clicking on the word "Poisonous" then links the user to the document *toads.html* and to the location marked by the <A NAME="poison">...</A> anchor. This need not be a full URL, but can also be a partial URL should the two documents lie on the same server. These issues are discussed in more detail in Chapter 2 (Example 6) and Chapter 8.

REL="*string*" (optional; valid with HREF only; not currently supported) REL attribute values describe the relationship(s) associated with the hypertext link—consequently, REL is only valid if HREF is also present. The relationship is defined between the two entire documents and is not just associated with the particular link. As an example, REL could indicate that the linked document is an index for the current one or is an annotation to the current one (which a browser might want to display as a pop-up). It is a pity that the REL (and REV, which is the converse of REL) attribute is so little used, as it can impart significant meaning and organization to large sets of related documents.

The value for REL is a space-separated list of case-insensitive relationship values (preferably a collection of name tokens). Some examples are:

```
<A HREF="http://foo.edu/fe.html" REL="next">sdfsddf</a>
```

This would mean that the document *fe.html,* at the given URL, is the next document in some author-defined document sequence. Values for the relationships and their semantics are currently being defined. Some other examples are:

```
<A HREF="http://foo.edu/note1.html" REL="annotation">related notes</a>
```

The information in the document *note1.html* is additional and subsidiary to the current document. A browser might display this as margin notes.

```
<A HREF="http://foo.edu/vers2.html" REL="supersedes">previously</a>
```

The document *vers2.html* is an earlier version of the document.

At present, the REL and REV attributes are rarely used, and most browsers do not understand them. They will be of growing importance as HTML documents and document development environments become more sophisticated.

REV="*string*" (optional; valid with HREF only; not currently supported) REV is like REL but with the relationship reversed. For example,

```
<A HREF="http://foo.edu/vers2.html" REV="supersedes"> later </a>
```

means that the document *vers2.html* is a later version of the document containing this link. Most browsers do not understand **REV** or **REL**.

SHAPE="circle," "default," "poly," "rect" (optional; used inside OBJECT only; If present, then COORDS is also mandatory; not currently supported) SHAPE is valid only for anchor elements within OBJECT elements, as discussed previously. SHAPE, in combination with the COORDS attribute, defines active regions of the image referenced by an OBJECT and attaches these regions to the remote resource indicated by the HREF attribute. SHAPE simply specifies the type of shape, the possible values being "circle," "default," "poly," and "rect."

TABINDEX="*number*" (optional; Internet Explorer 4 only)   Specifies the *tabbing order* for the linked region. By default, a user can use the **tab** key to switch between the various anchor elements, active images, and **FORM** input elements, starting from the top of the document and working down. **TABINDEX** lets an author change this default order and explicitly set the order of tabbing. This attribute is not supported on Netscape Navigator 4.

TABINDEX can apply to **A, AREA, OBJECT, INPUT, SELECT, TEXTAREA,** and **BUTTON** elements. The value assigned to **TABINDEX** is an integer: The smaller the integer, the higher the element is in the tabbing order. If two elements have the same **TABINDEX** value, then they are accessed in the order in which they appear in the document. Elements without a **TABINDEX** are accessed, sequentially, after all the elements with specified **TABINDEX** values. Elements with negative **TABINDEX** values are not accessed via tabbing, nor are any form input elements marked with a **DISABLED** attribute.

For example, consider the following elements and the associated **TABINDEX** values: The column to the right shows the order in which the elements will be accessed should the user employ the tab key to switch from element to element:

Element Markup	Tabbing Order
`<A TABINDEX="5" ....> ...`	3
`<INPUT TABINDEX="3" ...>...`	1
`<INPUT TABINDX="23" ...> ...`	5
`<A HREF="foo.org"> ...`	6
`<A HREF="foo.org" TABINDEX="-1"> ...`	*not accessible via Tab*
`<SELECT TABINDEX="12" ...>...`	4
`<A TABINDEX="4" ...> ...`	2

TARGET=*"string"* (optional)   This attribute is part of the Netscape frames technology that supports multiple browser windows and multiple *frames* within a given browser window—each frame with its own *name*. In this event, the **TARGET** attribute lets a document author direct data to be returned, upon selecting a hypertext link, to one of these *named* windows. If a window of the given name does not exist, the browser will create it. For example:

```
<A HREF="/path/file.html" TARGET="win-2">anchor text</A>
```

indicates that the retrieved document, upon accessing the anchor, should be directed to the window named "win-2." If a window or window frame with this name does not yet exist, the browser will clone a new copy of the browser, assign the name "win-2" to this new window, and direct the returned data to it.

In the absence of a **TARGET**, a document is retrieved to the window from which the link was accessed, as per standard practice.

TARGETs are most often *named frames* or panes within a given browser window. These are created by the **FRAMESET** and **FRAME** elements, which permit multiple, independent document viewing panes within the same browser window. If a frame is declared via <FRAME SRC="url" NAME="frame1">, then an anchor of the form:

```
<A HREF="/path/file.html" TARGET="frame1">anchor text</A>
```

will direct the returned document to the designated **FRAME**. **FRAME**s are discussed in Chapter 7.

Several target names are predefined, with specific meanings. These names (all beginning with the underscore character) and the associated meanings are defined in Table 6.10.

TITLE=*"string"* (optional; Internet Explorer 4 only)   Gives a title for the linked resource—valid only if **HREF** is present. This can be used by a browser to *preview* the title before retrieving a document—but note that you cannot guarantee that the **TITLE** is correct until you actually access the resource. Alternatively, **TITLE** can provide a title for a document that would otherwise not have a title, such as a plain text file, an image file, or a directory. Internet Explorer will display the content of the **TITLE** as a tool-tip pop-up when the mouse rests on top of the anchored text.

TYPE=*"mime-type"* (optional; not currently supported)   Gives a MIME content-type of the resource referenced by the **HREF** attribute.

Table 6.10 Predefined Target Names and Their Meanings

TARGET Value	Meaning
_blank	Load the referenced data into a new, unnamed window.
_self	Load the referenced data in place of the current document.
_parent	Load the referenced data into the window containing (or that contained) the *parent* of the current document (the document from which the current document was accessed). If there is no parent document, default to TARGET="_self."
_top	Load the referenced data into the window containing (or that contained) the "top" document (the document obtained by iteratively searching through successive parent documents until arriving at the initial, starting document). If there is no top document, default to TARGET="_self."
NOTE:	All other names beginning with an underscore (_) are ignored by the browser.

Phrase-Level Markup

Phrase-level markup elements specify special properties for a phrase or a string of characters—such elements do not cause line breaks or otherwise affect block layout of the text. HTML supports two types of phrase-level markup: *logical* (also called information-type formatting or idiomatic phrase markup) and *physical* (also called character or typographic formatting). Logical markup is more in keeping with the markup language model and marks blocks of text as pieces of typed computer code, variables, or as something to be emphasized. The rendering details are then left to the browser, although hints as to appropriate renderings are part of the HTML specifications. You are strongly encouraged to use logical elements rather than physical ones, whenever possible.

Physical markup requests a specific physical format, such as boldface or italics. This, of course, gives no clue to the underlying meaning behind the marked-up phrase. Thus, if a browser is unable to implement the indicated markup (e.g., if it is a dumb terminal that cannot do italics), it cannot easily determine an alternative highlighting style.

Logical styles may not be rendered in distinct ways (i.e., different logical styles may be rendered in the same way). Also, some browsers do not support all physical styles. For example, lynx does not support italics and renders it as underlined.

The different logical formatting elements are summarized in Table 6.11 and the physical formatting elements in Table 6.12. Figures 6.47 through 6.50 illustrate their use.

Table 6.11 Logical Highlighting Elements and Recommended Formatting

Element	Meaning	Recommended Formatting
ABBR	abbreviation	no recommended formatting
ACRONYM	acronym	no recommended formatting
BDO	bi-directional override of text	lay out the flow of text as specified by the DIR attribute value
CITE	citation	italics
CODE	example of typed code	fixed-width font
DFN	definition	italics
EM	emphasized text	italics
KBD	keyboard input; for example, in a manual	fixed-width
Q	short quotation	surround text with appropriate punctuation
SAMP	sequence of literal characters	fixed-width
STRONG	strong emphasis	boldface
VAR	variable name	italics

Content Model for Phrase-Level Elements

The content model for all the character highlighting elements is largely the same, so to avoid needless repetition, it is given once here. In the following content model, NAME is one of ABBR, B, BIG, BDO, CITE, CODE, DFN, EM, FONT, I, KBD, Q, S, SAMP, SMALL, SPAN, STRIKE, STRONG, SUB, SUP, TT, U, or VAR.

Usage:	<NAME> ... </NAME>
Can Contain:	characters, character highlighting, A, APPLET, *BASE-FONT*, BR, *BUTTON*, *IFRAME*, IMG, INPUT, *LABEL*, MAP, *OBJECT*, SCRIPT, SELECT, TEXTAREA
Can Be Inside:	ADDRESS, BLOCKQUOTE, BODY, CAPTION, ~~CENTER~~, DD, DIV, DT, *FIELDSET*, FORM, Hn, LI, *NOFRAMES*, *NOSCRIPT*, P, PRE, TD, TH, character highlighting, A, APPLET, *BUTTON*, *IFRAME*, *LABEL*, *LEGEND*, *OBJECT*
Attributes:	*CLASS, DIR, ID, LANG, STYLE, TITLE, standard event handlers*

Table 6.12 Physical Highlighting Elements and Recommended Formatting

Element	Meaning
B	boldface
BIG	bigger text
~~FONT~~	font size, face, or color
I	italics
	strike-through (equivalent to STRIKE)
SMALL	smaller text
SPAN	style sheet-specified formatting information
~~STRIKE~~	strike-through (equivalent to S)
SUB	subscript
SUP	superscript
TT	fixed-width font
~~U~~	underlined

There are four important exceptions to this content model:

1. The elements **BIG, FONT, SMALL, SUB,** and **SUP** are not allowed inside **PRE.**
2. The **FONT** element takes a different set of attributes. These attributes are discussed in the **FONT** element description.
3. The **BDO** element takes a different set of attributes. These attributes are discussed in the **BDO** element description.
4. The **Q** element takes an additional **CITE** attribute, discussed later in the **Q** element description.

You can nest highlighting modes inside one another. However, this is often not sensible with logical highlighting elements, given the rather specific meanings assigned to them—be careful that you are nesting things in a meaningful way! Note also that different browsers may interpret complicated nestings in different ways and that the resulting rendering can be unpredictable.

Physical highlighting elements can be nested; and these nestings (unlike those involving logical highlighting elements) often make sense. Therefore, requesting that a block of text be rendered in *underlined, boldface italics* is entirely reasonable.

Examples of the different elements are shown in Figures 6.47 and 6.48.

Figure 6.47 HTML example document illustrating the different phrase markup elements. Figure 6.48 shows this document as displayed by the Internet Explorer 4 browser.

```
<HTML><HEAD>
<TITLE> Example of Phrase-Level Markup Elements </TITLE>
</HEAD>
<BODY BGCOLOR="#ffffff">
<UL>
  <LI> <FONT SIZE="+1" COLOR="red"><B>A) Logical
        Phrase-Level Markup </B></FONT>
  <LI> ABBR - An example abbreviation is <ABBR>abbr</ABBR>
  <LI> ACRONYM - An example acronym is <ABBR>radar</ABBR>
  <LI> BDO - This is <BDO DIR="rtl">bi-directional overriden</BDO> text
  <LI> CITE - This is <CITE>citation</CITE> text
  <LI> CODE - This is <CODE>typed computer code</CODE> text
  <LI> DFN - This is <DFN>a defining instance</DFN> text
  <LI> EM - This is <EM>emphasized</EM> text
  <LI> KBD - This is <KBD>keyboard input</KBD> text
  <LI> Q - Here is an <Q>inline quotation</Q> inside a sentence.
  <LI> SAMP - This is <SAMP>literal character</SAMP> text
  <LI> STRONG - This is <STRONG>strongly emphasized</STRONG> text
  <LI> VAR - This is <VAR>a variable</VAR> text
</UL>

<UL>
  <LI> <FONT SIZE="+1" COLOR="red"><B>B) Physical
        Phrase-Level Markup </B> </FONT>
  <LI> B - This is <B>boldfaced</B> text
  <LI> BIG - This is <BIG>bigger</BIG> text
  <LI> I - This is <I>italicized</I> text
  <LI> S - This is <S>strike-through</S> text
  <LI> SMALL - This is <SMALL>small</SMALL> text
  <LI> SPAN - This is an example of <SPAN>spanned</SPAN> text.
  <LI> STRIKE - This is <STRIKE>strike-out</STRIKE> text
  <LI> SUB - This is sub<SUB>script</SUB> text
  <LI> SUP - This is super<SUP>script</SUP> text
  <LI> TT - This is <TT>fixed-width typewriter font</TT> text
  <LI> U - This is <U> underlined </U>text
</UL>
```

Continued

Figure 6.47 Continued.

```
<UL>
  <LI> <FONT SIZE="+1" COLOR="red"><B>C) Special-Meaning
       Markup </B></FONT>
  <LI> INS - This is <INS>some inserted</INS> text
  <LI> DEL - This is <DEL>some deleted</DEL> text
</UL>
</BODY> </HTML>
```

Logical Phrase-Level Elements

ABBR Element: An Abbreviation (Not Currently Supported)

ABBR marks an abbreviation, such as "Ont." (for Ontario) or "Fr." (for France). There is no special rendering associated with this element, although the TITLE attribute can be used to describe the origin of the acronym. For example:

```
<ABBR LANG="en" TITLE="Millisecond">ms</ABBR>
```

This element is not currently supported.

Figure 6.48 Display, by the Internet Explorer 4 browser, of the document shown in Figure 6.47.

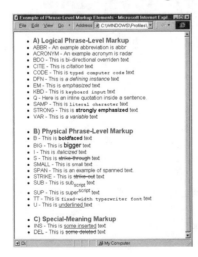

ACRONYM Element: An Acronym (Internet Explorer 4 only)

ACRONYM marks an acronym, such as HTTP or NATO. There is no special rendering associated with this element, although the **TITLE** attribute can be used to describe the origin of the acronym. For example:

```
<ABBR LANG="en" TITLE="HyperText Transfer Protocol">HTTP</ABBR>
```

The HTML specification does not recommend any special formatting for this element. This element is currently supported by Internet Explorer 4, which can set special rendering using a style sheet.

BDO Element: Bi-Directional Override (Not Currently Supported)

Attributes: *CLASS, DIR, ID, LANG, STYLE, TITLE*

BDO marks an inline section of text for *bi-directional-override*. The purpose is to force a particular directionality to the characters within the element, regardless of their intrinsic (or language-implied) directional properties. **DIR** is thus a mandatory attribute for **BDO**, while all other attributes are optional.

Note that **BDO** does not support any of the event-handler attributes. Note also that **BDO** is not supported by either Netscape Navigator 4 or Internet Explorer 4.

CITE Element: Citation

CITE marks a small *citation*—for example, a book or other document reference. Typically, this block of text will be rendered in italics, subject to the capabilities of the browser.

CODE Element: Typed Code

The **CODE** element marks a selection of typed computer code—for example, a single line of code from a program. Large selections of code should be displayed using a **PRE** element, which properly reproduces space characters and line breaks. **CODE** element contents should be rendered in a fixed-width typewriter font.

DFN Element: Defining Instance or Definition

DFN marks a selection of text as the *defining instance* of a term. The text content should be rendered in italics, as demonstrated by Internet Explorer. Netscape Navigator, however, renders **DFN** content with an unmodified font.

EM Element: Emphasis

EM marks a block of text for *emphasis*. Typically, the marked block of text is rendered in italics, subject to the capabilities of the browser. For example, lynx represents EM emphasized text by an underline.

KBD Element: Keyboard Input

KBD marks a block of text as *keyboard input*. Typically, this is displayed with a fixed-width typewriter font.

Q Element: Short Inline Quotation (Internet Explorer 4 Only)

Additional Attribute: *CITE*

Q marks an inline sequence of text that is a *quotation*. A browser should render this appropriate to the language, for example by surrounding the text with appropriate punctuation symbols, such as quotation marks. Q also supports an optional CITE attribute, which takes as its value a URL referencing the source of the quotation. This element is supported by Internet Explorer 4, although this browser does not assign any special formatting to the element—special formatting must be assigned, by the author, via a style sheet.

SAMP Element: Literal Characters

SAMP marks a block of text as a sequence of literal or *sample* characters. Typically, this is rendered in a fixed-width typewriter font.

STRONG Element: Strong Emphasis

STRONG marks a block of text for **strong** emphasis. Typically, this is rendered in boldface, although text-only browsers, such as lynx, use an underline (with lynx, EM and STRONG emphasis are displayed in the same way).

VAR Element: A Variable

VAR marks a *variable name*. This is typically rendered in italics or bold italics.

Physical Phrase-Level Elements

B Element: Boldface

B marks an inline block of text to be rendered in **boldface**. If this is impossible, the browser can render it in some other way (lynx uses an underline).

BIG Element: Text with Enlarged Font

Can Be Inside: Not allowed inside **PRE**

BIG marks text that should be rendered, when possible, with a font slightly larger than the font of the surrounding text. Enclosed images are not affected. **BIG** is ignored if a larger font is not available. **BIG** is equivalent to a **FONT** element with `<FONT SIZE="+1">`. Note that **BIG** is not allowed inside **PRE**. **BIG** is supported by Netscape Navigator 3, Internet Explorer 3, and later.

FONT Element: Select Text Font Size and Color

Can Be Inside: Not allowed inside **PRE**

Attributes: *CLASS, DIR, ID, LANG, STYLE, TITLE,*

COLOR, <u>FACE</u>, SIZE, (<u>POINT-SIZE</u>, <u>WEIGHT</u>: Netscape Navigator 4 only)

FONT marks text that should be rendered in modified color, size, or font face. **FONT** has no effect on enclosed **IMG** elements. **FONT** can take three attributes: **SIZE** for the font size, **COLOR** for the font color, and **FACE** for the font face. Note that **FONT** is not allowed inside **PRE**.

TIP: Use Style Sheets Instead of FONT

If you are really worried about obtaining absolutely precise control over formatting and presentation by using the **FONT** element, then you should be reading the style sheets section in Chapter 7 instead. **FONT** is a very crude tool for typesetting documents, and the style sheet mechanisms provide much better ways of accomplishing the same things.

Examples showing the use of **FONT** are shown in Figures 6.49 and 6.50. The supported attributes and their meanings are:

COLOR=*"#rrggbb,"* or *"color"* (optional)   Specifies the desired color for the text, either as a hexadecimal RGB code or as a named color. If using this attribute, be careful that the text color contrasts well with the display background.

<u>FACE</u>=*"string"* (optional)   This attribute, introduced by Microsoft but now widely supported, lets an author specify the desired typeface (**FACE**="Arial," "Times," etc.) to be used for the displayed text. Supported names depend on the fonts installed on the user's computer and on the browser; for example, on a typical Windows 95 system, the name "Helvetica" works with Netscape Navigator 3 but not Internet Explorer 3. Note also that the names are tied to the Microsoft font

names, and many fonts by these names are not found on other platforms (Macintosh or UNIX) or other PC operating systems (OS/2). On any system, **FACE** only works if the designated font is installed on the system.

FACE names are *space sensitive*. Thus to request the Arial black font you need **FACE**="Arial black" and not **FACE**="Arialblack." Names are not, however, *case sensitive*.

You can specify multiple fonts by separating the font names by commas. Thus **FACE**="Arial,helvetica,times" asks the browser to first try the Arial font, followed by Helvetica (if Arial is not present), and finally the times font (if Helvetica is not present).

Some font names are shown in Table 6.13 and are shown rendered in Figure 6.50.

POINT-SIZE="*number*" (optional; Netscape Navigator 4 only)
Specifies the desired font size for the text, in points. This allows for precise specification of font size and is an adjunct to the **SIZE** attribute. Equivalent functionality is available using style sheets, so authors should avoid this attribute and use style sheet rules instead.

SIZE="+*number*," "-*number*," or "*number*" (optional)   Specifies the desired font size for the text, either as an absolute size ("*number*") or as a size relative to the size of the surrounding font —"+*number*" for a bigger font, "-*number*" for a smaller font. Absolute font sizes range from 1 (the smallest) to 7 (the largest), with the default value being 3. For example, <FONT SIZE="1"> requests the smallest possible font, while <FONT SIZE="-2"> requests a font two sizes smaller than the current font. The default font size (with respect to which relative sizes are calculated) can be reset via the **BASEFONT** element.

Table 6.13 Some Supported Font Face Names with Examples

Font Name	Example	Font Name	Example
Arial	example	Arial black	**example**
Book Antiqua	example	Bookman	example
Courier	example	Garamond	example
Helvetica	example	Helvetica-narrow	example
Modern	example	Palatino	example
Times (Times New Roman)	example		

<u>WEIGHT</u>="100," "200," "300," . . . "900" (optional; Netscape Navigator 4 only)   Specifies the font weight or degree of boldness. There are nine allowed values, ranging from "100" (lightest weight) to "900" (heaviest weight) in steps of 100. Equivalent functionality is available using style sheets, so authors should avoid this attribute and use style sheet rules instead.

I Element: Italics

I marks a section to be rendered in *italics*. If this is impossible, the browser can render it in some other way (lynx uses an underline).

S Element: Strike-Through

S marks a section to be rendered with a line ~~struck-through~~ the text and is a synonym for **STRIKE**. If this is impossible, the browser can render this in some other way (lynx currently ignores this element). Note that HTML 4 marks this element as deprecated, indicating that this element is likely to be dropped in a future version of HTML. It should therefore be avoided as much as possible in new documents.

SMALL Element: Text with Smaller Font

Can Be Inside: Not allowed inside **PRE**

SMALL marks text that should be rendered, when possible, with a font slightly smaller than the font of the surrounding text. Enclosed images are not affected. **SMALL** is ignored if a smaller font is not available. **SMALL** is equivalent to a **FONT** element with `<FONT SIZE="-1">`. Note that **SMALL** is not allowed inside **PRE**. **SMALL** is supported by Netscape Navigator 3, Internet Explorer 3, and later.

SPAN Element: Generic Container for Inline Text

SPAN is a generic container for inline text or markup and is essentially the inline equivalent of the block element **DIV**. There is no special formatting associated with **SPAN** content. However, style sheets can be used to apply specific formatting to spans of text. Indeed, this is the main intent of **SPAN**—to provide markup whereby a style sheet can apply formatting to specific blocks of inline text. In this sense, you can think of **SPAN** as a general-purpose successor to the **FONT** element.

STRIKE Element: Struck-Out Text

STRIKE marks a block of text to be ~~struck-out~~ for some logical reason (typically, to indicate text that has been deleted). Lynx may render this is reverse-video. Note that HTML 4 marks this element as deprecated, indicating that it is likely to be dropped in a future version of HTML. It should therefore be avoided in new documents. The new **INS** and **DEL** elements, discussed later in this chapter, are designed for marking inserted or deleted sections of a document.

Figure 6.49 Example HTML document illustrating the use of the FONT element. Browser rendering of this document is shown in Figure 6.50.

```
<HTML><HEAD>
<TITLE> The FONT Element </TITLE>
</HEAD><BODY>
<H2 ALIGN="center"> The FONT Element </H2>

<FONT SIZE="+1"><B>Font Size</B> --</FONT>
You can use <B>FONT</B> to control font size. For example,
<FONT SIZE=2>t<FONT SIZE=3>h<FONT SIZE=4>i<FONT SIZE=5>s
<FONT SIZE=6>i</FONT>s </FONT>o</FONT>d</FONT>d </FONT>
looking, as I adjusted the size of each letter.
You can use this for large capital letters in
headings:
<p><FONT SIZE="+1">I</FONT>AN <FONT SIZE="+1">G</FONT>RAHAM'S
   <FONT SIZE="+1">H</FONT>OME
   <FONT SIZE="+1">P</FONT>AGE -- (with size change on
   leading letters)
<HR SIZE=4>
<FONT SIZE="+1"><B>Font Color -- </B></FONT>
You can can also control text color. For example,
the default text is black, but the following words are
<FONT COLOR="red">bright red</FONT>,
<FONT COLOR="#00ff00">bright green</FONT>, and
<FONT COLOR="#cccccc">light gray</FONT>. This of course, loses
some of its impact when printed in black and white....
<HR SIZE=4>
<FONT SIZE="+1"><B>Font Face -- </B></FONT>
Some browsers support font face control. This is nonstandardized,
and depends on (a) browser support for this extension, and (b) the
presence of the font on your computer. Here is a table of
some examples:
<BR><BR>
<CENTER>
<TABLE WIDTH="80%" CELLPADDING=2 CELLSPACING=3
       BGCOLOR="#cccccc" BORDER>
<TR>
  <TD><FONT FACE="arial">Arial</FONT>
  <TD><FONT FACE="Book antiqua">Book antiqua</FONT>
  <TD><FONT FACE="Helvetica">Helvetica</FONT>
```

Figure 6.49 Continued.

```
</TR>
<TR>
   <TD><FONT FACE="modern">modern</FONT>
   <TD><FONT FACE="times">times</FONT>
   <TD><FONT FACE="arial black">arial black</FONT>
</TR>
<TR>
   <TD><FONT FACE="bookman">bookman</FONT>
   <TD><FONT FACE="garamond">garamond</FONT>
   <TD><FONT FACE="helvetica-narrow">helvetica-narrow</FONT>
</TR>
<TR>
   <TD><FONT FACE="palatino">palatino</FONT>
   <TD><FONT FACE="lucida sans">lucida sans</FONT>
   <TD><FONT FACE="helvetica narrow">   </FONT>
</TR>
</TABLE>
</CENTER>
</BODY> </HTML>
```

Figure 6.50 Rendering, by the Netscape Navigator 3 browser, of the document shown in Figure 6.49. Note that these font names are not supported on all browsers, as discussed in the text.

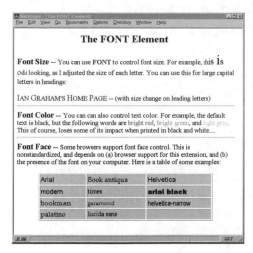

SUB Element: Subscript

> Can Be Inside: Not allowed inside **PRE**

SUB marks text that should be rendered as a subscript relative to the preceding text. The content of **SUB** may also be rendered in a smaller font, if possible. This is an unsafe element for browsers that do not support it, since subscripted text will be incorrectly presented by a browser that does not understand **SUB**. An example is

CaCO₃

Note that **SUB** is not allowed inside **PRE**. **SUB** is supported by Netscape Navigator 3, Internet Explorer 3, and later.

SUP Element: Superscript

> Can Be Inside: Not allowed inside **PRE**

SUP marks text that should be rendered as a superscript relative to the preceding text. The content of **SUP** may also be rendered in a smaller font, if possible. This is an unsafe element for browsers that do not support it, since superscripted text will be incorrectly presented by a browser that does not understand **SUP**. An example is:

x²

Note that **SUP** is not allowed inside **PRE**. **SUP** is supported by Netscape Navigator 3, Internet Explorer 3, and later.

TT Element: Fixed-Width Typewriter Font

TT marks a section to be rendered with a fixed-width typewriter font.

U Element: Underline

U marks a section to be rendered with an <u>underline</u>. This element is understood by some, but not all, browsers. Note that HTML 4 marks this element as deprecated, indicating that it is likely to be dropped in a future version of HTML. It should therefore be avoided as much as possible in new documents.

Phrase-Level Meta-Information Elements

Meta-information elements provide information used by the document, but not explicitly presented to the reader/user. The four relevant elements are: **MAP** and **AREA**, which provide imagemapping data used by client-side imagemaps; **BASEFONT**, which toggles default font characteristics; and **SCRIPT**, which includes a program script within an HTML document. Note that **SCRIPT**s that do not write any content into the document body should be placed in the **HEAD**. This element was thus described previously in this chapter in the **HEAD** element section.

BASEFONT Element: Set Default Font Characteristics

Usage:	`<BASEFONT>`
Can Contain:	empty
Can Be Inside:	ADDRESS, BLOCKQUOTE, BODY, CAPTION, ~~CENTER~~, DD, DIV, DT, *FIELDSET*, FORM, Hn, LI, *NOFRAMES, NOSCRIPT*, P, PRE, TD, TH,
	character highlighting, A, APPLET, *BUTTON*, *IFRAME, LABEL, LEGEND, OBJECT*
Attributes:	*COLOR, FACE, ID SIZE*

BASEFONT specifies the default font characteristics—primarily font size—for all text following. However, it does not affect the size of text within heading elements or inside table cells. Internet Explorer also supports text color and font face control; these are not supported by other browsers. With Internet Explorer, **BASEFONT**-specified colors and faces override any settings set by **BODY** element attributes. In addition, **BASEFONT** has some odd behaviors under Internet Explorer 3/4: With this browser, **BASEFONT** does not affect the size of the text inside headings or tables, but it can change the font family (**FACE**) or color (**COLOR**) of the text inside these elements!

The attribute specifications are:

SIZE="*number*" (optional)   Specifies the default font size, as a value from 1 to 7 (the default is 3), relative to the "default" size on the browser. Note that **BASEFONT** does not affect the size of text inside heading elements.

COLOR="*#rrggbb*," "*color*" (optional; Internet Explorer only)   Specifies the default text color, either as an RGB value or as a named color.

FACE="*string*" (optional; Internet Explorer only)   Specifies the default font face for the document, either as a font name or as a sequence of comma-separated font names. The browser will try all fonts from left to right and will choose the first possible font.

BASEFONT should ideally appear prior to any displayed text in the **BODY** of the document. Localized changes to the font size should be implemented using **SPAN** and style sheets, as discussed in Chapter 7.

MAP Element: Client-Side Imagemap Database

Usage:	`<MAP> ... </MAP>`
Can Contain:	**AREA**
Can Be Inside:	ADDRESS, BLOCKQUOTE, BODY, CAPTION, ~~CENTER~~, DD, DIV, DT, *FIELDSET*, FORM, Hn, LI, *NOFRAMES, NOSCRIPT*, P, PRE, TD, TH,
	character highlighting, A, APPLET, *BUTTON*, *IFRAME, LABEL, LEGEND, OBJECT*

Attributes:	*CLASS, DIR, ID, LANG, STYLE, TITLE, standard event handlers,*
	NAME

A **MAP** element contains *client-side imagemap* mapping data. Each **MAP** must be uniquely identified by the **NAME** attribute: for example, `<MAP NAME="map1">`. The value for NAME is an arbitrary string. A map is then referenced from an **IMG** element using the **USEMAP** attribute, for example:

```
<IMG SRC="image.gif" .... USEMAP="#map1">
```

A single document can contain any number of **MAP** elements, each uniquely identified by a **NAME**. In principle, a **MAP** need not be in the same document as the **IMG** from which it is referenced, so that the above reference should also be possible via:

```
<IMG SRC="image.gif" ... USEMAP="http://some.where.ca/maps/maps.html#map1">
```

where the file *maps.html* contains **MAP** elements used in several different documents. There are, however, no browsers that currently support such external **MAP** elements.

In addition to the mandatory **NAME** attribute, **MAP** also supports the standard "generic" and "event-handler" attributes described earlier in this chapter. Note that the event handlers are only partially supported by current browsers.

A **MAP** element must contain **AREA** elements—these are the only elements allowed within a **MAP**. **AREA** elements mark out the regions of an image and the URLs to which these regions are linked, for example:

```
<MAP NAME="map1">
  <AREA SHAPE="rect" COORD="10,20,50,50" HREF="stuff.html">
  <AREA SHAPE="rect" COORD="30,40,60,60" HREF="otherstuff.html">
...
</MAP>
```

SHAPE and coordinate specifications are discussed in the next section.

AREA Element: Client-Side Imagemap Mapping Areas

Usage:	`<AREA>`
Can Contain:	empty
Can Be Inside:	**MAP**
Attributes:	*CLASS, DIR, ID, LANG, STYLE, TITLE, standard event handlers,*
	onBlur, onFocus,
	ACCESSKEY, ALT, COORDS, HREF, <u>NAME</u>, NOHREF, SHAPE, *TABINDEX,* TARGET

The **AREA** element specifies shaped regions in a mapped image and the URLs associated with the shape. The meanings and uses of the attributes are:

ACCESSKEY="c" (optional; Internet Explorer 4 only)   Specifies a typeable character that can be used to access the area. For example, areas in an image could be labeled, using **ACCESSKEY**, by the letters "a," "b," and "c." If the user then selects the letter "c" on the keyboard, the browser will access the **HREF** referenced by the **AREA** with **ACCESSKEY**="c." This functionality is not supported by Netscape Navigator 4 or earlier, but is supported by Internet Explorer 4: With Internet Explorer 4, keys are selected by simultaneously typing the characters ALT-*c*, where *c* is the character to select and ALT is the ALT key

ALT=*"string"* (optional; not widely supported)   Gives a text description of the mapped region that can be presented to the user as a description of the linked region or can be used by browsers that cannot display the image. This attribute is not widely supported.

COORDS=*"x1,y1,x2,y2....."* (mandatory if **SHAPE** is not equal to "default")   Specifies the comma-separated coordinates of the defined **SHAPE**, as a sequence of *(x,y)* pairs—the required number of pairs depends on the specified **SHAPE**. Coordinates are specified in pixels measured from the upper left-hand corner of the image. The coordinate specifications for each of the four different **SHAPE**s are:

SHAPE	COORDS	Description
"rect"	*"x1,y1,x2,y2"*	where *(x1,y1)* are the coordinates of the upper left-hand corner and *(x2,y2)* are the coordinates of the lower right-hand corner
"circle"	*"xc,yc,r"*	where *(xc,yc)* is the circle center, and *(r)* is the circle radius
"poly"	*"x1,y1,x2,y2 ... xn,yn"*	where *(x1,y1)* ... *(xn,yn)* are the coordinates of the vertices of the polygon
"default"	N/A	the default behavior if the mouse is clicked in an undefined region.

AREAs can overlap—in this case, the browser searches sequentially down through the different **AREA** elements, and selects the first acceptable entry.

HREF=*"url"* (one of **HREF** and **NOHREF** is required)   Specifies the URL to which the region is linked. Note that partial URLs are evaluated relative to the URL of the **MAP** file—recall that the **MAP** need not be in the same document as the **IMG** element referencing the **MAP**. Similarly, if the document containing the **MAP** element also contains a **BASE** element, relative URLs specified by the **HREF** will be evaluated relative to the base URL.

<u>NAME</u>="*string*" (optional)   Specifies a name identifier for the area. This area is then accessible, via this name, by a JavaScript program. JavaScript (as of Netscape Navigator 3) can then modify the URL referenced by this **AREA** element.

NOHREF (one of **HREF** and **NOHREF** is required)   Indicates that the browser should take no action if the user clicks inside the specified region and should continue to display the current document.

SHAPE="rect," "circle," "poly," "default" (optional)   Indicates the type of shape being specified in the **AREA** element. If **SHAPE** is not specified, a browser assumes the default **SHAPE**="rect." "Default" specifies no area, and corresponds to the default behavior should none of the specified regions be selected.

NOTE: Problem with Internet Explorer 3 and 4

The Internet Explorer 3 browser does not support the **SHAPE** values "circle," "poly," or "default" (it only supports "rect"), while Internet Explorer 4 does not support the value "default." All four values are supported by Netscape Navigator 3 and 4.

TABINDEX= "*number*" (optional; Internet Explorer 4 only)   Specifies the *tabbing order* for the linked region. By default, a user can use the tab key to switch between the various anchor elements, active images, and **FORM** input elements, starting from the top of the document and working down. **TABINDEX** lets an author change this default order and explicitly set the order of tabbing. Please see the anchor element section for further details. Internet Explorer 4 supports the **TABINDEX** attribute, but Netscape Navigator 4 does not.

TARGET= "*string*" (optional)   Specifies the name of the *frame* or window to which the returned data should be sent. This attribute is used to the same purpose with the **A** (anchor element). Please see the anchor element section for further details.

Character-Like Elements

These elements provide character-like behavior within the document. The only such element defined in HTML 4 is **BR**. The proprietary HTML extensions **WBR** (word break) and **SPACER** (an arbitrary text spacing) are described in Chapter 7.

BR Element: Line Break

Usage:	` `
Can Contain:	empty
Can Be Inside:	**ADDRESS, BLOCKQUOTE, BODY, CAPTION,** ~~**CENTER**~~**, DD, DIV, DT,** *FIELDSET,* **FORM, Hn, LI,** *NOFRAMES, NOSCRIPT,* **P, PRE, TD, TH,**
	character highlighting, A, APPLET, *BUTTON, IFRAME, LABEL, LEGEND, OBJECT*
Attributes:	*CLASS, ID, STYLE, TITLE,* **CLEAR**

BR indicates a line break. This is fundamentally different from a paragraph element—`<BR>` is treated as a character (like a *hard* carriage return), while **P** defines a text block as a paragraph. An example of **BR** is shown in Figure 6.9 and 6.10, where it is used to break lines in an **ADDRESS**. **BR** can also break lines in a poem, with **P** elements marking the different verses.

BR takes the standard "generic" attributes **CLASS, ID, STYLE,** and **TITLE,** but does not take **LANG** nor the "event-handling" attributes. These attributes were described earlier in this chapter.

In the case of text flow around right- and left-aligned images, tables, or other objects, an author must be able to specify how the text should break; that is, should the text simple continue at the next line that runs alongside the image, or should it break until the next line can be flush with the left, right, or both margins? In HTML, **BR** with an optional **CLEAR** can make this specification. The possible **CLEAR** values and their meanings are:

CLEAR="left," "right," "all," "none" (optional) `<BR CLEAR="left">` breaks the line and moves the following text down until the text can be flushed with the left margin. `<BR CLEAR="right">` breaks the line and moves the following text down until the right margin is clear. `<BR CLEAR="all">` breaks the line and moves the following text down until both margins are clear. Last, `<BR CLEAR="none">` is simply the default value, and is rarely specified in a document. It may, however, be useful to override a default text flow specified in an associated style sheet.

Note that HTML 4 recommends the use of style sheet rules, in place of a **CLEAR** attribute. For example, to implement a BR element that clears to the right margin, the **STYLE** element could contain:

```
<STYLE>
BR.rightimage  {clear: right}
</STYLE>
```

with the body of the document containing BR elements of the form:

```
Here is some text .... <BR CLASS="rightimage">
```

Some example of **BR** elements are shown in Figures 6.43 and 6.44.

Special Markup: DEL, INS, and NOSCRIPT

There are two special elements, **INS** and **DEL**, used to denote inserted and deleted blocks of a document. These are designed for use in document management and revision, where it is important to track the various changes that have taken place in the document and either display these changes or let the reader toggle between different versions.

Because of this purpose, **INS** and **DEL** are neither inline nor block elements: These elements can, in fact, contain either block or inline elements, depending on what content has been inserted or deleted. Figure 6.48 illustrates a possible rendering for the content marked up by these elements. Note, however, that this rendering can (and probably should) be altered using style sheet rules.

HTML 4 permits **INS** and **DEL** elements anywhere inside the **BODY**—including anywhere within any nonempty element lying inside the **BODY**, with the exception of **SCRIPT** and **TEXTAREA**. Most commonly, INS and DEL are used to indicate inserted or deleted blocks of text, but the markup model lets you also use **INS** and **DEL** to delimit inserted and deleted table rows, or inserted or deleted **LI** list items. Note, however, however, that Internet Explorer 4—the only browser to currently support **INS** and **DEL**—does not support these elements around **TD**, **TR** or other table-markup elements.

You must not use these elements to break the distinction between block-level and inline elements. For example, you cannot use markup of the form:

```
<EM> emphasized text
<INS>
<DIV> here is a block of text
</DIV>
</INS>
and some more emphasized text
</EM>
```

Although the content model formally permits this, it is nevertheless illegal, and **EM** element cannot contain a **DIV**. A general rule is to look at the document with the **INS** or **DEL** elements removed: If the resulting markup is illegal, then the **INS** or **DEL** elements are illegally placed in the document. This is why this book does not mention **INS** and **DEL** elements in the content rules listed earlier in this chapter, and also in Chapter 7.

Last, the **NOSCRIPT** element contains HTML markup to be displayed by browsers that do not support scripting.

NOSCRIPT is supported by most current browsers. DEL and INS are supported by Internet Explorer 4, but not Netscape Navigator 4.

DEL Element: Deleted Text

Usage:	`<DEL> ... </DEL>`
Can Contain:	ADDRESS, BLOCKQUOTE, ~~CENTER~~, *COLGROUP*, DD, ~~DIR~~, DIV, DL, DT, *FIELDSET*, FORM, Hn, HR, [ISINDEX], LI, ~~MENU~~, *NOFRAMES*, *NOSCRIPT*, OL, P, PRE, TABLE, TD, *TBODY*, *TFOOT*, TH, *THEAD*, TR, UL,
	DEL, *INS*,
	characters, character highlighting, A, APPLET, *BASEFONT*, BR, *BUTTON*, CAPTION, *IFRAME*, IMG, INPUT, *LABEL*, MAP, *OBJECT*, *OPTGROUP*, OPTION, SCRIPT, SELECT, TEXTAREA
Can Be Inside:	ADDRESS, BLOCKQUOTE, BODY, ~~CENTER~~, *COLGROUP*, ~~DIR~~, DIV, DD, DL, DT, *FIELDSET*, FORM, Hn, LI, ~~MENU~~, *NOFRAMES*, *NOSCRIPT*, OL, P, PRE, TABLE, TD, *TBODY*, *TFOOT*, TH, *THEAD*, TR, UL,
	DEL, *INS*,
	character highlighting, A, APPLET, *BUTTON*, CAPTION, *IFRAME*, *LABEL*, MAP, *OBJECT*, *OPTGROUP*, OPTION, SELECT
Attributes:	*CLASS, DIR, ID, LANG, STYLE, TITLE, standard event handlers*,
	CITE, DATETIME

This element marks text that has been deleted. The browser should display this in a distinctive way, for example by rendering it in a different color or with a line struck through it. This behavior can, of course, be modified using a style sheet. This element is supported by Internet Explorer 4 (by default, the text is rendered with an underline), but is not supported by Netscape Navigator 4.

DEL supports the standard "generic" and "event-handler" attributes described earlier in this chapter. Note that the event handlers are only partially supported by Internet Explorer 4 and are not supported by Netscape Navigator 4. In addition, DEL supports the two optional attributes CITE and DATETIME to provide details related to the insertions and deletions. The meanings of these attributes are:

CITE="url" (optional) Specifies a URL that references a document that explains the reasons for the change, or the source of the change. Current browsers do not support this attribute.

DATETIME="*string*" (optional)   Specifies the time and date when the change was made. The value of this attribute must be of the format:

`YYYY-MM-DDThh:mm:ssTZD`

The meanings of these fields are defined in Table 6.14.

INS Element: Inserted Text

Usage:	`<INS> ... </INS>`
Can Contain:	ADDRESS, BLOCKQUOTE, ~~CENTER~~, *COLGROUP*, DD, ~~DIR~~, DIV, DL, DT, *FIELDSET*, FORM, Hn, HR, [ISINDEX], LI, ~~MENU~~, *NOFRAMES*, *NOSCRIPT*, OL, P, PRE, TABLE, TD, *TBODY*, *TFOOT*, TH, *THEAD*, TR, UL,
	DEL, *INS*,
	characters, character highlighting, A, APPLET, *BASE-FONT*, BR, *BUTTON*, CAPTION, *IFRAME*, IMG, INPUT, *LABEL*, MAP, *OBJECT*, *OPTGROUP*, OPTION, SCRIPT, SELECT, TEXTAREA
Can Be Inside:	ADDRESS, BLOCKQUOTE, BODY, ~~CENTER~~, *COLGROUP*, ~~DIR~~, DIV, DD, DL, DT, *FIELDSET*, FORM, Hn, LI, ~~MENU~~, *NOFRAMES*, *NOSCRIPT*, OL, P, PRE, TABLE, TD, *TBODY*, *TFOOT*, TH, *THEAD*, TR, UL,
	DEL, *INS*,
	character highlighting, A, APPLET, *BUTTON*, CAPTION, *IFRAME*, *LABEL*, MAP, *OBJECT*, *OPTGROUP*, OPTION, SELECT
Attributes:	*CLASS, DIR, ID, LANG, STYLE, TITLE, standard event handlers,*
	CITE, DATETIME

This element marks text that has been inserted. The browser should display this in a distinctive way, for example by rendering it in a different color or with an underline. This behavior can, of course, be modified using a style sheet. This element is supported by Internet Explorer 4 (by default, the text is rendered with an underline), but is not supported by Netscape Navigator 4.

INS supports the standard "generic" and "event-handler" attributes described earlier in this chapter. Note that the event handlers are only partially supported by Internet Explorer 4 and are not supported by Netscape Navigator 4. **INS** supports the two optional attributes **CITE** and **DATETIME**, which provide details related to the insertions. The meanings of these attributes are described in the **DEL** element section.

Table 6.14 Meanings of Fields for Time Specifications in a DATETIME Attribute

Field	Meaning
YYYY	The year (four digits are mandatory)
MM	The month (from 01 [January] to 12 [December]; must have two digits)
DD	The day of the month (from 00 to 31; must have two digits)
hh	The hour on a 24 hour clock (00-24, AM and PM not permitted; must have two digits)
mm	The minutes (00-59; must have two digits)
ss	The seconds (00-59; must have two digits)
TZD	Time Zone Displacement. The three possible values are:
Z	Indicates UTC (Coordinated Universal Time)
+hh:mm	Indicates that the time is in *local time* and that local time is hh hours and mm minutes ahead of UTC
-hh:mm	Indicates that the time is in *local time* and that local time is hh hours and mm minutes behind UTC

NOSCRIPT Element: Alternative to SCRIPT Content

Usage:	`<NOSCRIPT> ... </NOSCRIPT>`
Can Contain:	ADDRESS, BLOCKQUOTE, ~~CENTER~~, ~~DIR~~, DIV, DL, *FIELDSET*, FORM, Hn, HR, [ISINDEX], ~~MENU~~, *NOFRAMES*, *NOSCRIPT*, OL, P, PRE, TABLE, UL,
	characters, character highlighting, A, APPLET, *BASEFONT*, BR, *BUTTON*, *IFRAME*, IMG, INPUT, *LABEL*, MAP, *OBJECT*, SCRIPT, SELECT, TEXTAREA
Can Be Inside:	BLOCKQUOTE, BODY, ~~CENTER~~, DD, DIV, *FIELDSET*, FORM, LI, *NOFRAMES*, *NOSCRIPT*, TD, TH,
	APPLET, *BUTTON*, *IFRAME*, *OBJECT*
Attributes:	*CLASS, DIR, ID, LANG, STYLE, TITLE, standard event handlers*

The **NOSCRIPT** element contains regular HTML markup to be displayed by browsers that do not understand **SCRIPT** or that have script interpretation disabled. In the former case, the browser will ignore both the **SCRIPT** and **NOSCRIPT** tags, and will render the **NOSCRIPT** element content. (However, the content of the **SCRIPT** element will also be displayed unless, as has been previously discussed, it is placed inside an HTML comment `<!-- ... -->`.) In the latter case, a properly designed browser will hide the content of **NOSCRIPT** if script support is enabled, but will display the **NOSCRIPT** content if script support is disabled.

References

Web-Based SGML Resources

etext.lib.virginia.edu/sgml.html   (Simple guide to SGML)
etext.virginia.edu/bin/tei-tocs?div=DIV1&id=SG   (Gentle SGML Introduction)
ftp://www.ucc.ie/pub/sgml/p2sg.ps   (The above, but in PostScript)
www.sil.org/sgml/sgml.html   (Collection of SGML references)
www.w3.org/XML/Activity   (W3C's SGML/XML activities overview)

ftp://ftp.ifi.uio.no/pub/SGML/   (Eric Naggum's SGML archive)

Books on SGML

Special Edition Using SGML, by M. Colby and D.S. Jackson, Que Corp., 1996
The SGML Implementation Guide, by B. Travis and D. Waldt, Springer-Verlag, 1995
The SGML Handbook, by Charles F. Goldfarb, Oxford University Press, 1990 (the SGML "bible"—not for the tame of heart!)

HTML Specifications (See also Chapter 7)

ds.internic.net/rfc/rfc1866.txt   (HTML 2.0 specification)
www.w3.org/TR/REC-html32.html   (HTML 3.2 specification)
www.w3.org/TR/PR-html40/   (HTML 4 — proposed standard)
www.w3.org/MarkUp/html3/   (Expired HTML 3 draft)
www.w3.org/MarkUp/   (W3C's HTML overview)

PICS Document Rating System

www.w3.org/PICS/   (W3C PICS information and specifications)

HTML Document Type Definitions—DTDs

(Used by programs such as *sgmls* to validate HTML document syntax)

HTML 2.0

www.java.utoronto.ca/DTDs/HTML/HTML.decl	(SGML declaration for HTML)
www.java.utoronto.ca/DTDs/HTML/HTML2.dtd	(HTML 2.0 DTD)
www.java.utoronto.ca/DTDs/HTML/HTML2.catalog	(HTML 2.0 catalog)
www.java.utoronto.ca/DTDs/HTML/ISOlat1.sgml	(Entity definitions)

"Strict" HTML 2.0—Restricted Use of Elements

www.java.utoronto.ca/DTDs/HTML/HTML.decl	(SGML declaration for HTML)
www.java.utoronto.ca/DTDs/HTML/HTML2-strict.dtd	(Strict HTML 2.0 DTD)
www.java.utoronto.ca/DTDs/HTML/HTML2-strict.catalog	(Catalog for strict DTD)
www.java.utoronto.ca/DTDs/HTML/ISOlat1.sgml	(Entity definitions)

HTML 3.2

www.java.utoronto.ca/DTDs/HTML/HTML.decl	(SGML declaration for HTML)
www.w3.org/MarkUp/Wilbur/HTML32.dtd	(HTML 3.2 DTD)
www.w3.org/MarkUp/Wilbur/HTML32.cat	(HTML 3.2 catalog)
www.w3.org/MarkUp/Wilbur/ISOlat1.ent	(Entity definitions)

HTML 4

www.java.utoronto.ca/DTDs/HTML/HTML4.decl	(SGML declaration for HTML)
www.w3.org/TR/REC-html40/sgml/dtd.html	(HTML 4 DTD)
	(This reference contains links to several HTML 4 DTDs, as well as to the HTML 4 entity definition files.)

ADVANCED HTML—PROPRIETARY

EXTENSIONS AND NEW FEATURES

Chapter 6 provided an overview of HTML and detailed descriptions of the most commonly implemented, standards-based markup elements. However, there is more to practical HTML authoring than that. Most commercial browsers support popular proprietary extensions, such as **EMBED**, while some of the newer HTML 4 elements, such as **OBJECT**, are now being implemented. A Web author needs to know how to use these newer elements, but also needs to be aware of their status—after all, there's no point using an element if it is not supported by browsers in common use.

This chapter describes these newer HTML features. The topics covered range from proprietary elements, such as **FRAME, EMBED,** and **MARQUEE**, to proposed standards-based elements such as **OBJECT** and **SPAN**. Also covered are more advanced issues, such as styles sheets, internationalization, and document scripting.

Note that the descriptions of the new elements presented here follow the layout used in Chapter 6, and you are referred there for details. The main difference is in the elements grouped under the name "Character Highlighting." In Chapter 6, this group consisted of the physical (**B, I, U,** etc.) and logical (**EM, STRONG, CITE,** etc.) highlighting elements. In this chapter, the definition is extended to include the appropriate proprietary elements. The revised definition is:

Character highlighting:
ABBR, ACRONYM, BDO, CITE, CODE, DFN, EM, KBD, *Q,* SAMP, STRONG, VAR; and B, BIG, ~~FONT~~, I, ~~S~~, SMALL, *SPAN,* ~~STRIKE~~, SUB, SUP, TT, ~~U~~, and <u>BLINK</u>, <u>NOBR</u>, <u>MARQUEE</u>

where the additional, proprietary elements are underlined, and at the end of the list.

As in Chapter 6, the **INS** and **DEL** elements are not mentioned in the element descriptions. In general, you can assume that any of the elements mentioned here can be contained within an **INS** or **DEL** element.

Chapter Organization

For ease of use, the material in this chapter is divided into twelve sections. These are:

1. **FRAME and Framed Documents.** Describes the **FRAMESET, FRAME, IFRAME,** and **NOFRAMES** elements used to create framed documents. These elements let a single browser window contain multiple, independent frames, each frame containing a different HTML document. Most—but not all—commercial browsers support these elements. These elements are part of the HTML 4 standard.

2. **Common Proprietary HTML Extensions.** Describes other elements currently in common use but not part of the HTML standard. These include the Netscape-specific **BLINK, MULTICOL,** and **SPACER** elements; the Microsoft-specific **MARQUEE** and **BGSOUND** elements; and the nonstandard **EMBED, NOBR,** and **WBR** elements. As Netscape Navigator and Microsoft Internet Explorer are the most popular browsers, the section notes cases where an element in not supported by both.

3. **Advanced HTML FORMs.** Describes the new **BUTTON, FIELDSET, LABEL, LEGEND,** and **OPTGROUP** elements, as well as the form-related attributes, introduced with HTML 4. These elements are not supported by Netscape Navigator 4, but are largely supported by Internet Explorer 4.

4. **Embedding Objects in HTML.** Covers the **OBJECT** element, introduced in HTML 4 and designed to replace and augment the elements **APPLET, EMBED,** and **IMG.** This section also covers related changes to **A** and **PARAM. OBJECT** is partially supported by Internet Explorer 3 and is more fully (but still incompletely) supported by Netscape Navigator 4 and Internet Explorer 4.

5. **Netscape LAYER Elements.** Covers the **LAYER, ILAYER,** and **NOLAYER** elements supported by Netscape Navigator 4. These elements allow for floating layers of content that lie "above" the regular page. These elements are only supported by Netscape Navigator 4, and you are best advised not to use them in new applications: Much the same functionality is available via style sheet formatting.

6. **Style Sheets and HTML.** Describes the concept behind style sheets and how style sheets are linked to the text of an HTML document. This section also introduces some of the details of the cascading style sheets (CSS) language now being deployed in Web applications. Netscape Navigator 4 and Internet Explorer 4 both support CSS.

7. **Scripting in HTML Documents.** Describes the new attributes and elements added to HTML to allow interaction between HTML elements and script programs, and briefly describes the nature of these document scripting languages, using JavaScript as an example. This sections also covers dynamic HTML, as well as the new document object model (DOM).

8. **Internationalization of HTML.** A description of the new elements and attributes to be added to HTML in support of non-European languages. These features are not widely supported, but will be incorporated into the next generation of Web browsers.

9. **Fonts and Font Embedding.** This section discusses how Netscape and Microsoft now support the distribution of fonts along with documents.

10. **Missing Features: Mathematics.** This section discusses the special problems of including mathematical symbols and expressions in HTML documents.

11. **Other Missing Features.** This section discusses some of the other obvious missing features of HTML, and describes some efforts underway to resolve these limitations.

12. **References.** The references section provides a list of books, URLs, and other resources where you can find additional information on the technologies and languages mentioned in this chapter.

At present, few browsers support the more advanced multilingual or next-generation HTML features, although this situation will soon change. If you want to experiment with these more advanced aspects of HTML, you should obtain the non-commercial emacs-w3, amaya, or grail browsers. Information about these browsers is provided in the references.

FRAME and Framed Documents

With Navigator 2, Netscape introduced a new form of Web page layout, known as a *frame* document. Such documents use special markup that lets a document author divide the browser window into a number of independent *frames*, where each frame can contains its own, unique HTML document. In a frame document, the traditional **BODY** element is replaced by a **FRAMESET**, which defines the layout of a set of frames within the browser window. The initial *content* of these frames is defined by **FRAME** or **FRAMESET** elements located inside the **FRAMESET**. **FRAME** elements within **FRAMESET** reference an HTML document to be inserted within the frame (and also define certain properties about the frame), while a **FRAMESET** element within **FRAMESET** simply divides a frame into additional subframes.

The only other element allowed inside a frame document is **NOFRAMES**. This nonempty element can contain a **BODY** element that, in turn, contains regular body content HTML markup. Browsers that understand **FRAMESET** will load the content referenced by the **FRAME** elements and will hide any content placed inside the **NOFRAMES**. On the other hand, browsers that do not understand **FRAMESET** simply ignore all of the **FRAMESET**, **FRAME**, and **NOFRAMES** tags and take the **BODY** element and its content as the document to be displayed.

Figure 7.1 shows an example of a frame document, illustrating these basic parts. Figure 7.2 shows the rendering by a frame-capable browser, while Figure 7.3 shows the rendering by a nonframe browser: Note how the latter displays the **NOFRAMES** content.

An HTML document containing a **FRAMESET** cannot contain **BODY** content, other than within **NOFRAMES**. If you include regular **BODY** element tags prior to the first **FRAMESET** element, Netscape Navigator will entirely ignore the **FRAMESET** elements and will display the **NOFRAMES** content instead. Internet Explorer 4 behaves in the same way. Unfortunately, Internet Explorer 3 and 4 do the opposite, rendering the framed version even if there is body content ahead of the first **frameset**. Thus, care must be taken to ensure that a frame document displays properly under both browsers.

Figure 7.1, a simple frame document example (*fig7-1.html*) with markup that specifies four framed regions—the resulting document is shown in Figure 7.2, while Figure 7.3 shows the same document viewed by a browser that does not understand frames.

First, a few words about the content of Figure 7.1 and about how the frames are created.

Frames are created by the **FRAMESET** elements. The first **FRAMESET** divides the window horizontally into two frames, the top one 90 pixels high, the second occupying the remainder of the window height. A second **FRAMESET** subsequently divides the second of these frames vertically into three parts, the first occupying 10% of the available width, the remaining two 45% each, for a total of 100%. Note how a **FRAMESET** can divide a region either horizontally (**ROWS**) or vertically (**COLS**), but not both at the same time. The **FRAME** elements indicate, via the **SRC** attributes, which HTML documents should be loaded and displayed in each of these frames—the resulting document is shown in Figure 7.2. Also note how each frame is given a unique name via the **NAME** attribute. This allows each frame to be uniquely addressed by elements invoking hypertext links. This is discussed in more detail later in this section.

Some browsers do not understand frame elements and ignore all these elements and attributes. An example is shown in Figure 7.3: The noncommercial Mosaic browser does not understand frames and displays the **NOFRAMES** content instead.

Targeting Data to Named Frames

Frames are only useful if their content (such as the placeholders shown in Figure 7.2) can be updated or replaced by other documents or data. This is only possible given a way of *identifying* each frame, so that you can direct a retrieved document to a specific location. This identifier is provided by the **FRAME** element **NAME** attribute value. These names, which must be unique within a collection of framed documents, *identify* each individual frame. In the example in Figures 7.1 and 7.2, the top frame is named "topbar," the right hand frame "main-r," and so on.

Figure 7.1 A simple example document illustrating the use of the FRAMESET, FRAME, and NOFRAMES elements. Also listed are the contents of the documents initially referenced by the FRAME elements.

fig7-1.html

```html
<HTML>
<HEAD><TITLE>Simple Frame Test Document</TITLE></HEAD>

<FRAMESET ROWS="90, *">
  <FRAME NAME="topbar" SRC="direct.html">
  <FRAMESET COLS="10%, 45%, 45%">
    <FRAME NAME="navi-bar" SRC="left.html">
    <FRAME NAME="main-l" SRC="middle.html">
    <FRAME NAME="main-r" SRC="right.html">
  </FRAMESET>
</FRAMESET>

<NOFRAMES>
  <BODY>
  <H2 ALIGN="center">So, You Don't Support Frames, Eh?</H2>
  <BLOCKQUOTE>
    <P>So you don't like frames. Well, too bad for you!
  </BLOCKQUOTE>
  <HR>
  <DIV ALIGN="right">
    <EM>Stupid Document Trick Number 13</EM>
  </DIV>
  </BODY>
</NOFRAMES>
</HTML>
```

direct.html

```html
<HTML>
<HEAD><TITLE>Simple Frame Test Document</TITLE></HEAD>
<BODY>
<DIV ALIGN="center">
<TABLE CELLPADDING=0 CELLSPACING=0 WIDTH="100%">
<TR><TD COLSPAN="6" ALIGN="center">
    <B><FONT SIZE="+1">C</FONT>ATEGORIES</B>
</TR><TR>
  <TD ALIGN="center">Beasts
  <TD ALIGN="center"><A HREF=".">Birds</A>
```

Continued

Figure 7.1 *Continued*.

```
    <TD ALIGN="center"><A HREF=".">Fish</A>
    <TD ALIGN="center"><A HREF=".">Parrots</A>
    <TD ALIGN="center"><A HREF=".">Cheese</A>
    <TD ALIGN="center"><A HREF=".">Piston Engines</A>
</TR>
</TABLE>
</DIV></BODY></HTML>
```

left.html

```
<HTML>
<HEAD><TITLE>Category Navigation</TITLE></HEAD>
<BODY>
<B>Beasts</B><BR><BR>
<A HREF="dogs.html" TARGET="main-l">Dogs</A><BR><BR>
<A HREF="cats.html" TARGET="main-r">Cats</A><BR><BR>
<A HREF="nada.html">Frogs</A><BR><BR>
<A HREF="nada.html" TARGET="blobby">Deer</A><BR><BR>
<A HREF="nada.html">Snakes</A><BR><BR>
<A HREF="nada.html">Mice</A><BR><BR>
<A HREF="nada.html">Rats</A><BR><BR>
<A HREF="nada.html">Snakes</A><BR><BR>
</BODY></HTML>
```

middle.html

```
<HTML>
<HEAD><TITLE>Middle Frame Placeholder</TITLE></HEAD>
<BODY>
<BR><BR><BR><BR><BR><BR><BR><BR>
<H2 ALIGN="center">Placeholder For Middle Frame</H2>
</BODY></HTML>
```

right.html

```
<HTML>
<HEAD><TITLE>Right Frame Placeholder</TITLE></HEAD>
<BODY>
<BR><BR><BR><BR><BR><BR><BR><BR>
<H2 ALIGN="center">Placeholder For Right Frame</H2>
</BODY></HTML>
```

These names are arbitrary, but are generally chosen to be easy to remember—an author will refer to these names often, so it is best to choose ones that are meaningful.

Figure 7.2 Display, by Netscape Navigator 3, of the documents listed in Figure 7.1. Note how the frames are laid out, each frame containing its own distinct document.

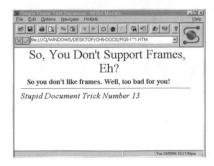

Individual frames can be *targeted* by **A** (hypertext anchor) or **FORM** elements taking a **TARGET** attribute. This attribute takes, as its value, the *name* of the frame to which the data should be sent. Looking to Figure 7.1, you will note that the anchor surrounding the word "Dogs" in the file *left.html* contains the attribute **TARGET**="main-l." Selecting this anchor retrieves the document *dogs.html* and displays it in the leftmost large frame. Similarly, selecting the link "Cats" retrieves the file *cats.html*, but directs this file to the frame labeled "main-r."

The document resulting from selecting these two links is shown in Figure 7.4. Figure 7.5 shows the HTML listing for the documents referenced by the activated hypertext links. Indeed, the two documents were retrieved and placed into the specified named frames.

Figure 7.3 Display, by the NCSA Mosaic 2.1.1 browser, of the documents listed in Figure 7.1. NCSA Mosaic does not understand frames, and displays the NOFRAMES content instead.

Figure 7.4 Display, by Netscape Navigator 3, of the documents listed in Figure 7.1, after selecting the links underlying the words "Dogs" and "Cats." Note how the returned documents are retrieved to the named frames as indicated in Figure 7.1. The listings for the linked documents *dogs.html* and *cats.html* are given in Figure 7.5.

Figure 7.5 HTML documents *dogs.html*, *cats.html*, and *nada.html* referenced by the hypertext links in the framed document listed in Figure 7.1.

dogs.html

```
<HTML>
<HEAD><TITLE>My Wife Loves Dogs</TITLE></HEAD>
<BODY>
<H1 ALIGN="center"><FONT FACE="arial black">
My Wife Loves Dogs!</FONT></H1>
<BLOCKQUOTE>
<FONT FACE="arial">
She loves dogs, and I want to get a cat. This leads
to enormous debates over the advantages and disadvantages
of each of these wonderful animals. But as yet, there is
no resolution to this difficult question.
</FONT>
</BLOCKQUOTE>
</BODY></HTML>
```

Figure 7.5 *Continued*.

cats.html
```
<HTML>
<HEAD><TITLE>Cats are Best</TITLE></HEAD>
<BODY BGCOLOR="#cccccc">
<H1 ALIGN="center"><FONT FACE="verdana">
Cats are King</FONT></H1>
<BLOCKQUOTE>
<FONT FACE="courier">
So what's the problem with cats? They eat mice,
which is probably good, given all the mice in
our house. They purr and like to sleep by the
hot radiators. They are generally friendly.
So -- what's the problem?
</FONT>
</BLOCKQUOTE>
</BODY></HTML>
```

nada.html
```
<HTML>
<HEAD><TITLE>Nothing</TITLE></HEAD>
<BODY>
<BLINK><CENTER><B><FONT FACE="arial">
N<BR>O<BR>T<BR>H<BR>I<BR>N<BR>G<BR>
<BR><BR>
H<BR>E<BR>R<BR>E<BR>
</FONT></B></CENTER><BLINK>
</BODY></HTML>
```

No TARGET Specified

If no **TARGET** is specified, the retrieved document replaces the frame from which the hypertext anchor (or **FORM** submission) was sent. Thus, if the link "Frogs" is selected, the document *nada.html* is retrieved and replaces the left-hand side navigational bar. The document resulting from selecting this link is shown in Figure 7.6.

Specifying an Empty FRAME

A frame can be "emptied" using the special *about:blank* URL. On Netscape Navigator 3/4 and Internet Explorer 4, this URL produces a blank browser page, filled with the browser's default background color. Thus, from within a frame, the URL *about:blank* will empty the frame and leave it empty.

Figure 7.6 Document generated by selecting the link to the word "Frogs" in the document shown in Figure 7.4. The selected anchor had no TARGET attribute, so the retrieved page simply replaces the frame from which the link was selected—and hence replaces the left-most framed window.

Nonexistent TARGET Name

If an anchor or **FORM** references an undefined **TARGET** name, then the browser will create a frame with this name and place the document in this newly created frame. However, there is no way to create a new frame within a framed document, so the browser creates a new browser *window* and gives this entire window the new name. For example, the anchor surrounding the word "Deer" references the target name "blobby," which was not defined in *fig7-1.html*. Thus, when this link is accessed there is no frame defined for this document, so it is retrieved and placed in a new browser window, as shown in Figure 7.7.

Predefined TARGET Names

The frame specifications define four special target names. These values, all of which begin with the underscore (_) character, were defined in Table 6.10. To reiterate, these values are:

Value	Meaning
_blank	Load the referenced data into a new, unnamed window.
_self	Load the referenced data in place of the current document.
_parent	Load the referenced data into the window containing (or, that contained) the *parent* of the current document (the document from which the current document was accessed). If there is no parent document, default to **TARGET**=" _self."

Value	Meaning
_top	Load the referenced data into the window containing (or, that contained) the "top" document (the document obtained by iteratively searching through successive parent documents until arriving at the initial, starting document). If there is no top document, default to TARGET="_self."
NOTE:	All other names beginning with an underscore (_) are ignored by the browser.

Appropriate Use of Frames

Frame documents can be quite useful, as they allow for easy separation of the various components of a page. However, this utility comes at a price, and an author must be aware of the problems associated with frames before diving wholeheartedly into frame-based design.

One problem relates to browser bookmark or "favorites" lists. The problem is that, in general, frame documents cannot be bookmarked. This is because the URL of a frame document simply gives the starting point for the collection of framed pages—if the user selects links that change the content of the different frames, the URL referencing the collection of frames does not change. Thus, if users bookmark one of these later "views," accessing the bookmark will return them to the very first framed document, which may be very different from the intended page.

Figure 7.7 Document generated by selecting the link "Deer" in Figure 7.4. The target name is not defined, so a new window with this name is created.

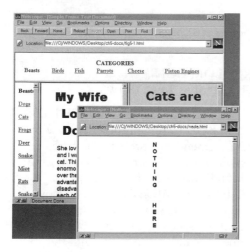

The only way to avoid this problem is to ensure that any pages likely to be bookmarked are either nonframed or are documents that themselves contain all the frameset and frame elements that create the view. This can be done, but only using very complicated Web site designs. It is thus important to decide early on which pages need to be bookmarked, so that you can properly plan ahead and budget your resources.

A second problem is *accessibility*. Many visually impaired users employ screen readers to "dictate" the page content and navigate between pages. Unfortunately, such software does not work well with frame documents, often because it is unclear which frame should be read first or even which frames are important. Thus, if accessibility is important, you should avoid frames.

By this point, you must be wondering when frames should be used! The answer is that framed documents are most useful when designing search interfaces (the different panes can represent different components of the search tool or returned results) or when building interfaces to complex software applications. In these cases, bookmarking is usually unimportant, while the use of frames can make it easier to design the application from a collection of "framed" parts.

There are several efforts underway to improve on the **FRAME** approach, by using style sheets to specify the structure and orientation of page content or by adding into the URL syntax structural information associated with a set of frames. However, none of these approaches is close to being implemented.

The next sections provide detailed specifications for the frame-related elements.

FRAMESET Element: Declare a FRAME Document

Usage:	`<FRAMESET> ... </FRAMESET>`
Can Contain:	*FRAME, FRAMESET, NOFRAMES*
Can Be Inside:	**HTML**
Attributes:	*CLASS, ID, STYLE, TITLE, onLoad, onUnload,* <u>onBlur</u>, <u>onFocus</u>,
	<u>BORDER</u>, <u>BORDERCOLOR</u>, COLS, <u>FRAMEBORDER</u>, <u>FRAMESPACING</u>, ROWS

FRAMESET divides a region of a framed document into frames. An HTML document containing a **FRAMESET** cannot contain **BODY** content, other than within a **NOFRAMES**. If you include regular **BODY** element tags prior to the first **FRAMESET**, Netscape Navigator browsers will entirely ignore the **FRAME** and **FRAMESET** elements and will display the **NOFRAMES** content (if any).

The layout and size of the frames defined by a **FRAMESET** are specified by the **COLS** or **ROWS** attribute. **COLS** indicates that the frames are laid out in columns, with the comma-separated values assigned to **COLS** specifying the number and sizes of the columns. **ROWS** indicates that the frames are laid out in rows, with the comma-separated value assigned to **ROWS** specifying the number and sizes of the rows. A **FRAMESET** must have one of **ROWS** or **COLS**, but not both.

The *number* of comma-separated values assigned to **ROWS** or **COLS** specifies the number of frames contained within the **FRAMESET**, while the *values* determine the frame sizes. The values can take the three possible forms described in Table 7.1.

The **TITLE** attribute is nonfunctional in Netscape Navigator 4. However, Internet Explorer 4 uses the **TITLE** text as a pop-up text description of a frameset, should the mouse hover above the border between the frames.

The *CLASS, ID,* and *STYLE* attributes can assign style sheet formatting rules to the **FRAMESET** (e.g., borders, sizes, etc.). Note that these rules only affect the layout and formatting of the frames and not the formatting of the document referenced by a **FRAME**. Care should be taken with such rules, due to possible interaction between properties specified by a **FRAMESET** and those specified by a style sheet. Also, an author should note that there are several bugs in Netscape Navigator 4 implementation of style sheets with frames, so that it is best to avoid using style sheets with **FRAME** and **FRAMESET**.

The four listed event handlers are implemented by both Internet Explorer 4 and Netscape Navigator 3 and 4, as discussed in the scripting section later in this section. Only **onLoad** and **onUnload** are defined in the HTML 4 specifications. Thus, the event-handling attributes **onBlur** and **onFocus** are proprietary in this context: Although they will work under current browsers, you should avoid using them here. The meanings of the commonly implemented event handlers are given in Table 7.5.

Finally, the attributes **BORDER, BORDERCOLOR, FRAMEBORDER,** and **FRAMESPACING** control presentation aspects of the frame borders, as described below:

BORDER=*"number"* (optional; Netscape Navigator 3+ and Internet Explorer 4+ only)   Specifies the width of the frame border, in pixels, the default being 5. **BORDER** can only be set on the outermost **FRAMESET** element. Scrollbars, if needed in a frame, are placed inside the frame border. This attribute is not supported by Internet Explorer 3. Figure 7.8 shows an example of a borderless frame document.

BORDERCOLOR=*"#rrggbb," "color"* (optional; Netscape Navigator 3+ and Internet Explorer 4+ only)   Specifies the color of the frame borders. This is overridden by a **BORDERCOLOR** specification of a **FRAMESET** lying inside another **FRAMESET** or by the **BORDERCOLOR** specification of a specific **FRAME**. This only affects true borders (**FRAMEBORDER**="yes"). If **FRAMEBORDER**="no," then the border is invisible, and always takes the default background color of the browser window, independent of the color of the pages loaded into the frames. This attribute is not supported by Internet Explorer 3.

COLS=*"comma-separated frame widths"* (one of **ROWS** or **COLS** is mandatory)   Specifies the widths of a selection of vertically oriented frames, where the terms specifying the widths of the different columns are separated by commas. Widths are specified as described in Table 7.1, while the *number* of comma-separated entries equals the number of frames within the

Figure 7.8 The same document as displayed in Figure 7.4 but with BORDER="0" applied to the outer FRAMESET (see Figure 7.1). Note that the frame borders are now invisible. In addition, the frames are not resizable—the user cannot use the mouse to grab and move the frame edges.

FRAMESET. An example (see Figure 7.1) is COLS="10%, 45%, 45%," which declares three columnar frames—the first frame occupies 10% of the available width, and the second and third occupy 45% each.

FRAMEBORDER="yes" or "1," "no," or "0" (optional)   Specifies how the frame borders should be drawn. FRAMEBORDER="yes" (or "1") draws three-dimensional borders (the default), while "no" (or "0") draws a plain border. If BORDER="0," then no borders are drawn regardless of the FRAMEBORDER setting. The default is to draw borders.

TIP: Internet Explorer 3 vs. Netscape Navigator Incompatibility

Internet Explorer 3 supports **FRAMEBORDER**, but only accepts the values 0 or 1 and not the values "yes" or "no." The following procedure will ensure the correct type of border on all browsers: For three-dimensional borders, omit the **FRAMEBORDER** attribute, since the default is to to have 3-D borders. For plain borders, use **FRAMEBORDER**="no," which eliminates borders on all browsers.

FRAMESPACING="*number*" (optional; Internet Explorer only)
Specifies the spacing to leave between internal frames, in pixels. This attribute is not supported by Netscape Navigator. On Internet Explorer 4, this overrides any BORDER value.

Table 7.1 Frame Size Value Specifications for FRAMESET, COL, and ROW Attribute Values

Type	Format	Description
Fixed Pixel	*number*	Specifies the absolute frame size, in pixels, where *n* is the integer number of pixels.
Percentage	*number*%	Specifies the frame size as a percentage of the total available height or width, where *n* is an integer. If the total of all specified frames is greater than 100%, then all frames are rescaled until the total is 100%. If the total is less than 100% and there are no relative frames (see below), then all frames are rescaled until the total is 100%. If the total is less than 100% and there are relative-sized frames, the remaining space is assigned to the relative frames.
Relative Size	*number**	Specifies the size as a free-floating, relative value—all space remaining after allocating fixed pixel or percentage frames is divided amongst all relative-sized frames. An optional integer preceding the asterisk weights the space contribution; thus, the string "2*,3*,*" would allocate 2/6 of the remaining space to the first frame, 3/6 to the second frame, and 1/6 to the third frame.

ROWS="*comma-separated frame heights*" (one of **ROWS** or **COLS** is mandatory)   Specifies the heights of a selection of *horizontally* oriented frames. Heights are specified as described in Table 7.1, and are separated by commas, while the number of entries gives the number of **FRAME**s within the **FRAMESET**. An example is **ROWS**="80, 3*, *, 100" which declares four frame rows. The first (top) frame is 80 pixels high, and the fourth (bottom) frame is 100 pixels high. The second frame will occupy 3/4 of the remaining height, while the third frame will occupy the final 1/4 of the remaining height.

FRAME Element: A FRAME Within a FRAMESET

Usage:	<FRAME>
Can Contain:	empty
Can Be Inside:	**FRAMESET**
Attributes:	*CLASS, ID, STYLE, TITLE,* (**onBlur**, **onFocus**, **onLoad**, **onUnload**: Internet Explorer 4 only)

Attributes: <u>BORDERCOLOR</u>, *FRAMEBORDER, LONGDESC, MARGINHEIGHT, MARGINWIDTH, NAME, NORESIZE, SCROLLING, SRC*

FRAME defines the content of a frame within a **FRAMESET** element—the **SRC** attribute references the HTML document to be placed within the **FRAME**. The attributes **MARGINWIDTH, MARGINHEIGHT, NORESIZE,** and **SCROLLING** define the physical properties of the frame. The **NAME** attribute assigns a specific name to the **FRAME** and allows the frame to be targeted using the **TARGET** attribute of anchor elements. All attributes are optional, including **SRC**; if **SRC** is absent, the frame is simply left empty. **FRAME** is an empty element, as the content of the frame is defined via the SRC attribute.

The **ROWS** or **COLS** attribute specifies the number of frames that must be inside the **FRAMESET**. It is an error if a **FRAMESET** does not actually contain this number of **FRAME** and/or **FRAMESET** elements.

The **CLASS, ID,** and **STYLE** attributes can assign style sheet formatting rules to the **FRAME** (e.g., borders, sizes, etc.). Note that these rules only affect the layout and formatting of the frame, not the formatting of the document referenced by a **FRAME**. Care should be taken with such rules, due to possible interaction between properties specified by a **FRAMESET** and those specified by a style sheet. Also, an author should note that there are several bugs in Netscape Navigator 4 implementation of style sheets with frames, so that it is best to avoid using style sheets with **FRAME** and **FRAMESET**.

The following is an example of correctly defined **FRAME**s (comments in italics):

```
<FRAMESET ROWS="10%, 80%, 10%>          3 rows, narrow top and bottom
  <FRAME SCROLLING="no" SRC="logo+buttonbar.html">   1st frame
  <FRAMESET COLS="20%, 80%">            2nd frame is a FRAMESET
    <FRAME NAME="navigation" SRC="navigate.html">   containing 2 frames
    <FRAME NAME="main" SRC="main/start.html">
  </FRAMESET>
  <FRAME SCROLLING="no" SRC="credits.html">   3rd frame
</FRAMESET>
....
```

In this example, the display is first divided into three rows: The top and bottom rows are narrow (10% of the available height) and contain nonscrolling documents, while the middle row takes up the remaining 80% of the window height. The middle row is further divided by the second **FRAMESET** into two columns: The first takes up 20% of the window width, the second taking up the remaining 80%. Both these frames are scrollable, and are named using **NAME** attributes.

The following is an example of incorrectly defined **FRAME**s (comments in italics)

```
<FRAMESET ROWS="10%, 80%, 10%>          3 rows, narrow top and bottom
  <FRAME SCROLLING="no" SRC="logo+buttonbar.html">   1st frame
```

```
<FRAMESET COLS="20%, 80%">              2nd frame is a FRAMESET
  <FRAME NAME="navigation" SRC="navigate.html">  containing 2 frames
  <FRAME NAME="main" SRC="main/start.html">
</FRAMESET>
<FRAME SCROLLING="no" SRC="credits.html">    3rd frame
<FRAME SRC="oops.html">                 ERROR -- FRAMESET declares
                                        3 rows, but this is the
                                        fourth FRAME!!

</FRAMESET>
```

The **TITLE** attribute should contain a **TITLE** for the frame, for use by non-visual (e.g., text-to-speech) browsers. The attributes **CLASS, ID,** and **STYLE** are also allowed. None of these attributes are supported by current browsers.

Note that event-handling attributes are not allowed (however, Internet Explorer 4 does support **onBlur, onFocus, onLoad,** and **onUnload**). In general, event handling for a specific frame should be implemented within the document loaded into the frame.

The next sections describe the remaining attributes, and their meanings.

BORDERCOLOR=*"#rrggbb," "color"* (optional)   Sets the color for the frame borders. This overrides any border colors specified by a surrounding **FRAMESET** element. The color is undefined if two neighboring **FRAME**s try and set different colors to an adjacent boundary. **BORDERCOLOR** is only valid with 3-D frame borders—if **FRAMEBORDER**="no," then the borders are invisible.

FRAMEBORDER="yes" or "1," "no" or "0" (optional)   Sets the display mode for the frame border—the value "yes" or "1" (the default) creates borders with a three-dimensional effect, while "no" or "0" produces plain borders. The border width is set by the **BORDER** attribute of the outermost **FRAMESET** element. Note that Internet Explorer and Navigator treat frame bordering differently, so make sure to test your frame designs on both browsers.

MARGINHEIGHT=*"number"* (optional)   Specifies the height, in pixels, of the top and bottom margins for the frame: The default value is approximately 10 and is browser-specific. **MARGINHEIGHT** cannot be less than 1 to ensure that there is some blank space left between the frame content and the frame borders. If this attribute is absent, the browser will itself determine a (hopefully) appropriate margin height.

LONGDESC=*"string"* (optional; not currently implemented) Specifies a long text description of the frame. This is intended for use by text-only or non-graphical browsers, and to supplement the value of **TITLE**. There are no current browsers that support this attribute.

MARGINWIDTH="number" (optional)   Specifies the width, in pixels, of the left and right margins inside the frame: The default value is approximately 10 and is browser-specific. **MARGINWIDTH** cannot be less than 1, to ensure that there is some blank space left between the frame content and the frame borders. If this attribute is absent, the browser will hopefully determine an appropriate margin width.

NAME="name" (optional)   Assigns a *symbolic name* to the particular frame: The **TARGET** attribute of a **FORM** or **A** element can then direct retrieved documents or data to this named frame. If **NAME** is absent, the frame name is undefined.

NORESIZE (optional)   Informs the browser that the frame size is fixed and cannot be modified by the user—this also restricts resizing of adjacent frames in the same window. If this attribute is absent, the frame can be resized, usually by using the mouse to drag a border of the frame.

SCROLLING="yes," "no," "auto" (optional)   Specifies the status of scrollbars for the frame. A value of "yes" means that the frame must always have scrollbars, while "no" means that the frame should never have scrollbars. If you use this latter value, you must be sure that the frame is large enough to contain the desired document. The value "auto" lets the browser include scrollbars when necessary. The default value is "auto."

SRC="url" (optional)   Specifies the URL of the HTML document to be displayed within the frame. **SRC** can be absent, in which case the frame is initially blank.

NOFRAMES Element: Markup for FRAME-Incapable Browsers

Usage:	`<NOFRAMES> ... </NOFRAMES>`
Can Contain:	ADDRESS, BLOCKQUOTE, BODY, ~~CENTER~~, ~~DIR~~, DIV, DL, *FIELDSET*, FORM, Hn, HR, [ISINDEX], ~~MENU~~, <u>MULTICOL</u>, <u>NOEMBED</u>, *NOFRAMES*, <u>NOLAYER</u>, *NOSCRIPT*, OL, P, PRE, TABLE, UL, characters, character highlighting, A, APPLET, *BASEFONT*, BR, *BUTTON*, <u>EMBED</u>, *IFRAME*, IMG, <u>ILAYER</u>, INPUT, <u>KEYGEN</u>, *LABEL*, <u>LAYER</u>, MAP, *OBJECT*, SCRIPT, SELECT, <u>SPACER</u>, TEXTAREA, <u>WBR</u>
Can Be Inside:	BLOCKQUOTE, BODY, CENTER, DD, DIV, *FIELDSET*, FORM, <u>MULTICOL</u>, *NOEMBED*, *NOFRAMES*, *NOSCRIPT*, TD, TH,

APPLET, *BUTTON*, *IFRAME*, *OBJECT*,
FRAMESET, HTML
Attributes: *CLASS, DIR, ID, LANG, STYLE, TITLE, standard
event handlers*

NOFRAMES contains HTML markup to be displayed by browsers that do not understand the **FRAMESET** and **FRAME** elements. **NOFRAMES** content is not displayed by a **FRAME**-capable browser. A **FRAME**-incapable browser, however, ignores the **FRAMESET, FRAME,** and **NOFRAMES** elements and displays the **NOFRAMES** content as if it were the **BODY** of a regular HTML document.

NOFRAMES was initially introduced to delimit, within a frameset document, markup alternative to the **FRAMESET** for frame-incapable browsers. In this model, the **NOFRAMES** element must appear after the last **FRAMESET** and should contain a **BODY** element and regular **BODY** content. The following is an example:

```
<HTML>
<HEAD>
<TITLE>Test of the NOFRAMES Element</TITLE>
</HEAD>
<FRAMESET ROWS="50%, 50%">
    <FRAME SRC="top_part.html" NAME="wind1">
    <FRAME SRC="bot_part.html" NAME="wind2">
</FRAMESET>
<NOFRAMES>
    <BODY BACKGROUND="greywhale.gif">
    <H1 ALIGN="center"> Warning! </H1>
    <P ALIGN="center"><EM>If you are reading this text, you are viewing this
        document with a FRAMEs-incapable browser--this document was designed
        to be viewed by a FRAME-capable browser, such as Netscape Navigator
        2.0. If you do not have such a browser, please access the alternative
        <A HREF="noframes.html">noframes</A> collection.
    </BODY>
    </NOFRAMES>
</HTML>
```

HTML 4 also allows **NOFRAMES** content within the **BODY** of nonframed documents. This, in principle, allows for regular documents to display certain blocks of markup only when loaded by browsers incapable of displaying frames. Thus, the individual documents loaded into each frame of a "framed" page can contain markup that is hidden when the document is presented in a framed view. Unfortunately, only Internet Explorer 4 supports **NOFRAMES** elements within the body of a document—Netscape Navigator does not understand **NOFRAMES** in this way and always displays **NOFRAMES** content when the element appears inside the body of a regular document.

> **NOTE: Use NOFRAMES Only after Last FRAMESET in a Frame Document**
>
> Netscape Navigator improperly renders documents that contain **NOFRAMES** elements inside the **BODY** of an HTML document. For reliable documents, you should therefore only place **NOFRAMES** elements after the last **FRAMESET** of a frameset document.

IFRAME Element: A Floating FRAME (Internet Explorer Only)

Usage:	`<IFRAME> ... </IFRAME>`
Can Contain:	ADDRESS, BLOCKQUOTE, ~~CENTER~~, ~~DIR~~, DIV, DL, *FIELDSET*, FORM, Hn, HR, [ISINDEX], ~~MENU~~, MULTICOL, NOEMBED, *NOFRAMES*, NOLAYER, *NOSCRIPT*, OL, P, PRE, TABLE, UL,
	characters, character highlighting, A, APPLET, *BASEFONT*, BR, *BUTTON*, EMBED, *IFRAME*, LAYER, IMG, INPUT, KEYGEN,*LABEL*, LAYER, MAP, *OBJECT*, SCRIPT, SELECT, SPACER, TEXTAREA, WBR
Can Be Inside:	BLOCKQUOTE, BODY, CENTER, DD, DIV, *FIELDSET*, FORM, MULTICOL, NOEMBED, *NOFRAMES*, *NOSCRIPT*, TD, TH,
	character highlighting, A, APPLET, *BUTTON*, *IFRAME*, *LABEL*, *LEGEND*, *OBJECT*
Attributes:	*CLASS, ID, STYLE, TITLE,* (onBlur, onFocus: Internet Explorer 4 only)
	ALIGN, FRAMEBORDER, HEIGHT, HSPACE, *MARGINHEIGHT, MARGINWIDTH, NAME, SCROLLING, SRC,* VSPACE, *WIDTH*

After Netscape introduced frameset documents, Microsoft introduced additional markup for *floating frames*. A floating frame is just that: a frame that can float anywhere inside an HTML document. Thus, **IFRAME** is placed inside the regular document **BODY** and, in a sense, acts like an embedded object or image. Figures 7.9 and 7.10 illustrate such an **IFRAME**.

The content of a floating frame is specified by an **SRC** attribute. The attributes **FRAMEBORDER, MARGINWIDTH, MARGINHEIGHT, NORESIZE,** and **SCROLLING** define the physical properties of the frame, while **HEIGHT** and **WIDTH** define the size, and **ALIGN** the alignment on the display. The **NAME** attribute assigns a specific name to the **FRAME**, which allows the frame to be targeted (using the **TARGET** attribute) by **A** or **FORM** elements.

The **CLASS**, **ID**, and **STYLE** attributes can be used to assign style sheet formatting rules to the element. Note that these rules only affect the layout and formatting of the element on the page and do not affect the formatting of the document referenced by **IFRAME**.

The content of an **IFRAME** element is alternative markup, displayed by browsers that do not understand **IFRAME**. Since Netscape Navigator does not understand **IFRAME**, it is always a good idea to include content inside this element. Figure 7.11 shows the rendering of the document listed in Figure 7.9 by an **IFRAME**-incapable browser.

Figure 7.9 An example document illustrating the use of the IFRAME element. Figures 7.10 and 7.11 show the rendering of this document by Internet Explorer 3 and Netscape Navigator 3, respectively.

```
<HTML>
<HEAD><TITLE>Test of Microsoft IFRAME</TITLE></HEAD>
<BODY>
<H2>A Test of Microsoft's IFRAME</H2>
This is not a terribly exciting example -- which is
not suprising, given that I am writing this at
around 2:30AM, afterapproximately 14 hours at the
computer. Book writing seems to take forever....
<IFRAME   SRC="dogs.html" BORDER="20"
          FRAMEBORDER="1" ALIGN="left"
          WIDTH="350" HEIGHT="200">
<HR NOSHADE>
<H3>Alternative Content</H3>
Ok, So you don't understand <B>IFRAME</B>. Well, this
block of text is for you!
<HR NOSHADE>
</IFRAME>
</DIV>
<P> Writing a book is a slow process, much slower than I
first expected -- there are always small things to do,
such as correcting Figure numberings, checking spelling, or
fixing poor wordings and explanations. The truth, however
is that most writers <em>enjoy</em> this process.
Perhaps 14 hours at a stretch is a bit too much -- and I will
admit that I would prefer less onerous hours (a publisher's
deadline does tend to focus one's efforts) -- but I do enjoy
the process, and feel great satisfaction at producing
informative, readable, and accurate prose.
</BODY>
</HTML>
```

Figure 7.10 Internet Explorer 3 rendering of the document illustrated in Figure 7.9. Note how the IFRAME is left-aligned with surrounding text flow, just as if it were an embedded image.

Currently, only Internet Explorer supports **IFRAME**. The attributes are:

ALIGN="top," "middle," "bottom," "left," "right" (optional)   Specifies the alignment for the floating frame on the page. The meanings are the same as for the **IMG** element. The values "left" and "right" produce floating frames. The default value is "bottom."

FRAMEBORDER="1," "0" (optional)   Sets the display mode for the floating frame border. The value "1" (the default) creates borders with a three-dimensional effect, while "0" produces no borders.

HEIGHT="*number*," "*number*%" (optional: must be specified if **WIDTH** is specified)   Specifies the height of the displayed floating frame, either in pixels or as a percentage of the available window height. If **HEIGHT** is specified, then **WIDTH** must also be specified, otherwise Internet Explorer will improperly display the document.

NOTE: You must specify *both* HEIGHT and WIDTH

If you specify a floating frame **WIDTH**, you must specify a **HEIGHT**.

<u>HSPACE</u>="*number*" (optional)   Specifies a spacing margin, in pixels, to leave to the left and right of the floating frame. The default margin is zero pixels. This is only relevant for "left" and "right" aligned frames.

LONGDESC="*string*" (optional; not currently implemented)   Specifies a long text description of the frame. This is intended for use by text-only or nongraphical browsers, and to supplement the value of **TITLE**. Support for this attribute is not implement on current browsers.

Figure 7.11 Netscape Navigator 3 rendering of the document illustrated in Figure 7.9. Navigator does not understand the IFRAME element, and instead displays the alternate content contained inside the IFRAME.

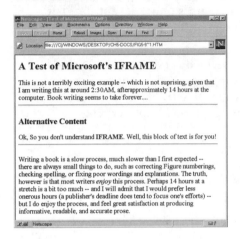

MARGINHEIGHT="*number*" (optional)   Specifies the height, in pixels, of the top and bottom margins within the frame: The default value is approximately 10 and is browser-specific. **MARGINHEIGHT** cannot be less than 1, to ensure that there is some blank space left between the frame content and the frame borders. If this attribute is absent, the browser will itself determine a (hopefully) appropriate margin height.

MARGINWIDTH="*number*" (optional)   Specifies the width, in pixels, of the left and right margins within the frame: The default value is approximately 10 and is browser-specific. **MARGINWIDTH** cannot be less than 1, to ensure that there is some blank space left between the frame content and the frame borders. If this attribute is absent, the browser will hopefully determine an appropriate margin width.

NAME="*name*" (optional)   Assigns a *symbolic name* to the particular frame: The **TARGET** attribute of a **FORM** or **A** element can then direct retrieved documents or data to this named frame. If **NAME** is absent, the frame name is undefined. Values for names must be name tokens, as defined previously.

SCROLLING="yes," "no," "auto" (optional)   Specifies the status of scrollbars for the frame. A value of "yes" means that the frame must always have scrollbars, while "no" means that the frame should never have scrollbars. If you use this latter value, you must be sure that the frame is large enough to contain the desired document. The value "auto" lets the browser include scrollbars when necessary. The default value is "auto."

SRC="url" (optional)   Specifies the URL of the HTML document to be displayed within the frame. **SRC** can be absent—in which case the frame is initially blank.

<u>VSPACE</u>*="number"* (optional)   Specifies a spacing margin, in pixels, to leave above and below the floating frame. This is only relevant for "left" and "right" aligned frames. The default margin for floating frames is zero pixels.

WIDTH="number" (optional: must be specified if **HEIGHT** is specified) Specifies the width of the displayed floating frame, either in pixels, or as a percentage of the available window width. If **WIDTH** is specified, then **HEIGHT** must also be specified, otherwise Internet Explorer will improperly render the document.

Common Proprietary HTML Extensions

Netscape and Microsoft have implemented a number of proprietary HTML elements, many of which have not been incorporated into the HTML standard. Some of these (e.g., **WBR, NOBR**) are widely adopted by other browser vendors, while others (e.g., **BLINK, MARQUEE**) are less widely supported and are unlikely to be supported in the future. These elements can be useful in certain contexts, but you should always be aware of their lack of universality. If you do use them, be sure to check your documents on several different browsers, to make sure that users will see the content you intend.

BGSOUND Element: Inline Audio Snippets (Internet Explorer Only)

Usage:	<BGSOUND>
Can Contain:	empty
Can Be Inside:	**HEAD**
Attributes:	**CLASS, ID, LANG, TITLE,**
	BALANCE, LOOP, SRC, VOLUME

BGSOUND is a **HEAD**-level element that references an audio file to be played as the document is being viewed—the URL location of the audio file is specified by the mandatory **SRC** attribute. By default, the sound is loaded and played once—this can be modified by the **LOOP** attribute. For example, LOOP="10" instructs the browser to play the sound file 10 times before stopping. The attributes, in detail, are:

BALANCE="*number*" (optional; Internet Explorer 4 only)   Specifies the volume balance between the left and right speakers. The allowed values range from -10,000 to +10,000, with the value 0 corresponding to sound balanced between the speakers.

LOOP=*"number"* (optional)   Specifies how often the audio file is looped before play is stopped. The values **LOOP**="-1" or **LOOP**="infinite" cause the sound file to loop endlessly. The default values is -1.

SRC=*"url"* (mandatory)   Specifies the URL for the audio file. Note that the file should be in one of the supported formats: AIFF (audio/aiff), Sun/Macintosh (audio/au), or WAV (audio/wav).

VOLUME=*"number"* (optional; Internet Explorer 4 only)   Specifies the playing volume for the background sound. Values can lie in the range 10,000 to 0. The value 10,000 corresponds to the maximum possible volume.

The following is an example of **BGSOUND**.

```
<BGSOUND SRC="/project1/sounds/bubbles.wav" LOOP="-1">
```

BGSOUND is not supported by Netscape Navigator, so it should be avoided in documents that must work across multiple browsers. An alternative is to use **EMBED** or **OBJECT**—Netscape Navigator and Internet Explorer can both play audio files using a plugin, so that invoking audio playback by this approach ensures maximum utility of the page.

BLINK Element: Blinking Text (Netscape Navigator Only)

Usage:	`<BLINK> ... </BLINK>`
Can Contain:	Unspecified, probably: **characters, character highlighting**, **A**, **APPLET**, *BASEFONT*, **BR**, *BUTTON*, <u>EMBED</u>, *IFRAME*, <u>ILAYER</u>, **IMG**, **INPUT**, <u>KEYGEN</u>, *LABEL*, <u>LAYER</u>, **MAP**, *OBJECT*, <u>SPACER</u>, **SCRIPT**, **SELECT**, **TEXTAREA**, <u>WBR</u>
Can Be Inside:	Unspecified, probably: **ADDRESS**, **BLOCKQUOTE**, **BODY**, **CAPTION**, ~~CENTER~~, **DD**, **DIV**, **DT**, *FIELDSET*, **FORM**, **Hn**, **LI**, <u>MULTICOL</u>, <u>NOEMBED</u>, *NOFRAMES*, <u>NOLAYER</u>, *NOSCRIPT*, **P**, **PRE**, **TD**, **TH**, **character highlighting**, **A**, **APPLET**, *BUTTON*, *IFRAME*, <u>ILAYER</u>, *LABEL*, <u>LAYER</u>, *LEGEND*, *OBJECT*
Attributes:	none

BLINK marks the enclosed text as blinking—browsers generally flash this text on and off. **BLINK** affects only enclosed text and has no effect on enclosed images, **FORM** input elements (although regular text inside a **FORM** can be rendered as blinking), or list item markers (bullets, numbers, etc.).

In principle, you should explicitly mark each block of text (paragraph, list item, etc.) for blinking, as opposed to marking large blocks (several paragraphs and lists) of the document. In practice, you can use a single <BLINK> tag to mark an entire document as blinking and thereby drive your readers crazy.

The slightest mention of the **BLINK** element causes formal HTML language designers to pull out crosses, garlic, and/or wooden stakes and begin chanting, in rising voices, "Evil, evil, horrible evil!!" It is, therefore, unlikely that **BLINK** will be integrated into the official HTML specification.

For obvious reasons, there are no **BLINK** examples in the figures.

EMBED Element: Embed an Arbitrary Data Object

Usage:	<EMBED>
Can Contain:	empty
Can Be Inside:	Unspecified, probably: **ADDRESS, BLOCKQUOTE, BODY, CAPTION,** ~~CENTER~~, **DD, DIV, DT,** *FIELD-SET*, **FORM, Hn, LI,** MULTICOL, NOEMBED, *NOFRAMES,* NOLAYER, *NOSCRIPT,* **P, PRE, TD, TH,** character highlighting, **A, APPLET,** *BUTTON, IFRAME,* ILAYER, *LABEL,* LAYER, *LEGEND, OBJECT*
Attributes:	(*CLASS, ID, STYLE*: Netscape Navigator 4 and Internet Explorer 4 only), (*onBlur, onFocus*: Internet Explorer 4 only), **ALIGN, BORDER, FRAMEBORDER, HEIGHT, HIDDEN, HSPACE, NAME, PALETTE, PLUGINSPAGE,** (**PLUGINSURL** Netscape Navigator 4 only) **SRC, TYPE, VSPACE, WIDTH,** *P_NAME* (arbitrary name value)

EMBED specifies an arbitrary data object to be embedded within the document—for example an audio file, a special-format graphic file, or a spreadsheet. Display of embedded objects requires extra functionality on a browser, usually provided by browser *plugins*—these are product- or data-format-specific modules that are loaded into the browser whenever the corresponding data format is accessed.

The **NOEMBED** element provides an HTML alternative to the embedded data, for use by browsers that do not support the **EMBED** element or that cannot process the specified embedded data type. The use of **NOEMBED** is described later in this section.

NOTE: EMBED Being Replaced by OBJECT

The **EMBED** element design has many problems, in particular its violation of important SGML syntax rules, and the inability to specify alternative or preferred plugins for handling a given data type. **EMBED** will very soon be replaced by the more sophisticated **OBJECT** element, described later in this chapter.

Note that the HTML 4 **CLASS**, **ID**, and **LANG** attributes are supported by Netscape Navigator 4 and Internet Explorer 4. This allows for binding of style sheet properties to **EMBED** elements.

Some examples of plugins were shown in Example 11 in Chapter 2. The attributes supported by **EMBED** are:

ALIGN="absbottom," "absmiddle," "baseline," "bottom," "left," "middle," "right," "top" (optional)   Specifies the alignment of the embedded object on the page. The meanings are the same as for the **IMG** element, as described in Chapter 6.

BORDER="*number*" (optional; not supported)   Specifies the size, in pixels, of the border to be drawn around the displayed object. The default is to have no border. Although defined in the Netscape documentation, there are no browsers that currently support this attribute.

FRAMEBORDER="no," "yes" (optional; not supported)   Specifies whether or not a border should be drawn around the displayed object: The default value is "no." Although defined in the Netscape documentation, there are no browsers that currently support this attribute.

HEIGHT="*number*" (mandatory if **HIDDEN**="false")   Specifies the height of the embedded object, in pixels. This is mandatory if the object is not hidden, as the browser has no other way of knowing the size of the object. Most standard plugin modules are distributed with recommended heights and widths—if you don't know the correct size, just try experimenting until you find appropriate values.

HIDDEN ="false," "true" (optional)   Specifies whether the plugin is displayed in the document ("false") or is hidden from view ("true"). The default value is "false." If the value is "false," then the **HEIGHT** and **WIDTH** must be specified.

HSPACE="*number*" (optional; Netscape Navigator only)   Specifies a horizontal spacing, in pixels, to leave at the left and right of the plugin. The default value is zero. This is only relevant if "**ALIGN**="left" or **ALIGN**="right."

NAME="*string*" (optional)   Specifies a *symbolic name* for the embedded object. This allows the object to be referenced by other objects, scripts, or applets embedded in the document, thereby allowing objects to communicate with each other.

PALETTE="background," "foreground" (optional)   Specifies the color palette to use in rendering the object, in terms of the default colors used by the browser. This is relevant only for Microsoft Windows platforms.

PLUGINSPAGE="*url*" (optional)   Specifies the URL of a document containing instructions as to how to obtain the plugin required by the **EMBED**ded object. If the browser does not have an appropriate plugin, it will inform the user of this fact and will give the user the option of visiting this location.

PLUGINSURL=*"url"* (optional; Netscape Navigator 4 only)   Specifies the URL of a Java Archive (JAR) file containing the desired plugin. The browser should run the JAR Installation Manager (JIM), which will ask users if they wish to install the specified JAR plugin. Plugins can be digitally signed, for security. For plugins that only come in the JAR format (and thus that only run on Netscape 4), **PLUGINSURL** should be used instead of **PLUGINSPAGE**.

P_NAME=*"string"* (optional)   Specifies names and values required by the embedded object: **P_NAME** corresponds to an arbitrary attribute name (e.g., **STARTURL, LOOPDELAY**, etc.) understood by the particular plugin being invoked, while *"string"* is a value to associate with the name. These names and values are passed to the plugin when it starts running. so that the names and values must have meaning understood by the plugin. This mechanism is typically used to define plugin startup configuration parameters.

Formally, arbitrary attribute names are not allowed by the syntax rules of SGML, so that this mechanism is illegal—this is one of the reasons why **EMBED** is not part of the HTML standard. The **PARAM** element, used by **APPLET** and **OBJECT**, provides an SGML-valid mechanism for passing arbitrary parameter names and values to an embedded applet or plugin.

SRC=*"url"* (mandatory if **TYPE** not specified)   Specifies the URL for the data object to be inserted into the document. This can be omitted if **TYPE** is specified and if the plugin does not need to download data.

TYPE=*"mime-type"* (mandatory if **SRC** not specified)   Specifies the MIME type for the embedded object. This is used in place of SRC when the plugin requires no data or when the plugin obtains the data itself. In these cases, **TYPE** simply indicates to the browser which plugin should be started.

VSPACE=*"number"* (optional; Netscape Navigator only)   Specifies a vertical spacing, in pixels, to leave above and below the plugin. The default value is zero. This is only relevant if "**ALIGN**="left" or **ALIGN**="right."

WIDTH=*"number"* (mandatory if **HIDDEN**="false")   Specifies the height of the embedded object, in pixels. This is mandatory if the object is not hidden, as the browser has no other way of knowing an object's size. Most standard plugin modules are distributed with recommended heights and widths—if you don't know the correct size, just try experimenting until you find appropriate values.

MARQUEE Element: A Scrolling Text Marquee (Internet Explorer Only)

Usage:	`<MARQUEE> ... </MARQUEE>`
Can Contain:	Unspecified, probably: **characters, character highlighting**, **A**, **APPLET**, *BASEFONT*, **BR**, *BUTTON*, <u>EMBED</u>, *IFRAME*, **IMG**, **INPUT**, <u>KEYGEN</u>, *LABEL*, **MAP**, *OBJECT*, <u>SPACER</u>, **SCRIPT**, **SELECT**, **TEXTAREA**, <u>WBR</u>
Can Be Inside:	Unspecified, probably: **ADDRESS**, **BLOCKQUOTE**, **BODY**, **CAPTION**, ~~CENTER~~, **DD**, **DIV**, **DT**, *FIELD-SET*, **FORM**, **Hn**, **LI**, <u>MULTICOL</u>, <u>NOEMBED</u>, **NOFRAMES**, <u>NOLAYER</u>, *NOSCRIPT*, **P**, **PRE**, **TD**, **TH**, **character highlighting**, **A**, **APPLET**, *BUTTON*, *IFRAME*, <u>ILAYER</u>, *LABEL*, <u>LAYER</u>, *LEGEND*, *OBJECT*
Attributes:	*CLASS, ID, LANG, STYLE, TITLE, standard event handlers,* <u>onBounce</u>, <u>onFinish</u>, <u>onStart</u>, **BEHAVIOR, BGCOLOR, DIRECTION, HEIGHT, HSPACE, LOOP, SCROLLAMOUNT, SCROLLDELAY, TRUESPEED, VSPACE, WIDTH**

MARQUEE delimits a text string to be scrolled on the display—the content of the element is the scrolling text. **MARQUEE** takes a number of attributes to control the size and placement of the marquee on the page (**ALIGN, HEIGHT, HSPACE,** and **VSPACE**) and the behavior of the scrolled text (**BEHAVIOR, DIRECTION, LOOP, SCROLLAMOUNT, SCROLLDELAY**). **BGCOLOR** specifies a background color specific to the marquee text. It also takes three special event handling attributes, related to the scrolling nature of the element. The following is a simple example of a **MARQUEE**:

```
<MARQUEE ALIGN="middle" HSPACE="10" LOOP="-1"
    SCROLLAMOUNT="1"
    SCROLLDELAY="4">Look out -- Falling Aardvarks!!</MARQUEE>
```

This marquee is shown in Figures 7.12 through 7.14—Figure 7.14 catches the scrolling marquee in action—pretty boring in print, isn't it? Figure 7.13 shows what happens when a browser does not understand **MARQUEE**. In this case there is no marquee, but the browser can use any surrounding emphasis elements (here **B** and **I**) to mark the marquee text in a special way. The **BR** after the **MARQUEE** helps ensure that the text is put on a line separate from any subsequent text.

Note also that, although form input elements can appear inside a MARQUEE, the resulting form will be almost impossible to use!

BEHAVIOR="alternate," "scroll," "slide" (optional)   Specifies how the marquee text should scroll. The value "scroll" means that the text should start from beyond one margin (left or right) and scroll completely across to the other margin, and disappear completely, while "slide" means that the text will start from beyond one margin (left or right) and will scroll onto the screen until it touches the other margin, whereupon it should cease scrolling. "Alternate" means that the text will bounce back and forth between the left- and right-hand margins of the **MAR-QUEE**. The default is **BEHAVIOR**="scroll."

BGCOLOR="*#rrggbb*," "*color*" (optional)   Specifies the background color for the marquee, either as an RGB code or by using a color name.

DIRECTION= "down," "left," "right," "up" (optional)   Specifies the scrolling direction for the text: "left" means that the text will scroll from right to left , while "right" means the text will scroll from left to right. Similarly, "down" means the text will scroll down, and "up" that the text will scroll upwards. The default is "left." Note that, with "up" and "down," an author must be sure to set an appropriate value for the **HEIGHT**, as the browser will default to **HEIGHT**="1."

HEIGHT=" *number*," " *number%*" (optional)   Specifies the height of the marquee. This height can be specified either in pixels or as a percentage of

Figure 7.12 Demonstration HTML document illustrating the MULTICOL, SPACER, NOBR, WBR, and MARQUEE elements. These elements do not work on all browsers.

```
<HTML>
<HEAD><TITLE>Common HTML Extensions</TITLE></HEAD>
<BODY>
<H2>Common HTML Extensions</H2>
<B><I><MARQUEE ALIGN="middle" HSPACE="10" LOOP="-1"
        SCROLLAMOUNT="3"
        SCROLLDELAY="4"
        BGCOLOR="yellow">
 Look out -- Falling Aardvarks!!</I></B>
</MARQUEE></I></B><BR>


Here is some regular text -- note how the lines are
broken to best fit the page. This is not an exciting
example but, as I have pointed out, the imagination
starts to fade at around 3:00AM.
```

Figure 7.12 Continued.

```
<HR WIDTH="80%" ALIGN="left">
<NOBR>
Here is some regular text, but placed inside a <B>NOBR</B>
so that lines are<WBR><EM>*wbr*</EM> not broken, except
at BR or WBR elements -- I have placed the string
<EM>*wbr*</EM> right after every ocurrence of an &lt;WBR>
tag. This is rather  boring but, hey -- <WBR><EM>*wbr*</EM>
whadaya want at these prices?</NOBR>
<HR NOSHADE SIZE=4>
<H3>MULTICOL Example</H3>
<MULTICOL COLS=2 GUTTER=15>
<P>There are three types of spacers, "block", "horizontal",
and "vertical". The first exmaple is a block spacer, with a
height of 40 pixels, a width of 60 pixels, and left-alignment.
Here it is --
<SPACER ALIGN="left" WIDTH="60" HEIGHT="40" TYPE="block">
-- and there it was. Notice how it floats like an image, with
text flowing around it. Of course, a blank, fully transparent
image works just as well--and also works on other browsers.
<H3>Horizontal and Vertical</H3>
Horizontal spacers are like tabs: here is one of SIZE=40
(40 pixels long)--|
<SPACER TYPE="horizontal" SIZE="40">|--
see how it tabs across. Vertical spacers moves text down
and also cause a line break. Here is an example
with a vertical spacing of 40 pixels.
--|<SPACER TYPE="vertical" SIZE="20">|--there it was.
</MULTICOL>
</BODY>
</HTML>
```

the display window height. You should be careful to make the **MARQUEE** sufficiently high that the text is clearly visible. For left- and right-scrolling text, the default will be just tall enough to contain the text in the selected font and font size.

HSPACE="*number*" (optional)   Specifies the margin, in pixels, to leave to the left and right of the **MARQUEE**. The default value is 0.

onBounce="*event-handling script*" (optional; Internet Explorer 4 only) Specifies the script to run when the content of the **MARQUEE** has scrolled to one side, and switches to scroll in the opposite direction— valid only with **BEHAVIOR**="alternate."

Figure 7.13 Rendering, using Netscape Navigator 3, of the HTML document shown in Figure 7.12. This browser does not understand the MARQUEE element.

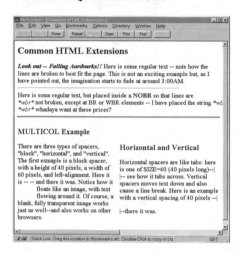

onFinish=*"event-handling script"* (optional; Internet Explorer 4 only) Specifies the script to run when the marquee content has finished scrolling.

onStart=*"event-handling script"* (optional; Internet Explorer 4 only) Specifies the script to run when the marquee starts scrolling, or when it finishes a scrolling pattern (such as a bounce) and restarts the same pattern.

LOOP=*"number,"* "infinite" (optional)   Specifies the number of times the marquee will loop before stopping. The values **LOOP**="-1" or **LOOP**="infinite" cause the marquee to loop forever. The default is "-1."

SCROLLAMOUNT=*"number"* (optional)   Specifies the number of pixels between subsequent redraws of the marquee text—a large value yields a marquee that jumps rapidly across the screen, while a small value yields smoothly scrolled text.

SCROLLDELAY=*"number"* (optional)   Specifies the time delay, in milliseconds, between subsequent redraws of the marquee text—a small value implies a rapidly scrolling marquee.

TRUESPEED (optional; Internet Explorer 4 only)   Specifies that the scroll delay should be exactly the number specified in the **SCROLLDELAY** attribute. If absent, values less than 59 are rounded up to 60 (milliseconds).

VSPACE=*"number"* (optional)   Specifies the margin, in pixels, to leave above and below the **MARQUEE**. The default value is 0.

WIDTH=*" number,"* " *number%"* (optional)   Specifies the width of the marquee. This width can either be specified in pixels or as a percentage of

Figure 7.14 Rendering, using the Internet Explorer 3 browser, of the HTML document shown in Figure 7.12. This browser does not understand the MULTICOL and SPACER elements.

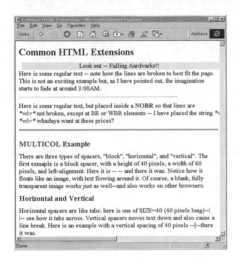

the display window width. You should be careful not to make the **MARQUEE** too narrow, as the content may then be hard to read.

MULTICOL Element: Multicolumn Text (Netscape Navigator Only)

Usage: `<MULTICOL> ... </MULTICOL>`

Can Contain: Unspecified, probably: ADDRESS, BLOCKQUOTE, ~~CENTER~~, ~~DIR~~, DIV, DL, *FIELDSET*, FORM, Hn, HR, [ISINDEX], ~~MENU~~, <u>MULTICOL</u>, <u>NOEMBED</u>, *NOFRAMES*, <u>NOLAYER</u>, *NOSCRIPT*, OL, P, PRE, TABLE, UL,

characters, character highlighting, A, APPLET, *BASEFONT*, BR, *BUTTON*, <u>EMBED</u>, *IFRAME*, <u>ILAYER</u>, IMG, INPUT, <u>KEYGEN</u>, *LABEL*, <u>LAYER</u>, MAP, *OBJECT*, SCRIPT, SELECT, <u>SPACER</u>, TEXTAREA, <u>WBR</u>

Can Be Inside: Unspecified, probably: BLOCKQUOTE, BODY, ~~CENTER~~, DD, DIV, *FIELDSET*, FORM, LI, <u>MULTICOL</u>, <u>NOEMBED</u>, *NOFRAMES*, <u>NOLAYER</u>, *NOSCRIPT*, TD, TH,

APPLET, *BUTTON*, *IFRAME*, ILAYER, LAYER, *OBJECT*

Attributes:	CLASS, *ID*, *STYLE*, COLS, GUTTER, WIDTH

MULTICOL specifies text to be displayed in multicolumn format. The attributes specify the number of columns to use and the spacing between columns. Almost any **BODY** element can appear inside **MULTICOL**, but some, such as **BLOCKQUOTE**, can lead to odd formatting due to the browser's miscalculation of text lengths within the columns. Embedding images or objects within columnar text will also cause problems if the object is larger than the column width.

MULTICOL is allowed inside **MULTICOL**—but don't get carried away or the text will look ridiculous!

An example of **MULTICOL** is shown in Figures 7.12 and 7.13. Figure 7.14 shows how this document looks when viewed by a browser that does not understand **MULTICOL**. The text is still easy to read, although only in one column.

COLS="*number*" (mandatory)   Specifies the number of columns to use. The default value is 1.

GUTTER="*number*" (optional)   Specifies the space to leave between the columns, in pixels. The default value is 10.

WIDTH="*number*," "*number%*" (optional)   Specifies the width for the collection of columns, including the gutter, either as an absolute width in pixels (*number*) or as a percentage of the available width (*number%*).

NOBR Element: No Line Break

Usage:	`<NOBR> ... </NOBR>`
Can Contain:	Unspecified, probably: **characters, character highlighting**, A, APPLET, *BASEFONT*, BR, *BUTTON*, EMBED, *IFRAME*, ILAYER, IMG, INPUT, KEYGEN, *LABEL*, LAYER, MAP, *OBJECT*, SPACER, SCRIPT, SELECT, TEXTAREA, WBR
Can Be Inside:	Unspecified, probably: ADDRESS, BLOCKQUOTE, BODY, CAPTION, ~~CENTER~~, DD, DIV, DT, *FIELDSET*, FORM, Hn, LI, MULTICOL, NOEMBED, *NOFRAMES*, NOLAYER, *NOSCRIPT*, P, PRE, TD, TH, **character highlighting**, A, APPLET, *BUTTON*, *IFRAME*, ILAYER, LAYER, *LABEL*, *LEGEND*, *OBJECT*
Attributes:	CLASS, *ID*, *STYLE*, *TITLE*

NOBR marks a block of text that cannot contain line breaks. Thus, a block of text enclosed by a **NOBR** will be presented as a single line of text with no word wrapping, even if it scrolls off the edge of the screen. This is useful for strings of text that you do not wish broken at word spaces, regardless of the page layout.

You may wish to allow word breaks, but only at specific locations. This is the role of the **WBR** element, which is used inside **NOBR** to mark places where line breaking is allowed. **WBR** is essentially a conditional **BR** element, in that it does not force a line break, but instead permits one where a break would otherwise be forbidden.

NOEMBED Element: HTML Alternative to EMBED

Usage:	`<NOEMBED> ... </NOEMBED>`
Can Contain:	Unspecified, probably: ADDRESS, BLOCKQUOTE, ~~CENTER~~, ~~DIR~~, DIV, DL, *FIELDSET*, FORM, Hn, HR, [ISINDEX], ~~MENU~~, MULTICOL, NOEMBED, *NOFRAMES*, NOLAYER, *NOSCRIPT*, OL, P, PRE, TABLE, UL,
	characters, character highlighting, A, APPLET, *BASEFONT*, BR, *BUTTON*, EMBED, *IFRAME*, IMG, ILAYER, INPUT, KEYGEN, *LABEL*, LAYER, MAP, *OBJECT*, SCRIPT, SELECT, SPACER, TEXTAREA, WBR
Can Be Inside:	Unspecified, probably: BLOCKQUOTE, BODY, ~~CENTER~~, DD, DIV, *FIELDSET*, FORM, LI, MULTICOL, NOEMBED, *NOFRAMES*, NOLAYER, *NOSCRIPT*, TD, TH,
	DEL,INS,
	APPLET, *BUTTON*, *IFRAME*, ILAYER, LAYER, *OBJECT*
Attributes:	none

When the Netscape programmers introduced the **EMBED** element, they realized that many browsers would be unable to process the element, or might not have a plugin capable of processing the embedded object or data type. Consequently, they introduced a second element, **NOEMBED**, to contain HTML markup to be used should the browser be unable to process **EMBED**. A browser that understands **EMBED** and that can process the referenced data will display the **EMBED**ded object and will hide the content of **NOEMBED**. On the other hand, a browser that does not understand **EMBED** will ignore the **EMBED** and **NOEMBED** tags, and will treat the content of the **NOEMBED** element as HTML markup to be displayed with the document.

NOEMBED should be placed just after the associated **EMBED**—for example:

```
<EMBED SRC="screaming-penguins.au" HEIGHT="100" WIDTH="200">
<NOEMBED>
   <H3> The Sound of The Screaming Penguins</H3>
   <P>If you are reading this text, then your browser does not
     support EMBED, and is unable to play the embedded audio
     snippet. You are missing the exciting musical texturings
     of the new jazz quintet <EM>The Screaming Penguins</EM>.
   You can pick up their debut album at a record store near you.
</NOEMBED>
```

Recall that **EMBED** will soon be replaced by **OBJECT**. **OBJECT** provides much better mechanisms for embedding arbitrary data or program objects, plus better mechanisms for providing alternative HTML content for browsers that do not support the specified object.

SERVER Element: Server-Side JavaScript (Netscape Navigator Only)

Usage:	`<SERVER> ... </SERVER>`
Can Contain:	characters (JavaScript code)
Can Be Inside:	**ADDRESS, BLOCKQUOTE, BODY, CAPTION, ~~CENTER~~,** DD, DIV, DT, *FIELDSET*, FORM, Hn, LI, **MULTICOL,** **NOEMBED,** *NOFRAMES,* **NOLAYER,** *NOSCRIPT,* P, PRE, TD, TH, **character highlighting,** A, APPLET, *BUTTON, IFRAME,* **ILAYER,** **LAYER,** *LABEL, LEGEND, OBJECT*
Attributes:	**ALIGN, HEIGHT, SIZE, TYPE, WIDTH**

SERVER is a container for JavaScript code to be executed on the Web server, prior to sending the document to a browser—at present, this is only supported by Netscape servers. Netscape servers support a special server-side JavaScript package, called *LiveWire*, which consists of a JavaScript interpreter, plus a special set of JavaScript functions designed for server-side processing, such as database querying. **SERVER** element content is processed before a document is sent to a browser, and the enclosed code (plus the `<SERVER>` and `</SERVER>` tags) are removed from the document before it is sent. Thus, a user should never see **SERVER** elements in served documents.

SPACER Element: Horizontal and Vertical Spacing (Netscape Navigator Only)

Usage:	`<SPACER>`
Can Contain:	empty

Can Be Inside: ADDRESS, BLOCKQUOTE, BODY, CAPTION, ~~CENTER~~, DD, DIV, DT, *FIELDSET*, FORM, Hn, LI, <u>MULTICOL</u>, <u>NOEMBED</u>, *NOFRAMES*, <u>NOLAYER</u>, *NOSCRIPT*, P, PRE, TD, TH

character highlighting, A, APPLET, *BUTTON*, *IFRAME*, <u>ILAYER</u>, <u>LAYER</u>, *LABEL*, *LEGEND*, *OBJECT*

Attributes: ALIGN, HEIGHT, SIZE, TYPE, WIDTH

SPACER introduces arbitrary horizontal or vertical spacing within typed text. TYPE="block" spacing is analogous to inserting a transparent (invisible) image of size HEIGHT and WIDTH, and allows insertion of horizontal and vertical space at the same place. TYPE="horizontal" spacers introduce simple horizontal tab-like spacings of length specified by SIZE. TYPE="vertical" introduces a vertical tab, again with size specified by SIZE. In this case, however, the tab also implies a line break.

Some examples of SPACER are shown in Figures 7.12 through 7.14. Note in particular Figure 7.14, which shows the page as displayed by a browser that does not understand SPACER. Because SPACER so strongly affects formatting, pages that depend on SPACER can be almost unreadable by browsers that do not understand this element.

TIP: Use Fully Transparent Images Instead of SPACER

A fully transparent image can be used to create indents similar to **SPACER**, but in a way that is better understood on a wide range of browsers. Simply create a fully transparent (blank) GIF image of some small size, for example 1-by-1 pixel. Then use **IMG** elements to create spacers of any size, simply by using the **HEIGHT** and **WIDTH** attributes to reshape the image. For example, to create a horizontal spacer 60 pixels long, use the tag

```
<IMG SRC="blank.gif" HEIGHT="1" WIDTH="60">
```

which shrinks the image to be 1 pixel high and 60 pixels wide.

The allowed SPACER attributes are:

ALIGN="top," "middle," "bottom," "left," "right" (mandatory: TYPE="block" only)   Specifies the page alignment for the spacer, relevant for TYPE="block" spacers only. Such spacers are treated in the same manner as images, so that the alignment options have the same meanings as for the IMG element.

HEIGHT="*number*" (mandatory with TYPE="block")   Specifies the height, in pixels, of the spacer. This is relevant only for TYPE="block," and should not be specified for other TYPEs.

SIZE="*number*" (mandatory with TYPE="horizontal" or "vertical") Indicates the horizontal or vertical width of the spacer, in pixels: this attribute relevant only for TYPE="horizontal" or "vertical" spacers. The effect is similar to a horizontal or vertical tab. This is relevant only for TYPE="horizontal" and TYPE="vertical," and should not be specified for TYPE="block."

TYPE="block," "horizontal," "vertical" (mandatory)   Specifies the type of the spacer. A "block" spacer is analogous to an invisible image—you must also specify the HEIGHT, WIDTH, and desired ALIGNment of this type of spacer. TYPE="horizontal" or TYPE="vertical" are analogous to tabs—in these cases, the only required attribute is SIZE, which specifies the tab size. Note that a "vertical" spacer also introduces a line break (BR).

WIDTH="*number*" (mandatory with TYPE="block")   Specifies the width, in pixels, of the spacer. This is relevant only for TYPE="block," and should not be specified for other TYPEs.

WBR Element: Word Break

Usage:	<WBR>
Can Contain:	empty
Can Be Inside:	Unspecified, probably: ADDRESS, BLOCKQUOTE, BODY, CAPTION, ~~CENTER~~, DD, DIV, DT, *FIELD-SET*, FORM, Hn, LI, <u>MULTICOL</u>, <u>NOEMBED</u>, *NOFRAMES*, <u>NOLAYER</u>, *NOSCRIPT*, P, PRE, TD, TH **character highlighting**, A, APPLET, *BUTTON*, *IFRAME*, <u>ILAYER</u>, <u>LAYER</u>, *LABEL*, *LEGEND*, *OBJECT*
Attributes:	none
Attributes:	CLASS, ID, LANG, STYLE

WBR marks a word space, within a NOBR element, where a word break is allowed. WBR does not force a break, but simply tells the browser where a word break is allowed, should one be needed.

Advanced HTML FORMs

HTML 4 introduces five new elements for structuring content within a FORM. These new elements are largely designed to be backward-compatible with existing FORM elements, so that documents that use these elements will be usable with browsers that do not support the elements. The following sections note where this is not the case.

BUTTON is a new input mechanism. Similar to an INPUT element, BUTTON provides for push-button controls, but supports more complex button labeling, such as labeling by images or even paragraphs. **OPTGROUP** is used to subgroup **OPTION** elements inside a **SELECT** list: On a browser, the resulting **SELECT** element might be presented as a *cascading* menu. The **FIELDSET** element provides a way of grouping form elements together, with an associated **LEGEND** element yielding a label for the set. Finally, **LABEL** is used to define text labels for any of the form input elements.

There are also four important new attributes: **READONLY** (for read-only elements), **DISABLED** (for disabled elements), **ACCESSKEY** (for defining keyboard bindings to input elements), and **TABINDEX** (for defining the order in which tabbing will access the elements).

Netscape Navigator 4 provides no support for these new elements or attributes. On the other hand, Internet Explorer 4 supports all, with the exception of **OPTGROUP**. The next few sections define in detail how each of these new elements and attributes works, and provides suggestions for ways to define forms that will function in the absence of support for these new mechanisms.

The document listed in Figure 7.15 illustrates the new **BUTTON**, **FIELDSET**, and **LEGEND** elements and the **DISABLED** and **READONLY** attributes. Browser rendering of these examples is shown in Figure 7.16 (Internet Explorer 4) and Figure 7.17 (Netscape Navigator 4). Note that Netscape does not support these new elements and attributes. For backward and cross-platform compatibility, it is best to avoid **BUTTON** elements (nonfunctional on Netscape Navigator), and to avoid the attributes **DISABLED** or **READONLY**.

BUTTON Element: Defining Push Buttons

Usage:	<BUTTON> ... </BUTTON>
Can Contain:	ADDRESS, BLOCKQUOTE, ~~CENTER~~, ~~DIR~~, DIV, DL, Hn, HR, ~~MENU~~, MULTICOL, NOEMBED, *NOFRAMES*, NOLAYER, *NOSCRIPT*, OL, P, PRE, TABLE, UL,
	characters, character highlighting, APPLET, *BASEFONT*, BR, EMBED, ILAYER, IMG, KEYGEN, LAYER, MAP, *OBJECT*, SCRIPT, SPACER, WBR
Can Be Inside:	ADDRESS, BLOCKQUOTE, BODY, CAPTION, ~~CENTER~~, DD, DIV, DT, *FIELDSET*, FORM, Hn, LI, MULTICOL, NOEMBED, *NOFRAMES*, NOLAYER, *NOSCRIPT*, P, PRE, TD, TH
	character highlighting, A, APPLET, *IFRAME*, ILAYER, LAYER, *LABEL*, *LEGEND*, *OBJECT*
Attributes:	*CLASS, DIR, ID, LANG, STYLE, TITLE, standard event handlers,*
	onBlur, onFocus,
	ACCESSKEY, DISABLED, TABINDEX, TYPE, VALUE

Figure 7.15 HTML document illustrating the BUTTON, FIELDSET, and LEGEND elements and the DISABLED and READONLY attributes. Browser renderings of this document are found in Figure 7.16 and 7.17.

```
<HTML><HEAD><TITLE>Example of HTML 4 FORMS </TITLE></HEAD>
<BODY BGCOLOR="#ffffff">
<FORM ACTION="ex-form.html">

<H3><FONT COLOR="green">(A) DISABLED and READONLY Elements</H2>
<BLOCKQUOTE>
<TABLE BORDER="0" CELLSPACING="2" CELLPADDING="3">
<TR BGCOLOR="#cccccc">
    <TH>Element Type</TH> <TH>Active</TH>     <TH>DISABLED</TH>
</TR><TR>
    <TD ALIGN="right"><B>BUTTON</B>                          </TD>
    <TD><BUTTON NAME="but1" VALUE="x1">Label
                                                text</BUTTON></TD>
    <TD><BUTTON NAME="but2" VALUE="x2" DISABLED>Label
                                                text</BUTTON></TD>
</TR><TR>
    <TD ALIGN="right"><B>INPUT TYPE="Checkbox"</B>           </TD>
    <TD><INPUT TYPE="checkbox" NAME="n1" VALUE="ok" CHECKED> </TD>
    <TD><INPUT TYPE="checkbox" NAME="n1" VALUE="ok" CHECKED
                                                DISABLED></TD>
</TR><TR>
    <TD ALIGN="right"><B>INPUT TYPE="text"</B>               </TD>
    <TD><INPUT TYPE="text" NAME="n1" VALUE="flopsy">         </TD>
    <TD><INPUT TYPE="text" NAME="n1" VALUE="flopsy" DISABLED></TD>
</TR><TR>
    <TD ALIGN="right"><B>INPUT TYPE="text"</B>               </TD>
    <TD ALIGN="right">                                       </TD>
    <TD><INPUT TYPE="text" NAME="n1" VALUE="flopsy" DISABLED></TD>
</TR><TR>
    <TD ALIGN="right"><B>INPUT TYPE="text"</B>               </TD>
    <TD ALIGN="right"> <B>READONLY:</B>                      </TD>
    <TD><INPUT TYPE="text" NAME="n1" VALUE="flopsy" READONLY></TD>
</TR></TABLE>
</BLOCKQUOTE>

<H3><FONT COLOR="green">(B) Button Containing a BLOCKQUOTE</FONT></H3>
<BLOCKQUOTE>
<BUTTON NAME="f2">
```

Figure 7.15 *Continued*.

```
  <P>Here is a button containing text, paragraphs, etc.</P>
  <P>Here is a button <FONT COLOR="green" SIZE="+2">containing
  text</FONT>, paragraphs, etc.</P>
</BUTTON>
</BLOCKQUOTE>

<H3><FONT COLOR="green">(C) Button Containing a Single IMG</FONT>:
    <BUTTON NAME="f4"><IMG SRC="button.gif"></BUTTON>
</H3>

<H3><FONT COLOR="green">(D) A FIELDSET</FONT></H3>
<BLOCKQUOTE>
<FIELDSET  STYLE="width: 50%; margin-left:auto; margin-right: 0;
            background: #ffffcc; border:solid double blue" >
   <LEGEND STYLE="color:blue; font-weight: bold;"
            ACCESSKEY="m"> Personal Information </LEGEND>
   <TABLE STYLE="margin-left: 1em">
   <TR>
      <TD ALIGN="right"><B>Last Name: </B></TD>
      <TD><INPUT NAME="personal_lastname" TYPE="text"> </TD>
   </TR><TR>
      <TD ALIGN="right"><B>First Name:</B></TD>
      <TD><INPUT NAME="personal_firstname" TYPE="text"> </TD>
   </TR><TR>
      <TD ALIGN="right"><B>Address:</B></TD>
      <TD><INPUT NAME="personal_address"   TYPE="text"> </TD>
   </TR>
   </TABLE>
</FIELDSET>
</BLOCKQUOTE></FORM></BODY></HTML>
```

The **BUTTON** element delimits text or other content to be displayed as a push button. There are three possible types: **TYPE**="button" (the default), "**TYPE**="submit," and **TYPE**="reset," which are functionally equivalent to **INPUT** elements of the same type. The difference is in the allowed content of the displayed button—with **INPUT** elements, this content is given by the **VALUE** attribute, while with **BUTTON,** this content is defined by the content of the button element, which can be any form of HTML markup. As a result, the rendered buttons can be far more complex. An example is shown in Figures 7.15 and 7.16, where the button contains paragraphs, blockquoted and enlarged-sized text, and images. **BUTTON** does take a **VALUE** attribute, which defines the value to associate with the button—and send to the server or JavaScript program—when the button is pressed.

Figure 7.16 Rendering, by Internet Explorer 4, of the document listed in Figure 7.15. Note how the disabled input elements are grayed out, while the FIELDSET (at the bottom of the page) is surrounded by a border and is labeled by the value of the LEGEND attribute.

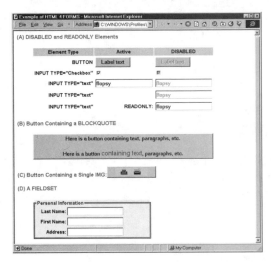

Figure 7.17 Rendering, by Netscape Navigator 4, of the document listed in Figure 7.15—this browser does not support the new form-related elements and attributes. Note, however, how the FIELDSET content is acceptably displayed, because the markup is designed to work in the absence of support for FIELDSET and LEGEND.

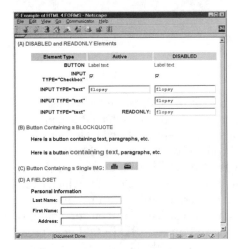

There are some important restrictions to **BUTTON** content: **BUTTON** cannot contain the elements **A, BUTTON, FIELDSET, FORM, IFRAME, INPUT, ISINDEX, LABEL, SELECT,** or **TEXTAREA. BUTTON** elements can contain images, but these cannot be active or client-side imagemapped images. If you want a button image that is imagemapped, use the **INPUT TYPE**="image" element.

BUTTON is not supported by Netscape Navigator 4 and is not compatible with older browsers that do not support **BUTTON**.

KEYGEN Element: Generate Encryption Key (Netscape Navigator Only)

Usage:	<KEYGEN>
Can Contain:	empty
Can Be Inside:	Undefined, probably: **ADDRESS, BLOCKQUOTE, BODY, CAPTION,** ~~CENTER~~, **DD, DIV, DT,** *FIELDSET*, **FORM, Hn, LI,** *NOFRAMES*, NOLAYER,*NOSCRIPT*, **P, PRE, TD, TH,**
	character highlighting, **A, APPLET,** *IFRAME*, ILAYER, LAYER, *LABEL*, *LEGEND*, *OBJECT*
Attributes:	NAME, CHALLENGE

KEYGEN generates encrypted public key certificates for submission, via a **FORM,** to a remote site—the remote site can use this key to authenticate the data sent to the server and the identity of the sender. The mandatory **NAME** attribute defines the name to use when sending the data to the server. The optional **CHALLENGE** attribute is assigned a challenge string, which is encrypted along with the user's public key when the value for the **KEYGEN** is calculated; the decrypted **CHALLENGE** value can determine the identity of the document that sent the request. The default value for **CHALLENGE** is an empty string.

When present, **KEYGEN** produces a user-selectable list of key sizes. When the form is submitted, a key pair of the selected size is generated: The public key and challenge string are encoded, digitally signed with the private key, and encoded (base64) to produce the *value* part of the *name/value* pair. The private key is encrypted and is stored locally in a database of valid keys.

NAME="*string*" (optional)   Defines the name to be associated with the encrypted key. This is the name that is associated with the encrypted key when the name/value pair is sent to the sever.

CHALLENGE="*string*" (optional)   Specifies the challenge string, which is encrypted along with the user's defined public key. The encrypted pair is sent as the value associated with the element's **NAME.**

LABEL Element: Labeling Input Elements

Usage:	`<LABEL> ... </LABEL>`
Can Contain:	characters, character highlighting, A, APPLET, *BASE-FONT*, BR, *BUTTON*, EMBED, *IFRAME*, ILAYER, IMG, INPUT, KEYGEN, LAYER, MAP, *OBJECT*, SPACER, SCRIPT, SELECT, TEXTAREA, WBR
Can Be Inside:	ADDRESS, BLOCKQUOTE, BODY, CAPTION, ~~CENTER~~, DD, DIV, DT, *FIELDSET*, FORM, Hn, LI, MULTICOL, NOEMBED, *NOFRAMES*, NOLAYER, *NOSCRIPT*, P, PRE, TD, TH,
	character highlighting, A, APPLET, *IFRAME*, ILAYER, LAYER, *LEGEND*, OBJECT
Attributes:	*CLASS, DIR, ID, LANG, STYLE, TITLE, standard event handlers, onFocus, onBlur,* *ACCESSKEY, FOR*

The **LABEL** element defines a label for a specified input element. This relationship is defined using the **FOR** attribute of the **LABEL**, which takes, as its value, the **ID** value of the input mechanism with which the label is associated. For example, the markup

```
<TD> <LABEL FOR="id23"> Set As Default: </LABEL> </TD>
<TD> <INPUT TYPE="checkbox" ID="id23" NAME="fname" VALUE="yes"> </TD>
```

associates the given label with the associated text input box—the **ID** value linking the two is highlighted in boldface. Note that this does not affect the rendering of the text or input mechanism and merely provides a way of logically linking these two components. Furthermore, the **ACCESSKEY** attribute of a **LABEL** lets an author tie a keyboard character to the input element, as discussed later in the section describing the **ACCESSKEY** attribute. For example, the markup:

```
<TD> <LABEL ACCESSKEY="d" FOR="id23"> Set As Default: </LABEL> </TD>
<TD> <INPUT TYPE="checkbox" ID="id23" NAME="fname" VALUE="yes"> </TD>
```

means that the author can type a special acceleration key sequence (ALT-d under Microsoft Windows) to access and "check" the associated checkbox. For more details, please see the *ACCESSKEY Attribute* section, later in this chapter.

Formally, a label can also be bound to an input element by placing the input element *inside* the **LABEL**, for example:

```
<LABEL> First Name:
   <INPUT TYPE="checkbox" NAME="fname" VALUE="yes">
</LABEL>
```

However, this limits the way in which the label and associated input mechanism can be formatted (note that tabular layout of the two items is not possible). Given this limitation, plus the fact that this notation is not supported by Internet Explorer 4, you should avoid this approach.

FIELDSET Element: Grouping Input Elements

Usage:	`<FIELDSET> ... </FIELDSET>`
Can Contain:	Unspecified, probably: ADDRESS, BLOCKQUOTE, ~~CENTER~~, ~~DIR~~, DIV, DL, *FIELDSET*, FORM, Hn, HR, [ISINDEX], ~~MENU~~, <u>MULTICOL</u>, <u>NOEMBED</u>, *NOFRAMES*, <u>NOLAYER</u>, *NOSCRIPT*, OL, P, PRE, TABLE, UL,
	characters, character highlighting, A, APPLET, *BASEFONT*, BR, *BUTTON*, <u>EMBED</u>, *IFRAME*, <u>KEYGEN</u>, <u>LAYER</u>, IMG, INPUT, *LABEL*, <u>LAYER</u>, *LEGEND*, MAP, *OBJECT*, SCRIPT, SELECT, <u>SPACER</u>, TEXTAREA, <u>WBR</u>
Can Be Inside:	Unspecified, probably: BLOCKQUOTE, BODY, ~~CENTER~~, DD, DIV, *FIELDSET*, FORM, LI, <u>MULTICOL</u>, <u>NOEMBED</u>, *NOFRAMES*, <u>NOLAYER</u>, *NOSCRIPT*, TD, TH,
	APPLET, *IFRAME*, <u>ILAYER</u>, <u>LAYER</u>, *OBJECT*
Attributes:	*CLASS, DIR, ID, LANG, STYLE, TITLE, standard event handlers*

FIELDSET groups together a related set of input elements and labels, so that they can be formatted and treated as a group. The content of a **FIELDSET** is simply a collection of input elements and labels, plus other HTML markup that structures the elements. Also allowed is a **LEGEND** element, which provides a label or title for the **FIELDSET**—this is the **FIELDSET** equivalent of a **LABEL**. For compatibility with older browsers, the **LEGEND** should appear just after the **FIELDSET** start tag.

The following is an example of **FIELDSET** markup: This is included in Figure 7.15 and is shown rendered by a browser in Figures 7.16 and 7.17. Note that this example uses style sheet instructions to format the **FIELDSET**—with Internet Explorer 4 (the only browser to currently support this element), this is the only mechanism for controlling **FIELDSET** element formatting.

```
<FIELDSET
      STYLE="width: 50%; margin-left:auto; margin-right: 0;
            background: #ffffcc; border:solid double blue" >
<LEGEND STYLE="color:blue; font-weight: bold;"
      ACCESSKEY="m"> Personal Information </LEGEND>
<TABLE STYLE="margin-left: 1em">
<TR>
   <TD ALIGN="right"><B>Last Name: </B></TD>
   <TD><INPUT NAME="personal_lastname" TYPE="text"> </TD>
</TR>
<TR>
   <TD ALIGN="right"><B>First Name:</B></TD>
```

```
<TD><INPUT NAME="personal_firstname" TYPE="text"> </TD>
</TR>
<TR><TD ALIGN="right"><B>Address:</B></TD>
  <TD><INPUT NAME="personal_address"  TYPE="text"> </TD>
</TR>
</TABLE></FIELDSET>
```

FIELDSET is not understood by Netscape Navigator 4.

LEGEND Element: Label for a FIELDSET

Usage:	`<LEGEND> ... </LEGEND>`
Can Contain:	characters, character highlighting, A, APPLET, *BASE-FONT*, BR, *BUTTON*, <u>EMBED</u>, *IFRAME*, <u>ILAYER</u>, IMG, INPUT, <u>LAYER</u>, MAP, *OBJECT*, <u>SPACER</u>, SCRIPT, SELECT, TEXTAREA, <u>WBR</u>
Can Be Inside:	*FIELDSET*
Attributes:	*CLASS, DIR, ID, LANG, STYLE, TITLE, standard event handlers,*
	ACCESSKEY, ALIGN

LEGEND specifies a label to associate with a **FIELDSET**. A **LEGEND** can only appear inside a **FIELDSET**, and there can be at most one **LEGEND** for each **FIELDSET**. A browser will use the **LEGEND** content to label the fieldset in some way, for example by embedding the text in the border around the fieldset.

In addition to the standard attribute set, **LEGEND** can also take the attributes **ACCESSKEY** and **ALIGN**. **ACCESSKEY** defines the access key for the associated **FIELDSET**, and allows for keyboard-based access of the element—once accessed via a key sequence, focus is transferred to the first input element inside the **FIELDSET**. **ALIGN** defines the alignment of the legend label relative to the fieldset, with possible values "top," "bottom," "left," and "right," with the obvious meanings. Internet Explorer 4, the only current browser that supports **FIELDSET** and **LEGEND**, only supports the values "left" and "right."

Figure 7.15 and 7.16 illustrate the appropriate use and rendering of a **LEGEND**.

OPTGROUP Element: Subgroups of OPTIONs

Usage:	`<OPTGROUP> ... </OPTGROUP>`
Can Contain:	*OPTGROUP, OPTION*
Can Be Inside:	*OPTGROUP, SELECT*
Attributes:	*CLASS, DIR, ID, LANG, STYLE, TITLE, standard event handlers,*
	DISABLED, LABEL

OPTGROUP defines a group of **OPTION** elements within a **SELECT** list and is used to define *hierarchical* or collapsible lists. For example, the list:

```
<SELECT NAME="region">
    <OPTGROUP LABEL="Canada">
        <OPTION>Alberta
        <OPTION>British Columbia
        ...
    </OPTGROUP>
    <OPTGROUP LABEL="United States">
        <OPTION>Alabama
        <OPTION>Arkansas
        ...
    </OPTGROUP>
...
</SELECT>
```

would be presented as a cascading list, with the first level in the cascade being the country names (Canada, United States, etc.) and the second level (once a country is selected) being the names of the provinces or states. Note how the **LABEL** attribute defines the label to associate with a particular **OPTGROUP**.

If an **OPTGROUP** is marked as **DISABLED**, then the content of the element—namely, all **OPTION** or **OPTGROUP** elements inside the **OPTGROUP**—are disabled and cannot be accessed or selected by the user.

The **OPTGROUP** element is not supported on Internet Explorer 4 or Netscape Navigator 4. However, these browsers simply ignore the **OPTGROUP** elements and display all the **OPTION** elements as a single (possibly long) list. Thus, a selection list may still be usable, even if the **OPTGROUP** elements are not displayed. Of course, this may present problems if **DISABLED** were used to disable an entire **OPTGROUP**, so it is best to avoid using **DISABLED** for this purpose.

New FORM Attributes

As mentioned earlier, the four new attributes **ACCESSKEY**, **DISABLED**, **READONLY**, and **TABINDEX** play an important role in the structure and design of HTML 4 forms. The following sections describe each of these attributes in detail, and explain how they are used. Table 7.2 lists the elements that support them.

DISABLED Attribute (Internet Explorer 4 Only)

Under HTML 4, *every* input element (**BUTTON**, **INPUT**, **OPTION**, **OPTGROUP**, **SELECT**, and **TEXTAREA**) supports a **DISABLED** attribute. When this attribute is set, the item is treated as disabled, and cannot be selected or changed by the user. Also, the data content of a **DISABLED** element is never sent when the associated **FORM** is sent to a server. On a graphical browser, a disabled item should be rendered in gray or in some other way that distinguishes the item from an active one.

Table 7.2 New Form Input Element Attributes, and Associated Elements

ATTRIBUTE	SUPPORTED ELEMENTS
ACCESSKEY	A, AREA, BUTTON, LABEL, INPUT, LEGEND
DISABLED	BUTTON, INPUT, OPTION, OPTGROUP, SELECT, TEXTAREA
READONLY	INPUT TYPE="text," INPUT TYPE="password," TEXTAREA
TABINDEX	A, AREA, BUTTON, OBJECT, INPUT, SELECT, TEXTAREA

Internet Explorer 4 supports the **DISABLED** attribute on all the above elements except **OPTION** and **OPTGROUP** (the browser does not support **OPTGROUP**). In most cases, the disabled items are grayed out, as illustrated in Figure 7.16. This is not done, however, with **INPUT TYPE**="image," **INPUT TYPE**="file," and **BUTTON** elements having **IMG** elements as their only content: these elements when disabled look the same as when they are active. This can be somewhat confusing to users, so authors should be careful when disabling these input mechanisms.

READONLY Attribute (Internet Explorer 4 Only)

The **INPUT** (**TYPE**="text" and **TYPE**="password") and **TEXTAREA** elements support a **READONLY** attribute. When this attribute is present, the associated element is treated as read-only: The element can be selected (for example, by tabbing or clicking on the element), but the content cannot be changed. Also, the data of a **READONLY** element are sent when the form is submitted.

READONLY does not affect the rendering of the displayed element, as illustrated in Figure 7.16. This should be contrasted with the effect of **DISABLED**, which leads to a graying-out of the element.

ACCESSKEY Attribute (Internet Explorer 4 Only)

ACCESSKEY, valid with the elements **A, AREA, BUTTON, LABEL, INPUT**, and **LEGEND**, defines a single-character keyboard shortcut for accessing these elements. The attribute value must be a single character available on the keyboard, for example **ACCESSKEY**="q." Since **ACCESSKEY** binds a specific character to a specific element, the values for the **ACCESSKEY** must be unique within a given document—no two elements should have the same value.

The manner in which keys are accessed varies from computer to computer. On Microsoft Windows platforms, the keys are accessed using the sequence ALT-*char* (ALT here means the keyboard ALT key), where *char* is the access key value: For example, a user would type "ALT-q" to access the element with attribute **ACCESSKEY**="q." Macintoshes in general use the sequence CMD-*char*, where CMD is the command key.

Typing the access key sequence on a browser will *activate* the referenced element, where possible. For example, if the referenced item is a checkbox, button, or radio button, accessing the item will cause it to be toggled or pressed; if it is a hypertext anchor, accessing the item will access the hypertext reference. However, when an access key references an item that requires editing (such as a reference to a **LABEL** that labels a **TEXTAREA**), the access key sequence simply moves the cursor to the region to be edited.

TABINDEX Attribute (Internet Explorer 4 Only)

The **A, AREA, BUTTON, OBJECT, INPUT, SELECT**, and **TEXTAREA** elements also support a **TABINDEX** attribute, which specifies the order in which these elements should be accessed when the user viewing the document presses the tab key. The value for **TABINDEX** can be any positive integer, including zero. Negative values are not allowed. Elements that support **TABINDEX**, but that are not assigned an explicit value, are assigned a default **TABINDEX** value of zero. Zero is considered to be the lowest priority in the tabbing sequence—all positively indexed elements are accessed before those assigned a value of zero. Unlike the case with **ACCESSKEY**, using TAB to select an item does not modify or activate the item—the user must still activate the selected item to change the value.

The tabbing sequence is as follows: Starting at the top of the document, the browser first tabs through all elements assigned positive **TABINDEX** values, starting with the smallest non-zero integer value and working upwards. If two elements have the same integer value, they are tabbed through in the order in which they appear in the document. Note that the tabbing index values need not be consecutive—a set of values such as 1, 3, 8, 25 is acceptable.

Once all the positive values are completed, the browser next tabs through all elements with zero (or unassigned) values, starting at the top of the document, and working downwards. Once all these items are finished, the browser goes back to the start and recommences the sequence.

Internet Explorer 4 supports **TABINDEX**, but Netscape Navigator 4 does not. Note that with a collection of **TYPE**="radio" buttons that share the same **NAME**, **TABINDEX** will only select the first button in the group, and the user must use another method to navigate and choose the desired button.

Embedding OBJECTs in HTML

OBJECT is designed to augment and replace the current embedding elements **IMG, EMBED**, and **APPLET**. It supports functionality similar to these elements, plus additional features not possible with any of them, as outlined below. Indeed, HTML 4 designates the **APPLET** element as deprecated, with the intention of using **OBJECT** for all object embedding in HTML.

As is apparent from the content model presented later, **OBJECT** can contain most HTML elements. Of particular importance are **PARAM** elements, which specify parameters to be passed to the object when it is run, as was the case for **PARAM** elements inside an **APPLET**. Almost all other markup inside **OBJECT** is ignored by a browser that supports **OBJECT** and that supports the object being embedded. However, if a browser does not understand **OBJECT** or does not support the particular *type* of embedded object, it should take the HTML content of the element and display it instead. Thus, the content of **OBJECT** serves as an HTML alternative for users who are unable to view the object itself.

In principle, you should be able to code documents using the **OBJECT** element, while including the pre-**OBJECT** markup inside. Thus if you already have markup using **EMBED** or **APPLET** elements, you can include these elements inside an **OBJECT**. Browsers that do not understand **OBJECT** will then, if capable, implement the **EMBED** or **APPLET** instructions.

In practice, however, this does not work—both Internet Explorer and Netscape Navigator have many bugs in their **OBJECT** implementation, making nesting of **EMBED** or **APPLET** elements inside an **OBJECT** a rather risky endeavor. Some illustrations of these problems are given in the following sections. The result is that you will need to very carefully test all uses of **OBJECT**, to make sure that things work as you want!

It is easiest to give a flavor for the **OBJECT** element using some simple examples, and that is the approach we shall take here. A detailed description of the **OBJECT** element and attributes follows this overview.

NOTE: Poor Support for OBJECT

OBJECT is not supported By Netscape Navigator 3, is only partially supported by Internet Explorer 3, and is "fully" supported—but with many bugs!—by Netscape Navigator 4 and Internet Explorer 4. In particular, Internet Explorer 3 does not support **OBJECT** embedding of simple data types (e.g., video or images) and does not support **OBJECT**-based client-side imagemaps.

OBJECT-Based Inclusion of Data

OBJECT is intended to replace three elements, **EMBED**, **IFRAME**, and **IMG**, which each take an external piece of data of a particular type (or types) and embed it in place within the document. However, there are many kinds of data one might wish to insert (images, video, text, HTML, PostScript, CAD files, etc.), and it is clearly impossible to create new HTML elements for each case.

With **OBJECT**, generic external data can be included via markup such as:

```
<OBJECT HEIGHT="100" WIDTH="100" DATA="button.tiff" TYPE="image/tiff">
  <P><I>An image of an example button, to be used ...
  </P>
</OBJECT>
```

Here, the **DATA** attribute gives the URL of the data file, and the new **TYPE** attribute specifies the MIME type of the data. **TYPE** is optional, but is useful information that lets the browser know the type of data to expect when it retrieves the **DATA**. It can then, for example, choose not to retrieve the data, should it not be able to process the indicated **TYPE**. The **HEIGHT** and **WIDTH** attributes define the size for the displayed object. If the referenced data can be rescaled, they will be rescaled to fit the defined region. If not, then **HEIGHT** and **WIDTH** simply define the size of a window through which the underlying object is viewed.

As mentioned previously, the content of **OBJECT** is HTML markup to be displayed by browsers that do not understand **OBJECT** or that are unable to display the referenced type of data (e.g., they do not have an appropriate plugin). Thus, in the preceding example, if the browser were unable to display TIFF images, it would instead display the paragraph text indicated.

This latter fact allows for nested **OBJECT**s, with the inner **OBJECT** being used if the browser cannot process the outer one. For example, the preceding code could be generalized as follows:

```
<OBJECT HEIGHT="100" WIDTH="100" DATA="button.tif" TYPE="image/tiff">
   <OBJECT HEIGHT="100" WIDTH="100" DATA="button.gif" TYPE="image/gif">
     <P><I>An image of an example button, to be used ...
     </P>
   </OBJECT>
</OBJECT>
```

Now if the browser cannot view TIFF images, it will process the HTML markup inside the **OBJECT**. But, just inside lies another **OBJECT**, referencing a GIF image. Then, if the browser is also unable to display the GIF image, it will bypass the second, nested object and display the HTML markup nested within. Indeed, you can place **EMBED**, **IMG**, and **IFRAME** elements within the **OBJECT**, to provide functionality for older browsers that do not support **OBJECT**.

Such markup is illustrated in Figure 7.18, with browser renderings in Figures 7.19 (Internet Explorer 4), 7.20 (Netscape Navigator 4), and 7.21 (Netscape Navigator 3).

Problems with OBJECT-Based Data References

Figures 7.19 through 7.21 illustrate some of the problems with **OBJECT**-based data embedding, as currently implemented. Indeed, these problems are so severe that **OBJECT**-based data embedding should, for the most part, be avoided. The main problems are:

- As demonstrated by the first inclusion example (OBJECT 1), Internet Explorer 4 improperly handles nested **OBJECT** elements and attempts to render *all* of the nested **OBJECT**s, instead of the first supported instance.

- Internet Explorer 4 renders inline data objects with scrollbars. Thus, the **HEIGHT** and **WIDTH** values required to fully display the object are not related in an obvious way to the actual size of the embedded object.
- Netscape Navigator 4 does not support **OBJECT**-based embedding of image or other displayable data content, but does properly render the **OBJECT**-element content in place of the referenced data.

Additional problems appear when other data are referenced from **OBJECT**—recall that **OBJECT** can in principle reference any types of data, not just images or HTML documents. For example, the markup:

```
<OBJECT DATA="sound.au" HEIGHT="60" WIDTH="160">
    <P>Audio recording of <A HREF="sound.au">Marc Andreesen</A></P>
</OBJECT>
```

references an audio file. Both Internet Explorer 4 and Netscape Navigator 4 come with plugin modules capable of playing this type of audio file, so that this should work. Indeed, Netscape Navigator understands this markup and displays a control panel for playing the audio file. Internet Explorer 4, however, crashes whenever it tries to load the file—and on occasion, completely crashes the Windows 95 operating system!

Imagemaps and OBJECT-Embedded Images

Since **OBJECT** elements can embed images, it is important that these images can be imagemapped in the same manner as **IMG** elements. Indeed, the **OBJECT** specification supports two mechanisms for imagemapping embedded objects, outlined in the following sections. Note, however, that **OBJECT** does not support server-side imagemaps, only client-side ones—if you want server-side imagemaps, you must use **IMG** elements or form **INPUT** elements of **TYPE**="image."

Note: OBJECT-Based Imagemaps Not Currently Supported

OBJECT-based imagemaps are *not* supported by Internet Explorer 4 or Netscape Navigator 4, since neither of these browsers properly supports **OBJECT**-based embedding of images.

OBJECT Imagemaps (1)—The SHAPES Attribute

The recommended form for adding imagemaps to **OBJECT**-embedded images makes use of a proposed extension to the anchor element. An example of this is shown in the HTML document listed in Figure 7.22—the attributes associated with the imagemap are shown in boldface.

As with **IMG**, the **ALIGN** attribute specifies the desired alignment for the displayed object (the image). The **SHAPES** attribute tells the browser that this object is an imagemap—as a result, the browser looks, within the HTML markup inside the

---

Figure 7.18 Document illustrating the use of OBJECT to embed data. Browser renderings of this document are found in Figures 7.19, 7.20, and 7.21.

```
<HTML><HEAD>
<TITLE>Test of OBJECT-based DATA Inclusions</TITLE>
</HEAD><BODY BGCOLOR="#ffffff">

<P><B>OBJECT 1 (.gif inside .tiff) </B><BR>
<OBJECT HEIGHT="25" WIDTH="100" DATA="button.tif" TYPE="image/tiff">
  <OBJECT HEIGHT="25" WIDTH="100" DATA="button.gif" TYPE="image/gif">
    <IMG SRC="button.gif">
  </OBJECT>
</OBJECT>

<P><B>OBJECT 2 (.html)</B><BR>
<OBJECT HEIGHT="100" WIDTH="300" DATA="demo.html" TYPE="text/html">
  <IFRAME SRC="demo.html" HEIGHT="100" WIDTH="300">
    <P>Alternative text for browsers that don't support
       <B>OBJECT</B> inclusion of HTML, or <B>IFRAME</B>.</P>
  </IFRAME>
</OBJECT>
</BODY></HTML>
```

OBJECT, for anchor elements containing the **SHAPE** and **COORDS** attributes—these contain the map coordinate information. If a browser does not support **OBJECT,** the user then sees the enclosed list of hypertext anchors as regular HTML markup. Thus the approach provides fully functional links or imagemaps, regardless of the browser's capabilities.

Figure 7.19 Rendering, by Internet Explorer 4, of the document listed in Figure 7.18. Note how, with the first example (OBJECT 1), this browser mistakenly tries to display *both* nested OBJECTs.

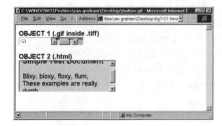

Figure 7.20 Rendering, by Netscape Navigator 4, of the document listed in Figure 7.18. This browser does not understand OBJECT elements that include data in this manner and instead displays the content of the OBJECT.

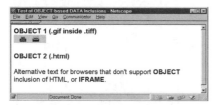

Figure 7.21 Rendering, by Netscape Navigator 3, of the document listed in Figure 7.18. This browser does not understand OBJECT.

A Elements Inside an OBJECT

As noted, A elements within an **OBJECT** support two new attributes relating the anchor reference to regions within the **OBJECT**-referenced image. The attributes and their meanings are:

SHAPE="circle," "default," "poly," "rect" (optional: only valid inside **A** within **OBJECT**)   **SHAPE** is valid only for anchor elements inside **OBJECT** elements, as discussed previously. **SHAPE**, in combination with the **COORDS** attribute, defines active regions of the image referenced by an **OBJECT** and attaches these regions to the remote resource indicated by the **HREF** attribute. **SHAPE** simply specifies the type of shape, the possible values being "circle," "default," "poly," and "rect."

COORDS="*string*" (optional: mandatory if **SHAPE** is present and if **SHAPE** is not equal to "default")   Specifies the coordinates associated with the designated **SHAPE**, measured from the upper left-hand corner of the image. Coordinates can either be integer quantities, in which case they are measurements in pixels from the upper-left hand corner or percentage values in the range (0%,0%) (the upper left-hand corner) to (100%, 100%) (lower right-hand corner).

Figure 7.22 Client-side imagemaps using OBJECT and special A element attributes.

```
<OBJECT DATA="activeimage.gif" SHAPES  ALIGN="left" HEIGHT="200" WIDTH="180">
  <A HREF="intro.html" SHAPE="rect"
     COORDS="20,20,60,40">Introduction</A> |
  <A HREF="welcome.html" SHAPE="circle" COORDS="70,70,10">Welcome</A> |
  <A HREF="blobby.html"  SHAPE="poly"
     COORDS="100,100, 100,110, 110, 120, 90, 130">Visit Mr. Blobby!</A> |
  <A HREF="help.html"     SHAPE="default">Help</A>
</OBJECT>
```

The following table describes appropriate **COORDS** values for the different **SHAPE**s.

SHAPE	COORDS
"circle"	"*x, y, r*"—A circle centered at (*x,y*) and of radius *r*.
"rect"	"*x_top, y_top, x_bot, y_bot*"—A rectangle with upper-left hand coordinates (*x_top*, *y_top*) and lower right-hand coordinates (*x_bot*, *y_bot*).
"poly"	"*x1, y1, ... xn, yn*"—A polygon, where the coordinates (*x1,y1*) .... (*xn,yn*) are the *vertices* of the polygon (minimum of three vertices). The polygon is closed by connecting the point (*x1,y1*) to (*xn, yn*).

OBJECT Imagemaps (2)—The USEMAP Attribute

For compatibility with the **MAP** element approach to client-side imagemaps (see Chapter 6), **OBJECT** also supports a **USEMAP** attribute, equivalent to the **USEMAP** attribute of the **IMG** element. Figure 7.23 shows a **USEMAP** equivalent to the client-side imagemap first given in Figure 7.22—once again, the attributes associated with the imagemap are highlighted in boldface. Although similar to the approach described in the previous section, this method does not provide a simple HTML text alternative for browsers that do not support **OBJECT**.

OBJECT Embedding of Applets

Of course, **OBJECT** can embed many things, not just images or simple data files. As an example, external applets can be included using **OBJECT**, illustrating that this element is a general-purpose successor to **APPLET**. Consider the **APPLET** markup example from Figure 2.32. The **APPLET** element was:

```
<APPLET
   CODEBASE="http://www.dgp.toronto.edu/people/JamesStewart/378/notes/"
   CODE="bst.class" WIDTH="321"
   HEIGHT="151" VSPACE="10" HSPACE="10"ALIGN="right">
   <PARAM NAME=keys value="50 42 43 15 6 23 17 30">
   <PARAM NAME=action value="rotate">
   <PARAM NAME=alternate_nodes value="15 42">
   <BLOCKQUOTE>
   <HR> If you were using a Java-enabled Web browser, you would
   see a binary search tree instead of this paragraph. <HR>
   </BLOCKQUOTE>
</APPLET>
```

where **CODEBASE** referred to the location of the class libraries, and **CODE** was the name of the class to run. The following illustrates the same applet embedding, but using **OBJECT**—the changes are shown in boldface.

```
<OBJECT
   CODEBASE="http://www.dgp.toronto.edu/people/JamesStewart/378/notes/"
   CLASSID="java:bst.class" WIDTH="321"
   HEIGHT="151" VSPACE="10" HSPACE="10" ALIGN="right">
   <PARAM NAME=keys value="50 42 43 15 6 23 17 30">
   <PARAM NAME=action value="rotate">
   <PARAM NAME=alternate_nodes value="15 42">
   <BLOCKQUOTE>
   <HR> If you were using a Java-enabled Web browser, you would
   see a binary search tree instead of this paragraph. <HR>
   </BLOCKQUOTE>
</OBJECT>
```

With **OBJECT**, **CLASSID** specifies the class ID for the applet to be run—here, this is a special class-related URL specifying a generic class ID for the desired code. In this case, the actual location of the code is given by the **CODEBASE** attribute, which is assigned the URL for the library or other resource containing the **CLASSID**-specified class. If **CODEBASE** is not given, then the code base takes, as its default value, the URL used to retrieve the document containing the **OBJECT**. Note, however, that the browser may not need to access the **CODE-BASE** resources—the **CLASSID** may contain sufficient information that the browser can find the required code on the local filesystem, without accessing it remotely. This is not true for the **java** URL example given above, but is true in other cases—an example is given below.

   CLASSID can also be a URL pointing to the program or class file, in which case **CODEBASE** may not be necessary, since the object is probably located in the same directory as the required, associated class files. When this is not the case,

Figure 7.23 Client-side imagemaps using OBJECT and MAP elements.

```
<OBJECT DATA="activeimage.gif" USEMAP="#mapref" ALIGN="left"
        HEIGHT="200" WIDTH="180"> >
... alternative markup ...
</OBJECT>
..... additional markup ....
<MAP NAME="mapref">
   <AREA HREF="intro.html" SHAPE="rect" COORDS="20,20,60,40"
         ALT="Introduction">
   <AREA HREF="welcome.html" SHAPE="circle" COORDS="70,70,10"
         ALT="Welcome">
   <AREA HREF="blobby.html" SHAPE="poly"
         COORDS="100,100, 100,110, 110, 120, 90, 130"
         ALT="Visit Mr. Blobby!">
   <AREA HREF="help.html" SHAPE="default"
         ALT="help">
</MAP>
```

CLASSID often must specify, via special URL scheme names, the *type* of the code. The names and meanings for some of these special schemes are given in Table 7.3.

OBJECT also can take the optional **CODETYPE** attribute, which gives the MIME type of the program code. A browser can use this information to skip loading the referenced applet, should the browser not support the indicated type of code. For example, **TYPE**="application/com" could indicate a Microsoft COM object—browsers unable to run COM objects could then skip loading the object and instead display the HTML content of the **OBJECT**.

OBJECT Reference to Active-X Objects

Microsoft first implemented **OBJECT** to support Active-X embedding—that is, to use **OBJECT** to embed a variety of Active-X plugins and downloadable code libraries into HTML documents. Active-X objects have **CLASSID** values of the form:

Table 7.3 Some Special CLASSID URLs

URL Prefix	Type of Code	Example
java:	Java class	java:myprogs.bst.bst.class
javabean:	A JavaBean class	javabean:netscape.open.flyby
clsid:	A Microsoft Active-X object	clsid:D27CDB6E-AE6D-11CF-96B8-444553540000

```
clsid:class-identifier
```

where *class-identifier* is a global identifier that unambiguously identifies the object. In this case, **CODEBASE** indicates the location from which the object (and any required supporting code) can be obtained. However, if the Active-X object with the indicated class ID is installed on the browser, the Active-X handler is smart enough to check to see if the local version is up-to-date and use the local version if it is current.

Here is an example **OBJECT** reference to an Active-X object (some of the URLs have been shortened to reduce the lengths of the lines):

```
<OBJECT ID="pilot"
     CLASSID="clsid:D27CDB6E-AE6D-11CF-96B8-444553540000"
     CODEBASE="http://..../flash/cabs/swflash.cab#version=2,1,0,7"
     ALIGN="top" BORDER="0" WIDTH="90%" HEIGHT="100%">

 <PARAM NAME="Movie" value="whatson/whatson_new.spl">
 <PARAM NAME="Play" value="true">
 <PARAM NAME="loop" value="false">
 <PARAM NAME="Quality" value="best">
 <PARAM NAME="bgcolor" VALUE="#000000">

 <EMBED SRC="whatson/whatson_new.spl" BGCOLOR="#000000" BORDER="0"
      TYPE="application/x-shockwave-flash"
      PLUGINSPAGE="http://../index.cgi?P1_Prod_Version=ShockwaveFlash"
      ALIGN="left" WIDTH="90%"  HEIGHT="100%"
      NAME="pilot" VALIGN="top" QUALITY="best"
      PLAY="true"  LOOP="false">

</OBJECT>
```

This reference is to a Macromedia Shockwave Splash player, accessible from the indicated **CODEBASE**. Note how the **PARAM** element with **NAME=**"Movie" references the movie file to be played. This URL is passed to the Shockwave player, which retrieves the data and displays it on the page.

Note also how the **OBJECT** contains an **EMBED** element, so that older browsers that do not understand **OBJECT** can fall back to this earlier embedding format.

Referencing Both Data and Data Handler

Finally, an object can reference both the code to be executed and the data to be processed by the code. For example, the following **OBJECT** element specifies both a data file and a special Java applet that should process the data:

```
<OBJECT   DATA="http://www.whoopee.com/test/frogs.cpt"
          TYPE="application/hdf"
          CLASSID="java:dataanal.hdf.start"
          CODBASE="http://hdf.ncsa.uiuc.edu/java-apps/"
          CODETYPE="application/java-vm">
   <PARAM NAME="resolution" VALUE="fine">
   <P>Sorry, but the browesr was unable to load the Java applet that
   processes the referenced HDF data file. If you have local software
   to analyze HDF data files, please select
   <A HREF=" http://www.whoopee.com/test/frogs.cpt">here</A>
   to directly download the data.</P>
</OBJECT>
```

In this case, the referred handler (a Java program) is located on one remote server, while the data to be viewed is located on another.

Nested OBJECTS

OBJECT elements can be nested, allowing a cascade of possible object embeddings and handlers. An example of the associated **OBJECT** markup is (commentary in italics):

```
<OBJECT  ... (preferred data/handler) >
   <OBJECT ... (second choice ...) >
      <OBJECT ... (third choice ...) >
          HTML alternative to OBJECT ...
      </OBJECT>
   </OBJECT>
</OBJECT>
```

The browser would then work its way in through the **OBJECT**s, stopping when it finds one it can successfully process and ignoring any subsequent **OBJECT**s. Note that this is not properly supported by current browsers, so that for now you should avoid nesting **OBJECT**s.

Backwards Compatibility

To a large extent, **OBJECT** elements *should* be compatible with browsers that do not understand **OBJECT**. For example, **OBJECT** elements used to invoke imagemaps can contain, as an alternative, the regular **IMG** element markup, while more complex **OBJECT**s might contain **EMBED** elements with similar or equivalent functionality. This, however, hinges on proper support of **OBJECT**—unfortunately, current implementations are buggy and incomplete, such that this approach is not feasible.

The specification for **OBJECT** is presented below. This is followed by an overview of the changes to the **PARAM** and **A** elements introduced in support of **OBJECT**.

OBJECT Element: Embed an Arbitrary Data/Program Object

Usage:	`<OBJECT>...</OBJECT>`
Can Contain:	ADDRESS, BLOCKQUOTE, ~~CENTER~~, ~~DIR~~, DIV, DL, *FIELDSET*, FORM, Hn, HR, [ISINDEX], ~~MENU~~, <u>MULTICOL</u>, <u>NOEMBED</u>, *NOFRAMES*, <u>NOLAYER</u>, *NOSCRIPT*, OL, P, PRE, TABLE, UL,
	characters, character highlighting, A, APPLET, *BASE-FONT*, BR, *BUTTON*, <u>EMBED</u>, *IFRAME*, <u>ILAYER</u>, IMG, INPUT, <u>KEYGEN</u>, *LABEL*, <u>LAYER</u>, MAP, *OBJECT*, SCRIPT, SELECT, <u>SPACER</u>, TEXTAREA, <u>WBR</u>,
	PARAM
Can Be Inside:	ADDRESS, BLOCKQUOTE, BODY, CAPTION, ~~CENTER~~, DD, DIV, DT, *FIELDSET*, FORM, Hn, LI, <u>MULTICOL</u>, <u>NOEMBED</u>, *NOFRAMES*, <u>NOLAYER</u>, *NOSCRIPT*, P, PRE, TD, TH
	character highlighting, A, APPLET, *BUTTON*, *IFRAME*, <u>ILAYER</u>, *LABEL*, :<u>LAYER</u>, *LEGEND*, *OBJECT*
Attributes:	*CLASS, ID, LANG, STYLE, TITLE, standard event handlers,* (*onBlur, onFocus*: Internet Explorer 4 only),
	ALIGN, ARCHIVE, BORDER, CLASSID, CODEBASE, CODETYPE, DATA, DECLARE, HEIGHT, HSPACE, NAME, STANDBY, TABINDEX, TYPE, USEMAP, VSPACE, WIDTH

ALIGN="absbottom," "absmiddle," "baseline," "bottom," "left," "middle," "right," "texttop" (optional)   Specifies the desired alignment of the object. The values are the same as those used for the **IMG** element, and you are refereed there (Chapter 6) for a description of the meanings.

ARCHIVE="*space-separated URLs*" (optional; not currently supported) Contains a space-separated list of URLs that reference resources relevant to the object. Such URLs could reference resources specified by the **CLASSID** or **DATA** attributes. A browser may use these URLs to *pre-load* the declared archives, prior to actually using them. Thus, one **OBJECT** may be used to pre-load archives that are needed by subsequent **OBJECT**s. Relative URLs are allowed and are interpreted relative to the URL specified by the **CODEBASE** attribute.

BORDER="length" (optional; not supported by Netscape Navigator 4) Specifies the thickness of the border to be drawn around the object, should it be within an active anchor element. The thickness can be specified in any of the supported length units—at present, the only supported units are pixels (the default), in which case the height is simply given as an integer. The value of "0" indicates that the object should be drawn without borders.

CLASSID= "url" (optional; one of **DATA** or **CLASSID** is required) Specifies the URL of the program code that will implement the object: The URL can either reference an Internet-accessible resource, or it can reference a class name using a class-type specific URL naming scheme. An example of the former is a URL that references a remote java class object, such as:

CLASSID="http://www.server.org/path/dir/myapplet.class"

An example of the latter is the **clsid** URL scheme introduced by Microsoft for identifying Component Object Model (COM) objects. For example:

CLASSID="clsid:D27CDB6E-AE6D-11CF-96B8-444553540000"

Clsid URLs are discussed in more detail in Chapter 8.

CODEBASE="string" (optional)   Specifies a URL that references program code required by the code specified by **CLASSID**, and which otherwise cannot be located by the **CLASSID** value. An example is a **CLASSID** that references an applet, with a **CODEBASE** that references the associated class/code library.

CODETYPE="string" (optional; not supported by Netscape Navigator 4) Specifies the MIME type of the code referenced by the **CLASSID** attribute (**CLASSID** references the program object to be loaded). This is a hint to the browser—a browser can use this information to avoid downloading objects it does not support.

DATA="string" (optional; one of **DATA** or **CLASSID** is required) Specifies the URL of the data to be loaded. This can, for example, be an image file, a spreadsheet data set, or a VMRL world scene. **TYPE** can specify the MIME type of the data referenced by **DATA**. If **CLASSID** is absent, the browser will use the MIME type specified by **TYPE** or the type determined by downloading the actual data file to establish a program to handle the data type. In other words, the data type is used to determine an appropriate default value for **CLASSID**.

DECLARE (optional; not currently supported)   Indicates that the object should be declared, but not *instantiated*. That is, the object is made available to the system, but is not started until invoked by some other resource. This allows objects to be loaded for future use.

HEIGHT="length" (mandatory)   Specifies the desired height of the box enclosing the object, in pixels. In principle, **HEIGHT** can be used to rescale the object to the specified height. Whether or not this is possible depends on the object being embedded.

HSPACE="length" (optional)   Specifies the desired horizontal spacing to leave to the left and right of the object, in pixels.

ID="name" (optional)   Specifies a name token identifier for the object. This identifier can be used by the browser, script programs, or other objects embedded in the document to identify and communicate with the **ID**-labeled object.

NAME="string" (optional)   Specifies a variable name, analogous to the **NAME** attribute of **SELECT, INPUT,** and **TEXTAREA** elements. This is only relevant if the **OBJECT** is inside a **FORM.** In this case, the presence of a **NAME** tells the browser that data from the object should be included with the form data when the form is submitted (it is the responsibility of the object author to ensure that the data are made available to the **FORM,** and in the correct format). If **NAME** is absent, then the object and the form are unrelated.

STANDBY="string" (optional; not currently supported)   Specifies a short text string (including character and entity references, but not HTML markup) that can be displayed to the user while the object is loading.

TYPE="string" (optional)   Specifies the MIME type of the data referenced by the **DATA** attribute. This is a hint to the browser—a browser can in principle use this information to avoid downloading data types it does not support. In practice, however, a browser cannot definitively know the type until the data are actually accessed.

CLASSID can reference the code to properly handle the indicated data type. If **CLASSID** is absent, then **TYPE** is used to select an appropriate data handler.

USEMAP="string" (optional; not currently supported)   Specifies the URL of a client-side imagemap **MAP** element, as described in Chapters 3 and 6. This gives **OBJECT** the same functionality as client-side imagemapped **IMG** elements.

VSPACE="length" (optional)   Specifies the desired vertical spacing to leave above and below the object, in pixels.

WIDTH="length" (mandatory)   Specifies the desired width of the box enclosing the object, in pixels. In principle, **WIDTH** can be used to rescale the object to the specified width. Whether or not this is possible depends on the object being embedded.

PARAM Element: Parameter Inside an OBJECT

Usage:	<PARAM>
Can Contain:	empty
Can be Inside:	**APPLET**, *OBJECT*
Attributes:	*NAME, TYPE, VALUE, VALUETYPE*

The advanced **OBJECT** model supports extra attributes to **PARAM** elements inside an **OBJECT**. VALUETYPE specifies the type of the string being assigned to **VALUE**, and can take the three possible values "data," "object," or "ref." "Data" means that the **VALUE** string is data to be passed to the object, and that HTML entity and character references must be replaced by the referenced characters before the string is sent. The value "object" means that the assigned string is a reference pointing to another (possibly running) **OBJECT** within the same document. The value "ref" indicates that the value is a proper URL referencing a resource. If **VALUETYPE**="ref," then the optional **TYPE** attribute can be used to specify the MIME type of the referenced object.

NOTE: TYPE and VALUETYPE Not Widely Supported

At present, Microsoft Internet Explorer 3, the only browser to support **OBJECT**, does *not* support the **TYPE** and **VALUETYPE** attributes.

Netscape LAYER Elements

With Navigator 4, Netscape introduced three proprietary HTML elements: **LAYER**, **ILAYER**, and **NOLAYER**. These elements allow for *layered* content on the displayed page—that is, for content that appears "above" the standard page, rather like a "floating" block of text or graphic. In the Netscape approach, such floating content is defined by the **LAYER** or **ILAYER** elements (the two elements define the different ways in which elements can "float," as discussed below), or within an external document referenced by a **SRC** attribute of a **LAYER** or **ILAYER**. The **NOLAYER** element was introduced as a container for markup to be displayed by browsers that do not understand **LAYER** elements. Thus, **NOLAYER** is similar in purpose to **NOFRAMES**, **NOSCRIPT**, and **NOEMBED**.

Just after Netscape introduced the layer elements, the World Wide Web Consortium introduced a style sheet approach for element positioning and z-indexing—that is, for elements positioned above the plane of the regular HTML document. This is equivalent to the functionality provided by layer elements, and is now the recommended mechanism for creating layers in HTML documents. At present, Netscape Navigator 4 supports both layer elements and CSS positioning, while Internet Explorer 4 and other browsers do not support **LAYER** elements—thus, you must use CSS if you wish your pages to work on non-Netscape browsers.

However, many Netscape (and other) documents are composed using the layer elements, so it is important to understand the elements and how they work. In addition, there are some aspects of the layer approach (for example, using **SRC** to reference external content for the layer) that are not possible with CSS.

LAYER and ILAYER: Absolutely and Relatively Positioned Layers

The different layers are defined by **LAYER** and **ILAYER** elements. A **LAYER** element defines an *absolutely positioned* layer—such layers are positioned *independent* of the location of the **LAYER** element within the HTML document. In addition, layers defined by **LAYER** do not affect the flow of the non-layered text in the rest of the document. Figure 7.24 shows one such layer, here consisting of the text "ABSOLUTE" in bold, light red (which appears, in this figure, as light gray) text. Note how, in Figure 7.25, this layer is physically positioned where it would have appeared if it had not been in a layer—this is simply the default placement for a positioned layer, should no specific position be specified. Note also that this layer does *not* affect the positioning of the other text in the paragraph—the regular document text continues underneath the layer, as if the layer were not present. Note that the background of the layer element is transparent, and the text of the underlying window shows through. This is the default behavior of a layer element. However, layer elements can be assigned background colors (**BGCOLOR**) or images (**BACKGROUND**), which are opaque and fully obscure the underlying content.

ILAYER, or *inflow* layer, defines *relatively positioned* content—such elements appear as part of the regular flow of the text, and are not separated from it. Figure 7.24 illustrates a simple example **ILAYER** element, here containing the single word "RELATIVE" in bold, light red text (light gray in the figure). Note how the text appears inline with the regular content, and the surrounding text is displaced from the region occupied by the layer.

Figures 7.24 and 7.25 illustrate the *default* positions of layers—that is, the positions occupied by the layers if no positioning information is given. Most of the time, layer elements are displaced to positions defined by the **LEFT**, **TOP**, **PAGEX**, or **PAGEY** attributes. Figure 7.26 illustrates this positioning, applied to the document in Figure 7.24—here, both elements are positioned to start at **TOP**="50" and **RIGHT**="50," which define the position of the layers, relative to an upper left-hand corner, in pixels (percentage values are also supported).

The location of this upper left-hand corner depends on the type of the element, as illustrated in the browser rendering of this document in Figure 7.27—note the important difference between the resulting positions of the **LAYER** and **ILAYER**. The **LAYER** element is positioned 50 pixels down and 50 pixels in from the upper-left corner of the browser window, whereas the **ILAYER** element is positioned 50 pixels down and 50 pixels in from the position it occupied as an *inline* element. This illustrates the difference between *absolute* positioning of a **LAYER**—absolutely positioned relative to the enclosing frame and relative positioning of an **ILAYER**—positioned *relative* to the position the element would have if it were not positioned.

Figure 7.24 Example HTML document illustrating the Netscape LAYER and ILAYER elements. Figure 7.25 shows the rendering of this document by Netscape Navigator 4.

```
<HTML><HEAD>
<TITLE> Test of LAYER Elements</TITLE>
</HEAD>
<BODY TEXT="black"  BGCOLOR="white">

<P>This paragraph contains an absolutely positioned
<LAYER ID="o1">
<B><FONT SIZE="+1" COLOR="#ffaaaa">ABSOLUTE</FONT></B>
</LAYER>
layer. Note how the rest of the paragraph
is formatted as if the layer was not there.
</P>

<P>This second paragraph contains a relatively positioned
<ILAYER ID="i1" >
<B><FONT SIZE="+1" COLOR="#ffaaaa">RELATIVE</FONT></B>
</ILAYER>
layer. Note how the a relative layer affects the
formatting of the remaining paragraph text.
</P>
</BODY></HTML>
```

Figure 7.25 Rendering, by Netscape Navigator 4, of the document listed in Figure 7.24. Note the placement of the layer element content (bold, light gray text).

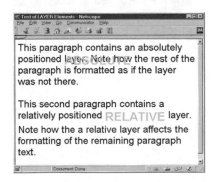

Figure 7.26 Example document illustrating *positioned* layers. Figure 7.27 shows the rendering of this document by Netscape Navigator 4.

```
<HTML><HEAD>
<TITLE> Test of LAYER Elements</TITLE>
</HEAD>
<BODY TEXT="black"  BGCOLOR="white">

<P>This paragraph contains an absolutely positioned
<LAYER ID="o1" LEFT="50" TOP="50">
<B><FONT SIZE="+1" COLOR="#ffaaaa">ABSOLUTE</FONT></B>
</LAYER>
layer. Note how the rest of the paragraph
is formatted as if the layer was not there.
</P>

<P>This second paragraph contains a relatively positioned
<ILAYER ID="i1" LEFT="50" TOP="50">
<B><FONT SIZE="+1" COLOR="#ffaaaa">RELATIVE</FONT></B>
</ILAYER>
layer. Note how the a relative layer affects the
formatting of the remaining paragraph text.
</P>
</BODY></HTML>
```

Figure 7.27 Rendering, by Netscape Navigator 4, of the document listed in Figure 7.26. Note how the LAYER is positioned relative to the upper left corner of the window, while the ILAYER is positioned relative to its "unpositioned" location.

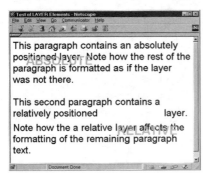

Nested, Overlapping Layers

By default, layers take on the height and width required to contain the layer content. This default size can be changed by **HEIGHT** and **WIDTH** attributes, which specify a desired size, in pixels, for the layer. Furthermore, layers can be nested one within the other—such nesting in turn affects the origin for absolute positioning of the enclosed layers. Finally, layers that are adjacent can *overlap*—the **Z-INDEX** attribute (or, alternatively, **ABOVE** and **BELOW**) then defines the z- or depth-ordering of the layers—that is, the order in which they lie one atop the other.

These aspects of layer elements are illustrated in Figures 7.28 and 7.29. This document contains a large, light gray layer, 350 pixels wide and 150 pixels high, set 150 pixels down and 100 pixels in from the left. This layer, in turn, contains three additional layers (labeled A, B, and C). Note the **LEFT** and **TOP** values of these nested layers—since these layers are nested, their positions are defined relative to the upper left-hand corner of the *parent layer* and not relative to the browser window.

Figure 7.28 Example document illustrating nested and stacked layers. Figure 7.29 shows the rendering of this document by Netscape Navigator 4.

```
<HTML><HEAD>
<TITLE> Test of Nested Layer Elements</TITLE>
</HEAD>
<BODY TEXT="black"  BGCOLOR="white">

<DIV>This block contains an absolutely positioned
<LAYER ID="o1" LEFT="100" TOP="150"
   HEIGHT="130" WIDTH="350" BGCOLOR="#cccccc">
   Here is the content of the first layer element.
   This element contains, in turn another layer.
   <LAYER ID="o2" TOP="20" Z-INDEX="2" LEFT="20" BGCOLOR="#666666"
       WIDTH="245">
      <FONT COLOR="white"><B>Layer A</B></FONT>
   </LAYER>
   <LAYER ID="o3" TOP="40" Z-INDEX="3" LEFT="130" BGCOLOR="#333333">
       <FONT COLOR="yellow"><B>Layer B...... .</B></FONT>
   </LAYER>
   <LAYER ID="o4" TOP="10" Z-INDEX="1" LEFT="250" BGCOLOR="white"
       HEIGHT="100" WIDTH="30"><B>..C.</B>
   </LAYER>
</LAYER>
layer that. in turn, contains three other absolutely
positioned layers.
</DIV>
</BODY></HTML>
```

Figure 7.29 Rendering, by Netscape Navigator 4, of the document listed in Figure 7.28. Note how the various smaller layers are stacked, one atop the other, all within (and on top of) the parent LAYER element.

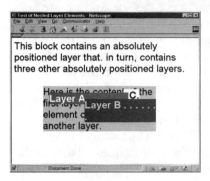

Note also the order in which the layers are "stacked" on the display. As shown in Figure 7.29, layer B is stacked above layer A, while layer C is actually *below* both layers A and B. The ordering of layers A and B reflects the normal stacking order—layers that appear later in the HTML document are simply stacked on top of layers that appear before. However, the **Z-INDEX** attribute can change this default ordering, as done in Figure 7.28. The layers A, B, and C are assigned the **Z-INDEX** values 2, 3, and 1 respectively. The stacking order is defined by these values, with layers with larger values appearing on top of layers with smaller values. Thus, this set of assignments places the third layer (C) on the bottom and layers A and B on top.

Clipping and Visibility

Finally, layers can be "clipped" using the **CLIP** attribute, or can have their visibility controlled using the **VISIBILITY** attribute. Both attributes are illustrated in Figure 7.30—here, **CLIP** is used to clip the parent layer containing the three sublayers, while the **VISIBILITY** attribute is used to hide (**VISIBILITY**="hidden") the layers labeled B and C. The resulting rendering is shown in Figure 7.31—notice how the layers are clipped according to the specified clipping box and that layers B and C are not longer visible.

LAYERs Versus Style Sheets

All of the layering mechanisms discussed in the preceding sections can be defined using cascading style sheets—indeed, Figures 7.36 and 7.37 demonstrate how the layer markup in Figure 7.30 can be rewritten to use the CSS notation. Since CSS is the defined standard for Web page formatting, it is best to use CSS to define layer positioning and layout, whenever possible. There are, however, a few attributes that have no standard CSS equivalent. For example, a layer can use the **SRC** attribute to reference a document to include in the layer. This is not supported by CSS, although Netscape does support a proprietary CSS property of the form:

include-source: url("*url-to-document*")

where *url-to-document* is a URL that references the document to include. This property is not supported by other browsers and is not likely to be incorporated into the CSS specifications.

Also, layer elements support the **PAGEX** and **PAGEY** attributes for specifying the positions of the layers (similar to **TOP** and **LEFT**) and the **ABOVE** and **BELOW** attributes for specifying the stacking order for layers (similar to **Z-INDEX**). These attributes have no CSS equivalents.

Figure 7.30 Example document illustrating layer *clipping*—the change from Figure 7.29 is shown in boldface. Figure 7.31 shows the rendering of this document by Netscape Navigator 4.

```
<HTML><HEAD>
<TITLE> Test of Nested Layer Elements</TITLE>
</HEAD>
<BODY TEXT="black"  BGCOLOR="white">

<DIV>This block contains an absolutely positioned
<LAYER ID="o1" LEFT="100" TOP="150"
   HEIGHT="130" WIDTH="350" BGCOLOR="#cccccc"
   CLIP="15,5,300,80">
   Here is the content of the first layer element.
   This element contains, in turn another layer.
   <LAYER ID="o2" TOP="20" Z-INDEX="2" LEFT="20" BGCOLOR="#666666"
       WIDTH="245">
       <FONT COLOR="white"><B>Layer A</B></FONT>
   </LAYER>
   <LAYER ID="o3" TOP="40" Z-INDEX="3" LEFT="130" BGCOLOR="#333333"
       VISIBILITY="hidden">
       <FONT COLOR="yellow"><B>Layer B ... ... .</B></FONT>
   </LAYER>
   <LAYER ID="o4" TOP="10" Z-INDEX="1" LEFT="250" BGCOLOR="white"
       HEIGHT="100" WIDTH="30"><B>..C.</B>
   </LAYER>
</LAYER>
layer that. in turn, contains three other absolutely
positioned layers.
</DIV>
</BODY></HTML>
```

Figure 7.31 Rendering, by Netscape Navigator 4, of the document listed in Figure 7.30. Note how the layers are "clipped" to the window defined by the CLIP attribute.

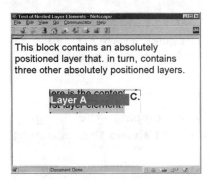

JavaScript Control of Layer Positions

Layer elements can create sidebar text and other positioned text content, although they are rarely used for this purpose—it is hard to get the positioning just right, particularly when a user can simply change the font size or select fonts that don't work with the desired positioning.

Layers are more commonly used to create *movable* layers. In Navigator 4, JavaScript programs can interact with layers, can toggle the value of the VISIBILITY attribute (to "hide" or "display" the element), or can change the position of a layer, causing it to move. Indeed, JavaScript code can let the user drag layered windows using the mouse to move and reposition layers. This is well demonstrated at the Netscape home page (www.netscape.com)—provided you have Netscape Navigator 4, of course.

LAYER and ILAYER Elements: Vertically Positioned Display Layers

Usage:	`<LAYER> ... </LAYER>`
	`<ILAYER> ... </ILAYER>`
Can Contain:	ADDRESS, BLOCKQUOTE, ~~CENTER~~, ~~DIR~~, DIV, DL, *FIELDSET*, FORM, Hn, HR, [ISINDEX], ~~MENU~~, <u>MULTICOL</u>, <u>NOEMBED</u>, *NOFRAMES*, *NOSCRIPT*, OL, P, PRE, TABLE, UL,
	characters, character highlighting, A, APPLET, *BASEFONT*, BR, *BUTTON*, <u>EMBED</u>, *IFRAME*, IMG, INPUT, <u>KEYGEN</u>, *LABEL*, MAP, *OBJECT*, SCRIPT, SELECT, <u>SPACER</u>, TEXTAREA, <u>WBR</u>,
	PARAM

Can Be Inside: **ADDRESS, BLOCKQUOTE, BODY, CAPTION,** ~~**CENTER**~~**, DD, DIV, DT,** *FIELDSET,* **FORM, Hn, LI,** <u>**MULTICOL**</u>**,** <u>**NOEMBED**</u>**,** *NOFRAMES, NOSCRIPT,* **P, PRE, TD, TH**

character highlighting, A, APPLET, *BUTTON, IFRAME, LABEL, LEGEND, OBJECT*

Attributes: **ABOVE, BACKGROUND, BGCOLOR, BELOW, CLIP, HEIGHT, ID, LEFT, NAME, PAGEX, PAGEY, SRC, TOP, VISIBILITY, WIDTH, onBlur, onFocus, onMouseover, onMouseout**

ABOVE=*"layer-ID"* (optional; only one of **BELOW, Z-INDEX,** or **ABOVE** is allowed)   Specifies the **ID** value of the layer *above* the current layer—that is, when the layer is created, it is created just below the layer referenced by **ABOVE.** The referenced layer must already exist. If it does not, then the layer is stacked in its natural order—that is, it appears on top of all layers that precede it in the document and under any subsequent layers.

BACKGROUND=*"url"* (optional)   Specifies the URL of an image to tile on the background of the layer. This is placed on top of any background color assigned to the layer. If the image is transparent and the background color is not specified, then the content of the main document or any underlying layer shows through the transparent regions of the image.

BGCOLOR=*"color"*(optional)   Specifies the background color for the layer. If a color is not specified, then the layer is transparent.

BELOW=*"layer-ID"* (optional; only one of **BELOW, Z-INDEX,** or **ABOVE** is allowed)   Specifies the **ID** value of the layer *below* the current layer—that is, when the layer is created, it is created just above the layer referenced by **BELOW.** The referenced layer must already exist—if it does not, then the layer is stacked in its natural order—that is, it appears on top of all layers that precede it in the document and under any subsequent layers.

CLIP=*"num1, num2, num3, num4,"* or *"num3, num4"* (optional) Specifies the clipping box for the layer: Regions of the layer inside the clipping box are displayed, while regions outside the box are invisible, and do not obscure underlying layers or content. The value is a set of four numbers, representing the position of the left edge (*num1*), top edge (*num2*), right edge (*num3*), and bottom edge (*num4*) of the clipping region, in pixels, relative to the top and left edge of the layer. If only two numbers are present, then these represent the position of the right and bottom edges, the top and left edges being assigned the default value zero.

HEIGHT=*"number," "number%"* (mandatory)   Specifies the height of the layer. This can be an integer, which gives the height in pixels, a percentage, which gives the height as a percentage of the height of the parent layer, or as a height of the window height if the attribute applies to a top-level layer. The default height is the minimum size required to contain the layer content.

ID=*"layer-ID"* (optional)   Specifies the **ID** value of the layer. This allows the layer to be referenced by **ABOVE** or **BELOW** attributes. Note that you cannot use **ID**-based CSS selectors to define formatting properties for a layer element.

LEFT=*"number," "number%"* (optional; only one of **PAGEX** or **LEFT** may be present)   Specifies the position of the left-hand edge of the layer, relative to the left edge of the parent layer (if the layer is within another layer) or relative to the inner-left border of the browser window for a layer within the document body. If not specified, the default position places the element at the position it would occupy if the content were not inside a **LAYER**. If no *x* position is specified (either by **PAGEX** or **LEFT**), the default position places the left-edge element at the position it would occupy if the content were not inside a **LAYER**.

NAME=*"layer-ID"* (optional)   Specifies a name for the layer. This allows for JavaScript access to the properties of the layer, and in that role is a synonym for **ID**. JavaScript can be used to hide, reveal, or move the layer, as discussed in the section on document scripting.

PAGEX=*"number"* (optional; valid with **LAYER** only; only one of **PAGEX** or **LEFT** may be present)   Specifies the position of the left-hand edge of the layer relative to the left edge of the parent document. This is similar to **LEFT**, except that the position is always measured away from the edge of the browser window, regardless of any parent layers. If no *x* position is specified (either by **PAGEX** or **LEFT**), the default position places the left edge of the element at the position it would occupy if the content were not inside a **LAYER**.

PAGEY=*"number"* (optional; valid with **LAYER** only; only one of **PAGEY** or **TOP** may be present)   Specifies the position of the top edge of the layer, relative to the top edge of the parent document. This is similar to **TOP**, except that the position is always measured away from the edge of the browser window, regardless of any parent layers. If no *y* position is specified (either by **PAGEY** or **TOP**), the default position places the top edge of the element at the position it would occupy if the content were not inside a **LAYER**.

SRC=*"url"* (optional)   Specifies a URL containing HTML markup to display in the layer. If **SRC** is specified, the content of the **LAYER** or

ILAYER is hidden, and the resource referenced by the URL is displayed. However, if the URL is invalid, then the **SRC**-specified resource is ignored, and the browser displays the content of the **LAYER** or **ILAYER**.

TOP="*number*," "*number%*" (optional; only one of **PAGEY** or **TOP** may be present)   Specifies the position of the top edge of the layer, relative to the top edge of the parent layer (if the layer is within another layer) or relative to the top inner edge of the browser window for a layer within the document body. If no *y* position is specified (either by **PAGEY** or **TOP**), the default position places the top edge of the element at the position it would occupy if the content were not inside a **LAYER**.

VISIBILITY="hidden ", "inherit," "show" (optional)   Specifies the display property of the element. The value "hidden" hides the layer (it is not visible, and does not hide other layers). The value "inherit" means that the layer has the same visibility as the layer's parent (a **LAYER** can nest within a **LAYER**). The value "show" causes the layer to be displayed. The default is "show."

WIDTH="*number*," "*number%*" (mandatory)   Specifies the width of the layer. This can be an integer, which gives the width in pixels, a percentage, which gives the width as a percentage of the width of the parent layer, or a percentage of the window width if the attribute applies to a top-level layer. The default width is the minimum size required to contain the element content.

Z-INDEX="*number*" (optional)   Specifies the *z-index*, or "depth"-position, for the layer relative to other layers within the same layer, with layers of larger z-index value lying above layers with smaller values. This essentially defines the order in which the layers are stacked one above the other. Values must be positive integers. This relative positioning only applies to layers that are siblings—that is, that are contained within the same layer or that are contained directly within the same parent document as the current layer.

NOLAYER Elements: Content for Layer-Incapable Browsers

Usage:	`<NOLAYER> ... </NOLAYER>`
Can Contain:	ADDRESS, BLOCKQUOTE, ~~CENTER~~, ~~DIR~~, DIV, DL, *FIELDSET*, FORM, Hn, HR, [ISINDEX], ~~MENU~~, MULTICOL, NOEMBED, *NOFRAMES*, *NOSCRIPT*, OL, P, PRE, TABLE, UL,
	characters, character highlighting, A, APPLET, *BASEFONT*, BR, *BUTTON*, EMBED, *IFRAME*, IMG,

	INPUT, <u>KEYGEN</u>, *LABEL*, MAP, *OBJECT*, SCRIPT, SELECT, <u>SPACER</u>, TEXTAREA, <u>WBR</u>,
Can Contain:	PARAM
Can Be Inside:	ADDRESS, BLOCKQUOTE, BODY, CAPTION, ~~CENTER~~, DD, DIV, DT, *FIELDSET*, FORM, Hn, LI, <u>MULTICOL</u>, <u>NOEMBED</u>, *NOFRAMES*, *NOSCRIPT*, P, PRE, TD, TH
	character highlighting, A, APPLET, *BUTTON*, *IFRAME*, *LABEL*, *LEGEND*, *OBJECT*
Attributes:	none

NOLAYER is a container for content to be displayed by browsers that do not understand **LAYER** or **ILAYER** elements. Browsers that understand layer elements will hide all **NOLAYER** content.

Style Sheets and HTML

Style sheets are a mechanism for adding formatting and other typographic information to an HTML document, but in such a way that the HTML markup is largely unaffected. Style sheets are supported by HTML through the addition of two new elements and three new general-purpose attributes. This section describes the style sheet mechanism and how it is related to an HTML document. However, style sheets are complex, and this chapter does not cover all the details! If you are interested in knowing more about style sheets, you should consider purchasing a book on the subject—my own *HTML Stylesheet Sourcebook* would, of course, be an excellent choice!

Summary of Relevant Elements and Attributes

Style sheet support requires the following new HTML elements and attributes. The use of these new elements and attributes are discussed later in this section.

New HTML Elements	STYLE and SPAN
New HTML Attributes	CLASS, ID, STYLE
Attribute Function	CLASS="*string*" (optional)—*Subclasses* the element. ID="*name*" (optional)—Gives an element a unique name token identifier. STYLE="*string*" (optional)—Provides style sheet instructions for an element
Special Attribute	REL="stylesheet;" supported by **LINK** element
Special Attribute	HTTP-EQUIV="Content-style-type;" supported by **META** element

Style Sheets Overview

As mentioned throughout this book, HTML is a semantic markup language designed to describe the *meaning* and structure of a document and not the physical presentation. And, as noted repeatedly, there are many advantages to this approach. First, semantic markup *adds* information about the text, by explaining what the text is for (e.g., headings, figures, or paragraphs) or what the text means (e.g., block quotations, address, or emphasis). In addition, the language model allows for alternate information content, for presentation by nongraphical or nonvisual displays—some examples are the **ALT** attribute content of **IMG** elements or text contained within an **APPLET**. The net result is that carefully crafted HTML documents can, in principle, be presented by many different technologies, ranging from graphical displays to Braille readers to text-to-speech converters, with little loss of information content.

At the same time, no author wants to be limited to a semantic description alone. Authors and readers alike care how a document is presented or what it looks like, be it on paper, a computer display, or any other format. Each author or designer has preferred ways of representing things such as headings, quotations, or emphasis, as well as background colors or textures, graphics, and so on. These issues fall under the general category of *style*—how do the different parts of the document look or feel? To be a fully functional markup language, HTML must support a mechanism whereby authors (or readers!) can specify the styles they want applied to the written words.

Until recently, HTML largely ignored these issues. Browser software often gave the user limited control over the display (for example, users could select preferred background colors, font faces and sizes, and so on), while limited author-side control was possible through elements such as **FONT** or **BASEFONT** or through attributes such as **ALIGN**, **BGCOLOR**, and so on. However, using elements and attributes to specify formatting details is not a good long-term solution—the documents soon become big, cumbersome, and impossible to maintain, largely because HTML is simply the wrong place to specify the page layout descriptions required for detailed layout control.

The solution is to create a *second* mechanism for specifying formatting, separate from the markup. This is known as the *style sheet* approach and, in practice, involves a second document that contains instructions specifying how to format and display the elements of a given marked-up document. Since a style sheet is a separate piece of information, it can be maintained separately. Indeed, multiple, different style sheets can be written, with each display device (graphic display, printer, text-to-speech, etc.) selecting the style information appropriate for its display format.

As an example, a style sheet can contains instructions such as:

```
H1 { font-size: 24pt;    font-family: arial;  text-align: center; }
H2 { font-size: 18pt;    font-family: arial;  text-align: left; }
EM { font-style: italic; }
```

which says:

> "Center **H1** headings on the page and display them using 24 point Arial font"

"Left-align **H2** headings and display them using 18 point Arial font"

"Format text inside **EM** using an italics version of the current font"

If a browser understands the style sheet mechanism, it takes an HTML document, accesses the associated style sheet information (mechanisms for finding this information are discussed later), and applies the style sheet instructions as it formats the document. This lets authors specify, through author-specified style sheets, the preferred formatting prescriptions for their documents. I use the word "preferred" because the browser, or the user, always has the option of ignoring the style information should it be inappropriate for some reason.

There are additional benefits to the style sheet approach. First, an author can develop a single style sheet and apply it to all documents in a given collection. As a result, the work of developing a style can be shared amongst a number of documents, making life easier for the author, and giving the collection a common look and feel. Also, separating the style information from the HTML documents means that the HTML documents stay compact and easy to understand—they do not become cluttered with multiple, device-specific formatting tags. It is far more difficult to write an HTML document if the author, each time, has to add all sorts of physical formatting hints. Using style sheets, the author need only create a single style sheet and can then forget about this part of the problem and get back to creating the desired content.

Style Sheet Languages

So if style sheets are so good, why are they not in common use? The answer is a bit like the chicken and the egg. First, until recently, there was no accepted Web style sheet language. Second, there was a lack of browser support for a style sheet language—which makes sense, given the lack of such a language. These issues have finally been resolved, with both major browser vendors supporting a single, relatively simple style sheet language.

The language now being implemented is known as *cascading style sheets* or *CSS*. CSS was designed to be very simple to use and understand, so that most HTML authors should find it easy to construct style sheets with CSS. This language is supported by Netscape Navigator 4 and Internet Explorer 4, albeit with some bugs.

Linking Style Sheets to HTML Documents

There are two ways to include style sheet information in a document: either by using **LINK** to reference an external style sheet or by including style sheet information within a **STYLE** element inside the document itself.

Linking to an External Style Sheet

In this approach, the style sheet is placed in a file separate from the HTML document. An HTML document then references the desired style sheet using a **LINK** element. The markup is

```
<LINK REL="stylesheet" TYPE="mime/type" HREF="url">
```

where the value **REL**="stylesheet" indicates that the target resource is a style sheet, *url* is the URL pointing to the style sheet document, and *mime/type* is the MIME type for the style sheet. This allows for different style sheet languages, each with its own MIME type. The CSS language has the MIME type text/css.

Style Sheets within the Document HEAD

Style sheets can be also placed inside a **STYLE** element lying inside the document **HEAD**. A simple example is:

```
<STYLE>
<!--
BODY      {
                font-family:  times, serif;
                color:        black ;
                margin-left:  10%;
                margin-right: 10%;      }
A:link    { color: black; text-decoration: underline }
A:visited { color: black; text-decoration: none }
-->
</STYLE>
```

Note the use of the HTML comment delimiters (<!-- and -->) to surround the style sheet—this ensures that older browsers that do not understand CSS will not display the content as regular markup.

As far as formatting is concerned, there is no difference between placing the style sheet in a separate file or in the **HEAD** of an HTML document. The advantage of the former, of course, is that the same style sheet can be used by many different files, without the need to duplicate the information in the **HEAD** of every document.

META Specification of a Default Language

Of course, the **STYLE** element does not indicate the style sheet language used by the enclosed data. **META** elements can be used to indicate this language, using the markup:

```
<META HTTP-EQUIV="Content-style-type" CONTENT="type/subtype">
```

where *type/subtype* is the type of the style sheet language. For CSS, this is simply:

```
<META HTTP-EQUIV="Content-style-type" CONTENT="text/css">
```

In the absence of this element, a browser may guess at the language, with unpredictable results. For now, of course, there is only one language (CSS), so that this is not required.

Note that this **META** format implies that the default style sheet type can be indicated by an HTTP server response header field of the form:

```
Content-style-type: type/subtype
```

See Chapter 9 for more information about HTTP headers and the HTTP protocol.

Attaching Formatting to Elements

There are then several ways to associate style sheet formatting information with HTML elements. Typically, style sheet instructions specify the element to which the style should be applied. For example, the statement EM {font-style:italic;} says that all **EM** elements should be rendered in italics, while the statement A:visited {color:purple} says that the text inside *visited* hypertext anchors should be in the regular font, but purple in color. This simple mechanism lets style sheets easily specify generic characteristics for all elements of a particular type.

Style Sheets and the CLASS Attribute

In some cases, however, an author may wish to specify formatting specific to one particular instance of an element and not another. For example, text within standard **DIV** elements may have no special formatting, whereas text within **DIV** elements serving a particular purpose should be indented and in a slightly smaller font to mark the fact, for example, that the enclosed text is part of an abstract.

In HTML, such element-specific variation is supported through element *subclassing,* made possible by the new **CLASS** attribute. **CLASS** is supported all **BODY** content elements except **BASEFONT, PARAM, SCRIPT,** and **STYLE. CLASS** is intended for defining special logical characteristics associated with an element. For example, to indicate that a block of text is part of an abstract, the markup could be written:

```
<DIV CLASS="abstract">
    <P>The spiny-bifurcated oyster is one of the most
       interesting, if poorly understood mollusks of the
       Eastern seaboard. In this overly long and tedious
       paper, we ....
</DIV>
```

In a style sheet, the author can specify abstract-specific formatting with the style sheet rule

```
DIV.abstract {
    font-size:     10pt;
    color:         black ;
    margin-left:   15%;
    margin-right:  15%;
}
```

where the notation DIV.abstract ties these rules to **DIV** elements of **CLASS**="abstract."

Nested Elements and Inheritance

An important feature of CSS is *inheritance*—unless a style sheet states otherwise, an element *inherits* the characteristics of the element it is inside. Thus, in the preceding example, **P** elements (paragraphs) inside the **DIV** inherit the extra indents and 10 point font size specification from the surrounding **DIV**. This is possible because, in general, default formatting for elements is specified as rules *relative to* the elements they are contained within. For example, the default specification for **EM** is EM {font-style:italic}, which just italicizes whatever font face, size, and color the surrounding text may have.

Style Sheets and the ID Attribute

Style sheets also support the **ID** attribute. **ID** specifies a unique *name token* identifier for an element (no two **ID** values in a given document can be the same) and is actually intended as a general-purpose replacement to the **NAME** attribute of anchor elements. However, **ID** is also used by CSS to provide a second way of associating style specifications with a specific element.

The mechanism is as follows. If an element is marked by an **ID** attribute, for example

```
<P ID="nut12"> A nutty paragraph, which will be
    rendered in a nutty way ....
...</P>
```

then style information can be tied to this specific paragraph through a CSS instruction of the form:

```
#nut12 { font-size:  42pt; color: #22FF3b;
      text-decoration: underline;
}
```

Note how similar this is to the URL fragment-identifier notation—the hash character, followed by the name, denotes an element **ID** value and relates the associated style sheet instruction to a particular and unique **ID**-labeled element.

ID is supported by all **BODY**-content elements except **SCRIPT** and **STYLE**. The more general purpose of **ID** is to act as a general-purpose element label. In principle, a hypertext anchor can link to any **ID**-labeled element by using the **ID** value as a URL fragment identifier. For example, a paragraph labeled with the start tag <P ID="gfx23"> could be referenced by the URL http://some.where/path/document.html#gfx23. This functionality is not supported by most current browsers, but is supported by Internet Explorer 4.

STYLE Attribute—Element-Specific Formatting

Sometimes an author wants to apply a style to just one element and does not have the luxury of modifying the style sheet. In this case, the author can use a **STYLE** attribute to add element-specific formatting information within the element itself. An example is:

```
<P STYLE="font-family: times; font-size: 12pt">
    paragraph text ....</P>
```

The value of **STYLE** is simply a set of applicable style sheet instructions, to be applied to the content of the element. **STYLE** is supported by all body-content elements except for those (**BASEFONT, PARAM, SCRIPT,** and **STYLE**) that are not associated with page content.

Cascading Style Sheets Overview

The CSS specification is long, and this brief discussion is not intended as a replacement for the full CSS specification. However, some simple examples will help to give a feel for how the system works, and are useful for understanding how the CSS mechanism relates to HTML documents. An example style sheet is shown in Figure 7.32.

Figure 7.32 Portion of a demonstration *cascading style sheet* (CSS). The meanings of the various lines are discussed in the text. The italicized line numbers on the left are not part of the style sheet and are there for reference purposes only.

```
1      BODY {
2         font-family:    Garamond, "times new roman", Times, serif;
3         color:          black ;
4         margin-left:    10%;
5         margin-right:   10%;
6      }
7      A:link           { color: black; text-decoration: underline }
8      A:visited        { color: gray;  text-decoration: none;    }
9      H1 H2 H3         { font-family:  arial, sans-serif;        }
10     H2 H3            { margin-left:  2%      }
11     H1               { text-align:   center  }
12     DIV.abstract{ margin-left:   15%;
13                        margin-right: 15%;
14                        font-size:    smaller }
15     .goofy           { color:        #FFFF00;
16                        font-family:  arial;
17                        background:    blue;
18                                              }
19     @import url(http://www.java.utoronto.ca/styles/special.css)
```

Lines 1 through 6 of Figure 7.32 set the default document properties: left and right margins 10% in from the full width of the display and black text. The font-family specification gives a list of preferred fonts, from left to right. Thus this style sheet requests Garamond font, followed by Times New Roman (if Garamond is not available), Times (if Times New Roman is not available), or serifed font (if none of the preceding are available). These font family names are specified in the CSS specifications. Lines 7 and 8 specify properties of anchored text: Line 7 indicates that unvisited links should be black and with an underline, while line 8 indicates that visited links should be gray and without an underline.

Lines 9 through 11 specify properties for headings. Line 9 states that **H1**, **H2**, and **H3** headings should all be in Arial font or alternatively in a sans-serif font should Arial not be available. Line 10 states that **H2** and **H3** headings should have only a 2% indent, so that they will hang to the left of the regular text, while line 11 states that **H1** headings should be centered between the margins.

Lines 12 through 14 specify the properties for text within **DIV**isions of **CLASS**="abstract." Inside such a **DIV**, the margins should be wider (15% of the display width), while the text should be in a font smaller than that of the regular font. Lines 15 through 18 state that *every* element of **CLASS**="goofy" should have text in the indicated color (as an RGB value—this is bright yellow), should be rendered in the arial font, and should have the indicated background color (blue). Finally, line 19 imports an external style sheet from the indicates URL, for inclusion with the current style specifications.

Figure 7.33 Simple HTML document that includes the style sheet listed in Figure 7.32. Rendering of this document is shown in Figures 7.34 and 7.35.

```
<HTML>
<HEAD>
<STYLE> <!--
BODY {
     font-family:  Garamond, "times new roman", Times, serif;
     color: black ;
     margin-left: 10%;
     margin-right:10%;
}
A:link       { color:        black; text-decoration: underline }
A:visited    { color:        gray; text-decoration: none }
H1,H2,H3     { font-family:  arial,  sans-serif }
H2,H3        { margin-left:  2% }
H1           { text-align:   center }
DIV.abstract{ margin-left:  15%;
              margin-right: 15%;
```

Continued

Figure 7.33 Continued.

```
                font-size:      smaller; }
.goofy        { color:          #FFFF00;
                font-family:    arial, helvetica, sans-serif;
                background:     blue;
              }
    @import url(http://www.java.utoronto.ca/styles/special.css)
--> </STYLE>
<TITLE>Test Of Stylesheets Document </TITLE>
</HEAD>
<BODY>
<H1>Big Stylesheets test</H1>
<DIV CLASS="abstract">
<P>This document tests stylesheet support. There are
    various stylesheet elements to modify presentation
    based on CLASS, or simply SPANning a group of letters.
<P>For example, if
    <A HREF="test.html">stylesheets are working</A>, this
    abstract should be in a slightly smaller font, with
    a slightly larger indent than the following paragraphs.
</DIV>
<H2>Level 2 Heading</H2>
<P>So, what did we get there?  Now, we will try doing some
    word specific formatting with the goofy style, as in
    <EM CLASS="goofy"> this line of text </EM>
<P>Was that interesting, or not?
<H3>A Level 3 Heading</H3>
<P>At this point, I will bring this example to an end. It
    is nothing terribly fancy, but it should illustrate the
    main features of stylesheets. We will see
    <SPAN STYLE="{font-family: arial; font-size:60pt;
     background: url('testimg.gif'); "> HELLO</SPAN>
</BODY>
</HTML>
```

The HTML document in Figure 7.33 helps to demonstrate the effect of this style sheet. Figure 7.34 shows this document formatted without the benefit of style sheet formatting instructions, while Figure 7.35 shows the effect of the style sheet instructions. Notice how the headings and indents in Figure 7.35 are just as specified by the style sheet.

The last feature of interest is the word "Hello" at the bottom of Figure 7.35. This is in a large Arial font on an image background. Looking to Figure 7.33 you will see that this is accomplished using a SPAN element with local, STYLE-attribute style sheet instructions.

Figure 7.34 Rendering, by the Netscape Navigator 3 browser, of the document listed in Figure 7.33. This browser does not support style sheets.

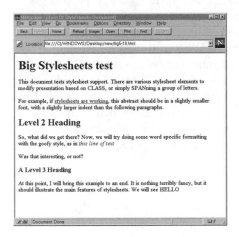

Figure 7.35 Rendering, by the Internet Explorer 4 browser, of the document listed in Figure 7.33. This browser does support style sheets.

Positioning Elements with CSS

A recent extension to CSS allows for positioning of elements, in a manner similar to that allowed by the Netscape layer elements. This is illustrated in Figure 7.36, which is the same as Figure 7.30, but formatted using CSS—notice how the HTML markup is much simpler than in Figure 7.30, as all the formatting-specific information is now in the style sheet. The CSS `top`, `left`, `height`, `width`, and `z-index` properties are equivalent to the layer attributes of the same name, while the `clip` property is similar to the layer attribute but uses a different syntax. The `position` property defines the type of positioning for the element—the values `absolute` and `relative` provide formatting equivalent to the **LAYER** and **ILAYER** elements, while the value `static` formats an element as a standard on-the-page component. Finally, the `visibility` property can take the values `hidden` (for a hidden element), `visible` (for a displayed element), and `inherit` (the element inherits the visibility of the element it lies within). Note also that this document uses **CLASS** attributes to define the CSS formatting and not **IDs**—Netscape Navigator 4 does not properly support **ID** attributes for assigning positioning formatting properties to layers.

Figure 7.37 shows the rendering of Figure 7.36 by both Netscape Navigator 4 and Internet Explorer 4. Both browsers provide formatting essentially equivalent to that shown in Figure 7.31, although Netscape does not properly color the entire background region of the elements—this is a bug in Netscape Navigator 4.

Figure 7.36 Example HTML document illustrating CSS positioning properties—these positioning properties are equivalent to the LAYER-based positioning defined in Figure 7.30. Rendering of this document by Netscape Navigator 4 and Internet Explorer 4 is shown in Figure 7.37.

```
<HTML><HEAD>
<TITLE> Test of Nested Layer Elements</TITLE>
<STYLE>
<!--
SPAN.o1 {position: absolute;    background-color: #cccccc;
         top:       150px;      left:              100px;
         height:    100px;      width:             350px;
         clip: rect(5px,300px,80px,15px);                    }
SPAN.o2 {position: absolute;    background-color: #666666;
         top:       20px;       left:              20px;
         width:     245px;      z-index:           2;        }
SPAN.o3 {position: absolute;    background-color: #333333;
         top:       40px;       left:              130px;
         visibility: hidden;    z-index:           3;        }
SPAN.o4 {position: absolute;    background-color: #fffffc;
         top:       10px;       left:              250px;
         height:    100px;      width:             30px;
```

Figure 7.36 Continued.

```
        z-index:   1;                                        }
--></STYLE>
</HEAD>
<BODY TEXT="black"  BGCOLOR="white">

<DIV>This block contains an absolutely positioned
<SPAN CLASS="o1">
   Here is the content of the first layer element.
   This element contains, in turn another layer.
   <SPAN CLASS="o2">
       <FONT COLOR="white"><B>Layer A</B></FONT>
   </SPAN>
   <SPAN CLASS="o3">
       <FONT COLOR="yellow"><B>Layer B ... ... .</B></FONT>
   </SPAN>
   <SPAN CLASS="o4"><B>..C.</B>
   </SPAN>
</SPAN>
layer that. in turn, contains three other absolutely
positioned layers.
</DIV>
</BODY></HTML>
```

Figure 7.37 Rendering, by Netscape Navigator 4 (top) and Internet Explorer 4 (bottom), of the document listed in Figure 7.36. Note how both browsers properly place and stack the positioned HTML elements, although Netscape Navigator 4 does not properly color the element background regions.

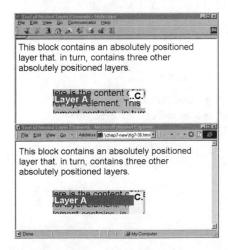

Cascading Properties

The above sections illustrated some of the cascading properties—styles cascade down from one element to other elements contained within it (e.g., from a **DIV** to all paragraphs within the **DIV**), until overridden by a specific declaration relevant to one of the interior elements (e.g., **DIV** content may be in Times-Roman, while a paragraph-specific instruction may override this font to Arial).

However, this does not cover the case where there are multiple style sheet specifications for the same element. There are several ways this might happen. First, there may be an external style sheet linked to the document, as well as internal style sheet information within a **STYLE** element. Also, individual users may have their own default style sheets, specified via a browser configuration file. Finally, there may be element-specific style information specified by **STYLE** attribute content or by an **ID** label with corresponding style information in the style sheet.

The CSS handles this kind of conflict through a sequence of complex cascading rules, which involve weighting different types of specifications and applying the formatting instructions in the order of increasing weights. In general, the instructions closer to a specific block of text override those further from it—that is, text-specific instructions will override block-specific instructions, which override generic document instructions. If two equivalent instructions are found, then the last one found is used. Finally, author-specified formatting instructions will override reader-specified style sheet instructions, which in turn override a browser's default behavior.

There are many aspects of CSS that have been omitted from this brief discussion: CSS also supports style specifications for nested elements (e.g., how to format list items within a list that lies within another list), drop-caps lettering, horizontal and vertical spacing control, backgrounds, floating elements, boxing of elements, and so on. For details, you are referred to the CSS specifications, referenced at the end of this chapter.

Scripting in HTML Documents

Scripting-Related HTML Elements and Attributes

Script-Related Elements	SCRIPT, NOSCRIPT, SERVER
Event-Handler Attributes	onBlur, onChange, onClick, onFocus, onLoad, onMouseOver, onMouseOut, onReset, onSelect, onSubmit, onUnload, onAbort, onError; see Tables 7.5, 7.6, and 7.7 for descriptions of these attributes and the events they are associated with.

Continued

Scripting-Related HTML Elements and Attributes *Continued*

Special Attribute	NAME; valid with **APPLET**, <u>EMBED</u>, **FORM**, **FRAME**, and **OBJECT**—identifies the item for access from a script program.
Special Attribute	HTTP-EQUIV="Content-script-type"; supported by **META**, used to indicate a document's default scripting language.

With the Navigator 2 browser, Netscape introduced the concept of *scripted* HTML documents. These are documents that contain, in addition to regular HTML markup, script programs that can process data passed from the HTML document (i.e., from **FORM** input, hypertext anchor selections, etc.) and that can also produce output for inclusion within the HTML document, as it is rendered for display. To implement this functionality, Netscape developed a new scripting language, called *JavaScript*. This is an object-derived language, similar in look and feel to Java or C++ but designed expressly for Web and HTML document-related scripting—the object model of JavaScript is based on the component structure of the browser (windows, status bars, document URLs, etc.) and of HTML documents (applets, embedded objects, forms, anchors, document body, images, etc.).

Microsoft quickly followed up Netscape's launch of scripted HTML, by implementing JavaScript support in their Internet Explorer 3 browser. However, Microsoft did not have access to all the details of the JavaScript language, so that their browser was not entirely compatible with the version of JavaScript supported by Netscape—indeed, Microsoft formally named their language *Jscript* to denote this difference. Thus, if you are working in a mixed-platform environment, it is important to check your JavaScript programs with all possible browsers.

Microsoft also implemented a second scripting language, known as VBScript (or Visual Basic Script). In terms of functionality, VBScript is similar to JavaScript, although the language is closer in design to Visual Basic, from which it is derived. However, the *interaction* between a document and a scripting language is largely independent of the language, so that the information presented here is also largely applicable to VBScript programs.

With the release of Netscape Navigator 4 and Internet Explorer 4, script compatibility became both better and worse. It became better in that both browsers support a similar core functionality, which is more or less the functionality of Netscape Navigator 3, plus some extensions. This "compatible" scripting component is the main topic of this section. However, both companies then added significant scripting capabilities that allow for much richer interaction between script programs and the HTML document. Unfortunately, the enhancements are entirely incompatible— the new Microsoft extensions do not work with Netscape's browser and vice versa. These scripting extensions are commonly called Dynamic-HTML and we briefly review the issues associated with this at the end of the section.

Please note that this is *not* a guide to JavaScript programming—the language is far too complex for this short section to do it justice. For details about the language, you are referred to the references listed at the end of the chapter.

General Scripting Issues

As mentioned in Chapter 4, document scripts are included within an HTML document via the HTML **SCRIPT** element. These elements can be in the **HEAD** or **BODY** of a document, but it is strongly recommended that the bulk of the code appear in the **HEAD**. This is because of they way scripts are interpreted and executed. When a browser parses a document for script components, it starts at the beginning of the file and works downwards. As a result, any required functions must be defined *before* they are used—if this is not done and the function is not defined at the time of its intended invocation, then the script will fail, claiming that the function is undefined. Consequently, function definitions are best placed in the **HEAD** of a document—that way they are guaranteed to be defined before the browser begins to layout the document **BODY**.

Script programs can be included directly within an HTML document, or they can be included from external files. Some examples illustrating these two mechanisms are given in the following sections.

Including a Script Within a SCRIPT Element

Figure 7.38 illustrates a simple JavaScript function definition, defined in a **SCRIPT** element that typically would lie in the document **HEAD** (since it defines a general-purpose function). This simple example illustrates a few of the important points which are relevant whenever a script is included within an HTML document.

There are three critical things to note in Figure 7.38:

1. **JavaScript comment lines.** Comments in JavaScript begin with two successive forward slashes. All text following these slashes *and on the same line* is a comment and is ignored by the JavaScript parser.

2. **Hiding a script using an HTML comment.** A script can be placed inside an HTML comment, safely hiding it from any browsers that do not understand **SCRIPT** elements. Note that the string --> ending the comment must be placed at the end of a JavaScript comment line, as otherwise it is interpreted as JavaScript program code.

3. **Use of single quotes For strings.** In JavaScript, single quotes can be used to delimit strings (e.g., 'this is a string'). This allows HTML markup inside a string, as any double quotes in the HTML markup will not prematurely end single quote-delimited JavaScript strings.

With respect to the actual JavaScript language, this example illustrates how variables (`var`) and functional methods (`function()`) are defined and shows how alerts (pop-up alert notifications) are invoked (`alert()`). JavaScript variables are *untyped*—as with several other scripting languages (e.g., Perl), variable type is determined by context.

Figure 7.38 Example SCRIPT element containing a single function definition. Note the use of an HTML comment (the tag is in bold-face) to "hide" the element content from old browsers that do not understand the SCRIPT element.

```
<SCRIPT LANGUAGE="JavaScript">
<!--  Use Comments to "hide" script from old browsers
//     that don't understand scripts
//     The symbol // starts a comment line
function validate(obj, minV, maxV)) {
  var value = parseInt(obj.value);
  if( value < minVal || value > maxVal) {
     alert(obj.name + ' Not in range ('+minV+','+maxV+')' );
  }
}
//  End HTML comment that hides the script from old browsers  -->
</SCRIPT>
```

Using SCRIPT Within the BODY

Script components in the document **BODY** can actually print out text for inclusion with the displayed HTML. A simple HTML document example that uses the JavaScript `Date()` function to print the current time and date is shown in Figure 7.39. Figure 7.40 shows the resulting document displayed by Netscape Navigator, while Figure 7.41 shows the document displayed by a browser that does not understand **SCRIPT** elements.

Figure 7.39 A simple HTML document containing a JavaScript block that prints a line of HTML into the displayed document.

```
<HTML><HEAD>
<TITLE>Scripting Test</TITLE></HEAD>
<BODY>
<H2>Scripting Test</H2>
<SCRIPT>
  <!--
document.write('<H3 ALIGN="right">' + Date() + '</H3>');
  // -->
</SCRIPT>
<NOSCRIPT>
  <P>Sorry, no Scripting Support...
</NOSCRIPT>
</BODY></HTML>
```

Figure 7.40 Netscape Navigator 3 rendering of the document listed in Figure 7.39. Note the JavaScript-produced date on the right of the page.

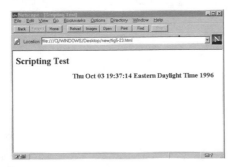

Looking to Figure 7.39, you should note how the single-quote string delimiters allow HTML elements to be easily included in the `write` statement. Note also the presence of a new element, **NOSCRIPT**, just following the **SCRIPT**. **NOSCRIPT** can contain regular HTML markup, as an alternative to **SCRIPT** for those browsers that do not understand the scripting language or the **SCRIPT** element. Browsers that understand both **SCRIPT** and **NOSCRIPT** will hide the **NOSCRIPT** content. Figure 7.40 shows the utility of this new element. **NOSCRIPT** is understood by Netscape Navigator 3 and Internet Explorer 3, but not by earlier versions of these browsers—these early versions display the **NOSCRIPT** content in addition to that produced by **SCRIPT**.

Dynamic Scripting

Usually, scripting programs are more dynamic than the example shown in Figures 7.39 and 7.40, with many script programs including a level of user interaction. However, the dynamic character of the document is actually quite limited. Using

Figure 7.41 NetManage WebSurfer 5 rendering of the document listed in Figure 7.39. This browser does not understand JavaScript and hence displays the alternative NOSCRIPT content.

the "standard" version of JavaScript (that is, the components understood by both Netscape Navigator and Internet Explorer), text—once drawn to a frame or window—can only be modified by replacing the entire frame or window with a new document. Fortunately, **FORM** element text input fields can be dynamically updated by JavaScript programs, without reloading the entire document.

External Script Files

Script programs can be kept in external files and then included into an HTML document. Remote script programs are included using **SCRIPT** elements of the form:

```
<SCRIPT LANGUAGE="lang_name" SRC="URL">
</SCRIPT>
```

where *lang_name* is the name of the scripting language (JavaScript or VBScript), and *URL* is the URL referencing the script file. Note that the end tag </SCRIPT> is required—if you leave it out, the script will not load properly. Figure 7.42 shows how the document listed in Figure 7.39 can be rewritten to use an external script and also shows the content of the referenced script file *script.js*.

The language names that are actually understood depend on the browser, and on the version of the browser. For example, Netscape Navigator 3 understands the names "Javascript1.1" and "Javascript," the first name corresponding to

Figure 7.42 HTML document illustrating external JavaScript files. This document is equivalent to the one listed in Figure 7.39, except for the placement of the JavaScript program in the external file *script.js*.

script1.html
```
<HTML><HEAD>
<TITLE>Scripting Test</TITLE></HEAD>
<BODY>
<H2>Scripting Test</H2>

<SCRIPT LANGUAGE="javascript" SRC="script.js">
</SCRIPT>
<NOSCRIPT>
  <P>Sorry, no Scripting Support...
</NOSCRIPT>
</BODY></HTML>
```

script.js
```
document.write('<H3 ALIGN="right">' + Date() + '</H3>');
```

JavaScript as implemented in Navigator 3, and the second to JavaScript as implemented in Navigator 2. Navigator 4 supports the additional value "JavaScript 1.2," to correspond to the newest incarnation of JavaScript (note that these strings are case-insensitive). Internet Explorer, on the other hand, understands the values "javascript," "jscript," and "vbscript," but will interpret any of the "javascript1.x" values as indicating a JavaScript program.

Browsers should ignore scripting languages that they do not understand. Thus, Netscape Navigator (all versions) ignores scripts with **LANGUAGE=** "jscript" or "vbscript," while Netscape Navigator 3 ignores script sections labeled by **LANGUAGE=**"javascript1.2."

Note in Figure 7.42 how the external script file does not place the script inside an HTML comment—obviously this hiding mechanism is not needed for a script outside an HTML document. However, you can include the HTML comment delimiters within a script file, as they are ignored by a script parser. This is convenient if you are copying scripts between HTML documents and external script files.

MIME Types for Script Files

An HTTP server distributing script files must be configured to send the correct MIME type associated with the script—otherwise the browser will not know the language of the arriving program. The currently supported MIME types are listed in Table 7.4. Note that browsers support multiple names for the languages, with or without the leading "x-."

Mixing Local and Remote Scripts

A document can contain both local and remote **SCRIPT** declarations. This can make for sensible separation of program modules, with generic script libraries included via external files and document-specific scripting placed within the documents. However, you cannot use the *same* **SCRIPT** element to simultaneously reference local and remote script components. To employ both external and internal scripts, you must use a different **SCRIPT** element for each.

Table 7.4 Scripting Languages and Associated MIME Types

Language	Typical Filename Extension	MIME Type
JavaScript	.js	text/x-javascript; text/javascript; text/x-jscript (Microsoft)
VBScript	.vb	text/x-vbscript; text/vbscript

Proposed Changes to SCRIPT: The TYPE Attribute

The World Wide Web Consortium recommends dropping the **LANGUAGE** attribute and replacing it by **TYPE**, the value of **TYPE** being the MIME type of the associated local or remote script. This makes **SCRIPT** consistent with other type-labeling mechanisms used on the Web, and eliminates the need to develop two different naming schemes (language names and MIME types) for the same things. As an example, a script element would take the form:

```
<SCRIPT TYPE="text/javascript" SRC="/path/to/prog.js"></SCRIPT>
```

This mechanism is supported by Netscape Navigator 4 and Internet Explorer 4. However, there is no defined mechanism for giving the language *version*—the traditional way would be to include the version as a parameter, as in

```
text/javascript; version=1.2
```

but this is not supported by either browser. Thus, for now, it is best to use both **TYPE** and **LANGUAGE** attributes, until proper support for **TYPE** is available.

Using META to Specify A Default Script Language

If neither **TYPE** nor **LANGUAGE** is given, then the browser needs to guess at the language used by the document script. To avoid the possible confusion that may arise from this process, an author can use a **META** element to specify the default scripting language in a document. The form is:

```
<META HTTP-EQUIV="Content-Script-type" CONTENT="type/subtype">
```

where *type/subtype* is the MIME type of the default document scripting language. Note that this format indicates that the default script type can also be indicated by an HTTP server response header field of the form:

```
Content-script-type: type/subtype
```

See Chapter 9 for more information about HTTP headers and the HTTP protocol.

Script Interaction with HTML Elements

Scripting languages become much more dynamic when they are bound to user input elements. In HTML, the basic user input elements are the anchor element **A** and the various **FORM** elements. Both JavaScript and VBScript provide bindings to these elements via the *event handlers* listed in Table 7.5—these event handlers are triggered by the events described in the table. For example, an *onClick* event can be triggered when a hypertext link is "selected" (clicked), while the *onLoad* event is triggered whenever a document or frame is loaded onto the display.

Event handlers are attached to specific elements via special event handling *attributes*. These attributes have names matching the events they handle (the attribute names are *case insensitive*) and take as their value the *function* that should be invoked when the event takes place. Consider, for example, the following markup:

```
<INPUT TYPE="button" NAME="butt1" VALUE="foo"
     ONCLICK="alert('Uh oh -- you pressed the Foo Button!' );">
```

The **ONCLICK** attribute binds this button (named "butt1") to the indicated JavaScript—here a simple alert pop-up window. When the user presses this button, the *onClick* event is triggered, and the browser will pop up an alert window containing the given message string.

To support client-specific form processing and user interaction, Netscape introduced a **TYPE="button" INPUT** element. This is used for client-side actions only—the name and value associated with a **TYPE="button"** element are *never* sent with the form data when a **FORM** is submitted to a remote server. This is illustrated in Figure 7.43, which shows a **FORM** containing two **INPUT** elements: one of **TYPE="button,"** (taken from our previous example) and the other of **TYPE="submit."**

Figure 7.44 shows the document displayed after the user has selected the button labeled "foo." This button is tied by the *onClick* event handler to the JavaScript alert() function, so that pressing this button causes the visible pop-up alert menu. If, instead, the user presses the submit button, the accessed URL is (omitting the leading part of the URL)

```
..../cgi/prog.pl?submit=Submit+It%21
```

which contains only the encoded data from the **TYPE="submit"** button—the name and value from the **TYPE="button"** element are absent.

Figure 7.43 Example HTML document illustrating the TYPE="button" input element and event handling. The display of this form by Internet Explorer 3 is shown in Figure 7.44.

```
<HEAD><TITLE>
Scripting Test</TITLE></HEAD>
<BODY>
<H2>Buttons and More Buttons</H2>
<BLOCKQUOTE>
<FORM ACTION="/cgi/prog.pl" METHOD="get">
  <H3> A Simple FORM Example</H3>
  <INPUT TYPE="button"
    NAME="butt1" VALUE="foo"
    ONCLICK="alert('Uh oh -- you pressed the Foo Button!' );" >
   -- <B>The FOO BUTTON!</B><BR>
  <INPUT TYPE="submit" NAME="submit" VALUE="Submit it!">
</FORM>
</BODY></HTML>
```

Figure 7.44 Display, by the Internet Explorer 3 browser, of the document listed in Figure 7.43. Note the JavaScript alert window displayed as a result of clicking on the button labeled "foo."

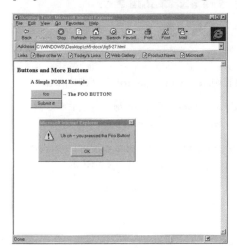

HTML Elements and Event Handlers

With Netscape Navigator 4 and Internet Explorer 4, there are 12 commonly supported event handlers (listed in Table 7.5) and 19 different HTML elements that accept event handling attributes. However, only a few event handlers are appropriate for any given element—for example, the *onUnload* event, triggered when the user leaves document, is irrelevant to the **AREA** (client-side imagemap data) element, but appropriate to **BODY** and **FRAMESET**. To help keep track of which handlers go where, Table 7.6 lists elements that take event handlers, alongside the supported handler types. Note that support for these handlers may be buggy, or nonexistent, depending on the browser. Some common version-specific limitations are indicated in the table captions, but more definitive information is found in the book *JavaScript, The Definitive Guide*, by David Flanagan.

Internet Explorer 4 supports all these event handlers, plus many others that will be discussed later, in the section titled "Advanced Scripting and the Document Object Model."

Dynamic Scripts

As mentioned, HTML output generated by scripts is static—once it is displayed on the page, it can in general only be modified by erasing the page and starting again. More dynamic interaction is possible using **FORM** text-level elements—script programs can dynamically update the value content of **INPUT TYPE**="text" and **TEXTAREA** elements (they can actually modify the content of any **VALUE**

Table 7.5 Commonly Supported HTML Event Handling Attributes. Italicized event handlers were introduced in Netscape Navigator 3. These event handlers are supported by Netscape Navigator 3 and 4 and also by Internet Explorer 3 and 4. See also Table 7.6.

Attribute	Description
onAbort	Triggered when loading of images is aborted, for example by the user pressing the "Stop" button. This is relevant only for **IMG** elements.
onBlur	Triggered when the associated form input element *loses focus* (i.e., the user selects text outside the element or selects another input element).
onChange	Triggered when a form element both loses focus *and* has been modified (for example, by user-input of text, or by selecting a button).
onClick	Triggered when a form-element button, or a hypertext link, has been selected ("clicked").
onError	Triggered when there is a problem loading an image, as when the image file or other reference is invalid or corrupted.
onFocus	Triggered when a form input element is selected, usually by clicking the mouse button within the element or by using the tab key to advance to a new item.
onLoad	Triggered when the document is loaded.
onMouseOut	Triggered when the associated *hypertext link* is deselected (e.g., the mouse moves off the link).
onMouseOver	Triggered when the cursor is moved onto the associated hypertext link.
onReset	Triggered when a form reset button is pressed.
onSubmit	Triggered when a form is submitted.
onUnload	Triggered when the document is unloaded (e.g., the user selects to move to another page).

attribute). This allows for auto-tabulating forms (for example, summing a column of elements, as in a spreadsheet) or dynamic generation of form field data using data derived from user input or other sources.

This dynamic functionality is illustrated by the simple JavaScript example listed in Figure 7.45. This small script uses a **FORM** text input element to display the local time and date, updated every second. Figure 7.46 shows the result of this script as rendered by the Netscape Navigator 3 browser, while Figure 7.47 shows the script rendered by Internet Explorer 4.

Table 7.6 HTML Elements and Associated, Commonly Supported Event Handling Attributes
Support for italicized handlers/elements was added in Netscape Navigator 3; LAYER/ILAYER elements were added to Navigator 4.

Element Type	Supported Event Handlers
AREA	*onClick, onMouseOut, onMouseOver*
A	onClick, *onMouseOut, onMouseOver*
IMG	*onAbort, onError, onLoad*
FORM	onSubmit, *onReset*
INPUT TYPE="button"	onBlur, onFocus, onClick
INPUT TYPE="checkbox "	onBlur, onFocus, onClick
INPUT TYPE="radio"	onBlur, onFocus, onClick
INPUT TYPE="submit"	onBlur, onFocus, onClick
INPUT TYPE="reset"	onBlur, onFocus, onClick
INPUT TYPE="text"	onBlur, onChange, onFocus
INPUT TYPE="password"	onBlur, onChange, onFocus
INPUT TYPE="file"	onBlur, onChange, onFocus
INPUT TYPE="image"	N/A
SELECT	onBlur, onChange, onFocus
TEXTAREA	onBlur, onChange, onFocus
FRAMESET	onLoad, onUnload
BODY	*onBlur, onFocus*, onLoad, onUnload, *onError*

Netscape Navigator 4 Only

LAYER/ILAYER	onBlur, onFocus, onLoad, onMouseOut, onMouseOver

The script inside the document **HEAD** defines three methods: `start()` (lines 26 to 31), called when the page is loaded; `stop()` (lines 32 to 34), called when the page is unloaded (the user moves to another page); and `updater()` (lines 10 through 25), which actually runs the timer.

How are these invoked? When the document is loaded, the **BODY** element **ONLOAD** attribute (line 43) invokes the start() method, to start the timers. The argument of start() is the object name for the **FORM** element with which the timer output will be associated. The notation `document.forms.clock` references the **FORM** element, lying in the current document, with the attribute **NAME**="clock."

The start() method first assigns a reference variable to this object (the variable `form_name`) and then calls updater(). Updater() does all the work. The first line (line 21) calls the window method `window.setTimeout()`, with two arguments, the first being the name of a method to run (`updater()`), the second being the time delay (`delay`) before the next call. As a result, the system will awaken after one second and re-invoke updater()—this procedure then continues until this timer, labeled by `timer_id`, is explicitly deleted.

After setting the wake-up call, the function creates a new instance of the Date() object (line 22) and assigns this to the **VALUE** attribute of one of the **FORM** input elements. The particular element attribute is addressed as an object; for example, line 22 references the **FORM** with **NAME** given by the form_name variable ("clock") and references the particular **FORM** input element with **NAME**="result." This is simply the first of the three text input elements, starting at line 52. Lines 23 and 24 assign this same object to the two other input elements within the **FORM**.

When the document is generated, the contents of these elements are replaced by the Date() object, giving rise to the dates displayed in Figures 7.46 and 7.47. This field is updated every second for every invocation of the updater() method.

Server-Side Scripting—Netscape LiveWire

Document scripting is a powerful tool for creating dynamic and interactive documents. It is also useful to have similar scripting capabilities at the HTTP server. This would allow servers to process documents and to dynamically include content, client-side scripts, and data generated by a script run on the server. This is similar to the facilities offered by server-side includes and CGI programs, although a well-designed scripting language, designed with the nature of browsers, HTML documents, and the Internet in mind, would provide an easier framework for writing Web-related applications.

Netscape supports this type of scripting in their *Netscape LiveWire* server packages. In LiveWire, documents delivered by the server can contain scripts that are preprocessed by the server, prior to the delivery of the document. These scripts are placed inside a special Netscape-specific element called **SERVER**. **SERVER** acts just like **SCRIPT** (that is, it is a container for a JavaScript program), except

Figure 7.45 Example HTML JavaScript document illustrating dynamic updating of a text input element. This example creates a single text input element that acts as a real-time clock. The line numbers, in italics, are not part of the document.

```
1    <HEAD>
2    <TITLE>Clock Test Script</TITLE>
3    <SCRIPT>
4    <!--  hide the script
5
6    var timer_id   = 0;                  // reference to timer
7    var form_name  = 0;                  // Instance label for form
8    var delay      = 1000;               // Delay between updates (1 sec)
9
10   function updater(){
11                                         // Initialize timer interrupt
12                                         // to re-call clock_updater()
13                                         // after 'delay' milliseconds
14                                         // Then calculate new time/date,
15                                         // and put results in the VALUE
16                                         // attribute of the FORM
17                                         // field with NAME="result".
18                                         // Then copy time/date into the
19                                         // form field with NAME="result2"
20                                         // and NAME="result3"
21       timer_id=window.setTimeout("updater()", delay);
22       form_name.result.value  = new Date();
23       form_name.result2.value = form_name.result.value;
24       form_name.result3.value = form_name.result.value;
25   }
26   function start(element_id) {
27       form_name = element_id;          // Attach time_field to
28                                         // form element named as argument.
29       updater();                       // Then call clock_updater()
30                                         // to start the clock
31   }
32   function stop() {
33       window.clearTimeout(timer_id); // Remove Timer reference
34   }
35
36   // End script -- end of comment that hides the script -->
37
```

Continued

Figure 7.45 Continued.

```
38   </SCRIPT></HEAD>
39
40   <!--        ONLOAD   triggers    start(), passing the named form
41               ONUNLOAD triggers    stop (), which deletes the timer
42   -->
43   <BODY ONLOAD="start(document.forms.clock)"
44         ONUNLOAD="stop()">
45
46   <H2 ALIGN="center">Dynamic Clock Script</H2>
47
48   <FORM NAME="clock">
49     <CENTER>
50     <B>Clock Output</B> (updates every second)<BR>
51     <BR>
52     <INPUT TYPE="text" NAME="result"  SIZE=18>   <BR><BR>
53     <INPUT TYPE="text" NAME="result2" SIZE=39>   <BR><BR>
54     <INPUT TYPE="text" NAME="result3" SIZE=50>
55     </CENTER>
56   </FORM>
57   </HTML>
```

that the content is executed on the server and not on the client. For instance, the following example document contains both client and server scripts:

```
<HTML>
<HEAD>
<SERVER>
    .... JavaScript to be executed by the server
```

Figure 7.46 Rendering of the document listed in Figure 7.45 by the Netscape Navigator 3 browser.

Figure 7.47 Rendering of the document listed in Figure 7.45 by the Internet Explorer 4 browser.

```
</SERVER>
<SCRIPT>
<!--  Begin hiding
    .... JavaScript to be passed through to, and executed on,
         the client
//  end hiding -->
</SCRIPT>
<TITLE> Some title -- may be generated by Script </TITLE>
</HEAD>
<BODY>
    .... body HTML content ...
<SERVER>
    .... additional server-executed script ...
</SERVER>
</BODY></HTML>
```

When this document is requested, the server executes the JavaScript contained within the **SERVER** elements, which can result in the dynamic generation of document content, the modification of server database entries, and so on. LiveWire includes special methods for database access on the server and for communicating with custom-written server modules authored in Java or other languages.

Microsoft supports similar scripting capabilities with their Web servers, using their Jscript language and special server-side extensions to that language. Once again, of course, these extensions are incompatible with those introduced by Netscape, so that server-side scripts written for LiveWire do not function with Microsoft's servers and vice versa.

Advanced Scripting and the Document Object Model

The preceding scripting technology is rather limited, as it supports only one mechanism for controlling page layout—namely, the generation of HTML content prior to displaying the page. In addition, there is no connection between scripting and style sheet formatting properties. Netscape and Microsoft software engineers both recognized the need for additional control over the page layout to allow for the following features:

- Script access to style sheet properties, so that scripts not only could generate HTML markup, but also could generate and modify the formatting properties for the markup.
- Ability to dynamically interact with the HTML markup, for example by creating a draggable "layer" or a selectable table cell.
- Ability to dynamically modify the HTML markup or page content, without the need to regenerate the entire document.

Netscape's Dynamic HTML

As you probably expected, Microsoft and Netscape took entirely different approaches in addressing these needs. Netscape developed several extensions to JavaScript, including a JavaScript mechanism for defining style sheets, known as *JavaScript Accessible Style Sheets* or *JASS*, and also introduced several JavaScript enhancements to the **LAYER** and **ILAYER** elements, such that layers can be moved, exposed, and revealed under the control of a JavaScript program. Netscape named this technology dynamic-HTML, since it allowed for dynamic access to page properties (via JASS) and since the **LAYER** and **ILAYER** elements allowed for dynamic repositioning of page content.

Microsoft's Dynamic HTML

Microsoft's approach was similar, but much more extensive. Microsoft decided to reengineer the entire mechanism by which an HTML document is rendered to the display and create an underlying object model for the document and all its parts. They then defined an abstract software interface to these objects and finally created a way for Jscript/VBScript programs to access this interface. Then, using this scripting interface, a script program can dynamically modify the appearance of an element (for example, change some text to boldface when a mouse brushes over it) or even rearrange the content, by reordering table rows or hiding/revealing content.

As a result, Internet Explorer 4 browser supports event handlers for a whole variety of elements, not just those listed in Table 7.5. Indeed, Internet Explorer 4 essentially supports all the "generic" event handlers defined as part of HTML 4, listed in the element descriptions given in Chapters 6 and 7. These attributes, along with brief descriptions of the events that "trigger" these attributes, are shown in Table 7.7. Note that Internet Explorer 4 also supports some proprietary event handlers that allow for dynamic updating and modification of the actual *content* of HTML elements. Please consult the Internet Explorer scripting references at the end of this chapter for additional details.

Table 7.7 Event Handling Attributes Defined in HTML 4 and Their Meanings
Most of these event handlers are understood by Internet Explorer 4, but not by Netscape Navigator 4.

Attribute	Conditions for Event
(A) Generic Event Handling Attributes *Supported by most elements*	
onClick	Event occurs when the mouse button is clicked over an element.
onDblClick	Event occurs when the mouse button is double clicked over an element.
onMouseDown	Event occurs when the mouse button is pressed over an element.
onMouseUp	Event occurs when the mouse button is released over an element.
onMouseOver	Event occurs when the mouse is moved onto an element.
onMouseMove	Event occurs when the mouse is moved while it is over an element.
onMouseOut	Event occurs when the mouse is moved away from an element.
onKeyPress	Event occurs when a key is pressed and released while the element has focus.
onKeyDown	Event occurs when a key is pressed down while the element has focus.
onKeyUp	Event occurs when a key is released while the element has focus.
(B) Special-Purpose Event Handlers *Apply only to specific elements*	
onBlur	Event occurs when an element loses focus, either by selecting another element using the mouse or by using tabbing navigation to select another element. This attribute is supported by the form-specific elements **LABEL, INPUT, SELECT, TEXTAREA** and **BUTTON**.
onFocus	Event occurs when an element receives focus either by the mouse selection or by selection using tabbing navigation. This attribute is supported by the same form-specific elements as **onBlur**.
onLoad	Event occurs when the browser finishes loading a window or when it finishes loading all the frames within a frameset. This attribute is thus supported by **BODY** and **FRAMESET**.
onUnload	Event occurs when the browser removes a document from a window, or e removes an entire set of frames within a specified frameset. This attribute is thus supported by **BODY** and **FRAMESET**.

Continued

Table 7.7 *Continued*

Attribute	Conditions for Event
onSubmit	Event occurs when a form is submitted. This attribute is supported by the **FORM** element.

(B) Special-Purpose Event Handlers
Apply only to specific elements

onReset	Event occurs when a form is reset. This attribute is supported by the **FORM** element.
onSelect	Event occurs when a user selects some text in a text field, for example by using the mouse to mark a text selection. This attribute may be used with the **INPUT** and **TEXTAREA** elements, although it is relevant only for **INPUT** elements of **TYPE**="text" and **TYPE**="password."
onChange	Event occurs when a form input mechanism loses the input focus *and* has also had its value modified since the element gained focus. This attribute is supported by the **INPUT**, **SELECT**, and **TEXTAREA** elements.

The Document Object Model

The Microsoft and Netscape approaches are similar in goal, but very different in implementation. However, both approaches depend on a model for the browser and the displayed page as a collection of objects that can be manipulated and processed. This model has come to be know as the Document Object Model, or DOM. Unfortunately, Netscape and Microsoft employ slightly different models, so that it is becoming practically impossible to write scripting software for one browser that will also work on the other.

Fortunately, the World Wide Web Consortium has formed a DOM working group, which is working towards defining an open DOM model to be used by all browser vendors. Both Microsoft and Netscape are active participants in the DOM working group, and with much hard work and some luck, it is likely that this group will define an "open" DOM standard sometime in mid-1998. If this standard is adopted by both Netscape and Microsoft, we can look forward to a much more exciting future of compatible scripting and dynamic HTML content in all browsers.

Internationalization of HTML

Internationalization refers to the process of modifying software and software systems to support the world's languages and to operate with an interface customized for any of these languages. For HTML, this means the ability to use character sets other than ISO Latin-1, as well as the ability to support truly multilingual documents—that is, documents containing more than one language.

Elements and Attributes Related to Internationalization

HTML Elements	*BDO*
Attributes	*DIR, LANG*
Attribute Function	DIR="ltr", "rtl" (optional; mandatory for **BDO**)—specify directionality of text flow**LANG**=*"lang-code"* (optional)—specify language for text within the element

---

HTML 4 incorporated several major changes in support of internationalization. First, the *document character set* for HTML was changed from ISO Latin-1 to another set that supports more of the characters used by the world's languages. The required characters or symbols (*glyphs*) number in the tens of thousands, a far cry from the 200-odd characters possible with ISO Latin-1. The character set is known as Unicode. When Unicode is the selected character set, every character reference refers to a Unicode character— thus the reference δ refers to the 948th character in the Unicode character set, which is the Greek lowercase letter δ. Second, new elements and attributes were added to specify the language used within a particular element or the direction in which the characters should be drawn on the display.

Internationalized Character Sets

To support truly international applications, HTML must support a character set that in turns supports all the characters and symbols of all the world's languages. This is a tall order! Unfortunately, the specified character set of HTML 3.2 was ISO Latin-1, an 8-bit character set that only supports some 200-odd characters common in Western European languages. This is, to say the least, insufficient—ISO Latin-1 is useless for non-European languages, while any standard 8-bit character set is clearly insufficient for languages, such as Chinese or Japanese, where the required repertoire of characters far exceeds the 256 character limit of an 8-bit character set.

There is a character set that does support the world's languages, and it goes by the romantic name ISO 10646. The most important part of ISO 10646 is contained within a 16-bit (65,536-character) subset known as the *Basic Multilingual Plane* or *BMP*. As noted in Appendix A on the companion Web site, this subset is equivalent to the Unicode 2.0 character set. The HTML internationalization effort chose this character set as the *document character set* for HTML. The phrase "document character set" means that the rules for processing HTML documents are composed using this character set and that a document must in some way be convertible into this character set to be properly processed. It further means that HTML character references in HTML (for example, ֘) refer by default to the character at this "position" in the UCS/Unicode character set.

However, this does not mean that a document need be *encoded* using this character set (although that would be the preferred choice). Documents can still be written in any desired character set, known as a *character encoding* (in reflection of the fact that a digital document is simply an encoding of the characters as binary data), but any entity references must be defined as part of HTML, while numeric character references must refer to the Unicode character at the indicated numerical position. This is discussed in more detail in Appendix A on the companion Web site.

Communicating Character Encoding

When an HTML document is sent by a server to a browser, the server should indicate the character set encoding for the document being sent. The mechanism for this is to send, with the header that precedes the document, a MIME content-type header of the form

```
Content-type: text/html; charset=charset_name
```

where `charset_name` is the name of the character set in which the document is encoded.

Unfortunately, most browsers do not understand charset strings and assume that the string is part of the MIME type declaration. They consequently think the document is of some unknown type and cannot display it. To circumvent this problem, HTML 4 supports a special **META** element for indicating a document's character encoding. An example is:

```
<META HTTT-EQUIV="Content-type"
    CONTENT="text/html; charset=charset_name">
```

A browser can search for this header to determine the charset encoding of the document. Of course, this is a bit of a chicken and egg problem, as the browser must first assume a character set (typically ISO Latin-1) in order to start reading the text. This will work provided the document, up to the afore-mentioned **META** element, is encoded in bytes that correspond to ASCII characters, since then the text can be understood assuming the standard default encoding. This mechanism is implemented on Internet Explorer 4 and Netscape Navigator 4.

The general algorithm used by a browser to determine the character encoding is as follows:

- Use the character set specified in the header sent by the server.
- If there is no charset value sent by the server, check for META element content specifying a character set.
- If there is no detectable META element, use heuristic algorithms to determine the character set (i.e., guess).

Issues Related to Language and Character Set

Once you have an internationalized document, you confront several important formatting problems not encountered with simple European text. For example, several languages read from right to left and not left to right—and in a truly international document, many languages may appear in the same document, even in the same paragraph! Thus internationalized HTML needs a way of specifying both the language of a particular piece of text and the desired directionality for the layout of the characters.

These features are enabled through the attributes **LANG** and **DIR**. **LANG** specifies the language for a block of text, while **DIR** specifies the text directionality. Browsers that understand these attributes use **LANG** to control text formatting and **DIR** to change the direction of the text layout. There may also be a need to locally override the directionality of a block of text, and this fine control is provided by the **BDO** or *Bi-Directional Override element.*

Last, the internationalization efforts introduced a new element, **Q**, for use with short inline quotations. The purpose is similar to **BLOCKQUOTE**, except that text inside **Q** will be inline with the regular text flow and will be surrounded by quotation symbols appropriate to the language. **Q**, discussed in Chapter 6, is not yet widely supported.

Added Entity References

To support certain special relationships between adjacent characters, HTML 4 adds four new entity references corresponding to four special Unicode characters. These are:

Entity Reference	Character Reference (UCS)	Description
&zwnj;	&#8204;	zero width non-joiner
&zwj;	&#8205;	zero width joiner
&lrm;	&#8206;	left-to-right mark
&rlm;	&#8207;	right-to-left mark

The first two entities control cursive joining behavior between adjacent letters: an ‌ after a letter means that the cursive joining form of the letter should be used, regardless of the following letter, while an &znj; after a letter means that the cursive non-joining form should be used, again regardless of the letter that follows. The second two entity references specify text directionality in situations where the directionality is not obvious—for example, for a double quotation mark between an Arabic (right-to-left) and a Latin (left-to-right) character. In this case, it is unclear if the mark should belong with the Arabic or Latin letter, whereas if the double quote is surrounded by characters of the same directionality (one of these characters being either ‎ or ‏), then this deadlock is broken, and the quotation mark knows which way to point.

The details of internationalized text are complex, and the preceding discussion has only touched on some of the main issues. For detailed information, you are referred to the HTML 4 specifications and the references quoted therein.

Fonts and Font Embedding

One problem with producing quality typography on the Web is the lack of fonts—an author may design a page using dozens of elegant typefaces, but the user viewing the document only has access to the fonts on his or her machine—and this is usually a small number of rather uninteresting fonts! Ideally, it would be nice if a document could reference font information, so that fonts too could be delivered via the Web and loaded into a document when needed.

Both Microsoft and Netscape recognized this need and—as you might expect—have developed two different and entirely incompatible technologies for accomplishing the job. Netscape, in conjunction with Bitstream, has implemented a technology called *TrueDoc*. TrueDoc is a technology that lets authors create a Web page using any fonts they desire (for example, PostScript or TrueType). When the document is saved, the software saves it along with TrueDoc-format descriptions of the fonts—these descriptions are stored in compressed, encrypted files known as Portable Font Resources, or PFR filed. The HTML document references these PFR files using style sheet rules or HTML link elements. For example, the CSS font reference might be:

```
@fontdef  { url('http://www.site.com/dir/fontfile.pfr' }
```

while the HTML font reference might be:

```
<LINK REL="fontdef" SRC="http://www.site.com/dir/fontfile.pfr">
```

The Microsoft approach is similar, but different. Microsoft has implemented an extension of their TrueType font format, called *OpenType*. This contains compressed TrueType fonts, which can be distributed and referenced in a manner similar to TrueDoc fonts, although the font file formats and the underlying technologies are incompatible. With Microsoft's technology, the desired, downloadable fonts must be referenced using style sheet rules of the form

```
@font-face {font-family: family-name;
         src: url(http://domain.zz.com/fonts/fontfile.eot');
      }
```

where *family-name* is the name to use in the document to reference this font.

Once again the two approaches are incompatible. The Netscape approach has the advantage of font flexibility, since any font can be used when authoring. The disadvantage is rendering speed, since the software that draws the fonts is built into Netscape Navigator 4 and is not terribly fast. Microsoft's approach is much faster at drawing text, as the downloaded OpenType fonts are converted into

TrueType fonts, which are rendered very quickly directly by the operating system. The major limitation is that the fonts used must be TrueType or OpenType, as other formats are not supported.

Missing Features: Mathematics

HTML is currently missing a number of useful hypertext document description features. Notably absent is a way of expressing mathematical symbols and equations. The absence of mathematical expressions is particularly surprising, given the origin of HTML in the scientific community. At present, mathematical equations can only be included by using a separate application to create GIF images of mathematical expressions, which are then included within the HTML document.

Using TeX and LaTeX on the Web

In the mathematics and scientific community, the LaTeX typesetting/document formatting language is almost universal for preparing scientific and mathematical texts. For this community, Nikos Drakos of the University of Leeds has produced a sophisticated program that can convert a LaTeX document into a hypertext collection of HTML documents, automatically converting mathematical expressions into inline GIF images. This remarkably useful package is called latex2html and is available at:

cbl.leeds.ac.uk/nikos/tex2html/doc/latex2html/latex2html.html

Of course, this means you need to learn LaTeX as well. For less sophisticated needs, there is a convenient collection of GIF-format Greek letters and other mathematical symbols, which authors can include in their documents to create simple mathematical equations or scientific expressions. A crib sheet for these icons plus access and licensing information (there is a charge for commercial use—read the license agreement for more information) can be found at:

donald.phast.umass.edu/latex/tutorials/kicons.html

www.anachem.umu.se/graphics/symbols/symbols.html

donald.phast.umass.edu/kicons/license.html

TeX/LaTeX Viewer Plugin

A third alternative is to use a browser plugin that can format and display TeX/LaTeX documents. IBM has developed such a tool, named *techexplorer*, available for download and evaluation at:

www.ics.raleigh.ibm.com/ics/techexp.htm

This package does not support the full set of TeX/LaTeX markup commands; rather, it supports a large subset, plus special extensions for hypermedia and windowing support. Thus, LaTeX documents originally prepared for print publication often need some reworking to be viewed via techexplorer. The documentation at this URL describes the techexplorer-supported TeX/LaTeX language and some of the steps that this adaptation process may entail.

Other Mathematical Alternatives

The current preference of the HTML language design community is to leave mathematical expressions out of HTML. The goal is then to create a separate markup language that is mathematically parsable—that is, a markup language that contains sufficient understanding of the meaning of the expression that the expression can be used as input to mathematical analysis programs, such as Mathematica or Maple, or spreadsheets, such as Lotus 1-2-3 or Excel. The World Wide Web Consortium has been actively pursuing this approach and recently announced a working draft of the proposed MathML mathematical markup language. Interested readers should obtain the working draft listed in the references at the end of the chapter.

Other Missing Features

Other annoyingly missing features are page banners (nonscrolling headers or footers for documents—these can be mimicked by frame documents, but not completely reproduced), footnotes (perhaps displayable as pop-up items above the regular text), tabbing control, and the ability to mark arbitrary spots in a document (for linking or referencing purposes), or a range of text in a document (for selective retrieval of document fragments). Several elements (**FN**, **TAB**, **SPOT**, **RANGE**) in support of these functions were proposed in HTML 3, but have subsequently been dropped from the W3C proposals for the next generation of HTML. With luck they will be reintroduced in the future, as such functionality is often needed in a general-purpose markup language such as HTML. For additional reading on these topics, you are referred to the expired HTML 3 draft document and to the *Next Generation HTML Starting Points* listed in the references.

XML—A Successor to HTML?

One problem with HTML is its inflexibility—every change to the language must be approved by a large, unwieldy committee, such that even the slightest extension to the standard can take years to approve and implement.

Recently, however, a new language was developed that foreshadows the possibility of *customized* markup, tailored to each application. This new language is known as XML, for the eXtensible Markup Language. Unlike HTML, XML does not define a set of tags or elements. Instead, it defines a scheme whereby authors can create their own elements and attributes, allowing them to define document structure as they wish, without the limitations implicit in the element structure of HTML. This document can then be distributed and processed by any software equipped with an XML parser (the software that structurally processes the markup). To make this latter step easy, XML was designed to be simple so that such parsers are easy to write.

Indeed, simplicity was one of the main goals of XML. In some ways, one can think of XML as a "simplified" version of SGML, retaining all the best features of SGML while discarding those features that are rarely used and overly complex to implement.

XML is already widely used on the Web—for example, the Channel Definition Format (CDF), used by Microsoft's "push" channel to distribute HTML content to subscribers, is written in XML. In the future, when XML documents can be distributed along with a style sheet to specify how the XML elements should be displayed, one can expect to see XML being distributed in much the same way as HTML.

Keeping Up-to-Date

Many of the details about upcoming features of HTML are found at the World Wide Web Consortium Web site, listed at the beginning of the references section. If you're burning to know what's up and coming, or you're just being thorough, this is the place to look.

References

Next-Generation HTML Starting Points

www.w3.org/MarkUp/MarkUp.html	(W3C HTML Notes)
www.w3.org/TR/	(W3C Technical Reports/Publications)

Netscape Frame Documentation

home.netscape.com/assist/net_sites/frames.html

Microsoft and Netscape HTML Documentation

developer.netscape.com/library/documentation/ htmlguid/index.htm	(Netscape HTML)
developer.netscape.com/library/documentation/ index.html	(General Netscape documentation)
www.microsoft.com/workshop/author/other/ htmlfaq1.htm	(HTML FAQ for Internet Explorer 3)
www.microsoft.com/workshop/author/newhtml/	(HTML in Internet Explorer 3)

www.microsoft.com/msdn/sdk/inetsdk/help/dhtml/   (HTML in Internet Explorer 4)
   references/htmlrefs.htm

www.microsoft.com/workshop/author/dhtml/   (Microsoft Dynamic HTML)

Object Embedding and Mobile Code Issues

www.w3.org/MobileCode/   (Mobile code proposals)

www.camb.opengroup.org/tech/dce/   (Open Software Foundation DCE—Distributed Computing Environment)

java.sun.com/   (Java programming language)

www.microsoft.com/intdev/sdk/   (Microsoft Active-X)

Cascading Style Sheets

www.w3.org/pub/WWW/Style/   (General style sheet information)

www.w3.org/TR/REC-CSS1/   (CSS1 specification)

www.w3.org/TR/WD-CSS2/   (CSS2 working draft)

www.htmlhelp.com/reference/css/   (Web Design Group CSS references)

   members.aol.com/sjacct/index.html   (List of CSS resources)

HTML Stylesheet Sourcebook, by Ian Graham, John Wiley and Sons, 1997

www.utoronto.ca/ian/books/style/   (Supporting Web site for preceding book)

Cascading Style Sheets: Designing for the Web, by Håkon Wium Lie and Bert Bos, Addison-Wesley, 1997

SCRIPT and HTML-Related Scripting Languages

www.w3.org/pub/WWW/TR/WD-script.html   (SCRIPT Element Discussion paper)

home.netscape.com/eng/mozilla/3.0/handbook/   (JavaScript 1.1)
   javascript/index.html

developer.netscape.com/library/documentation/   (Javascript 1.2)
   communicator/jsref/index.htm

developer.netscape.com/library/documentation/   (Netscape dynamic HTML)
   communicator/dynhtml/index.htm

www.microsoft.com/workshop/author/dhtml/   (Microsoft Dynamic HTML)

www.microsoft.com/vbscript/default.htm   (VBScript/JScript documentation)

developer.netscape.com/library/wpapers/ beanconnect/index.html	(Bean Connect program model)
www.w3.org/DOM/	(Document Object Model)
www.w3.org/TR/WD-DOM/	(DOM—working draft)
www.w3.org/TR/WD-dom	(DOM—requirements list)

Internationalization and Character Sets (See also Appendix A on the companion Web site)

| www.w3.org/pub/WWW/International/ | (Overview and notes) |
| ds.internic.net.rfc/rfc2070.txt | (HTML internationalization) |

Fonts and Font Embedding

www.bitstream.com	(TrueDoc font format)
developer.netscape.com/library/documentation/ communicator/dynhtml/webfont1.htm	(Netscape font embedding)
www.microsoft.com/typography/web/embedding/ weft/default.htm	(OpenType font embedding)

Mathematical Markup

| www.w3.org/Math/ | (Mathematical Markup Language) |
| www.w3.org/TR/WD-math/ | (Math Markup Language working draft) |

XML—eXtensible Markup Language

www.w3.org/XML/	(Notes and specifications)
www.w3.org/TR/WD-xml	(Draft specification)
www.w3.org/TR/WD-xml-link	(Draft specification—XML linking)
www.w3.org/TR/NOTE-XSL-970910	(Proposal—XML style sheet language)

Experimental Web Browsers

www.w3.org/pub/WWW/Amaya/	(Amaya browser)
moose.cs.indiana.edu/pub/elisp/w3/	(Emacs-w3 browser)
monty.cnri.reston.va.us/grail/	(Grail browser)

Uniform Resource Locators

(URLs)

Uniform Resource Locators, or *URLs*, are a set of schemes for specifying Internet resources using a single line of typed ASCII characters: A URL simply indicates where a resource is and how to access it. The syntax for URL schemes is very flexible, and schemes exist for all the major Internet communications protocols, including FTP, Gopher, e-mail, HTTP, and WAIS. Within HTML documents, URLs reference the targets of a hypertext link. However, URLs are not restricted to the World Wide Web and can be used to communicate information about Internet resources in e-mail letters, handwritten notes, or even books.

This chapter begins with a general overview of URL properties and the rules for constructing valid URLs. This is followed by a detailed specification of the currently supported URL schemes. The chapter concludes with a discussion of some proposed, but not widely implemented, schemes, along with more general addressing issues relevant to the World Wide Web.

URL Overview and Syntax Rules

As mentioned, a URL is simply a scheme for referencing a particular Internet resource. In general, A URL generally contains the following four pieces of information, some of which are optional depending on the protocol:

- The *protocol* to use when accessing the server (e.g. HTTP, Gopher, WAIS). This is always required.

- The Internet *domain name* of the site on which the server is running, along with any required username and password information. This is not required for some protocols.

- The *port number* of the server, which can be present (it is optional) only if the URL requires a domain name. If absent, the browser assumes a default value dependent on the protocol. For example, the default value for HTTP is 80.

- The *location* of the resource on the server—often a file or directory specification. This is sometimes optional, depending on the protocol.

Here is a typical example, in this case for the HTTP protocol:

```
http://www.w3.org/pub/WWW/People/W3Cpeople.html
```

This references the file *W3Cpeople.html*, in the directory */pub/WWW/People*, accessible at the server *www.w3.org* using the HTTP protocol.

NOTE: Book Notation for http URLs

In this book, **http** URLs that reference Internet-accessible resources are given without the *http://* portion of the string: for example

```
www.w3.org/pub/WWW/People/W3Cpeople.html
```

This takes advantage of the fact that most current browsers interpret strings typed into the "Location" text field at the top of the browser window or into the "Open File..." or "Open Page..." pop-up text input windows, as **http** URLs, if no other protocol is specified.

However, this is *not true* for **http** URLs embedded within HTML documents, and authors *must not* leave out the *http://* portion when specifying a full HTTP address. The reasons for this are discussed in the section on "Relative URLs" later in this chapter.

Allowed Characters in URLs

A URL can, in principle, contain any ISO Latin-1 character, but must be *written* using only the printable ASCII characters from the bottom half of the ISO Latin-1 character set (as discussed on the companion Web site in Appendix A, excluding control characters). This restriction ensures that URLs can be sent by electronic mail, as many electronic mail programs cannot properly transmit messages containing characters from the upper half of the ISO Latin-1 character set. In a URL, non-ASCII characters (or, indeed, any ISO Latin-1 character) can be represented via a *character encoding* scheme. This is analogous to the character entities used with HTML. However, the schemes are distinctly different—the URL encoding scheme is understood as one of the rules for writing URLs, whereas character entities are only understood inside an HTML document.

The encoding is simple: any character can be represented by the encoding

```
%xx
```

where the percent sign is the special character indicating the start of the encoding and where *xx* is the *hexadecimal code* for the desired ISO Latin-1 character (the *x* represents a hexadecimal digit in the range [0-9,A-F]). Table A.1 (on the companion Web site in Appendix A) lists all the ISO Latin-1 characters alongside their hexadecimal codes. As an example, the encoding for the character "é" (the letter "e" with an acute accent) is %E9.

Disallowed ASCII Characters

Several ASCII characters are disallowed in URLs and can be present only in encoded form. This is because these characters often have special meanings in a non-URL context. For example, HTML documents use the double quotation mark (") to delimit a URL in a hypertext anchor, so that a quotation mark inside the URL would cause the browser to end the URL prematurely. Therefore, the double quote is disallowed. The space character is also disallowed, since many programs will consider the space as a break between two separate strings. For example, space characters often appear in Macintosh or Windows 95 file or folder names, as in the filename "Network Info" (there is a single space between the words "Network" and "Info"). In a URL, this name must be encoded as:

```
Network%20Info
```

Finally, all 33 control characters (hex codes 00 to 1F, and 7F) are disallowed.

Table 8.1 summarizes the disallowed printable characters, including TAB (although TAB, formally, is a control character). You will sometimes see disallowed characters (e.g., the tilde, "~") in a URL, without any special encoding. Such URLs will often work correctly, but to avoid possible problems you should use their encoded forms.

"Special" ASCII Characters

In a URL, several ASCII characters have special meanings. In particular, the percent character (%) is special, since it starts a URL character encoding sequence, while the forward slash character (/) is also special, denoting a change in hierarchy, such as a directory change. These special characters must be encoded if you

Table 8.1 ASCII Characters That Are Disallowed in URLs

Character	Hex	Character	Hex
TAB	09	SPACE	20
"	22	<	3C
>	3E	[	5B
\	5C	]	5D
^	5E	`	60
{	7B			7C
}	7D	~	7E

want them to appear as regular characters and not be interpreted as special. Thus, to include the string

`ian%euler`

in a URL, you must encode it as:

`ian%25euler`

where `%25` is the encoding for the percent character. If you do not do this, a program parsing the URL will try to interpret `%eu` as a character encoding. Conversely, you must *not* encode a special character if you require its special meaning. For example, the string

`dir/subdir`

indicates that `subdir` is a subdirectory of `dir`, while:

`dir%2Fsubdir`

is just the character `string dir/subdir` (`%2F` is the encoding for the slash).
The most common special characters are:

The percent sign (%) This is the escape character for character encodings and is special in all URLs.

The hash (#) This separates the URL of a resource from the *fragment identifier* for that resource. A fragment identifier references a particular location within a resource. This character is special in all URLs.

The slash (/) This indicates hierarchical structures, such as directories.

The question mark (?) This indicates a *query string*; everything after the question mark is query information to be passed to the server. This character is special only in Gopher, WAIS, and HTTP URLs.

Other characters that are special in certain URL schemes are the colon (:), semicolon (;), at (@), equals (=), and ampersand (&). These special cases will be noted as they arise.

TIP: URL Encoding Rule

Encode any character that might be special if you do not want to use its special meaning.

Examples of Uniform Resource Locators

Figure 8.1 illustrates three typical URLs, showing the different parts and the associated meanings. The parts are:

Protocol Specifier. The first string in the URL, of the general form *string:*, specifies the Internet *protocol* to use in accessing the

Figure 8.1 Three example URLs (here http, telnet, and mailto URLs), showing the main components. Not all URLs follow these models, as discussed in the text.

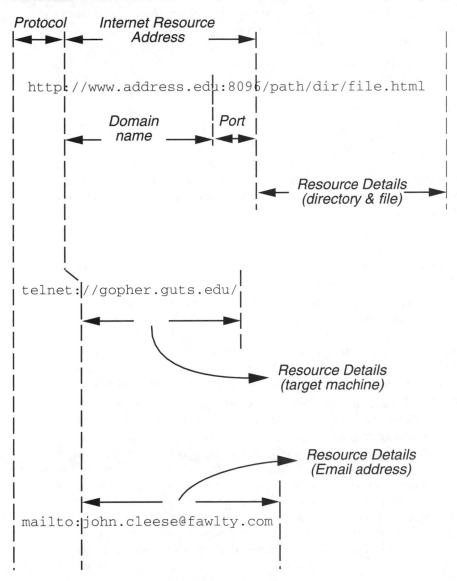

resource—the examples here being for the HTTP (`http:`), Internet mail (`mailto:`), and telnet (`telnet:`) protocols. The protocol is indicated by the name before the colon. The string specifying the protocol can contain only *lowercase letters* (`a-z`). URL schemes are defined for most Internet protocols. The details of the different schemes are presented later.

Domain Name and Port Number (Address). The second part of a URL is usually the Internet address of a server; this information lies between the double forward slash (*//*) and a terminating forward slash (*/*). This region contains the *domain name* of the server and, optionally, the *port number* to contact, the general form being `//dom.name.edu:port/`. Omitting the port number (and the colon before it) implies the default port for the given protocol. Numeric IP addresses can be used instead of domain names, for example:

```
//132.206.9.22:1234/
//128.100.100.1/
```

You can sometimes (depending on protocol) include username and password information, if this is needed to access a resource. The form is then:

```
//username:password@www.address.edu:port/
```

Note that the password can be read by anyone who sees the URL, so this is not a secure way to allow access to a resource.

Some URL schemes do not require Internet domain names. This is the case for protocols that do not depend on a specific server, such as those for sending electronic mail (**mailto**) or accessing USENET newsgroup (**news**) articles. In these cases, users have, and must somehow specify, their own default mail or news server. The domain names for these servers are usually set using a browser's configuration menus.

Resource Location. The forward slash after the host and port number field indicates the end of the address field and the beginning of the information required to locate the resource on the server. This field varies considerably, depending on the service being accessed. Often, it resembles a directory path leading down to a file, as in the **http** URL in Figure 8.1. In this context, the forward slash character (*/*) defines a change in hierarchy or directory and is used in place of *all* system-dependent symbols defining such relationships, such as the backslash (\) on DOS, OS/2, or Windows computers, the colon (:) on Macintoshes, and the `[dir.subdir.subsubdir]` expressions on VAX/VMS systems.

Query Strings in URLs

The URL syntax allows you to encode query strings to be passed to the designated Internet resource, in situations (typically Gopher, HTTP, or WAIS) that support queries. This is accomplished by appending the query strings to the URL, separated from it by a question mark. Two examples are (the query string is in boldface):

```
gopher://gopher.somewhere.edu/77/searches.phone?bob+steve
http://www.somewhere.edu/cgi-bin/srch-data?archie+database
```

The question mark is a special character in HTTP, Gopher, and WAIS URLs and must be encoded if you do *not* want to indicate a query string.

Encoding of Query Strings

Of course query strings, since they are part of a URL, must also be encoded. However, query string data take an additional level of encoding, over and above the encodings discussed to this point. By way of illustration, space characters in a query string are encoded as plus (+) signs and not via hex character encodings (as illustrated in the previous two examples). Query string encodings are specific to the protocol being used, and also to the mechanism used to gather data from the user (**ISINDEX, FORM,** or **ISMAP** active image). These mechanisms are discussed in the section on **http** URLs.

Some Simple URL Examples

The following examples illustrate basic URL structure:

```
http://www.w3.org/pub/WWW/Addressing/URL/Overview.html
```

> References the file *Overview.html* in the directory */pub/WWW/Addressing/ URL/* obtainable from the server *www.w3.org* using the HTTP protocol at the default port number (80 for HTTP).

```
gopher://gumby.brain.headache.edu:151/7fonebook.txt
```

> References the searchable index *fonebook.txt* from the Gopher server at *gumby.brain.headache.edu* running on port number 151.

```
news:alt.rec.motorcycle
```

> References the newsgroup *alt.rec.motorcycle*, to be accessed from a new server. The identity of a news server must be specified elsewhere. With Web browsers, this is usually accomplished via the browser's configuration menus.

```
mailto:ross@physics.mcg.ca
```

> References sending an electronic mail message to the indicated e-mail address.

In general, a browser sends mail to a designated *mail server*, which then forwards the mail to the final destination. The name of this mail server must be specified by the user, usually via the browser's configuration menus.

Relative URLs—Within an HTML Document

From within an HTML document, you do not always need to specify the full URL of a second resource. This is because being *in* a document implies knowledge of the current URL, which lets you reference neighboring documents or resources using a *relative* URL (also called a *partial* URL), which gives the location *relative* to that of the current document. To put it another way, the URL need only indicate the part of the URL *different* from that used to access the current document.

For example, suppose a user accesses the document *file.html* using the full URL

```
http://www.stuff.edu/main/docs/file.html
```

and that, within this document, there is a hypertext reference containing the *relative* URL:

```
<A HREF="stuff.html">anchor text</A>
```

Where is this file? Any information not present in a URL reference is considered to be the *same* as that used to access the current document. Thus, the partial URL `stuff.html` is transformed into a full URL by appropriating the required URL components from the URL that was used to access *file.html*. The completed URL is then:

```
http://www.stuff.edu/main/docs/stuff.html
```

which indicates, as expected, that *stuff.html* is on the same server and in the same directory as *file.html*. Other, equivalent, relative URLs would then be:

```
/main/docs/stuff.html
//www.stuff.edu/main/docs/stuff.html
```

The former appropriates `http://www.stuff.edu` from the current URL to complete the reference, while the latter appropriates only the `http:` part from the *base* URL of the current document.

You can also use relative URLs to reference resources at other locations on the same server. For example, from within the file *file.html*, the relative URL

```
../../main.html
```

references the file *main.html* in the root HTTP directory, namely:

```
http://www.stuff.edu/main.html
```

Note how, with relative URLs, the special symbol ".." indicates a location one up in the directory hierarchy, just as it does in DOS or UNIX.

Relative URLs are also discussed in Example 2 from Chapter 1.

Relative URLs and the BASE Element

Relative URLs are very useful when constructing large collections of documents that will be kept together. However, relative URLs become invalid for a single document that is moved to a new directory or a new Internet site. This problem can be mitigated by using a **BASE** element within the moved document. **BASE** records the *base*—or original—location of the document. Relative URLs are evaluated relative *to* this recorded base URL. Thus, when the document is moved, all relative URLs are determined relative to the URL recorded by **BASE**, and the linked resources are correctly accessed from the original server. For example, suppose a document contains the **head**-level element

```
<BASE HREF="http://www.flopsy.com/dir1/path/file2.html">
```

and also the **body**-level hypertext reference:

```
<A HREF="../stuff.html">link to some stuff</A>.
```

Then, this hypertext link references the URL

```
http://www.flopsy.com/dir1/stuff.html
```

regardless of the actual location of the document containing the reference, since the **BASE** always directs relative URLs to an address relative to the base location.

Fragment Identifiers

In some cases, you will see locator strings of the form:

```
http://some.where.edu/Stuff/Path/plonk.html#location
```

The portion of the URL following the hash (#) character is called a *fragment identifier* and references a particular location *within* the designated URL. Within the targeted HTML document, this location must be marked by an anchor element of the form:

```
<A NAME="location">text marker</A>
```

where the string `location` is the text string marking the location.

When a browser accesses a resource specified by a URL, it first strips off *all* characters following and including an unencoded hash (#) and uses the remaining string as the resource URL. Consequently, for the "stripped" URL to be valid, a fragment identifier must be the very last substring on a URL. The browser preserves the fragment identifier as local information and, after retrieving the indicated resource, looks for the indicated location. The browser will present the document to the user, such that the location is prominently displayed, either by placing the location at the top of the screen or by highlighting it in some way.

You can also reference named locations from within the document that contains the location. The general form for this is:

```
<A HREF="#location">anchor text</A>
```

That is, you reference just the fragment identifier, and nothing else. A browser should then scroll the document to prominently display the targeted location.

The use of fragment identifiers was discussed in detail in Example 6 of Chapter 2.

URL Specifications

We now look at the details of the different URL schemes. The protocols that can be referenced by URLs are listed in the Table 8.2; italicized entries indicate schemes that are not widely supported, while "Pseudo"-URLs lists URL schemes that are not formal resource locators, but that are commonly encountered in Web browsers and Web applications.

Table 8.2 Description of URL Protocol Specifier Strings. Italicized entries are not widely supported. "Supported By" column indicates level of browser support. "Special" schemes are only used for OBJECT element CLASSID values. "Pseudo"-URLs do not reference well-defined internet resources.

Protocol Specifier	Protocol or Function	Supported By
castanet:	*Apparent synonym for HTTP urls (Netscape Navigator 4 only)*	NS 4
cid: (see also mid:)	*Content-ID resource reference; for mail and USENET messages*	NS 4 Mail/News Client
data:	Inclusion of inline data	MSIE 4; NS 4
file:	Local file access (various protocols)	All
ftp:	FTP protocol	All
gopher:	Gopher protocol	All
http: (https:)	HTTP protocol	All
https:	Secure HTTP	All
ldap: (ldaps:)	*Lightweight Directory Access Protocol*	MSIE 4; NS 4 Calendar client
mailto:	Internet mail address	All
mid: (see also cid:)	*Message-ID resource reference; for mail and USENET messages*	NS 4 Mail/News Client
news: (snews:)	NNTP USENET protocol	All
nntp:	*NNTP USENET protocol*	All
prospero:	*Prospero directory services protocol*	None
telnet: (rlogin:, tn3270:)	Telnet protocol	All
wais:	WAIS protocol	Most (via a proxy)

Table 8.2 *Continued*

Protocol Specifier	Protocol or Function	Supported By
"Special" URLs		
clsid:	Microsoft COM class identifier	MSIE 3/4
java:	Java classes	NS 4; MSIE 4
javabean:	A Javabean class	NS 4
"Pseudo"-URLs		
about:	References information about the browser	MSIE 4 (partially); NS
javascript:	References inline JavaScript code	MSIE 3/4; NS
mailbox:	References Access to local mail client	NS 4
res:	References a resource accessible from a loadable (DLL) module	MSIE 4
view-source:	References a source listing of a resource	NS 4
wysiwyg:	References JavaScript-derived HTML output	NS 4

Key to Table: NS: Netscape Navigator (Versions > 1); NS 4: Netscape Navigator 4; MSIE: Microsoft Internet Explorer (Versions > 2); MSIE 4 Microsoft Internet Explorer 4.

Castanet URLs (Netscape Navigator 4 Only)

Castanet URLs were apparently intended as a reference to Marimba *Castanet* resources—I use the word "apparently," as little documentation on this URL scheme is available. Netscape Navigator 4, the only browser to understand this scheme, treats **castanet** URLs as equivalent to **http** URLs. Thus, the references

```
castanet://www.utoronto.ca
http://www.utoronto.ca
```

are equivalent. Authors should thus avoid **castanet** URLs, since they are not understood by other browsers and **http** URLs provide exactly the same functionality.

Cid URLs

Cid URLs refer to a specific part of a MIME-encoded multipart message. In particular, **Cid** URLs are designed for use within multipart HTML (M-HTML; see Appendix B on the companion Web site) messages—such messages contain HTML documents and images, all within the same message body. The general form for a **cid** URL is

```
cid:content-id
```

where *content-id* is the URL-encoded versions of the MIME Content-ID for the desired part of the message. The format for Content-IDs in a multipart message is defined in the MIME specifications, listed at the end of Appendix B on the companion Web site. As an example, a typical ID might be:

```
part3-12%d7f4@flopsy.org
```

which identifies the machine from which the message was sent (`flopsy.org`) and contains a generated string (`part3-12%d7f4`) chosen to ensure that all IDs in the message are unique. The corresponding **cid** URL would be

```
cid:part3-12%25d7f4@flopsy.org
```

where the percent character in the Content-ID has been URL-encoded.

    Cid URLs permit links between parts of a multipart message. For example, a single message could contain multiple HTML documents, with links between them or could contain an HTML document along with the associated images files. In this case, the images would be referenced from the document using IMG elements of the form

```
<IMG SRC="cid:content-id">
```

where *content-id* is the Content-ID for the image.

    Cid URLs are supported by the Netscape Communicator mail, news, and HTML authoring clients, but only within the mail or news viewing client (Netscape Messenger); they are not understood by the Navigator 4 browser. Indeed, if a user clicks on a hypertext link referencing a **cid** URL in the Netscape Messenger mail client the resulting string displayed in the Navigator "Location" window is actually a **mailbox** URL. **Cid** URLs are not supported by Internet Explorer 4.

    An author would only rarely type a **cid** URL, since they are typically generated by the tool that assembles a mail message or newsgroup posting. **Cid** URLs are related to **mid** (Message Identifier) URLs, discussed later in this chapter.

Data URLs

Data URLs allow for inclusion of small pieces of data within a URL—that is, instead of referencing a data resource, **data** URLs actually contain the data. This is useful for including small chunks of data within a document, such as **OBJECT** parameters or a small, inline image.

The form for a data URL is rather complex, and you are referred to the specification document listed in the references section for details. In general, **data** URL have the form

`data:`*`mime/type`*`;base64,`*`data-content`*

where *`mime/type`* give the MIME type (and any optional parameters, such as the character set or encoding); the optional `;base64` parameter indicates that the data content is URL-encoded; and a comma separates the data URL parameters from the data content. Some typical forms are illustrated in the following, where *`datastring`* corresponds to the data content of the URL.

`data:,`*`datastring`*

> A string of data, by default of type text/plain and in the US-ASCII character set.

`Data:image/gif;base64,`*`datastring`*

> A string of data that is BASE64 encoded and that corresponds to a GIF image.

`data:text/html;version=4.0;charset=utf8,`*`datastring`*

> A string of data that corresponds to HTML content, encoded using the Unicode UTF-8 character set.

Internet Explorer 3/4 and Netscape Navigator 4 understand **data** URLs that specify data to be passed, via HTML **OBJECT** elements, to Java or Active-X components. Netscape Navigator 4 can handle **data** URLs in almost any context; for example, to encode small images (as an argument to an **IMG** element **SRC** attribute) or to encode small documents (as an argument to an **A** element **HREF** attribute).

File URLs

File URLs specify the location of resources relative to the local filesystem. Since such references are valid only for computers with direct access to the local filesystem (e.g., connected to the same Novell, UNIX, or Windows NT file server), **file** URLs should not be used in documents to be publicly accessed over the Internet.

NOTE: Do Not Use File URLs for Internet Publishing

Since **file** URLs are designed to specify local files, and the general public will not have access to your filesystem, **file** URLs should not be used for documents to be published on the Internet.

The general form for a **file URL** is

```
file://int.domain.nam/path/file
```

where `int.domain.nam` is the domain name for the system and `path/file` is the locator of the file. Note that there is no specified port number. **File URLs** are designed to represent local file access. All browsers allow local file access, often with a pull-down menu, and represent the location using a **file** URL. The domain name for local file access can either be the special string `localhost` or an empty field (i.e., `file:///...`). For example, if you are accessing the local file */big/web/docs.html*, the **file** URL could be either of the following:

```
file://localhost/big/web/docs.html
file:///big/web/docs.html
```

where the file could be on a local disk or on a filesystem mounted on the local system from elsewhere.

FTP URLs

Ftp URLs designate files and directories accessible using the FTP protocol. In the absence of any username and password information, anonymous FTP access is assumed (implying a connection to the server as username *anonymous*, using the user's Internet mail address as the password). The general form for this type of **ftp** URL is

```
ftp://int.domain.nam:port/resource
```

where `int.domain.nam` is the domain name to access, `:port` specifies the optional port number (the default is 21), and `resource` is the local resource specification. Here is a typical example, referencing the file *splunge.txt* located in the directory *stuff* at the Internet site *ftp.mysite.com* at the default port:

```
ftp://ftp.mysite.com/stuff/splunge.txt
```

You can specify FTP access of a directory using a URL such as:

```
ftp://ftp.mysite.com/path/
```

in which case the server returns a listing of the directory contents. Browsers display this information as a menu, allowing the user to navigate through the filesystem or select particular files for downloading.

Special Characters in FTP URLs

The forward slash (/) and semicolon (;) characters are special in an **ftp** URL. The forward slash indicates directory or other hierarchical structures, while the semicolon is used to indicate the start of a *typecode* string. Typecode strings, discussed later in this section, must be the last string of the URL (not including any fragment identifier).

Non-Anonymous FTP Access

You can reference non-anonymous FTP resources by specifying, within the URL, the username and password of the account you wish to access. For example, the URL

```
ftp://joe_bozo:bl123@internet.address.edu/dir1/Dir2/file.gz
```

references the indicated file on the machine *internet.address.edu*, accessible by logging in as user *joe_bozo* with password *bl123*. This is obviously not a secure way of giving access, since anyone who reads the URL knows *joe_bozo*'s password. A more secure alternative is to give only the username, as in:

```
ftp://joe_bozo@internet.address.edu/dir1/Dir2/file.gz
```

Netscape Navigator browsers (versions 2 and up) will connect to the remote machine using the indicated username and will prompt the user for an appropriate password. Similarly, Netscape Navigator browsers will prompt for the username and password when the server explicitly requires these quantities and does not accept *anonymous* user access.

Unfortunately, this does not work with Internet Explorer. Internet Explorer 3 and 4 do not prompt the user for an appropriate password, even if the URL contains only a username, and not a password. Instead, these browsers always use the return e-mail address, configured into the browser, as the password.

A Note about FTP Directory Paths

Directory locations during FTP accesses are defined relative to a well-defined *home directory*, with the actual location of this home directory depending on the identity of the user making the connection. A user who connects via anonymous FTP is placed in a special "anonymous FTP" home directory and has restricted access to the server filesystem. This security feature permits making certain files publicly available without exposing the rest of the system to unauthorized users. On the other hand, if a visitor connects to the same machine as a registered user, the home directory will be that of the registered user, entirely different from that attained via anonymous FTP.

Modes for File Transfers

The FTP protocol supports several modes for transferring files. The most important is *image* or *binary* mode, which makes a byte-by-byte copy of the file. This is the mode to use when transferring programs, compressed data, or image files. Also important is *ASCII* or *text* mode, which is designed for transferring plain, printable text files. This mode is useful because it "corrects" for the fact that PCs, Macintoshes, UNIX, and other operating systems use different characters to mark the end of a line of text. In particular, Macintoshes use the carriage-return character CR; UNIX computers use the line-feed character LF; and DOS/Windows computers use both CR and LF (often written CRLF).

In ASCII mode, FTP automatically converts between these three end-of-line markers to ensure that the received file has the new line codes appropriate to the local system. You cannot use this mode to transfer programs, however, since programs and data files contain bytes with the same codes as CR or LF characters—under ASCII mode, these codes are converted into the new-line codes appropriate to the local system, thereby corrupting the content of binary files.

The FTP protocol has no knowledge of the data content of a file and must be told what mode to use in a file transfer. Thus, your WWW browser must have some way of determining the data type of a file being accessed via an **ftp** URL. Some browsers "guess" the type from the suffix of the filename, using a browser database that maps filename suffixes onto data types. This is not ideal, since the true type is only known by the author who constructed the URL and who created the resource referenced by the URL.

TIP: Troubleshooting FTP URLs

At times, an **ftp** URL request will fail. This may occur because the network is down or because the machine being accessed is overloaded with FTP requests and refuses your connection. Alternatively, the remote server may be configured to limit access to a restricted set of Internet sites. Web browsers are very terse when handling FTP connections and say very little when a connection fails. You can often diagnose the source of a problem by using an FTP program, independent of your Web browser. A stand alone FTP session provides more commentary on the state of the connection and will often explain why a connection cannot be made.

FTP Typecode Strings

Authors can use URL *typecode strings* to specify the desired transfer mode. For example, the following URL

```
ftp://ftp.mysite.edu/path/splunge.txt;type=a
```

indicates that the designated resource (the file *splunge.txt*) should be retrieved using ASCII mode. The special semicolon character is used to separate the end of the resource locator string from the type indicator. Other possible type indicators are `type=i` for image (binary) transfers and `type=d` for directory listings. Typecode strings are optional, the default being binary data transfers. Fragment identifiers, if used, must be placed after the typecode string—for example:

```
ftp://ftp.somesite.edu/path/goof.html;type=a#location
```

TIP: Problems with Typecode Strings?

Typecode strings are supported by Netscape Navigator 3.0 and Microsoft Internet Explorer 3, but not by some other browsers or by earlier versions these programs. These older browsers assume the typecode string to be part of the filename, and thus do not locate the resource. If your URLs use typecode strings, you may wish to warn users about this possible problem.

Gopher URLs

Gopher servers can be accessed via URLs in a manner that looks superficially similar to **ftp** or **http** URLs but that is, in fact, quite different. This is because Gopher resources are referenced using a combination of *resource identifier* codes and *selector strings*, and not directories and files. Resource identifiers are single-digit codes that specify the *type* of the Gopher resource—for example, that it is a text file, a directory, or a searchable index. The Gopher selector string is just a symbolic name associated with this resource. This can be a directory or file name, but can also be a redirection to a database search procedure or to a Telnet session. Sometimes the selector string has, as its first character, a duplicate of the single-character resource type identifier. This can lead to hair-pulling confusion, with resource identifiers appearing alone or in pairs, seemingly at random. Table 8.3 summarizes the Gopher resource identifier codes.

Table 8.3 Gopher Resource Identifier Codes

Code	File or Resource Type
0	Text file
1	Directory
2	CSO name/phone book server
3	Error
4	Macintosh binhexed (*.hqx) file
5	Dos binary file of some type
6	UNIX uuencoded file
7	Full-text index search
8	Telnet session
9	Binary file

General Form of a Gopher URL

The general form for a basic Gopher URL is

`gopher://int.domain.nam:port/Tselector_string`

where the port number is optional (the default value is 70), *T* is the Gopher type code from Table 6.3, and `selector_string` is the Gopher selector string. The root information of a Gopher server can be obtained by leaving out all type and selector string information. Thus, the root information of the Gopher server at *mr.bean.org* is available at:

`gopher://mr.bean.org/`

Hierarchical relationships are possible. For example:

`gopher://mr.bean.org/1stuff`

indicates that `stuff` behaves like a directory and will retrieve the Gopher contents of `stuff`, while the URL

`gopher://mr.bean.org/7stuff/index`

indicates access to the *index* search in the directory *stuff*. Accessing this URL would cause the browser to ask the user for query string information to be used in the search.

Query Strings for Searches

Search information is sent to the Gopher server by appending the search strings to the URL, separated from the URL by a question mark. Thus, to pass the strings `tad`, `jill`, and `joanne` to the Gopher search index noted in the previous section, the URL is:

`gopher://mr.bean.org/7stuff/index?tad+jill+joanne`

Note that the URL syntax for Gopher queries uses a plus (+) sign to separate different search strings. Therefore, if you want to include a literal plus sign within a string, it must be encoded (the encoding for a plus sign is `%2B`).

Client Construction of Query Strings

Inserting plus sign separators and converting plus signs in query strings into encoded values is done by the Web browser. When a user accesses a Gopher search from a Web browser, he or she is prompted for search strings. These are generally entered in a text box, using space characters to separate the different strings. When the search information is submitted, the search strings are appended, with appropriate encodings, to the URL. The client software is responsible for replacing space characters by plus signs and for encoding characters in the user's search string that might be incorrectly interpreted.

The Gopher protocol supports additional features not discussed here. Please see the references at the end of this chapter for additional information.

HTTP URLs

Http URLs designate files, directories, or server-side programs accessible using the HTTP protocol. An **http** URL must always point to a file (text or program) or a directory. The general form is

```
http://int.dom.nam:port/resource
```

where the port number is optional (the default value is 80) and where *resource* specifies the resource. Resources are usually (but not always) files or directories. A directory is indicated by terminating the directory name with a forward slash, as in:

```
http://www.utoronto.ca/webdocs/HTMLdocs/
```

The following reference to this directory is an error, since it implies a reference to a file and not a directory:

```
http://www.utoronto.ca/webdocs/HTMLdocs
```

Most HTTP servers can detect this type of error and realize that the user wants to view the directory listing. In these cases, the server returns a *server redirect* HTTP response header, which contains the correct URL (with the trailing slash) and instructs the browser to try this URL instead. Server redirects are discussed in Chapter 9.

Note, however, that you can omit the trailing slash when referencing the *root* of a Web site. Thus, the following two URLs are both equivalent and correct:

```
http://www.utoronto.ca/
http://www.utoronto.ca
```

Special Characters in HTTP URLs

The forward slash (/), semicolon (;), question mark (?), and hash (#) are special characters in the path and query string portions of an **http** URL. The slash denotes a change in hierarchy (such as a directory), while the question mark ends the resource location path and indicates the start of a query string. The hash denotes the start of a fragment identifier. The semicolon is reserved for future use and should therefore be encoded in all cases where you intend a literal semicolon.

URL Encoding of Query Strings

Http URLs can contain query data to be passed to the server—these data are appended to the URL, separated from it by a question mark. Besides the character encodings required within URLs, query strings undergo additional levels of encoding to preserve information about the *structure* of the query data. This is necessary because certain characters in a query string are assigned special encoded meanings as part of the query—for example, the plus character (+) used to encode spaces, as noted earlier. There are several different ways these encodings are done, depending both on the mechanism by which the data are input by the user and on the mechanism by which the data are sent to the server.

Document authors do not usually have to worry about the encoding phase; browsers take **ISINDEX** or **FORM** data and do the encoding automatically. However, a gateway program author must explicitly *decode* these data to recover the original information; thus, he or she must understand the encoding in order to reverse the procedure. The following is a brief review of the encoding steps; you are referred to Chapters 6 (discussion of **FORM** elements) and 10 for more details.

URL Encoding for ISINDEX and FORM Data

The following steps outline the query string encoding process, elaborated to illustrate the important points. If the data are from an **ISINDEX** query, these steps apply to the encoding of the entire query input string; if the data are from **FORM**-based input, the encoding steps apply to each name and value string from the form's user-input elements.

1. Percent characters (%) are converted into their URL encodings (`%2f`).
2. Plus signs (+) are converted into their URL encodings (`%2b`).
3. Ampersands (&) are converted into their URL encodings (`%26`).
4. Equals signs (=) are converted into their URL encodings (`%3d`).
5. The possibly special characters—namely # ; / ? : $! , ' ( )— are converted into their URL encodings.
6. Space characters are encoded as plus signs (+).
7. All non-ASCII characters (hex codes greater than `7f`), all ASCII control characters (hex codes `00-1f`, and `7f`), and the unsafe ASCII characters listed in Table 6.1 are converted into their URL encodings (note that spaces have already been converted into plus signs).

At this point, all ASCII punctuation characters are encoded, except for the five characters:

`_ - . * @`

If the data are from an **ISINDEX** query, the encoding is complete. If they are from a **FORM**, only the individual *name* and *value* strings from each **FORM** input element have been encoded, as described in steps 1 through 7. These strings are then combined according to the following rules:

1. Each *name* and *value* pair is combined into a composite string of the form *name=value*. Note that the first encoding phase (steps 1–7) encoded

all equals signs in the *name* and *value* strings, so that the only *un*encoded equals signs in the string are those used to separate a name from its associated value.

2. The `name=value` strings from all the **FORM** elements are combined into a single string, separated by ampersand (&) characters. For example:

`name1=value1&name2=value2`

Note that the first encoding phase (steps 1–7) encoded all ampersands in the name and value strings, so that the only unencoded ampersands in the query string are those that separate name/value pairs.

Query-String Encoding MIME Type

Query string data encoded according to this algorithm are said to be *URL-encoded*. In fact, this encoding mechanism is assigned its own MIME type, namely:

`Content-type: application/x-www-form-url-encoded`

Note that you can easily tell if the data are from a **FORM** or **ISINDEX** query just by checking for unencoded equals signs. For example, the first of the following two URLs is from an **ISINDEX** query, the second from a **FORM** (the query string portion is in boldface):

`http://some.site.edu/cgi-bin/foo?arg1+arg2+arg3`
`http://some.site.edu/cgi-bin/program?`**`name1=value1&name2=value2`**

NOTE Proposed Replacement of Ampersand (&) by Semicolon (;)

The FORM encoding use of the ampersand (&) to separate name/value strings was an unfortunate choice, given the use of this character to denote character and entity references. The current URL specification recommends using an unencoded semicolon (;) in query strings instead of ampersands. Thus, strings would be combined as:

`name1=value1;name2=value2`

There are no current browsers that do this when processing **FORM** data. However, a gateway program author should write programs to interpret either the ampersand or semicolon character as delimiting characters, so that the program is compatible with next-generation browsers.

URL Encoding for ISMAP Active Image Queries

A typical active image is written, in an HTML document, as:

```
<A HREF="http://some.where.edu/cgi-bin/program"><IMG
     SRC="funny_image.gif" ISMAP>
</A>
```

The **ISMAP** attribute makes the **IMG** element active, while the surrounding anchor element gives the URL to which the image coordinates should be sent. **ISMAP** active image queries are composed by taking the integer (x,y) pixel coordinates of the mouse click, with respect to the upper left-hand corner of the active image, and appending them to the URL of the enclosing anchor, using the format (query string in boldface italics):

```
http://some.where.edu/prg-bin/program?x,y
```

The only valid characters in the query string are the integer coordinates (x, y) and the comma separating the two values. An example is:

```
http://some.where.edu/prg-bin/program?56,312
```

Server Issues: Server Processing of Queries

In general, HTTP servers do not handle queries themselves, but instead pass query data on to other "gateway" programs for further processing—the path /cgi-bin/ in a URL often indicates that process is taking place. The name, however, need not be /cgi-bin/—this is a configurable symbolic name, and other names (or many different names) may be used. This book generally uses the name cgi-bin to indicate this functionality.

The name following the path /cgi-bin/ is the name of the program to be run by the server. Any information following this name and preceding any query string data (i.e., after any slash following the program name and before a question mark) is known *as extra path* information. This is an additional parameter that, like the query string, is passed to the CGI program.

When a server is contacted via a URL referencing a *gateway* program, the server launches the program and passes to it any data sent from the client (if any) for further processing. In addition, it passes on any query string data, along with any extra path information. This is discussed in more detail in Chapter 10. Here are two simple examples, with brief explanations—the part lying after the program specification is marked in boldface, with the query string portion also in italics:

```
http://some.site.edu/cgi-bin/srch-example
```

> The server executes the program *srch-example* found in the *cgi-bin* directory. Any output from *srch-example* is sent back to the client.

```
http://www.site.edu/cgi-bin/srch-example/path/other?srch_string
```

> The server again executes the program *srch-example* found in the *cgi-bin* directory. The *extra path* information path/other is passed as a parameter to *srch-example*, as is the query information srch_string.

Server Issues: Personal HTML Directories

Users who have accounts on a machine running the NCSA, Apache, Netscape, and most other servers can have world-accessible HTML documents in their own home directories. These "personal" HTTP document directories are indicated in a URL by a tilde (~) character prepended in front of the path information (the first item in the path hierarchy following the tilde must be the account name of the user). The tilde tells the server that this is not a regular directory, but a *redirection* to a personal document archive of the user with the indicated account. For example, if the user `iang` has a personal document directory, this could be accessed using the URL

```
http://site.world.edu/%7Eiang/
```

where `%7E` is the encoding for the tilde character. You will often see a real tilde in such URLs, since the tilde is safe in most situations.

HTTP URL Examples

The following are some simple example HTTP URLs, illustrating the points mentioned in the previous discussion.

```
http://www.myfrog.com:3232/crunchy/frog/bolt.html#cheeks
```

References the document *bolt.html* in the directory *crunchy/frog/* accessible from the server *www.myfrog.com* at port 3232 via HTTP. Once retrieved, the browser will look for an anchor with the **NAME** attribute value "*cheeks*" and will render the page such that the text labeled by this anchor is prominently displayed, usually by placing it at the top of the browser window.

```
http://mr.grumpy.edu/cgi-bin/barf.pl/bad/mood?bad-day#greeting
```

References the program *barf.pl* accessible via the HTTP server running on the machine *mr.grumpy.edu*. When accessed, the extra path information *bad/mood* is passed to the program, along with the query string `bad-day`. Once the data from the gateway program are returned to the browser, the browser will look for an anchor with the **NAME** attribute value "*greeting*" and will display the text labeled by this anchor.

```
http://www.utoronto.ca/
http://www.utoronto.ca
```

Accesses the root directory of the indicated HTTP server. A server can be configured to deliver a standard HTML document, a listing of the directory contents, or an error message. Since there is no directory or file specified in the URL, the trailing slash is optional.

HTTPS URLs—Secure HTTP

Many commercial Web browsers (in particular, those from Netscape) support **https** URLs. Such URLs are composed—and behave—in exactly the same way as **http** URLs, the only differences being the default port number (443 for **https**) and the fact that the connection between client and server is encrypted using the

Secure Sockets Layer encryption technology. As a result, data can pass securely between client and server, without being intercepted and read by a third party. The general form for a URL referencing a resource exported by a secure Web server is:

```
https://int.domain.nam:port/resource
```

where the port number is optional and where `resource` specifies the resource on the server. Note that a single machine can run both secure and unsecure Web servers at the same time, since they use different ports. SSL is discussed in more detail in Chapter 9.

LDAP URLs

LDAP, or Lightweight Directory Access Protocol, is a technology that provides corporate directory services—it allows for directory-like information about staff, resources, facilities, addresses, et cetera, accessible from directory servers that can be searched using LDAP requests. As a component of their implementation of LDAP, Netscape developed a now-standardized URL scheme for referencing LDAP directory information from an LDAP server. The general form is:

```
ldap://int.domain.nam:port/ldap-query
```

where *int.domain.nam* is the machine running the LDAP server at the indicated *port* (default value is 389) and *ldap-query* is a query string requesting information from the server. The syntax for such queries is complex and is not reproduced here—in general, a query is composed by the software creating the URL, and not by the user. An example query is:

```
ldap://ldap.utoronto.ca/o=University%20of%Toronto,c=CA
```

which requests directory information about the University of Toronto in Canada.

Ldap URLs are supported by Netscape Navigator 4 and Internet Explorer 4 and later, but are not supported by earlier versions of these (or other) browsers.

LDAPS URLs—Secure LDAP

Ldaps URLs are equivalent to **ldap** URLs, except that the request is addressed to port 636 instead of 389, and the connection to the LDAP server is encrypted. **Ldaps** URLs are supported by Netscape, but only via the conferencing and address book components of Netscape Communicator.

Mailto URLs

The **mailto** URL designates an Internet-format mail address to which mail can be sent. The format is

```
mailto:mail_address
```

where *mail_address* is the Internet mail address (as specified in RFC 822, the document that specifies the format for Internet mail) to which a message can be mailed. Typically, this is of the form *name@host*, where *name* is the user mail account name of the person and *host* is the name of the machine at which the user receives mail. A browser that supports **mailto** will provide a mechanism for users to compose and send a letter to this destination.

Some mail addresses contain the percent character. This character must be encoded, since it is a special character (marking the beginning of a character encoding string). As an example, the e-mail address:

```
jello%ian@irc.utoronto.ca
```

must be converted into the **mailto** URL:

```
mailto:jello%25ian@irc.utoronto.ca
```

A **mailto** URL does not indicate how the mail should be sent. In general, a client mail program must contact a *mail server*—a program which validates the mail and forwards it to its destination. **Mailto** URLs do not specify a mail server—this information must be separately configured into a browser. Web browsers usually provide a configuration menu for this purpose.

Specifying Subject and Other Mail Message Information

When composing a URL to send a mail message, authors often want to include information beyond just the destination address. For example, the author may want to specify a default subject line or perhaps give alternate (CC'd) mail destinations for the letter.

One proposed approach for specifying the subject line is to place the message subject in a **TITLE** attribute of the element containing the **mailto** reference (typically an **A** or **FORM**). Thus elements of the form

```
<A HREF="mailto:address" TITLE="Message title">.....</A>
<FORM ACTION="mailto:address" ... TITLE="Message title"> ...
```

would use the **TITLE** value as the subject when composing the message. This approach, within the context of **A**, is supported by some versions of the lynx browser.

Netscape Navigator developers took a different approach and decided to include the information as query string information within the **mailto** URL itself. This is done by appending any required mail header in URL-encoded format, using strings of the form *header=value*, where *header* is the mail header name (URL-encoded) and *value* is the (URL-encoded) string to associate with the name. For example, to send a message to the address *address*, specifying a given title and a list of CC recipients, the URL would be

```
mailto:address?subject=test%20mail%20message&cc=address1%2caddress2
```

which associates the subject line "test mail message" to the indicated address, as well as the two indicated CC'd addresses. Notice how the different values are separated by the ampersand character (as with **FORM** data encoding) and that all special characters in the fields are encoded via their URL-encoded values.

If a **mailto** URL appears in a hyperlink, then any headers that do not correspond to headers that can be edited in a mail authoring tool are ignored and are not added to the letter. On the other hand, if the **mailto** appears within a **FORM** that is using the POST method to send mail, then all headers present in the URL are generated, even if they are not understood by the mail client. However, headers that should not be altered (return address, content type, etc.) cannot be changed by the **mailto** URL, and in these cases the information in the URL is ignored. The list of mail headers that cannot be overridden is:

Apparently-to	BCC	Content-encoding
Content-length	Content-transfer-encoding	Content-type
Date	Distribution	FCC
Followup-to	From	Lines
MIME-version	Message-ID	Newsgroup
Organization	Reply-To	Sender
X-UIDL	XREF	

Netscape 4 also allows for the inclusion of the actual message *body* within the URL, via the syntax:

```
mailto:address@domain.com?subject=xxxx?body=body-of-message
```

where the special keyword *body* is equal to the content of the message. This is not supported by Netscape Navigator 3 or earlier.

There is an obvious problem with this approach— it does not work with other browsers, in particular Internet Explorer 4, which assume the extra text to be part of the mail address. Fortunately, the address fields can be hand-edited before sending the letter—provided the user understands the problem and how to fix it.

Mid URLs

Mid URLs reference specific mail or USENET messages, or can reference a specific body part of a specific message. Thus, **mid** URLs can be thought of as a generalization of **cid** URLs, which reference parts within a given message. A **mid** URL takes one of the following two forms:

```
mid:message-id
mid:message-id/content-id
```

The first form references an entire message (identified by the Message-ID), while the second form references a particular part (identified by the Content-ID) of a specific multipart message (identified by the Message-ID). Here the *message-id* and *content-id* strings are the URL-encoded versions of the appropriate Message-ID and Content-ID headers, respectively, as defined by the MIME and USENET message protocols.

Mid URLs are supported by the Netscape Communicator mail, news, and HTML authoring clients, but only within the mail or news viewing client (Netscape Messenger). They are not understood by the Navigator 4 browser. However, the clients ignore the Message-ID portion of the URL and assume that the reference is internal within the displayed document. Essentially, then, Netscape treats **mid** URLs as equivalent to **cid** URLs. **Mid** URLs are not supported by Internet Explorer 4.

The following are two examples:

```
Mid:12311-123124123@flopsy.org
mid:12411-123124123@flopsy.org/part3-12432-1212@flopsy.org
```

An author would only rarely type a **mid** URL, as they are typically generated by the tool that assembles a mail message or newsgroup posting.

Mid URLs are related to **cid** (Content Identifier) URLs, discussed earlier in this chapter.

News URLs

News URLs reference USENET newsgroups or individual USENET news articles. There are several ways to compose **news** URLs. Particular newsgroups are specified using the form

```
news:news.group.name
```

where *news.group.name* is the name of a particular newsgroup. The special form

```
news:*
```

references *all* available newsgroups. Note that this does not specify an NNTP server from which news can be accessed. This must be specified elsewhere, in a browser-specific manner. Most browsers let the user set the name of the news server using a pull-down menu, while on UNIX systems it is set by defining the server domain name in an NNTPSERVER environment variable.

Referencing Particular News Articles

An alternative form is used to request particular news articles. The form is

```
news:message_id@domain.name.edu
```

where *message_id* is the unique ID associated with a particular article originating from the machine *domain.name.edu* (this is all discussed in gruesome detail in

RFC 1036, referenced at the end of the chapter). The at (@) character is special in a **news** URL and indicates this alternative form of reference. This format is not generally useful, since most news servers delete articles after a few days or weeks, so that any referenced article is soon unavailable.

Referencing Both Server and Newsgroup

A third form, not part of the official URL standard but widely supported, references both the newsgroup and the server from which the articles should be retrieved or both the server and a particular article. The two forms are

```
news://int.domain.nam:port/news.group.name
news://int.domain.nam:port/message_id@domain.name.edu
```

where *int.domain.nam* is the domain name of the server to be contacted, *:port* is the optional port number (the default value is 119), *news.group.name* is the desired newsgroup, and *message_id* and *domain.name.edu* form the message ID for a specific message posted from the machine at *domain.name.edu*.

Snews URLs—Secure News

Many commercial Web browsers (in particular, those from Netscape) support **snews** URLs. Such URLs are composed—and behave—in exactly the same way as **news** URLs, the only difference being the default port number (563 for **snews**) and the fact that the connection between client and server is encrypted using the Secure Sockets Layer encryption technology. As a result, data can pass securely between client and server, without being intercepted and read by a third party. To access summary listings for a newsgroup accessible via a secure news server, the URL would be:

```
snews:news.group.name
```

The identity of the news server is in general set using browser Configure menus. SSL is discussed in more detail in Chapter 9.

NNTP URLs

In principle, the **nntp** URL scheme provides a way of explicitly referencing a news article from a particular NNTP news server. An example **nntp** URL might be

```
nntp://news.server.com/alt.rubber-chickens/12311121.121@foo.org
```

which references article number *12311121.121@foo.org*, in the newsgroup *alt.rubber-chickens*, from the NNTP server running on the machine *news.server.com* (at the default port number 119). The NNTP protocol is described in RFC 977, should you want additional details.

NOTE: Nntp Functionality Within News URLs

Essentially all the functionality of **nntp** URLs has been added to **news** URLs by allowing server domain name specification in the **news** URL, as described above. It is thus unlikely that **nntp** URLs will be widely implemented. At present, few browsers support this URL scheme.

Prospero URLs

This scheme references resources accessible using the Prospero Directory Service, which acts as a sophisticated caching and proxying service for directory, file, and other data. Prospero URLs take the form

```
prospero://int.domain.nam:port/string/stuff
```

which references a prospero server running at the indicated machine and port (the default port is 1525), the remaining portion of the string indicating the desired resource.

NOTE: Prospero URLs Are Not Widely Supported

Very few Web browsers (i.e., practically none) support **prospero** URLs, so that this form is not discussed in detail here. Further information is found in the references at the end of the chapter.

Telnet URLs

Telnet URLs reference a Telnet link to a remote machine. An example is

```
telnet://int.domain.nam:port
```

where *int.domain.nam* is the machine to which a connection should be made, and the optional *:port* specifies the desired port (the default value is 32). A more general form is

```
telnet://username:password@int.domain.nam:port/
```

to indicate the *username* and *password* that the user should employ (the *:password* is optional). The colon (:) and at (@) characters are special in a **telnet** URL, since they designate the different fields in this form. In general, the username and password information are not directly used by a browser to complete the connection. Rather, this information may be presented to users as a hint as to what they should do once the connection is made. Obviously you do not want to use this more general form if you want to keep a password secret!

Tn3270 and Rlogin URLs

Some browsers support a variant of a **telnet** URL, called a **tn3270** URL, which references a connection requiring IBM 3270 terminal emulation on the part of the client. In general, this is only useful if the client computer supports a tn3270 client program (tn3270 clients are rarely built into Web browsers) and provided the browser knows about this program. If not, most browsers default to a regular Telnet connection.

A few browsers support rlogin connections via **rlogin** URLs. The specification is

```
rlogin://username@int.domain.nam
```

where *username* is the account name for the rlogin. The user will be prompted for a password in the resulting window unless one is not required. Most browsers that support this emulate **rlogin** URLs using a Telnet connection. As these are not widely supported, it is best to stick to **telnet** URLs.

WAIS URLs

WAIS servers can be accessed via URLs in a manner similar to HTTP servers. The major difference is in the file specification: The URL must pass the correct search instructions to the WAIS server, in addition to information about what is to be searched.

The standard form for accessing a WAIS server is

```
wais://int.domain.nam:port/database?search
```

where *int.domain.nam* is the Internet domain name of the host running a WAIS server at the indicated port (the default port is 210); *database* is the name of the WAIS database to be searched; and *search* is a list of search instructions to pass to the database. Another form is (leaving out the port number for brevity)

```
wais://int.domain.nam/database
```

which designates a particular searchable database. A browser will understand that this URL references a searchable database and will prompt for query string input.

Finally, **wais** URLs can reference individual resources on a WAIS database. The form for this URL is:

```
wais://int.domain.nam/database/wais_type/resource_path
```

where *wais_type* is a type indicator, which gives the type of the object being accessed, and *resource_path* is the document ID, used internally by the WAIS database. In general these strings are generated by the WAIS server itself, and it is rare that a user (or document author) will actually compose the *wais_type* and *resource_path* fields.

Most browsers do not support **wais** URLs directly, and instead must forward WAIS queries through a WAIS proxy, identified via a browser's proxy configuration menu.

Special Class ID URLs

There are several special URL formats that currently are only used as **CLASSID** attribute values of **OBJECT** elements. These URLs define class **ID** values for special classes of executable objects, so that the syntax of the URL schemes varies widely depending on the object type. In addition, the URL syntax does not, in general, specify the location of the object—this must be obtained from an object catalog, maintained by the browser, or from the **CODEBASE** attribute.

Clsid URLs

Clsid URLs were introduced by Microsoft, and are used, within an **OBJECT** element, to reference an Active-X/COM class to be *instantiated* (loaded and run) when the object is created. The general form for a **clsid** URL is

```
clsid:class-id
```

where *class-id* is the identifier for the desired COM class. An example is:

```
clsid:EFE6733J-1321-43Cf-J43B-08113F412501
```

Clsid URLs are only valid within an **OBJECT** element, as the value of the **CLASSID** attribute. They are currently only supported by Internet Explorer 3 and 4.

Java URLs

Java URLs were introduced by Netscape and are used, within an **OBJECT** element, to reference a Java class to be instantiated and run. The general form is

```
java:packagelocation.packageobject
```

where *packagelocation* is the location of the package containing the desired class, and *packageobject* is the name of the class to be run. An example is:

```
java:myjava.applet.start.class
```

which references an applet from my personal applet collection. **Java** URLs are only valid within an **OBJECT** element, as the value of the **CLASSID** attribute.

Javabean URLs

Javabean URLs were introduced by Netscape to identify java objects built using the special *JavaBean* library. Thus, referencing a JavaBean tells the browser which other supporting classes will be required. The general form is:

```
javabean:packagelocation.packageobject
```

where *packagelocation* is the location of the package containing the desired class and *packageobject* is the name of the class to be run. An example is:

```
javabean:netscape.application.Button
```

which references a Netscape Internet Foundation Class (IFC) button object. Note that **javabean** URLs are only valid within an **OBJECT** element, as the value of the **CLASSID** attribute. They are only supported by Netscape Navigator 4.

"Pseudo"-URLs

Last, there are several, often proprietary, "pseudo"-URLs frequently seen in a browser's Location window. The most common such schemes are **about, javascript, mailbox, res, view-source**, and **wysiwyg**. There are no formal specifications for these URLs: Indeed, the **about** URL was initially introduced—partly as a practical joke—by the Netscape development team, while the **javascript** URL was introduced to allow for easy testing of typed-in strings of JavaScript code. In general, these schemes are not of use to an author, although it is always nice to know what they mean! However, the special `about:blank` URL turned out to have several practical uses, such that this form is now supported by most browsers. Similarly, **javascript** URLs proved to be a simple (if not ideal) way of binding script programs to hypertext anchors, so that this URL form is also widely supported by browser vendors.

About URLs

About URLs reference general information about the browser. This URL format was invented by Netscape as a tool for displaying information about the browser and also for presenting personal information about the browser developers. For example, the URL `about:mozilla` references (only on Netscape Navigator) a brief page that reflects the youthful enthusiasm of the Netscape developers (just try it!), while the URLs `about:marca` and `about:ebina` provide information about Marc Andreessen and Eric Bina, two of the co-founders of Netscape Inc. Needless to say, these three URLs do not work on Internet Explorer!

There are, however, four **about** URLs with practical uses. These are:

`about:` (Netscape Navigator only) Provides some practical information about the browser, such as the version number, or the list of software packages licensed, by Netscape, for use within the browser. This is equivalent to the "Help...About" menu item.

`about:blank` (Netscape Navigator and Internet Explorer) Requests that the browser render a blank page, using the browser's default background color. This is useful for creating a blank window or a blank frame within a **FRAME** document. The latter can be accomplished, for example, via **FRAME** elements of the form:

```
<FRAME SRC="about:blank" NAME="frame-name">
<FRAME SRC="about:"      NAME="frame-name">
```

The above elements are identical and simply illustrate the two ways in which **about** can create a blank frame.

About:cache (Netscape Navigator only) Requests that the browser list the files stored in the browser cache. Note that for large cache sizes, this can cause the computer (in particular, Windows 95 or Macintosh machines) to "freeze" for several minutes as the cache is processed.

About:plugins (Netscape Navigator only) Requests that the browser list all the plugins installed on the Web browser. This lists the MIME types, the name of the company providing each plugin, and the typical filename suffixes associated with the MIME type.

Javascript URLs

Javascript URLs encode JavaScript program code within a URL. The general form is

```
javascript:javascript-statements
```

where *javascript-statements* is a semicolon-separated list of valid JavaScript statements. This URL can, on Netscape Navigator and Internet Explorer 4 (but not Internet Explorer 3), be typed directly into the "Open File" or "Location" window, thereby providing an easy way to test simple JavaScript expressions. For example, typing the URL

```
javascript:alert('Hi Mom!')
```

into the browser's "Location" window will tell the browser to pop up a JavaScript alert window with the associated text.

With Netscape Navigator, the special URL `javascript:`—that is, a **javascript** URL without any JavaScript statements—causes the browser to display a special JavaScript type-in field at the bottom of the browser window. This is useful for testing small pieces of JavaScript code. The results of running the typed-in JavaScript commands are displayed in the portion of the browser window above the type-in field.

Javascript URLs can be used, within a hypertext anchor, to invoke a JavaScript program when the hypertext link is accessed. Example markup is:

```
<A HREF="javascript:anchor_handler()">anchored text</a>
```

where the function *anchor_handler()* is a JavaScript function to run when the link is accessed. Similarly, the **SRC** element of an **IMG** element can take a **javascript** URL value, but note that the script must then pass an image to the **IMG** element object so that the element has something to display.

Of course, using **javascript** URLs in these contexts means that the documents will be improperly rendered—or will not function at all—if JavaScript is disabled or is not supported by the browser. A more reasonable approach is to use the **onClick** (or other) event-handling attributes for the **A** and **IMG** elements, as discussed in Chapter 7.

NOTE: JavaScript URLs Not Fully Supported in Internet Explorer 3

Internet Explorer 3 does not support JavaScript URLs that are typed directly into the Location window of the browser. However, the browser does support JavaScript URLs that are present as values of hypertext anchor HREF attributes.

Mailbox URLs (Netscape Navigator 4 Only)

Mailbox URLs reference the local mail client on the browser. With Netscape Navigator 4, a **mailbox** URL causes the browser to launch the mail client (usually Netscape Messenger) and open the mailbox defined in the body of the URL. For example, the URL

```
mailbox:inbox
```

will open the folder named "Inbox," which, with Netscape *Messenger*, is the default name for the folder containing incoming, unread mail. If no folder is specified (i.e., `mailbox:`), then the mail client is launched, and the user must choose a mailbox to open. If the URL specifies a mailbox that does not exist, then the mail client is not launched. Netscape Navigator 4 also uses **mailbox** URLs to display, on the Navigator browser, resources that are referenced within mail or newsgroup messages via **cid** or **mid** URLs.

Res URLs (Internet Explorer 4 Only)

Res URLs reference a resource that can be retrieved from a software module, or *DLL* (Dynamic Load Library), accessible to the browser. The general form is:

```
res://resource-file/res-type/res-id
```

where *resource-file* is the path to and name of the file containing the module, *res-type* is an optional string that defines the resource type, and *res-id* is the specific identifier for the resource within the module. An example is:

```
res://mymodule.dll/doc23.html
```

The use of **res** URLs requires a detailed understanding of the Active-X model for data storage within DLLs. For those interested, this information is available at the Microsoft Web site, at:

www.microsoft.com/msdn/sdk/inetsdk/help/itt/protocols/protocols.html

View-Source URLs (Netscape Navigator 4 Only)

View-source URLs cause a Netscape browser to render a source listing of the referenced resource. The value for the **view-source** URL must be the URL of the resource to be displayed, for example:

```
view-source:http://www.utoronto.ca/home.html
```

View-source URLs are used internally by the Netscape Navigator software to generate source listings and should not be used in HTML documents.

Wysiwyg URLs (Netscape Navigator 4 Only)

Wysiwyg URLs are used internally by Netscape Navigator's JavaScript engine and denote certain cases where JavaScript code produces the document content being displayed by the browser. Authors should never themselves code (or need to code) **wysiwyg** URLs—but it is always nice to know where they came from!

Coming Attractions

Several other special-purpose URL schemes have recently been defined and are being deployed in a variety of applications. For example, the **imap** scheme designates IMAP mail servers, mailboxes, messages, and search programs on Internet hosts, and is used to locate mail messages on IMAP servers. This serves as a useful complement to the **cid** and **mid** URLs.

The **nfs** URL scheme has been proposed as the foundation of a distributed, Web-based filesystem. NFS is a distributed filesystem architecture, commonly used on UNIX systems, and **nfs** URLs provide a way of referencing NFS-accessible resources. Netscape Navigator supports **nfs** URLs, but only via specially equipped proxy servers.

Also of interest are the various **z39.50** URL schemes. Z39.50 is an information retrieval protocol commonly used by indexed databases such as libraries. **Z39.50** URLs provide a standard syntax for encoding Z39.50-format database queries within a URL.

Other schemes, such as **irc** (for Internet Relay Chat sessions), **vemmi** (for a distributed multimedia/videotex standard), **whois++** (for referencing WHOIS++ servers), and **tv** (for referencing TV broadcasts!), have also been proposed. These schemes are not discussed here—information about these proposals can be found in the references at the end of the chapter.

Naming Schemes for the Web

The URL scheme is the only naming scheme currently used on the Web, but it is not the only such scheme—several others have been proposed and are likely to be implemented in the future. This brief section summarizes the names and general features of the different proposed schemes. The "Proposed URL Schemes and Updates" portion of the "References" section at the end of this chapter provide pointers to additional discussions on these topics.

Uniform Resource Names: URN

Uniform Resource Names, or URNs, are designed to be a location-independent way of referencing an object. Thus, a URN would not specify the location of the desired resource, but would specify a generic name. The software processing the name would then locate the named object at the closest or most accessible location, using a name lookup service.

The specification of URNs is still being developed by the URN working group of the IETF; the working group home page, at www.ietf.org/html-charters/urn-charter.html, lists the standards documents arising from this group's efforts. You should visit this site for up-to-date information.

Uniform Resource Locator: URL

Uniform Resource Locators, or URLs, are protocol- and location- specific schemes for referencing resources on the Internet. This is currently the only implemented mechanism for referencing resources on the Internet.

Uniform Resource Identifier: URI

Uniform Resource Identifiers, or URIs, generically represent any naming schemes used to reference resources on the Internet. Thus, both URLs and URNs fall under the category of URIs. The names URI and URL are often used synonymously, but this is only correct in the absence of a defined naming scheme for URNs.

Uniform Resource Citation: URC

Uniform Resource Citations, or URCs, were designed to be collections of attribute/value pairs that describe a particular object (referenced using a URI). Some of the values in these pairs could also be URIs. A URC can act in many ways, for example as a cross-indexing resource for a large resource collection or simply as a collection of references to related data. The specification for URCs is not complete, so that they are not in current use. Indeed, the URC idea is being completely rethought, with the intention of using the new eXtensible Markup Language (*XML*) as the tool for recording URC-like data within an XML catalog document. Additional information can be found in the *Addressing* and *XML* sections of the World Wide Web Consortium (W3C) site, at www.w3.org.

References

The URI specifications originate from the various working groups currently developing Internet and Web standards. In most cases, the Internet protocols or standards are formalized in documents known as Requests for Comments, or RFCs. Once approved by the appropriate Internet Engineering Task Force (IETF), these documents are officially numbered, giving rise to the referenced RFC numbers quoted here. Note that the draft documents that precede an RFC, with names like "draft-masinter-url-data-03.txt," evolve with time, each new version having a new version number (e.g., "draft-masinter-url-data-04.txt," and so on). Thus, if you cannot locate the draft document listed here, try looking for an updated version with a higher version number.

Overviews and Defined URL Schemes

www.w3.org/Addressing/Addressing.html	(Overview of issues)
www.w3.org/Addressing/schemes	(List of proposed URL schemes)
ds.internic.net/rfc/rfc1738.txt	(Standard URL specification)
ds.internic.net/rfc/rfc1808.txt	(Relative URL specification)
ds.internic.net/rfc/rfc2056.txt	(Z39.50r & X39.50s URLs)
ds.internic.net/rfc/rfc2111.txt	(Cid and Mid URLs)
ds.internic.net/rfc/rfc2192.txt	(IMAP URLs)
ds.internic.net/rfc/rfc1959.txt	(LDAP URLs)
ds.internic.net/rfc/rfc2224.txt	(NFS URLs)
ds.internic.net/rfc/rfc2122.txt	(VEMMI URLs)
ds.internic.net/internet-drafts/ draft-masinter-url-data-03.txt	(DATA URLs)

Proposed URL Schemes and Updates

www.w3.org/Addressing/clsid-scheme	(CLSID URLs)
developer.netscape.com/library/wpapers/ beanconnect/index.html	(JavaBean URLs)
www.w3.org/Addressing/ draft-mirashi-url-irc-01.txt	(IRC URLs)
ds.internic.net/internet-drafts/ draft-zigmond-tv-url-00.txt	(TV URLs)
ds.internic.net/ draft-ietf—asid-whois-url-01.txt	(Whois++ URLs)
www.utoronto.ca/ian/books/html4ed/chap8/ mail.html	(Netscape mailto URL extensions)
ds.internic.net/internet-drafts/ draft-hoffman-mailto-url-01.txt	(Mailto URL update)
ds.internic.net/internet-drafts/ draft-casey-url-ftp-00.txt	(FTP URL update)

Protocol and Data Format Specifications

ds.internic.net/rfc/rfc822.txt	(Internet Mail messages)
ds.internic.net/rfc/rfc1036.txt	(Usenet messages)
ds.internic.net/rfc/rfc977.txt	(NNTP protocol)
www.sco.com/skunkprev/Skunk96/src/Tools/ freeWAIS-sf-2.1/doc/original-TM-wais/	(WAIS documentation)

ds.internic.net/rfc/rfc1625.txt   (WAIS protocol)
ftp://prospero.isi.edu/pub/prospero/doc/   (Prospero documentation)

URI Specification

ds.internic.net/rfc/rfc1630.txt

URNs: Uniform Resource names

ds.internic.net/rfc/rfc1737.txt   (Functional requirements for URNs)
www.ietf.org/html.charters/   (IETF URN working group
   urn-charter.html   information)

THE HTTP PROTOCOL

To develop truly interactive HTML-based applications, a Web designer must understand how a Web client program, such as a browser, interacts with an HTTP server. This interaction involves two distinct but related issues. The first is HTTP—the protocol by which a client program sends information to an HTTP server and vice versa. HTTP supports mechanisms for communicating information about the transaction, such as the transaction status (successful or not) and the nature of the data being sent (i.e., what is the MIME type of the data) on top of mechanisms for sending data from client to server or from server to client. The protocol also supports several communication *methods* (for example, *GET, POST,* or *HEAD*) for specifying *how* message data is being sent by the browser or how the request should be handled by the server. This chapter presents a detailed description of these mechanisms and of how they work.

The second issue is the manner in which servers *handle* a request. If the requested resource is a file, the server locates the file and sends it back to the client or sends an appropriate error message if the file is unavailable. However, the requested resource (specified by the URL) in some cases is not a file, but rather a request for special processing at the server end of the transaction, such as a database query. In most cases, the Web server does not do this processing, since such tasks are specific to the applications running at the Web site and do not reflect "generic" functionality that can be easily incorporated in a "universal" server. Instead, most servers "hand off" these application-specific tasks to other programs, called *gateway programs*. These programs run independent of (but can communicate with) the HTTP server and are designed explicitly for the special processing required at a Web site. The *Common Gateway Interface* (CGI) specification, described in Chapter 10, defines how HTTP servers communicate with these gateway programs.[1]

---

[1] Most servers now support compiled modules that can be dynamically linked to the server and that support gateway-like functionality, with significant performance improvements over the CGI approach. This mechanism and the advantages and disadvantages of this approach are also discussed in Chapter 10.

This chapter first outlines the general principles of the HTTP protocol and then illustrates its operation using seven example transactions. The chapter concludes with a detailed list of the control messages that can be sent from client to server, and vice versa.

Like HTML, HTTP is evolving, with new features being added in later versions of the protocol. This chapter primarily discusses HTTP 1.0, as this is the current, universally supported protocol—Netscape Navigator 4 does not support HTTP 1.1, while Internet Explorer 4 only supports HTTP 1.1 for certain types of client-server connections. Note, however, that a few HTTP 1.1 features, particularly important for controlling the client-server connection, were incorporated as "extensions" to HTTP 1.0 and are supported by most Web browsers and HTTP 1.0 Web servers. These extensions are also discussed here. A brief description of the other major differences between HTTP 1.1 and 1.0 are presented later in this chapter.

HTTP Protocol Overview

HTTP, or HyperText Transfer Protocol, is an Internet client-server protocol designed for the rapid and efficient delivery of hypertext materials. HTTP is a stateless protocol, which means that once a server has delivered the requested data to a client, the client-server connection is broken, and the server retains no memory of the event that just took place.

All HTTP communication transmits data as a stream of 8-bit characters or *octets*. This ensures the safe transmission of all forms of data, including images, executable programs, and HTML documents.

A typical HTTP 1.0 session has four stages:

Client opens the connection. The client program (for example, a Web browser) contacts the server at the specified Internet address and port number (the default port is 80).

Client makes the request. The client sends a message to the server requesting service. The request has either one or two parts. The first part is an HTTP *request header,* specifying the *HTTP method* to be used during the transaction and providing information about the capabilities of the client and about the data being sent to the server (if any). Typical HTTP methods are *GET*, for getting an object from a server, and *POST*, for posting (sending) data to a resource (e.g., a gateway program) on the server. The second part of the message consists of the data being sent by the client to the server—this part is absent if no data are being sent.

Server sends a response. The server sends a response to the client. This consists of either one or two parts. The first part is the *response header* describing the state of the transaction (e.g., was the transaction successful, or not) and the type of data being sent (if any), and the second part is the data being returned (if any).

Server closes the connection. The connection is closed; the server does not retain any knowledge of the transaction just completed.

This procedure means that each connection processes a single transaction and can therefore download only a single data file to the client, while the stateless nature means that each connection knows nothing about previous connections. The implications of these features are illustrated in the following two illustrations.

NOTE: HTTP 1.0 Extension—HTTP Keep-alive

Most HTTP 1.0-capable browsers and servers support an HTTP 1.0 extension known as *keep-alive*, which keeps the client-server connection open whenever a client requests multiple resources from the same server. In terms of the preceding model for HTTP transactions, this means that step 4 (the closing of the connection) is deferred—instead, the next request starts at step 2 and does not require the reopening of the connection. Note, however, that the server still does not retain knowledge of a transaction after it sends its response (step 3). Keep-alive is an integrated core feature of HTTP 1.1.

Illustration: Single Transaction per Connection

Assume that HTTP is used to access an HTML document that contains, via **IMG** element references, 10 inline images. Displaying the document requires 11 distinct connections to the HTTP server—one to retrieve the HTML document itself and 10 others to retrieve the 10 image files.

If this transaction is repeated using keep-alive, the browser still retrieves 11 distinct files, but the connection between browser and server is only broken after the last image has been downloaded. This can significantly speed up the downloading of composite documents, since the connection is only opened and closed once, not 11 times. However, as far as the browser and server are concerned, each request is a single transaction, and the server does not retain knowledge of each transaction after it is completed, even if the connection to the client is still open.

Illustration: Stateless Connections

Assume that a user retrieves, from a server, an HTML **FORM** containing a fill-in field for a user name—by typing in a name, the user is able to access name-specific information in a personnel database. When the user submits the **FORM**, the name (and any other information gathered by the **FORM**) is sent to a gateway program residing on the server that processes of the request; the URL that references this gateway program is specified as a **FORM** element attribute, as discussed in Chapter 6.

This gateway program processes the data and returns a second HTML document containing the results, along with another **FORM** allowing further requests of the database. But, in this case, the **FORM** does not contain a place to type a name. Since the server is stateless and has no memory of the first connection, how will it know the name of the person when data from this second form are sent to the server?

The answer is that the server does not know the name. Rather, the application designer must write software such that the gateway programs explicitly keep track of this information. One way to do so is to hide the name information *inside* the **FORM** returned to the user. This can be accomplished using special *hidden* input elements of the form `<INPUT TYPE="hidden" ...>`. In the case of this simple example, the element might be:

```
<INPUT TYPE="hidden" NAME="name_of_person" VALUE="user_name">
```

Then, when the user submits the second **FORM**, the content of the hidden element is sent along with any new input, thereby returning the user name to the server.

Information that tracks the history of a sequence of transactions is often called *state information*. Using hidden elements, state information can be passed back and forth between client and server, preserving knowledge of the name for each subsequent transaction.

Example HTTP Client-Server Sessions

The easiest way to understand HTTP is through simple examples. The following sections present seven examples covering the most common HTTP methods. Each presentation shows both the data sent from the client to the HTTP server and the data returned from the server to the client. First, a few words about how this "eavesdropping" was accomplished.

Monitoring Client-Server Interaction

It is easy to monitor the interaction between HTTP servers and Web clients, since the communication is entirely in character data sent to a particular port (a port is a bit like a telephone extension, at which data can be sent or received). Consequently, all you need do is *listen* at a port or *talk* to a port. You can listen at a port using the program *listen* or *backtalk*,[2] while you can talk to a port using *backtalk* or the standard Internet program *telnet*.

Client Sending to Server

You can use *listen* to find out what a Web client sends to a server. To do this, you run the *listen* program on a computer and make a Web client talk to *listen*. As an example, suppose *listen* is started on the computer with domain name *leonardo.subnet.ca*. When started, *listen* indicates the port number it is listening at by printing a message such as:

---

[2] The programs *listen* and *backtalk* are available, in source code form, from the book's supporting Web site, available at www.wiley.com/compbooks/graham/.

```
listening at port 1743
```

It then falls silent, waiting to print any data that arrive at this port. The next step is to configure a Web client so that it sends HTTP requests to this port. This is done by accessing a URL that *points* to port 1743 on *leonardo.subnet.ca*, for example:

```
http://leonardo.subnet.ca:1743/Tests/file.html
```

where the port number is marked in boldface. The client dutifully sends the HTTP request headers to port number 1743 on *leonardo.subnet.ca, w*hereupon *listen* receives the data and prints them to the screen.

Server Sending to Client

Determining what the server sends back to the client takes a bit more work. In this case, you can use Telnet to connect to the server, but you must now enter by hand the HTTP request headers that are sent by a "real" client (and which you fortunately intercepted using the *listen* program, using the procedure described in the previous section). Suppose, for example, that a server is running at port 80 on *leonardo.subnet.ca*. You can connect to this server by simply making a telnet connection to this port. On a UNIX system, you would type (the typed command string is in boldface):

```
telnet leonardo.subnet.ca 80
Trying 128.100.121.33...
Connected to leonardo.subnet.ca
Escape character is '^]'.
```

Telnet gives three lines of information to explain what it is doing and then falls silent. Whatever you now type is sent to the server running on *leonardo.subnet.ca*, so you now type in the required request headers. Whatever the server sends in response is sent to the *telnet* program and printed on the screen.

Another useful tool is the program *backtalk*. *Backtalk* is a derivative of *listen* that allows you both to monitor data arriving at a port and send data to the remote program talking to that port. When launched, *backtalk* allocates a port and, like *listen*, prints out the port number, for example:

```
listening at port 1743
```

Thereafter, *backtalk* prints to the display anything that a remote program sends to port 1743, while anything typed into the console is sent out through port 1743 back to the remote program. Thus you can use *backtalk* to mimic the response of an HTTP server, albeit by hand. This is useful for examining client response to special server response headers, such as a request for user authentication.

Overview of Examples

The tools just described were used to determine the information passed between the client and server in several typical HTTP transactions. The examples that follow look at:

13. a simple GET method request

14. a simple GET method request, illustrating some newer header fields

15. a HEAD method request for file meta-information

16. a GET method request with a query string within the URL

17. a GET method request arising from an HTML **FORM** submission

18. a POST method request arising from an HTML **FORM** submission

19. a file access request requiring "Basic" user authentication

To get the most out of these examples, you will need a basic understanding of URLs and of the way data are gathered by an HTML form and composed as a message for the server. These topics were covered in Chapters 6 (**FORM**s) and 8 (construction of query strings).

Basic Elements of an HTTP Session

When a client contacts a server, it sends a *request header* defining the details of the request, followed by any data the client may be sending. In response, the server returns a *response header* describing the status of the transaction, followed in turn by any data being returned. The first example illustrates the basics of this flow of information.

Example 13: A Simple GET Method Request

This example looks at how a client makes a GET request for a document resource from an HTTP server and at how a server responds to the request. In practice, such a transaction would be initiated on a browser by clicking on a hypertext anchor pointing to the server and the desired file—for example:

```
<A HREF="http://smaug.middle.earth.ca:2021/Tests/file.html">anchor text</A>
```

For this example (and for Examples 14 and 15), we assume this anchor was accessed from a document previously retrieved from the URL:

```
http://www.utoronto.ca/webdocs/webinfo.html
```

That is, the user first accessed the document *webinfo.html* and within this page selected the anchor that retrieved the test file. The analysis is broken into the two basic parts: the passing of the request to the server and the response sent by the server back to the client.

The Client Request Header

Figure 9.1 shows the actual data sent by an old client (Netscape Navigator 1.01!) to the server. Other clients send qualitatively the same information (we will look at some others later on). The dots indicate `Accept` header fields omitted to save space.

This request message consists of a *request header* containing several *request header fields*. Each field is a line of ASCII text, terminated by a carriage-return linefeed character pair (CRLF). A blank line containing only a CRLF pair marks the end of the request header and the beginning of any *data* being sent from the client to the server. This example transaction does not send data to the server, so the blank line is the end of the request.

The request header contains two parts. The first part—the first line of the header—is called the *method* field. This field specifies the HTTP *method* to be used, the location of the desired resource on the server (as a URL), and the version of the HTTP protocol the client program would like to use. This is followed by several HTTP *request* fields, which provide information to the server about the client and about the nature of the data (if any) being sent by the client to the server.

Client Request: Method Field

The method field contains three text fields, separated by whitespace (whitespace is any combination of space and/or tab characters). The general form for this field is:

```
HTTP_method   identifier   HTTP_version
```

which, in our example, was:

```
GET /path/file.html HTTP/1.0
```

Figure 9.1 Data sent from a Netscape Navigator 1.01 client to an HTTP server during a simple GET request. Comments are in italics.

```
GET /Tests/file.html HTTP/1.0
Accept: text/plain
.

.
Accept: */*
If-Modified-Since: Wed, 25 Sep 1996 17:23:31 GMT
Referer: http://www.utoronto.ca/webdocs/webinfo.html
User-Agent: Mozilla/1.01
          [a blank line, containing only CRLF ]
```

The three components of this method field are:

HTTP_method The HTTP method specification—GET in this example. The method specifies what is to be done to the object specified by the URL. Some others common methods are HEAD, which requests header information about an object, and POST, which is used to send information to the object.

identifier The identifier of the resource. In this example, the identifier, /path/file.html, is the URL stripped of the protocol and Internet domain name strings. If this were a request to a *proxy server*, it would be the entire URL. Proxy servers are discussed later in this chapter.

HTTP_version The HTTP protocol version used by the client; HTTP/1.0 for Netscape Navigator 4 and earlier.

Client Request: Accept Field

The example shows several additional request headers. The Accept fields contain a list of data types, expressed as MIME content-types, which tell the server what type of data the client is willing to accept. MIME types are discussed in more detail later in this chapter; see also Appendix B, "Multipurpose Internet Mail Extensions," available at the companion Web site at www.wiley.com/compbooks/ graham. The meanings for simple requests are relatively straightforward. For example, Accept: text/plain means that the client can accept plain text files, while Accept: audio/* means that the client can accept any form of audio data.

A client can include information in accept headers stating the relative desirability of particular types of data. This is expressed through two quantities: the q or quality factor (a number in the range 0.0 to 1.0, where 0.0 is equivalent to not accepting a type, and 1.0 is equivalent to always accepting a type) and mxb, which stands for the maximum size in bytes. If the resource is bigger than the mxb value, then it is not acceptable to the client. The default values are q=1.0 and mxb=undefined (that is, any size is acceptable). Thus the following

```
Accept: image/*
Accept: image/jpeg; q=0.7; mxb=50000
Accept: image/gif; q=0.5
```

mean that the client prefers image/jpeg files, provided they are smaller than 50 KB. If there is a JPEG file, but it is too big, then the client would prefer a GIF. If there are no GIF files, then the client will take any available image file.

Accept types can be combined in a single field if they are separated by commas. For example, the above three fields could be written:

```
Accept: image/*, image/jpeg; q=0.7; mxb=50000, image/gif; q=0.5
```

NOTE: Unreliability of Accept Header Information

In principle, a server or a server-based gateway program can use `Accept` information to decide what type of data to send back to the client. However, very few servers have this capability, while many browsers send the field `Accept: */*`, which indicates that they will accept anything.

Client Request: User-Agent Field

There are several other common request header fields. The `User-agent` field, of the form `User-agent: ascii_string`, provides information about the client making the request. The example gave

```
User-Agent: Mozilla/1.01
```

to indicate the Netscape 1.01 browser (code-named "Mozilla"). Some other examples are:

```
User-Agent: Mozilla/2.02 (Windows 3.1)
User-Agent: Mozilla/3.02 (Win95; I)
User-Agent: Mozilla/4.03 [en] (Win95; I)
User-Agent: Mozilla/2.0 (compatible; MSIE 3.0; Windows 95;1024,768)
User-Agent: Mozilla/4.0 (compatible; MSIE 4.0; Windows 95)
```

The first three correspond to different versions of the Netscape Navigator browser, with the text inside the parentheses providing additional information about the platform (typically, the operating system). This is the correct syntax for including additional browser specific information. The fourth and fifth examples are from Microsoft Internet Explorer 3 and 4, respectively—note how these browsers claim to be a Netscape equivalents, and properly identify themselves only via the text inside the parentheses. Many server gateway programs use the browser identity string to select the type of data to return, and thus Microsoft uses the Mozilla name so that server software will treat the Microsoft product as equivalent to Netscape's.

Client Request: If-Modified-Since Field

A second common header is `If-modified-since`. This contains a time and date, in Greenwich Mean Time, and is used to conditionally retrieve a document (or data) only if the requested resource has been modified since the specified time and date. This is sent by browsers that *cache* local copies of data they have retrieved and records the date and time at which the file was cached. The browser then only needs a new copy of the file if it has changed since the browser last retrieved it. In Figure 9.1, the client sent the header:

```
If-Modified-Since: Wed, 02 Aug 1995 17:23:31 GMT
```

If the requested resource */path/file.html* has been modified since this time and date, then the server sends a new copy to the client. If the resource has not been modified since this time and date, the server does not send a new copy and instead sends a special message indicating that the resource has not changed and that the client should use its existing copy. These messages are discussed in the upcoming section on server response.

Client Request: Referer Field

Another common field is `Referer`, which takes the general form `Referer:` *URL*. This field gives the URL of the document from which the request originated. In our example, we noted in the discussion that the user first accessed the document

www.utoronto.ca/webdocs/webinfo.html

and from there accessed the link producing the request shown in Figure 9.1. Thus, the header field

```
Referer: http://www.utoronto.ca/webdocs/webinfo.html
```

is part of the request header sent to the server. This header is sent by Netscape Navigator 3 and greater and by Internet Explorer 3 and greater.

Request Headers and Gateway Programs

In this example, the request headers are used by the server to determine whether a data file should be sent to the server, and if so, what type of data to send. (Servers can use the `Accept:` fields to decide from amongst a variety of different possible files to return. At present this feature, known as *content* or *format negotiation*, is implemented on several servers.) If the request references a gateway program, then the server cannot make this decision. Instead, the server passes *all* the request header information to the gateway program (as a collection of environment variables) and lets the gateway program decide what to do. Thus, a gateway program author must understand the meanings of these header fields, since he or she will have to write gateway programs that interpret them. A complete list of the possible request headers is given at the end of this chapter, in the section entitled "HTTP Request Header Field Specifications."

The Server Response: Header and Data

When the server receives the request, it tries to apply the designated method (e.g., GET or POST) to the specified object (file or program) and passes the results of this effort back to the client. The returned data are preceded by a *response header* consisting of *response header fields*, which communicate information about the state of the transaction back to the client. As with the request header fields sent from client to server, these are single lines of text terminated by a CRLF, while the end of the response header is indicated by a single blank line containing only a CRLF. The data of the response follow the blank line.

Figure 9.2 shows the data returned by the server in response to the request of Figure 9.1.

The first six lines are the response header. The end of the response header is indicated by the single blank line. The data response of the request (in this case, the requested HTML document) follows this blank line.

Server Response: The Status Line

The first line in the response header is a status line, which lets the client know what protocol the server uses and whether or not the request was successfully completed. The general format for this line is:

```
HTTP/version  status_code  explanation
```

which in the example was:

```
HTTP/1.0 200 Document follows
```

The three components of this status line are:

> HTTP/*version* The protocol version being used by the server, HTTP/1.0 in the example in Figure 9.2. If a client requests HTTP/1.1 but the server is only capable of HTTP/1.0, then the server should return HTTP/1.0 to indicate this fact.

> *status_code* The *status code* for the response, as a number between 200 and 599. Values from 200 through 299 indicate successful transactions, while values 300–399 indicate *redirection*—the resource at the requested URL has moved. In this case, the server must also send the

---

Figure 9.2 Data returned from the server to the client subsequent to the GET request of Figure 9.1. Comments are in italics.

```
HTTP/1.0 200 Document follows
Date: Sat, 13 Dec 1997 16:04:09 GMT
Server: NCSA/1.5.2
Content-type: text/html
Last-modified: Thu, 03 Oct 1996 16:03:27 GMT
Content-length: 139
     [a blank line, containing only CRLF ]
<html><head>
<title> Test HTML file </title>
</head><body>
<h1> This is a test file</h1>
<p> So what did you expect, art?
</body></html>
```

new URL of the object, if it is known (sent within a `Location` response header field). Numbers 400–599 are error messages. When an error occurs, the server usually sends a small HTML document explaining the error to help the user understand what happened and why. The status codes and their meanings are summarized in Table 9.2 at the end of this chapter.

Explanation A text string that provides descriptive information about the status. Explanation strings vary from server to server, whereas `status codes` and their meanings are explicitly defined by the HTTP specification.

In this example, the code 200 means that everything went fine and that the server is returning the requested data.

The remaining response header fields contain information about the server and about the response being sent. The example in Figure 9.2 returns six lines of response header information. The first two, the `Date` and `Server` fields give the date at which the message was sent and identify the server software, respectively, while the `Content-type`, `Last-modified`, and `Content-length` fields pass information specific to the document or data being returned. The formats and meanings of these header fields are described in the following sections.

Server Response: Date Field

This field, of the format `Date: date_time`, contains the time and date when the message was assembled for transmission. Note that the time *must* be Greenwich Mean Time (GMT) to ensure that all clients and servers share a common time zone. In the example, this field was:

```
Date: Sat, 13 Dec 1997 16:04:09 GMT
```

Note that this is *not* the date at which the data being returned was created or last modified—that information is contained in the `Last-modified` header field. Details about supported time formats are given at the end of the chapter.

Server Response: Server Field

This field, of the format `Server: name/version`, returns the name and version of the server software, with a slash character separating the two. Some examples are:

```
Server: Netscape-Enterprise/2.01
Server: Apache/1.2.4
Server: Microsoft-IIS/4.0
```

Server-Response: Content-Type

This field, of the format `Content-type: type/subtype`, indicates the MIME `Content-type` of the data being sent from the server to the client. In this example, the returned data is an HTML document, so the returned header field is:

```
Content-type: text/html
```

MIME types are discussed in more detail in Appendix B, "Multipurpose Internet Mail Extensions," available at the companion Web site at www.wiley.com/compbooks/graham. If no data are returned, this field is absent.

Server Response: Last-Modified

This field, of the format `Last-modified:` *date_time*, gives the date and time that the document was last modified. As with the `Date` field, the information must be given in Greenwich Mean Time. In the example, this field was:

```
Last-Modified: Thu, 03 Oct 1996 16:03:27 GMT
```

If the server does not know the date at which the resource was last modified, this field is absent.

Server Response: Content-Length Field

This field, of the format `Content-length: length`, gives the length in bytes of the data portion of the message. In some situations, the length is unknown (for example, if it is output from a gateway program), in which case this field is absent. In this event, the client will continue to read data until the server breaks the connection. If no data are returned, this field is absent. In the example, the message is 139 bytes long, so the header field is:

```
Content-length: 139
```

Server Generation of Response Header

How is the response header generated by the server? If the requested resource is a file, the HTTP server constructs the header itself. If the request is to a gateway program, then the gateway program must provide information about the details of the returned data, such as the `Content-type`, since only this program knows what is to be returned. There are two mechanisms that can be used by gateway programs to providing response header information. In the first, the gateway program returns *server directives* to the server—these are used by the server to create appropriate header fields, which are included with the full response header generated by the server. In the second mechanism, the gateway program returns a complete response header, which is sent directly to the remote client, bypassing processing by the server. This is called the *non-parsed header* gateway approach. Both methods are described in detail in Chapter 10.

Server Response If a File Has Not Changed

How does a server respond if the requested file was not modified subsequent to the time specified in the `If-modified-since` request header field? The resulting response is a short message of the form:

```
HTTP/1.0 304 Not Modified
Date: Sat, 13 Dec 1997 16:04:09 GMT
```

```
Server: NCSA/1.5.2
MIME-version: 1.0
   [Blank line, containing CRLF]
```

This contains the status code 304, which tells the client that the file was unchanged and that the client should use its cached copy of the data.

Lessons from Example 13

1. When a client contacts an HTTP server, it sends a *request header* composed of *request header fields*. The first of these fields is the *method field*, which specifies the HTTP method being requested by the client and the *location* on the server of the resource being requested. This is followed by other header fields that pass information about the capabilities of the client. The request header is terminated by a single blank line, containing only a carriage-return linefeed (CRLF) character pair.

2. The server responds with a message consisting of a *response header* followed by the requested data. The response header fields communicate information about the state of the transaction, including a MIME *content-type* header that explicitly tells the client the type of data being sent. The response header is terminated by a single blank line. The data being sent to the client follows this blank line.

Example 14: Other Common Request Header Fields

Modern browsers have extended the repertoire of request header fields, incorporating some fields proposed in HTTP 1.1 and others not part of the "official" HTTP 1.0 specification. For example, Figure 9.3 shows the request header produced by the Microsoft Internet Explorer 3.0 browser when making a request identical with that shown in Figure 9.1, while Figure 9.4 shows the header sent by the Netscape Navigator 3.0 browser. Both cases assume the request is made as described at the beginning of Example 13. New header fields are shown in boldface.

Figure 9.3 Request headers sent by the Microsoft Internet Explorer 3.0 browser as per the access described at the beginning of Example 13. New fields are shown in boldface.

```
GET /Tests/file.html HTTP/1.0
Accept: */*
Referer: http://www.utoronto.ca/webdocs/webinfo.html
Accept-Language: en-US, fr
User-Agent: Mozilla/2.0 (compatible; MSIE 3.0; Windows 95;1024,768
Host: smaug.middle.earth.ca:2021
   [a blank line, containing only CRLF ]
```

Aside from somewhat cleaner header presentation (there are fewer superfluous accept header fields), there are three new fields as well as extra information in one of the `User-agent` fields. The purpose of these additions is described in the following sections.

Client Request: Accept-Charset Field

The `accept-language` field, of the form `Accept-language:` *charset1,* *charset2,* ..., gives a list of character sets supported by the browser; very few servers, however, support this field. Character set specifications are discussed in more detail in Appendix A, "Characters and Computer Character Sets," available through the companion Web site at www.wiley.com/compbooks/graham. In Figure 9.4 the field `accept-charset: ISO-8859-1,*,UCS-2` means that the client will accept the ISO-8859-1, UCS-2, or any character set. This header is currently sent by Netscape Navigator 4.

Client Request: Accept-Language Field

The `accept-language` field, of the form `Accept-language:` *lang1,* *lang2* ..., gives a list of languages supported by the browser. This is similar to `accept` headers, but allows, in principle, for selection of different language versions of the same document. Some servers support this field, depending on how the request is made. Here, the field `accept-language: en-Us, fr` means that the client will accept English language (American version) or French language documents. This header is sent by Internet Explorer 3 and greater as well as Netscape Navigator 2 and greater. Language specifications are discussed in more detail in Appendix E, "Tags for Identifying Languages," available through the companion Web site at www.wiley.com/compbooks/graham.

Figure 9.4 Request headers sent by the Netscape Navigator 4.0 browser as per the access described at the beginning of Example 13. New fields are shown in boldface.

```
GET /Tests/file.html HTTP/1.0
Referer: http://www.utoronto.ca/webdocs/webinfo.html
Connection: Keep-Alive
Cookie: good=bad; apples=oranges
User-Agent: Mozilla/3.0b5 (Win95; I)
Host: smaug.java.utoronto.ca:2021
Accept: image/gif, image/x-xbitmap, image/jpeg, image/pjpeg, */*
Accept-Language: en-US, fr
Accept-Charset: ISO-8859-1,*,UCS-2
    [a blank line, containing only CRLF ]
```

Client Request: Host Field (HTTP 1.0 Extension; HTTP 1.1)

The host field, of the form Host: *domain_name*:*port* gives the domain name and port to which the client has directed its request—if the port is absent, the default value (80) is assumed. This field may seem superfluous, but is useful if the request passes through a proxy server or is directed to a server that has more than one domain name. This header is sent by Internet Explorer 3 and greater, and Netscape Navigator 3 and greater.

This header was adopted as an HTTP 1.0 extension. Its use in HTTP 1.1 is the same as that described above. In HTTP 1.1, it is an error if a request header does not have this field.

Client Request: User-Agent Field

Note how the user-agent field in Figure 9.3 indicates that the browser (MSIE 3.0B) is compatible with Netscape 2.0 (Mozilla). The field also gives the display resolution of the computer (1024 by 768). The placement or inclusion of such data is nonstandardized, so you cannot count on this information being present—indeed, this information is not found in the Internet Explorer 4 user-agent field.

Client Request: Connection Field (HTTP 1.0 Extension; also HTTP 1.1)

Figure 9.4 illustrates the connection header field of the form Connection: *keep-alive*. This is used to keep the TCP/IP connection open after the requested resource has been sent to the client. As mentioned in the introduction, HTTP 1.0 was designed to break this connection as soon as the data were sent. This can be very inefficient if a browser requests several subsequent files from the same server (such as an HTML document plus all the inline graphics). If the browser sends an HTTP 1.0 keep-alive header field, servers that understand this header will keep the connection open for a short time (usually 10–15 seconds) in preparation for the next request.

As seen in Figures 9.3 and 9.4, not all browsers support keep-alive. Similarly, not all servers support this feature, and instead simply ignore this field. Finally, a server will use keep-alive *only if* it can return a content-length response header field for the data it returns—with keep-alive, the content-length field is the only way a client can determine if all the data have been sent by the server, whereupon it can make another request.

The connection field was introduced as an extension to HTTP 1.0, but the mechanism used for maintaining a connection led to a number of problems that could only be resolved by significantly modifying the keep-alive mechanism. Thus, while HTTP 1.1 supports the connection field and the value "keep-alive," the mechanism used is very different from that in HTTP 1.0—in HTTP 1.1, the default is to keep the connection "open," and the connection field is used to close it. You are referred to the HTTP 1.1 standard for the details.

Client Request: Cookie Fields (HTTP 1.0 Extension)

Netscape introduced a special header field mechanism commonly called *Netscape cookies*—this is a mechanism that lets a server store small pieces information on a browser. This information is sent to the client using a `Set-cookie` server response header. A browser that understands cookies will store the data on the client machine's hard disk and will return these data to the server from which the cookie originated, within a `cookie` request header field.

Cookies are useful for storing state information (e.g., the time at which the user last visited the site, which resources the user last used, etc.) on the browser in such a way that the information is not lost when the user leaves the site or shuts down his or her browser. However, note that not all browsers support cookies, while browsers that do support cookies give the user the option of disabling this feature.

Detailed information about the cookie mechanism is found in Chapter 10.

Lessons from Example 14

1. Most browsers send a `Host` request field, which gives the domain name and port number to which the request is being directed. Some also send an `accept-language` field, to indicate the language(s) preferred by the user.

2. The `User-agent` field may contain browser-specific information, such as the monitor display resolution. There is no standardized way for including this information.

3. Some browsers also send a `Connection: keep-alive` header field to stop the server from breaking the connection after the server has sent the requested data. Not all browsers or servers support this feature. Note that the HTTP 1.1 implementation of keep-alive is very different from the implementation in HTTP 1.0.

4. Using the `Set-cookie` response header fields and the Netscape cookie mechanism is a useful way of storing state information about the client-server session. However, not all browsers support this mechanism.

HEAD Method: Information about a Resource

In some cases, it is useful to gather information about a resource without retrieving the resource itself. For example, a link-checking program does not always need to retrieve a resource to verify that the resource exists, while an indexing package may only want to know if a resource has changed since it was last catalogued, prior to deciding if it should be retrieved.

This role is satisfied by the HTTP HEAD method, which requests that a server send the response header relevant to the requested URL, but not the content of the referenced object. As the following example indicates, this is a quick way of seeing if a document or gateway program is actually present and of obtaining some general information about it, such as its MIME content-type or the date it was last modified, without downloading the entire resource.

Example 15: Using the HEAD Method

In this example, we suppose that the user (or some automated program, such as a robot or spider) wants to access HEAD information about the document referenced in Example 13. The request that would be sent to the server is simply:

```
HEAD /Tests/file.html HTTP/1.0
User-Agent: HEAD Test Agent
From: name@domain.name.edu
```

The request does not need `accept` header fields, since no data are being retrieved. The `From` field gives the server the electronic mail address of the user making the HEAD request—it is important to give this information if the request comes from an automated program. A typical response (in this case, from an Apache 1.1.1 HTTP server) is:

```
HTTP/1.0 200 OK
Date: Wed, 09 Oct 1996 23:10:55 GMT
Server: Apache/1.1.1
MIME-version: 1.0
Content-type: text/html
Content-length: 139
Last-modified: Fri, 20 Sep 1996 19:44:28 GMT
```

This indicates that the document exists (the status code 200 indicates a valid URL) and includes information about the document type and the date it was last modified. If this URL referenced a dynamic resource, such as a program or a parsed HTML document (see Chapter 10), the `content-length` and `last-modified` headers would be absent to indicate that the length is unknown *a priori* and that the document is essentially new every time it is accessed.

If the HEAD request references an HTML document, some servers will parse the document **HEAD** and extract **META** element information for inclusion in the response header. This server feature is not widely implemented.

Lessons from Example 15

1. A HEAD request retrieves only the response header for the indicated URL—the document itself is not retrieved. If the HEAD request targets an HTML document, some servers parse the document **HEAD** for

information to include in the response header. This feature is not widely implemented.

Sending Data to a Server: GET and POST

The HTTP protocol supports several methods for sending data from client to server. The most common are GET and POST, which are used as the interface between HTML **FORM**s or **ISINDEX** queries and server-side processing programs. The PUT method, on the other hand, is used to create new resources (such as files) on a server. PUT is described later in this chapter.

Example 16: GET Method with a Query String

This example illustrates a GET method request, but with query information appended to the URL. As discussed in Chapters 2 and 8, query information is appended to the URL following a question mark. This encoding is done automatically by Web browsers when an **ISINDEX** query or, depending on the mechanisms used, when an HTML **FORM** is submitted. An example URL is

```
http://www.stuff.ca/cgi-bin/srch-example?item1+item2+item3+item4
```

which passes four items from an **ISINDEX** query to the program *srch-example*.

Figure 9.5 shows the request headers sent by the Internet Explorer 3.0 browser when accessing this URL. This request header is essentially the same as that in Figure 9.3, the only important difference being the query string appended to the locator string. The server's handling of query strings is described in the next chapter.

Lesson from Example 16

1. Query data appended to a URL during a GET request to a server are passed as part of the locator string in the HTTP *method field* of the request header. All other request header fields are the same as those for a standard GET request, as described in Examples 13 and 14.

Figure 9.5 Data sent from the Internet Explorer 3.0 Beta 1 browser to an HTTP server during a GET request that has a query string appended to the URL. Comments are in italics.

```
GET /cgi-bin/srch-example?item1+item2+item3+item4 HTTP/1.0
Accept: */*
Accept-Language: en
User-Agent: Mozilla/2.0 (compatible; MSIE 3.0B; Windows 95;1024,768)
Host: smaug.middle.earth.ca
    [a blank line, containing only CRLF ]
```

Example 17: Submitting a FORM Using the GET Method

This example examines how an HTML **FORM** sends form data to a server when the GET method is used. The example **FORM** is shown in Figure 9.6. The actual rendering of this form by a Web browser is shown in Figure 9.7.

The **FORM** element was discussed in detail in Chapter 6. This **FORM** defines the three variable names: *srch*, *srch_type*, and *srvr*. These have been assigned, by user input, the values *srch=dogfish*, *srch_type=Exact Match*, *srvr=Canada,* and *srvr=Sweden*. Figure 9.8 shows the data sent by the Netscape Navigator 3 to the server when the **FORM** is submitted.

As discussed in Chapters 6 and 8, the default method of submitting a **FORM** sends the data to the server as a collection of encoded *name/value* pairs. The names and values from each FORM input element are encoded and composed into strings of the form `name=value,` with ampersand characters (`&`) separating the composite strings (e.g., `name1=value1&name2=value2...`). With the GET method, this string is appended to the URL as a *query string*, separated from the base of the URL by a question mark. When the HTTP server receives these data, it forwards the entire query string to the gateway program *form1* referenced by the URL. These details are discussed in Chapter 10.

Figure 9.6 Example HTML FORM that uses the GET method to submit data to a server.

```
<FORM ACTION="http://smaug.java.utoronto.ca:2021/cgi-bin/form1"
      METHOD=GET>
<p> Search string: <INPUT TYPE="text" NAME="srch" VALUE="dogfish">
<p> Search Type:
  <SELECT NAME="srch_type">
    <OPTION> Insensitive Substring
    <OPTION SELECTED> Exact Match
    <OPTION> Sensitive Substring
    <OPTION> Regular Expression
  </SELECT>
<p> Search databases in:
  <INPUT TYPE="checkbox" NAME="srvr" VALUE="Canada" CHECKED> Canada
  <INPUT TYPE="checkbox" NAME="srvr" VALUE="Russia"  > Russia
  <INPUT TYPE="checkbox" NAME="srvr" VALUE="Sweden" CHECKED> Sweden
  <INPUT TYPE="checkbox" NAME="srvr" VALUE="U.S.A."  > U.S.A.
  <em>(multiple items can be selected.)</em>
<P> <INPUT TYPE="submit"> <INPUT TYPE=reset>.
</FORM>
```

Figure 9.7 Netscape Navigator 3 browser rendering of the FORM example in Figure 9.6.

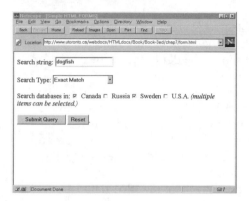

Figure 9.8 Data sent from a client to an HTTP server during a FORMs-based GET request.

```
GET /cgi-bin/form1?srch=dogfish&srch_type=Exact+Match&srvr=Canada&srvr=Sweden HTTP/1.0
Connection: Keep-Alive
User-Agent: Mozilla/3.02 (Win95; I)
Host: smaug.java.utoronto.ca:2021
Accept: image/gif, image/x-xbitmap, image/jpeg, image/pjpeg, */*
Accept-Language: en-US, fr, fr-CA
    [a blank line, containing only CRLF ]
```

Lesson from Example 17

1. When an HTML **FORM** submits data to an HTTP server using the GET method, the **FORM** data are appended to the URL as a query string. Consequently, the **FORM** data are sent to the server in the query string part of the locator string, in the request header method field. The **FORM** data are encoded according to the **FORM-URL** encoding scheme discussed in Chapters 6 and 8.

Example 18: Submitting a FORM Using the POST Method

This example uses the **FORM** shown in Figure 9.7 to submit the same data to the server, but with one subtle modification: The form requests the POST method instead of GET. This is done by changing the first two lines in Figure 9.6 to:

```
<FORM ACTION="http://smaug.java.utoronto.ca:2021/cgi-bin/form1"
      METHOD=POST>
```

(The change is noted in boldface.)

As in Example 16, this form has variable names *srch*, *srch_type*, and *srvr*. These have been assigned values *srch=dogfish*, *srch_type=Exact Match*, *srvr=Canada*, and *srvr=Sweden*. Figure 9.9 shows the data sent to the server, again from the Netscape Navigator 3.0 browser.

The POST method sends data in a message body and not in the URL. The difference is indicated in Figure 9.9 in the four places noted in boldface: the method header, which now specifies the POST method and which has no data appended to the URL; the additional request header fields `Content-type` and `Content-length`, which give the type and length of the data message being sent; and last, the actual data following the header.

There are currently two valid content-types for sending **FORM** data to a server. In this example, the type is

```
Content-type: application/x-www-form-urlencoded
```

which indicates that the data is from a **FORM** and that it is encoded in the same manner as when appended to a URL. You can compare the message body at the bottom of Figure 9.9 with the data appended to the URL in Figure 9.8 to verify this equivalence. The details of how the data are passed from the server to a CGI program are described in Chapter 10.

Alternatively, **FORM** data sent via the POST method can be encoded as a MIME *multipart/form-data* message. On a browser, this encoding is selected by changing the first two lines in Figure 9.6 to (the changes are noted in boldface):

```
<FORM ACTION="http://leonardo.utirc.utoronto.ca:8080/cgi-bin/form1"
      METHOD=POST ENCTYPE="multipart/form-data">
```

Figure 9.9 Data sent from a client to an HTTP server during a FORMs-based POST request. Fields and data specific to the POST method are shown in boldface.

```
POST /cgi-bin/form1 HTTP/1.0
Connection: Keep-Alive
User-Agent: Mozilla/3.0b5 (Win95; I)
Host: smaug.java.utoronto.ca:2021
Accept: image/gif, image/x-xbitmap, image/jpeg, image/pjpeg, */*
Accept-Language: en-US, fr, fr-CA
Content-type: application/x-www-form-urlencoded
Content-length: 58
     [a blank line, containing only CRLF]
srch=dogfish&srch_type=Exact+Match&srvr=Canada&srvr=Sweden
```

Figure 9.10 Data sent from a client to an HTTP server during a FORMs-based POST request using the multipart/form-data encoding mechanism.

```
POST /cgi-bin/form1 HTTP/1.0
Connection: Keep-Alive
User-Agent: Mozilla/3.02 (Win95; I)
Host: smaug.java.utoronto.ca:2021
Accept: image/gif, image/x-xbitmap, image/jpeg, image/pjpeg, */*
Accept-Language: en-US, fr, fr-CA
Content-type: multipart/form-data; boundary=-----------------80006273428
Content-Length: 443
    [a blank line, containing only CRLF]
-------------------80006273428
Content-Disposition: form-data; name="srch"
    [a blank line, containing only CRLF]
dogfish
-------------------80006273428
Content-Disposition: form-data; name="srch_type"
    [a blank line, containing only CRLF]
Exact Match
-------------------80006273428
Content-Disposition: form-data; name="srvr"
    [a blank line, containing only CRLF]
Canada
-------------------80006273428
Content-Disposition: form-data; name="srvr"
    [a blank line, containing only CRLF]
Sweden
-------------------80006273428--
```

Figure 9.10 shows the data sent to the server by the Netscape Navigator browser. The important changes from Figure 9.9 are noted in boldface. Once again the method is POST—content-type and content-length header fields are again present, and data is sent following the header. Note, however, the encoding of the data: The FORM data are encoded as a special multipart MIME type, with each block of the message corresponding to a different form input element.

This encoding has several advantages. First, you can use multipart/form-data to upload data files from a client to a server—indeed, if a form contains **INPUT TYPE**="file" elements (for selecting a file to upload with the form data), then multipart/form-data is the only supported encoding. Second, the multipart/form-data allows for text input that is not coded in the ISO Latin-1 character set (recall that URLs must use ISO Latin-1). These issues are discussed in more detail in

Chapter 10; see also the MIME types appendix (Appendix B) available at the book's companion Web site at www.wiley.com/compbooks/graham.

Lesson from Example 18

1. When an HTML **FORM** submits data to an HTTP server using the POST method, the **FORM** data are sent to the server as a *message body* that follows the request header. This message body is encoded in the same manner as when appended to the URL. Additional request header fields tell the server the content-type of the arriving message, as well as the length of the message. No data are appended to the URL.

Sending Data to a Server: PUT and DELETE

The methods PUT and DELETE are designed for sending data to and deleting data from an HTTP server. For example, the HTTP request

```
PUT /project/dir1/file.html HTTP/1.0
Content-type: text/html
Content-length: 103
    [a blank line, containing only CRLF]
<HTML><HEAD><TITLE>Silly Test Stuff</TITLE></HEAD>
<BODY><H1>Really Silly Test Stuff</H1></BODY><HTML>
```

instructs the server to create the file *../project/dir/file.html* (the root location is determined by the server configuration files) and *put* the sent message data into this file. If this file already exists, it should be replaced by the new file. If successful, the response status field line should be

```
HTTP/1.0 201 created
```

to indicate that the resource was created.

The DELETE method is the converse of PUT. Thus, the request

```
DELETE /project/dir1/file.html HTTP/1.0
    [a blank line, containing only CRLF]
```

asks that the server delete the resource at the indicated URL.

There are currently no major browsers that implement PUT or DELETE. Some servers do implement these methods, usually through special gateway programs or application-specific server plug-ins. Obviously PUT and DELETE are not terribly practical without mechanisms for controlling how objects are put onto, modified, or deleted from a server. In this regard, there are several document management systems (e.g., Microsoft FrontPage or MKS Web Integrity) that use PUT and DELETE methods to manage document archives on Web servers.

Access Control, User Authentication, and Data Encryption

So far, we have not discussed the control of access to an HTTP server or the encryption of data transmitted between client and server. This section briefly discusses those mechanisms that are currently supported by most Web browsers and/or servers.

For low-level security, most servers can be configured to restrict access to machines in an authorized Internet domain or subdomain. For example, servers can be configured such that only machine domain names (or numeric IP addresses) belonging within a particular domain (e.g., for example, all machines with domain name ending in *.middle.earth.edu*) are permitted access. In general, this restriction can be applied on a per directory basis, although some servers can apply restrictions file-by-file. This is not very secure, however, since a clever cracker can *spoof* (mimic) a domain name and access the data. It is also not very specific, since anyone who can log in on a machine inside the domain can access the restricted material.

Finer, user-specific control is possible via *user authentication*. The "Basic" user-authentication scheme is part of the HTTP 1.0 protocol, and lets a server restrict access to users who can provide verifiable usernames and passwords. When users request a password-protected file, the browser prompts them for username and password information, which is sent to the server with the request. The server then checks the name and password against a designated password file. However, in the Basic authentication scheme, the username and password are sent over the Internet in an essentially unencrypted format, so that it is easy for anyone sniffing the network traffic to extract the username and password. Thus, the Basic scheme is not secure, unless the underlying data are also encrypted in some way. And, of course, you need some other mechanism for getting the usernames and passwords onto the server in the first place.

A second method, known as *digest authentication*, has recently been developed and is implemented experimentally by NCSA's Mosaic browser and the NCSA HTTP server. This is similar to the Basic scheme, but passes usernames and passwords in an encrypted string. This is a significant improvement over Basic authentication, but still requires that a username/password database exist on the server. Although experimental in HTTP 1.0, digest authentication is an integral part of HTTP 1.1.

Secure communication and user authentication requires encryption of the data being sent between client and server. The most common mechanisms employ *negotiated encryption*. Negotiated encryption means that the server and client exchange information, usually encryption keys, that allows each to send encrypted information that can only be decoded by the other. This requires that both client and server support the same encryption and decryption software and that they both understand the encryption protocol used to send messages between the two.

There are two main encryption schemes currently in use, but as yet no common standard. In addition, all of the encryption algorithms used by these schemes are regulated by U.S. trade and security restrictions (the algorithms are considered "munitions," with tight export controls), which place severe limits on the quality of encryption software that can be exported outside the United States. This significantly restricts the deployment of highly secure Web-based applications, although the medium grade encryption that can be exported is sufficient in many cases.

Example 19: The "Basic" Authentication Scheme

The Basic authentication scheme is the only user authentication scheme universally available on the World Wide Web. This scheme is *not* secure, as username and password information are not encrypted when sent from client to server (they are encoded, however, which at least hides them from nonexperts). You should, consequently, not think of this as a secure authentication scheme, unless it is combined with an encryption mechanism such as the Netscape SSL technology (discussed later).

The Basic scheme uses special HTTP request and response header fields. The following example follows a request for a resource that requires user authentication and illustrates how these fields negotiate the request for authentication information.

Step 1: Client Requests the Resource

The client first makes a regular request for the resource (here, an HTML document). A typical request header is shown in Figure 9.11.

Step 2: Server Response—Authentication Required

The response message is shown in Figure 9.12. The server status message

```
HTTP/1.0 401 Unauthorized
```

tells the client that the resource was not returned because the resource requires user authentication. In this regard, the server sends the additional header field:

```
WWW-Authenticate: Basic realm="SecRealm1@server.dom.edu"
```

Figure 9.11 Typical GET request from the Netscape Navigator browser.

```
GET /SecDir1/foo.html HTTP/1.0
User-Agent: Mozilla/1.1N (X11; I; IRIX 5.3 IP22)
Accept: */*
Accept: image/gif
Accept: image/x-xbitmap
Accept: image/jpeg
```

Figure 9.12 HTTP server response upon a request for a resource protected by the Basic authentication scheme. The authentication-related fields are shown in boldface.

```
HTTP/1.0 401 Unauthorized
Date: Thursday, 03-Aug-95 14:38:57 GMT
Server: NCSA/1.3
MIME-version: 1.0
Content-type: text/html
WWW-Authenticate: Basic realm="SecRealm1@server.dom.edu"
<HEAD><TITLE>Authorization Required</TITLE></HEAD>
<BODY><H1>Authorization Required</H1>
     Browser not authentication-capable or
     authentication failed.
</BODY>
```

WWW-Authenticate: tells the client which authentication scheme to use (Basic), and also what *realm* is involved, here realm="SecRealm1@server.dom.edu" (realms are discussed a bit later on). The response message includes a short HTML document that is displayed by a browser if the user chooses not to provide authentication information, or if the browser does not understand WWW-Authenticate headers.

Step 3: Client Requests Resource

The client, upon receipt of a 401 HTTP response header, prompts the user for his or her username and password. The client takes the username and password and forms the string:

username:password

This strings is then *uuencoded* into a pseudo-encrypted string (I say pseudo-encrypted, because it is trivial to decode). The client then tries, once again, to access the resource, this time passing the encoded username and password information within an Authorization request header field, of the form

Authorization: Basic aWFuOmJvb2J5

where the string aWFuOmJvb2J5 is the encoded username and password. Figure 9.13 shows a typical request header containing this authentication information.

The server takes the contents of the Authorization field, unpacks the contents to obtain the username and password, and checks these values against its own list of usernames and passwords. If there is a match, then the user is authenticated, and the server returns the resource. If there is no match, then the server indicates the failure by again returning the response shown in Figure 9.12, which causes the browser to once again prompt the user for a username and password.

Figure 9.13 Typical client request for a resource protected by the Basic authentication scheme—the `Authorization:` **field indicates the authentication scheme being used (**`Basic`**) along with the encoded username and password. The authentication-related fields are shown in boldface.**

```
GET /SecDir1/foo.html HTTP/1.0
User-Agent: Mozilla/1.1N (X11; I; IRIX 5.3 IP22)
Accept: *.*
Accept: image/gif
Accept: image/x-xbitmap
Accept: image/jpeg
Authorization: Basic aWFuOmJvb2J5
```

The Meaning of a Realm

A *realm* is simply a way of grouping username and password information, so that the browser need not prompt the user for this information if subsequent requests access the same realm. For example, suppose that a server administrator creates two secure directories, *SecDir1* and *SecDir2*, and controls access to them using the password files *pass1* and *pass2*, respectively. The administrator must also assign realm names to these directories so that, in communicating with a client, the server can inform the client which realm is involved, without giving away the name of the password file. In this example, we assume the administrator assigned the name "SecRealm1@server.dom.edu" to the directory *SecDir1* and the name "SecRealm2@server.dom.edu" to the directory *SecDir2*.

The first time a user accesses a document in *SecDir1*, he or she is prompted for a username and password. The browser stores this name/password string under the realm name "SecRealm1@server.dom.edu." On subsequent accesses to this directory or to any subdirectory of this directory (e.g. *SecDir1/subdir2/*), the browser sends an `Authentication` header field containing the authentication username and password already stored under this realm name and does not prompt the user for this information.

If, on the other hand, the user requests a document from *SecDir2*, then the browser does not sent the Authentication: header, since the password under the "SecRealm1@server.dom.edu" realm does not apply to this directory. As a result, the server sends back a header containing a second `WWW-Authenticate` field:

```
WWW-Authenticate: Basic realm="SecRealm2@server.dom.edu"
```

to tell the browser that authentication is required for this new, as yet unentered, realm. As the browser has never accessed this realm, it has no record of an appropriate username and password and therefore prompts the user for this information. This information is then stored on the browser under the second realm keyword.

Note how all the realm names in these examples contained the domain name of the server housing the access-controlled documents. This is not required, but is useful in that it guarantees unique realm names.

NOTE: Security Issues with the Basic Password Scheme

With most browsers, usernames and passwords are preserved until the user exits the browser. This can create security concerns when browsers are running on public-area workstations, since once a user has entered his or her username, this information can be reused by the next user of the machine.

Client-Server Data Encryption

As mentioned in the previous section, any authentication scheme is insecure if the messages and data passed between client and server are unencrypted: If the username and password are not encrypted, then they can be copied and used by someone else; if the transported data are not encrypted, then the data can be intercepted and read regardless of any password protection. There are two main approaches to encryption currently being deployed on the Web, and these are summarized in the following sections. Detailed information about these schemes is found in the references at the end of this chapter.

Netscape's Secure Sockets Layer (SSL)

The *Secure Sockets Layer* protocol is designed as an encryption layer *below* the HTTP protocol. Thus, HTTP messages are unaffected, with encryption occurring just prior to converting the messages into TCP/IP packets for transmission over the Internet. To indicate the special nature of this connection, Netscape created the new URL **https** (HTTP-Secure) scheme, identical to **http** URLs save for the initial string `https:`. The default port for **https** URLs is 443, and not 80, so that a single machine can run secure and non-secure HTTP servers at the same time.

In principle, SSL can be used for any Internet tool that uses the underlying TCP/IP protocol for data communications. For example, Netscape markets NNTP news and LDAP directory servers employing SSL and intends to implement SSL widely in the future.

SSL works at several levels. At the encryption level, SSL employs a sophisticated security handshake protocol: When a client contacts a secure server, they exchange encryption keys, which are subsequently used to encrypt all data passed between the server and client. Encryption keys are never reused, to ensure that keys cannot be intercepted and used by an unauthorized party. The server also sends the client a cryptographic certificate that tells the client which server it is in contact with and that is used to validate that the server is indeed who it claims to be. Finally, the client and server send, ahead of the transmitted data, a message digest calculated from the data; the receiving party uses this message digest to ensure that the data content has not been modified by any intervening party.

Version 3 of the SSL protocol includes mechanisms for client certificates, which allow users to authenticate themselves using digital signatures just as servers are currently authenticated.

At present, almost all commercial browsers and servers support SSL.

Secure HTTP Protocol (S-HTTP)

Secure HTTP, or *S-HTTP*, is a second Web encryption and authentication scheme. S-HTTP is implemented as part of the HTTP protocol and involves additional HTTP request and response headers that *negotiate* the type of encryption being used, the exchange of encryption keys, the passing of message digest information, and so on. This is roughly similar to the Basic authentication scheme, except that S-HTTP allows the client and server to exchange cryptographic certificates and encryption keys within the HTTP headers, so that each party can authenticate the other and encrypt data being sent to the other.

S-HTTP and SSL are complementary schemes. SSL has the advantage of encrypting all underlying communication, but the disadvantage that the same encryption is applied to all messages. There is no easy way to change the encryption scheme based, for example, on the personal encryption key of a user (some variation is possible in SSL version 3, however). S-HTTP, on the other hand, allows for this type of flexible encryption, since the keys can be passed in the HTTP headers. With luck, the various vendors will arrive at a compromise that adopts the best features of both approaches.

S-HTTP is not widely supported and in particular is not supported by Netscape Navigator or Microsoft Internet Explorer.

Security Enhanced Transactions—SET

Financial transactions over the Web require additional levels of encryption and authentication, to allow users to send credit information—or even digital money—over the network safely and reliably. Visa and MasterCard, in association with Microsoft, Netscape, and others, are developing a secure transaction technology called SET. This scheme will allow for secure use of credit cards on the Net, with automatic validation of the card information and debiting of the transaction from the user's account—Using SET, users will never need to give their actual credit card number to the merchant from whom they are buying a product or service. Other efforts are underway to develop digital cash—the ability to send real money, in digital format, over a computer network. These technologies are in the development and testing stages and are likely to be deployed sometime over the next two years. The references section at the end of this chapter provides links to additional readings on these subjects.

Proxy Servers and Server Caching

Proxy servers are often used by local area networks (LANs) who want to protect their network from unauthorized entry via the Internet. Such protection can be accomplished by installing *firewall* software on the gateway machine that links the local network to the outside world. A firewall keeps TCP/IP packets from entering the local network from outside and thereby protects the LAN from intruders.

Unfortunately, a firewall means that users inside the LAN cannot access WWW resources outside the LAN, since incoming data are blocked at the firewall. The solution is to install a *proxy server* on the firewall, and to configure the users' Web browsers to refer all outgoing requests to the proxy server instead of to the real servers outside the LAN. A proxy server has access to both the inside and outside worlds and can safely pass information back and forth across the firewall. When a browser wants to request information from outside the firewall, it instead sends the request to the proxy server on the firewall. The proxy server then *proxies* the request—that is, it makes the request on the user's behalf and returns the *proxied* results.

This two-stage process can be slow. To speed up service, proxy servers can *cache* retrieved files. Thus, the first time a user requests a document, the server goes to the outside world and fetches it. But, the server then keeps a copy of the file on its own local disk. If a user then makes a subsequent request for the same file, the proxy server returns the locally cached copy and does not need to access the original server to re-fetch it. This saves time and can also significantly reduce the load on the network connection.

This can be a problem, however, if the file changes with time. This is the case for pages containing periodically updated data, or for documents created dynamically by CGI programs: Obviously, such files either should not be cached or should be removed from the cache after some fixed time. With HTTP 1.0, these problems are mitigated somewhat by using Expires and pragma server response header fields. Expires contains an expiry time and date (in one of the standard time/date formats described at the end of this chapter), which tells a proxy server (or a browser) how long it can keep a cached copy of a document before it expires and should be discarded or replaced. An even stronger statement is made by the Pragma field, which takes the form:

Pragma: no-cache

When a client (or a proxy server) sends a request header containing this field to a server, the targeted server must always access a new copy of the requested URL and can never use a cached version. This ensures that the requesting client always gets the most up-to-date version, regardless of which proxy server(s) the requests pass through.

Finally, most servers do not send a last-modified header for documents that should not be cached. A browser that retrieves a document that does not contain a last-modified header field will assume that the document is not cacheable and will not save a local copy. For example, dynamic, rapidly changing documents generated by CGI programs are often sent to a browser without a `last-modified` header field, so that the browser will always contact the server for a fresh copy of the document.

For a variety of reasons, HTTP 1.0 is very poor at handling proxy transactions and the proper maintenance of cached files. Indeed, HTTP 1.1 contains a number of protocol enhancements designed to make proxy-server caching more effective, efficient, and reliable. You are referred to the references at the end of the chapter for additional information on this subject.

HTTP Proxy Servers

There are two ways of implementing proxy support. The first is to use an HTTP server that has proxying and caching capabilities. Several commercial HTTP servers from Netscape, Microsoft, and others support proxying and caching, as does the freeware Apache server. A second alternative is to use the *Squid* cache, which is a caching proxy server that can handle HTTP, FTP, and NNTP transactions. URLs referencing these different packages are provided at the end of the chapter, should you be interested in further investigating these options.

SOCKS Proxy Support

An alternative is to employ a general-purpose Internet proxying package. Many such packages are available commercially, from various firewall and software security vendors. A useful, freeware alternative is the package known as SOCKS. SOCKS does not have caching capabilities and ignores all the HTTP header messages relevant to proxy HTTP servers. However, SOCKS is a useful choice if you do not need an HTTP server, and is significantly easier to implement and maintain than a full caching, proxy server. A further advantage for a secure environment is that SOCKS can proxy all standard Internet protocols, including FTP, NNTP, Telnet, and others. Additional information about SOCKS is found at:

ftp://ftp.nec.com/pub/socks/

A proxy server is of course useful only if a browser can be configured to use it. Today, almost all browsers have this capability.

Format Negotiation

The last topic for this chapter is *format negotiation*. As mentioned in the discussion of `accept` request headers, a client can send information to a server explaining the types of data it prefers and the order of preference. The example request headers given were

```
Accept: image/*
Accept: image/jpeg; q=0.7; mxb=50000
Accept: image/gif; q=0.5
```

which indicates a preference for image/jpeg files, provided they are smaller than 50 KB; followed by GIFs (if the JPEGs are too big), followed by any format of image if the first two are unavailable. However, the HTTP requests described in this chapter were directed at specific files and not a collection. So, how can a server be configured to return alternative format-versions of the same resource?

The Apache server implements format negotiation using two non-CGI-based mechanisms. One method requires that the Web or document administrator create a special map file containing information about the different data variants. As an example, consider the following map file *monty_python.image*:

```
URI: monty_python; vary="type"

URI: monty_python.jpeg
Content-type: image/jpeg; qs=0.85

URI: monty_python.gif
Content-type image/gif; qs=0.5

URI: monty_python.xpm
Content-type: image/xpm; qs=0.2
```

The content indicates that there are three different image variants for this file, accessible at the indicated Uniform Resource Identifier (*URI*, equivalent here to a URL, as discussed at the end of Chapter 8), and describes the relative qualities of the images (through the parameter qs). A URL pointing to the file *monty_python.image* will retrieve the appropriate image file from amongst the three possible formats, depending on the accept headers sent by the client.

The map file can also contain content-language, content-encoding, and content-length fields to define the language, encoding, and length of each resource variant.

The second method of format negotiation implemented on the Apache server is known as *MultiViews*. This method lets a user request a generic resource *minus* the filename extension, for example http://.../path/monty_python, whereupon the server locates all files with this suffix in the indicated directory, and dynamically creates a map file similar to the one above (but without qs parameters). The server then uses the accept headers to determine which file to return to the client.

HTTP Methods and Header Fields Reference

The following sections summarize the HTTP methods, request headers, response headers, and server error messages currently defined and in use. These are predominately HTTP 1.0 values, but some HTTP 1.1 values are in common use on experimental HTTP servers and are also presented here.

HTTP Methods Specification

Table 9.1 summarizes the defined HTTP methods—the commonly implemented methods are GET, HEAD, and POST, which were discussed in detail in this chapter.

HTTP Request Header Field Specifications

Request header fields can be divided into two broad categories: (A) those that describe the status and properties of the server and of the client-server connection and (B) those describing the status and properties of the data (if any) being sent by the client.

(A) Client and Connection Status Header Fields

These header fields define the properties of the requesting client and of the client-server connection, such as the client capabilities, authentication information, required by the connection, and so on.

Accept: *type/subtype, type/subtype2 ...*

> Contains a list of MIME content-types acceptable to the client, separated by commas. Types can also contain parameters describing their relative merit (q=0.0 to q=0.1) and the maximum allowed size for a resource (mxb=*num_bytes*). The use of these terms was discussed earlier in this chapter.

Accept-Charset: *charset1, charset2 ...*

> Lists the character sets preferred by the browser, other than the default (ASCII or ISO Latin-1). Thus the server, if capable, can deliver the resource using the character set preferred by the browser. This is sent by Netscape Navigator 4.

Accept-Encoding: *enc_type1, enc_type2 ...*

> Lists the data encoding types acceptable to the client. For example,
>
> Accept-Encoding: x-compress
>
> tells the server that the client can accept compressed data in the compress format. Currently understood encoding types are x-compress and x-gzip, which may also be seen under the names compress and gzip. Other possible (but largely unimplemented) encoding types are base64 and quoted-printable. If a server sends a document in one of these encodings, it must include the appropriate Content-encoding response header.

Accept-language: *lang1, lang2 ...*

> This field lists the languages preferred by the browser. (For the schemes used to specify the languages, see Appendix E available from the

Table 9.1 HTTP Methods and Their Meanings

Method	Description
HTTP 1.0 Methods	
GET	Retrieve the indicated URL. Data can also be sent to the URL by including a query string with the URL. This is the situation for data sent from ISMAP active imagemaps, from ISINDEX queries, and from FORM elements with the FORM attribute METHOD="GET."
HEAD	Retrieve the HTTP header information for the indicated URL.
POST	Send the data to the indicated URL.The URL must already exist: It is an error to POST to a nonexistent URL. This method is used by HTML FORM elements with the attribute value METHOD="POST."
PUT	Place the data sent by the client in the indicated URL, replacing the old contents if the URL already exists. Many, but not all, servers support PUT.
DELETE	Delete the resource located at the indicated URL. Many, but not all, servers support DELETE.
Largely Unimplemented HTTP 1.0 Methods	
LINK	Link an existing object to another object. For an HTML document, this would imply editing the document and adding LINK information to the document HEAD. This method is not implemented on most servers.
UNLINK	Remove the link information inserted, for example, by a LINK method. This method is not implemented on most servers.
HTTP 1.1 Methods	
OPTIONS	Similar to HEAD, this requests that the server return a list of all communication or processing options available for the requested object. The server should return a list of all such options, without actually accessing the object. This method is not implemented on most servers.
PATCH	Like PUT, but the data consists of a list of differences with respect to the referenced object. The server should apply these differences and update the object. This method is not implemented on most servers.
TRACE	This method requests that the server receiving the request should simply return the entire request header within the body of a `message/http` MIME-type message. This is intended for diagnosing HTTP communications problems. This method is not implemented on most servers.

companion Web site at www.wiley.com/compbooks/graham. For example, the field

Accept-language fr-ca, fr, en

would mean that the browser prefers Canadian French, will accept standard French if Canadian French is not available, and lastly, will accept English if the other two are not available.

Authorization: *scheme scheme_data*

This passes user authentication and encryption scheme information to the server. Scheme indicates the authorization scheme to be used, with scheme_data containing scheme-specific authorization data. If authentication is not required, this field is absent.

Connection: *connection_state*   (HTTP 1.0 extension, and HTTP 1.1)

Several HTTP 1.0 servers support *keep-alive* connections. If a browser sends the header field

Connection: keep-alive

a server that supports keep-alive will *not* close the client-server link, allowing the client to send several requests down the still-open connection.

In HTTP 1.1, *all* connections are by default kept-alive and are consequently called *persistent connections*. Thus, in HTTP 1.1, the connection field is used to *close* the connection rather than keep it open. The connection header field that closes a connection is:

Connection: close

Only browsers that understand HTTP 1.1 will send this header.

Cookie: *name=value cookie_info*   (HTTP 1.0 extension)

This passes stored state information from the client to server. Servers can use a special Set-Cookie: response header to place state information, in the form of name/value pairs, on a client. The client will then return this information, but only to the server that originally sent the "cookie." This Netscape extension is supported by some but not all clients. Details of the mechanism are found in Chapter 10.

Date: *date_time*

Gives the time and date when the current object was assembled for transmission. Note that the time must be Greenwich Mean Time (GMT) to ensure that all servers share a common time zone. Possible formats for the date_time string are discussed at the end of this chapter.

From: *mail_address*

Contains the address, in Internet mail format, of the user accessing the server. In general, a browser does not send this information out of concern for a user's privacy.

Host: *server.domain.name:port*   (HTP 1.0 extension; HTTP 1.1)

> Contains the domain name and port number (optional if port 80) to which the request is being directed. This is useful if the request is passing through a proxy server or if the request is to a server that has more than one domain name or IP address. This is not sent by all browsers.

If-Modified-Since: *date_time*

> Sent with a GET request to make the GET conditional—if the requested document has not changed since the indicated time and date, the server does not send the document. Possible formats for the *date_time* string are discussed at the end of this chapter. If the document is not sent, the server should send the response header message 304 (not modified).

Pragma: *server_directive*

> Pragma directives pass special-purpose information to servers. Currently, there is only one server directive, Pragma: no-cache, which tells a proxy server (or servers, if it takes multiple proxy servers to reach the resource) to always fetch the document from the actual server and to never use a locally cached copy.

Referer: *URL*

> Gives the URL of the document from which the request originated. This can be a partial URL, in which case it is interpreted *relative* to the URL of the document being requested. If a document contains an HTML BASE element, then the URL referenced by this element should be sent instead.

User-Agent: *program/version comments*

> Provides information about the client software making the request.

(B) Message Properties Header Fields

These header fields define specific properties of the message being sent (or about the requested resource, if the request method is HEAD). Certain fields may be absent, if they are inappropriate for the response data (e.g., content-language is irrelevant for an image file).

Content-language: *lang*

> Gives the language in which the document is written. Note that this is not the same as the character set. At present, this field is not widely used with request headers.

Content-length: *length*

> Gives the length, in bytes, of the message being sent to the server. If no message is sent, then this field is absent.

Content-type: *type/subtype; parameters*

> Gives the MIME content type of the message being sent to the server, with optional parameters for this type. If no message is sent, then this field is absent.

MIME-version: *version_number*

> Gives the MIME protocol version used to encode the message, the current version being 1.0. Many browsers, unfortunately, send this even if the message is not MIME-compliant.

Other, Uncommon Message Property Header Fields

In principle, a client could also send the message property header fields `allow`, `content-encoding`, `expires`, `last-modified`, `link`, `title`, or `URI`. However, these are rarely used in a request header and so are not described here.

HTTP Response Header Field Specifications

The following is a list of currently implemented HTTP response headers. A more detailed list can be found in the references listed at the end of this chapter.

(A) Server and Connection Status Header Fields

These headers define properties about the server and about the client-server connection, such as the server capabilities, the date the message was sent, requests for authentication data required by the connection, and so on.

Date: *date_time*

> Contains the time and date when the current object was assembled for transmission. The following example illustrates the format:
>
> Thu, 03 Aug 1995 16:04:09 GMT
>
> The time must be Greenwich Mean Time (GMT) to ensure a common time zone for all users and servers. Possible time formats are discussed at the end of this chapter.

Location: *URL*

> Contains a URL to which the client should be redirected. This is returned by a server if the requested document was not found on the server, but the server knows the correct (moved) location of the resource. A `Location` header is included when a *redirection* HTTP status field (status 301 or 302) is returned.

Public: method1, method2, ...   (HTTP 1.1)

> Contains a comma-separated list of nonstandard (experimental) methods supported by the server. This header is not implemented on most current servers.

`Retry-after:` *date_time* (or *seconds*)

Contains a time and date (or a time in seconds) after which a client should retry to access a resource that was temporarily unavailable. This field is appropriate when the status header 503 (service unavailable) is being returned. It might be returned by a server or gateway program that is temporarily unable to comply with a request. Typical forms are:

`Retry-after:` Thursday, 10-Aug-95 12:23:12 GMT

`Retry-after:` 60

The latter indicating that the client should retry after a 60 second wait. Most browsers (and proxy servers) do not understand the `retry-after` field.

`Server:` *program/version*

Contains information about the server software from which the resource originated. The program and version information fields are separated by a slash.

`Set-cookie:` *cookie-information*   (Netscape Extension; HTTP 1.1)

Contains cookie data sent by the server. A browser that supports cookies will save these data to disk, and will return them to the server that originally deposited the data. The mechanism is discussed in detail in Chapter 10.

`WWW-Authenticate:` *scheme scheme_message*

Tells the client about the user authorization scheme the server wants to use. This is returned following any browser request that requires user authentication. `Scheme` gives the name of the authorization scheme (e.g. `Basic`), while *scheme_message* gives data, related to the scheme, that is required by the browser..

(B) Message Properties Header Fields

These headers define specific properties of the message or resource being sent. If no message is sent, these fields will be absent.

`Allow:` *method1, method2, ...*

Contains a comma-separated list of HTTP methods supported by the resource. This must be returned if the status code 405 (HTTP method not allowed) is being returned. It can contain any supported method, including nonstandard ones supported by the server. In principle, the browser can then attempt to re-contact the server using one of the supported methods. This is not implemented by current browsers or servers.

`Content-Encoding:` *encoding_type*

Specifies the encoding type mechanism appropriate to the data. The only currently valid types are `compress` and `gzip` and their synonyms `x-compress` and `x-gzip` (the latter are obsolete, and are being phased out). You can only have one content-encoding type per header. This allows compressed files to be uncompressed on-the-fly by the client.

`Content-language:` *lang*

Gives the language of the message being sent to the client.

`Content-length:` *length*

Gives the length, in bytes, of the message being sent to the client.

`Content-type:` *type/subtype; parameters*

Gives the MIME content-type of the message being sent to the client. The content-type can contain optional parameter fields, separated from the type/subtype by a semicolon. For example

`Content-type: text/html; charset=ISO-10646-1`

indicates that the message is an HTML document, written using the ISO 10646-1 character set. Parameter fields are ignored by most current browsers.

`Content-Version:` *version_info*   (HTTP 1.1)

Indicates the version of the resource being sent. This is used in version control for document management purposes. It is implement by some version control systems, but is not implemented by most current browsers.

`Derived-From:` *version_info*   (HTTP 1.1)

Indicates that the version of the resource from which the enclosed data (being sent by the client to the server) were derived. This is used in version control of collaboratively developed resources, and, under HTTP 1.1, is mandatory if data are being sent to the server using the PUT method. This field is not implemented on current browsers (which also do not support PUT).

`Expires:` *date_time*

Gives the time and date after which the information being sent should be considered invalid. This tells clients when to refresh data in their local cache. Proxy servers can use this field to determine when a cached copy of a document should be refreshed.

`Last-modified:` *date_time*

Gives the date and time that the document was last modified, here in the format `Thu, 03 Aug 1995 16:02:27 GMT`. As in the `Date` field, the date must be given in Greenwich Mean Time.

Link: *link_information*

> This is similar to the HTML **LINK** element and defines relationships between the data being returned by the server and other resources. If derived for an HTML document, this field (or multiple fields) should contain the information from the **LINK** elements in the document. This allows the HTTP header to contain **LINK** information about a resource, and allows a client, using HEAD methods, to access information about the document that is useful for cataloguing, organizational, or indexing purposes. Link is not currently implemented.

MIME-version: *version_number*

> See same entry in the preceding section, "HTTP Request Header Fields Specifications."

Title: *title*

> The title of the document. This should be identical to the contents of the document's **TITLE** element.

URI: *uri_of_resource*

> Contains a URL for the resource being sent—sometimes this is an alternate URL (as per the Location field). In general, the meaning of the URI header is not well defined, and it will be dropped in HTTP 1.1 in favor of other headers with better-defined meanings.

HTTP Status Codes Specification

Table 9.2 lists the meanings of the different HTTP status codes. In general, codes 200–299 indicate a successful transaction, while codes 400–599 indicate an error of some type. Codes 300–399 imply redirection: Either the resource has moved, and the server is returning the URL of the new location to the client or the resource has not changed since it was last requested by the client, in which case the server does not need to resend the document.

Time and Date Format Specification

The HTTP protocol defines a preferred format for specifying times and dates—this format is described here. HTTP must also support two other commonly used formats, also described here. In this context, support means that HTTP servers (or gateway programs) should *understand* these two alternative time formats. However, all Web applications, including CGI programs, should always *provide* time information using the preferred syntax.

Table 9.2 HTTP Status Codes. Codes introduced in HTTP 1.1 are in boldface italics

Successful Transactions

200	The request was completed successfully.

201 The request was a POST (or PUT) method and was completed successfully. 201 indicates that data were sent to the server and that the server created a new resource as a result of the request.

202 The request has been accepted for processing, but the results of this processing are unknown. This would be returned, for example, if the client deposited data for batch processing at a later date.

203 The GET (or HEAD) request was fulfilled, but has returned partial information.

204 The request was fulfilled, but there is no new information to send to the client. The browser should do nothing and should continue to display the document from which the request originated.

Redirection Transactions

300 The requested resource is available from more than one location, but the server could not determine which version to return to the client. The response should contain a list of the locations and their characteristics. The client should then choose the one that is most appropriate. This is not currently supported.

301 The resource requested has been permanently moved to a new URL. If this status is returned, the server should also send the client the URL of the new location via the header

`Location: URL comments`

where `URL` is the new document URL. Browsers that understand the `Location` field will automatically connect to the new URL.

302 The resource was found but it actually resides at a different URL. If this status is returned, the server should also send the client the correct URL via the header

`Location: URL comments`

Browsers that understand the `Location` field will automatically connect to the new URL. You will get a 302 Redirection if a URL pointing to a directory is missing the trailing slash character.

303 The response is available at a different URL and should be retrieved using a GET method. This lets a server, accessed via a POST method request, redirect the client to a second resource that should be accessed using the GET method.

Table 9.2 *Continued*

Redirection Transactions

304   A GET request was sent that contained the `If-Modified-Since` field, and the server found that the document had not been modified since the date specified in this field. Consequently, the server responds with this code and does not re-send the document.

305   The request must be accessed through a proxy server; the response must also contain a `Location:` field specifying the location of the proxy. This is not currently supported.

Client Error Messages

400   The request syntax was wrong.

401   The request required an `Authorization:` field, and the client did not specify one. The server also returns a list of the allowed authorization schemes using a `WWW-Authenticate` response header. This mechanism is used by a client and server to negotiate data encryption and user authentication schemes.

402   The requested operation costs money and the client did not specify a way to pay. There is no specification for payment methods, so this is not currently implemented.

403   The client has requested a resource that is forbidden. No explanation is provided for this refusal.

404   The server cannot find the requested URL.

405   The client tried to access a resource using a method that is not allowed for that resource. The response must include a list of allowed methods, contained within an `Allow:` field. This is not widely implemented.

406   The resource was found, but could not be delivered because the type of the resource is incompatible with the acceptable types indicated by the `accept:` or `accept-encoding:` headers sent to the server by the client.

407   The request was to a proxy server, and the proxy server requires authentication information; the proxy server must also return a `Proxy-authenticate` header field to indicate the authentication scheme required by the server. This is not currently supported.

408   The client did not produce a request in a timely manner, and the server has timed out and is breaking the connection. This is not currently supported.

409   The request could not be completed due to a conflict; for example, a PUT is not allowed because someone else has locked the resource. This is not currently supported.

Continued

Table 9.2 *Continued*

Client Error Messages

410   The resource is no longer available at the server and no forwarding information is available.

411   The server is refusing access because the client tried to access the server and send data to the server, but did not use a content-length header to give the size of the data stream. This is not currently supported.

412   The server is refusing access because one of the conditions in the request header field was not satisfied. This is not currently supported.

413   The server is refusing access because the request is too large in some way. The server should include a `Retry-after` response header field to indicate when the client should try again. This is not currently supported.

414   The server is refusing access because the URI of the request is too long. This is not currently supported.

415   The server is refusing access because the client is trying to send data in a MIME type not supported by the server. This is not currently supported.

Server Error Messages

500   The server has encountered an internal error and cannot continue with the request.

501   The request made is legal, but the server does not support this method.

502   The client requested a resource from a server that, in turn, attempted to access the resource from another server or gateway. In this case, the secondary server or gateway did not return a valid response to the server.

503   The service is unavailable, because the server is too busy. The server may also send a `Retry-After:` header, which tells the client how long to wait before trying again.

504   The client requested a resource from a server that, in turn, attempted to access the resource from another server or gateway. This is similar to 502, except that in this case, the transaction failed because the secondary server or gateway took too long to respond.

505   The server does not support the HTTP protocol version in which the request was posed. This is not currently supported.

Preferred Format

The preferred format is specified in RFC 1123. An example is:

```
Wed, 09 Aug 1995 07:49:37 GMT
```

where the first field is the day of the week (Mon, Tue, Wed, Thu, Fri, Sat, or Sun), the second is the day of the month (01 to 31), the third is the month (Jan, Feb, Mar, Apr, May, Jun, Jul, Aug, Sep, Oct, Nov, or Dec); the remaining hours (0 to 24), minutes, and seconds fields are obvious. The time must be in Greenwich Mean Time (GMT), so that all Web applications share a common time zone.

First Alternative Format

An alternative format is defined in RFC 850. An example is:

```
Wednesday, 09-Aug-94 07:49:37 GMT
```

where the first field is the day of the week (Monday, Tuesday, Wednesday, Thursday, Friday, Saturday, or Sunday), the third is the month (as given above), and the remaining fields are obvious. This second format will clearly cause chaos at the end of December 31, 1999, and therefore should be avoided.

Second Alternative Format

This format is defined by the ANSI C language asctime() format. An example date is:

```
Wed Aug 9 07:49:37 1994
```

Note that this format does not specify a time zone—the assumption is that the time is in GMT.

References

HTTP Overviews and Specifications

www.w3.org/Protocols/	(Overview)
ds.internic.net/rfc/rfc1945.txt	(HTTP 1.0 specification)
ds.internic.net/rfc/rfc2068.txt	(HTTP 1.1 specification)
www.w3.org/Protocols/HTTP-NG/Overview.html	(HTTP—Next Generation)

Caching and Proxy Servers

squid.nlanr.net/Squid/	(Squid caching proxy server)
www.w3.org/Daemon/	(CERN/W3C caching proxy server)

www.netscape.com/download/index.html   (Netscape caching proxy server /
                                              software catalog)

www.microsoft.com/proxy/   (Microsoft caching proxy server)

ftp://ftp.nec.com/pub/socks/   (SOCKS Internet services proxy)

User Authentication, Data Encryption, and Security

www.w3.org/Security/   (Overview)
www.netscape.com/info/security-doc.html   (Netscape SSL)
ds.internic.net/rfc/rfc2069.txt   (HTTP 1.1 digest authentication)
ds.internic.net/internet-drafts/   (Secure HTTP—S-HTTP)
    draft-ietf-wts-shttp-05.txt
www.genome.wi.mit.edu/WWW/faqs/   (Web Security FAQ)
www-security-faq.html

Secure Financial Transactions

ganges.cs.tcd.ie/mepeirce/project.html   (Digital cash overview)
www.visa.com/cgi-bin/vee/nt/ecomm/main.html   (Security Enhanced Transactions—
                                              SET)
www.mastercard.com/set/set.htm   (Security Enhanced Transactions—
                                              SET)

Browser and Server Comparisons and Benchmarks

webcompare.internet.com/   (Server comparisons and bench-
                                              marks)
website-1.openmarket.com/browsertest/   (Browser tests and benchmarks)
www.browsercaps.com/   (BrowserCaps browser capabilities)
www.yahoo.com/Computers_and_Internet/   (Yahoo list of Web servers)
    Software/Internet/World_Wide_Web/Servers/

Apache Server Content Negotiation

www.apache.org/docs/content-negotiation.html

Time and Date Formats

ds.internic.net/rfc/rfc1123.txt
ds.internic.net/rfc/rfc850.txt

DATA PROCESSING ON AN HTTP

SERVER

Having an HTTP server to deliver documents is all well and good, but the true power of the Web is only unleashed when you add dynamic content and user interaction. This means that the server must do more than just deliver data: It must be able to dynamically process and deliver content and respond to complex data sent to the server by a user.

The HTTP protocol, through the GET, POST, and PUT methods, provides many mechanisms for sending user-selected data to the server. But, what to do with the data when it arrives? As mentioned earlier, an HTTP server generally does not itself process these data; in fact, it would be impossible to write a server that came prepared to do all the special processing everyone would want. Instead, servers come with generic tools that let local server administrators add data processing functionality in a locally customizable way. The traditional method is via the *Common Gateway Interface* (CGI), which is a mechanism that can link a running HTTP server with completely separate programs, known as *gateway programs*, that do this second level of processing. This is still the most commonly used mechanism and is the main topic of this chapter. Many modern servers also support server programming interfaces, which allow for special processing modules that can be compiled and linked to the server. This is a bit like adding CGI right into the server, eliminating the separation between server and gateway processes. The comparative advantages and disadvantages of this alternate approach are also discussed in this chapter.

The Common Gateway Interface

The Common Gateway Interface (CGI) is the specified Web standard for communication between an HTTP server and server-side gateway programs. When a URL is accessed that references a gateway program, the server launches this gateway program *as a separate running process* and passes to it any **ISINDEX**, **FORM,** or other data sent by the client. When the gateway program finishes processing the data, it sends the results back to the server, which in turn forwards these data to the client that made the initial request. The CGI specifications define how these data are passed from the server to the gateway program, and vice versa. This data flow is schematically illustrated in Figure 10.1.

Server Applications Programming Interfaces

Gateway programs are ideal for many problems, as they can be easily added without modifying the HTTP server software. However, flexibility comes at the expense of speed and *scalability*: Starting up a gateway program involves significant operating system overhead, which can slow server response, particularly when the demand for a CGI program rises and the system tries to run a number of CGI programs in parallel. Most modern servers support linked-in modules, written in C or other compiled languages, to incorporate gateway-like processing right into the server. In a similar vein, certain Netscape HTTP servers support compiled Java modules, through a special Java interface incorporated into the server, while Microsoft servers support server-side Active-X components.

In all cases, these modules are written using a special server *applications programming interface*, or *API*, which is the software interface that links the modules to the underlying server. Unfortunately, the APIs used by each server vendor (Netscape,

Figure 10.1 Schematic diagram illustrating the data flow between a client, an HTTP server, and a server-side CGI program.

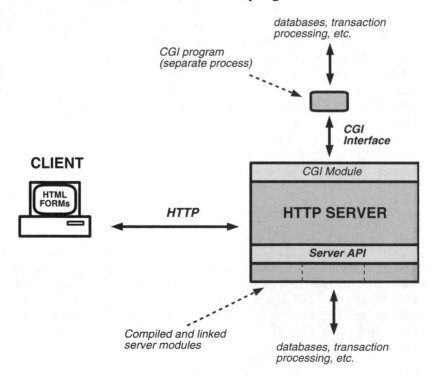

Microsoft, Apache, or other) are different and incompatible, so that modules written for one server do not work with another. However, this is the approach to use if you want fast server response for things like transaction processing or if you have generic and commonly used CGI functionality (such as imagemapping) that can be easily incorporated into the server. This chapter does not discuss module programming and design—the "References" section lists online documentation on these topics.

Gateway Programming Languages

Gateway programs can be compiled programs written in languages, such as C, C++, or pascal, or they can be executable scripts written in languages such as perl, tcl, and the various shell programs. In fact, many gateway programs are perl scripts, since these are easy to write and modify and are easily transportable from machine to machine. In addition, execution speed is often not an important factor with gateway programs, since the slowest component is often the resource the gateway connects to and not the gateway program itself. After all, if a database takes many seconds to complete a query, it does not matter if the gateway program takes an extra millisecond to start up. Even when this is not the case, speed is usually not an issue, since most CGI programs are actually quite small and very fast to start.

This chapter first reviews how data are communicated between a client and server (using the HTTP protocol) and then discusses how data are communicated between a server and a gateway program (the CGI mechanisms). This is followed by five examples that explore the details of the CGI mechanisms for the relevant HTTP methods, namely GET and POST, and for different HTML user input tools, namely **ISINDEX** and **FORM** elements. Lastly, there are brief discussions of how data sent by a client are decoded in gateway programs and of security issues you should be aware of when writing gateway programs.

Chapter 11 follows up this overview with several CGI programming examples and also provides a list of CGI utility programs and libraries available over the Internet.

Communication with Gateway Programs

The CGI mechanisms describe what data are passed from a server to a server-side gateway program, and vice versa, and how they are passed. In general, all data that a client sends to an HTTP server are made available, using *three* CGI mechanisms, to a referenced gateway. In turn, a gateway program has two CGI mechanisms for returning data to the server and from there to the client. These mechanisms are discussed below.

Client Sends to Server (HTTP)

There are three ways data can be sent from a client to a server. These are:

As a URL query string. An example URL is:

```
http://some.site.edu/cgi-bin/ex_prog?query_info
```

This passes the query string query_info to the server. The server, in turn, places the query string within an *environment variable* and then launches the gateway program ex_prog, which, in turn, obtains the query string from the environment variable.

As *extra path* information in the URL. *Extra path* information is placed in the URL by adding directory-like information to the URL, just after the name of the gateway program. An example is (extra path in boldface):

http://some.site.edu/cgi-bin/ex_prog**/dir/file**?query_info

If the server knows that /cgi-bin/ex_prog references a gateway program, then the string /dir/file is interpreted by the server as extra path information, while query_info is again the query string. When the server launches the gateway program ex_prog, it passes both the query string query_info and the extra path string /dir/file to ex_prog. In both cases, these data are passed to the gateway program within environment variables.

As data sent to the server in a message body. This is possible with the HTTP POST method and is commonly used with HTML FORMs. When a server receives a POST method message from a FORM, it sends the POSTed data to the designated gateway program. The gateway program reads the data from its standard input.

Server Sends to Gateway (CGI)

The CGI specifications define the mechanisms by which data are forwarded by a server to a gateway program. There are three mechanisms:

Command-line arguments. The server launches the gateway program and passes data to the program as command-line arguments. This occurs only with a GET method request arising from an **ISINDEX** query.

Environment variables. The server puts information in *environment variables* before starting the gateway program—the gateway program can then access these variables and obtain their contents. *Everything* contained in the HTTP headers sent by a client is placed in these environment variables. Thus, environment variables contain the query string and the extra path information discussed previously, as well as the content of *every* request header field sent by the browser. There are also environment variables containing information about the server, such as the home directory for the documents, the type of server, and the server's domain name.

Standard input. The gateway program reads data from standard input. This is how message data, sent by a browser using the POST method, are passed to the gateway program.

The mechanisms relevant during a particular transaction depend on the HTTP method used (GET or POST) and on the nature of the query string appended to the URL (**ISINDEX** versus non-**ISINDEX** queries). Examples illustrating typical cases are given later in this chapter.

Gateway Sends to Server (CGI)

There are two mechanisms by which a CGI program sends information back to the server:

By writing to standard output. A gateway program passes results back to the server by writing to standard output—this is the *only* way a gateway program can return data. In general, the returned data are in two parts. The first part is a collection of *server directives*, which are parsed by the server and are used by the server to compose the response header that the server sends ahead of the returned data. The second part is the actual data being returned by the gateway program. The two parts are separated by a blank line containing only a CRLF (carriage return linefeed) pair.

By the *name* of the gateway program. Gateway programs with names beginning with the string nph- are called *non-parsed header* programs and are treated specially by the server. As just mentioned, the server usually parses the output of a gateway program and uses the *server directives* to create the HTTP response header that is sent to the client ahead of the returned data. If a gateway program name begins with nph-, the server sends the gateway program output directly to the client without this extra processing, which means the server does *not* add any header information. In this case, a gateway program must itself provide *all* required HTTP response header fields.

These methods are illustrated in the following five examples. Example 20 looks at an HTML **ISINDEX** document request. Example 21 demonstrates non-parsed header gateway programs, which send data directly back to the client, bypassing any server processing. Example 22 shows how environment variables are passed to the gateway program and explains the contents of these variables. Examples 23 and 24 show how data from HTML **FORM**s—using the GET and POST methods, respectively—are passed to a gateway program. These examples also explain how these data are decoded by a gateway program.

Example 20: ISINDEX Searches

ISINDEX is the *only* query method that passes data to a gateway program as command-line arguments. It is a simple technique, and a useful starting point for understanding client-server-gateway interactions.

This example accesses the gateway program *srch-example* listed in Figure 10.2, which is a Bourne-shell script designed to search a phone-number database via the search program *grep*. The script searches for names in a phone-number database and uses the **ISINDEX** element to prompt for the search string. In this example, the search string is just the list of names you want to search for. When the script receives these data, it searches the database for the indicated names and returns the names and phone numbers of any matches. The script is designed both to prompt for search strings and return the results of the search.

Chapters 2 and 6 discussed how **ISINDEX** queries send data to the server by appending the query data to the URL of the document being viewed and then accessing the newly composed URL. An example of such a URL is:

```
http://some.where.edu/cgi-bin/srch_program?string1+string2
```

When this information reaches the server, and if it is an **ISINDEX** query, the server decodes the URL (converts plus (+) signs back into spaces, and converts URL character encodings back into the correct 8-bit characters), uses the space characters to break the query string into individual terms, and then passes these terms to the indicated gateway program as command-line arguments.

Detecting ISINDEX Queries

How does the server know if a GET method request comes from an **ISINDEX** query? The answer is that an ISINDEX query string *never contains* unencoded equals signs (=). As pointed out in Chapter 8 (which gave the details of the URL encoding mechanism) and in Example 16 of Chapter 9, **FORM** data are encoded as a collection of strings of the form *name=value*, which always contains at least one unencoded equals sign (any equals signs originally present in the name or value strings are encoded as %3d). Therefore, the presence of a "real" equals sign in the query string means that the data came from a **FORM** and not from an **ISINDEX**.

Step 1. First Access of the URL

In this example, we assume that the script *srch-example* is initially accessed via the URL:

```
http://leonardo.utirc.utoronto.ca:8080/cgi-bin/srch-example
```

Note that there is no query information attached to the URL; this is an important factor in the initial behavior of the script.

Line 1 tells the computer to interpret this script using the */bin/sh* program, which is the traditional location and name for the Bourne shell. The lines 2 and 3 echo information to standard output (echo is the Bourne-shell command that prints to standard output). Standard output is sent back to the server and, from there, back to the client.

Server Directives in Gateway Programs

The second line prints an HTTP *server directive*, which gives the server information about the data to come. This is absolutely necessary, as the server has no

---

Figure 10.2 Bourne-shell script CGI gateway program *srch-example*.

```
01 #!/bin/sh
02 echo Content-TYPE:   text/html
03 echo
04
05 if [ $# = 0 ]          # is the number of arguments == 0 ?
06 then                   # do this part if there are NO arguments
07     echo "<HEAD>"
08     echo "<TITLE>Local Phonebook Search</TITLE>"
09     echo "<ISINDEX>"
10     echo "</HEAD>"
11     echo "<BODY>"
12     echo "<H1>Local Phonebook Search</H1>"
13     echo "Enter your search in the search field.<P>"
14     echo "This is a case-insensitive substring search: thus"
15     echo "searching for 'ian' will find 'Ian' and Adriana'."
16     echo "</BODY>"
17 else                           # this part if there ARE arguments
18     echo "<HEAD>"
19     echo "<TITLE>Result of search for \"$*\".</TITLE>"
20     echo "</IIEAD>"
21     echo "<BODY>"
22     echo "<H1>Result of search for \"$*\".</H1>"
23     echo "<PRE>"
24     for i in $*
25     do
26           grep -i $i /vast/igraham/Personnel
27     done
28     echo "</PRE>"
39     echo "</BODY>"
40 fi
```

other way of knowing what type of data the program will return. This line prints the header

```
Content-TYPE: text/html
```

to tell the server that the data to follow is an HTML document. The next line prints a blank line. This denotes the end of the header—subsequent output is the actual data being returned.

Several other server directives are possible—they are summarized in Example 21.

Line 5 tests the *number* of command-line arguments. In this case, there was no query string, so there are no command-line arguments and the first branch of the `if` is executed. This branch prints, to standard output, a simple HTML document explaining the nature of the search; this is shown in Figure 10.3. This document contains an **ISINDEX** element, to tell the browser to prompt for search information—this gives rise to the query box in Figure 10.3. I have typed the names `ian` and `bradley` into this box (the author always likes to look for his own name), separated by a single space. These are the names that will be used in the search.

Step 2: Second Access of the URL

Submitting this **ISINDEX** search information accesses the same URL, but appends the names *ian* and *bradley* to the URL as query strings. Thus, in this second phase, the accessed URL is

```
http://leonardo.utirc.utoronto.ca:8080/cgi-bin/srch-example?ian+bradley
```

where the space between *ian* and *bradley* has been encoded as a plus sign, as required by the URL query string encoding scheme described in Chapter 8.

When the server receives this URL, it parses the query string and finds that there are no unencoded equals signs, so it knows that this is an **ISINDEX** query. It therefore takes the query string and breaks it into individual strings, using the plus signs to mark the string separators. This yields the two strings `ian` and `bradley`. The server next launches the gateway program *srch-example*, using the names `ian` and `bradley` as command-line arguments. The equivalent command, typed by hand, would be:

```
srch-example ian bradley
```

Figure 10.4 shows the results of this second access to the Bourne-shell program; by following Figure 10.2, you can see how it was generated. As before, the first two lines print the MIME content-type of the message and the blank line separating the HTTP headers from the data. At line 5, the program checks for

Figure 10.3 Document returned from the script *srch-example* when accessed *without* a query string appended to the URL.

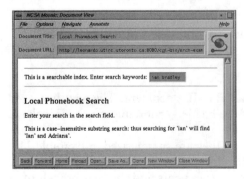

Figure 10.4 Document returned from the script *srch-example* when accessed *with* a query string appended to the URL.

command-line arguments. This time there are arguments, so the second branch of the script is executed, starting at line 18. This section prints a different HTML document, this time including output from the program grep. Lines 24 through 27 loop the variable *i* through all the command-line arguments. The content of the variable *i* (denoted by $i) is used as an argument to the program grep, which scans the file */vast/igraham/Personnel* for names matching the pattern given by $i. Grep prints the matches to standard output. The result of the searches is shown in Figure 10.4. Note that there is no query box, as the second branch of the script in Figure 10.2 did not return an **ISINDEX** element.

Example 21: Gateway Program Server Directives

The second example looks at how HTTP servers compose a response header for data returned by a gateway program. Consider first the actual data sent by a server (here, the Apache 1.1.1 server) upon the client's first access of the program *srch-example* (Figure 10.5; these are the data that produced Figure 10.3).

Comparing Figure 10.5 with Figure 10.2, you will see that the headers are *not* those returned by the script: The content-type headers are typographically different (`Content-TYPE` versus `Content-type`). In fact, the headers returned to the client were generated by the HTTP server, with help from server directives returned by the gateway program.

Server Directives

The server takes the header data returned by the gateway program and parses each of the header fields. Most of these headers are passed through unaltered and are included as part of the server response header returned to the client. Some, however, are treated as *server directives* and are used by the server to *modify* the HTTP response header fields the server normally returns in the response. The three valid server-directive headers are listed and described in Table 10.1.

Figure 10.5 Data returned to the client upon accessing the URL:

`http://leonardo.utirc.utoronto.ca:8080/cgi-bin/srch-example`
These are the data that produce Figure 10.3.

```
HTTP/1.0 200 OK
Server: Apache/1.1.1
Date: Thu, 01 Aug 1996 16:43:53 GMT
Content-type: text/html

<HEAD>
<TITLE>Local Phonebook Search</TITLE>
<ISINDEX>
</HEAD>
<BODY>
<H1>Local Phonebook Search</H1>
Enter your search in the search field.<P>
This is a case-insensitive substring search: thus
searching for 'ian' will find 'Ian' and Adriana'.
</BODY>
```

In addition to these special server directives, a gateway program can return most regular server response header fields—they will simply be forwarded to the client as part of the response header, following those headers generated by the server itself. For example, if a gateway program returns results from a database that is updated on a regular basis, the program could return an `Expires` header as part of the server directives to indicate when the data will be stale, thereby allowing clients to reliably cache copies until the specified expiration date.

Limitations of Server Directives

You *must not* use server directives to produce duplicates of the headers ordinarily returned by the server—such headers usually describe generic characteristics of the server and cannot be altered by a gateway program. For example, the `Server`, `Date`, and `MIME-Version` header fields are server-specific and should never be returned by a gateway program. But, as with spelling, there is an exception to every rule—and the exception here is for *non-parsed header* gateway programs.

Non-Parsed Header Gateway Programs

It is possible to return gateway program output directly to the client without any processing by an HTTP server—in this case, the gateway can return any header fields it wants, regardless of the rule presented above. This is accomplished by appending the string nph-, for *non-parsed header*, to the beginning of the name of the script. When the server sees a gateway program name beginning with nph-, it passes the

Table 10.1 CGI Server Directives and Their Allowed Content

`Content-type:`
`type/subtype`
`(; parameters)`
	Gives the MIME type for the data being returned by the gateway program. The server will use this value to compose the `content-type` header field returned with the HTTP response header.

`Location: URL`	Specifies a URL to which the client should be *redirected*. A server will add this `Location:` field to the server response header and will also modify the server response status line to be: `HTTP/1.0 302 Redirection`
`Status: code string`	Contains an HTTP status code (`code`) and arbitrary descriptive status string (`string`) to be used by the server in place of the standard value. A server will modify its default status field to return the server response header field: `HTTP/1.0 code string`

gateway program output directly to the client, without any processing. For example, Figure 10.6 shows the data returned from the gateway *program nph-srch-example:* This is an exact duplicate of the program *srch-example* listed in Figure 10.2, the only change being the string nph- added to the front of the filename.

Comparing Figure 10.6 with the program listing in Figure 10.2 shows that the response now contains just the data printed by the gateway program, with

Figure 10.6 Non-parsed header output returned upon accessing the URL.

`http://leonardo.utirc.utoronto.ca:8080/cgi-bin/nph-srch-example`

```
Content-TYPE: text/html

<HEAD>
 <TITLE>Local Phonebook Search</TITLE>
<ISINDEX>
</HEAD>
<BODY>
<H1>Local Phonebook Search</H1>
Enter your search in the search field.<P>
This is a case-insensitive substring search: thus
searching for 'ian' will find 'Ian' and Adriana'.
</BODY>
```

nothing added or modified by the server. The advantages of non-parsed header gateway programs is speed and flexibility, since the server is not required to parse the returned data and generate appropriate headers and the programmer is not limited in what can be placed within the response header. In exchange, the gateway program itself must produce *all* the required headers fields. Note how the returned data in Figure 10.6 are an *invalid* server response, as the response does not contain a status line nor does it indicate the date or server type. Thus an nph- script must print, at a minimum, the following response headers, with values appropriate to the script and the data being returned (the portions that must be customized to the situation are shown in italics; these are just example values):

```
HTTP/1.0 200 OK
Date: Thu, 01 Aug 1996 16:50:57 GMT
Server: NCSA/1.5.2
Content-type: text/x-babelfish
```

Custom Response Fields

Of course, a CGI program can return any manner of response fields—with non-parsed header scripts, these are passed right through to the client, while if the server parses the response, it will generally pass along any well-formed field that does not conflict with a field the server normally returns.

This can be useful, as some browsers understand nonstandard fields in the response header. For example, Netscape Navigator understands *content-disposition* fields of the form:

```
content-disposition: attachment; filename=name-of-file
```

Such fields tell the browser that the downloaded data is an attached file and that it should be assigned the indicated filename. For example, the message:

```
content-type: application/x-gzip
content-length: 1232123
content-disposition: attachment; filename=archive.gz
```

tells the browser that the downloaded file (a GZIP archive) has the name *archive.gz*. Since Netscape cannot view this type of file, it will prompt the user to save the file and will offer to save it under the name *archive.gz*.

If the content-disposition field is not present, the browser generally uses the last part of the URL (minus the query string) as the default filename, which in this case would likely be the name of the program that generated the response.

This is a convenient way to use a single CGI program for downloading a variety of stored archive files. However, there is an important caveat—the content-disposition header field is only understood by Netscape Navigator, and is not understood by Internet Explorer.

Example 22: Environment Variables

The preceding examples would imply that the server passes very little information to a gateway program. In fact, the server is not so ungenerous. Before launching a gateway program, the server initializes several *environment variables* that are subsequently accessible to the gateway. In particular, this mechanism passes any extra path and query string information to a gateway program. Table 10.2 lists the environment variables defined as part of the CGI standard, while Figures 10.7 and 10.8 illustrate the most common variables in an example application. Figure 10.7 shows the gateway script srch-example-2; this is the same **ISINDEX** script listed in Figure 10.2, modified to print out environment variable contents. The HTML document generated upon accessing this script at the URL

```
http://leonardo.utirc.utoronto.ca:8080/cgi-bin/srch-example-2/dir/file?ian+bradley
```

is shown in Figure 10.8. Accessing this URL passes both query string (ian+bradley) and extra path information (/dir/file) to the referenced gateway program.

Most of the environment variables in Figure 10.8 are easy to understand. Some are set by default and do not depend on the nature of the request, while others are set only when particular client-server-gateway interactions are involved.

Standard Environment Variables

Table 10.2 lists the standard environment variables that are passed to a gateway program by an HTTP server. Not all variables are defined in all cases; for example, the variables associated with user authentication are only defined when authentication is being used.

Request Header–Based Environment Variables

As noted in Table 10.2, *every* piece of information in the HTTP request header (the headers sent from the client to the server) not contained within a standard CGI environment variable is passed to the gateway program within an environment variable of the form HTTP_*NAME*, where *NAME* is related to the *name* of the request header fields. These environment variable names are constructed by:

1. *capitalizing* the name in the request header field (e.g., User-agent to USER-AGENT)
2. *converting* dash (-) characters into underscores (_) (e.g., USER-AGENT to USER_AGENT)
3. *adding* the prefix HTTP_ (e.g., USER_AGENT to HTTP_USER_AGENT)

Some of the more common environment variables of this type are listed in Table 10.3. Note, in particular, the construction of the HTTP_ACCEPT header.

Figure 10.7 Bourne-shell script *srch-example-2*. This is essentially the same script shown in Figure 10.2, but modified to explicitly print out the environment variables and the command-line arguments.

```
#!/bin/sh
echo Content-TYPE:  text/html
echo
 if [ $# = 0 ]    # is the number of arguments == 0 ?
then             # do this part if there are NO arguments
     echo "<HEAD>"
     echo "<TITLE>Local Phonebook Search</TITLE>"
     echo "<ISINDEX>"
     echo "</HEAD>"
     echo "<BODY>"
     echo "<H1>Local Phonebook Search</H1>"
     echo "Enter your search in the search field.<P>"
     echo "This is a case-insensitive substring search: thus"
     echo "searching for 'ian' will find 'Ian' and Adriana'."
     echo "</BODY>"
else             # this part if there ARE arguments
     echo "<HEAD>"
     echo "<TITLE>Result of search for \"$*\".</TITLE>"
     echo "</HEAD>"
     echo "<BODY>"
     echo "<P> Number of Command-line Arguments = $#.    They are:"
     for i in $*
     do
          echo " <code> $i </code> "
     done
     echo "<h2> The Environment Variables </h2>"
     echo "<pre>"       # print the environment variables
     echo " SERVER_SOFTWARE = $SERVER_SOFTWARE"
     echo " SERVER_NAME = $SERVER_NAME"
     echo " GATEWAY_INTERFACE = $GATEWAY_INTERFACE"
     echo " SERVER_PROTOCOL = $SERVER_PROTOCOL"
     echo " SERVER_PORT = $SERVER_PORT"
     echo " REQUEST_METHOD = $REQUEST_METHOD"
     echo " HTTP_ACCEPT = $HTTP_ACCEPT"
     echo " PATH_INFO = $PATH_INFO"
     echo " PATH_TRANSLATED = $PATH_TRANSLATED"
```

Figure 10.7 *Continued*

```
        echo " SCRIPT_NAME = $SCRIPT_NAME"
        echo " QUERY_STRING = $QUERY_STRING"
        echo " REMOTE_HOST = $REMOTE_HOST"
        echo " REMOTE_ADDR = $REMOTE_ADDR"
        echo " REMOTE_USER = $REMOTE_USER"
        echo " AUTH_TYPE = $AUTH_TYPE"
        echo " CONTENT_TYPE = $CONTENT_TYPE"
        echo " CONTENT_LENGTH = $CONTENT_LENGTH"
        echo "</pre>"
        echo "<H2>Result of search for \"$*\".</H2>"
        echo "<PRE>"
        for i in $*
        do
            grep -i $i /vast/igraham/Personnel
        done
        echo "</PRE>"
        echo "</BODY>"
fi
```

Figure 10.8 Document returned from the script in Figure 10.7 after accessing the URL.

http://leonardo.utirc.utoronto.ca:8080/cgi-bin/srch-example-2/dir/file?ian+bradley

Table 10.2 Environment Variables Available Within a Gateway Program

(A) Server Properties

SERVER_SOFTWARE — The name and version of the server software answering the request, in the format *name/version*: for example, NCSA/1.5.2 or Apache/1.1.1.

SERVER_NAME — The Internet domain name of the server; if the domain name is not known, this is the numerical IP address.

GATEWAY_INTERFACE — The version of the CGI specification used by the server in the format CGI/*version*. The current version is 1.1, so this should be CGI/1.1.

SERVER_PROTOCOL — The protocol being used and the version number, in the format *protocol/version*. This permits gateway programs that support different protocols (e.g., Gopher and HTTP) or different protocol versions, as the program can use this variable to select appropriate code sections. The current HTTP protocol version is 1.0, so this is usually HTTP/1.0.

SERVER_PORT — The port number used in a transaction (typically 80).

(B) Client Properties

REMOTE_HOST — The Internet domain name of the host making the request. If the domain name is unavailable, this variable is undefined. The numerical IP address is always available in the *REMOTE_ADDR* variable.

REMOTE_ADDR — The numeric IP address of the remote host accessing the server. This is always defined.

HTTP_*NAME* — The contents of *all* the request header fields sent by the client. The environment variable name is composed of the string HTTP_*NAME*, where *NAME* is capitalized *header field name*, with all dashes in the name converted to underscores: for example, HTTP_USER_AGENT for the User-Agent field.

(C) Request Properties

REQUEST_METHOD — The method associated with the request. For HTTP server access this will be GET, HEAD, POST, PUT, and so on.

PATH_INFO — Extra path information present in the URL; undefined if there is no such information in the URL.

PATH_TRANSLATED — The PATH_INFO path translated into an *absolute path* on the server's filesystem; undefined if PATH_INFO is undefined. For example, if the server document directory is /vast/igraham/WebDocs, and PATH_INFO=dir/file, then PATH_TRANSLATED=/vast/igraham/WebDocs/dir/file This is often used to reference gateway

Table 10.2 *Continued*

	program configuration files. Note that this is *not* related to the location of the gateway program.
SCRIPT_NAME	The *path* and *name* of the script being accessed as it would be referenced in a URL: for example, /cgi-bin/prog.pl. This can be used to construct URLs that refer back to this same gateway program, for insertion in script-generated HTML documents. For example, the string http://$SERVER_NAME:$SERVER_PORT$SCRIPT_NAME gener-ates the full URL to the program using information contained in the environment variables ($NAME refers to the *content* of the environment variable NAME).
QUERY_STRING	The query string portion of the URL, in encoded form. A gate-way program must decode this string to extract the data sent by the client. If this string results from an ISINDEX search request, the query string data are also passed to the program as *decoded* command-line arguments.

(D) Authentication Information

AUTH_TYPE	The *authentication method* required to authenticate the user requesting access. This is defined only for scripts that are access protected. The only currently implemented value is Basic, for the Basic authentication scheme.
REMOTE_USER	The *authenticated name* of the user; defined only when authen-tication is required. This is undefined if authentication is not required.
REMOTE_IDENT	The remote user name, retrieved by the server from the client machine using the *identd* protocol and the remote identification daemon. This is largely unused.

(E) Client Data Properties

CONTENT_TYPE	The MIME content-type of the data sent by the client to the server (POST or PUT method). This is undefined if no data are sent. The actual data are available to the gateway program by reading from standard input. The currently implemented types for POST requests are application/x-www-form-urlencoded and application/form-data.
CONTENT_LENGTH	The length, in bytes, of the data message sent to the server by the client (POST or PUT methods). If no data are being sent, this is undefined. A gateway program does not have to read all the data before returning a response or before exiting.

Table 10.3 Common Gateway Environment Variables Derived from HTTP Request Header Fields

Variable	Content
HTTP_ACCEPT	A comma-separated list of all MIME types acceptable to the client, as indicated by the Accept headers sent to the server. An example is shown in Figure 10.8. Gateway programs can use this to determine which type of data to return to the client.
HTTP_COOKIE	A semicolon-separated list of *Netscape cookies*. Netscape cookies are described later in this chapter.
HTTP_IF_MODIFIED_SINCE	Gives the time and date, in the standard format described at the end of Chapter 9, of data held by the client. The gateway program can then decide if the server has data that are newer than this and if it should forward updated data or not.
HTTP_REFERER	Contains the URL which referred the user to the current request; undefined if there is no Referer header field.
HTTP_USER_AGENT	The contents of the User_Agent request header field. An example is shown at the bottom of Figure 10.8.

Server-Side Include Environment Variables

Several servers support a feature known as *server-side includes*, or SSI. SSI allows for parsable HTML documents: The documents contain special server directives that are processed by the server and are replaced by text from a second document, or by the output of a designated CGI program. SSI supports additional environment variables not mention in Tables 10.2 and 10.3. Chapter 11 contains a thorough discussion of SSI, while Tables 11.2 and 11.3 list the special environment variables provided by the SSI mechanism.

NOTE: Customized Environment Variables

Some servers permit local customization of CGI environment variables. You should check with your local server administrator to find out about any special-purpose CGI environment variables available at your site.

Example 23: HTML FORMs via a GET Request

This example examines the data passed by an HTML **FORM** to the program shown in Figure 10.9. The **FORM** used is the same one employed in Example 16 in Chapter 9, which uses the GET method to send the data to the program (the **FORM** document is shown in Figure 9.6 and, as rendered by a browser, in Figure 9.7). The Bourne-shell program in Figure 10.9 prints out the relevant environment variables and also reads in data from standard input (the `read var` command, on the fourth line from the bottom) and prints this input data to standard output.

The data sent to the server (and to the gateway program listed in Figure 10.9) by the form listed in Figure 9.6 are:

```
GET /cgi-bin/form1?srch=dogfish&srch_type=Exact+Match&srvr=Canada&srvr=Sweden HTTP/1.0
Accept: text/plain
Accept: application/x-html
Accept: application/html
Accept: text/x-html
Accept: text/html
Accept: audio/*
   .

   .
Accept: text/x-setext
Accept: */*
User-Agent: NCSA Mosaic for the X Window System/2.4 libwww/2.12 modified
    [a blank line, containing only CRLF ]
```

The dots indicate Accept headers omitted to save space. You will note that these data were sent by the Mosaic for X-Windows browser.

Figure 10.10 shows the document returned by the script listed in Figure 10.9. You will note that there are no command-line arguments. In parsing the URL, the server detected "real" equals signs within the query string. This indicates a non-**ISINDEX** query, so the server does not create command-line arguments. The remaining quantities are obvious. The `REQUEST_METHOD` environment variable is set to GET, and the query string is placed in the `QUERY_STRING` environment variable. The `CONTENT_TYPE` and `CONTENT_LENGTH` variables are empty, since there is no data sent in a GET method, while the `PATH_INFO` and `PATH_TRANSLATED` variables are also empty, since there was no extra path information in the query.

Further processing requires more sophisticated programming tools to parse the `QUERY_STRING` and break it into its component parts. This is not difficult, recalling that the ampersand character divides the different segments; the equals sign relates FORM variable names to the assigned values; and spaces in the query strings are encoded as plus signs. Finally, you must decode all the special characters that may have been encoded using the URL encoding scheme discussed in Chapter 8. The perl code extract in Figure 10.11 illustrates how this decoding can be done.

Some useful collections of CGI utilities are listed in Chapter 11.

Example 24: HTML FORMs via a POST Request

This example again accesses the program shown in Figure 10.9 using a **FORM** equivalent to the one in Figure 9.6, but this time, using the POST

Figure 10.9 Test script *form1* accessed by the HTML FORM in Figure 9.6. This script returns an HTML document listing the script command-line arguments (if there are any), the contents of all the environment variables, and any data read from standard input (if any exists).

```
#!/bin/sh
echo Content-TYPE:  text/html
echo
# is a FORMs test script -- it prints the environment variable
# contents generated by a FORM access to this script.
echo "<HEAD>"
echo "<TITLE>FORMs Test Page </TITLE>"
echo "</HEAD>"
echo "<P> Number of Command-line Arguments = $#. They are:"
for i in $*
do
    echo " <code> $i </code> "
done
echo "<h2> The Environment Variables </h2>"
echo "<pre>"
echo "SERVER_NAME = $SERVER_NAME"
echo "SERVER_PORT = $SERVER_PORT"
echo "REQUEST_METHOD = $REQUEST_METHOD"
echo "PATH_INFO = $PATH_INFO"
echo "PATH_TRANSLATED = $PATH_TRANSLATED"
echo "SCRIPT_NAME = $SCRIPT_NAME"
echo "QUERY_STRING = $QUERY_STRING"
echo "CONTENT_TYPE = $CONTENT_TYPE"
echo "CONTENT_LENGTH = $CONTENT_LENGTH"
echo
if [ -n "$CONTENT_LENGTH" ]; then # Read/print input data (if any).
    echo "<H2>data at Standard Input is:</h2>"
    echo "<PRE>"
    read "var"  # read data from standard input into "var"
    echo "$var" # print var to standard output
    echo "</PRE>"
else
    echo "<h2> No Data at standard input </h2>"
fi
echo "</BODY>
```

Figure 10.10 Data returned from the script shown in Figure 10.9 when accessed, using the GET method, by the FORM shown in Figure 9.6.

method. The data sent to a server (again using the Mosaic for X-Windows browser) are:

```
POST /cgi-bin/form1 HTTP/1.0
Accept: text/plain
Accept: application/x-html
Accept: application/html
Accept: text/x-html
Accept: text/html
Accept: audio/*
       .

       .
Accept: text/x-setext
Accept: */*
User-Agent: NCSA Mosaic for the X Window System/2.4 libwww/2.12 modified
Content-type: application/x-www-form-urlencoded
Content-length: 58

srch=dogfish&srch_type=Exact+Match&srvr=Canada&srvr=Sweden
```

In this case, the data are sent to the server as an encoded message following the headers. There are two extra header fields: the content-length field, which tells the server the length of the following message; and the content-type field, which tells the server that this is an application/x-www-form-urlencoded MIME type—this is the MIME type that indicates **FORM** data that have been encoded using the URL encoding scheme.

Figure 10.11 Perl code extract for decoding FORM data passed in a query string. Note that this is not a functional piece of code and that the extracted name and value strings must be place in a permanent storage location (such as an associative array or hash table) for subsequent processing.

```perl
if( !defined($ENV{"QUERY_STRING"})) {      # Check for Query String environment
    &pk_error("No Query String\n");        # Variable -- if absent, then error.
}
$input=$ENV{"QUERY_STRING"}                # get FORM data from query string

                                           # Check for unencoded equals sign -- if
                                           # there are none, the string didn't
if( $input !~ /=/ ) {                      # come from a FORM, which is an error.
    &pk_error("Query String not from FORM\n");
}
                                           # If we get to here, all is OK. Now
@fields=split("&",$input);                 # split data into separate name=value
                                           # fields(@fields is an array)


#   Now loop over each of the entries in the @fields array and break
#   them into the name and value parts. Then decode each part to get
#   back the strings typed into the form by the user

foreach $one (@fields) {
    ($name, $value) = split("=",$one);     # split, at the equals sign, into
                                           # the name and value strings. Next,
                                           # decode the strings.
    $name  =~ s/\+/ /g;                    # convert +'s to spaces
    $name  =~ s/%(..)/pack("c",hex($1))/ge; # convert URL hex codings to Latin-1
    $value =~ s/\+/ /g;                    # convert +'s to spaces
    $value =~ s/%(..)/pack("c",hex($1))/ge; # convert URL hex codings to Latin-1


    #   What you do now depends on how the program works. If you know that each
    #   name is unique (your FORM does not have checkbox or SELECT items that
    #   allow multiple name=value strings with the same name) then you can place
    #   all the data in an associative array (a useful little perl feature!):

    $array{"$name"} = $value;

    #   If your form does have SELECT or <INPUT TYPE=checkbox..> items,
    #   then you'll have to be a bit more careful...


}
```

Figure 10.12 Data returned from the script shown in Figure 10.9 when accessed by the FORM shown in Figure 9.6 and modified to use the POST HTTP method.

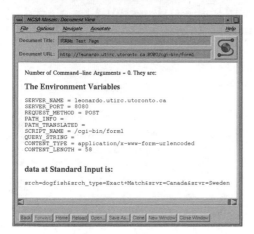

Figure 10.12 shows the results returned by the script in Figure 10.9 and displays the data that arrived at the script. There are no command-line arguments this time, because there is no query string. Most of the environment variables are the same as with the GET request shown in Figure 10.10. Obvious differences are the REQUEST_METHOD variable, which is now POST instead of GET, and the null QUERY_STRING. In addition, the CONTENT_TYPE and CONTENT_LENGTH are not empty but contain the length of the message and the content-type, as indicated in the fields sent by the client.

Where are the **FORM** data? With the POST method, these data are sent to the gateway program as an input stream, which the program reads from standard input. The script in Figure 10.9 reads data from standard input and prints the results back to standard output. The result is printed at the bottom of Figure 10.12, which clearly shows the query data sent by the client. These data are encoded using the same URL encoding mechanisms employed with the GET query in Figure 10.10. To further process these data, you must parse it and separate the fields. Figure 10.13 shows an extract of a perl program that illustrates how this decoding can be done. This is similar to the code in Figure 10.11—the differences occur only at the beginning of the script and are marked in italics. Again, there are CGI libraries, mentioned in Chapter 11, that can help in the processing of these data.

Example 24 may seem similar to Example 23, but it is, in fact, different in important ways. First, many computer operating systems limit the size of environment variables, so that large messages passed via GET URLs may be truncated. In addition, the POST method allows for complicated MIME messages to be sent from client to server, something that is impractical, if not impossible, with the

Figure 10.13 Perl code extract for decoding FORM data passed to the program via standard input. Differences from the extract in Figure 10.11 are shown in italics. Note that this is not a functional piece of code and that the extracted name and value strings must be placed in a permanent storage location (such as an associative array) for subsequent processing.

```perl
$input=<STDIN>;                         # read FORM data from stdin
chop($input); chop($input);             # chop CR/LF trailing characters:
                                        # recall that the data sent by a client
                                        # is always terminated by a single line
                                        # containing only a CRLF pair. This
                                        # must be removed, since it is not
                                        # part of the message body.
                                        # Check for unencoded equals sign -- if
                                        # there are none, the string didn't
if( $input !~ /=/ ) {                   # come from a FORM, which is an error.
    &pk_error("Query String not from FORM\n");
}
                                        # If we get to here, all is OK. Now
@fields=split("&",$input);              # split data into separate name=value
                                        # fields(@fields is an array)

#   Now loop over each of the entries in the @fields array and break
#   them into the name and value parts. Then decode each part to get
#   back the strings typed into the form by the user

foreach $one (@fields) {
    ($name, $value) = split("=",$one);  # split,at the equals sign,into
                                        # the name and value strings. Next,
                                        # decode the strings.
    $name  =~ s/\+/ /g;                 # convert +'s to spaces
    $name  =~ s/%(..)/pack("c",hex($1))/ge; # convert URL hex codings to Latin-1
    $value =~ s/\+/ /g;                 # convert +'s to spaces
    $value =~ s/%(..)/pack("c",hex($1))/ge; # convert URL hex codings to Latin-1

    #   What you do now depends on how the program works. If you know that each
    #   name is unique (your FORM does not have checkbox or SELECT items that
    #   allow multiple name=value strings with the same name) then you can place
    #   all the data in an associative array (a useful little perl feature!):

    $array{"$name"} = $value;
```

Figure 10.13 *Continued*

```
#     If your form does have SELECT or <INPUT TYPE=checkbox..> items,
#     then you'll have to be a bit more careful...


}
```

GET method. In this regard, data can be POSTed to a server using the *multipart/form-data* encoding scheme, discussed in Example 18 in Chapter 9. This scheme supports file upload (the ability to upload arbitrary data files from the client to the server) as well as the encoding of text input using any character set— recall that URLs, and hence URL-encoded FORM data, are restricted to the ISO Latin-1 character set.

Relative Advantages of GET and POST

The GET and POST methods for handling **FORM** input have different strengths and weaknesses. POST is clearly superior if you are sending large quantities of data to the server or data encoded in character sets other than ISO Latin-1. If you are sending small quantities of data, and only ISO Latin-1 characters, the choice is less clear. One useful criterion is to ask if you want the user to be able to store ("bookmark") a URL that will return the user to this particular resource. If the answer is yes, then you must use the GET method, since the relevant data will be placed in the query string portion of a URL, which is stored when a URL is recorded. If, on the other hand, you do not want the user to be able to quickly return to this resource or you want to hide the **FORM** content as much as possible, you should use POST.

HTML Encoding of Text Within a FORM

With gateway programs, you often need to place data inside the **FORM** sent to the client—this might be initial field values assigned to the **VALUE** attributes of **INPUT** or **OPTION** elements or within the body of a **TEXTAREA** element, or it might be *state information* (information describing the state of the interaction between the user and the server-side application) preserved within the **VALUE** attributes of **TYPE**="hidden" **INPUT** elements. However, in doing so, you must remember that the text received by the client will be *parsed*. This means that any entity or character references embedded in the **VALUE** (or **NAME**) strings or within the body of a **TEXTAREA** element will be automatically expanded into the correct ISO Latin-1 characters. For example, if a document sent to a client contains the hidden element

```
<INPUT TYPE="hidden" NAME="stuff" VALUE="&lt;BOO&quot;&gt;">
```

the client will *parse* the **VALUE** string and convert it into the string `<BOO">`. When the **FORM** containing this hidden element is submitted, the string `<BOO">` will be URL-encoded and sent to the server, so that the entity references in the original data are lost.

This is sensible if you recall that, as far as the browser is concerned, entity references and character references *are* no different from the characters they represent. This can be a problem, however, if the data within the hidden form contains HTML markup, since you often need to *preserve* entity references distinct from the characters they represent; for example, so that simple character strings (`&lt;tag&gt;`) do not get converted into markup tags (`<tag>`) by the conversion process. Thus, if you need to preserve entity references, you must do the following encodings of the string prior to placing it within a **VALUE** or **NAME** attribute or inside a **TEXTAREA** element:

1. encode all ampersand characters in the text string as `&amp;`
2. encode all double quotation symbols as `&quot;`
3. encode all right angle brackets as `&gt;`

The second and third steps are necessary, as any raw double quote characters (`"`) will prematurely terminate a **VALUE** or **NAME** string, while some browsers mistakenly use an unencoded greater-than symbol (`>`) to prematurely end **INPUT** elements. The first step encodes the leading character of each entity or character reference: For example, the original string `&eacute;` becomes `&amp;eacute;`. This is processed by the client browser back to the string `&eacute;`, which brings you full circle when the data are returned to the server.

State Preservation in CGI Transactions

In a complex gateway application, a complete session may require a series of interactions between the client and server. Since the HTTP protocol is stateless, the server—and any gateway program on the server—retain no knowledge of any previous transaction. Thus you, the gateway program designer, must build in mechanisms for keeping track of what happened in any previous stage. There are two strategies for doing this. The traditional way is to use **TYPE**="hidden" **INPUT** elements within HTML forms, to pass state information back and forth between client and server. A second, newer method is to use Netscape cookies to store state information on the client.

State Preservation by Hidden Elements

There are two ways to use **TYPE**="hidden" **INPUT** ("hidden," for short) elements to preserve state information. First, the gateway program can place all the data received from the client inside "hidden" elements returned with the **FORM** used for the next stage of a transaction. Then, the subsequent access to a server resends the data from the previous interaction(s), since all the data are preserved in the "hidden" elements. The second method is to create a temporary file on the server and store the transaction data within this file. In this case, the gateway program need only return a single "hidden" element containing the *name* of this temporary file, so that the gateway program, on subsequent requests, is told where to find the state information. This reduces the amount of data that must be sent from client to server (and back again), but also means that the gateway programs must carefully manage these temporary files. For example, many remote users may not complete the transaction, which will leave temporary files in place unless there are auxiliary routines for deleting "stale" entries.

State Preservation by Netscape Cookies

The "hidden" form element mechanism works, but is not ideal. Problems arise if a user does not move through the sequence exactly as planned and in a single session. For example, a user might get halfway through a process, shut off his or her computer and go home, hoping to resume the next morning. This is not possible with "hidden" form elements, since all the state information is lost when the browser is turned off.

As a partial solution to this problem, Netscape introduced a mechanism commonly known as *Netscape cookies*. The idea behind cookies is to have the browser store, on its local hard disk, specific state information sent by the server. In a sense, this is like storing "hidden" element data, but outside the document and in such a way that they can be retrieved whenever needed. The cookie content is then sent to the server, as part of the HTTP request header, when appropriate.

Cookies are sent to a browser using a `Set-Cookie` HTTP response header field or fields (the server can send multiple cookies in a single transaction). In turn, the browser sends cookies to a server using a `Cookie` HTTP request header field.

Putting a Cookie on the Browser

An HTTP server places cookie information on a browser by sending a special `Set-Cookie` HTTP response header field—which is often returned by CGI programs within a server directive. The `Set-Cookie` field contains the cookie content as a name/value pair and can also contain information explaining when the cookie will no longer be valid (*expires*), the Internet domain for which the cookie is valid (*domain*), and the path portion of the URL within this domain for which the cookie is valid (*path*).

Cookie Parameter Values

The general form of a `Set-Cookie` header field is:

```
Set-Cookie: name=value; expires=date; path=val_path; domain=dom_nam; secure
```

Note that the different parts of the cookie header are separated by semicolons. Most of these parameters are optional. The meanings and uses of the parameters are described in Table 10.4.

Table 10.4 Definition of Parameters for Set-Cookie Fields

name=value
(mandatory)

This mandatory parameter specifies the name and value for the cookie. Both name and value must be strings of printable ASCII characters and cannot contain semicolons (;), commas (,) or space characters. There is no encoding mechanism specified for cookies. Both the name and value are arbitrary, given the above restrictions. The similarity to the name and value portions of a form INPUT element is intentional.

domain=*domain.name*
(optional)

This parameter specifies the Internet domain for which the cookie is valid and to which the cookie content can be sent. This can be a *subdomain*, for example .java.utoronto.ca, in which case the valid domains will be any domain names ending in this string. For domain names ending in country codes (e.g., .ca, .us—see Appendix E, "Tags for Idenfity Languages", available from the companion Web site at www.wiley.com/compbooks/graham), the *subdomain* specification must contain at least three periods, as in this example. In the case of the special top-level domains .com, .edu, .net, .org, .gov, .mil, and .int, only two periods are needed. Thus an example subdomain specification would be .netscape.com.

The server sending the Set-Cookie request must reside in the domain specified by the domain parameter. Thus the machine home.netscape.com can specify domain=.netscape.com, while the machine smaug.java.utoronto.ca cannot.

If not specified, the default value is the full domain name for the server sending the Set-Cookie request.

path=*valid/path*
(optional)

Specifies the set of URLs at the allowed domain(s) for which the cookie is valid.

If not specified, the default value is the URL path to the resource being returned with the Set-Cookie header.

expires=*time_date*
(optional)

Sets the date at which the cookie expires and should be deleted. The allowed value is a date string of the format

Day, dd-Mon-yyyy hh:mm:ss GMT

or any of the date formats described at the end of Chapter 9. If absent, the cookie expires when the user exits the browser session (or when the browser crashes).

Table 10.4 *Continued*

secure (optional) Indicates that the cookie content should only be communicated down a secure HTTP connection, such as **https**. If this parameter is present and the connection is not secure, then the cookie content is not sent. If this parameter is absent, the cookie is sent regardless of security issues.

TIP: No Quotation Marks in Parameter Fields

Unlike HTML attributes, cookie parameter values must not be enclosed in quotation marks. Thus, you must type `domain=.sub.domain.edu` and not `domain=".sub.domain.edu"`—the latter will not work. Similarly, you must not surround the `name=value` portion with quotes, as the quotation marks will be taken as the first character of the name and the last character of the value.

Sending Cookies to a Server

When a browser that supports cookies accesses a URL, it checks in its cookie jar for all cookies that are appropriate to the specified domain and path. If there are no relevant cookies, the transaction proceeds normally. If there are relevant cookies, then the browser combines all the cookie *name=value* strings together, separated by semicolons, and modifies the request to include an HTTP request header field of the form

```
Cookie: name1=value1; name2=value2; ...
```

A CGI program parsing this request must look to the `HTTP_COOKIE` environment variable and extract the cookie information.

Finite Number of Cookies

Cookies do not live forever, nor do browsers support an infinite number of them; for example, Netscape Navigator allows at most 300 cookies, each cookie no longer than 4 KB. At the same time, there can be no more than 20 cookies per server or domain. If these limits are exceeded, the client will delete cookies, starting with the one least recently used. A gateway program can delete unneeded cookies by sending a new `Set-Cookie` header that contains an `expires` value that has already "expired." This is a useful way of cleaning up cookies that are no longer required. Note that this will only work if the replacement header uses the same name for the cookie value.

Cookies and JavaScript

Cookies and cookie content can also be modified, created, or destroyed by JavaScript programs within HTML documents. This is useful for recording user actions from within navigational tools. However, a JavaScript program can only modify cookies that arrived from the same server as the JavaScript program.

Support for Cookies and Refusing Cookies

Cookies would seem an ideal way of preserving state during a transaction. This would be true—if one could guarantee that they work. However, not all browsers support cookies, while browsers that support cookies let the user *disable* cookie storage. Netscape Navigator, for example, can be configured to prompt the user whenever a server tries to send a cookie and gives the user the option of refusing the cookie data.

CGI Program Security Issues

There is always a security risk associated with running a gateway program, since a rogue program can easily corrupt the files located on the server. Most HTTP servers are configured such that executable CGI programs are restricted to special URLs (typically those pointing to the directories /cgi-bin or /htbin) and do not permit executable gateway programs in areas where regular documents are kept. The server administrator can then maintain strict control over the installation of gateway programs, and can verify that installed programs are not dangerous to the integrity of the server.

The details of security management depend on the server that you are using. In general, most servers allow significant customization of these features. You should check with your server manager—or with your server documentation if you are the server manager—to determine how your server can be customized.

Designing Safe Gateway Programs

Of course few people set out to write unsafe gateway programs. Nevertheless, it is easy to do so unless careful when writing the programs. Although it is hard to give definitive rules for writing safe programs, here are three points you should particularly consider:

Guard system information. Gateway programs should never return to the client any information about the local system that could compromise system security, such as absolute paths to files, system usernames, password information, and so on. If you must return directory information, pass it as a path *relative* to a location unknown to outside users—this reveals only limited information about the server's filesystem.

Never trust client data. A gateway program should never trust data sent by a client—the data could be in error, either due to a simple typing mistake or due to an intentional effort on the part of the client to break into your system. As a relatively benign example, you should never blindly trust the e-mail address (either *From*: or *To*:) typed into a fill-in HTML **FORM**, since you could be mailing data to the wrong user, or to a nonexistent mail address.

More importantly, you should be extremely careful about using strings that are derived from user input as arguments to system calls; examples include the C or perl `system()` and `popen()` calls or the perl or shell `eval` commands. Blindly passing strings to these calls or commands is a classic mistake, since commands executed by these calls can easily delete files, mail your password file to a remote user, and commit other venial sins. If you must execute strings passed by the user, be sure to check them for dangerous commands and to *unescape* special shell characters that can cause grievous problems. The possibly dangerous shell characters are:

```
` ~ ! # $ ^ & * ( ) = | \ { } [ ] ; : ' " < > , . ?
```

Execute in a secure environment. You can often run a script under a secure or restricted shell that take proactive action to prevent problems. For example, if you are using perl gateway programs you should use *taintperl* instead of perl. This version of perl treats all quantities that come from environment variables or external input as *tainted* and refuses to pass these quantities, unprocessed, to system calls.

Chapter 11 describes some CGI programming tools that can help protect you from these sorts of security problems. However, you should still strive to design your own programs to be as secure as possible.

Server Application Programming Interfaces

The gateway mechanism is simple and effective. However, it can be slow, since the gateway program must be started up, as a distinct running process, each time it is referenced. As mentioned earlier, this is often not a problem, particularly if the resource behind the gateway program is not speedy. Nevertheless, there are many occasions when speed is of the essence and where it would be useful if the gateway designer could bypass the CGI mechanisms completely and build the interface routines directly into the server.

A few servers support this feature through custom-designed gateway *application programming interfaces*, or *APIs*. Notable among these are the Netscape Netsite server's NSAPI (Netscape API), the Microsoft IIS Web server ISAPI, and an API under development as part of the Apache server project. The Netscape home page (`http://www.netscape.com`) maintains some on-line documentation on the API (just search for the string "nsapi"), but this is badly organized and poorly written (Netscape does, however, sell an NSAPI manual, should you be so bold!). On the other hand, the apache documentation site (www.apache.org/) maintains somewhat better on-line information on their own API, which is distinctly different from the Netscape variant.

Gateways built using an API are much faster than those built using the CGI interface. However, they gain this speed at the expense of portability—APIs are strongly server-specific, so if you write an API-based gateway for the Netscape Netsite server, you will be forever tied to that server as no other vendor supports that interface specification.

References

The following URLs provide documentation on CGI, Netscape cookies, and server-specific APIs. References to CGI utilities and libraries and to on-line CGI tutorials are given at the end of Chapter 11.

CGI Specification

hoohoo.ncsa.uiuc.edu/cgi/overview.html

hoohoo.ncsa.uiuc.edu/cgi/examples.html   (CGI demo scripts)

Netscape Cookies

developer.netscape.com/   (Netscape developer resources: search for "cookie")

CGI Security

www.go2net.com/people/paulp/cgi-security/   (Resource list)

www.genome.wi.mit.edu/WWW/faqs/   (Web security FAQ)
www-security-faq.html

Server APIs

www.apache.org/docs/API.html   (Apache API)

solo.dc3.com/wsapi/index.htm   (O'Reilly WebSite WSAPI)

developer.netscape.com/   (Netscape developer resources: search for "NSAPI")

www.microsoft.com/support/isapi/   (Microsoft ISAPI)

CGI Examples, Programs,

and Tools

This chapter discusses some practical issues associated with CGI. The first section covers the Netscape *client-pull/server-push* HTML and HTTP extensions, which are currently implemented on most browsers. These extensions allow for rudimentary animation of Web presentations—examples are provided that illustrate how these extensions work. The second section is a discussion of *server-side includes*. This is a special feature of many HTTP servers that allows for *parsable* HTML documents which are processed, by the server, prior to being delivered to a client. The third section gives a detailed presentation of six gateway programming examples, illustrating some of the important issues in gateway program design.

The remaining seven sections are a guide to useful CGI resources. The topics covered include FastCGI (a tool for significantly speeding up CGI program execution), CGI and generic Web application programming libraries, security wrappers for enhanced CGI security, tools that support sophisticated server-side document parsing, "utility" CGI programs for handling common tasks, and CGI packages for connecting Web pages to databases. The chapter concludes with a list of references useful for obtaining additional or updated information.

Netscape CGI Animation Techniques

Most modern browsers support mechanisms that allow for slide show-like presentations and for a rudimentary form of "pushed" animation. The animation scheme, called *server-push*, uses a special *multipart* MIME type to let a server send a client a series of images or documents, which in turn are displayed by the browser as an animated sequence. To use this technique, a Web designer must use a gateway program that sends the data to the client using this special MIME type. The "slide-show" mechanism, more properly called *client-pull*, uses a special HTTP response header, `Refresh`, which instructs the browser after a defined delay, to either actively refresh the displayed document, or access another document at a specified URL. Again, a gateway program must produce the `Refresh` HTTP header field. However, HTML authors can include, in their documents,

META elements containing the `Refresh` header field content (using the **HTTP-EQUIV** attribute value, as discussed in Chapter 6). The browser parses the documents for the **META** element and understands `Refresh` header information. This method is particularly useful for creating document slide shows.

The following sections look in detail at these two animation techniques.

Client-Pull

In *client-pull*, the server sends the client a special HTTP `Refresh` response header field. The field has the general form

```
Refresh: xx; URL=url_string
```

where *xx* is an integer giving the time, in seconds, that the browser should wait before *refreshing* the document, and `url_string` is the *full* (not relative) URL that the browser should access when it is time to do the refresh. For example, the header

```
Refresh: 10; URL=http://www.utoronto.ca/home.html
```

tells a browser to wait 10 seconds and then access the indicated URL. The URL portion can be left out, in which case the browser will re-access the URL it just retrieved. Thus, the header

```
Refresh: 30
```

tells a browser to refresh the currently displayed URL, after a 30-second delay. The refresh time can be set to zero, in which case the browser will refresh the display as soon as the currently requested data are fully loaded.

There are several things to note about this procedure. First, this response header field is understood by most, but not all, browsers (it is understood by Netscape Navigator 2 and greater, and Internet Explorer 3 and greater); those that do not understand it will simply ignore the header, display the accessed document, and then stop. Second, the `Refresh:` field must be returned by a gateway program—servers themselves do not return refresh header fields. Third, each request by the client counts as a separate HTTP transaction—in particular, the connection will be broken between requests unless HTTP keep-alive headers are sent by the CGI program sending the documents.

Client-Pull via META Elements

As an alternative to using a CGI program, `Refresh` can be placed inside an HTML document **META** element. This lets authors add refresh capability into already existing parsed HTML documents (parsed HTML documents are discussed later in this chapter) or build slide shows into a sequence of regular HTML documents, using the URLs in the `Refresh` fields to reference consecutive pages. The **META** element equivalent to the general form of the `Refresh` HTTP response header is

```
<META HTTP-EQUIV="Refresh" CONTENT="xx; URL=url_string">
```

while **META** elements equivalent to the two examples just given are:

```
<META HTTP-EQUIV="Refresh" CONTENT="10;
      URL=http://www.utoronto.ca/home.html">
<META HTTP-EQUIV="Refresh" CONTENT="30">
```

Most browsers understand these **META** elements and interpret their content as HTTP response header fields (this is the purpose of the **HTTP-EQUIV** attribute, as discussed in Chapter 6). This is, of course, only possible with HTML documents; if you are returning other forms of data, such as images, you need to use the gateway program approach.

Server-Push

Server-push is a second and fundamentally different way of creating dynamic documents. When a client accesses a resource delivered using server-push, the client-server connection remains open, and the server sends a sequence of data objects, one after the other, over an open connection—the connection does not close until the sequence is finished. This is done using a special MIME *multipart* message format, discussed next. There are two advantages to this method. First, it is faster than client-pull, since the browser does not need to recontact the server to get the second (or subsequent) piece of data. Second, the method can be used not just for a document, but also for the images within a document—you can use server-push to download a sequence of images into an <IMG SRC="..."> element. This allows for embedded *animation sequences* created by referencing, from an **IMG** element, a gateway program that delivers a sequence of image files via server-push. The disadvantage is that you absolutely need to write a special-purpose gateway program—unlike client-pull, you cannot implement server-push using **META** elements.

NOTE: Efficiency of Server-Push

Although faster than client-pull, server-push animation is far less efficient than an animated GIF—you should use the latter whenever possible. Server-push is appropriate when the animation must be dynamically generated by a gateway program such as an animated GIF that is dynamically generated by the server or an HTML page that lists the users of a system and is "pushed" whenever a user logs in or out.

Server-push is implemented using the MIME type *multipart/x-mixed-replace*. By employing this MIME type, a server can deliver a sequence (in principle, an endless sequence) of data files, one after the other. This is done by defining a *boundary* string as part of the MIME type header. A boundary string is a string of ASCII characters used to separate each part of a multipart message from the preceding and following parts. The MIME content-type declaration takes the form:

```
Content-type: multipart/x-mixed-replace;boundary=String
```

where `String` is a string of ASCII characters used as the separator between the different parts of the message. This string of characters must consist only of letters (a–z, A–Z) and numbers (0–9), and it must not appear anywhere within the message parts being sent. This ensures that the software receiving the data will not detect the string within a part of the message and prematurely end the message part. The general format for this MIME message type is shown in Figure 11.1.

Note how the boundary between different parts of the multipart message are denoted by the string SpecialAsciiString preceded by two dashes, that is:

--SpecialAsciiString

The end of the message is denoted by the same string but with two additional trailing dashes:

--SpecialAsciiString--

In practice, you can leave out this termination string and send an unending sequence of messages. A user can end this sequence by selecting the browser's "Stop" button, or by explicitly selecting an alternate URL.

Figure 11.1 Structure of a *multipart/x-mixed-replace* MIME message. Here, SpecialAsciiString represents the string of ASCII characters used as the the separator between message parts, and type/subtype is the data type of the data being sent. Comments are in italics.

```
Content-type: multipart/x-mixed-replace;boundary=SpecialAsciiString
                         [blank line, containing a CRLF pair    ]
--SpecialAsciiString     [marker denoting boundary between parts]
Content-type: type/subtype
   [blank line, containing a CRLF pair ]
.... content of first chunk ....
.... and more content ....
--SpecialAsciiString
Content-type: type/subtype
   [blank line, containing a CRLF pair ]
.... content of second chunk ....
.... and more content ....
--SpecialAsciiString
Content-type: type/subtype
   [blank line, containing a CRLF pair ]
.... content of third chunk ....
.... and more content ....
--SpecialAsciiString
.

. [and so on... any number of parts can be present...]
.
--SpecialAsciiString--   [The end of the multipart message]
```

The following two gateway program examples illustrate how server-push works.

Example 25: A Simple "Server-Push" Shell Script

This simple shell script, listed in Figure 11.2, repeatedly returns a document listing the "top" process running on the computer.

This first thing to note is that this is a *non-parsed header* script—this is usually necessary with server-push, as many servers *buffer* the data returned from a gateway program, and only forward data when the buffer is full or when the gateway program stops running. Here, however, we want each part of our multipart message to be immediately delivered to the client. We ensure this by using a non-parsed header script, which bypasses the server buffering and dumps data directly down the port to the client.

As a result, lines 2 through 6 return *all* the required HTTP response headers, namely, the status header (response 200, implying success), the date (the format

Figure 11.2 The Bourne shell script nph-top-list.sh, which returns a list of the top 10 processes running on the computer every 10 seconds. *Line numbers are in italics.*

```
1   #!/bin/sh
2   echo "HTTP/1.0  200 OK"                    # [ Server
3   date -u '+Date: %A, %d-%b-%y %T GMT'       #   Response
4   echo Server: $SERVER_SOFTWARE              #   Headers ]
5   echo MIME-Version: 1.0
6   echo "Content-type: multipart/x-mixed-replace;boundary=a1lpRf5fgFd1dr"
7   echo ""
8   echo "--a1lpRf5fgFd1dr"       # [initial boundary for first part]
9   while true
10  do
11        echo "Content-type: text/html"
12        echo ""
13        echo "<HTML><HEAD>"
14        echo "<TITLE> Top Running Processes </TITLE></HEAD><BODY>"
15        echo "<H1 ALIGN=center> Top Running Processes at time: <BR>"
16        date                       # [prints the current time and date]
17        echo "</H1><HR>"
18        echo "<PRE>"
19        /usr/local/bin/top -d1  # [Print out "top" running processes]
20        echo "</PRE></BODY></HTML>"
21        echo echo "--a1lpRf5fgFd1dr"
22        sleep 10
23  done
```

instructions provide a date in the correct format), the server type (obtained from the environment variable), and the MIME version, followed by the content-type declaration for the type multipart/x-mixed-replace. In this example, the multipart boundary string is `allpRf5fgFd1dr`. Note that there are no space characters in this content-type header. Ordinarily, you can have spaces before and after the semicolons separating the type/subtype from the associated parameters, but this is incorrectly processed by some servers (in particular, early versions of the NCSA HTTP server), so it is safest to remove all unnecessary whitespace. Finally, line 7 returns a blank line, which indicates the end of server directives and the start of the data being returned to the client.

Line 8 prints the first boundary marker—this indicates the start of the first *part* of the message. The script then executes a loop, starting from line 10, which is executed every 10 seconds (see the `sleep 10` command at the bottom of the loop). The loop returns a content-type header (here text/html) followed by a blank line—the mandatory blank line marks the end of the headers and the beginning of the data. This is followed by the HTML document which includes, inside a **PRE**, the output from the program *top*. The last thing returned is the boundary marker "`--allpRf5fgFd1dr`" that tells the client that the message is complete and that it can stop waiting for more data. It also tells the client to keep the connection to the server open, in anticipation of the next part of the message.

This program will in principle run forever, sending information every 10 seconds. A user can interrupt this by simply pressing the "Stop" button, or by selecting another URL. The server should detect the broken connection and issue a kill signal to the gateway program. Unfortunately, this does not work on some servers, so it is a good idea to have gateway programs check for a broken connection and gracefully quit if this has occurred. Shell languages, such as the Bourne shell used in this example, are notoriously bad at this—they often "forget" to die—so you should write server-push scripts in languages such as perl or C, which properly terminate when the connection breaks. The script in Figure 11.2, for example, does not always terminate when the client breaks the connection—this has, on occasion, left a dozen of these scripts happily running on our server, long after the browser that started them has broken the connection to the server.

Example 26: A C Program for "Pushing" Images

The example C program *nph-doit-2*, shown in Figure 11.3, uses server-push to send a sequence of GIF images. Assume that this CGI program is located in the server's *cgi-bin/* directory. Then, to insert an animated image in an HTML document, you would write the following HTML markup:

```
<IMG SRC="/cgi-bin/nph-doit2">
```

which assumes that the HTML document and gateway program are on the same server. The client will access the indicated URL to download the requested image. A browser that understands multipart messages will play the image sequence as a simple animation. Browsers that do not understand the multipart MIME type will display nothing or will display a symbol representing a missing or broken image link.

Figure 11.3 Simple C program *nph-doit2.c*, for pushing a sequence of images to a client. The files are read from the indicated directory. Commentary not originally in the program listing is in boldface italics.

```c
/*
 * doit-2.c
 * Based on doit.c --
 *    Quick hack to play a sequence of GIF files, by Rob McCool.
 *    This code is released into the public domain. Do whatever
 *    you want with it.
 *
 * Doit-2.c Modifications by By Ian Graham, July 23 1995
 * to make it a simpler demonstration example -- or so I thought!
 */

#include <sys/types.h>
#include <unistd.h>
#include <stdlib.h>
#include <fcntl.h>
#include <sys/stat.h>
#include <dirent.h>
#include <stdio.h>

/* Define the server directives and response headers            */

#define HEADER1  "HTTP/1.0 200 OK\r\n"    /* Nph-response header  */
#define HEADER2 \
   "Content-type: multipart/x-mixed-replace;boundary=aRd4xBloobies\r\n"

/* Define the boundary strings, the Content-type header, and the  */
/* path to the directory containing the images                   */

#define BOUNDARY      "\r\n--aRd4xBloobies\r\n"
#define END_BOUND     "\r\n--aRd4xBloobies--\r\n\r\n"
#define CONTENT       "Content-type: image/gif\r\n\r\n"
#define IMG_DIR       "/abs/path/image_dir"   /*  where the files are   */

int main(int argc, char *argv[])
{
    static char    *file;
    char           *files[1024], *tmp, buf[127];
    caddr_t         fp;
    int             fd, i, ndir=0;
    DIR            *dirp;
```

Continued

Figure 11.3 *Continued*

```
struct dirent *dp;
struct stat    fi;

/* Get list of all files in image directory -- we will       */
/* spit them out in alphabetical order                       */
                                        /* ** GET LIST    ** */
dirp = opendir(IMG_DIR);
while ( ((dp = readdir(dirp)) != NULL) && (ndir < 1024) ) {
    if( strncmp(dp->d_name,".", 1)) {
        files[ndir] = malloc(strlen(dp->d_name)+1+strlen(IMG_DIR));
        sprintf(files[ndir], "%s/%s", IMG_DIR, dp->d_name);
        ndir++;
    }
}
closedir(dirp);
                                        /* ** GOT LIST    ** */
/* Write out server directives, and first multipart boundary      */

                        /* ** PRINT SERVER RESPONSE HEADERS    ** */
if(write(STDOUT_FILENO, HEADER1, strlen(HEADER1)) == -1)   exit(0);
if(write(STDOUT_FILENO, HEADER2, strlen(HEADER2)) == -1)   exit(0);
if(write(STDOUT_FILENO, BOUNDARY, strlen(BOUNDARY)) == -1) exit(0);

/* Now loop over all files, and write to client              */
for (i=0; i<ndir; i++)   {
    fprintf(stderr, "Doing output loop -- i=%i\n", i);
    sleep(1);
                            /* ** WRITE PART CONTENT-TYPE    ***/
    if(write(STDOUT_FILENO, CONTENT, strlen(CONTENT)) == -1) exit(0);
    if( ( fd=open(files[i],O_RDONLY)) == -1 ) {
        fprintf(stderr,"Unable to open file %s\n", files[i]);
        continue;
    }
    fstat(fd, &fi);                      /*  find size of file and  */
    tmp=malloc(fi.st_size*sizeof(char));  /*  allocate memory for it */
    read(fd, tmp, fi.st_size);
                            /* ** WRITE THE IMAGE DATA ** */
    if(write(STDOUT_FILENO, tmp, fi.st_size) == -1) exit(0);
                            /* ERROR: unable to write image    */
    free(tmp);
    close(fd);
                            /* ** WRITE THE PART BOUNDARY ** */
```

Figure 11.3 *Continued*

```
        if(write(STDOUT_FILENO, BOUNDARY, strlen(BOUNDARY)) == -1) exit(0);
                                    /* ERROR unable to write boundary   */
    }

    /* Write out the boundary marking the end of the multipart        */
    /* message. Then we are done.                                     */

    write(STDOUT_FILENO, END_BOUND, strlen(END_BOUND));
    exit(0);
}
```

The first part of the program (between the **GET LIST** and **GOT LIST** comments) gets a list of all the image files in the directory */abs/path/image_dir* and creates an array (`files[]`) of absolute path filenames pointing to these files. The program then writes out the necessary server response headers, as well as the initial multipart headers and message dividers required by the multipart message (just after the **PRINT SERVER RESPONSE HEADERS** comment). The subsequent loop iterates over the different image files, sending them one after the other to the client, and each file is followed by the required multipart boundary marker (after the **WRITE THE PART BOUNDARY** comment). When finished with the list, the program exits, writes out the final boundary marking the end of the multipart message, and ends the connection.

Because this is a gateway program, you can pass variables to the program using the usual tricks. Thus you can use extra path information in a URL (the PATH_INFO environment variable) to pass the location of the image directory to the CGI program, instead of using a hard-wired location as done in this example.

Both client-pull and server-push are simple, but not terribly flexible techniques for automatically updating page content. For example, client-pull can be mimicked by a JavaScript program, but with added functionality such as user control of the time delay between pages. Similarly, server-push is a rudimentary way of pushing data to the browser and is being supplanted by animated GIFs, Java applets, Macromedia Shockwave plug-ins, and push-channel technologies.

Server-Side Includes

A recurring HTML authoring question is: "Can I include a file within my HTML document in the same way I include an image?" Generally, the answer is no, as there are no elements in HTML that allow arbitrary document inclusions (other than for frame elements, of course). If you want to have documents that are created *dynamically* (which is what is implied by inclusion), you are supposed to use a CGI program. Needless to say, this is overkill if all you want to do is patch a small piece of text into an otherwise stable document. Some kind of *include* HTML command would be far easier than a full CGI program.

Most HTTP servers support file inclusion via a mechanism called *server-side includes*, or *SSI*. With SSI, a server parses specially marked documents (called *parsable* HTML documents, often with the filename extension *.shtml*), looking for specially encoded HTML comment strings containing SSI *directives*. The server replaces these special comments with the output generated by processing the directive. There are several different directives: some that "include" other text or HTML files into the document, and others that can execute server-side programs and include the program output within the document.

This powerful feature should not be overused, however, as every parsable file must be specially processed by the server, which can significantly slow server response. As a result, most servers come with this feature initially disabled—you have to explicitly turn it on. Each server's documentation explains how this is done, if it is supported.

Server-side includes are well documented in the NCSA HTTPD server on-line manuals, referenced at the end of this chapter. Also referenced are several sites on the Web that provide useful interactive tutorials illustrating server-side includes.

Include Command Format

The server-side include mechanism is framed inside an HTML comment string:

```
<!--#include_command -->
```

When parsed by a server supporting this feature, the entire comment string is replaced by the output of `include_command`. Because the command is inside a comment string, this will not cause problems if the document is processed by a server that does not support this feature or that has this feature disabled. Such servers will simply deliver the document, including the comment line, and the client will treat the string as a comment and ignore it.

The general form for the include command is:

```
<!--#command arg1="value1" arg2="value2" -->
```

where `command` is the name of the command to be executed and `arg1` and `arg2` are arguments passed to the command. There must be no space between the hash sign (#) and the command name, or between the hash sign and the leading double dash (--#). The number and name of the argument(s) depend on the actual command; most commands take a single argument. Note that, despite its structure, this is *not* a comment statement. You *cannot* include comment descriptions inside an include command. Consequently, lines like

```
<!--#command arg1="value1" This prints the time of day -->
```

are invalid.

There are six SSI commands: `config`, `include`, `echo`, `fsize`, `flastmod`, and `exec`. `Config` configures the way the server parses the document. `Include` includes another document (*not* a CGI program) at the indicated location, while echo includes the contents of one of the special environment variables that are set for parsed documents. Fsize and flastmod are similar to echo; fsize prints the size of a specified file, while flastmod prints the last modification date of a specified file. Finally, exec executes a single-line Bourne-shell command, or a CGI program. For security reasons, the exec facility can be disabled in the server configuration files, while leaving the other features operational.

The next sections describe each of these commands, and how they work; entries in italics are variables to be set by the document author. Table 11.1 summarizes the commands and the allowed forms.

Include—Include Another Document

This directive includes another document (or another parsed document) at the given location in the current document—it cannot include CGI program output. Include takes two arguments to specify the file to be included. These are:

virtual="*virtual-path/file*"

> Specifies the *virtual* path to the document, relative to the server's document directory or to a user's personal server directory. For example, user fosdick with his or her own public HTML area would access files in this area with the virtual path:
>
> `<!--#include virtual="~fosdick/path/file.html" -->`

file="*relative-path/file*"

> Specifies the path to the document relative to the current URL. For example, to include the file *junk.html* from the same directory, or the file *blog.html* from the subdirectory *muck*, you would use:
>
> `<!--#include file="junk.html" -->`
> `<!--#include file="muck/blog.html" -->`
>
> You cannot use this form to move up in the hierarchy, only down (e.g., you can't use ../stuff.html).

Echo—Include Value of a Variable

This includes the contents of a named environment variable. The variable is indicated by the argument var="*var_name*", where *var_name* can be any of the CGI environment variables listed in Tables 10.2 and 10.3 (except QUERY_STRING and PATH_INFO—see the discussion of the *exec* include mechanism later in this section) or one of the special environment variables listed in Table 11.2, valid only in parsable files or in CGI programs called from a parsable file.

Fsize—Include Size of Listed File

This includes the size, in bytes, of a file—the file can be specified using either the file or virtual arguments, as described in the include command section.

Table 11.1 Server-Side Include Commands. Strings in italics are set by the document author.

Include Command	Function and Behavior
`<--#config errmsg="`*err_str*`" -->`	Set error message to be return upon error
`<--#config timefmt="`*format_str*`" -->`	Set format for times and dates
`<--#config sizefmt="bytes" -->`	Set format for printing file sizes to "bytes"
`<--#config sizefmt="abbrev" -->`	Set format for printing file sizes—Bytes, KBytes of MBytes, depending on size
`<--#echo var="`*variable*`" -->`	Print contents of listed environment variable
`<--#exec cmd="`*cmd_string*`" -->`	Execute the given Bourne shell command string and include the output inline
`<--#exec cgi="`*path/cgi_prog*`" -->`	Execute the indicated CGI program and include the output inline
`<--#flastmod virtual="`*virt/file*`" -->`	Print last-modification date of the file at the indicated *virtual* location
`<--#flastmod file="`*path/file*`" -->`	Print last-modification date of the file at the indicated relatve location
`<--#fsize virtual="`*virt/file*`" -->`	Print size of the file at the indicated *virtual* location
`<--#fsize file="`*path/file*`" -->`	Print size of the file at the indicated relative location
`<--#include virtual="`*virt/file*`" -->`	Include document from the indicated virtual location
`<--#include file="`*path/file*`" -->`	Include document from indicated relative location

`Fsize` is useful for presenting information about a file to be downloaded, particularly when the size varies often. For example:

```
...Download</A> the mail
archive: (<!--#fsize file="main.html"  --> bytes)
```

The output format is set by the `sizefmt` argument of the `config` command.

Table 11.2 Environment Variables Defined Only Within Parsed HTML Documents. These variables are also available to CGI programs executed from within a parsed HTML document.

Variable Name	Content
DOCUMENT_NAME	The name of the document being parsed. This is the raw name, stripped of any leading path information, extra path information, or query string data. For example, if the accessed URL were of the form /path/to/file.shtml/extra/path?foo, DOCUMENT_NAME would simply be file.shtml.
DOCUMENT_URI	The virtual (relative to server document directory) path to the document, such as ~fosdick/path/file.shtml, or /path/subpath/templates/template2.html. This will include any extra path information in the requesting URL, but not appended query string data.
DATE_LOCAL	The current date using the local time zone. The format of this date is controlled using the timefmt argument of the config command.
DATE_GMT	Same as DATE_LOCAL, but in Greenwich Mean Time.
LAST_MODIFIED	The last modification date of the current document. The format is specified by timefmt.

The following variable is not available on all HTTP servers

DOCUMENT_PATH_INFO	Contains any extra path information in the requesting URL. For example, if the requesting URL were /path/to/file.shtml/extra/path?foo, the DOCUMENT_PATH_INFO would be /extra/path.

Flastmod—Include Last Modification Time of Listed File

This includes the last modification time of a file specified using the file or virtual arguments, as described in the include command section. Like fsize, flastmod is useful for providing up-to-date information about files that are periodically changed. For example:

```
This file was last changed on:
<!--#flastmod virtual="/path/dir1/dir2/main.html"  -->
```

The output format is determined by the timefmt argument of the config command.

Exec—Execute Shell Script of CGI Program

This directive executes the indicated Bourne-shell command or CGI program and includes the program output inline in the document. The two possible arguments are:

cmd="*cmd_string*"

Causes the string "*cmd_string*" to be executed using the Bourne shell (*sh*). *Cmd_string* can be a simple one-line shell program that does simple tasks, such as listing directory contents or running a program to filter data for inclusion. The SSI directive is replaced by the output of the shell program.

cgi="*cgi_program*"

Executes the given CGI program, where the location of the program is given by the *virtual* path to the program; recall that the SSI directive is replaced by the output of the program. Also note that the script must return a valid MIME type. You cannot pass query strings or path information to the script using the standard URL mechanisms. Thus expressions like

```
<!--#exec cgi="/cgi-bin/script.cgi/path1/path2?query" -->
```

are invalid. The only way you can access the script is with the command:

```
<!--#exec cgi="/cgi-bin/script.cgi" -->
```

However, suppose the parsable script *stuff.shtml* contained the command

```
<!--#exec cgi="/cgi-bin/script.cgi" -->
```

and you access the file *stuff.shtml* via a URL of the form:

```
.../stuff.shtml/extra/path?query_string
```

In this case, the query_string and /extra/path information *are* available to the script *script.cgi* called from *stuff.shtml*. This is illustrated in an example at the end of this section.

Environment Variables Within Exec'ed CGIs

The variables defined in Table 11.2 are also available within gateway or shell programs that are executed using the exec command. In addition, any extra path or query information appended to the parsed HTML document name are passed to the CGI program within the PATH_INFO and QUERY_STRING variables, as per standard practice. At the same time, several servers define additional environment variables to provide information about the executing script. The most common of these additional variables are given in Table 11.3. These variables are defined by the Apache servers (Version 1 and greater), but not by NCSA servers prior to version 1.5.

NOTE: Possible Problems with Environment Variables

Some servers do not set the environment variables listed in Table 11.3 or at the bottom or Table 11.2, while others improperly set their content. To be safe, you should verify the accuracy of all environment variables prior to installing any CGI programs invoked via server-side includes.

Table 11.3 Environment Variables Defined Only Within CGI Programs Invoked by a Parsed HTML Document. These variables are not universally available on all servers.

Variable Name	Content
SCRIPT_NAME	The name of the script being executed, including the virtual path information needed to locate the script.
SCRIPT_FILENAME	The complete absolute name of the file, including the path to the file from the root of the filesystem.

Config—Set SSI Configuration Settings

This directive controls aspects of the output of the other parsed commands, such as the formats of the date and size output strings, or the error message string to include if parsing fails. Config can take three different arguments, one argument per command. These are:

errmsg="*error_string*"

> Sets the error message to use if there is an error in parsing the parsable commands.

timefmt="*format*"

> Sets the format for printing dates. This format is specified as per the C strftime library call (strftime is commonly found on UNIX computers).

sizefmt="bytes","abbrev"

> Sets the format for the specification of file sizes. The value bytes prints file sizes in bytes, while abbrev uses kilobytes or megabytes as abbreviated forms, where applicable.

> Some examples of config format specifications are:

```
<!--#config sizefmt="abbrev" -->
<!--#config timefmt="%m%d%y" -->
<!--#config errmsg="Unable to parse scripts" -->
```

Example 27: Server-Side Includes

The following example (shown in Figures 11.4 and 11.5) illustrates the use of server-side includes. The example consists of a main document *stuff.shtml* (the suffix *.shtml* indicates parsable HTML documents) that includes a second parsable document *inc_file.shtml* and that also executes the CGI program *test_script.cgi*. The listings for these examples are shown in Figure 11.4, while the browser rendering of the document *stuff.shtml* is shown in Figure 11.5.

In this example the document *stuff.shtml* is accessed using the URL:

```
http://leonardo:8080/stuff.shtml/extra/path/info?arg1+arg2
```

Note that this passes query strings and extra path information to *stuff.shtml*, as if it were a gateway program (see Chapter 10 for more information about CGI programs and passed variables)—thus this information is available, within the HTML parsing phase, via environment variables. All the example documents are designed to print these environment variables and display them within the returned document. As seen in Figure 11.4, these variables are empty inside the parsable HTML document. However, the bottom of Figure 11.5 shows that these variables *are* present inside the CGI program (in the environment variables QUERY_STRING and PATH_INFO) executed from within the parsable document. You can, therefore, access a parsable document and, through it, pass query information to a CGI program, just as if you were accessing the CGI program directly.

Figures 11.4 and 11.5 also illustrate the include and echo commands. These are useful for printing information about local files. However, you really want to do this as sparingly as possible, as every such request slows down the server. For example, it is a waste of server resources to use the LAST_MODIFIED variable to display the last time you edited a simple HTML document, since you could just as easily add this information while editing it.

For additional information about server-side includes and how to configure the NCSA server to support server-side includes, please consult the NCSA online documentation at:

hoohoo.ncsa.uiuc.edu/docs/tutorials/includes.html

Some Example CGI Programs

This section presents a few example CGI programs, representing some of the common uses of the CGI facility. The first example is a program that returns a document containing a count of the number of times the page was accessed. The second uses a gateway program and server-side includes to insert a randomly selected HTML snippet into an HTML document. The third and last example looks at WebNotice, a large-scale gateway-program application, designed by the author. This package integrates 28 gateway programs, 19 HTML document templates, and 10 HTML documents to create a Web-based system for depositing and viewing notices to be made available to the public.

Example 28: Page Access Counter

The simple perl script of this example answers the common question, "How do I include, within my page, a number indicating how many times the document has been accessed?" This program reads in the document to be returned to the client and edits it, replacing a dummy comment string in the document (the string <!-- counter -->) with the desired count. The count is obtained from a log file that

Figure 11.4 Example of server-side includes, showing the listings for three example documents. The main file is *stuff.shtml*, which *includes* the file *inc_file.shtml* and also the output of the CGI program *test_script.cgi*. The resulting HTML document, upon accessing the URL
```
http://leonardo:8080/stuff.shtml/extra/path/info?arg1+arg2
```
is shown in Figure 11.5.

1. *stuff.shtml*

```
<html>
<head>
<title> Test of NCSA Server-side Includes </title>
<body>
<h1> Test of NCSA Server-side Includes </h1>
<pre>
Stuff.shtml was last modified:    <!--#flastmod virtual="/stuff.shtml"  -->.
Size of stuff.shtml is:           <!--#fsize file="stuff.shtml"  -->.
DOCUMENT_NAME =                    <!--#echo var="DOCUMENT_NAME" -->
DOCUMENT_URI =                     <!--#echo var="DOCUMENT_URI" -->
DATE_LOCAL =                       <!--#echo var="DATE_LOCAL" -->
QUERY_STRING =                     <!--#echo var="QUERY_STRING" -->
PATH_LOCAL =                       <!--#echo var="QUERY_STRING" -->
DATE_GMT =                         <!--#echo var="DATE_GMT" -->
LAST_MODIFIED =                    <!--#echo var="LAST_MODIFIED" -->
</pre>

<!--#config errmsg="Unable to parse scripts"  -->

<p><em>....now include inc_example.shtml....</em>

<!--#include file="inc_file.shtml" -->

<p> <em>..... now include test_script.cgi CGI program output...... </em>

<!--#exec cgi="/cgi-bin/test_script.cgi" -->
</body>
</html>
```

2. *inc_file.shtml*

```
<pre>
Inc_file.shtml last modified:     <!--#flastmod virtual="/inc_file.shtml"-->.
Size of inc_file.shtml is:        <!--#fsize file="inc_file.shtml"  -->.
DOCUMENT_NAME:                    <!--#echo var="DOCUMENT_NAME" -->
```

Continued

Figure 11.4 *Continued*

```
DOCUMENT_URI:                    <!--#echo var="DOCUMENT_URI" -->
DATE_LOCAL:                      <!--#echo var="DATE_LOCAL" -->
DATE_GMT                         <!--#echo var="DATE_GMT" -->
LAST_MODIFIED                    <!--#echo var="LAST_MODIFIED" -->

</pre>
```

3. *test_script.cgi* (in the cgi-bin directory)

```
#!/bin/sh

echo "Content-type: text/html"
echo
echo "<pre>"
echo "This is  CGI script output."
echo "QUERY_STRING is \"$QUERY_STRING\"."
echo "PATH_INFO =  \"$PATH_INFO\". "
echo "</pre>"
```

tracks the number of times the file has been accessed. The gateway program opens this log file and increments the counter by 1. The program listing is found in Figure 11.6.

Figure 11.5 Browser rendering of the server-side executable document stuff.shtml when accessed using the URL

```
http://leonardo:8080/stuff.shtml/extra/path/info?arg1+arg2
```

To use this gateway program, you must access a document using a URL of the form

```
http://some.where.edu/cgi-bin/counter.pl/path/file.html
```

where `path/file.html` is the path to the document, relative to the root of the server document directory.

The specific location of the file to be returned is contained within the `PATH_TRANSLATED` environment variable; this value is placed into the local variable `$path` at line 3. Line 2 checks to make sure this variable actually exists—if it does not, there was no extra path information in the URL, meaning the author forgot to reference a file. Lines 8 through 11 process the variable `$path`, to extract the path to the directory containing the document being returned (`$path`) as well as the name of the file being returned. The count file is given the same name as the file, but preceded by a dot. Thus if the file being returned is *home.html*, then the count file will be named *.home.html*. Every file has its own distinct count file, with a matching name.

Line 15 checks to see if the count file exists—if it does not, lines 16 through 19 create it and give it an initial value of 0.

Lines 22 through 29 attempt to *lock* the file (`flock($cntfile,2)`). Locking the file means that the running perl program is the *only* program that can modify the file and ensures that two users cannot simultaneously attempt to change the file. The program tries four times to lock the file, waiting one second between attempts. If it fails, it sets a default value for the string containing the counter value (`$cnt`) and skips the part of the program that actually reads the count file. If it succeeds in locking the file, it proceeds to the next phase, beginning at line 30, where the count file is opened, the count is read and incremented by 1, and the count is rewritten to the file, overwriting the old value. The file is then closed and the lock is released (`flock($cntfile, 8)`), freeing it for use by other users.

Line 39 begins the processing of the file returned to the client. The file is opened at line 40 and read in at line 42, into the array `@array`. When finished, the file is closed (line 43).

Line 45 prints the required content-type header. Lines 46 through 48 print the data to standard output, replacing *every* occurrence of the string `<!-- counter -->` by the counter string (line 47)—this is either the counter value from line 33 or the error string from line 25.

And that is it. The count is inserted, the document is returned, and the counter has been incremented by 1.

There are several limitations to this program. First, it is slow, since the program has to check every line for the string `<-- counter -->`. A second problem is associated with file permissions: The server that launches a gateway program usually runs with very limited ability to create and modify files in the directories on the server; thus this gateway program, when launched by the server, will probably not be able to create or modify the count file. If this is the case, the document author will have to create the count file by hand and change the

Figure 11.6 Listing of the perl gateway program *counter.pl*, which inserts an access count into a designated HTML document. The path to the designated HTML document is passed as *extra path* information in the URL used to access this program. Line numbers, in italics, are added for reference purposes only—they are not present in the original program.

```
1   #!/usr/local/bin/perl
2   if (defined($ENV{"PATH_TRANSLATED"}) ) {
3       $path = $ENV{"PATH_TRANSLATED"}   # get file from extra path info
4   }
5   else {
6       &f_error("No file specified\n");
7   }
8   $file    = $path;                    # Path to file to be processed
9   $cnt_file = $path;
10  $cnt_file =~ s/.*\///;               # Extract substring for counter filename
11  $path     =~ s/\/[\w-.;~]*$/\//;     # get path to directory
12
13  $cnt_file = $path.".".$cnt_file;     # counter filename = path/.filename
14
15  if( !(-e $cnt_file) ) {              # If count file doesn't exist, create it
16     open(CNTFILE, "> $cnt_file") ||
17            &f_error("Unable to create count file\n");
18     print CNTFILE "0";
19     close(CNTFILE);
20  }
21  $loops = 0;                          # try 4 times to lock the count file
22  while ( flock($cnt_file,2) == -1 )  {
23     $loops++;
24     if( $loops > 4) {
25        $cnt = "-1 (Unable to lock counter)\n";
26        goto PROCESS;                  # If unable to lock, skip it.
27     }
28     sleep 1;
29  }
30  open(CNTFILE, "+< $cnt_file")        # open the counter file
31          || &f_error("Unable to open counter file\n");
32  $cnt = <CNTFILE>;                    # get the current count
33  $cnt++;                              # increment count by one
34  seek(CNTFILE, 0, 0);                 # rewind to start of file
35  print CNTFILE "$cnt";               # write out new count
36  close(CNTFILE);                     # close the count file
37  flock($cntfile, 8);                 # Unlock the count file
```

Figure 11.6 *Continued*

```
38
39  PROCESS:
40  open(FILE, $file)                       # Open file to process
41      || &f_error("Unable to open file for processing\n");
42  @array= <FILE>;                         # Read in the file
43  close(FILE);
44                                          # Print out the document
45  print "Content-type: text/html\n\n";
46  foreach (@array) {                      # scan for special string, and
47    s/<!-- counter -->/ $cnt /i;          # replace it by the count
48    print $_;
49  }
50  # Error Handling Subroutine
51  sub f_error {
52    print "Content-type text/plain\n\n";
53    print "<HTML><HEAD>\n<TITLE>Error In Counter Script</TITLE>";
54    print "\n</HEAD><BODY>\n<h2>Error</h2>\n<P>Error message: $_[0]";
55    print "\n<P> Please report this problem to someone.";
56    print "\n</BODY></HTML>";
57    die;
58  }
```

file characteristics so that the gateway program can modify it. Finally, we note
that this program only counts accesses that pass through the gateway program.
If the document is accessed via the URL

```
http://some.where.edu/path/file.html
```

then the access is not counted. In this regard, it is far better to invoke a counter
using a parsed HTML document and a server-side exec.

There are several useful features you might want to add. For example, you
might want to exclude your own machine or domain from the counting process,
or you may prefer keeping all the count values in a single counter database file as
opposed to having one file per document.

These and other variations on page counters are available in a number of
counter programs, many of which are far more sophisticated than this example.
The latter part of this chapter lists sites where such resources can be found.

Example 29: Inserting a Randomly Selected HTML Fragment

One useful parsed HTML trick is to use a gateway program to insert a randomly
selected HTML text snippet into an HTML document. The perl program *rot-new.pl*

is a simple implementation, which selects a file at random from a specified directory and inserts it inline within the parsed document. Assuming that the program is located in the server's *cgi-bin/* directory, the relevant server-side include instruction is:

```
<!--#exec cgi="/cgi-bin/rot-new.pl" -->
```

When the server parses this document, it replaces this string by the output of the program *rot-new.pl*.

Figure 11.7 gives the listing for the program *rot-new.pl*.

The ideas are very simple. At line 8, the program prints a text/html content-type header—recall that this is required of CGI programs returning data to a parsed HTML document. The second block, at lines 12 to 14, retrieves a directory listing for the directory /svc/www/InsTest—this is the directory that contains the insertions. Lines 15 to 17 convert the filenames into absolute paths, excluding non-data files (i.e., directories), and store the list of files in the array @filenames. The subsequent if statement at line 22 checks to see if there are any files in this list—the program exits if there are none. The alternate block of the if, beginning at line 25, selects a filename at random (line 28), opens the file (line 29), reads in the file content and then closes the file (line 31), and prints the content to standard output (line 32). The output is the text included within the HTML document.

Figure 11.7 Listing for the program *rot-new.pl*, which randomly selects an HTML document segment for insertion within an HTML document. Line numbers (in italics) are added for illustration only and are not present in the original program. The boldfaced comments are referred to by the text.

```
1    #!/usr/local/bin/perl
2    # rotator.pl
3    # Author:  Ian Graham
4    #           Information Commons, University of Toronto
5    #           <ian.graham@utoronto.ca>
6    # Version: 0.1b.    Date:    July 13 1995
7
8    print "Content-type: text/html\n\n";      # print content-type header
9
10   $include_path="/svc/www/InsTest";         # Directory containing include files
11                                             # Second Block: Get listing for
12   if( !opendir(DIR, $include_path)) {       # the directory containing the inserts
13       &f_error("Unable to open notices directory\n", __LINE__, __FILE__); }
14   @tmp = readdir(DIR);                       # Read list of filenames; then check
15     foreach (@tmp) {                         # to see if they are files, and not
```

Figure 11.7 *Continued*

```
16                                    # directories (-T tests for "real" files
17        push(@filenames, $include_path."/".$_) if -T $include_path."/".$_; }
18   close(DIR);
19   $last_index = $#filenames;          # Get index of last entry
20   $last_index += 1;                   # in array of filenames
21
22   if($last_index < 0) {
23     print " no files to insert ....\n"; die; # no stuff, so don't do nuthin'
24   }
25   else {                             # If there are files to be
26                                       # inserted, select one at random
27     srand(time);                      # and print it to stdout.
28     $rand_index = int(rand($last_index));
29     open(TEMP, $filenames[$rand_index]) ||  # Open selected file --
30        &f_error("Unable to open insertion file.\n", __LINE__,__FILE__);
31     @insertion = <TEMP>; close(TEMP);
32     print @insertion;                 # Print contents to standard output
33   }
34   # -------------- FINISHED ----------- FINISHED --------------
35   # Error Handling Subroutine
36
37   sub f_error {                       # What to do if there is an error
38     print "Content-type text/html\n\n";
39     print "Fatal error  at line $_[1] in file $_[2].\n";
40     print "Please send mail to: <BR>\n";
41     print "<A HREF=\"mailto:webmaster@comm.ut.ca\">webmaster@comm.ut.ca</A><BR>\n";
42     print "to inform us of this error. If you can please, quote the URL\n";
43     print "of the page that gave this error.\n<HR>\n";
44     die "Fatal Error: $_[0] at line $_[1] in file $_[2] \n";
45   }
```

Example 30: WebNotice—A Web-Based System for Distributing Notices

WebNotice is a Web-based package for posting and distributing notices on the World Wide Web. WebNotice uses the **FORM** interface to collect information from users, and uses gateway programs to process the submitted data, to archive that data in a server-side database, and to extract data from the database for return to the user. Any user can access the database to retrieve posted notices, but only authorized users can add new notices to the system—authorization is accomplished using the Basic authentication scheme, discussed in Chapter 9. The stored notices are organized into *groups*, so that notices can be posted under different group categories (in this example, the groups are different university departments). Each group has its own distinct set of authorized users, and a user can only post under groups for which he or she is authorized.

WebNotice consists of 28 gateway programs, 19 HTML document templates (read in by the gateway programs, and processed into complete HTML documents), 10 HTML documents, and a 30-page instruction manual, making it impossible to explain the whole package in this short section. The following will simply give an outline of the package, with an explanation of how the important parts work. The intent here is not to explain the detailed functioning of any particular component, but to give an idea of the overall design of a large gateway programming system.

The WebNotice system is currently running at a number of sites. To see how it works, you can visit the original home of the package at:

www.utoronto.ca/reg/notices_main.pl

Figure 11.8 shows the organization of the different gateways, with the arrows showing the flow as the user traverses the system. Everything begins with the program *notices_main.pl*, which returns a simple HTML document describing the various options. The program generates this document by reading in a simple HTML template document, which it customizes according to the local configuration of the WebNotice system. An example of the resulting document is shown in Figure 11.9.

Adding a Notice with WebNotice

There are several possible options shown in Figure 11.9—as an example, we follow the link to "Add a notice." Selecting this link accesses the gateway program *add_notices.pl*. This program checks a server-side database to obtain a list of all the groups registered with the system and returns a page containing this list. This page is shown in Figure 11.10. The list of groups (here, a list of university departments) is presented as a list of selectable items (radio buttons) in a fill-in **FORM**. The user selects the group under which he or she wishes to submit a notice, and presses the *Submit* button—in this example, the user has selected the *Department of Statistics*. Pressing the *Submit* button sends the **FORM** data to the server, and to the program *deposit_form.pl* (see Figure 11.8 to follow the flow).

The Notice Fill-in FORM—deposit_form.pl

Figure 11.11 shows the document returned by the program *deposit_form.pl*. Note how this gateway program was accessed using the GET method—you can tell this by the encoded group information appended to the URL. This lets the user *bookmark* this page, so that he or she can return here without having to restart at *notices_home.pl*. This judicious choice of the GET method makes it possible for users to bookmark pages they are likely to access often.

Figure 11.8 A schematic diagram showing some of the different perl programs in the WebNotice notice distribution system. The arrows show the possible hypertext links that relate the different documents. The loops following the *process_form.pl* and *process_modify.pl* programs indicate that the results returned by these programs can produce HTML FORMs that have ACTIONs linked to either of the two destinations, depending on the data.

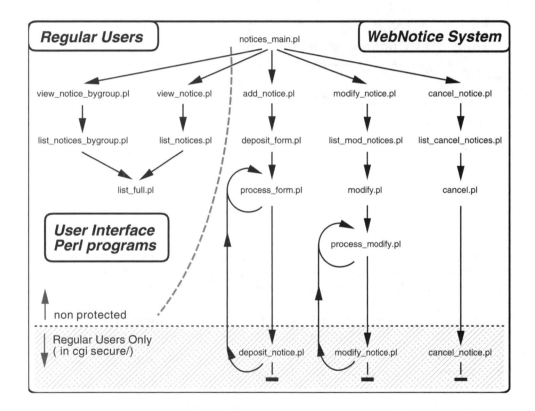

The document returned by *deposit_form.pl* contains an extensive fill-in **FORM**, into which the user enters the information required for a notice announcement (an announcement of events such as concerts or seminars)—there are fields for the time, date, and location of the event, the name of the presenter, and so on. Not obvious here is that the **FORM** also contains the "hidden" input element:

```
<INPUT TYPE="hidden" NAME="dept" VALUE="stats">
```

Figure 11.9 The HTML document returned by the program
***notices_main.pl*. This is the home page for the WebNotice system and**
provides links to all the functional components of the system.

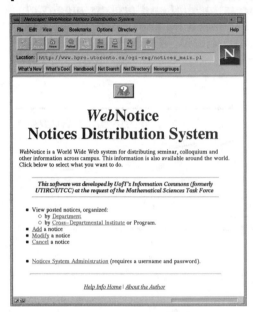

This was inserted into the **FORM** by the program *deposit_form.pl*. Thus, when
the data in this new **FORM** are sent the server, they will include the name of the
group under which the notice is to be recorded.

Processing and Checking the FORM Data—process_form.pl

When the user completes the **FORM**, he or she presses the *Submit* button at the bottom of the page. This **FORM** uses the POST method to send the data to the gateway
program *process_form.pl*. This program processes the data and checks for obvious
errors, such as missing fields, errors in the time and date, and so on. If there are no
errors, the program returns a preview of the posted notice for confirmation by the
user—an example preview document is shown in Figure 11.12. Notice the "Accept?"
yes-or-no checkboxes and the associated *Submit* button. The *entire* data content of
the notice is stored within `<INPUT TYPE="hidden" ...>` elements contained
inside the "Yes/No" acceptance **FORM**. The **ACTION** of this **FORM** points to the
program *deposit_notice.pl*, which actually adds the notice to the notices database. If
the user decides the notice is acceptable, selects "Yes," and presses *Submit*, the data
contained within the hidden elements are sent to *deposit_notice.pl*.

Figure 11.10 The HTML document returned by the program
add_notice.pl. **This page lists, within an HTML FORM, all the groups**
under which notices can be deposited. The program *add_notice.pl*
obtains this information by reading a server database.

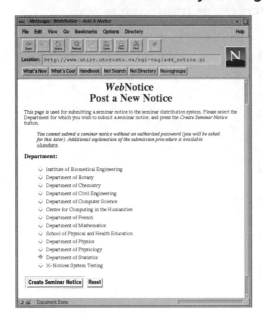

Processing an Error-Free FORM

As indicated in Figure 11.8, the program *deposit_notice.pl* is located in a directory
(here labeled *cgi-secure*) different from that containing *process_form.pl*,
deposit_form.pl, and so on—*deposit_notice.pl* is located in a directory *protected*
by the "Basic" authentication scheme. As soon as a user accesses *deposit_notice.pl*,
he or she is challenged for an authorization username and password. If the username and password information entered by the user are in error, access is immediately refused. If the username/password pair is acceptable because it is a valid
pair, the program *deposit_notice.pl* then checks to make sure this particular user
is authorized to deposit under the group being considered— the username and
password may be valid, but only for *another* departmental group (e.g., for the
Department of Physiology). The WebNotice system checks the username against a
database that matches usernames with groups—if the user is *not* authorized to
submit notices under the Department of Statistics, the program *deposit_notice.pl*
returns the server directive

```
Status: 401 Not authorized
```

Figure 11.11 The HTML document returned by the program *deposit_form.pl*. This document contains a FORM into which the user enters the required notice information. This program is accessed using the GET method (see the URL in the "Location" window), so that this document can be bookmarked for future reference.

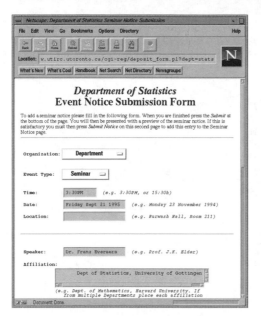

which is the HTTP status message indicating authorization failure. The server subsequently returns the 401 header message to the client. In general, the client will tell the user that authorization failed and will give the user the option of trying again with another username and password.

Finally, if the username/password pair is acceptable and the particular user is allowed to deposit notices under the given department, then the notices data are stored in the notices database. The deposited notice can then be retrieved for viewing (*list_notices.pl* and *list_notices_bygroup.pl*), modification (*modify.pl*), or deletion (*cancel.pl*). The processes of modification and cancellation both pass through programs in the *cgi-secure* directory, ensuring that authentication is again required before changes are permitted.

Processing a FORM Containing Field Errors—process_form.pl

It is also possible that the data passed to *process_form.pl* contained errors in the time, date, or other fields. In this case, *process_form.pl* creates a table of the errors and returns a document containing both a list of these errors and a duplicate fill-in FORM. The input fields of this duplicate FORM contain the data from the user's first attempt, so the user need only correct the mistakes and not re-enter the entire content. An example of such a document is shown in Figure 11.13.

Figure 11.12 If the FORM in Figure 11.11 is properly completed and submitted, the user is presented with this "preview" of the notice. It contains a small FORM, which the user uses to accept or reject the notice. This FORM contains `<INPUT TYPE="hidden"...>` elements that contain the entire data content of the fill-in FORM shown in Figure 11.11.

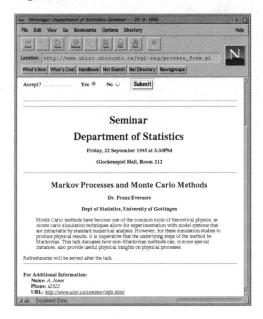

General Issues in Gateway Program Design

There are many problems that will crop up as you write gateway programs, as is the case with any programming project. This section describes ways to check for four of the more common errors, in this author's experience, that occur when writing gateway programs. Your list will assuredly be different, but hopefully this section will help you avoid some basic pitfalls!

Check for the Correct HTTP Method

The environment variable REQUEST_METHOD gives the method being used by the browser to access the script. If the method is incorrect (the request used the GET method, but the program expects POST), the program should return an appropriate error message.

Check for Input

The gateway program should always check for the existence of input (if input is expected), either in the QUERY_STRING environment variable or at standard input, depending on the HTTP method. Programs often behave very badly if they

Figure 11.13 The FORM returned by the program *process_form.pl* if there were errors in the FORM input fields. This document lists the errors at the top and then reproduces the fill-in FORM for correction by the user. This FORM, when submitted, once again accesses the program *process_form.pl*. The issues involved in assuring that FORM data are safely returned in this second form and in "hidden" elements within a FORM are discussed in the text.

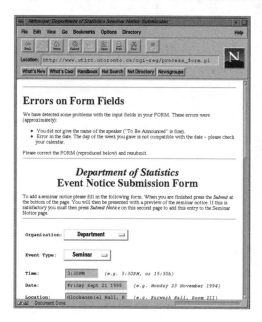

attempt to read nonexistent environment variables or an empty standard input stream. If data are missing, the program should return an appropriate error message.

Check for Errors in Input Fields

Check the input fields for obvious errors and never trust the data sent by a browser. Innocuous errors, such as an unexpected negative number where a positive one was anticipated, can lead to havoc if you haven't checked for all possible errors.

Remember: Browsers *Parse* Returned Text

Remember that text returned to a browser inside a **NAME** or **VALUE** string or inside a **TEXTAREA** region, will be parsed and that all character and entity references will be converted into the corresponding ISO Latin-1 characters. If you do not want this to happen, you must *encode* the ampersand characters in the original data prior to placing the data in the **FORM** being sent to the client. This issue was discussed in detail in Chapter 10.

Want to Obtain WebNotice?

The WebNotice software package is, like many World Wide Web applications, freely available over the Internet. If you want to find out more about WebNotice, and perhaps obtain your own copy of the software, just access the URL:

www.utoronto.ca/ian/Software/webnotice.html

FastCGI: A CGI Program Accelerator

www.fastcgi.com/

CGI programs are slowed by the fact that they need to be loaded into memory every time they are called—that is, they begin from a standing start, every time. This startup time can be almost eliminated by using FastCGI. FastCGI acts like a second server, running next to the HTTP server and acting as the general-purpose gateway between the Web server and the CGI programs. The difference is that, in this case, the CGI programs are incorporated into the FastCGI engine, using a special FastCGI API. Thus, writing FastCGI programs is like writing programs that bind to a server API, except that here the FastCGI API is independent of the server and was designed to work in a manner similar to traditional CGI. Indeed, there are FastCGI interfaces to most servers, so that FastCGI applications are almost as portable as regular CGI programs.

FastCGI was developed by Open Market Inc., but is now a free public-domain package that can be openly used and ported to any server. FastCGI programs can be written in almost any language, including perl, C, python, and Java.

CGI Programming Libraries

One of the most tedious aspects of CGI programming is parsing the environment variables or standard input data—these data are encoded, and a gateway program must decode the information before it can be used. To help in this process, a programmer can use one of the many programming libraries, available in a variety of languages, that provide routines for doing these basic tasks. Many of these have additional tools for generating HTML content for the returned document or for accessing databases. This section describes the more popular libraries of this type. You should look to the references at the end of the chapter for information about newer resources.

CGI.pm: Perl 5 Library

www-genome.wi.mit.edu/ftp/pub/software/WWW/cgi_docs.html

CGI.pm, by Lincoln Stein, is the most complete of the perl 5 CGI programming libraries. There are modules for parsing and processing form data, including those sent using the multipart/form-data encoding, for generating FORM-based HTML documents to return to the client and for error checking and report generation. The package is complicated, complete, and highly recommended. The package can be thought of as a more sophisticated (and complicated) successor to the *cgi-lib.pl* package (see later). However, the library is large, and thus can be slow to start up—for smaller, faster perl applications, see *cgi-lite.pm*.

Cgic: ANSII C Library

www.boutell.com/cgic/

Cgic, by Thomas Boutell, is a free (non-commercial use only) library of C-language routines for parsing and manipulating **FORM** data. Cgic contains modules for exception and error handling, and for handling standard processing functions, such as bounds checking and multiple-choice selection; it can even check for well-known browser errors. There is also a debugging mode. The package can run under UNIX and also under DOS/Windows.

Cgi-lib.pl: Perl 4/5 Library

cgi-lib.stanford.edu/cgi-lib/

Cgi-lib.pl, by Steven Brenner, is one of the most popular perl libraries for CGI program development. It is simple, compatible with both perl 4 and 5, and can handle data sent using the multipart/form-data encoding. There are also modules for constructing standard HTML headers and footers for the returned data. Cgi-lib.pl is simpler than *CGI.pm*, but provides less functionality. It is also smaller and faster than *CGI.pm*, but not as fast as *cgi-lite.pm*.

Cgi-lite: Perl 5 Library

www.oasis.leo.org/perl/exts/infosys/www/cgi/

Cgi-lite.pm, by Shishir Gundavaram, is a small CGI library for processing form data. It is modeled, to some degree, after *CGI.pm,* but omits many of the advanced *CGI.pm* features. The advantage of cgi-lite.pm is speed—since it is much smaller, it is much faster to launch and is ideal when the CGI program needs to be fast.

Libcgi++: C++ Library

www.ncsa.uiuc.edu/People/daman/cgi++/

Libcgi++, by Dragos Manolescu, is a C++ library for parsing and processing data obtained from GET and POST requests. There are routines for parsing and decoding query strings, for encoding data for return to a client, and so on.

Uncgi

www.midwinter.com/ftp/pub/

Uncgi, by Steven Grimm, is a simple front-end package that handles form element parsing. Uncgi decodes all the **NAME** and **VALUE** attribute values sent by GET or POST methods, and places them in environment variables. Uncgi then calls the processing program (C, perl, or whatever), passing it these environment variables. Note that this may be a problem if the string being passed in an environment variable becomes too large, since some systems place limits on the size of environment variables.

Generic Web Application Libraries

There are two additional libraries that are useful for CGI programming, but that were originally designed for writing general-purpose Web applications, such as clients (browsers or other), servers, or Web indexing robots.

Libwww: W3C Sample Code Library

www.w3.org/Library/

Libwww is a general-purpose Web API written in C. Libwww is a highly modular, extensible API that is commonly used as the code base for Web clients and robots and for developing and testing experimental Web-based protocols and software.

Libwww-perl: Library for Web Applications

www.ics.uci.edu/pub/websoft/libwww-perl/

Libwww-perl, by Roy Fielding of the University of California at Irvine, is a perl library package of perl (Version 4 and 5) functions and provides a useful library and API for writing client and server Web applications. This package is highly recommended to any serious Web programmers. Note, however, that libwww-perl was *not* designed specifically for CGI programming and is not ideal for CGI applications. Development of the perl 4 package stopped in late 1994, so you should use the perl 5 version whenever possible.

CGIwrap: Security Wrapper

wwwcgi.umr.edu/~cgiwrap/

As mentioned previously, CGI programs pose a number of security risks. CGIwrap is a gateway program designed to reduce these security risks. With CGIwrap, CGI programs run with the permissions of the user who owns the program and not with those of the Web server that launches it. This makes it easier for users to write and run their own CGI programs, with reduced risk that these programs can damage other users' resources.

CGIwrap reduces, but does not eliminate, security problems. If you want to properly understand CGI security issues, you should read the security references listed at the end of Chapter 10.

Server-Side Document Parsing

The SSI mechanism works through a parsing module incorporated into the HTTP server. Of course, it is easy to build additional modules that support other forms of parsable markup within HTML documents. Indeed, most commercial Web servers support server-side scripting via proprietary scripting languages; for example, Netscape's *LiveWare* suite provides JavaScript-based server-side scripting, while Microsoft's Active Server Pages technology provides similar functionality on Microsoft servers.

However, there are also several shareware and freeware programs that are not bound to a particular server platform and that provide similar server scripting functions. Some of the more popular packages are:

Product Name	URL For Additional Information	Status
Cold Fusion	www.allaire.com	commercial
htmlscript	htmlscript.volant.com	commercial
NeoWebScript	www.neosoft.com/neowebscript/	commercial
META-HTML	www.metahtml.com	free (with license)
PHP/FI	php.iquest.net	free (GNU public license)

These tools are much more sophisticated than server-side includes and support parsed documents that are essentially programs, complete with branching and conditional execution. The corresponding document markup often resembles HTML, but with additional, special-purpose tags reflecting the "language" of the preprocessor. Most of these packages support database access commands, allowing for dynamic document generation based on server database content.

CGI Utility Programs

CGI Program Resource Sites

http://www.cgi-resources.com/

www.oac.uci.edu/indiv/ehood/perlWWW/

www.yahoo.com/Computers_and_Internet/Internet/World_Wide_Web/
CGI___Common_Gateway_Interface/

This section lists several commonly useful CGI gateway programs and utilities, such as mail forwarders or feedback form/guestbook utilities, document access counters, and UNIX man (manual) page-to-HTML converters. Of course, this is an incomplete list, and you should search the Web if you need a tool that is not listed here—the URLs at the start of this section provide some useful starting points. You should also look in many of the Web magazines currently in print, as many commercial CGI packages are advertised in such venues.

Email Handler

www.boutell.com/email/

This package, due to Thomas Boutell, is a simple C-language CGI program that lets browser users send e-mail messages to a restricted set of allowed recipients. This package is quite simple and has been used as a model for several other, more extensive, implementations.

Server-Side Include Page Counters

www.yahoo.com/Computers_and_Internet/Internet/World_Wide_Web/Programming/Access_Counts/

There are many CGI programs that, via the server-side include mechanism, can count the number of times a page is accessed. This URL references the page at Yahoo! where many of these CGI programs are listed.

CGI Database Gateways

Many Web applications are now designed as front-ends to sophisticated database systems. This requires gateway programs to take the **FORM** or **ISINDEX**-based query data and communicate them to the back-end SQL (or other) mechanisms used by databases such as Sybase, Oracle, and WAIS. The following is a very brief list of some such Web-database gateway tools, along with some hints as to where to find additional information.

If you are using a commercial database product, either on UNIX, Macintosh, or Windows platforms, then you should contact your vendor to obtain whatever Web interface software they provide. All database vendors now provide sophisticated gateway and server plug-in modules that connect their products to Web-based query interfaces. The following section is more likely to be of interest to those using freeware or shareware databases such as freeWAIS, mSQL, or postgres.

WAIS Gateways

WAIS, for Wide Area Information Servers, is an extremely popular text-database system. WAIS was designed as a client-server system, enabling WAIS clients to interrogate WAIS databases using a well-defined protocol and URL scheme. It is particularly popular because it is free—the *freeWAIS* software is a simple, yet powerful, text indexing tool and is often a good option when cost is a factor or when commercial software is not available or appropriate. This protocol is supported by some Web clients, so that it is often possible to directly interrogate a WAIS server by constructing a URL (with appropriate query strings) that points to that WAIS server.

However, most browsers do not support **wais** URLs. Furthermore, most users wish (and need) to design database queries using fill-in forms, so there is a need for software that can take the form data, convert it into an appropriate WAIS query, forward the query to the database, and then return the database results to the user. Indeed, there are now many gateway programs that support such interfaces to WAIS servers. The following section lists some of these packages.

KidofWAIS

www.cso.uiuc.edu/grady.html

Kidofwais.pl, by Michael Grady, is a perl script WAIS gateway program. Kidofwais.pl uses the simple **ISINDEX** query interface, but allows for pattern searches (`astro*` matches any word beginning with "astro") as well as complex Boolean searches. The program returns search results complete with useful information about the resulting items, such as document type and length. In addition, when the documents are retrieved, the search string is highlighted in boldface for easier location and identification.

SFgate

ls6-www.informatik.uni-dortmund.de/SFgate/SFgate.html

Sfgate, by Norbert Gövert and Ulrich Pfeifer, is another perl-based WAIS gateway program but is distinctly different from *wais.pl* or its derivatives. SFgate does not access a server-side WAIS query engine. Instead, WAIS client software is built into SFgate, so that it can itself query any Internet-accessible WAIS database. In addition, SFgate supports a form-based query interface, so that the user can select various databases (which can be searched at the same time) and enter complex query information into text input boxes. You can also create customized form interfaces to make it easier for users to access the database.

Although SFgate can work with any freeWAIS server, it is designed to work best with freeWAIS-sf. FreeWAIS-sf is a WAIS variant, modified, among other things, to allow for structured fields. Information about freeWAIS-sf is found at:

http://ls6-www.informatik.uni-dortmund.de/freeWAIS-sf/

ftp://ftp.germany.eu.net/pub/infosystems/wais/Unido-LS6/freeWAIS-sf/

WWWWAIS

www.eit.com/software/wwwwais/wwwwais.html

www.eit.com/software/wwwwais/

WWWAIS, by Kevin Hughes, is a small ANSI C program that acts as gateway between waisq and waissearch (the WAIS programs that search WAIS indexes) and a forms-capable browser. WWWWAIS supports customized form interfaces and a database access control mechanism (restricting access to certain Internet domains) and allows users to choose from amongst multiple searchable databases. As with the previously mentioned packages, WWWWAIS returns the search results as a hypertext document.

SQL Gateways

There are many packages for linking Web servers to commercial SQL database packages such as Oracle or Sybase. The following section lists public-domain packages. Most commercial vendors also provide gateway software, and you should consult with your vendor to obtain up-to-date information on their offerings.

GSQL Gateway

www.ncsa.uiuc.edu/SDG/People/jason/pub/gsql/starthere.html

GSQL, by Jason Ng, is a C program invoked from the HTTP server via a shell script. GSQL is a simple gateway to Sybase or other SQL databases. It parses an SQL-specification file (called a *PROC* file) to create an HTML form, and uses the user form input to call the database back-end program to process the SQL query. Search query results are then returned to the client. The PROC file maps components of the SQL string to widgets (fields, buttons, pull-down menus, etc.) for user input or selection. This is an older package (circa 1994) but still useful and simple to implement.

GSQL-Oracle Backend

ftp://ftp.cc.gatech.edu/pub/gvu/www/pitkow/gsql-oracle/oracle-backend.html

GSQL-Oracle Backend, by James Pitkow, is a CGI program for linking WWW applications to an Oracle database, using either **ISINDEX** or form interfaces. GSQL-Oracle Backend is written in PRO-C, the C language development environment for Oracle, so you need this development option to compile the software. The package comes with installation instructions and compiles easily on most UNIX machines.

Web/Genera

gdbdoc.gdb.org/letovsky/genera/

Web/Genera, by Stanley Letovsky, is a software toolset for integrating Sybase databases into the World Wide Web. Web/Genera can be used to retrofit a Web front-end (**FORM** or **ISINDEX**) to an existing Sybase database or to create customized interfaces. To use Web/Genera, you write a specification of the Sybase database and of the desired appearance of its contents on the Web, using a simple high-level schema notation. Various Web/Genera programs process this description file to generate SQL commands and formatting instructions, that together extract objects from your database and format them into HTML. Note that this package has not been updated since early 1996 and is not being actively maintained.

WDB—Sybase, mSQL, and Informix Gateway

arch-http.hq.eso.org/bfrasmus/wdb/wdb.html

www.dtv.dk/~bfr/wdb/intro.html

WDB, by Bo Frese Rasmussen, is a CGI package similar to Web/Genera and also based on perl and *sybperl*. Like Web/Genera, WDB allows you to use high-level description files to specify the structure of the database and the format of the responses, so that you can construct a generic WWW-SQL interface without writing a single line of code. Notable is the ability to turn data from the database into hypertext links, so that it is possible to access any database element directly via a URL. This package was last updated in the summer of 1996 and is not being actively maintained.

W3-mSQL

www.Hughes.com.au/

W3-mSQL, a product of Hughes Technologies of Australia, is a gateway to mini-SQL databases from World Wide Web documents. W3-mSQL is a single CGI program that provides full Web access to data stored within mini-SQL databases. The software is free for noncommercial uses and is being actively maintained.

Perl Database Interface Libraries

ftp://ftp.demon.co.uk/pub/perl/db/

ftp://ftp.demon.co.uk/pub/perl/db/README

There are many freeware perl interfaces to common commercial database systems. The URL identified here is an archive site of such software, where the README file provides an overview of the site content. This is an ideal place for locating freeware database interface libraries, which you can use along with a CGI library to create Web database applications.

References

General Starting Points

www.yahoo.com/text/Computers_and_Internet/Internet/World_Wide_Web/
    CGI___Common_Gateway_Interface/

CGI Programmer's Reference and FAQs

www.stars.com/Seminars/CGI/	(CGI tutorials and resources)
www.cgi-resources.com/	(Directory of CGI resources)
www.itg.lbl.gov/~clarsen/projects/htcl/ http-proc-args.html	(CGI using tcl)
starship.skyport.net/crew/davem/cgi_faq.html	(CGI using python)
www.comvista.com/lessons/START_HERE.html	(Macintosh applescript CGI)

Server-Side Includes

hoohoo.ncsa.uiuc.edu/docs/tutorials/includes.html   (Overview)

On-line CGI and FORM Tutorials

www.stars.com/Seminars/CGI/	(CGI tutorial)
agora.leeds.ac.uk/nik/Cgi/start.html	(CGI tutorial)
www.jmarshall.com/easy/cgi/	(CGI tutorial)
www.catt.ncsu.edu/projects/perl/index.html	(CGI and perl tutorial)
blackcat.brynmawr.edu/~nswoboda/prog-html.html	(HTML-based interfaces tutorial)
robot0.ge.uiuc.edu/~carlosp/cs317/cft.html	(FORMs tutorial)

CGI Program Archive Sites

www.worldwidemart.com/scripts/	(Matt's script archive)
www.extropia.com/Scripts/	(Selena Sol's script archive)
www.oac.uci.edu/indiv/ehood/perlWWW/	(Web perl scripts)
128.172.69.106:8080/cgi-bin/cgis.html	(C language CGI programs)
awsd.com/scripts/index.shtml	(CGI script archive)
www.cgi-resources.com/	(Scripts and CGI documentation)

Database-Web Gateway References

gdbdoc.gdb.org/letovsky/genera/dbgw.html	(List of software)
www.yahoo.com/Computers_and_Internet/ Internet/World_Wide_Web/ Databases_and_Searching/	(General information and software)
www.yahoo.com/Business_and_Economy/ Companies/Computers/Internet/ Databases_and_Searching/	(Commercial software)

ABOUT THE WEB SITE

www.wiley.com/compbooks/graham/

Instead of a CD-ROM, the *HTML 4.0 Sourcebook* is supported by a companion Web site, available by going to the URL above, and selecting the link to this book. This site provides functionality similar to a CD-ROM, but with several advantages. The first advantage is cost—the book is much less expensive than a book with a CD. (You thought those CD inserts were cheap?) Second, and more important, the Web site can (and will!) be updated with information about late-breaking changes to HTML, as well as corrections to the printed book. Thus, the book and its Web site will remain up-to-date long after other books are obsolete. Finally the Web site contents are available as an archive file, and can be downloaded and installed on your own machine—giving you the advantage of up-to-date material, without having to stay connected to the Internet.

The Web site contains the following material:

All example documents. Listings to all the HTML documents and CGI programs given as figures in the book.

Hypertext reference lists. A hypertext listing of all the book references.

Corrections and Updated Material. Corrections to the printed material, as well as updates on new features.

Additional supporting material. Useful information that didn't make it into the book, including:

- A glossary of Web and Internet terms
- Source code for the programs listen.c and backtalk.c
- Figures and tables illustrating HTML character and entity references
- "Appendix A," a description of the relationship between characters and computer character sets

- "Appendix B," a guide to the Multipurpose Internet Mail Extensions (MIME) mechanism, its application to Web application, and an extensive table listing commonly used Internet MIME types

- "Appendix C," tips for obtaining software over the Internet

- "Appendix D," a detailed description of TCP/IP communication

- "Appendix E," describing how human languages are identified over the Internet

- "Appendix F" describing the Web-supported color names (e.g., "red," "blanchedalmond") and color codes (e.g., #44eF3B), with example HTML documents illustrating those names and codes

- Descriptions of useful "Web Management and Maintenance Tools," with instructions for obtaining those tools

Additional HTML and Web resources are available from the author's Web sites, found at www.utoronto.ca/webdocs/ and www.utoronto.ca/ian/books/html4ed/. The Wiley and author's Web sites are linked together, just like every good Web application, so be sure to visit both!

Finally, it is important to realize that, to keep up with modern site design, you must get out there and continue to browse the Web. Reading a book in which an author spouts off his own ideas of good and bad design is all well and good; but you, as a writer and designer of documents and Web sites, will only appreciate how things look and feel by going out there and looking and feeling. The content of this book is merely a framework for appreciating what tens of thousands of creative individuals are already doing. So, go and see for yourself!

INDEX